BBC ENGINEERING
1922–1972

BBC ENGINEERING
1922–1972

Edward Pawley
OBE, MSc(Eng), C Eng, FIEE

BBC Publications

Published by the British Broadcasting Corporation,
35 Marylebone High Street, London W1M 4AA

ISBN 0 563 12127 0

First published 1972

© British Broadcasting Corporation 1972

Printed in England by The Broadwater Press Limited,
Welwyn Garden City, Hertfordshire

Contents

Contents

Illustrations

Foreword

This book is a survey of the development of BBC engineering during the fifty years since the British Broadcasting Company, the predecessor of the British Broadcasting Corporation, was founded. It is about the application of technology to the development of the BBC's services. BBC engineers have played a significant part in this continuing effort, but are far from claiming all the credit for it. A host of scientists and engineers in many countries, in the universities, in government establishments, and in industry, have helped to create the technical resources from which broadcasting derives its being and to which it has contributed its quota.

Many of the techniques used in broadcasting are common to other branches of electronics and especially to other forms of radio-communication. Broadcasting differs from them in one way that has had a profound effect upon its development: the receiving part of a broadcasting system – a vitally important part – is not under the control of the broadcasters, but is chosen and operated by members of the public. This fact makes it impossible to design the system as a whole and necessitates co-operation between a number of different interests to ensure that the various elements in the system fit together.

Another result of this peculiarity is that the problem of obsolescence imposes a severe constraint on development. No improvement can be made at the transmitting end unless either it is planned and announced so far ahead that existing receivers are worn out before the change occurs or it is carried out in such a way that it does not result in any deterioration in reception on existing receivers. A change may be introduced that will result in an improved service only to those listeners or viewers who equip themselves to take advantage of it, provided that those who do not do so are not penalised. Hence the frequency with which the word 'compatible' enters into discussions about development plans. Colour television could not be introduced until a system was evolved that would provide satisfactory reception in black-and-white on monochrome receivers. Stereophony could not be introduced until a method was developed that would enable listeners with ordinary VHF receivers to continue to receive the programmes in monophony.

Another effect of this constraint is that any development or extension of broadcasting services must be planned to last for a long time and errors may be impossible to rectify. If a high-power television station is put in the wrong place, it will be extremely difficult to move it, not only on account of the cost to the broadcaster, but also because many viewers will individually be put to the expense of altering their aerials, or even replacing them, to receive the transmissions from a new direction.

This book does not attempt to record the names and achievements of all those who have helped to create the broadcasting services and to keep them going. It concentrates rather on the efforts of the pioneers in the BBC and their immediate collaborators, in the hope that their dedication to the cause – and many of them were dedicated to an astonishing degree – will encourage their present and future successors.

In tracing the development of present-day techniques from the seeds sown at the beginning of the century, we shall perhaps be able to show the kinds of approach to engineering problems that have succeeded in the past and may, given the necessary flexibility to meet changing needs, be successful in the future. We shall try to examine not only the successes but the failures, and the reasons for them, by presenting a record based largely on first-hand evidence from people who were directly concerned in the march of events.

There is a particular reason for presenting this book to the public now. Its appearance in 1972 coincides with the fiftieth anniversary of broadcasting in this country. By a happy chance, the previous year, 1971, marked the centenary of the Institution of Electrical Engineers, with which BBC engineering has been linked in many ways. The Institution, formerly the Society of Telegraph Engineers, has done great service to electrical and electronic engineering in this country. One of the names that it honours is that of Michael Faraday, the father of electrical science, and the discoverer, in 1831, of the laws of electromagnetic induction, the application of which made broadcasting possible.

The fifty years with which we deal have seen the BBC expand from three small radio stations, each with a crude studio, to a complex of nearly six hundred transmitters providing two television programmes in colour, five radio programmes for audiences in this country, and programmes in forty languages for listeners overseas. The audience in the United Kingdom has grown from some 35,000 households, mostly equipped with crystal sets, to virtually the whole population, using highly sophisticated receivers. The tide of invention and development shows no sign of ebbing; television is advancing into the satellite age with rapid strides and, even in the long-established art of radio, new techniques are evolving at an increasing pace.

Engineers of today, who are able to call in aid a complex of computers, pulse techniques, solid-state devices, integrated circuits, and elaborate testing equipment, may think of the pioneers of the '20s as men living in an age not far removed from the abacus. The greater honour to them that they achieved so much with so little, that their vision was clear and their determination unfaltering.

The role of engineering in relation to programme production has changed over the years. Before 1922 broadcast programmes were little more than a means of exploiting the new wonder of 'wireless', and engineers helped to present them. During the early years of the Company, broadcasting gradually secured acceptance as a normal part of life. Its status was enhanced by the vital importance that broadcast news acquired during the Second World War. The change in the scope of broadcasting necessitated increasing specialisation and professionalism among its staff. Programme planning, production and presentation have become highly professional tasks in their own right, but engineers still have a voice in major discussions on policy, because so many policy decisions depend on technical factors. Engineering developments must be rated strictly according to their value in providing improved services or in reducing costs. The 'cost-effectiveness' of each decibel of signal-to-noise ratio must be compared with that of an extra hour of *Top of the Pops* or an extra instalment of *Civilisation*. An iron discipline indeed!

The Engineering Division, though not in the spotlight of public interest to which the programme producers are accustomed, forms a not inconsiderable part of the BBC staff, its numbers having grown from 37 in December 1923 to 7760 (out of a total staff of nearly 22,500) in 1969. (Since then a number of engineering staff have been transferred to the 'output' directorates, though still responsible to the Director of Engineering for their professional standards.)

The history of broadcasting in the United Kingdom falls naturally into six periods, namely:

1 The experimental era preceding the formation of the British Broadcasting Company in 1922.
2 The lifetime of the British Broadcasting Company: 1922–6.
3 The formative period of the British Broadcasting Corporation, from its foundation in 1927 until the outbreak of war.
4 The war years: 1939–45.
5 The period of post-war reconstruction: 1946–55.
6 The years of expansion, from 1956 onwards.

This book is divided roughly into these six periods, but it will not confine itself too rigidly to them where a particular line of development extends from one period into the next.

Most of the material for this history has been assembled by three retired BBC engineers: J. H. Holmes, who joined the BBC Lines Department in 1935 and retired as Head of that Department in 1962, W. E. C. Varley, who joined in 1933 and retired as Chief Engineer, Transmitters, in 1968, and P. E. F. A. West, formerly Head of Engineering in the South and West Region. The author cannot sufficiently acknowledge the devoted labours of these men who have carried out an enormous amount of research and have also interviewed more than seventy retired and present BBC engineers to obtain first-hand information about the developments in which they were personally engaged.

Thanks are due to Sir Harold Bishop, who kindly undertook to read through the text and has made valuable comments on it. Also to D. E. Todd for much useful information. Finally to Miss Eileen Tasker, who has tirelessly typed the manuscript, deciphered the author's crabbed writings and hesitant tape recordings, and generally organised order out of chaos.

A great deal of the information about the background in which engineering developments took place has been derived from Professor Asa Briggs's monumental work, *The History of Broadcasting in the United Kingdom*, of which the first three volumes had appeared at the time of writing. Acknowledgments are also due to the authors of the many other published works mentioned in the references.

It would be tedious to record here the names of all those who have contributed information and personal reminiscences; thanks are due to all of them. It is, however, permissible to single out four retired Heads of the BBC's Engineering Division. The first was Captain P. P. Eckersley, Chief Engineer from 1923 to 1929, who died in 1963 leaving on record a considerable amount of information in writing and in the form of sound recordings of lectures delivered in the breezy style that is associated with his name. Next, Sir Noel Ashbridge, appointed Chief Engineer in 1929 and later Director of Technical Services until his retirement in 1952; Sir Harold Bishop, appointed Director of Technical Services and later Director of Engineering until he retired in 1963; and Sir Francis McLean, Director of Engineering from 1963 to 1968; all of them consented to be interviewed at length and have allowed many of their papers to be studied. These four distinguished men, and their present successor Mr James Redmond, have left the imprint of their personal styles and of their professional interests on the ethos of the Engineering Division and have borne the responsibility for steering the ship through uncharted and sometimes dangerous waters and for keeping the crew in a state of readiness to meet the challenges recorded in these pages.

We have now reached a milestone, and the function of a milestone is to indicate a quantum of progress and not to provide a permanent resting place. So we cannot avoid speculating on the future. Men of vision are more than ever needed to choose the right road before the relentless machine – with its automatic steering, integrated power supply, constant acceleration, and no reverse gear – chooses it for us.

The Engineering Division of the BBC has created a great and intricate edifice during fifty years of effort; the author alone is responsible for the inadequacy of this presentation of its achievement.

CHAPTER I

The Begi⟋ ⟋ of Broadcasting

CASTING?

⟋en in existence, or at least in embryo, for some years before the
Company was formed in 1922. It is difficult to assign a date to
is impossible to do so without first deciding what broadcasting is.
of the power that broadcasting had, from the start, to catch the
on that it was able to secure for itself almost a monopoly in the use
d a quite different application in established usage.

portmanteau definition of a broadcasting service can be derived
everal of the internationally accepted definitions given in the Radio
68:[1]

g electromagnetic waves of frequencies lower than 3000 GHz, propa-
ce without artificial guide, for transmitting sound, television or other
transmission intended for direct reception by the general public.

ie object of mentioning the frequency limit of 3000 GHz in this definition is to
iclude all frequencies (see table, p. 2) that could conceivably be used for radio communication, but to exclude light and X-rays. (The frequencies of light waves are in
the region of 500,000 GHz, and those of X-rays much higher still.)

The definition gives a fair picture of the mechanism of broadcasting, though only
in terms of transmission and reception and without giving more than a hint of its
purpose. Broadcasting is, in fact, a means of publication, and the BBC has always
regarded itself as a source of entertainment, information and enlightenment available
to all. Since the definition applies to a broadcasting service and not to a broadcasting
system, it omits any clue to the complex operations that precede radio transmission –
the planning and production of the programmes, the operation of the equipment that
converts sound and scene into signals capable of being transmitted by radio, and the
running of all the ancillary services that constitute a broadcasting system.

The technical means of originating the programmes are at least as important as the
means of transmitting and receiving them; they are also more diverse and in some
ways more complicated. They will figure prominently in these pages. Electromagnetic
waves are all very well, but they must be kept in their place. It is the entertainment,
information and enlightenment that matter. In other words, the function of broadcasting is a social one.

Taking this aspect into consideration, a fairly adequate definition of 'broadcasting'
could be derived from the definition of a broadcasting service quoted above, by sub-

TABLE OF FREQUENCY BANDS

Band Number	Frequency Range	Designation	
4	3 to 30 kHz	Very low frequencies (VLF)	Myriametric
5	30 to 300 kHz	Low frequencies (LF)	Kilo...
6	300 to 3000 kHz	Medium frequencies (MF)	Hecto...
7	3 to 30 MHz	High frequencies (HF)	Decam...
8	30 to 300 MHz	Very high frequencies (VHF)	Metric ...
9	300 to 3000 MHz	Ultra high frequencies (UHF)	Decimeti...
10	3 to 30 GHz	Super high frequencies (SHF)	Centimetr...
11	30 to 300 GHz	Extra high frequencies (EHF)	Millimetric
12	300 to 3000 GHz or 3 THz	—	Decimillime...

Note 1
Hz = hertz (cycle per second, c/s)
k = kilo (10^3)
M = mega (10^6)
G = giga (10^9)
T = tera (10^{12})

Note 2
The frequency in kilohertz multiplied ...
wavelength in metres is always equa...
300,000 (the velocity of electromag...
waves in km/s).

Note 3
Low frequencies correspond to 'long waves', medium frequencies to 'medium waves' and high frequencies to 'short waves'.

Note 4
The band numbers mentioned in the table are not to be confused with the numbers of the broadcasting bands, which, in the United Kingdom, are:

Band I (VHF) 41 to 68 MHz Television
Band II (VHF) 87·5 to 100 MHz FM Sound Broadcasting
Band III (VHF) 174 to 216 MHz Television
Band IV (UHF) 470 to 582 MHz Television
Band V (UHF) 614 to 854 MHz Television

stituting the words 'a means of publication' for 'a service' at the beginning. It should be noted that the phrase 'other types of transmission' is all-embracing; it could be taken to include not only special signals (such as time signals) that are commonly regarded as appropriate to broadcasting, but also messages in the Morse code and even telecommand signals, which are not.

However, there are still two major difficulties in adopting this definition. First, what is meant by the 'general public'? Broadcasts are often, quite legitimately, intended for particular sections of the public, such as farmers or motorists. The broadcasting service as a whole is nevertheless intended for anybody who is in possession of an appropriate receiver and is within reach of the broadcast transmissions.

The other difficulty lies in the phrase 'intended for direct reception'. A broadcasting station does not forfeit that title merely because some members of its audience receive its programmes indirectly. They may, for instance, receive them via a community aerial, from which the programmes are distributed to a number of subscribers in a block of flats, or through a distribution system that picks up the programmes from broadcasting stations and distributes them by wire, possibly over a large area, to individual homes. Subscribers to such systems are members of the audience for broadcasting and responsible, as such, for paying any licence fees that may be levied upon users of ordinary radio or television receivers.

The definition in the Radio Regulations implies that the organisation responsible for a broadcasting service is the one that operates the transmitters. This can be misleading. In the United Kingdom, the broadcasting authorities are responsible both for originating the programmes and for operating the transmitters. In some countries these two functions are carried out by different organisations, but it is universally accepted that the broadcasting authority is the one responsible for originating the programmes, whether or not it is also responsible for transmitting them. Thus, the definitions given in the Radio Regulations, though reasonably adequate for distinguishing between a broadcasting service and other services using electromagnetic waves, is far from embracing the whole business of broadcasting. In the words of the statutes of the European Broadcasting Union: 'An organisation shall be deemed to operate a broadcasting service if it produces and has the general responsibility for the programmes broadcast by one or more transmitters permanently at its disposal.'

The implications of this concept are far-reaching. The use of satellites for transmitting programmes directly to the general public may be developed during the 1980s. The responsibility for originating the programmes must still lie with the broadcasting organisations, though a different authority may own and operate the satellites carrying the broadcasting transmitters. Other likely developments in the near future include various systems of distributing television programmes in recorded form to be played back in viewers' homes; several such systems are already coming into use. In sound broadcasting, distribution of gramophone records and magnetic tapes has long been commonplace. The paraphernalia required for producing recordings for distribution to the public is much the same as that required for producing programmes for broadcasting. The line of demarcation between broadcasting and other means of publication may thus become less clear-cut, but broadcasting must at least include the task of producing programmes that are primarily intended for direct reception by the general public by means of electromagnetic waves.

It would be rash, even if it were possible, to combine all these considerations into a single definition that would be universally valid and legally admissible, but perhaps enough has been said to constitute a rough guide to what is meant by 'broadcasting' for the purpose of inquiring into its origin and studying its progress.

The first attempts at broadcasting were naturally in the nature of experiments. This word has two dictionary meanings:[2]

1 'A procedure tried on the chance of success' (i.e. something that is always going wrong).
2 'A procedure tried as a test' (i.e. something done to check that all is well).

To these two meanings, the BBC has added a third. 'This is an experimental transmission' means 'we hope it will work, but please don't grumble if it doesn't.'

The earliest broadcasts were, discounting Morse transmissions and time signals, in the form of telephony. They constituted what was popularly known as 'the wireless' and this term was in common use for many years. It has recently, following American usage, been displaced by 'the radio'. Because people are accustomed to say 'Let's turn on the radio', the BBC has officially adopted the term 'radio' as synonymous with 'sound broadcasting'. We cannot follow this practice (except, perhaps here and there as a sop to Cerberus), because it will often be necessary to use the term 'radio' in its proper sense implying the use of 'electromagnetic waves of frequencies lower than 3000 GHz, propagated in space without artificial guide'. Some of these waves will be carrying sound broadcasting and some television broadcasting.

The term 'signal' also has a special significance. It refers to variations in some physical property that conveys information, for example, the position of a railway signal, the colour of a traffic light, the presence, absence, frequency or phase of an electric current as in telegraphy, the amplitude of a current as in telephony, or the amplitude, frequency or phase of a radio wave as in broadcasting. The signal may be a simple analogue of the original stimulus as in sound broadcasting, or it may result from a process of coding as in colour television. In recent years, methods have been developed for coding both sound and television signals in digital form, though so far digital signals have been confined within the broadcasting network and have not been broadcast.

The distinction between the 'signal' and the 'programme' that it represents may be an academic one to engineers, who frequently use the word 'programme' when referring to the signal. To our legal colleagues the difference is an essentially practical one. For the rights belonging to those who contribute to the creation of the programme, including the broadcasting organisation itself, must attach to the signal throughout all the vicissitudes through which it may pass on its way from the studio to the sitting-room – through wires, processes of recording and reproduction, distribution networks, satellites, transmitters and receivers.

2   EARLY STEPS

The engineering side of broadcasting thus comprises two elements: the origination and processing of signals corresponding to the programme material, and the transmission of those signals by radio for reception by the general public. Both these elements had to be combined before broadcasting became possible. Each of them has a great deal in common with techniques other than broadcasting. The first with telephony, closed-circuit television and sound distribution, and film production; the second with point-to-point radiocommunication (telegraph, telephone, data transmission) and with many other radio services that send messages to all the members of a designated class of recipients wherever they may be within the service areas of the transmitting stations (ships, police cars, taxis, ambulances).

It is only when these two elements are combined that broadcasting emerges. Of the two, the origination and processing of signals is the more complex and nowadays demands the greater part of the operational effort. We should therefore resist the impulse to trace the origin of broadcasting to Leyden jars and spark coils and consider first the development of means for producing signals.

The earliest efforts in this direction were confined to making a distinction between 'ON' and 'OFF'. Usually 'ON' meant 'DANGER!' or at least 'ATTENTION!', and 'OFF' meant 'RELAX!' The message could be conveyed by means of beacon fires, balloons, maroons, or anything else that could be seen or heard over a wide area. Such signals had been important from primitive times, through Homer's beacon fires to Drake's drum and Byron's 'tocsin of the soul – the dinner bell'. The ON/OFF principle was extended to convey more elaborate messages by using a form of coding ranging from smoke signals, drum beats and trumpet calls, to the Morse code and autotelegraphy.

The two great steps forward that made broadcasting possible were the production of an electrical analogue of a sound wave (the basis of the telephone) and the invention of the three-electrode valve (the key to amplification and oscillation). Both these discoveries were the culmination of a long series of inventive acts in the domains of electromagnetism and electronics respectively. The first can be traced through the work of the great unitary eponyms, Gilbert, Ohm, Ampère, Volta, Oersted, Henry, and Faraday, to the practical realisation of the telephone by Alexander Graham Bell, a Scottish immigrant to the USA in 1876. (Elisha Gray filed a notice making his own claim to the first telephone later on the same day as Bell filed his patent application.)[3]

In Graham Bell's original telephone, the 'transmitter' and 'receiver' were almost identical, both depending on electromagnetic induction. The transmitter had a diaphragm vibrating in sympathy with the sound waves and mechanically connected to a reed placed over one pole of an electromagnet. The currents induced in the coil were conducted to a similar coil in the receiver, where the resulting variations in magnetisation vibrated another reed connected to a diaphragm, the movements of which produced sound waves in the surrounding air. In the more practical forms of telephone developed shortly afterwards, notably by Edison in 1879, the transmitter, instead of generating an oscillatory current, produced oscillatory variations in the current provided by a battery by varying the resistance of carbon granules under varying pressure from the diaphragm. The receiver was improved later by using an iron diaphragm instead of a reed and a permanent magnet instead of an electromagnet. (The use of a magnet rather than an unmagnetised core increased the sensitivity at the expense of linearity.) These principles were applied many years later to microphones and loudspeakers for broadcasting and it was not until amplifiers became readily available that other forms of transducer (moving-coil, electrostatic and piezo-electric) could be generally adopted, so as to give greater fidelity, but with lower electro-mechanical efficiency.

The second of the fundamental discoveries was Fleming's diode of 1904, the potentialities of which were greatly increased by the addition of a third electrode in Lee de Forest's 'Audion' in 1906.

These inventions made it possible to transmit the sound of the human voice over long distances in the form of electric currents propagated along wires. As long ago as 1894 the possibilities of this form of communication were extended to the distribution of entertainment by the Electrophone Company of London. Musical performances, lectures, and church services were disseminated to subscribers in this way.[4] Even before this, transmissions from theatres and concert halls had been transmitted over telephone wires to an exhibition at the Crystal Palace. The Electrophone was not a great success, but it continued to operate for many years and the remains of the equipment were still to be seen in telephone exchanges as late as 1926.

The development of telephone communication over long distances led to the building up of a body of knowledge on the fundamental problems of communication through the study of the effects of noise and bandwidth, and the theory of transmission lines. These researches were later extended to embrace the fundamentals of broadcasting technology.

By the time it became possible to transmit signals by radio, signals corresponding to speech and music were already available—though still crude and distorted. At the receiving end, the telephone receiver, later enlarged into a loudspeaker, provided the means of reconstituting sounds corresponding roughly to those presented to the microphone at the transmitting end.

The possibility of conveying messages over a distance without wires emerged from a series of experiments starting with the discoveries of Hughes and Hertz. In 1879 Hughes produced electric sparks in his house at 40 Langham Street, London, near where Broadcasting House now stands, and detected them at distances up to 450 m, while walking up and down Great Portland Street, by means of a microphonic contact and a telephone earpiece.[5] The pundits of that time refused to accept that the effect was produced by 'aerial electric waves' and so Hughes's discovery remained unpublished until after Hertz had conclusively proved, in 1887, that electromagnetic waves at frequencies below those of light could be detected at a distance. He used an induction coil to produce sparks across a gap between two metal balls. At the receiving end, a few metres away, sparks appeared across a gap introduced into a metal loop. Hertz thus verified the existence of electromagnetic waves, of which Clerk-Maxwell had postulated the existence by mathematical reasoning in 1862. Hertz explained their properties and the differences between light and electricity in a lecture at Heidelberg in September 1889.[6] He himself said that his discovery could not be used for a practical purpose. At a meeting of the British Association in 1894 Sir Oliver Lodge demonstrated actual radiotelegraphy over a distance of 55 m, using Hertz's oscillator in conjunction with a receiver containing a Branly coherer. Because of his academic duties, Lodge failed to follow up this experiment and, like Hertz, he apparently thought that there was no future for radiocommunication because its range would be limited to a few hundred metres. (Fortunately, later experimenters were not deterred by these gloomy prognostications.)

Thus, before the end of the nineteenth century, many of the elements necessary for radiocommunication were available. Electromagnetic waves at what are now known as radio frequencies could be produced and could be detected at a distance of a few metres. It was already appreciated that this involved a mode of propagation different from the previously known electrical processes of conduction, electromagnetic induction and electrostatic induction. Means of producing both telegraphic and telephone signals were available. A detector, the coherer, which could at least respond to telegraphic signals was known. Three major problems remained to be solved before radiocommunication became of practical use:

1 The range had to be greatly increased. The use of high aerials and subsequently of amplifiers overcame this limitation.
2 Means had to be found to distinguish a wanted signal from all others that might be present at the receiver. This problem was solved by the invention of tuning, which provided a means of discriminating between signals carried by waves at different frequencies and also helped to discriminate against atmospheric noise.
3 Methods of modulation had to be developed to enable electromagnetic waves to carry signals more complex than telegraphic signals confined to the ON/OFF principle.

The first major step in solving these problems was taken by Marconi, an Italian whose mother was Irish; at the age of twenty he determined to put the earlier discoveries to practical use. His idea of using elevated aerials followed earlier experiments in the detection of thunderstorms by Mahlon Loomis in the USA in 1872, by Popov in Russia, and by Marconi himself during the closing years of the nineteenth century. The use of an aerial in conjunction with an earth connection at both the transmitter and the receiver greatly increased the range, and a rough approximation to tuning was achieved by making the transmitting and receiving aerials of similar dimensions. In this way, and by refinements in apparatus, Marconi had increased the range to $1\frac{1}{2}$ miles by 1894.

In the succeeding years Marconi used bigger and better aerials, with transmitters of higher power, to such remarkable effect that within seven years the range had been increased by three orders of magnitude. In 1901 he and the group of pioneers that he had gathered round him (notably G. S. Kemp who had been deputed by Sir William Preece, Engineer-in-Chief of the Post Office, to co-operate with Marconi) succeeded in bridging the Atlantic using Morse transmissions on a frequency of about 300 kHz, or perhaps somewhat lower.[7]

Marconi's persistence quickly led to the use of wireless telegraphy for communication with ships at sea. This was an extremely important application, because there was no other means of communicating over long distances with ships or, indeed, with vehicles in motion. It is interesting to note that although communication with ships usually demanded omnidirectional or at least wide-beam aerials, and therefore tended to favour developments that would later find their place in broadcasting, the military applications of radio that were soon to be developed demanded secrecy and hence the use of narrow beams – the reverse of what would be needed for broadcasting.

Marconi's experiments in England were paralleled by others undertaken by Prof. Adolf Slaby of Berlin, who had witnessed one of Marconi's demonstrations in 1897, and by Count Arco. Slaby gave full credit to Marconi for his discovery (which had been the subject of the first patent application for wireless telegraphy in June 1896), but he introduced some ideas of his own – including a receiving aerial arrangement that permitted the detector to be connected at an antinode of potential.[8] He soon succeeded in sending telegrams over a distance of 13 miles and in 1897 he already considered that 'wireless communication was fit for ordinary use', and would be especially important for military purposes.[9]

The experiments of Hertz must have produced waves at very high frequencies, but the practical application of radiocommunication started with the use of frequencies in the region of hundreds of kilohertz. (The first wave-meter did not appear until J. A. Fleming's cymometer of 1905.) Knowledge of propagation was greatly stimulated by the early experiments in transatlantic transmission. Their success appeared to be contrary to scientific theory, which assumed that radio waves being similar in essence to those of light would behave in a similar way and would travel in straight lines. It was only much later that the refractive properties of the ionosphere, which accounted for the possibility of transatlantic transmission, were discovered.

Sir Oliver Lodge drew attention to the importance of tuning and followed up his early experiments with 'syntonic jars' by patenting a tuned circuit in 1897. The practical application of this principle was made by Marconi in 1898 when he devised a transformer tuned by a fixed capacitor to couple the oscillator to the aerial circuit; a similar arrangement was used at the receiving end. More elaborate tuners using coupled circuits were developed by C. S. Franklin in 1907.

The spark transmissions that were used in the early days of radiotelegraphy and continued into the 1920s had the very serious defect that, being in the form of damped oscillations, they covered a wide band of frequencies, so that reception was extremely unselective, and much power was wasted. It was to overcome this defect that high-frequency alternators were developed, to produce continuous waves, though only at low radio-frequencies. Another approach resulted from the discovery by Duddell in 1900 that a carbon arc was capable of sustaining continuous oscillations, when shunted by a tuned circuit, by virtue of the negative slope of its current/voltage characteristic. The principle was applied to the production of rf oscillations by Poulsen in 1902 and the idea was followed up by Marconi. The production of continuous oscillations enabled telegraph transmissions to be confined to a narrow band and thus permitted a tuned receiver to accept any one of a number of transmissions in the same part of the radio-frequency spectrum.

The production of continuous waves afforded another possibility, which constituted an essential step towards radiotelephony and hence towards broadcasting. So long as radio transmissions were confined to telegraphy, there was no difficulty in modulating the radio-frequency output of a transmitter to enable it to carry the signal; it was merely necessary to interrupt the oscillations to produce the required signal. Telephone transmission required a more sophisticated approach for which the production of continuous waves was essential. If a continuous oscillation at radio frequency could be varied in amplitude in sympathy with an audio-frequency signal, radiotelephony would be possible.

In 1900 A. S. Popov of Russia communicated to an international congress in Paris a description of a method of radiotelephony using damped waves in conjunction with a coherer. He had operated from February to April of that year a radio link between the islands of Kuutsalo, near Kotka, and Suusaaren (Hogland) on a wavelength of 260 m.[10] In the same year Prof. R. H. Fessenden, a Canadian working in the USA, attempted radio transmission of speech by modulating a stream of sparks. The results were poor, but in 1903 he did better with a modulated arc, transmitting speech over a distance of about 20 km. In 1905 Ernst Ruhmer established two-way telephony over a distance of 15 km using a modulated light beam; this does not come within the definition of radio, but in 1906 the same experimenter demonstrated radiotelephony over a distance of 30 m to an international conference on radiotelegraphy in Berlin, using a microphone to modulate a continuous wave, produced by an arc, with speech and music. In 1906 also, Fessenden achieved considerable success with a high-frequency alternator with an output of $0 \cdot 5$ kW. He played gramophone records to listening ships' operators up to 80 km distant. In 1908 R.-B. Goldschmidt collaborated with Ruhmer and Maurice Philippson in a series of transmissions from the Palais de Justice in Brussels using a modulated arc for telephony on a wavelength of 1750 m. The transmissions were received in Liège at a distance of 110 km and aroused considerable interest. (This information comes from an unpublished paper by G. Gourski, Honorary Director-General of Technical Services, RTB/BRT.)

In this country H. J. Round demonstrated radiotelephony in 1908, using a modulated arc. In 1908, also, Slaby and Arco transmitted a Caruso record by radio in Berlin and in 1910 Lee de Forest 'broadcast' the same famous voice – live this time – to fifty amateurs in New York.[11] Neither the alternator nor the arc was really satisfactory for transmitting speech and music; moreover, it seems unlikely that the principles of modulation and the production of sidebands had been established at that time.

An interesting proposal for a public-address system was made by Father Lucas, S.J., of the Scientific Society of Brussels in 1902. He suggested that a singing arc could be modulated by means of a carbon microphone and that the arc lamps used for street lighting could thus take the place of the town-crier. (Visitors to BBC stations have sometimes been entertained by disembodied voices speaking from the sky, when an accidental arc on an aerial feeder was modulated by the programme.)

Although, in the first decade of the century, wireless transmissions were mostly in the form of telegraphy, it soon became apparent that the use of the medium would have to be regulated. The Berlin Conference of 1906 made provisions to avoid interference between stations and to safeguard distress calls, and also to ensure that installations on ships and on shore would be compatible with each other. It was evident that governments would have to take powers to enable them to control wireless transmissions in their own countries and the first Wireless Telegraphy Act had already been passed by the legislature in the United Kingdom in 1904.

Although Lee de Forest's triode valve proved to be a sensitive detector, it was not until 1912 that the inventor appreciated and exploited its possibilities as an amplifier. It could also be used to produce continuous oscillations at radio frequency; this discovery was made by A. Meissner in Germany in 1913 and almost simultaneously by Armstrong in the USA and by C. S. Franklin and H. J. Round in the United Kingdom. It was soon found that the oscillations produced in this way could be modulated at audio frequencies; one method of doing this was to apply the audio-frequency input to a choke in the anode circuit of the valve, so as to vary the anode voltage in sympathy with the modulation and thus to vary the amplitude of the radio-frequency output similarly.

Another important advantage of the triode oscillator was that the frequency could be kept reasonably constant, and later developments enabled a very high standard of frequency stability and accuracy to be attained.

At the receiving end, the coherer, the magnetic detector and the electrolytic detector gave place to the crystal detector (based on a series of discoveries leading to the carborundum detector, invented by General Dunwoodie of the US Army in 1906), to the diode rectifier and then to the triode valve, which could be used simultaneously as a rectifier and as an amplifier. The triode greatly increased the sensitivity and the selectivity of receivers. The rectified output derived from the anode circuit could be applied directly to a telephone headset after the radio-frequency components had been filtered out.

Once the problem of producing continuous waves and of modulating them with a telephone signal had been solved, a great deal of study was given to the process of modulation and to the inverse process of detection. The way in which sidebands were produced in the process of modulation and the way in which the original audio-frequency signal could be recovered by rectification were soon established.

The stage was now set for the development of radiotelephony, which pointed the way to broadcasting. In 1913 H. J. Round again demonstrated radiotelephony, this time using valve circuits. By the outbreak of the First World War it was thus possible to use valves in conjunction with continuously-tuned circuits in both the transmitter and the receiver for telephone communication. Developments were accelerated by the military demands of the war, particularly for ground-to-air communication with military aircraft and for the control of armoured fighting vehicles from the air. Among the engineers engaged on these developments were H. J. Round himself, P. P. Eckersley and R. T. B. Wynn,[12] all of whom were at that time in the Marconi Company and later became well known in the broadcasting field. N. Ashbridge was in the Royal Engineers in France working on radiocommunications for the army; he later transferred to research work and then joined H. L. Kirke (also of the Royal Engineers) in Marconi's.

Speech was first transmitted across the Atlantic in 1915 by the American Telephone & Telegraph Company in conjunction with the International Western Electric Company from a transmitter at Arlington, which is said to have used over three hundred valves, to the Eiffel Tower in Paris. After the First World War the knowledge and experience gained in the development of wireless telephony for military purposes was soon applied to peace-time uses. The first telephony transmission across the Atlantic in the east-west direction was made by H. J. Round in 1919 using a transmitter of 2·5 kW input power at Ballybunion in Ireland on a frequency of

79 kHz (3800 m). W. T. Ditcham of the Marconi Company, who spoke on that occasion, was the first European whose voice was heard by wireless telephony on the other side of the Atlantic.[13]

One of the first to visualise the potentialities of broadcasting was David Sarnoff (1891–1971) who in 1916, while employed by the American Marconi Company, foresaw the need to establish broadcasting stations and to make radio sets for home use. (This was the first of the many ambitious targets that he set himself – including the development of the gramophone, television, colour television and satellite communication. He made major contributions to all of these during his long career, for thirty-seven years of which he was president of the Radio Corporation of America. He also formed the National Broadcasting Corporation, the first of the American networks, in 1926.)

Developments in circuitry, in valve design and in aerials led to the setting up of an experimental telephony transmitter of 6 kW input power by the Marconi Company at Chelmsford using an aerial suspended between two 450-ft masts. This transmitter was replaced early in 1920 by one of 15 kW input power and this was used for a series of range trials. Reports of satisfactory reception were received from various places in the United Kingdom and also from as far away as Rome and Madrid. The first regular wireless telephone news service started on 23 February 1920, using this transmitter operating on a frequency of 107 kHz (2800 m).

During this period a number of improvements were made in receivers. In 1902 Fessenden had already proposed that a local oscillator could be used to produce a beat note at an audible frequency. The superheterodyne principle, using a local radio-frequency oscillator to heterodyne the incoming radio frequency so as to convert it to a lower frequency at which more efficient amplification and tuning could be used, was described by Armstrong in 1919. The use of positive feedback, or 'reaction', to increase the amplification had been introduced in 1913, and patented by H. J. Round.

A series of improvements in receiving valves quickly followed:

the improvement in stability brought about by using 'hard' vacuum, as in the 'R' valve (1915);

the reduction of inter-electrode capacitance, by bringing out the leads at different points in the envelope (the French horned valve and the Marconi 'Q' valve of 1916);

the use of dull-emitter filaments (Western Electric Company, 1918).[14]

The use of valves in receivers made it possible to employ loudspeakers. One of the first practicable types was the Brown loudspeaker of 1920, which had a conical metal diaphragm connected to an electromagnetically operated reed; it was produced by S. G. Brown, whose headphones were already well-known. Horn loudspeakers followed in 1920–3.

Thus, by the time the BBC* was formed in 1922, valve receivers with loudspeakers were already available to the public, although the majority of listeners at that time still had crystal sets with headphones. By this time also, transmitting valves able to

* The letters 'BBC' will be used indiscriminately for the British Broadcasting Company and the British Broadcasting Corporation, where there is no risk of ambiguity.

11

handle fairly high power had been developed. The use of glass bulbs limited the power rating to about 500 W, because of the problem of heat dissipation. One of the pioneers of transmitting valves in the United Kingdom was Stanley Mullard; he developed valves with silicon envelopes, which were the first products of the company he founded in 1920.[15] They were made for the Admiralty and were also used in a transmitter built by the Radio Communication Company which subsequently became the BBC station in Manchester. However, air-cooled glass valves were commonly used until the next major development was introduced by Marconi's in the mid-1920s. Improved means of sealing metal to glass then made it possible to use the copper anode itself as part of the envelope, so making it accessible to liquid coolants and avoiding losses caused by impurities in the glass. There followed the series of CAT (cooled-anode transmitting) valves that were subsequently widely used in BBC stations.

It is neither necessary nor appropriate to give further details of these basic developments in radiocommunication here. They have been fully explored elsewhere[16, 17-20] and this book is concerned with *BBC* Engineering, which did not come into existence until 1922.

3 THE FIRST BROADCASTS

The telegraphy transmissions to ships at sea, which developed rapidly from 1900 onwards, and the telephony transmissions mentioned in the last section could be received by anybody within range who possessed a suitable receiving installation, but they cannot properly be described as broadcasts. This term could, with more justification, be applied to the time signals that were regularly transmitted from the Eiffel Tower, starting in 1909; they contributed to the formation of a 'radio public', not only in France but also in neighbouring countries. This fact, together with the enthusiasm of Belgian amateurs, encouraged the start of the regular programmes of music that were transmitted from the grounds of the Royal Castle at Laeken in Belgium every Saturday afternoon from 28 March 1914. These transmissions have a strong claim to priority in the broadcasting field;[21] they continued until the transmitter was demolished before German troops entered Brussels in 1914.

The birth of broadcasting in Germany is held to date from May 1917 when Hans Bredov transmitted music and talks to the troops on the Western Front.[22]

On 6 November 1919 regular broadcasts started from station PCGG in Holland. These transmissions were made by H. H. S. à S. Idzerda, founder of the company 'Netherlands Radio Industry'. He had grasped the importance of the triode valve and in 1917 had persuaded the Philips Company to manufacture one to his own design. The broadcasts from PCGG on Sunday evenings followed a regular schedule and were advertised in advance. Many listeners in the United Kingdom became familiar with them as the 'Hague Concerts'. In 1921 the *Wireless World* appealed to listeners in this country for funds to help the station to carry on, and later the *Daily Mail* paid for the English-language broadcasts for a whole year.[23]

In the USA Dr Frank Conrad established a broadcasting station in Pittsburgh (KDKA), which was licensed on 27 October 1920; on 2 November it broadcast the results of the US Presidential Election. In that year the transmitter at Königswusterhausen in Germany was making daily transmissions of speech, and occasionally of music, on long waves.

In Russia Lenin had made an announcement about the success of the Bolshevik Revolution in 1917, using a radio transmitter in the cruiser *Aurora*, but regular broadcasting did not start in the USSR until 1924.[24]

In the United Kingdom interest in the transmission of music as well as speech was no doubt stimulated by the success of the Hague Concerts. On 15 June 1920 there took place the famous recital of songs by Dame Nellie Melba from the Marconi transmitter at Chelmsford under the sponsorship of the *Daily Mail*. Reception reports were received from many European countries and even from Persia and Newfoundland. This programme was announced in advance in the Press and was thus the first advertised programme to be broadcast in this country.[25]

On 20 July 1920 the SS *Victorian* sailed for Canada with delegates to the Ottawa Imperial Press Conference on board. One of the main subjects for discussion at this Conference was to be wireless communication and, as a practical demonstration of its possibilities, a programme of speech and musical items was transmitted from a long-wave telephone transmitter at Chelmsford on a frequency of 107 kHz (2800 m) and also from a 6-kW long-wave transmitter at Poldhu, Cornwall, on the same frequency. The ship was fitted with a 3-kW telephony transmitter and while the vessel was within range of Poldhu the delegates were able to conduct wireless telephone conversations with the shore station. Each evening, while on passage, the *Victorian* broadcast short gramophone concerts for the benefit of listeners in other ships in the vicinity.[26]

The transmissions from Chelmsford were made under a general licence from the Postmaster-General, which permitted the Marconi Company to 'conduct experimental wireless telephony transmission'. It was hoped that these transmissions would convince foreign countries of British knowledge and skill in this field in view of the interest being shown by American manufacturers at that time in the world market for wireless receivers. However, many complaints were made that the experimental transmissions were causing interference to aircraft and other communications and the licence was withdrawn on 23 November 1920.

Interest in broadcasting was fostered by the activities of radio amateurs. They had been working in several countries before the beginning of the First World War, when their activities were suppressed for reasons of national security. They resumed soon after the war and by March 1921, 150 amateur transmitting licences had been issued by the UK Post Office for stations up to 10 W in power. One of these amateurs used a transmitter mounted in a lorry to report the result of the Derby in 1921, and this was probably in a sense the first outside broadcast.[27]

After the withdrawal of the licence for the Marconi Company's test transmissions the Wireless Society of London (later to become the Radio Society of Great Britain) convened two conferences of wireless societies and the members agreed to support an application by the Marconi Company for a licence to transmit 'special calibration signals'.[28] This application was approved by the Post Office, but permission to broadcast telephony was still refused. In December 1921 a petition was drawn up by representatives of sixty-three wireless societies calling for a resumption of telephony test transmissions to 'serve the scientific purpose of improving the receiving arrangements'. This petition was presented to the Postmaster General and eventually resulted in the Marconi Company being authorised, on 13 February 1922, to include 15 minutes of telephony in the weekly half-hour test transmissions.

Meanwhile, the Marconi Company had formed a Department under R. D. Bangay called 'Field & Air', to meet the demands that could be foreseen for airborne wireless telephony as civil aviation developed. A part of this department was established at Writtle, near Chelmsford, the staff of which included a group of engineers all of whom were destined to make important contributions to broadcasting engineering in later years. The group included P. P. Eckersley, N. Ashbridge, R. T. B. Wynn, H. L. Kirke, and B. N. MacLarty, all of whom later became prominent in the BBC. They were instructed to build a transmitter to make weekly test transmissions in accordance with the licence issued by the Postmaster General. The equipment was assembled and tested during a single weekend. Members of the group regarded the transmissions as being of purely technical interest and admit that they did not foresee that broadcasting in this country would grow from this small beginning to the status and importance that it subsequently achieved.

The first of these transmissions from Writtle was made during the evening of 14 February 1922 using a power of 250 W and the call-sign 2MT ('Two Emma Toc' in signaller's phonetic language), which soon became widely known. The transmitter used a circuit similar to that of the telephony transmitters then built, and had a four-wire aerial about 200 ft long, supported by 110-ft masts. The carrier frequency used at first was 430 kHz (700 m), but this was soon changed to 750 kHz (400 m) to avoid interference from one of the many harmonics radiated by the arc transmitters at the Post Office station at Leafield, near Oxford.

2MT broadcast a programme of entertainment every Tuesday evening. P. P. Eckersley acted as compère for these transmissions and pioneered spontaneous microphone humour to great effect. (With or without a microphone, he was responsible for several dicta that have survived, e.g. 'It is more blessed to transmit than to receive', 'To "er" is human, to forgive divine'.) Letters of appreciation flooded in, and quite ambitious items were introduced into the programme. For example, one programme included the balcony scene from *Cyrano de Bergerac* in which Eckersley played Christian and Eileen Travers played Roxane. This was probably the first radio play to be broadcast. These transmissions continued from Writtle until they were closed down on 17 January 1923, to the regret of a wide circle of enthusiastic listeners.

Shortly after the Writtle transmitter began operating, with Eckersley and Ashbridge in charge, the Marconi Company received another permit, for an experimental station of 100-W power and call-sign 2LO to be located at Marconi House, London. This permit was for the transmission of speech only, between 11 am and noon, and between 2 pm and 5 pm daily. The station started operating on 11 May

1922, and after a while the broadcasting of musical items was permitted and the power limitation was increased to 1½ kW. Demonstration tests were later added to the public transmissions, but these were not advertised. They were timed and arranged for specific audiences at institutions, hospitals, wireless society meetings, private garden parties, and so on, at which the receiving apparatus was installed and operated by engineers of the Marconi Company. Each transmission was prearranged and was the subject of special Post Office authorisation. The station staff included H. Bishop (later Sir Harold Bishop, Director of Engineering of the BBC).

Capt. Round claimed to have designed the first 2LO transmitter and Franklin to have made it work. Eddy currents were a problem, and were reduced by sawing through the metal panelling at various points. The main oscillating valve was a Marconi-Osram MT2 and there was a modulator and sub-modulator. The dc mains supply from the Charing Cross power station was converted to ac and stepped up by a transformer to feed a full-wave valve rectifier with smoothing chokes and capacitors. The aerial consisted of two cages, each of four wires, supported by 50-ft masts on the roof of Marconi House about 100 ft apart. The lead roof and the steel framework of the building were bonded to the lightning conductors to provide the earth connection.

The frequency of 2LO was 840 kHz (360 m) and the authorisation included a requirement that the station should close down for three minutes at the end of each seven minutes of transmission to enable the 'operator' to listen on the working frequency for official messages ordering the transmission to cease 'for any reason'. No such messages were received and this requirement, which no doubt stemmed from the 'Silence Period' of marine operating practice, could well join the 'Red Flag' rule imposed on certain road users in an archive of restrictive practices.

Some of the evening programmes from 2LO were announced editorially in the Press, but mention of Marconi House was not allowed. Listeners registered with the Marconi Company were sent postcards notifying them of forthcoming programmes.

The content of the 2LO programmes was in striking contrast to that of the light-hearted Writtle performances and it must have been somewhat galling for the 2LO staff to receive requests to close down during the Writtle Tuesday-evening transmissions so that listeners to that station might hear their preferred programme, which by then was tending to satirise the slightly self-conscious sobriety of its London rival.[29] However, 2LO was not lacking in enterprise. In 1922 at least three outside broadcasts were made: a running commentary on the Lewis/Carpentier fight from Olympia, reports on the King's Cup Air Race, and a speech by the Prince of Wales from York House to Boy Scouts on the occasion of their rally at Alexandra Palace.

At first the studio was in the same room as the transmitter on the top floor of Marconi House. Heavy drapes constituted the acoustic treatment and the microphone had to be carefully placed in relation to the performer to avoid under-modulating or over-modulating the transmitter. (The word 'studio' was used from the beginning and has since been universally adopted in English-speaking countries and in many others. Those who performed before the microphone were known as 'artists';

15

people who preferred the Gallic form 'artistes' fought a rear-guard action for many years, but 'artists' was the official BBC term.)

Public relations were already seen to be important, because the broadcasts had to be brought to the attention of the public. This aspect was handled by A. R. Burrows, later to become 'Uncle Arthur' of the Children's Hour.

Although the Marconi Company was responsible for 2MT at Writtle and 2LO in London, it did not by any means have a monopoly of broadcasting in the United Kingdom. In 1922 Metropolitan Vickers in Manchester and the Western Electric Company in London were also active.

The Metropolitan Vickers Research Department under A. P. M. Fleming (later Sir Arthur Fleming) was located at Trafford Park, Manchester, and was conducting experiments in wireless telephony. In 1921 Fleming had visited the United States and inspected broadcasting stations in Detroit and Pittsburgh, and also factories turning out cheap radio receivers. On his return he set up an experimental transmitter (2ZY) of 50 W power in his Company's Research Department, and also a smaller transmitting and receiving station at his home at Hale, some six miles away. Successful tests were made and on 30 March 1922 Metropolitan Vickers applied to the Post Office for authorisation for a 3-kW transmitter at Trafford Park, and for a similar one at Slough, Bucks. It was proposed that these transmitters should broadcast afternoon and evening programmes for reception by the general public.

This application was, however, joined by twenty-one others between March and May 1922 and to all of them the Post Office gave a refusal on the grounds that 'the ether was already full'. The Metropolitan Vickers application was treated as one of a group of similar applications during the negotiations between manufacturers and the Post Office leading up to the formation of the British Broadcasting Company.[30]

Regular experimental transmissions from the Trafford Park station continued from 16 May 1922 until the station was taken over by the BBC on 15 November 1922, by which time the transmitter had been replaced by a 700-W transmitter built by the Radio Communication Company (the power of which was subsequently increased to $1\frac{1}{2}$ kW). The station had its own studio, and during this period many experiments were carried out to improve the performance of microphones and microphone techniques. Work was also done on the improvement of studio design and on methods of balance and control.

The other large concern to be engaged in early broadcasting in this country was the Western Electric Company. In October 1922 this Company built a 500-W transmitter (2WP) in its London laboratories. It also had an associated studio, which was particularly well-equipped to broadcast music, as it used an improved type of microphone with a better frequency response than the usual carbon-granule types of that time. Before much experimental work was done by Western Electric with this transmitter, it was transferred – by steam lorry – to the General Electric Company's works at Birmingham, where it operated with the call-sign 5IT on being taken over by the BBC on 15 November 1922. F. C. McLean (later Sir Francis McLean), who later became the fourth of the pioneers to direct the Engineering Division of the BBC, worked at the Birmingham station while with the Western Electric Company.

CHAPTER II

The British Broadcasting Company: 1922–6

I   THE COMPANY

In several ways the year 1922 was a favourable one for the start of a new era in broadcasting. The pioneers whose work has been touched upon in the previous chapter were still full of enthusiasm and those who had seen active service in the 1914–18 war had returned to civilian life with a mixture of relief and bewilderment and with a lighthearted camaraderie, which helped to establish the team-work that was essential to the development of a new technology. Among the public also there was great enthusiasm for scientific discoveries and their application. Inquiring minds and eager hands were ready to grapple with new ideas and make them work. In the new science of telecommunication they found a particularly fertile field. Many schools were encouraging interest in science, and the most popular hobbies were those requiring the use of induction coils, capacitors, rectifiers, and other heralds of the electronic age.

Interest in these things was fostered by a number of popular periodicals dealing with radio as a hobby. The first issue of *Wireless World*, then called *The Marconigraph*, had appeared in April 1911; its ownership was transferred from the Marconi Company to Iliffe & Sons in 1924 and it is now published by IPC Electrical-Electronic Press. Other magazines for the home constructor were *Modern Wireless* (with P. P. Eckersley as Radio Consultant), started in 1923, *Wireless Weekly* (1923), *The Wireless Constructor, Amateur Wireless, Popular Wireless* and later, *Practical Wireless*. The first three of these were published by the Radio Press; its proprietor was John Scott-Taggart, well known, among many accomplishments, for his receiver designs and textbooks. *Experimental Wireless*, which started publication in 1923, had Prof. G. W. O. Howe as technical editor and, for many years, Hugh S. Pocock as editor – he was also editor of *Wireless World* from 1920–41. The editor of *Experimental Wireless* (then called *Wireless Engineer*) from 1946 was W. T. Cocking (later editor-in-chief of that journal and of *Wireless World*). For many years the editorials by Prof. Howe lucidly expounded the fundamental principles of electronics, and contributed greatly to the understanding of those who were grappling with the subject. This periodical continued to flourish under various names and in October 1962 it was incorporated in *Industrial Electronics*, which finally ceased publication in 1969. Some of these magazines catered for 'do-it-yourself' enthusiasts; some were directed also to the professional engineer. They all helped to encourage those who wanted to know how 'the wireless' worked, to make the most of the equipment and components that were available and to appreciate the results.

At the beginning of the 1920s shops sprang up which found a ready market for thousands of stampings and washers for making variable capacitors, as well as wire, insulating sleeving, headphones, and other components for building receivers. Most receivers at this time were crystal sets with headphones, but valve receivers were beginning to come into use and loudspeakers were being advertised as early as November 1922. Valves had the disadvantage that cumbersome accumulators were needed for the filament supply and dry batteries for the ht supply, but their use greatly increased the interest that listeners and experimenters could get from their sets, because the greatly improved sensitivity and selectivity of the receivers enabled foreign stations, as well as those in the same country, to be received. (A number of broadcasting stations had by this time opened in other countries and by the middle of 1922 there were already over two hundred registered stations in the USA.)

Publication of the BBC's own programme journal, the *Radio Times*, was started by the Company in 1923. Interest in the reception of foreign programmes led to the publication of a supplement devoted to them, which started in July 1925 and a year later changed its name to *World Radio*.[1] Details of foreign broadcasts were obtained from broadcasting organisations abroad in exchange for advance information about BBC programmes. *World Radio* was naturally unpopular with other radio magazines, especially when it started to include technical articles. As a result of their objections the BBC agreed to discontinue the publication of articles concerned with home construction of receivers, but continued to include descriptions of equipment developed by the BBC (many of which have provided material for this book) until publication ceased with the issue of 1 September 1939.

The excitement lay in the ability to pick signals out of the air and to hear speech and music. This was an achievement in its own right, quite apart from any entertainment value that the programmes might have. In this atmosphere broadcasting grew up as a source of wonder rather than of 'entertainment, information and enlightenment'. It was clear, however, that to achieve a lasting impact on the public at large, it would need two things: programmes and money. Hence it had to be organised and all kinds of artists, administrators and businessmen became involved in its progress.

The slump of 1929 had not yet arrived to dampen enthusiasm for new ventures, and the prevailing mood was one of optimism and enterprise. A group of manufacturers interested in both what is now called the capital goods side of the radio industry and the production of receivers entered into discussions that led to the formation of the British Broadcasting Company. The course of the negotiations is fully described by Asa Briggs.[2]

On 4 May 1922 the Postmaster General made a statement on broadcasting in the House of Commons, in which he proposed, *inter alia*, that Great Britain should be divided for broadcasting purposes into eight areas, each to be served by one or more broadcasting stations sited within that area. The eight areas were to have as their centres London, Cardiff, Plymouth (later changed to Bournemouth), Birmingham, Manchester, Newcastle, Glasgow or Edinburgh, and Aberdeen. The output power of each station was not to exceed $1\frac{1}{2}$ kW and the hours of transmission were to be restricted to 1700 to 2300 hours on weekdays, but with no restriction on Sundays.

On 18 May 1922 a conference was held at the GPO London attended by twenty-eight representatives of companies interested in broadcasting, at which the Post Office outlined their proposals and asked the representatives to go away and agree amongst themselves on the formation of one or more organisations to give effect to the proposals. A meeting of manufacturers was accordingly held at the Institution of Electrical Engineers on 23 May 1922 under the Chairmanship of the then President of the Institution, Sir Frank Gill. Negotiations between the various manufacturers and the Post Office continued largely on financial matters and on patent rights, most of the receiver patents being owned by Marconi's. A further meeting was held at the IEE on 18 October 1922, at which it was decided to form a single company to be responsible for broadcasting.

The choice of venue for these meetings was significant, for the IEE itself has played an important role in the development of broadcasting and there has been a continuous relationship between the Institution and the BBC arising from their common interest in the field of electrical engineering. This relationship was further cemented by the fact that from April 1923 the BBC's London offices and studios were housed in a part of the IEE building at No. 2 Savoy Hill. These premises remained the headquarters of the Company and later of the Corporation, until Broadcasting House was opened in 1932. The Institution was careful to retain the right to close down the BBC programme if it interfered with the use of the nearby lecture theatre. This power does not appear to have been exercised and indeed the BBC maintained friendly and fruitful relations with the IEE, which have subsisted over fifty years.

The British Broadcasting Company started regular broadcasting on 14 November 1922, though it was not registered until 15 December 1922 and did not receive a formal licence from the Post Office until 18 January 1923. Such a licence was necessary, because the Post Office was authorised to regulate radio transmissions under the Wireless Telegraphy Act of 1904. (The first recorded prosecution for operating an unlicensed radio transmitter was on 27 August 1924.)[3]

The first Chairman of the Company was Lord Gainford and there were eight Directors representing firms, large and small, that were '*bona fide* manufacturers of wireless apparatus'. The formation of the Company was very much a co-operative venture. The 'Big Six' companies, which put up £60,000 of the total authorised capital of £100,000 and guaranteed to finance a broadcasting service for a period of two years,[4] were the Marconi Company, the Metropolitan Vickers Company, the Western Electric Company, the Radio Communication Company, the General Electric Company, and the British Thomson-Houston Company. A number of smaller firms, receiver manufacturers and retailers, also took part in the formation of the Company and subscribed to its capital.

The income of the Company was derived partly from a half-share in the ten-shilling fee for broadcast receiver licences, instituted on 1 November 1922, and partly from royalties paid by the member firms on all receiving sets sold by them. The royalty amounted to about 10 per cent of the selling price of receivers and also on certain components that could be used by home constructors.[5] Initially royalties on typical items were as follows:

	£	s.	d.
crystal set		7	6
crystal, plus one-valve, set	1	7	6
crystal, plus two-valve, set	2	2	6
one-valve set	1	0	0
two-valve set	1	15	0
multi-valve set			
10s. extra for each valve beyond two			
loudspeaker with or without trumpet		3	0
valve			2

Manufacturers undertook not to sell any apparatus for broadcast listening unless the components were British made. Their receivers were stamped 'BBC Type Approved by Post Master General'. The broadcast receiving licence required the listener to use a 'type-approved' set.

An experimental receiving licence had been in force since 1906 for radio amateurs.[6] This was quite distinct from the broadcast receiving licence and initially no fee was payable for it, but in 1913 a fee of one guinea was introduced. When war-time restrictions were relaxed in 1919 a new ten-shilling licence was introduced for receiving equipment for experimental work. Anybody who could convince himself and the Post Office that he was a *bona-fide* experimenter could build a receiver himself and take out an experimental licence for it. This licence carried no stipulation that the equipment must be 'type-approved' and so the holder was free to use any components he pleased, whether or not they were made by firms that were members of the Company or even whether they were of British manufacture. Although the BBC received a share of the fee for an experimenters' licence, it lost money on royalties, because home-construction quickly became popular and was cheaper than buying a complete 'type-approved' set. As a result, the number of experimental licences increased from about 7000 at the end of March 1922 to over 35,000 by March 1923, at which date the number of broadcast licences was about 88,000. Most of the home constructors who obtained experimental licences did not really qualify as '*bona-fide* experimenters'; they merely assembled their receivers with the aid of simple tools, a diagram and a set of components. There was also a large number of listeners, estimated at at least 200,000, who were evading the licence altogether – a foretaste of troubles to come!

These difficulties led the BBC to make strong representations to the Post Office and the negotiations had almost reached a deadlock when the Sykes Committee was set up on 24 April 1923.[7]

This Committee recommended that from 1 January 1925 there should be a single ten-shilling licence for all receivers, of which the BBC's share would be 7s. 6d. The prohibition of imported receivers was to be withdrawn and royalty payments to the BBC to cease. Some interim arrangements were recommended for constructors' and experimental licences, for the period 1 October 1923 to 31 December 1924. After the publication of the report, on 1 October 1923, the total number of licences increased in ten days from 180,000 to 414,000[8] – a striking indication of the degree of evasion that had existed. In fact, the interim arrangements ceased on 1 July 1924, so that, from that date, the single ten-shilling licence came into effect.

By the time the Company took over, the broadcasting facilities mentioned in the previous chapter were already available. The London station with its studio was taken over by the Company on 14 November 1922, although strictly speaking the Company did not yet exist and its affairs were managed by a Committee representing the founder members. The transmitters and studios in Birmingham and Manchester were taken over on 15 November. The BBC had not yet recruited any staff of its own and therefore had to rely on employees of the firms that were already operating the studios and transmitting stations to continue to run them.

The first task of the new Company was to appoint a General Manager; he was J. C. W. Reith (later Sir John Reith, and subsequently Lord Reith), who became Managing Director in November 1923, and, on the formation of the British Broadcasting Corporation, its first Director-General. Reith was an engineer and he set a standard of public service, the influence of which continues to be felt in this and many other countries. There will be occasion later to mention the influence that a series of Chief Engineers and Directors of Engineering had on the staff and achievements of the Engineering Division, under the leadership of Reith and his successors. At this point it is necessary only to pay tribute to the enduring influence that Reith's personality had on the ethos of the BBC from the beginning. Asa Briggs has surveyed his principles and the way in which he applied them during the formative years of the BBC in *The History of Broadcasting in the United Kingdom*, Volume I, *passim*.

2 TRANSMITTERS AND RECEPTION

The British Broadcasting Company took over the responsibility for the transmitters that had already been set up: one by the Marconi Company in London (2LO), one built by the Radio Communication Company and installed in the Metropolitan Vickers' works in Manchester (2ZY), and one built by the Western Electric Company, which had just been moved to the General Electric Company's works at Birmingham (5IT). The Company was also responsible for the programmes radiated by these stations and by the further stations that were to be built.

The range of each of the transmitters was about 25 miles during daylight hours, when a crystal receiver was used, and each station operated on its own exclusive wavelength. Thus from the very start the concept of regional or area broadcasting took shape, simply on account of the limited range of the transmitting stations; they were not interconnected and all the stations had therefore to be programmed independently. It is interesting to speculate on what would have happened if a high-power low-frequency station could have been built first so as to serve the whole country with a single programme.

By this time a good deal was known about propagation at medium frequencies through experience in communicating with ships at sea. Marconi and others had already, at the beginning of the century, disproved the theory of Guarini that a line-of-sight was essential to the transmission of radio waves and that they could (at least at the frequencies then in use) circumvent obstacles and reach beyond the horizon.

The fact that radio waves follow the curvature of the earth appeared to be contrary to the laws of physics and to normal experience with the more familiar type of electromagnetic waves, namely those of light. But in 1902, Heaviside in the UK and Kennelly in the USA had postulated the existence of layers of ionised gas in the upper atmosphere, having refractive properties capable of bending radio waves back towards the earth and thus acting as reflectors. Since the height and density of these layers depended on the sun, the properties of the ionosphere varied with the time of day and with the season of the year, and also with the eleven-year sunspot cycle.

The activities of amateurs had contributed a great deal to empirical knowledge of the behaviour of radio waves at different frequencies. On 2 February 1921 a series of attempts was made by amateurs in the United Kingdom, the USA and Canada to bridge the Atlantic using frequencies in the neighbourhood of 1500 kHz, but with inconclusive results; in December of the same year a further series of tests took place in which a number of signals from the USA were received in the UK.[9] In 1924 understanding of the properties of the ionosphere was put on a firm basis by the researches of Prof. E. V. (later Sir Edward) Appleton in a series of experiments that determined the height of the reflecting layers; he used the BBC station at Bournemouth and a receiving point near Oxford. In 1925 G. Breit and M. A. Tuve in the USA developed a pulsed system for ionospheric sounding. These studies were to prove invaluable when short-wave broadcasting was developed and they were reinforced in the early 1960s when 'topside sounders' carried by artificial satellites made it possible to examine the upper, as well as the lower, strata of the ionosphere.

When broadcasting came into being as a public service the effect of these phenomena immediately became apparent and of practical importance. The aerials used at each of the transmitting stations radiated a part of the energy along the ground (the ground wave) and a part at angles above the horizontal (the sky wave). The ground wave gave constant reception during daylight hours at all distances within the limiting range, which was determined by the power of the transmitter and the sensitivity of the receiving installation. At night the sky wave could be received at distances considerably beyond the daytime range of the station, but with some fading and distortion resulting from variations in the refractive properties of the ionosphere.

There was, however, an intermediate range of distances at which the ground wave and the sky wave could be received at night at roughly equal strength. Interference between the two produced serious fading in what became known as the 'mush area' surrounding each station at a distance somewhat less than that corresponding to the daytime range. Thus, the range of reliable reception was less at night than by day; on the other hand, reception at a lower standard was possible at night over much greater distances. The transitions between day-time and night-time conditions occurred about an hour after sunrise and an hour before sunset at the point where the sky wave was reflected by the ionosphere.

The characteristic behaviour of medium-wave transmissions has, through the years, provoked a stream of complaints from listeners that they cannot satisfactorily receive a BBC medium-wave station fifty miles away, although they can receive continental stations at much greater distances. Some of them are reluctant to accept the fact that this is a natural phenomenon and that if they lived on the Continent they could receive distant BBC stations better than nearer continental stations. Quite recently, serious consideration has been given in several countries to the possibilities of using sky wave transmission for domestic broadcasting. This is feasible only in countries that are large enough to have populated areas about a thousand miles apart, and the quality of reception cannot be as good as with ground wave propagation because of fading.

The sky wave not only made reception possible at night over considerable distances; it could also cause interference with the reception of other stations on the same or nearby wavelengths at distances of hundreds of miles.

These considerations have profoundly affected the development of broadcasting on medium frequencies (medium waves) to this day. The effect on low-frequency (long-wave) transmissions is less marked, and at the high frequencies that were later brought into use for short-wave broadcasting only sky-wave transmission is of practical use.

The engineers who operated the first three stations on behalf of the British Broadcasting Company were initially employees of the three owning companies, but shortly after P. P. Eckersley was appointed Chief Engineer, in February 1923, these engineers were offered direct employment in the BBC. For example, H. Bishop, who was at first employed by the Marconi Company and was operating the London (2LO) transmitter, joined the BBC on 10 May 1923.

The Engineering Department, as it was then called, soon began to expand as broadcasting spread to other provincial cities; additional staff were recruited and specialised sections were formed within the department during the four years of the Company's existence. The aims of the Engineering Department during these early years were:

(i) to maintain a high technical standard of broadcasting;
(ii) to spread the broadcasting service into areas of the country having either unsatisfactory reception or none at all;
(iii) to conduct research into all engineering aspects of broadcasting, as only a few of the firms in existence at that time were equipped to do such work and interested in undertaking it.[10]

In the original licence, the Post Office authorised the BBC to install and operate nine $1\frac{1}{2}$-kW main transmitting stations; these were the eight stations previously mentioned plus a ninth station at Belfast (see table). After all these main stations had been commissioned, many parts of the country still had poor reception or none at all. For example, reception was very poor in Sheffield, Leeds, Edinburgh and Plymouth. The state of the art at that time did not permit the production of high-power transmitters to alleviate this problem, even if permission could have been obtained in the

The British Broadcasting Company

MAIN AND RELAY STATIONS: 1922–4

Station	Call-sign	Wavelength (m)	Frequency (kHz)	Opening Date	Closing Date
Main Stations					
London (Marconi House)	2LO	363·7	825	11.5.22*	5.4.25
London (Selfridges)	2LO	363·7	825	6.4.25	4.10.29
Manchester	2ZY	378	793	16.5.22†	17.5.31
Birmingham	5IT	477	629	15.11.22	21.8.27
Newcastle	5NO	404·5	742	24.12.22	19.10.37
Cardiff	5WA	353	850	13.2.23	28.5.33
Glasgow	5SC	422	717	6.3.23	12.6.32
Aberdeen	2BD	496	605	10.10.23	9.9.38
Bournemouth	6BM	387·2	775	17.10.23	14.6.39
Belfast	2BE	440	682	24.10.24	20.3.36
Relay Stations					
Sheffield	6FL	306·1	980	16.11.23	16.5.31
Plymouth	5PY	338·2	887	28.3.24	13.6.39
Edinburgh	2EH	328·2	914	1.5.24	12.6.32
Liverpool	6LV	318·2	943	11.6.24	16.5.31
Leeds	2LS	346·2	866	8.7.24	16.5.31
Bradford	2LS‡	310	968	8.7.24	16.5.31
Hull	6KH	355·5	844	15.8.24	16.5.31
Nottingham	5NG	326·1	920	16.9.24	1.11.28
Dundee	2DE	331	906	12.11.24	12.6.32
Stoke-on-Trent	6ST	301·1	996	21.10.24	16.5.31
Swansea	5SX	482·2	622	12.12.24	28.5.33

Note
The addresses of these stations are given in the table in the next section.
The wavelengths and frequencies given are those on which the stations operated at the time when they opened or shortly after. A number of changes were made subsequently (see table in section 7).

* Taken over by the BBC on 14.11.22   † Taken over by the BBC on 15.11.22
‡ Bradford relayed Leeds

political climate of that time for such transmitters to be used. In any case, the selectivity of receivers was then very poor by modern standards and a high-power transmitter sited near a large city centre would have 'blanketed' reception for listeners living there, so that they would have been unable to tune to any other station.[11]

Of the nine transmitters, seven were manufactured by Marconi's and six of them were of the 'Q' type with choke modulation and independent drives to ensure frequency stability. The one at Marconi House, London, preceded the 'Q' set, but had about the same output power. (As already mentioned, the other two – at Birmingham and Manchester – were made by the Western Electric Company and the Radio Communication Company respectively.)

The transmitters used in the first group of stations survived in service for many years; the one at Bournemouth was in use for fifteen years and eight months. They were renovated from time to time and, as L. Hotine remarked of the transmitter at Aberdeen, after almost fifteen years it was like the everlasting hatchet, which had had six new handles and three new heads.

There were two variants of the 'Q' set, one rated at 6 kW and the other at 12 kW; these were the amounts of power supplied to the anode circuits of the valves and the filaments of the rectifiers. At that time various methods of rating were used and the 6-kW transmitter was alternatively rated at $1\frac{1}{2}$ kW, this being the power supplied to the oscillator anode, and at 1 kW, which referred to the radiated output. (This confusion was not finally cleared up until many years later when the Radio Regulations, issued by the ITU, laid down that the quoted power of an AM sound broadcasting transmitter should be the unmodulated carrier power, while that of an FM transmitter is the average power of the modulated transmission and that of a vision transmitter is the power at peak modulation. In each case the power quoted is that supplied by the transmitter to the aerial feeder and, for AM is averaged over one rf cycle. To obtain the effective radiated power (erp) the output power is multiplied by the net gain of the aerial in a particular direction.)

In the 6-kW 'Q' set power was drawn from the mains and converted by a motor-generator set to 300 Hz at 500 V, single-phase. The voltage was raised by a transformer for the high-tension supply. The transmitter comprised four panels, each composed of an open steel framework with interlocked barriers to prevent access to live parts. The first enclosed the valve rectifiers, which delivered 10 kV to a smoothing circuit consisting of capacitors and a large iron-cored inductance; the second panel contained the drive oscillator; the third an rf amplifier, and the fourth the modulator and sub-modulator.

Transmitters of this type were supplied to a number of other countries and became widely known. The range of the '6-kW' transmitter was claimed to be 25 miles for a crystal receiver and 125 miles for a two-valve receiver. The corresponding ranges claimed for the '12-kW' version were 35 and 200 miles respectively.

At this time all receivers sold to the public had to comply with specifications issued by the Post Office and to carry an authorisation stamp. Crystal sets usually employed a very simple circuit and tuning was achieved by means of a slider operating on a coil in the form of a helix on a tubular former, although there were other forms of tuning, such as the so-called 'spade tuning' of C. S. Franklin, in which a copper sheet could be moved relatively to a flat coil so as to vary its inductance. The coil was shunted by a fixed capacitor and followed by the headphones and a by-pass capacitor. Contact with the crystal was made with a 'cat's whisker', which was tricky to adjust and had to be reset frequently. Various expedients were tried to improve the performance of the crystal detector, e.g. by introducing dc bias to ensure that the detector worked on the most efficient point on its characteristic, by using an electrode held rigidly against the crystal (as in the carborundum-steel combination), or by using two crystals in permanent contact with each other instead of one with a movable contact.

With a crystal set the whole of the energy required to produce an audible signal in the headphones had to come from the rf input; it was therefore necessary to use an efficient aerial to deliver the maximum signal strength to the receiver. Listeners took a great deal of trouble to erect aerials as high as practicable and to insulate them carefully. The most usual form was an inverted 'L' aerial (the 'T' aerial was less common) slung between a chimney and a pole or tree with a string of insulators at each end and an insulated lead-in tube passed through the window-frame. The aerial wire and lead-in were usually of 7-strand 22-gauge bare wire, though there was a ready market for war-time surplus supplies of 'electron' covered wire. For many years, however, the Post Office restricted the total length of aerial wire to 100 ft.

Aerials of this kind were also used with the early valve receivers and there were special restrictions on aerials used with superheterodyne receivers to limit radiation at the oscillator frequency. Later, simple vertical rod aerials, with screened down-leads connected through transformers at each end, were found to be effective and the long outside aerials were largely replaced either by these rods or by frame aerials or, later still, by ferrite-rod aerials inside the receiver. Despite the increasing sensitivity of receivers, it was, and still is, necessary to use a sufficiently good aerial to provide an input to the receiver strong enough to override electrical interference, preferably an outside aerial so placed as to pick up the maximum signal and the minimim interference from electrical wiring in the house.[12]

Valve receivers, though much more expensive than crystal sets, were already becoming popular in 1922. The earliest of them had a single valve and tuning was varied by means of a slider operating on a helical coil. Variable inductances comprising two coils in series, one fixed and one rotatable, soon made their appearance under the name of 'variometers'. Plug-in coils first appeared in 1922; each covered a part of the broadcasting wavebands when shunted by a variable capacitor and this became the most popular form of tuning. A second coil was connected in the anode circuit of the valve to provide positive feedback when coupled to the tuning coil. Multi-valve sets, often having each stage of amplification in a separate box, had already appeared in 1922 with one or two transformer-coupled af stages and sometimes with an rf stage.[13] Rf amplification, though inefficient, improved both the sensitivity and the selectivity of the receiver; it relied for stability on the loading imposed by the aerial circuit or on judicious adjustment of the operating voltages.

The superheterodyne receiver, mentioned in the previous chapter, advanced in popularity in 1924–5. The invention of band-pass tuning and other improvements substantially enhanced its performance about 1930.

From the moment when it started broadcasting, the BBC prided itself on giving the best possible quality and this encouraged both the radio industry and home constructors to look for ways of improving the performance of receivers. Transformer coupling was used for the af stages and much care was taken to reduce losses in the transformers by making the cores of iron wire, and later of laminations. Resistance-capacitance coupling became popular in 1923. Horn-type loudspeakers began to replace headphones between 1922 and 1924. Cone-type loudspeakers were produced in 1924–5 and in 1925 the Rice-Kellogg moving-coil speaker appeared in America. The adoption of the moving-coil principle, first patented by Siemens in 1874, was a major advance over the use of diaphragms, such as those in telephone receivers, working on the moving-iron principle.[14] A Rice-Kellogg unit imported from the USA was tested by the BBC in 1925. Permanent magnets instead of heavy electromagnets became practicable in 1928.

The necessity for accumulators for filament supply and dry batteries for h.t. was a serious inconvenience; it led to the production of 'battery-eliminators', which incorporated a tapped transformer and a rectifier to derive the ht and lt supplies from ac mains. In 1926 the first receiver operating entirely from an ac mains supply was introduced. This development was assisted by the design of valves with indirectly heated cathodes; an all-mains set using such valves was marketed in 1928.

A major advance in receiver design resulted from the introduction of the screen-grid valve in 1926–7. The stability of this valve enabled it to give considerably more rf amplification than earlier types. A development of it was the 'variable-mu' valve, which became prominent about 1931; its amplification factor could be varied by altering the negative bias voltage applied to the grid. Automatic volume control had been applied to receivers about 1925, but did not become widespread until the 'variable-mu' valve became available. It was effected by means of a control voltage derived from the rectified carrier. The demand for high outputs to operate loudspeakers led to the development of push-pull circuits about 1927–8.

The introduction of an additional electrode between the screen grid and the anode resulted in the pentode valve of 1928. This could handle a relatively large output with a minimum of distortion and it was therefore particularly valuable in the output stage of a receiver.

From the very early days the BBC has felt an obligation to do its best to protect its audience from interference that might spoil reception of its programmes. Interference from atmospheric and galactic noise is a natural phenomenon; the broadcaster can do nothing about it except to provide as high a field strength as is reasonably practicable (for example, by supplementing the coverage of main stations by building relay stations) and to encourage listeners and viewers to use the best possible receiving aerials, taking advantage of their directional properties. Interference from transmitters other than the wanted one can be reduced by careful frequency-planning. A third, and important, kind of interference is that generated by electrical apparatus, the so-called 'man-made' interference. In the days of crystal sets this was not often a serious problem because receivers were insensitive and because relatively few electrical appliances capable of causing serious interference were in use. When valve receivers became popular from 1922 onwards, radio sets themselves became a major source of interference. This was because of the widespread use of variable 're-action', i.e. positive feedback applied to a tuning coil in the aerial circuit. It considerably increased the sensitivity of the receiver, but could easily cause the valve to oscillate. The oscillation was radiated by the aerial and, being at a frequency close to that of the station to which the receiver was tuned, produced a whistle in neighbouring receivers, the pitch of which varied as the tuning was adjusted. So great was this nuisance that the BBC received 15,000 complaints in a year and had to undertake a major publicity campaign to persuade listeners not to annoy their neighbours by excessive use of 're-action'. This campaign was conducted through the microphone and the Press and by the issue of a pamphlet on the subject. Eckersley himself made a spirited plea on the theme: 'Please don't do it'. In persistent cases the BBC obtained detailed information from the complainants and passed it to the Post Office, which used direction-finding vans to locate the source of the interference. The trouble was greatly reduced when a radio-frequency amplifying stage preceded the detector valve. This additional stage not only increased the sensitivity of the receiver and improved the sharpness of tuning but also acted as a buffer to prevent the oscillation from reaching the aerial.

However, this was not the end of the problem, because the superheterodyne receiver came into widespread use towards the end of the 1920s. This included an internal oscillator operating at a frequency corresponding to the difference between the fixed intermediate frequency incorporated in the design of the receiver and the frequency to which the set was tuned. The internal oscillator could radiate directly to an extent sufficient to cause interference to neighbouring receivers and the interference could be reradiated by the aerial to which the receiver was connected. The interference was usually within the broadcasting band and had to be reduced by careful design of the receiver, including the use of internal screening. Later, when television receivers were introduced they created a new problem: not only did they incorporate a frequency-changing oscillator but they had another oscillator to generate the line-scanning frequency. Both these oscillators could cause interference to neighbouring receivers. Through the years BBC engineers have co-operated with the receiver industry and with the Post Office in dealing with these troubles. Agreed limits for the interference generated by sound and television receivers are now included in British Standard 905 first published in 1940,[15] which, though not mandatory, is generally observed by British manufacturers.

Other forms of electrically generated interference became troublesome with the increased sensitivity of receivers and with the widespread use of domestic electrical equipment. By the end of the 1920s a considerable amount of attention was being given to this problem by the Post Office, the Electrical Research Association, the BBC Engineering Division, and the various interests responsible for producing the interference. The first steps were to produce measuring equipment and to standardise the methods of measurement so that the field strength (or, in the case of interference conducted by the mains wiring, the voltage) could be measured in such a way as to give some indication of the subjective effect on the listener when the interference was heard as a background to a broadcast programme. It was soon apparent that agreed limits for the acceptable maximum level of interference from various types of electrical apparatus would have to be fixed so that manufacturers would have some guide from which to work. A portable radio-interference measuring set was designed by the Post Office, which was in effect an idealised superheterodyne receiver incorporating an rf voltmeter with specified time constants. It covered a frequency range from 150 kHz to 25 MHz. The ERA also developed a measuring set of a somewhat different design.

Progress was also made in the design of interference suppressors. Since the interference from most kinds of domestic appliance was mains-borne, it could usually be sufficiently reduced by inserting a low-pass filter, or even one or more capacitors, at the mains terminal of the machine. It was, however, necessary to deal with both the symmetrical and asymmetrical components of the interfering voltage and it was not easy to design effective suppressors that were cheap enough to be applied to small appliances, such as hair-dryers, and at the same time small enough to be incorporated in them.

Developments in receivers and in coping with interference were paralleled by improvements in the broadcasting system. In the latter part of 1923 the BBC Board decided to build additional transmitters of low power sited in populated areas that could not be reached effectively by the main stations. The programming of these relay stations, for reasons of economy and local choice, was mainly from London and this raised problems of simultaneous broadcasting, which are described later in this chapter.

None of the large manufacturers could at this time offer a suitable low-power medium-frequency broadcasting transmitter, so the Development Section of the Engineering Department immediately set about designing a transmitter with an output of 100 W. The manufacture of these transmitters was co-ordinated by H. S. Walker (later head of the Valve Section).

Eleven relay stations were put into service at the remarkable rate of one each month, starting with the station to serve Sheffield (6FL), which went into service on 16 November 1923, and concluding with the installation at Swansea (5SX) on 12 December 1924.

The coverage given by the group of nine main and eleven relay stations was estimated at the time to be between 60 per cent and 70 per cent of the country's population, assuming that only crystal sets were in use by the majority of listeners.

The capital cost of the low-power stations was of the order of £2000 each and the running costs were about £1500 pa each. Eckersley estimated that one station could bring in 20,000 additional licences during the first year and a further 30,000 in the second year.[16] This forecast was more than amply fulfilled, for by 31 March 1924 the number of licences in force had already grown to nearly three-quarters of a million. The licence revenue received by the BBC in the sixteen months from 15 November 1922 to 31 March 1924 (that is, up to the time of commissioning the eighth of the main stations) was £176,934, but in the following financial year, which included the commissioning of the ninth main station and the eleven relay stations, the licence revenue increased to £488,881. The extension of the coverage contributed materially to the increase in the BBC's income.

The decision to use a number of low-power stations raised what is now the familiar limiting factor in the development of medium-frequency broadcasting, i.e. the shortage of wavelengths. In October 1923 the Government had accepted the recommendations of the Sykes Committee[17] that broadcasting should be given an extended waveband and that the BBC should have the exclusive use in this country of the band from 300 to 500 m (1 MHz to 600 kHz). At the same time, the BBC was asked to explore any technical innovations likely to have the effect of reducing the number of separate wavelengths required. At the end of 1924, when the last of the nine main stations and eleven relay stations had been opened, all the BBC's medium-wave assignments had been taken up. Interference from continental stations at night was increasing and the wavelengths of several stations were altered between 1924 and 1926 to combat it. In 1925 preparations were being made for the European Conference at Geneva that was to change the assignments (see section 7 of this chapter).

In accordance with the Geneva Plan (1926), all the relay stations except Leeds and Bradford had to operate on the UK Common Wave of 288·5 m (1040 kHz), and although their range was only five to ten miles with a crystal receiver, it was necessary to ensure that mutual interference, particularly during the hours of darkness, was minimised by adjusting their carrier frequencies to quasi-synchronism. If all the stations on the same frequency carried the same programme, the mutual interference between them could cause fading and distortion at night; if they carried different programmes the listener could also be troubled by a background of the unwanted programme. (The tolerable field-strength ratio was about 14 dB in the former case and 46 dB in the latter.)

At this time the development of quartz crystal oscillators had not reached a sufficiently advanced stage for them to be used for precision control of carrier frequencies; the BBC Development Section under H. L. Kirke, which included A. B. Howe, T. C. Macnamara and J. McLaren, designed a tuning-fork drive for these stations. (A patent for such a drive had been taken out by Dr W. H. Eccles in 1918.) The apparatus consisted of a tuning fork electrically maintained at a frequency of 1015·625 Hz, and a frequency multiplier having a ratio of $1:2^{10}$. The multiplier employed twenty-two type LS5 valves and produced an output at a frequency of 1040 kHz. The first tests were made in 1924 using the tuning fork in London and the frequency multiplier at the Sheffield relay transmitter, the output from the tuning fork being sent by Post Office line to the transmitter. Later, transmitter shutdowns caused by line breaks (phase changes in the driving tone do not seem to have been considered to be a problem in those early days) were obviated by providing each of the relay stations with its own local tuning fork; its frequency was adjusted against that of a 'master' tuning fork, the frequency of which was known with some precision. The frequency stability of these tuning fork oscillators was of the order of $\pm 1/10^5$.[18]

For the first nine main stations and the relay stations, Heising (i.e. choke) modulation at high level was universally used. For later stations other methods of modulation were evolved. The long-wave station at Daventry, 5XX, had transformer-coupled modulators for high-level modulation, but later the experimental medium-wave transmitter at Daventry, 5GB, which was the prototype for the transmitters used in the Regional Scheme, used choke modulation at low level. The advantages of low-level modulation preponderated and this method was used in the high-power stations introduced in the Regional Scheme at the beginning of the 1930s.

Choke modulation gave place to series modulation from 1934 onwards, starting with the long-wave station at Droitwich. From 1937 onwards the Class A type of modulator as hitherto used gave place to Class B, which was used in the medium-wave transmitters at Stagshaw and Start Point and in the later short-wave transmitters.

The differences between these various systems were as follows. In choke modulation the audio-frequency output from the modulating amplifier was passed through an inductance coil in the anode circuit of the modulated amplifier, so as to vary the anode voltage applied to that amplifier. In the simplest form of series modulation, the cathode-anode path of the final valve of the modulating amplifier was connected between the anode of the modulated amplifier and its ht supply, so as to present a resistance varying with the audio-frequency modulation applied to its input. The filament circuits of the modulating amplifier were at a high voltage above earth and the machines used to generate the power supply for the filaments had to be designed to withstand this voltage. Both methods had low power-conversion efficiency.

If modulation was applied at high level, the audio-frequency amplifying stages had to be capable of carrying relatively high power and had therefore to include large and expensive iron-cored components. If modulation took place at low level, i.e. in one of the earlier stages of the transmitter, the modulating amplifier had only to handle low power, but all the stages following the modulated amplifier had to be capable of dealing with the frequency range represented by the carrier and its sidebands and the adjustment of these stages could be difficult.

In these systems the modulated amplifier operated in Class C, but the modulating amplifier operated either in Class A or Class B. In Class A amplifiers the valve was biased so that the anode current, which varied with the signal applied between the grid and cathode, never reached zero. The negative grid bias had to be such as to ensure that the valve operated in the linear part of its anode current/grid voltage characteristic.

In a Class B amplifier, two valves were in push-pull, the grid bias of each being adjusted so that it operated on a non-linear part of its characteristic, but the combined effect of both valves was approximately linear. This system gave increased power output with a reduced feed and therefore a reduced power input. The power efficiency was thus substantially improved, but distortion was increased. Class B modulation was not therefore of much interest until the introduction of negative feedback (see chapter III, section 2).

Eckersley's aim had always been to achieve what he termed 'universal coverage' throughout the United Kingdom, but he knew that it would not be possible to obtain this economically on medium waves, particularly in the remoter rural areas. During 1923 he recalled the work of W. T. Ditcham of the Marconi Company on long waves at Chelmsford and conceived the idea of a high-power long-wave transmitter located in the centre of England, which he thought would provide a service to most of the country. This was a bold and imaginative concept; it led to the building, at Daventry, of the first long-wave transmitter in the world to be used exclusively for broadcasting.

In December 1923 the proposal for a high-power transmitter was raised at a Board Meeting when Reith submitted a memorandum proposing that there should be two stations in the London area, one of which should employ a 'high-power' transmitter

31

of 20 kW. A committee was appointed to investigate this proposal and it reported to the Board, on 24 January 1924, that such a station would 'solve once and for all the questions of jamming, that it would be possible to get crystal reception up to nearly a hundred miles and that it would enable the larger towns of England to be served by relay stations working off the main stations'. A wavelength between 1400 and 2000 m was proposed (150 to 215 kHz) and the committee gave a specification of the type of site needed for such a station. It was suggested, finally, that tests should be made before committing the Board to a site and to a wavelength.

The Board agreed with the committee's recommendation and requested the Post Office to grant the BBC a licence for temporary experiments to be carried out on a long-wave transmitter at the Chelmsford works of the Marconi Company. Unfortunately there were few long-wave channels available for broadcasting and in any case there were objections from the Services concerning the effect of long-wave broadcasting on other radio users. Also, some sections of the Radio Industry were not enthusiastic about the use of long waves for broadcasting owing to the increased cost of receivers covering two separate wavebands.

However, all these doubts and fears were eventually overcome and a licence was granted on 9 July 1924 for experimental transmissions of speech and music from a long-wave transmitter at Chelmsford.

The object of the experimental transmissions was to determine:

(i) the range of crystal set reception;
(ii) the extent of interference of a high-power long-wave station with other broadcasting stations;
(iii) the possible danger of interference with other radio users.

The transmitter operated on 1600 m (197·5 kHz) with the call-sign 5XX. (Both the call-sign and the frequency were subsequently taken over by the Daventry transmitter when it opened on 27 July 1925.) From 21 July 1924 Chelmsford broadcast the London programmes after 1900 hours each evening. BBC engineers co-operated with W. T. Ditcham and his staff in running the transmitter. Reports were received from all over the country indicating that these experimental transmissions were being very well received and on 7 August 1924 the Board decided to ask the Post Office for permission to open a permanent high-power long-wave station.

The Postmaster General called a meeting of the Wireless Telegraph Board on 26 September 1924 to consider this request and the Services objected, complaining that the Chelmsford test transmissions had caused disturbance to their communications. After much argument, it was finally agreed that a long-wave station should be built with a power not exceeding 25 kW, provided that it was sited north of a line joining the Severn to The Wash. Pending the building of the new station, it was agreed that the Chelmsford broadcasts should continue after 1900 hours each evening.

The Post Office pressed the BBC to avoid delay in transferring the transmissions from Chelmsford to the new site, but there was no need for such an exhortation as the BBC had decided in August 1924 to go ahead immediately once permission had been granted. Further it had decided to supervise the building of the new station itself rather than go out to tender for the complete project with one of the large companies. The masts and aerial were ordered from the Radio Communication Company, the transmitter from the Marconi Company, and the programme input equipment from the Western Electric Company. H. Bishop and L. W. Hayes immediately set out for the Northampton area to find a suitable site. This area was roughly on the Severn/Wash line and was centrally placed in England. Of some six sites examined, that at Borough Hill, near Daventry, appeared to be the most suitable.

The Daventry site was a plateau some fifty acres in extent at a height of 650 ft above mean sea level. The cost of the site was £2670 freehold, which amounted to £53 per acre. (This price compares with that of a recent land acquisition in the same area at £235 per acre.) As the site was some distance from the road a light railway had to be built to the top of the hill, using petrol-driven locomotives to transport the building materials.[19]

The Daventry station, with the call-sign 5XX and the frequency of 187·5 kHz, was the first high-power long-wave station designed for broadcasting. It had an output power of 25 kW, and used a T-aerial suspended between two stayed masts of triangular section, 500 ft in height and spaced 800 ft apart. The earth system consisted of a number of zinc plates buried on the perimeter of the area occupied by the transmitter building and connected to the earth point of the transmitter by overhead conductors run on short poles. The power supply – approximately 300 kW – was derived from the public mains via a sub-station on the site. No reserve engine-driven power supply was provided, but a ring main arrangement provided some protection against mains failure. Motor generator sets were installed to supply the filaments of the transmitting valves and the eht supply, at about 10 kV, was obtained from thermionic rectifiers; these derived their anode supply from transformers with primary windings fed at approximately 1500 V and 300 Hz from motor alternators. The rectifiers used type CAR 2 valves and two groups each of four of these, were used to supply the modulated amplifier and modulator respectively. The first rf stage consisted of a self-oscillating CAT 1 valve driving four CAT 1 valves in parallel in the modulated amplifier. This amplifier was stabilised by using negative feedback in the form of an anti-reaction coil, but this was later changed to a capacitative neutralising circuit, or 'neut'. The output of the modulated amplifier was inductively coupled to the aerial in the initial arrangement, but this was changed to capacity coupling later to reduce harmonic radiation. The modulator consisted of eight CAM 1 valves in parallel driven by sub-modulator and sub-sub-modulator stages.

Valves with water-cooled anodes using copper-glass seals (e.g. the CAT 1) were already available in 1922. The power rating had been increased to 20 kW by 1923, and within the succeeding ten years valves rated at 500 kW were being made. All water-cooled valves, such as those at Daventry, used mains water as the coolant in an open system. The insulation was obtained by using sprays fed from a header tank at the top of each unit. The coolant left the units by gravity and returned to a low-level pond outside the building whence it was raised by a pump to the high-level tank in the pump-room. The use of mains water necessitated frequent cleaning of the valve anodes, and the open circulating system was subject to obstruction by frogs and other foreign bodies caught in the suction pump inlet. Such obstructions, which precluded priming of the pump, resulted in traumatic problems when only one engineer was on duty to start up the transmitter.

The Control Room served as an SB sub-centre as well as housing the programme input equipment for the 5XX transmitter, and for the 5GB transmitter that was subsequently added.

Staff quarters were provided at the top of Borough Hill and a caretaker was employed to look after single staff. The cost of this accommodation to a single man was initially 35s. per week all found; to a married man it was £1 per week, but he had to provide his own food, electricity and 'attendance'. The subsidy from the BBC for the Daventry Staff Quarters was estimated to be about £300 pa. For many years they were the home of some of the resident staff and also provided temporary accommodation for generations of visiting engineers. They had something of the atmosphere of a residential club and in this respect remained unique in the BBC until the Second World War forcibly brought people closer together.

The Daventry 5XX station was opened by the Postmaster General on 27 July 1925 and reception reports soon confirmed that the range of the station was 150 to 200 miles for valve receivers, which at this time were becoming fairly common. In fact, the coverage confirmed the accuracy of Eckersley's predictions; it included 85 per cent of the population. The opening of this station was a significant event for the BBC as a whole, and for the Engineering Department in particular, because for the first time listeners were provided with an opportunity to receive an alternative programme if they were also within range of a medium-wave station; it also enhanced the status of the BBC in relation to the Services when negotiating frequencies for future stations.

For the radio receiver industry, the opening of the 5XX long-wave station provided some protection against the importation of American receivers as there was no home market for long-wave receivers in the USA. It also gave a welcome boost to the British home trade at a critical season of the year.

In April 1925 the 1-kW transmitter at Marconi House was superseded by a '12-kW' (double-Q) transmitter installed on the roof of Selfridges store in Oxford Street, London, giving an output of 2 kW. Its aerial was suspended about 250 ft above the ground between two 120-ft masts erected at opposite ends of the roof; the earth connection was made to the steelwork of the building. The range of this new transmitter was better than that of the Marconi House installation and extended the London coverage further into the Home Counties. A contemporary field-strength map shows the 1 mV/m contour passing through Bedford and beyond Tunbridge Wells, while the 0·3 mV/m contour embraced Coventry, Brighton and Hythe. There were some teething troubles with the new station, including a breakdown lasting $1\frac{1}{2}$ hours on 13 May 1925, but the quality was reported to be much improved and a listener wrote that 'At last Tchaikovsky by wireless is worth listening to'.[20] Reradiation from water-pipes aroused much interest in the Press – as it has continued to do at intervals ever since. This new 2LO transmitter remained in service until replaced by the high-power transmitter at Brookmans Park on 4 October 1929.

In July an internal memorandum entitled 'Reorganisation of powers and wave-lengths of BBC stations' stated that 'the public would soon demand the possibility of a choice of programmes' throughout the country.[21] Some listeners already had alternative programmes available – the National programme from Daventry 5XX and the local programme from their nearest medium-wave station – but Eckersley wanted to give everybody a choice. He conceived the idea of the 'Regional Scheme' during 1924 and it was being discussed early in 1925.[22] In December 1925 Reith formally expounded the main points of the scheme and asked the Post Office for approval to a network of alternative programme stations. Knowing by now the kind of reaction to be expected from the Post Office and the Services, the BBC made the point that all forms of interference that might result from the proposed high-power stations would be tackled energetically by the BBC and it was hoped that the scheme would not be dismissed because of hypothetical difficulties.

The transmitting stations had to work on frequencies assigned to them by the Post Office as the government department responsible for the control of frequency usage in this country. (Its responsibilities in this respect were taken over by the Ministry of Posts & Telecommunications in October 1969.) Since transmissions on long and medium waves could cause interference with broadcast transmissions in other countries, the assignment of channels to individual stations had to be planned internationally – as indicated in section 7 of this chapter.

The BBC's appeal for permission to initiate the Regional Scheme was backed by the Crawford Committee's recommendation that the Postmaster General should continue negotiations for new high-power stations.[23] The Post Office did not show much enthusiasm for the project, but in 1926 it did authorise the start of further experimental broadcasting from a new transmitter at Daventry 'as a preliminary to the development of the whole scheme'.

On 18 February 1926 Eckersley had written to Reith giving the proposed costs of an experimental transmitter at Daventry to serve as a prototype for the 50-kW transmitters needed for the Regional Scheme. Eckersley said that after this experimental work had been completed, the new building could probably be used for experiments in short-wave broadcasting. This proved to be a prophetic statement as the building was in fact used to house a short-wave transmitter (Sender 3, formerly G5SW) much later, in 1934.

At that time no high-power medium-wave transmitter design suitable for broadcasting purposes was available from any of the large manufacturers, so the BBC had to produce its own design. Ashbridge and Kirke had started some preliminary design and planning for the Daventry experimental station when B. N. MacLarty – formerly with the Marconi Company at Writtle – was appointed as their assistant.

MacLarty went to Daventry towards the end of 1926 to install the equipment, with only the part-time assistance of the station mechanic. Early in 1927 T. C. Macnamara and a full-time mechanic were sent to help. In spite of the very small staff, and of many technical difficulties and unexpected set-backs, progress was rapid and the complete transmitter was powered into the aerial for the first time on 5 May 1927. It became known as 5GB and will be mentioned further in the next chapter.

An event of special significance to the BBC occurred in 1926, namely the General Strike from 3 to 12 May. Arrangements were made for the protection of transmitting stations and studio centres; Daventry was protected, for example, by a force of twelve plain-clothes policemen. Immediately before the strike, there had been threats to cause jamming by mass oscillation of receivers. This would have been the first case of intentional jamming of broadcasts, but in the event the strikers were as anxious as the rest of the public to hear the frequent News Bulletins broadcast by the BBC and no cases of intentional jamming were reported. A further action taken during the strike by the Engineering Department was to over-modulate the transmitters during News Bulletins to increase the signal-to-noise ratio in areas of poor reception. This may be compared with the much more sophisticated methods of improving intelligibility used at short-wave transmitters immediately after the Second World War to counteract the effects of intentional jamming of broadcasts to countries beyond the Iron Curtain.

After the General Strike was over, the Prime Minister, Baldwin, wrote to Reith warmly congratulating him and his staff who deserved, he said, 'the greatest credit' for all they had done. In a later letter he added that 'the power of broadcasting triumphantly showed itself in a searching test'.[24]

The story of short-wave broadcasting belongs mainly to a later chapter, but it started during the life-time of the Company. It was one of Reith's ambitions to broadcast to India and other countries in what is now the British Commonwealth. His ideas were reinforced by G. C. Beadle (later Sir Gerald Beadle) who had been seconded to the South African broadcasting station at Durban as Station Director. He pressed the BBC to broadcast on short waves to South Africa so that he could relay the programmes from his station. After some delays, caused by technical and financial problems, the Post Office granted permission to the BBC, in May 1926, to set up an experimental short-wave transmitter at Daventry with a power not exceeding 20 kW. The object of the experimental transmissions was to 'establish whether it would be possible . . . to establish a wireless link for the purpose of transmitting British programmes to the Dominions and Colonies'.

Faced with shortages of money and man-power, Eckersley had to give priority to the experiments that were then in progress on the use of high-power transmissions on medium waves. Thus, short-wave transmissions did not start until after the Company had been dissolved and the Corporation had been set up.

3 STUDIOS

When the BBC took over the responsibility for broadcasting on 14 November 1922, it inherited the studio at Marconi House, London. By that time the transmitter had been moved to another room, its power and size having been increased, and the room occupied by the studio (about 20 ft square) was devoted exclusively to programme production. The BBC also took over the studios in Birmingham and Manchester.

The new London premises at Savoy Hill were opened on 1 May 1923. At first there was only one studio about 40 ft by 20 ft. The walls were heavily damped with six layers of Hessian felt, partly to provide insulation against sounds coming from outside and partly because the directional characteristics of the microphones made it necessary to eliminate reflections from the walls as far as possible. The intention was to provide an approximation to an anechoic chamber. Little was known about room acoustics, but they were already becoming important, because there was only one microphone and some of the artists were at a considerable distance from it. The result of the treatment used was that the response of the studio at the upper audio frequencies was extremely poor.

The original studio at Savoy Hill was later designated Studio 3, because it was on the third floor. It was followed by Studio 1 (a second general-purpose studio) in January 1924, and later by Studios 2 (drama), 4 (variety) and 5 (news and talks), so that by early 1926 five studios were in operation.

In Manchester the first studio was at Trafford Park, where the transmitter was also located. A new studio was opened at Dickenson Street in August 1923, where both the studio and the transmitter were housed in the upper part of a warehouse. The reason for choosing this otherwise unattractive site was that it was close to the Manchester Corporation power station, the chimneys of which were used to support the transmitting aerial. Access for engineers, artists and programme staff was by a goods hoist on which they had to pull themselves up and down; in the evenings the hoist was given a more decorous appearance, consistent with the dignity of the BBC, by draping it with curtains. On 12 December 1924 there was a move to Orme Buildings, The Parsonage, Manchester, where two studios were provided in the basement, one for orchestral and other music, and a smaller one, more heavily damped, for talks and drama. The control room was on the same floor, but the transmitter remained at Dickenson Street, being connected to the studios by Post Office line. Most of the technical wiring for the new studios was done by the local staff, the engineers working continuously during the night for a week or more before the opening.

In Birmingham the studio was located, with the transmitter, at the G.E.C. works at Witton until August 1923, when a studio, control room and offices were set up in New Street. The control room was connected to the transmitter by line. A further move was made to new studios in Broad Street, opened on 20 January 1926; they comprised a large main studio, 48 ft by 40 ft, and a talks studio, using Western Electric microphones. The engineers there carried out announcing duties as well as operating the equipment. At the conclusion of the day's programmes, the engineer on duty in the control room would make the closing announcement and then switch over to an electric pianola playing the National Anthem. This economical procedure was possible because the control room was adjacent to the studio and there was an observation window between the two. At centres where the transmitter was in the same building as the studio, the same engineer could also shut down the transmitter. (Engineers in those days were also valued as 'uncles' for the popular Children's Hour: in Glasgow L. Hotine (later Senior Superintendent Engineer), was Uncle Leslie and in Manchester R. H. Wood (later EiC London OBs) was Uncle Bob.)[25]

In Cardiff the studio premises were in Castle Street, remote from the transmitter.

There was one studio but no separate control room and this studio was used every evening for a local programme. There were four Peel-Conner microphones and the balance between their outputs was effected by means of slide-wire potentiometers on the wall. The BBC tenure of the Castle Street premises was short and on 17 May 1924 a move was made to 39 Park Place. The new studio was built in the garden at the back of the house and the control room equipment was brought up to date. The microphone was the new Round-Sykes and the amplifiers were made by Marconi's.

At Belfast the transmitter was remote from the studio centre, which was in Linen-hall Street in part of an early nineteenth-century linen mill. The control room consisted of a lean-to with a glass roof, at the side of the main building. The low ceiling and walls of the studio were heavily draped with curtains.

The development of broadcasting in Scotland is a story in itself.[26] Scottish broadcasting began at 202 Bath Street, Glasgow, on 6 March 1923, where J. M. A. Cameron was 'The Engineer'. The studio was about 30 ft square and draped with hessian. It was connected by line to the transmitter at the Port Dundas power station of the Glasgow Corporation Electricity Department. The transmitting aerial was in the form of a cage slung between two high chimneys above the glass roof of the power station. It withstood many gales, but succumbed to one of them. The control room adjacent to the studio was furnished with a Western Electric 8A amplifier.

Scotland was in the forefront in developing the potentialities of broadcasting. Glasgow made experiments in schools broadcasting on closed circuit in April 1924, before regular transmissions for schools had started. In November 1924 the Glasgow staff moved from Bath Street to 21 Blythswood Square and stayed there until 1930 when a move was made to 268 West George Street.

The second main station in Scotland was Aberdeen, opened on 10 October 1923; the studios were at 17 Belmont Street (renamed 15 Belmont Street in 1925). The Edinburgh relay station opened on 1 May 1924. (The original transmitter was replaced about the end of 1924 by one that had been used at the Wembley Exhibition and was transferred to Plymouth in December 1932.) The studios at Edinburgh were first at 79 George Street, then at 87 George Street, and from May 1930 at 5 Queen Street. An attempt was made there to adapt the acoustics of the various studios to their use by using light acoustic treatment for music and heavily damped studios for drama (reverberation being added artificially when required). In 1931 the Edinburgh transmitter was moved to a new site, where it was set to work in fifteen hours – but only just, a last-minute fault having been rectified twenty seconds before the first 'pip' of the Greenwich Time Signal, with which the programme started. The Dundee relay station opened on 12 November 1924 and the studio was at 1 Lochee Road until it was closed down in 1932.

Thus, each of the nine main stations was provided with its own local studio and each of the relay stations that were added in 1923 and 1924 also had their own small studios. There were at first no permanent lines to permit the stations to carry a common programme; nor was any recording equipment available. Each station had therefore to be programmed individually and this had the advantage of encouraging the broadcasting of programmes of local interest, with the result that the geographical shape of broadcasting bore a remarkable resemblance to the area broadcasting and local radio of recent times.

BBC STUDIO AND TRANSMITTER PREMISES 1922–1926

Station	Date	Studio(s)	Transmitter
1 MAIN STATIONS			
London	14.11.22	Marconi House, Strand	Marconi House, Strand
	1.5.23	*2 Savoy Hill	Marconi House, Strand
	6.4.25	2 Savoy Hill	Selfridges, Oxford Street
Birmingham	15.11.22	General Electric Company's Works, Witton	General Electric Company's Works, Witton
	11.8.23	New Street Picture House, 105 New Street	Power Station, Summer Lane
	20.1.26	282 Broad Street	Power Station, Summer Lane
Manchester	15.11.22	Metropolitan-Vickers Works, Trafford Park	Metropolitan-Vickers Works, Trafford Park
	3.8.23	57 Dickenson Street	57 Dickenson Street
	12.12.24	Orme Buildings, The Parsonage	57 Dickenson Street
Newcastle	24.12.22	Eldon Square	Co-operative Wholesale Society, West Blandford Street
	23.12.25	54 New Bridge Street	Co-operative Wholesale Society, West Blandford Street
Cardiff	13.2.23	Castle Street Cinema, Castle Street	Electricity Sub-station, Eldon Road†
	17.5.24	39 Park Place	Electricity Sub-station, Eldon Road†
Glasgow	6.3.23	202 Bath Street	Port Dundas Power Station
	7.11.24	21 Blythswood Square	Port Dundas Power Station
Aberdeen	10.10.23	‡17 Belmont Street	Aberdeen Steam Laundry Company, 40 Claremont Street
Bournemouth	17.10.23	72 Holdenhurst Road	Bushey Road
Belfast	24.10.24	Linenhall Street	East Bridge Power Station

* In September 1925 the 2 was dropped and the address became simply 'Savoy Hill'.
† Renamed Ninian Park Road in 1924.
‡ In May 1925 a separate entrance for the BBC was provided, and the address was changed to 15 Belmont Street.

Station	Date	Studio(s)	Transmitter
2 RELAY STATIONS			
Sheffield	16.11.23	Union Grinding Wheel Co., Alma Street	Union Grinding Wheel Co., Corporation Street
	Apr. 1925	Castle Chambers, Castle Street	Union Grinding Wheel Co., Corporation Street
Plymouth	28.3.24	Athenaeum Chambers, Athenaeum Lane	Sugar Refinery, Mill Street
Edinburgh	1.5.24	79 George Street	The Quadrangle, University Buildings, Teviot Place
	31.7.25	87 George Street	The Quadrangle, University Buildings, Teviot Place
Liverpool	11.6.24	Edinburgh Café, 85 Lord Street	Smithdown Lane
	Nov. 1924	Edinburgh Café, 85 Lord Street	Corporation Refuse Destructor, St Domingo Road
Leeds/Bradford	8.7.24	Cabinet Chambers, Basinghall Street, Leeds	Messrs S. H. Sharp & Sons, Claypit Lane, Leeds
	8.7.24	Cabinet Chambers Basinghall Street	Simes Street, Bradford
	Nov. 1924	Cabinet Chambers, Basinghall Street	Corporation Destructor, Stanley Road, Burmantofts, Leeds.
Hull	15.8.24	26–7 Bishop Lane	Wincolmlee
Nottingham	16.9.24	4 Bridlesmith Gate	Messrs Weldon & Wilkinson, Duke Street, Basford
Dundee	12.11.24	1 Lochee Road	Caldrum Jute Works, St Salvador Street
Stoke-on-Trent	21.10.24	Majestic Buildings, South Wolfe Street	Minton's Works, London Road
Swansea	12.12.24	Oxford Buildings, Oxford Street	Townhill

The microphones at many of the early stations were of the Peel-Conner carbon-granule type made by the General Electric Company. These had been used at Chelmsford and Writtle by the Marconi engineers and were similar to those used in telephones. They were inherently noisy and gave very poor quality; they were also insensitive so that it was necessary to place them very close to the speaker to achieve sufficient output, especially as in some cases there was no amplifier between the microphone and the line feeding the transmitter.

An improved microphone (type 373) supplied by the Western Electric Company had two carbon-granule buttons, which were mounted one on each side of a stretched steel diaphragm to give a push-pull output. This was a considerable improvement on the Peel-Conner microphone, but still suffered from background noise. It was used in Birmingham and Cardiff. Manchester, for a short time in 1923, used a 'photophone' in which a modulated light-beam was picked up by a selenium cell.[27]

Another microphone produced by the Western Electric Company was of a revolutionary type. Instead of relying upon the variable resistance of a carbon-granule button, it operated by the variation in capacitance between a metal diaphragm and the metal casing. There were high hopes of this type of microphone, because it gave promise of eliminating the noise that had always been associated with carbon-granule microphones. However, in practice, the 'condenser' microphone gave a great deal of trouble, because any moisture in the air-gap caused an alarming 'frying' noise. This was particularly apt to occur when an orchestra was playing in a studio in which there was little or no ventilation so that the atmosphere became more and more humid. Once the frying noise had started the only immediate cure was for an engineer to hurry into the studio and substitute a carbon microphone. To reduce this problem the microphone was taken out of the studio when not in use and hung in a cupboard containing a saucer of calcium chloride to absorb the moisture and keep the microphone dry until it was next required. Condenser microphones nevertheless continued to give trouble and the bad reputation they acquired was not dispelled until several years later.

The Round-Sykes moving-coil microphone was used in Studio 3 at Savoy Hill in May 1923, at Bournemouth and Aberdeen in October 1924, and subsequently at other studio centres. It was a considerable advance on the earlier types, because, being electromagnetic, it avoided the problems associated both with carbon-granule and with condenser microphones. It had been developed by Captain H. J. Round of the Marconi Company and became known as the 'Magnetophone'. It consisted of a large circular electromagnet taking a current of 4 A from an 8-V accumulator. A coil of fine-gauge aluminium wire was attached to the magnet by means of three pieces of cotton wool smeared with vaseline. (Some experts who had experience of this microphone claimed that four pieces of cotton wool were better than three – which goes to show the extent to which empirical methods came into the technology of those days.)

The output was weak and the associated amplifier had therefore to be located as close to the microphone as possible. This microphone operated on sound principles, which were later applied in a more practical manner. Though electrically satisfactory, it had a number of shortcomings. The coil had a tendency to fall off and the microphone had to be cradled in a thick layer of 'sorbo' rubber; the whole assembly was usually mounted on a massive wooden trolley, which made it an unwieldy piece of equipment. Since a rise in the temperature of the studio could melt the vaseline, it became a matter of routine to change the cotton wool just before a broadcast if the microphone had been in use for some time beforehand. Nevertheless, when at its best, this microphone gave remarkably good quality, as was shown a few years ago when comparative tests were made on a number of old microphones.

Towards the end of the life of the British Broadcasting Company the Marconi-Reisz microphone appeared. This originated in Germany but was manufactured in the United Kingdom. It was of the carbon-granule type and consisted of an octagonal block of marble with a cavity in one side in which the granules were placed. The diaphragms were at first made of thin rubber, but later of mica. A peak in response between 4 and 6 kHz caused violins to scream. Finally diaphragms made of rice-paper were used; these resulted in a considerable improvement and the Reisz microphone continued to be used at all stations for many years until it was displaced by the ribbon microphone of the 1930s. The output of the Reisz microphone was high, so that hum and other forms of interference were reduced. There was, however, a tendency for the microphone granules to pack together and the microphone could easily be overloaded. The packing was particularly likely to occur if the microphone had been used on a stand and moved about. It produced an increase in hiss and a decrease in sensitivity. It could be cured by taking the microphone out of circuit, tipping it upside-down and beating it gently with the fist until the feed current observed on a milliammeter was restored to the correct value. The electrodes were of carbon about $\frac{1}{4}$ in. in diameter and $1-1\frac{1}{2}$ in. long connected directly to the terminals at the back. Because of the high level of hiss, it was not advisable to use the Reisz microphone at a great distance from the performers, but this had to be done if the artists' voices contained strong components near the peak frequency of the microphone. On this account, the baritone Raymond Newall had to be placed about 14 ft from the microphone. Normally the artists were fairly close to the microphone and spoke at an angle to it to reduce the effect of the rising frequency characteristic. This microphone was used with success for OBs, but music in the studio tended to sound very hard – which was possibly the reason why studio carpets were used for so long. One of the advantages of this microphone was that it could be suspended from the ceiling at a height at which it could 'see' the performers at the back of the studio.

Already during this early period the long-standing controversy had started about whether engineers should be responsible for the balance and control of programmes and for the resulting quality. At first they were so responsible because they were familiar with the equipment and its potentialities and peculiarities. Towards the end of this era, however, discussions arose on the question whether orchestral music ought to be 'controlled' by a professional musician following the musical score.

It was then, as now, necessary to take care in the placing of the microphones in relation to the performers and it was necessary to control the volume of the programme output to keep it within fairly well-defined limits; excessive volume would over-modulate the transmitter, while background noise would become evident during periods of low volume. It was clear that, though such a control was essential, its use could defeat the intentions of the conductor and P. P. Eckersley, as Chief Engineer, pointed out the danger of having 'two conductors in series'. Nevertheless, a small unit was set up at Savoy Hill called 'Balance and Control' to be responsible for the microphone balance and for controlling the output. In the Regions, however, these functions continued to be performed for many years by engineers. It soon became evident

P. P. Eckersley, Chief Engineer, 1923–9

Studio 1, Savoy Hill, 1928

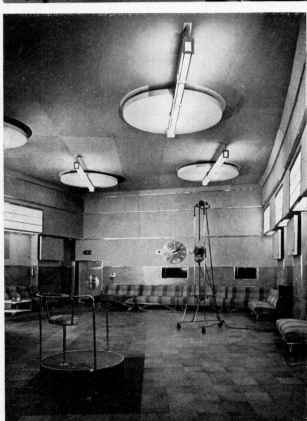

Left Studio 8A, Broadcasting House, London, 1932

Right Orchestral stereo studio at Birmingham Broadcasting Centre, 1971

Control table, Savoy Hill, 1928

Type A studio desk, 1947

Stereo control desk, 1971

Control room, Savoy Hill, 1928

Control room, the Parsonage, Manchester, 1924

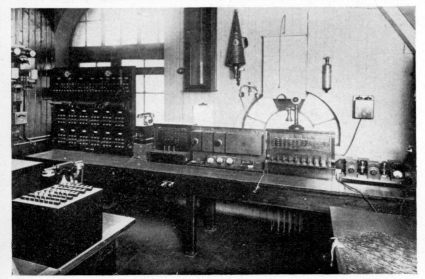

Control room, Aberdeen, 1929

Right Control room, Broadcasting House extension, 1961

Control room, Piccadilly,
Manchester, 1929

Below left Control room,
Broadcasting House,
London, 1932

Below right Temporary
wartime control room,
Broadcasting House, 1939
(Photo: H.M. Bonner)

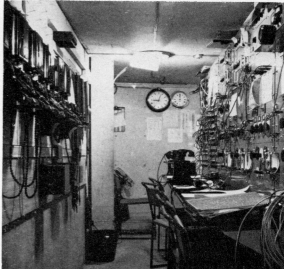

Top 2LO transmitter, Marconi House, 1922

Bottom VHF and UHF transmitters, Pontop Pike, 1969

Top left Aerial towers at Brookmans Park, 1929

Top right Short-wave aerials at Daventry, 1937

Bottom left Feeder-switching tower, Skelton, 1950

Bottom right Aerial feeders and switches, Daventry, 1963

Communications equipment, Glasgow, 1923

Below left Automatic selectors, Bush House, 1959

Above right Main distribution frame, Broadcasting House Extension, 1962

Communications Centre, Birmingham Broadcasting Centre, 1971

that the person responsible for controlling musical programmes, whether an engineer or not, should have at least some knowledge of music.

The origin of 'balance and control' as a special technique can be traced to the decision by H. Bishop, then Senior Superintendent Engineer, to appoint R. Haworth to the post of Programme Liaison Engineer in November 1926; Haworth was released from duties in the control room and for the first six months of his tenure of his new office he handled almost every programme, apart from OBs. He had been a transmitter engineer at Bournemouth, but had shown interest in the programme side, both his parents having been on the stage. He was therefore well qualified to co-operate with producers when he was transferred to the London control room in 1925. A test was held in 1926, in which musicians and engineers controlled orchestral programmes in turn and anonymously. Members of the Music Advisory Committee, who acted as assessors, voted overwhelmingly in favour of the control being done by musicians. As a result, Stanton Jefferies, who had been Musical Director, was appointed to be the first 'balance and control' expert, with one assistant. Haworth was transferred to this unit and it was expanded to a total of four people.

Haworth was the first to use two Round-Sykes microphones in one studio; this was for a revue called *Radio Radiance*, which had a dancing chorus of six girls. The two microphones were placed back-to-back and had to be connected in parallel because there were no arrangements for microphone mixing. A more ambitious programme followed on 21 November 1926 when James Elroy Flecker's *Hassan* was performed in Studio 1 at Savoy Hill.[28] Rehearsals were conducted before the microphone and the result was considered to be a great advance on any previous attempt. This was no doubt because the technical aspects of the production were in charge of the same man throughout the rehearsals and the actual transmission, and because a great deal of care was taken to secure the right balance. The importance of 'perspective' was already appreciated to the extent that the chorus of merchants at the end of the play took 'the golden road to Samarkand' by going out of the studio and up the back staircase, to the accompaniment of camel bells.

The demands of correct balance and perspective made it necessary to use more than one microphone and necessitated the use of a mixer. The first of these, introduced about 1925, had two channels and was used for the sole purpose of superimposing the chimes of Big Ben on the late-night dance music. An earlier attempt to achieve an artistic effect by fading down the music from the Savoy Hotel behind the chimes of Big Ben so as to tail off before midnight struck had been successful, but it required the services of two men operating two separate faders. The new mixer permitted one man to control the operation. The mixing was done, nominally at zero level, at the input of the 'B' amplifier.

The mixing technique put a powerful tool into the hands of drama producers, and in early 1927 there was a production of *Trilby* with an orchestra and singing cast in Studio 1, Savoy Hill, the action taking place in Studio 3. At the last moment it was decided to use artificial echo for the theatre scene, which involved mixing three channels, a feat not before attempted.

The need for sound effects arose very early, because of the demand for realism in dramatic performances. At first the effects were produced in the studio. In the 1926 production of *Hassan*, a fountain had to be provided in Studio 1; this was built up with water tanks, waterproof canvas and hoses, and was required to drip for half an hour at a time during the programme. As two-channel mixers were available by this time, it was natural that the next step should be to create the effects in a separate studio, the output from which could be mixed into the programme as required. This technique was much elaborated in later years and finally led to the dramatic control panel, which was to play an important part in drama and in other important productions, such as the Christmas Day programmes during the 1930s.

The application of acoustic treatment to studios was still in an elementary stage, although W. C. Sabine of Harvard University had already done fundamental work on sound absorption and reverberation. At first, several layers of materials were used on walls and ceilings to provide an approach to an anechoic chamber. At the end of 1925 A. G. D. West, then Head of the BBC Research Department, listed the following requirements:

i) there should be no echo to spoil the intelligibility of transmissions,
ii) no noise should come into the studio from outside, and vice versa,
iii) it should be possible to carry out the investigation of microphones without any of the disturbing factors caused by reflection from the surface of the walls and ceilings.

The last requirement was thought to be important, because at that time no really satisfactory microphones were available for transmitting speech and music at high quality. At the same time, West reported the results of tests made in various halls and public buildings. A heavily draped BBC studio was found to have a reverberation time of 0·25 s, whereas that of Gloucester Cathedral was 10 s.

By 1927 the basic principles of studio acoustics were being applied to BBC studios, and West wrote a series of articles on the subject.[29] It had already been grasped that the reverberation time must suit the size of the room, that it must not vary excessively with frequency, and that discrete echoes could be troublesome. It was also appreciated that the acoustics of the studio could affect the performers as well as the listeners and that a person with two ears could discriminate between sounds coming from different directions, whereas a microphone could not. As a result of these studies it was considered that the reverberation time should be between 2 and 4 s for a large orchestra, 1·5 s for an octet, and 1 s for a solo singer. When new studios were built at Savoy Hill in 1925 the internal walls were of light construction and the acoustics of Studio 4 were made variable by using draping mounted on runners. Studio 5, used for talks, exhibited a strong boom caused by vibration of the walls and they were therefore covered with a layer of hair felt behind a decorative draping. By the beginning of 1927 the studios had been brightened up, both visually and acoustically. Studio 6 was completed in the summer of 1926 for talks and piano music. The acoustic treatment was intended to reduce the reverberation time to about 0·8 s; it consisted of hair felt applied to the brick walls and covered with strong wallpaper, a combination giving absorption at low frequencies and reflection at the higher frequencies. A part of the wall surface was covered with wood to increase the reverberation at the upper end of the scale; this was rather overdone and was partly compensated by hanging pictures and tapestries on the walls.

Already in 1926 artificial echo was introduced following a suggestion from Captain Round of the Marconi Company. A loudspeaker and a microphone were mounted on the staircase outside Studio 1 at Savoy Hill. As the staircase was spacious and constructed of stone, it was admirably suited to the purpose, the loudspeaker being placed at the bottom and the microphone at the top. The reverberant sound was superimposed on the main output by means of the two-channel mixer already mentioned. From that time onwards artificial reverberation was used on nearly all musical programmes. Studio 2, used for drama, had an echo room adjacent to it; this was not provided with a loudspeaker – when echo was required, the door leading into the echo room from the studio was left open so that the echo room formed, in effect, a 'live' extension to the studio. Also alongside the studio was a 'noise' room for sound effects and inside this room was a silence cabinet for announcements and for switching the four microphones (studio, announcer, effects and echo). Until 1927 the silence cabinet was usually built inside the studio, but it was found more convenient to have a small room adjacent to the studio giving a view of it through a small window, 'rather like a lepers' squint in the walls of ancient churches'.[30] This room contained a microphone for the announcer, a microphone change-over switch, headphones for balancing the programme and a telephone communicating with the Control Room.

The Control Room at Savoy Hill was in the shape of a truncated L, and the whole of one limb of the L was occupied by batteries (300 V for ht, 6 V for filament heating, 24 V for grid bias and relay operation) and charging generators. The centre of the main part of the room was occupied by the SB switchboard and a 'line corrector' desk. Along, and on, the walls were amplifiers, relays, a fuse panel, receivers, time-signal equipment, a power switchboard, and four control positions. Each of these last comprised an input board with plugs, jacks and indicators, a 'B' amplifier with its volume controls, an output board, again with plugs, jacks and indicators, and an amplifier for 'miscellaneous operations' – all mounted on a table.[31] (Plate IV.)

As the same lines were used for programme and for PBX traffic, a complicated method of semi-automatic operation was introduced. Insertion of a plug in the line jack at a distant centre put a balanced earth connection on the line, which operated a series of relays at the SB centre and also a pilot lamp and a buzzer; this indicated that the distant centre was ready to accept the programme. Inserting a plug into a jack in the SB board operated a further series of relays, which, if the line was available, switched on the filaments of the appropriate amplifiers, connected the programme to line, and gave an 'engaged' signal to the PBX operator.

An important ancillary to studio operation was the system of signal lights. At first arrangements for cueing were primitive; instructions were given to artists by signalling through the window between the control room and the studio. The installation of red lights in the studios at Savoy Hill was done in the spring of 1925. Signalling methods had not yet been standardised; in Birmingham, for example, the engineer in charge installed two lamps in the studio that could be switched from the control room, one labelled 'come closer' and the other labelled 'move back'.

A large amount of paperwork accumulated in the form of station logs. Every item that was broadcast was logged, with the time of starting and finishing and with details of all faults, including line noise, momentary breaks, crosstalk, distortion and 'blasting'. The log sheets from all the stations and studio centres were scrutinised in the Superintendent Engineer's office.

Throughout this period a great deal was left to the self-reliance and ingenuity of the engineers on the spot, and their powers of improvisation were frequently called upon. This was possibly more evident in the studios than at the transmitting stations, because the design of transmitters had at first to be given priority and much of the skilled engineering effort available for research and design work had been devoted to them. On the studio side no corresponding body of knowledge had been built up and many problems in studio acoustics, the use of microphones, and transmission over lines had to be solved empirically. Nevertheless, the leaders of the Engineering Department quickly appreciated the need for research and development work in all these matters and it was started as soon as suitable staff were available for it. In this way a fund of knowledge about every aspect of broadcasting technology was built up before the great expansion of studio facilities took place in the 1930s, with a corresponding improvement in the quality of the output.

The spirit of improvisation was exemplified in the installation at Glasgow – the first in Scotland – where the switching equipment comprised a complex array of double-pole double-throw knife switches obtained from a local shop. These switches were capable of carrying a current of about 15 A and were screwed to a board and connected with heavy-gauge wire. (Plate VIII.) Their correct operation depended on local knowledge, especially when the labels fell off. These problems were resolved in 1924 when the Glasgow studio centre was moved to Blythswood Square, where it remained for fourteen years. Only about a fortnight was allowed between the date when the Blythswood Square premises were acquired and the deadline set for changing over from the old to the new equipment. Apparatus for the new station was sent up from London, but the engineers in Glasgow had to work continuously for three days and nights to meet the completion date.

Such dedication to the job in hand was by no means unusual; no doubt it was helped by the fact that those engaged in the pioneer work felt that they were helping to create something new and of potential worth.

By 1924 plugs and jacks began to be used for making inter-connections. They were apt to give trouble if dust and grit got into the contacts and the plugs had to be kept clean by frequent polishing. Some stations prided themselves on the gleaming appearance of their rows of plugs. At a later stage it became common for the input and output of each amplifier to pass through two break-jacks in tandem with a third jack connected in parallel for monitoring purposes; this arrangement made it possible to break the circuit on either side at will or to monitor across it without breaking the connection. A point was eventually reached at which the number of jacks used for the purpose of facilitating every kind of check introduced more hazards than it was intended to obviate.

Starting in 1924 there was a revolution in methods of wiring. Up to that time heavy wire capable of carrying currents of 10 A had been used. It was followed by a vast and ponderous amount of cabling in what was known as '1-pair 10', which persisted for many years in control rooms at both studios and transmitters. This was a standard type of Post Office cable, consisting of a single pair of enamelled copper wires, each insulated with wrappings of waxed cotton and the whole enclosed in a lead sheath. The gauge (0·63 mm diameter) corresponded to a weight of 10 lb per mile of single wire. All wiring, except for mains supplies, employed this type of cable.

The first attempts to broadcast gramophone records were made by wheeling a hornless acoustic gramophone up to the microphone, but an electromagnetic pick-up was introduced by Capt. Round in 1925. At first very few records were available and they were used only to fill gaps in the programme. In the Bournemouth studio, for example, there was, for several weeks, only one record, which carried the *Turkish Patrol* on one side. It is not known what was on the other side, but whatever it was listeners in Bournemouth must have become well acquainted with it and with the *Turkish Patrol* – perhaps almost as well as BBC engineers became acquainted with *The Teddy Bears' Picnic*, which was used for many years for test purposes.

The use of the acoustic gramophone called for a considerable degree of artistic judgment. One of the large knife switches of the type seen in the Glasgow photograph was labelled 'Integrating Condenser' and was used to reduce the response at the high audio frequencies, so as to eliminate the 'scratch' that was then a prominent concomitant of music from gramophone records. Immediately after the next gramophone record had been announced, the great switch would be closed, thereby substituting 'woof' for 'scratch', At the end of the record, the switch had to be pulled out again to permit the next announcement to be made at normal intelligibility.

The evolution of amplifiers was closely linked to that of microphones. The output of the original solid-back carbon microphone used in the studio at Marconi House was high enough to be applied directly to the line feeding the transmitter without any amplification. At Cardiff, the microphone output was fed directly to the line until August 1923 when a Western Electric Type A amplifier was installed. The introduction of microphones giving better sound quality, but with a lower output, made the use of amplifiers in the studio control rooms essential. The first microphone amplifier at Savoy Hill was huge – at least 6 ft long, 4 ft high and 2 ft deep. To reduce microphony the valves were suspended upside-down in beakers of thick oil.[32] This amplifier, designed by H. J. Round of the Marconi Company, had six stages of amplification, the last stage comprising four bright-emitter valves in parallel. When the first studio at Savoy Hill was brought into use on 1 May 1923 this impressive piece of equipment was housed in an amplifier room, which was near the studio and was the forerunner of the control room.

This amplifier was soon superseded by others of improved design, but still of massive proportions. The Western Electric Type 8A amplifier installed at Birmingham, Cardiff, Manchester and Glasgow in 1923 was rack-mounted and about 2 ft square and 8 in. deep. The lt supply for the filaments and the ht supply for the anodes came from separate batteries. The valves had bayonet-type bases and W-shaped filaments mounted between the two halves of the grid, which were flanked by the two halves of the anode. The gain control was a stud switch on the top of the amplifier and there was a pull-on/push-off switch. Two small windows were provided in the case; these were covered with gauze and made it possible to see whether the amplifier was switched on or off. The output from the microphone, or from an OB line, was applied directly to the input of the amplifier; its output was connected to the line feeding the local transmitter.

From this period onwards the design of audio-frequency amplifiers was directed towards the evolution of specific types adapted to different purposes. The broadcasting chain began to take shape in much the same form as it exists today.

The microphone amplifier, which had to have fairly high gain to increase the signal-to-noise ratio at a point as early as possible in the transmission chain, became known as the 'A' amplifier. In the control room, a second amplifier was needed to make it possible to adjust the level of the signal and send it over a Post Office line to the local transmitter. This was the 'B' amplifier. As soon as it became possible to undertake simultaneous broadcasting, a third type of amplifier was needed, known as the 'line amplifier'. It was normally used to increase the level at the sending end of outgoing lines and in that capacity was later called a 'C' amplifier. A fourth type, known as the 'D' amplifier, was used at the receiving end of incoming lines.

Some of the 'A' amplifiers were made by Marconi and others were the Western Electric type 8A, already mentioned. The Marconi 'A' amplifier of 1924 (type GA1) had five stages: the first originally contained a 'Wecovalve' (or 'peanut') and later a DEV valve; each of the remaining four stages had Marconi dull-emitter valves mounted in a spring holder with gold-plated contacts. The contacts were connected into the circuit by flexible leads and the valves were mounted on special stagings suspended by rubber bands. These precautions were necessary to reduce the prevailing bugbear of microphony. Since noise introduced in the early stages was amplified by later stages, the valves in the first stage were specially selected for low noise; those found to be quiet were marked with a white spot and put into a box so as to be readily available as replacements when an amplifier became noisy. The 'A' amplifier included a variable control operating on the grid circuit of the second valve to adjust the response at the upper frequencies, and another operating on the grid circuit of the third valve to adjust the response at the lower frequencies. These were provided 'to enable the operator to balance the sounds in the different items reproduced as best to suit the acoustic properties of the hall in which the microphone is installed' – and possibly also to compensate for variations in the characteristics of the microphone. Somewhat different forms of 'A' amplifier were used at different centres.

The Marconi 'B' amplifier (type GK1) had three stages, using LS5 valves throughout. The gain was about 28 dB and there were three valves in parallel in the output stage. There were two volume controls, the one at the input end being intended to prevent the first stage from overloading; to minimise noise it was set as high as possible short of overloading.

48

The 'C' amplifier was developed for feeding outgoing lines; as early as 1923 Western Electric loudspeaker amplifiers were used for this purpose. If it was necessary to feed two lines simultaneously, a second line amplifier had to be used. In London the output of the 'B' amplifier could be connected to a single input on the 'SB Board' and thence to all the outgoing line amplifiers in parallel, without regard to impedance matching.

A 'D' amplifier was brought into use in 1926. This had two stages, with LS5 valves, and was provided with a gain control; a tapped choke in the anode circuit of the first valve provided a tone control.

There were variations on these arrangements. At Bournemouth, for instance, the Round-Sykes microphone was in use from the opening of the station on 17 October 1923. There was one studio amplifier and a line amplifier, the latter being a two-valve model screwed to the wall. The control room, some $4\frac{1}{2}$ ft wide, also contained the batteries and a battery charger, but only natural ventilation was available. The studio, or microphone, amplifier had dull-emitter valves (DER) in the first two stages and LS5 valves in the middle stages. The output stages used bright-emitter LS2 valves. In a variation of this type of amplifier, the output stage consisted of six LS 3 valves in parallel. (Of the valves in the series LS1 to LS6, the LS5 was the best known, being the only one on sale to the public.)

Each of this series of amplifiers had input and output impedances appropriate to its function and the gains were such that the signal at the output of the 'B' amplifier could be brought to a standard level.

Audio-frequency amplifiers were normally provided with an input transformer and an output transformer, both somewhat heavy and bulky components, designed to give appropriate values of input and output impedance. The coupling between stages was either a transformer or tapped choke. The use of transformers and chokes tended to introduce distortion of the frequency response and also non-linearity distortion, but they enabled high gain to be achieved by taking advantage of the step-up ratio of the transformers. (When multi-grid valves became available some years later, sufficient gain could be achieved with resistance-capacity coupling, with a consequent improvement in performance and reduction in weight.)

There were two major problems with these amplifiers: noise and microphony. At Bournemouth, for example, the tramways in Holdenhurst Road produced spectacular sparks, the interference from which made it necessary to screen the first valve in the amplifier by wrapping it in copper gauze connected to earth. The importance of screening was thus appreciated quite early. Early attempts at screening prototype amplifiers included the use of tea chests lined with tinfoil, but most of the equipment in regular service was professionally designed and included the necessary screening. Similarly, early attempts to combat microphony included the suspension of the panels by 'aeroplane' elastic, but more sophisticated methods emerged at an early stage and the valves themselves became less prone to this trouble. The noise and microphony exhibited by the early amplifiers stimulated some research, as a result of which standards were established and a great improvement in performance was obtained.

The power supplies for audio-frequency amplifiers were provided by secondary cells: the filament supply at 6 V came from three cells in lead-lined teak cases, as used on ships, and the high-tension supply at 300 V was provided by 50-V units of smaller cells.

Measurement of programme volume was done by means of a 'slide-back' meter. This was a valve voltmeter with a centre-zero instrument. The reading was adjusted to zero by means of a potentiometer and the position of the potentiometer gave an indication of the voltage. A largely dc voltmeter was used for line testing, and by 1927 valve testers were also available. Control rooms were also provided with a check receiver for monitoring the output of the local transmitter.

In those days a visit to a broadcasting centre was in some ways more interesting to the casual visitor than it is nowadays. Modern trends in the housing of equipment and in styling and finish have reached a stage where a UHF transmitter, a standards converter, and a snack-vending machine look very much alike. In the 1920s the various assemblies and even individual components were separately mounted on desks, on racks, or on the walls, so that it was not difficult to appreciate the functions of each item. Expanses of rich mahogany, with highlights of gleaming brass, jostled with exposed coils, valves and heavy wires. Elegant cabinet work and rows of jack-strips reflected the influence of Post Office telephone switchboards. The general effect was of Victorian solidity with, here and there, a touch of the empirical style associated with the name of Heath Robinson.

From November 1922 time signals were regularly transmitted before the news bulletins at 7 pm and 9 pm by an announcer playing the Westminster Chimes on a piano or, later, on tubular bells installed for the purpose. This innovation was so well received that it became necessary to improve the clocks and a contract was placed with the Synchronome Company for master clocks and slave dials to be installed in studio centres. The loudness of the tick was adjustable and it could be arranged to start some seconds before the hour. An announcer could then begin counting and ring a gong at the hour.[33] At Aberdeen, Bournemouth and Manchester impulse clocks, made by Gent & Company, were installed.

In a broadcast on 21 April 1923 Frank Hope-Jones, a well-known radio amateur and horologist, concluded his talk by counting down the last five seconds to 10 pm. He afterwards suggested that a regular service of accurate time 'pips' might be provided by the Royal Observatory and broadcast by the BBC. Equipment was designed for reproducing the six pips accurately from a 1 kHz oscillator, the output of which was controlled by a switch operated directly by the escapement wheel of a chronometer at the Observatory, which was then at Greenwich. The Greenwich Time Signal (GTS) was regularly broadcast from 5 February 1924, the signal consisting of six pips starting five seconds before the minute and ending on the minute.[34]

4 SIMULTANEOUS BROADCASTING

We have long been accustomed to the idea of a radio programme being broadcast simultaneously from perhaps thousands of transmitting stations on a world-wide scale, but in the early 1920s even the small number of transmitters in this country could not, at first, be linked up for a simultaneous broadcast. Telephone repeaters, or amplifiers, which had become practicable as a result of the development of the three-electrode thermionic valve during the First World War, were only just beginning to make possible the use of long-distance underground cable circuits for commercial telephony. Before then the only way of achieving a low enough line loss to enable telephone conversations to take place over long distances was to use heavy-gauge copper wires carried overhead on poles. By spacing the wires 12 in. (30 cm) apart, and using gauges up to 600 lb per mile (4·92 mm diameter), it was possible to achieve the low resistance and capacitance and the high inductance necessary for low attenuation. The pairs of wires were transposed at intervals along the route to reduce crosstalk between them by offsetting the capacitance unbalances in successive sections against each other.

Open-wire lines, if well maintained, gave good-quality telephony over long distances (there had been such a line during the First World War between Berlin and Baghdad, portions of which were still in use during the 1930s), but bad weather, especially storm, snow or frost, could affect them severely. Moreover, the amount of space needed for an open-wire pair is so enormously greater than that required for a cable pair that the number of open-wire lines that could be carried on a trunk route was severely limited. Even commercial telephony therefore was still somewhat hazardous in the early years of British broadcasting, and first attempts to make use of the trunk line network to link up the transmitting stations were not very successful; the transmissions done in this way often suffered from noise, abrupt changes in level and other undesirable effects.

At first, use was made of trunk lines only occasionally, most of the programmes being produced locally, with the main stations in the Regions joining London only for the news. The importance of being able to link up all the transmitting stations for the radiation of a common programme was realised at an early date by the Chief Engineer, P. P. Eckersley; he also realised that it might be advantageous at times to make use of radio links for programme distribution. The first music test over an SB circuit was made on the night of 20 March 1923 from Birmingham to London. The results were judged to be 'very much beyond expectation, the only serious distortion being due to the loss of the higher harmonics of the violin and the top notes of the piano'.[35] A further test from Glasgow to London was made on 16 April 1923, using overhead lines. On 13 May of the same year a test was made from London simultaneously to the transmitters at Newcastle, Glasgow, Manchester, Birmingham and Cardiff. Each transmitter required an input of 0·25 W and was fed directly from the line; as the attenuation of the circuits was about 15 dB, a power of 7·5 W had to be applied to each line. A large Western Electric public-address amplifier had to be used to deliver this amount of power to each of the five outgoing lines simultaneously. The test was 'an unqualified success', except that the crosstalk into other telephone circuits was enormous. (The Post Office now limits the maximum power during programme peaks to just over 6 mW.) A few days later a further test was made with the power drastically reduced to 1 mW, but the crosstalk was still excessive and had to be

E

diminished by inserting repeating coils at the input of each line. (The power was determined by using a thermocouple; each one cost about £5 and one was burnt out when E. K. Sandeman, who was making the tests, coughed in front of the microphone.) At each end of the overhead lines, the circuits were brought into the cities on non-loaded cables and it was noted that this accounted for the rather 'hollow sound' obtained with speech and music. However, the tests had been so successful that programme transmission over long lines (then, and for many years later, referred to as 'land lines', even when they were in submarine cable) appeared to be feasible.

The first General News Bulletin read in Marconi House, London, by C. A. Lewis and broadcast by all transmitters was an adventure, not only for the engineers but also for the newsreader. The latter was overcome by the importance of the occasion and he concluded the bulletin with the audible *cri de coeur*: 'What the devil do I do next?'[36]

On 9 August 1923 'a rough programme given from 2LO' was scheduled, and in early September 1923 there occurred what was described by *The Sphere* as a 'Milestone in Radio Development', that is, an OB from Liverpool which was simultaneously broadcast by all the main stations then existing. The contemporary account is worth quoting:

'The experiment by which Sir Ernest Rutherford's address on the structure of the atom, delivered at the meeting of the British Association at the Philharmonic Hall, Liverpool, was heard from end to end of the British Isles simultaneously, is an achievement unsurpassed by any other country.

'Concealed among the flowers in front of the speaker was the microphone, a small gauze-covered disc 6 in. across. A wire from this led to a three-stage amplifier in the building. A tap line to a loudspeaker in the Technical Institute, Liverpool, supplied another packed audience. From Liverpool the current was carried by underground PO trunk line to Manchester, where it was tapped and broadcasted (*sic*), the remainder amplified, flowing to London by PO trunk line. At the London station, 2LO, the speech was put through the control board.

'The astonishing fact remains that all over England, Scotland and Ireland the speech would be heard in one-fiftieth of a second, whereas the voice, travelling through the atmosphere in the hall, would take one-fifth of a second to reach the seats at the back.'

An accompanying illustration showed the line routeing as Liverpool-Manchester-London, and then by separate lines to Glasgow, Newcastle, Birmingham, and Cardiff. Belfast and Bournemouth had not yet appeared in the network, but arrows drawn in by the artist suggest that not only was it possible to receive the programme in Belfast (from the Glasgow transmitter), but also in Dublin (from Manchester), Amsterdam, Brussels and Paris. The caption reads:

' "Speech like lightning" – how Sir Ernest Rutherford's speech to the British Association was broadcasted all over the country "within the twinkling of an eye".

'The above diagram shows the means employed to broadcast the President's address at the meeting of the British Association simultaneously all over the country.

The arrangements necessary to procure a successful result were in the hands of Mr H. W. Litt of the BBC, whose work at the control in the London station contributes to such uniformly successful results.'

On 4 October 1923 Eckersley wrote to the Post Office asking for terms for increased use of the lines, from 5 or 5.30 pm onwards, instead of from 6 pm. The lines that were handed over by the Post Office were non-repeatered open-wires, but with considerable lengths of 'entrance cable' at each end, which resulted in large variations of loss over the usable frequency range owing to impedance mis-match at the junctions between cable and open wire.

Much trouble was experienced with lines during the early years owing to bad quality and unreliability. Complaints were made to the Post Office Headquarters, but they were reluctant to admit any shortcomings in their lines. A politely worded request from the General Manager that the Post Office should give the BBC a definition of what they considered to be 'a suitable land wire', coupled with the modest suggestion that such a line should transmit frequencies up to 6000 Hz (no mention was made of the many other important requirements of a music line) drew a formal reply to the effect that the Post Office engineers were fully aware of the technical requirements for music circuits.

Only one line was used on any one route between two BBC stations and this had to be used as a programme and as a control line. The engineers would speak first to make all the necessary arrangements and then, at the appropriate time, both ends would switch over to programme. At junction points, such as Glasgow, where several lines had to be handled, this led at first to a rather untidy layout in which there was one hand-ringing telephone for each line. Glasgow was the simultaneous broadcast (SB) centre for the stations in Scotland and, later, also for Belfast. As stations were added to the network, more large knife switches were added, until a stage was reached when the system almost got out of hand owing to its sheer complexity.

In 1924 knife switches gave way to plugs and sockets for switching. A 'second generation' control room using this method is shown in the photograph of the one at 'The Parsonage', Manchester, where an engineer is operating one of the controls on the 'B' amplifier. To his left can be seen the switchboards with jacks and cords. (Plate IV.)

Each of the main stations was provided with an 'input board' and an 'output board'. At a typical provincial station the input board accepted all programmes incoming from the local studios, from outside broadcasts and from London. The output board carried the output from the 'B' or control amplifiers to the transmitters and to any other outgoing lines.

Gradually, as the necessary equipment became available and as the necessary techniques were acquired, more and more programmes were broadcast from some, though not necessarily all, stations simultaneously. There was, however, no permanent line network. Careful logging of all line phenomena was considered indispensable. Line faults were reported back to the previous station along the route and, if conditions became intolerable, the control room would telephone the local GPO

Trunk Test Clerk and ask him to change the line. Although the Post Office Engineering Department then, as now, was very helpful, the answer would often be that the BBC already had the best line available. An unorthodox method of clearing a line fault, which was sometimes at least temporarily successful, was to ring on the line during an interval in the programme.

By the summer of 1924 line operations in the Savoy Hill control room were on a fairly orderly basis. The Control Room was on the top floor, flanked on one side by a room containing the Development Section and on the other by a room containing the Research Section. Cynics declared that this was a convenient arrangement because the Development Section would produce equipment that would be tried out in the Control Room, and then the Research Section would find out why it would not work. In 1924 the Control Room was fairly small, and the most prominent piece of equipment was the SB board. Basically, this consisted of a kitchen table covered with American cloth, to which a vertical wooden framework had been added. On this wooden framework, which had a sheet of plywood across it, were hung Western Electric loudspeaker amplifiers in small boxes, one for each provincial station. The same amplifier served for both incoming and outgoing lines.

There was also a jackfield on which the lines and amplifiers terminated, and all switching was done manually by means of plugs and jacks. The immediate termination of the line as it entered the control room was a Standard Telephones and Cables type 4028 fuse mounting, which came into widespread use during the next ten to fifteen years, in Europe as well as in the UK. (The Western Electric Co. in the UK changed its name to Standard Telephones and Cables on its acquisition by the International Telephone and Telegraph Corporation in 1924). The circuit was then led via an intermediate distribution frame (IDF) to the SB board jackfield, where it appeared on 'Line', 'Listen', and 'Apparatus' jacks. As there was only a two-way line to each place, if anything went wrong during a programme stations had to get into touch with each other by outside telephone. Although the quality of transmission was poor in several respects, serious line trouble did not occur very often. The only station that seemed to have much difficulty was Plymouth, no doubt because of a long exposed open-wire route. Another trouble was that the Plymouth amplifier in the Savoy Hill control room was unstable, and would sometimes oscillate at a frequency above 15 kHz. Only young members of the staff were able to perceive frequencies as high as this; if one of them, when walking down the passage to the control room, heard the Plymouth amplifier oscillating, he would quickly switch it off and on, whereupon it would stop oscillating.

Since all the lines were two-way, attempts were made to exploit them as fully as possible while they were available. They could all be plugged through to the PBX for telephone traffic, though the control room retained priority and had to be asked for the line each time. There were keys for listening across each line, and there were one or two private lines, including one to the home of the Managing Director. Normally, any calling indicator operated a buzzer, but the Managing Director's indicator rang a bell, so that when Mr Reith called, extra prompt answering was assured.

There were normally two engineers on duty for SB work in the control room, because in the evening so many switching operations had to be done in a short time that they could not be managed by one pair of hands. Some of the staff were employed to work from 6 pm to close-down at about 10.30 pm. If stations were taking London programmes and then had five minutes of their own local news, the SB men in London had just five minutes in which to unplug everything, ring up each station individually to obtain clearance, and then plug back again. Even with two people, this had to be a brisk operation.

Technical wiring was done by control room staff; a particularly difficult operation, which actually occurred twice, was the removal of the SB board in the Savoy Hill control room. When the time came to expand the control room, the three rooms, occupied by Development Section, Control Room and Research Section, were merged into one larger control room. Ceilings as well as walls had to come down and the wiring was run on the upper side of the ceiling, so that for some weeks all the wiring, the jackfields and the distribution frame, had to be suspended by ropes. The SB board and the amplifiers had to be moved by night, first to an intermediate position and then to the final position; the process was assisted by supplies of sandwiches and beer, but without benefit of overtime payments. The main difficulty of the operation was in handling the masses of 1-pr. 10 lb cable, with their enormous weight of lead. As far as possible, the required lengths were laid out along the passage, tied up in bundles of a dozen and put into the ducts.

Because of the growing number of transmitting stations, including relay stations, the greater complexity of programme requirements (an alternative programme began with the opening of the Daventry long-wave transmitter on 27 July 1925) and the prospect of programme transmission over cable circuits, consideration was being given in 1926 to future methods of programme distribution, line switching, line testing and attenuation equalisation. An investigation was already in progress into the possibility of using trunk lines for the transmission of synchronising tone from a tuning-fork standard in London to the various transmitting stations.

The line routing provided for Birmingham, Bournemouth, Cardiff, Manchester and Newcastle to be fed direct from London; when Glasgow and Aberdeen, the last of the first eight main stations, came into operation, they received the programme from Newcastle. The ninth station, Belfast, was fed from Glasgow. Changes occurred when the relay stations began to be added. The first was Sheffield, which was originally intended to relay the Manchester programme, but the people of Sheffield objected and declared in favour of the London programme; their transmitter was therefore linked direct to London.[37, 38] The example of the people of Sheffield was followed in other places where stations were installed, with the result that the London programme had to be fed over long and expensive lines, and with considerable degradation of quality, to these stations.

The expensive and cumbersome nature of such a system of programme distribution gave an impetus to technical development in the line system. When the Leeds and Bradford transmitting stations were set up, they received their programme via the Leeds studio centre, and the fact that the latter was located in the same city as an important centre on the Post Office telephone network soon suggested the desirability of making the Leeds studio centre act as a distributing centre. The distribution was therefore rearranged so that the London programme was fed through Leeds to Manchester and separately to Newcastle for onward distribution to the various stations in Scotland, and to Belfast via Glasgow. Leeds thus became a BBC repeater station in 1926.

Shortly after this, it was decided that some saving in line rentals could be achieved by installing a BBC repeater station at another strategic point in the network. Gloucester and Derby were considered as possible sites for it, and it was finally agreed with the Post Office that it should be at Gloucester. Premises for it were taken on a five-year lease and the station was opened on 2 December 1926 and became fully operational early in the following year. The amplifiers at Leeds and Gloucester were similar to the line amplifiers used at Savoy Hill and were built by the Equipment Department. They used LS5 valves and had a gain of nearly 20 dB. The installation work at Gloucester was done by the Engineer-in-Charge (G. H. Daly), who was allowed to spend petty cash at the rate of about £80 per week. The Post Office co-operated willingly in this development, which proved highly successful. The repeater station could feed the programme to Cardiff (for Swansea), Plymouth and Birmingham (for the North). (An alternative route from London to these stations was provided via Leeds and Stoke as a protection against failure of the link between London and Gloucester.)[39]

The early long-distance lines were used as they were taken over from the Post Office, without any attempt at equalisation, but during the years 1924 and 1925 the problem of transmitting programmes over long distances by line was being studied by the Development Section under H. L. Kirke. A Lines Sub-Section was formed under A. S. Attkins, an ex-Post Office engineer, who concerned himself with line switching, testing and equalising equipment. The equalising work was done by A. C. Cameron. The design of an equaliser to improve the frequency response of long-distance circuits was originally suggested by J. S. Elston of the Post Office. It consisted of a parallel resistor and capacitor in *one* leg of the incoming pair, followed by a shunt consisting of a resistor in series with an inductor between the two legs, this being followed again, in the *other* leg of the line, by another parallel resistor and capacitor. The output was connected to the input of the 'B' amplifier. A variable equaliser according to this schematic was made up and became known as the 'Sullivan' equaliser, after the manufacturer. It was contained in a large wooden box with various values of resistance, capacitance and inductance which could be brought into circuit by means of plugs. A frequency run would first be done from London, readings being taken at the remote end of the line on the slide-back voltmeter, which was then the only equipment used to measure level. These readings were sent back to the Lines Engineer in London, who would work out what values should be used and instruct the remote control room accordingly. Another frequency run was then made. Some manipulation was necessary to make the levels at three or perhaps four frequencies approximately the same, though there must have been serious discrepancies in between. The equaliser presented a variable impedance to the line, so

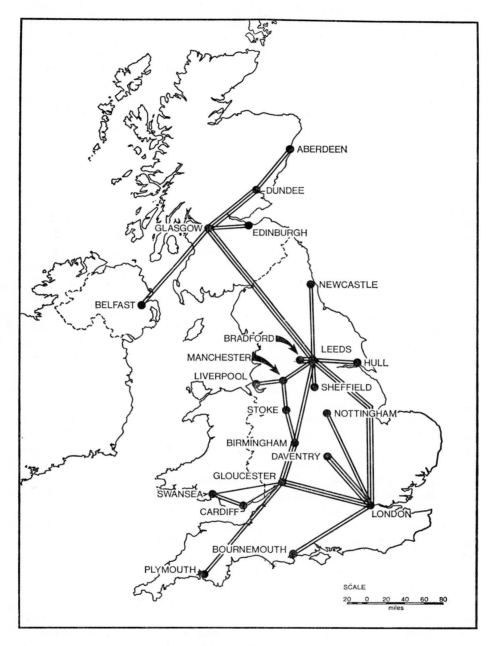

SB Line Network (1927)

that the results obtained depended on the impedance conditions and could therefore neither be controlled nor foreseen. This haphazard method of correction of the loss-frequency characteristics of the lines was to continue for some years, until the introduction of the constant-impedance equaliser in 1929 put line equalisation on a more systematic basis. The appearance of the 'Sullivan' equaliser can best be described by reference to the photograph of the Aberdeen control room, where it can be seen in the left foreground. This photograph also shows the 'B' amplifier (with three meters) and, on its left, the 'output board'. On the right of the 'B' amplifier is the 'input board' and on the extreme right is a 'line' amplifier. (Plate IV.)

5   OUTSIDE BROADCASTS

The BBC soon began to reach out beyond its own studios to collect programme material from outside. Within two months of its taking over the responsibility for broadcasting in Britain, there was an OB from the Royal Opera House, Covent Garden; this was a performance of Mozart's *The Magic Flute* on 8 January 1923.[40] Another OB in the early part of 1923 was of a political meeting in the Kingsway Hall – a fortunate choice as the acoustics of this hall are particularly good. The technical arrangements at these early OBs were made by the Western Electric Company, since that company possessed most of the technical knowledge needed to ensure good-quality transmission over the cable circuits from OB p hint to studio. Some OBs were not without excitement. Arthur Burrows recalls a broadcast in 1923 from the Regent Theatre, London, in which a pistol fired on the stage caused a choke coil in the transmitter to burst into flame.[41] From October 1923 a regular series of OBs from the Savoy Hotel provided dance music from the Savoy Orpheans and the Savoy Havana Band, of which even now 'the memory lingers on'.

The first OBs in the Regions are believed to have been from the Oxford Street cinema in Manchester. They usually consisted of music played by a sextet and the OB equipment was generally unattended. This was made possible by using an unorthodox 'passive' microphone consisting of a large loudspeaker base damped with vaseline, no amplifier being needed. It was the practice simply to telephone to the cinema and say that broadcasting would begin from there in, say, ten minutes' time. The first OB in Glasgow was of an opera from the Coliseum in March 1923.

Many OBs were done with Western Electric double-button microphones, which were used with a Western Electric two-valve amplifier using thoriated tungsten valves designed originally for use in a public-address system. An early engineering project in Birmingham was the construction in 1923 of an OB equipment known as the 'Cooper' amplifier, after its originator J. A. Cooper, who was the BBC Engineer-in-Charge at Birmingham at the time. This appears to have been the first attempt to systematise OB techniques. The equipment consisted of a large teak box, in which one of the Western Electric amplifiers was suspended by means of springs at the corners; the batteries, dry ht and wet lt were also installed in the box, together with a telephone and headphones. There was a carrying handle on the top, and the whole unit, which was very heavy, looked like a suitcase. A number of these amplifiers were made, not only for Birmingham but for other stations too. They were used for the series of open-air brass band concerts, broadcast during the summer from the bandstand in the gardens in Lord Street, Southport; a Western Electric double-button microphone was fixed high up in the bandstand and connected to the amplifier by a cable carried over the street to the nearby Cambridge Hall, where the Post Office lines terminated. A curious feature of the Western Electric amplifier was that a feedback circuit was employed to obtain the increased gain needed for certain applications, but when the amplifier was connected to Post Office overhead trunk circuits the feedback circuit had to be disconnected to keep the line noise within acceptable limits.

In the days of the Company there were no OB engineers or teams as such. The same engineers who looked after the control rooms, the studios and often the local transmitter also went out in a taxi with the OB equipment, rigged it up and carried out the whole operation, including, in most cases, the announcing. This was not always easy. A number of broadcasts of bells were done in the Midlands. One of these was from the Loughborough War Memorial, which consists of a tower erected in the middle of a park and carrying a large carillon installation, Loughborough having an important bell foundry. The opening recital was broadcast with one microphone, which was slung about halfway up a ladder below the bell-chamber. Between items in the programme the engineer had to climb up the ladder, lean over, and announce the next item.

Similar conditions prevailed in the other Regions. In Cardiff, for example, OBs also started quite soon, because here all the early programmes had to be of local origin; it was not until the late summer of 1923 that it became possible to receive programmes by line from London. The first OBs were from the Capitol Cinema where, as elsewhere, Western Electric microphones were used in conjunction with the amplifier described above. This was a standing OB, taking place every afternoon from Monday to Saturday inclusive, and consisted of a programme given by the Capitol Cinema Orchestra, conducted by Lionel Falkman. There were two engineers, one at the transmitter and one at the studio, and the usual procedure was that the studio engineer would switch on his control room equipment, plug the line from the Capitol into the amplifier, lock the control room door and go down to the Capitol Cinema. Here, he would switch on the amplifier, which was in the band room, switch over to a local microphone, announce the opening of the station from the band room and so start the programme. He would then go into the auditorium and see the film, five days running, and at the end of the hour or so during which the programme was on the air he would go back and make the closing announcement from the same microphone. There was a difference in procedure on Saturdays, because then it was the transmitter man who went first to the studio and switched on the studio equipment, then to the cinema to switch on the equipment there, then to the transmitter to run it up and finally to announce the opening of the programme from a microphone at the transmitting station.

Radio links began to play their part quite early. In 1924 the Development Section, under H. L. Kirke, designed a mobile transmitter installed in a unit like a tea trolley and called 'the Pram'. This was trundled around the London Zoo to get live OBs for the Children's Hour programme. It produced something like 10 W and used a large number of receiving-type valves, mostly LS5s. These sometimes had to be rapidly changed by a gloved hand, when they glowed brighter than 'cherry red'. Mechanical stability was assured by the weight of a 300-V lead-acid battery on the bottom shelf of the 'pram'. This transmitter was also used for a live OB from the zoo at Bellevue, Manchester, in 1925. As this was the first occasion of the kind in the North Region, the project received considerable publicity, with the result that when the engineers of the Research and Development Sections in London arrived at the old London Road railway station in Manchester they were met by the Stationmaster in his top-hat and given full VIP treatment.

At Bournemouth, as at the other centres, most of the programme was still coming from local sources in 1924. There was only one set of OB gear with which to do a number of local OBs, and when there was one it usually meant that somebody did not get a day off. Among the Bournemouth OBs there were the Bournemouth Municipal Orchestra under Dan Godfrey, a small light-music combination from the King's Hall Rooms, and the organ from the Boscombe Arcade. On one occasion in the spring of 1924 the programme planners had arranged for an organ programme from the Boscombe Arcade followed about 35 minutes later by music from the King's Hall Rooms. The OB team therefore had to finish at Boscombe Arcade, de-rig the equipment, sprint down the Arcade laden with ship-type lt accumulators, ht accumulators, the amplifier and the Western Electric double-button carbon microphone and load them all into a waiting Daimler. On arrival at the King's Hall Rooms the team hurried through the main entrance of the Hotel (there was no time to go round to the back) and through the tea room, connecting up the microphone on the way. The driver carried in the accumulators, the equipment was rigged again and the programme went on the air. The lines from such town OB points were in cable circuits and, as no equalisation was done on local circuits in those days, the quality, by modern standards, must have been noticeably 'woolly'.

The keynote of many of the early attempts at outside broadcasting was improvisation. Leeds claims to have had the first OB vehicle, which was an old motor-bicycle, a very heavy Triumph with a sidecar. Instead of the normal sidecar, however, the engineers fitted a large box in which they placed the whole OB equipment, microphones, batteries and amplifiers. The first broadcast of the 'Military Sunday' from York Minster took place at Christmas 1924, with brass bands and massed choirs. By the standards of those days this was a very large OB indeed, with some fifteen of the heavy Round-Sykes microphones slung in various positions round the Minster, and wired up by the BBC engineers in lead-covered 1-pr/10-lb cable. The switching of the microphones was done by porcelain-mounted switches and, since the wiring carried a dc supply from a battery to energise the microphone magnet, a loud click was heard every time a microphone switch was operated. The attempted solution was to buy some filament rheostats in a local radio shop and to wire one in series with each microphone, so that the microphone current could be gradually increased. Unfortunately, the operation of the rheostat produced a tearing noise instead of a click. This seems to have been the first time a microphone had ever been faded in.

The OB that made the maximum impact was undoubtedly the opening by King George V of the British Empire Exhibition at Wembley on 23 April 1924. This was the first broadcast by the Sovereign and also the first broadcast to be recorded (by a commercial company) for a repeat transmission later in the day. *Popular Wireless* reported: 'In the evening it was very instructive to listen to the gramophone broadcast. According to Captain Eckersley some twenty-nine valves were utilised before the speech was recorded at the HMV works at Hayes, and although some of it proved unintelligible, the result on the whole was remarkable.'[42] It was estimated that the King's speech was heard by at least ten million listeners, a fact that caught the imagination of the people and perhaps revealed to many for the first time the far-reaching possibilities latent in the medium. The *Daily Mail* made special arrangements for massed crowds to hear the King's speech in cities such as Manchester, Leeds and Glasgow.[43] The Marconi Company set up receivers in more than a hundred cities for this purpose. J. H. Holmes recollects the awestruck wonder with which country people in Northern Ireland heard the King's voice through headphones on a three-valve receiver.

The engineer responsible for the technical preparations was H. Bishop (later Sir Harold Bishop, Director of Engineering). The microphone used by the King was the Round-Sykes, which had recently been introduced as a replacement for the Peel-Conner carbon microphone. This occasion gave rise to an old story. Eckersley and Round were consulting with an equerry at the microphone point about where the King should be asked to stand, how loudly he should speak, etc. During the conversation the equerry said to Eckersley, 'You know, one day the King may command you to kneel and may tap you on the shoulder and say, "Arise, Sir Peter".' As Round had produced the microphone that was to be used, Eckersley replied, 'It would be better if he commanded Round here to kneel and said, "Arise, Sir Cumference!".'

An OB on a smaller scale, but one that lives in the memory of those who heard it, was the broadcast of the song of nightingales at midnight in the early summer of 1924. The broadcast came from the garden of Miss Beatrice Harrison's sixteenth-century home in Surrey. The birds were encouraged by Miss Harrison playing the 'cello and their song was picked up by a microphone and relayed by line to London. The birds responded so well to an Elgar Concerto that the broadcast was repeated on the night of 30–31 May 1925. Nature made a further sally into the world of technology when the sound of the sea was first broadcast from Bovisand Bay, near Plymouth, during the summer of 1925.[44]

The conduct of programme operations was sometimes made more difficult by the rigidity of rules about timing, especially when Regional stations were required to join London for SB transmissions such as the news at 9 pm. On one occasion, Glasgow was doing an OB from a conference that was to be taken by all Scottish transmitters and by Belfast. This OB had, as its last speaker, Lord Charlmont, then Minister of Education in Northern Ireland; the instructions were that, immediately after the speeches, stations must switch over to London for the time signal and news. At that time stations were given no discretion, and failure to radiate a time signal or even part of one was cause for disciplinary action. About ten minutes before the end of the OB, Glasgow telephoned to the engineer at the OB point to say that London was under-running and stations would have to be prepared to switch over to London two or three minutes early. It was agreed, however, that the OB programme would be left on the line until Glasgow control room confirmed that it was no longer required. When Mr Reith, the General Manager, appeared and wanted to know how the OB had gone, he was told that the end of the Minister's speech might perhaps have been cut on instructions from London. He was angry, but when he had a full report next morning and learned that London, in spite of the warning to the contrary, had in fact *over-run* by a few minutes, he was correspondingly delighted by the initiative shown by Glasgow. After this, some discretion was given to Regional Directors in these matters.

The attitude towards such aesthetic considerations as the visibility of the microphone at a public event was less permissive than it is today, when up to a dozen microphones (though of small and elegant design) can be seen at many music performances. The British National Opera Company allowed broadcasts from its performances, provided they were not transmitted locally: for example, when the BNOC was in Glasgow, the broadcast was carried by all transmitters *except* Glasgow. At one of these opera OBs, the engineer wanted to use a Reisz microphone slung above the orchestra pit, as he thought that a better balance would be obtained by such an arrangement. The conductor, however, would not allow it, saying that the microphone might distract the audience, who would need all their imaginative powers to visualise the principal soprano as a fairy. Fortunately, a Round-Sykes microphone in the footlights gave satisfactory results.

An important 'first' was the inauguration of the long series of broadcasts by Big Ben. This took place at midnight on New Year's Eve at the end of 1923 and was treated as an OB. It was followed by regular broadcasts twice a day from 9 March 1924. The microphone and amplifier were at first installed on the roof of Bridge Chambers, Bridge Street, Westminster. The microphone was a Round-Sykes, and it is thought that this may have been the first time that one of these was used on an OB, the Western Electric double-button type having been used hitherto. The microphone was enclosed in a biscuit tin filled with cotton-wool, but was later transferred (still wrapped in cotton-wool) to a football bladder sealed with rubber solution 'to guard against the inclemency of the weather' and suspended about 15 ft above the bells.[45] The amplifier was the prototype of the Marconi 'A' amplifier, which later became standard at most studios; it was contained in a teak case and was heavy and cumbersome. The 8-V 4-A supply for the microphone was obtained from four 60–Ah batteries. The 6-V lt and the 300-V ht supplies for the amplifier were also obtained from portable accumulators. The signal from Big Ben was fed to all stations, and the great bell was heard at midnight to the accompaniment of ships' sirens on the Thames and in the docks. When the Marconi-Reisz microphone became available in 1926, one was installed permanently in the Clock Tower.

The heights and the depths had been scoured for material during the lifetime of the Company. There were relays from aircraft of the popular entertainers, John Henry and Blossom, and on 9 May 1925 of Sir Alan Cobham teaching the actress Heather Thatcher to fly. A broadcast was made by a diver under the Thames on 5 July 1926 and, on a more exalted level, the first broadcast from the House of Lords on 26 May 1926.

6 THE KESTON RECEIVING STATION

The proposal that the British Broadcasting Company should set up a receiving station of its own stemmed from the work done by A. G. D. West, the Company's Senior Research Engineer, at the Biggin Hill aerodrome in 1923–4. Here he received signals from the American station broadcasting from Pittsburgh (KDKA) on 110 m (2·75 MHz). The aerial used was a simple one and the receiver comprised an rf amplifier, a detector, and an af amplifier. To reduce the effect of vibration on the tuning capacitors, they were mounted on sorbo rubber and the extremely critical tuning operation was helped by the provision of 15-in. extension handles to them. A programme from KDKA was picked up and relayed in the BBC programme in December 1923 – the first relay from a foreign station.[46]

It was felt that the Biggin Hill results could be improved upon and a search was made for a site for a new receiving station. West found a suitable location at Layham's Farm, about one mile to the west of the village of Keston in Kent. The fifty-acre site, which was leased by the BBC, consisted of a flat area, well clear of main roads and other sources of interference, at an altitude of about 520 ft AMSL. The receiving station was opened there in 1925. Its accommodation consisted of two wooden huts, the larger of which contained the receiver room, a small workshop, a store and an office. The smaller hut contained batteries and charging plant.

The original intention was that the Keston Receiving Station should be used to provide good-quality relays of programmes broadcast from European capitals, such as Paris, Berlin and Vienna; at this time, lines from the Continent were intended for telephony and their frequency response and noise level were unsatisfactory for the transmission of music. No recording equipment was provided at Keston and all relays were therefore taken 'live'. Shortly after the station opened, it took on the task of measuring the carrier frequencies of all BBC long-wave and medium-wave transmitters. Keston thus became the first frequency measuring station in the world to be set up by a broadcasting authority.[47]

The first Engineer-in-Charge was J. A. Partridge, a well-known amateur radio experimenter of that time. Partridge and his one assistant, L. G. Shuttleworth, worked day shifts for seven days a week and once each week spent an evening making frequency measurements of the Continental broadcasting stations then receivable at Keston.[48]

Simple aerials were used for reception on long and medium waves, but for long-distance work there was a Beverage aerial – a long wire connected to earth at the far end through its characteristic impedance, so as to have maximum sensitivity to signals coming from the direction of its length. This type of aerial was usually used for reception on long waves; the conductor was at least half a wavelength (sometimes several wavelengths) long and was supported between 10 ft and 20 ft above the ground. The receivers used between 1925 and 1927 were Marconi 'Straight 8' sets using dull-emitter V24 valves. These receivers covered the medium-wave band only and had six stages of neutrodyned rf amplification. The receiver used by West at Biggin Hill had also been transferred to Keston. In 1927 and 1928 a short-wave superheterodyne receiver was provided for the reception of the American station W2XAD at Schenectady operating on 31 m (9·7 MHz). A simple dipole aerial was used with this receiver, which consisted of an rf stage, a mixer stage and three stages of neutralised if amplification on a frequency of about 2·75 MHz, followed by conventional detector and af stages. In 1927 reception tests were made jointly by the BBC at Keston and the Marconi Company at Terling, in Essex, on the Schenectady transmissions. The Terling experiments included an investigation of spaced diversity reception and W. Proctor Wilson (later Head of Research Department) and H. V. Griffiths (later EiC Tatsfield) worked for the Marconi Company on this project. The signals from Schenectady received at Keston were relayed by the BBC transmitters during the late-evening programmes and the engineer at Keston was given the right to break into late-night dance programmes, announce the Schenectady programme and switch it into the network.

A number of enterprising relays were carried out at Keston. For example, in 1926 the Savoy Orpheans Band flew in an Imperial Airways 'Hannibal' that circled the Keston site at about 1000 ft while the station staff replenished a large bonfire and fired Verey lights at one-minute intervals to provide a navigational aid for the pilot. It appears that the aircraft's own transmitter was used, working on 900 m (330 kHz). The received signal, which included a large component of aircraft engine noise, was fed to Savoy Hill and transmitted over the network.

A regular relay provided by Keston was the broadcast of church bells by various European stations at Christmas and the New Year. These relays were embodied in quite complex productions.

The first frequency-measuring equipment provided at Keston was a calibrated absorption wavemeter, specially made for the work by the Marconi Company at a cost of about £5. This wavemeter covered the range 500 to 1500 kHz and when in use it was loosely coupled to the receiver input. Its accuracy was of the order of one part in 3000 (compared with the accuracy of two parts in 10^{11} achieved in present-day measurements at Tatsfield). All BBC transmitters then in service were measurable at Keston using this rudimentary apparatus, but the low-power relay stations sharing a wavelength had to come up one by one and identify themselves. This was done by modulating the transmitter after programme hours with a tone keyed with the call-sign of the station in Morse code. In 1927 a Sullivan heterodyne wavemeter, type 592, was supplied to Keston. Its range was 150 to 1500 kHz and it represented a considerable improvement in accuracy. In 1928 a type 81 heterodyne wavemeter designed by the International Broadcasting Union (UIR/IBU) was provided. During this period there was still no means of checking the accuracy of the wavemeters at Keston.

The frequency measurement charts produced at Keston were copied and used extensively by Raymond Braillard, Director of the UIR Technical Centre in Brussels.

Keston was used for general experimental field work at this time. L. W. Hayes carried out tests there to demonstrate to Post Office officials that it was possible with a simple crystal set to receive two programmes, without mutual interference, from two transmitters operating at the same site, if they were using the frequency separation planned for the Regional station at Brookmans Park. Two low-power transmitters were used at Keston for this demonstration. A. B. Howe carried out his original common-wave experiments there in 1928, the equipment used for carrier frequency synchronisation being transferred later to Bournemouth and Aberdeen to drive the transmitters at those places.[49]

The BBC hoped to purchase the Keston site, but the owner would not sell and a search was made for a new site on the North Downs. An area of about 3·75 acres was purchased at Tatsfield on the borders of Kent and Surrey at a height of 830 ft AMSL. A new Receiving Station was opened there in September 1929.

7 INTERNATIONAL RELATIONS

The chaos resulting from the unco-ordinated way in which broadcasting expanded in the USA from 1922 onwards stimulated the BBC to take a lead in organising the international control of broadcasting in Europe, in an attempt to avoid the pitfalls revealed by the haphazard development in America. Until 1922 the only international regulations concerning radiocommunications were contained in the International Radiotelegraphy Convention signed in London in 1912, well before broadcasting had been considered. A World Conference of Telecommunications was convened in Washington in 1920, but only the USA, the United Kingdom, France, Italy and Japan were represented and the results were of little consequence to broadcasting.

Although the power of broadcasting stations was limited to a few kilowatts, stations using the same frequency could interfere with each other at night over distances of hundreds of miles. As the number of stations operating in Europe increased, they took over all wavelengths in the available bands above 1000 m and below 600 m. Before long, mutual interference was becoming intolerable and the proper allocation of wavelengths was recognised as an international problem of major importance. Other matters such as copyright and the organisation of programme exchanges between countries also needed international discussion and agreement between broadcasters.[50]

In December 1923 Vice-Admiral C. D. Carpendale, then Assistant General Manager of the BBC, heard that a 'small committee of experts' had met in London in July 1923 and in Geneva in December 1923 and had suggested that an International Wireless Conference should be held during 1924 within the framework of the League of Nations. It was proposed that representatives of Governments and of private undertakings should be invited to attend. The Post Office did not agree that there was any need for the BBC to send a representative to this conference, as its terms of reference were not primarily concerned with broadcasting. Nevertheless, Reith pressed the case for setting up a body to organise the international control of broadcasting and stressed the urgency of doing so. In the event, no conference was convened under the aegis of the League of Nations in 1924 and in the absence of action by the League, private interests took a hand. In February 1924 C. A. Lewis, Deputy Director of Programmes, BBC, was told by an official of the Compagnie Française de Radiophonie in Paris of the formation of an international committee called 'le Comité International de la TSF.[51]

In March 1924 Reith was invited to send a representative to an international conference to be held in Geneva in April of that year. It was sponsored by the International Esperanto Office, and Reith did not consider that they were the right people to enforce order in the ether. He pointed out that, on the question of wavelengths, the conference could do no more than make recommendations – since the licensing of transmitting stations was the prerogative of governments, exercised through their Telegraph and Telephone Administrations. The conference – styled 'Preliminary Conference for an International Agreement on Wireless Telephony' – nevertheless took place in Geneva on 22 and 23 April 1924. Forty representatives attended from State Administrations, societies, radio clubs, firms connected with broadcasting and periodicals devoted to it. The Administrations of the United Kingdom and Germany – the two most active broadcasting countries in Europe at that time – were not represented. The conference resolved, *inter alia*,

'that certain bands of wavelengths should be exclusively reserved for wireless telephonic transmissions and that they should be clearly differentiated from those attributed to wireless telegraphy'; and
'that the use of damped waves should be exclusively confined to danger signals of shipping and to time signals.'

The conference requested the League of Nations and the Telegraph Union (now the International Telecommunications Union), to do their utmost to hasten the convening of a new intergovernmental conference to fill the gap resulting from the development of broadcasting since the signing of the London Convention of 1912 and the Washington Agreement of 1920. The conference also invited all the wireless telephony organisations to create a current of public opinion and to petition their Governments to intervene in Geneva and Berne to hasten the calling of this new conference. It was decided to form an Executive Committee with headquarters in Geneva to continue to press for an international agreement on wireless telephony. J. Rambert, President of the Swiss Radio-Electric Society, was the Chairman of the Executive Committee and he called for a conference to be held in Geneva at the end of 1924 for the purpose of setting up an International Broadcasting Union.

On 28 May 1924 a meeting was held at the Post Office in London to discuss the international status of 'wireless broadcasting'. Besides the representatives from the Post Office and the BBC (Eckersley), there were present representatives of the Armed

Forces, the Chairman of the Wireless Sub-committee of the Imperial Communications Committee, and spokesmen from some of the large commercial interests. After much argument, this meeting agreed to submit to foreign governments a proposal that the waveband from 300 to 500 m (1000 to 600 kHz) should be allocated internationally for the exclusive use of broadcasting. Neither Reith nor Eckersley wished to prejudice the international acceptance of this proposal by premature discussion with unofficial bodies. They considered that if international acceptance of an exclusive broadcasting waveband could be obtained, it would be a step towards internationally agreed assignments within the band, which was the BBC's urgent aim.

Reith wrote to Rambert urging that a fully representative conference should be called, which would, in effect, be a 'Union of all broadcasting stations and not solely an international office with contributing supporters'. In September 1924 Rambert visited the BBC in London and was, as he said, greatly impressed with the BBC as an organisation. On 26 September 1924 Reith, with the agreement of Rambert, wrote to other broadcasting authorities outlining the aims of a proposed Association of Broadcasters and stressed the need to set up an International Broadcasting Bureau. He suggested that a conference should be held in London on 1 December 1924 to be presided over by Lord Gainford, the Chairman of the BBC. This conference was deferred by the BBC until the spring of 1925 and the proposed venue was changed to Paris. Rambert was not enthusiastic about the deferment or about the change of venue and, with French support, he made a counter-suggestion that the conference should be held in Geneva in January or February 1925.[52] It was again postponed and finally a BBC proposal to hold it in London on 18 March 1925 was accepted.

The conference was held at No. 2 Savoy Hill on 18 and 19 March 1925 and it was there that the first international broadcasting organisation was created, with its headquarters in Geneva. The name given to the new organisation was Union Internationale de Radiophonie (UIR) or International Broadcasting Union (IBU). Reith insisted that it should not be governed by the principle that later became known as Parkinson's Law. Eckersley stressed the importance of the technical side of its work and expressed the opinion that programme exchanges in Europe would give a welcome stimulus to the development and expansion of broadcasting in all countries.

At this time considerable interest was being shown in the United Kingdom in the promotion of programme exchanges between countries and the Post Office drew the BBC's attention to a question to be raised in the House of Commons asking why the Company did not arrange more of these exchanges. Reith replied that direct reception by radio was not yet good enough and lines were not yet satisfactory for regular exchanges, although he hoped that the newly formed UIR would soon act to make occasional exchanges possible.

The constitution of the UIR (whose name was altered to Union Internationale de Radiodiffusion in 1929), was drafted in Geneva on 3 and 4 April 1925 and the Statutes were submitted to a meeting of its first General Assembly held at the League

F

of Nations building in Geneva on 4 April 1925. Admiral Carpendale of the BBC was the first president and remained in that office for eleven years until his retirement. Arthur Burrows was its Secretary-General.

One of the first acts of the UIR was to convene a 'European Conference of Wireless Engineers' in July 1925. Its purpose was to find a solution to the increasingly urgent problem of the assignment of wavelengths, and the success of this initiative may be gauged from the fact that thirteen broadcasting organisations representing fifty stations operating in Europe promptly joined the UIR. The complexity of the problems soon necessitated the creation of special committees. A technical committee of five members was appointed in December 1925 to prepare a European wavelength assignment plan and in March 1926 this Committee was placed under the chairmanship of Raymond Braillard, an able French engineer working in Belgium, who later became Director of the UIR Technical Centre in Brussels.

It was found that eighty-seven stations in Europe were already broadcasting in the band from 550 to 270 m (545 to 1110 kHz) and that thirty-seven new stations were planned. As the waveband could not be extended, a preliminary plan was made regrouping the stations with a carrier-frequency separation of 20 kHz. This relatively wide separation, which was thought necessary mainly because of the poor selectivity of the receivers then available, would have limited the number of separate channels that could be accommodated in the medium-wave band to twenty-seven.

A special wavemeter was specified for checking the maintenance of the allotted wavelengths, and tests to establish the minimum practical separation between stations were arranged for the early part of September 1925. The results of these tests, in which the BBC took full part, were considered by the Technical Committee at the end of September and in the middle of December 1925 a technical conference was held in Brussels presided over by Braillard. At this conference further tests were arranged resulting in a wavelength plan, based on a spacing of 10 kHz, which was submitted to the Council of the UIR on 25 March 1926. Eckersley and Braillard had worked closely together on the preparation of this plan, which allocated to each European country at least one exclusive wavelength and a number of other wavelengths according to the number of broadcasting stations in the country, and to its size, topography, and the state of its economic and cultural development.[53]

The plan made provision for eighty-three exclusive wavelengths and sixteen shared wavelengths in the band from 580 to 200 m (525 to 1500 kHz). The assignment of long-wave channels for broadcasting was deferred. The UIR submitted the plan to the Telegraph & Telephone Administrations of the countries concerned and it was implemented on 14 November 1926 as the Geneva Plan. (The delay was due to the lack of a sufficient number of internationally calibrated wavemeters.)

Before the Geneva Plan, the BBC was using twenty exclusive medium wavelengths and one long wavelength; under the Plan it was assigned eight exclusive wavelengths, one common wavelength for relay stations in the UK and two internationally shared wavelengths (as shown in the table). The allocation of long wavelengths was deferred at Geneva and the BBC continued to use the wavelength of 1600 m (187·5 kHz) until 3 July 1927 when it was changed to 1604·3 m (187 kHz).

BBC WAVELENGTHS 1926

Main Stations	In use immediately before Geneva Plan	Allocated in Geneva Plan 14.11.26	In use 12.12.26
	(m)	(m)	(m)
Aberdeen	495	491·8	500
Birmingham	479	491·8	491·8
Belfast	440	326·1	306·1
Glasgow	422	405·4	405·4
Newcastle	404	312·5	312·5
Bournemouth	386	306·1	326·1
Manchester	378	384·6	384·6
London	365	361·4	361·4
Cardiff	353	353	353
Daventry	1600	—	1600
Relay Stations			
Swansea	482·2	288·5	288·5
Plymouth	338·2	288·5	400
Hull	335	288·5	288·5
Liverpool	331	288·5	297
Edinburgh	328·2	288·5	294·1
Nottingham	326·1	288·5	275·2
Leeds	321	297	277·8
Dundee	315	288·5	288·5
Bradford	310	294·1	254·2
Sheffield	306·1	288·5	272·7
Stoke-on-Trent	301·1	288·5	288·5

Note:
A number of changes were made in the frequencies used in order to avoid interference.

After the Geneva Plan had been in use for about 10 days, it was found that the sharing of a channel by the Aberdeen and Birmingham transmitters was unsatisfactory and it was agreed that Aberdeen should change to the International Common Wave of 500 m (600 kHz). Bournemouth and Belfast exchanged wavelengths to provide better separation in Northern Ireland between the Belfast and Dublin transmitters; a further advantage of this change was that interference from Morse telegraphy to the Bournemouth transmitter was reduced. From 12 December 1926 some of the other relay stations changed to International Common Waves to improve reception.

The effect of the introduction of the Geneva Plan on listeners in this country was explained to them in advance by Eckersley in a series of articles published in the *Radio Times* in November 1926. He warned listeners in the Aberdeen, Newcastle upon Tyne, and Bournemouth areas that they might be worse off, and those in some other areas that they might have to retune their receivers, but pointed out that those in the London, Cardiff, Glasgow, and Manchester areas would not be affected at all.

The setting-up of the UIR had important consequences, since it provided a forum for discussion covering the whole field of broadcasting. The Geneva Plan was certainly one of its greatest achievements and it was the forerunner of a succession of frequency assignment plans that have continued to be made from time to time and have extended into all the frequency bands that have since become available for broadcasting.

Another of the UIR's main interests was the promotion of programme exchanges between broadcasting organisations in Europe. (The BBC's first relay from the Continent came by line from Paris on 30 December 1923.) In June 1926 L. W. Hayes went with Raymond Braillard and Arthur Burrows of the UIR to a meeting of the CCI (Comité Consultatif International des Communications Téléphoniques à Grande Distance) in Paris to discuss the possibilities of setting up international circuits for the exchange of programmes. The development of these exchanges will be followed up in the next chapter.

8 ENGINEERING FINANCE

The sources from which the BBC derived its income have been mentioned in section 1 of this chapter. Few financial records have survived from this period, doubtless because there was at that time no need for the complex financial procedures that are now essential to the running of a large organisation devoted to public service and financed by public money.

The total income of the Company was on the following modest scale.[54]

			£
15.12.22	to	31.3.24	£206,974
1.4.24	to	31.3.25	£538,529
1.4.25	to	31.3.26	£570,892
1.4.26	to	31.12.26	£646,467

The Company was perpetually short of money, and until the decisions resulting from the report of the Sykes Committee towards the end of 1923 there was continued uncertainty about the amount of the licence revenue. To quote Asa Briggs: 'Throughout the whole of the period... broadcasting was arbitrarily and inequitably financed.'[55] The Company had therefore to live from hand to mouth and modern costing methods hardly had a place in this environment.

Engineering spending was necessarily modest. In 1923, for example, salaries and wages and general expenses for the nine stations that had been commissioned by the end of the year amounted to only £6417, plus £8247 paid to the contractors to cover their operating costs. The estimated expenditure on transmitting stations for 1924, by which time all the main and relay stations were in service, was not much more ambitious:

	£
Engineers' salaries and wages	8160
Maintenance	6000
OBs	2000
	16,160

Capital expenditure, most of which related to engineering projects, increased steadily year by year:

	£
31.3.24	70,493
31.3.25	177,339
31.3.26	271,448
31.12.26	334,788

Short-term forecasts of capital and revenue expenditure were prepared from time to time. A forecast of capital expenditure for the last six months of the fiscal year 1924–5 was as follows:

	£
High-power station (Daventry)	40,000
New studios and equipment	12,000
New transmitting site, London	8,000
New plant	15,000
	75,000

This budget, in its simplicity and brevity, is typical of the time.

Schemes of quite modest magnitude had to be submitted to the Board of Directors for approval. In November 1923, for example, a proposal for an OB van was presented to them, the cost of which could hardly have exceeded two or three hundred pounds. In 1924 we find the Directors approving £500 capital and £200 pa revenue for an experimental receiving station. Lesser sums could be authorised by the Chief Accountant.

Despite the skeletal nature of the records, engineers were conscious of costs and more will be said about this later.

9   THE ENGINEERING DEPARTMENT: STAFFING AND ORGANISATION

> Did you ever expect a corporation to have
> a conscience, when it has no soul to be
> damned, and no body to be kicked?
> *Baron Thurlow*, 1731–1806

A brilliant epigram, but containing more wit than truth. The present author, having spent forty years in the BBC, can vouch for the fact that the Corporation has both a soul and a conscience. This is indeed to be expected, for the soul and conscience of a corporation must match its objectives; it must attract to itself people who are sympathetic to those objectives and will seek to achieve them.

The first engineering appointment in the Company was that of Capt. P. P. Eckersley, who took up his duties as the Chief, and only, Engineer on 5 February 1923. He has described the tasks with which he was faced during the first few weeks of his service.[56] During February and March 1923 he was responsible for an exchange of letters between the BBC and the Marconi Company concerning the terms upon which the latter would circularise its staff at the London, Cardiff, Newcastle upon Tyne, and Glasgow stations asking for volunteers for service with the BBC. The Marconi Company accordingly passed on an invitation from the BBC offering £250 pa for a senior man to be employed at each station and £200 pa for a second man. There would be no annual rises, but good work would be rewarded by bonuses given to maintenance staff who could show 'most efficient working from the point of view of cost and reliability'. There were also one or two openings for area maintenance engineers at £300 pa; they had to have a very good knowledge of up-to-date methods of wireless telephony. A number of staff transfers resulted from this approach: they were arranged in an amicable way, the Marconi Company being a partner in the BBC. A list of the first Engineers-in-Charge is given in Appendix A.

During the first six months of 1923 the Head Office staff of the Engineering Department was also increased, until, by 14 August 1923, it conformed to Eckersley's first organisation chart (Appendix B). The important posts of Southern Area Maintenance Engineer and Northern Area Maintenance Engineer were filled by H. Bishop and J. M. A. Cameron respectively. They were responsible for all aspects of the operation of the transmitting stations and studio centres in their areas. The Northern Area covered the stations in Scotland, Northern Ireland, and in England as far south as Stoke-on-Trent, while the Southern Area covered London and the remaining stations in England and Wales. A post of Personal Assistant to the Chief Engineer was filled by Cdr Carter, while Capt. Frost was put in charge of Equipment and Stores (including Engineering Buying).

By the end of 1923 Capt. A. G. D. West, who had worked under Rutherford at the Cavendish Laboratory, had been appointed Assistant Chief Engineer (Development) and Bishop had become Assistant Chief Engineer and Deputy to the Chief Engineer. H. W. Litt had taken over the Southern Area from Bishop. On 23 November 1923 the titles of engineering staff on stations was promulgated by Eckersley as follows:

'The engineer in charge of each station will be called the Engineer-in-Charge; the second in command of the station will be called the Maintenance Engineer; any other grade will be termed Assistant Maintenance Engineer. The normal strength of staff at each station will be one Engineer-in-Charge, one Maintenance Engineer, and two Assistant Maintenance Engineers.'

By 11 December 1923 the Engineering Department staff totalled forty-six.

The year 1924 was one of considerable engineering activity, since one main station was commissioned and ten new relay stations were brought into service. These required operational staff and the increase in responsibilities for the developing system also required additional Head Office staff. During 1924 about sixty-five additional engineering staff were recruited bringing the total at the end of the year to about 110. Notable engineering appointments during the year were:

1 February 1924, H. L. Kirke appointed Senior Development Engineer (with Kirke's appointment, Capt. West was redesignated ACE (Research)).

12 May 1924, A. B. Howe appointed Assistant in Development Section.

1 July 1924, L. W. Hayes appointed Administration and Finance Assistant to Kirke.

In 1925 F. M. Dimmock rejoined the BBC as Stores Auditor in Head Office after a short period of previous service (June–August 1924) as an Assistant to Frost in the Stores Section. In July 1925 the Daventry 5XX long-wave transmitting station was opened and H. W. Litt was appointed its first Engineer-in-Charge. His staff consisted of a Maintenance Engineer (L. Hotine), six Assistant Maintenance Engineers, a mechanic, a clerk, four labourers, a van driver and a nightwatchman. A caretaker and his wife were recruited to look after the staff living in the quarters on Borough Hill, Daventry, and this couple were reimbursed at the rate of £100 pa. all found.

Meanwhile, in Head Office, the Research and Development Sections of the Department had been expanded and reorganised. Three well-known radio amateurs were recruited to it in 1924; J. A. Partridge (2KF), H. S. Walker (2OM), and B. Honri (5HY). By the end of 1925 the Research and Development Sections were staffed as follows:

Assistant Chief Engineer (Research), A. G. D. West.

Head of Development Section and Senior Development Engineer, H. L. Kirke.

Assistant to SDE (Admin. & Finance), L. W. Hayes.

Radio Projects, Workshops & Drawing Office, H. S. Walker.

Test Room, R. C. Patrick.

Programme Input Equipment, Radio Receivers, CR Oscilloscopes, AF Test Equipment, A. B. Howe.

Lines & Switching, A. S. Attkins.

Keston Receiving Station, J. A. Partridge

By the end of 1925 the Engineering Department staff numbered 179.[57]

Although no new transmitting stations were commissioned during 1926, there was considerable development at studio centres and in SB activities, and during the year transmitters were being prepared for the changes in wavelengths resulting from the Geneva Conference, which were to be made in November. During that year the initial planning for the Regional Scheme was started, including transmitter development work at Daventry.

During 1926 notable additions to the Head Office staff of the Engineering Department were:

N. Ashbridge, who joined from the Marconi Company on 5 January as Assistant
  Chief Engineer (Bishop then became Senior Superintendent Engineer – as it
  turned out a case of *reculer pour mieux sauter*.)

M. T. Tudsbery, who joined on 11 January as the Civil Engineer.

R. T. B. Wynn, who joined from the Marconi Company on 19 April to take charge of
  the Technical Correspondence Section.

B. N. MacLarty, who joined from the Marconi Company on 3 August as Personal
  Assistant to Ashbridge and Kirke to work on the design and planning of the
  prototype high-power medium-wave transmitting station.

The staff of the Development Section remained virtually unchanged during 1926,
but the work of the Section increased very considerably and included the development of synchronising apparatus for transmitters.

The Lines & Switching Sub-section under A. S. Attkins had pioneered the line-
switching arrangements at Leeds and Gloucester and had developed uniselector
switching for Manchester while based in cramped premises at Savoy Hill, but in 1928
this group moved to nearby offices in Cecil Chambers. The remainder of the Development Section worked on in very restricted accommodation at Savoy Hill until the
move to Avenue House, Clapham, in 1927.

A further thirty-four staff joined the Department during 1926, bringing the total
number at the end of the year to about 213. The organisation chart on 26 July 1926
is given in Appendix C.

There was, during the 1922–6 period, a small group of staff having dual departmental responsibilities, and hence referred to as 'The Marines'. They were later
known as Education Engineers. The first engineer to be employed on these duties
was R. W. Blackwell, who undertook visits to Education Authorities and schools
in the London area and in the Home Counties, particularly in Kent where the Education Authority was interested in expanding school broadcasting as a teaching
medium. Maintenance effort was diluted by day-long visits to widely-scattered
schools, and it was decided to prepare a comprehensive estimate of the cost of putting
this work on a rational basis. A second post had been agreed in the meantime to
provide some assistance for Blackwell. The estimate was submitted in November
1926 for a force of eighteen Education Engineers to cover England, Scotland, and
Wales. The Control Board did not approve this estimate, but approval was given at
the end of 1926 for an increase to four Education Engineer posts. They remained the
responsibility of the Senior Superintendent Engineer until 1 April 1941, when they
were transferred to the staff of the Overseas & Engineering Information Department.

Although no references have been found to formal staff representation during the
lifetime of the Company, it is to be noted that in this patriarchal era spontaneous
demonstrations of loyalty by the staff were not unknown. The text of a 'Souvenir
Memo' sent to the Chief Engineer at Christmas 1924 by members of the Northern
Area of the Department is reproduced in Appendix D. As a guarantee of good faith,
each signatory added his thumb print after his name.

As a means of encouraging engineering staff to put forward ideas for technical improvements, an embryo Suggestion Scheme was started in July 1926 when Eckersley circularised all engineering staff informing them that suggestions would be considered on their merits for the grant of awards not exceeding £5 each. Eckersley wrote to Reith proposing that an amount of £100 pa should be set aside for distribution in this way. A Suggestions Committee was set up, consisting of Ashbridge, Bishop, West and Kirke, to adjudicate on the suggestions received. A Staff Circular of 10 July 1926 pointed out, however, that awards would be made only to staff working outside the 'Administration, Development and Research Sections'. (These latter were expected to develop ideas as part of their normal duties.) Eckersley remarked, in his proposal to Reith, that staff would be pleased not so much 'with the money, but in the pride they would feel in winning an award'.

Arrangements were also made for dealing with patents for inventions by members of the staff. Under these arrangements, which still subsist, the BBC is free to decide whether or not to apply for a patent for an invention by one of the staff; if it decides to do so, the inventor is required to assign his rights to the BBC. When letters patent have been issued a grant is paid to the inventor, which may be increased later if the patent proves to be of exceptional value. If the BBC does not wish to apply for a patent, the inventor is free to do so on his own account.

The first BBC patent was in the name of H. L. Kirke, and was applied for in 1926; it referred to a thermionic rectifier with two grids intended to have a linear characteristic over a wide range of input voltage. Many of the other inventions mentioned in this book have been patented through the years.

Appendices to Section 9

APPENDIX A

ENGINEERS-IN-CHARGE 1923–25

Station	*First Engineer-in-Charge*
London	A. C. Shaw
Manchester	P. A. Florence
Birmingham	J. A. Cooper
Newcastle	P. A. Florence
Cardiff	E. Chesterfield
Glasgow	V. A. M. Bulow
Aberdeen	C. G. Harding
Bournemouth	L. A. V. Everitt
Belfast	G. W. Ingram
Sheffield	A. Birch
Plymouth	D. A. G. Curd
Edinburgh	J. A. Beveridge
Liverpool	B. H. Vernon
Leeds/Bradford	L. Harvey
Hull	F. N. Calver
Nottingham	A. Fielder
Dundee	A. C. Cameron
Stoke-on-Trent	H. F. Humphreys

Station	First Engineer-in-Charge	
Swansea	C. H. Colborn	
Daventry	H. W. Litt	Transmitting station only
Keston	J. A. Partridge	Receiving station only

APPENDIX B

ENGINEERING DEPARTMENT: ORGANISATION AS AT 14 AUGUST 1923

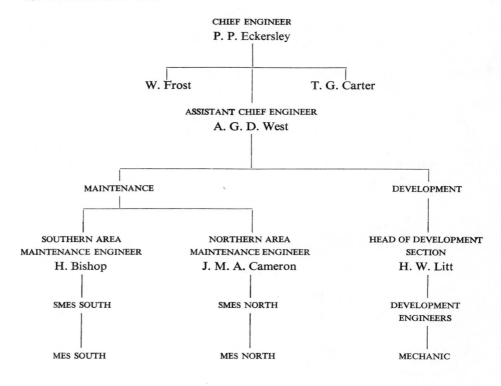

CHIEF ENGINEER
P. P. Eckersley

W. Frost   T. G. Carter

ASSISTANT CHIEF ENGINEER
A. G. D. West

MAINTENANCE   DEVELOPMENT

SOUTHERN AREA MAINTENANCE ENGINEER H. Bishop	NORTHERN AREA MAINTENANCE ENGINEER J. M. A. Cameron	HEAD OF DEVELOPMENT SECTION H. W. Litt
SMES SOUTH	SMES NORTH	DEVELOPMENT ENGINEERS
MES SOUTH	MES NORTH	MECHANIC

APPENDIX C

ENGINEERING DEPARTMENT: ORGANISATION AS AT 26 JULY 1926

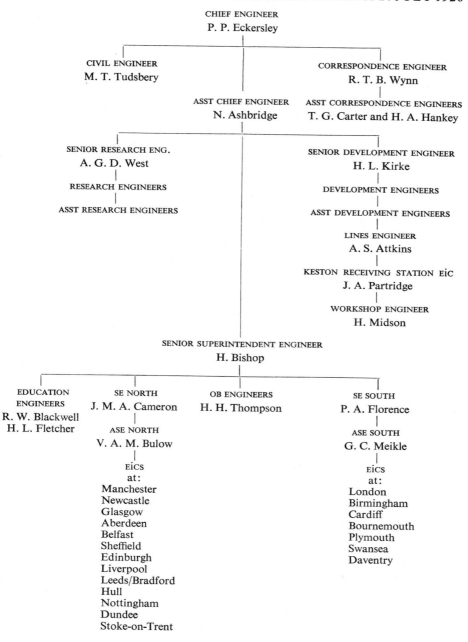

CHIEF ENGINEER
P. P. Eckersley

CIVIL ENGINEER
M. T. Tudsbery

CORRESPONDENCE ENGINEER
R. T. B. Wynn

ASST CHIEF ENGINEER
N. Ashbridge

ASST CORRESPONDENCE ENGINEERS
T. G. Carter and H. A. Hankey

SENIOR RESEARCH ENG.
A. G. D. West

RESEARCH ENGINEERS

ASST RESEARCH ENGINEERS

SENIOR DEVELOPMENT ENGINEER
H. L. Kirke

DEVELOPMENT ENGINEERS

ASST DEVELOPMENT ENGINEERS

LINES ENGINEER
A. S. Attkins

KESTON RECEIVING STATION EiC
J. A. Partridge

WORKSHOP ENGINEER
H. Midson

SENIOR SUPERINTENDENT ENGINEER
H. Bishop

EDUCATION
ENGINEERS
R. W. Blackwell
H. L. Fletcher

SE NORTH
J. M. A. Cameron

ASE NORTH
V. A. M. Bulow

EiCS
at:
Manchester
Newcastle
Glasgow
Aberdeen
Belfast
Sheffield
Edinburgh
Liverpool
Leeds/Bradford
Hull
Nottingham
Dundee
Stoke-on-Trent

OB ENGINEERS
H. H. Thompson

SE SOUTH
P. A. Florence

ASE SOUTH
G. C. Meikle

EiCS
at:
London
Birmingham
Cardiff
Bournemouth
Plymouth
Swansea
Daventry

APPENDIX D

Text of 'Souvenir Memo' to Capt. P. P. Eckersley from 'His Northern Staff' dated Christmas 1924.

Dear Sir,

For over two years since the inception of the British Broadcasting Company, with a nucleus of about three people, it is impossible retrospectantly [*sic*], to disregard the difficulties and trials interposed in all our paths. Such difficulties concerned even the most junior members, and after a job well done, the consummation in every case was an expression of appreciation or congratulation from yourself. It is felt by all concerned that appreciation is the stimulus of efficiency and that without it little can be accomplished. It is known by every individual that this appreciation was quickly forthcoming from you, but it is not known whether you in turn have been encouraged in the same way. It is therefore the unanimous desire of all your people in the Northern Section to express the value which they attach to the kind words of encouragement and cheerful exhortation to carry on, thereby attempting to show you that your acknowledgements of our efforts are quickly and thoroughly reciprocated by renewed assurance of continued endeavour. The BLACK SQUAD in the North do therefore hereby append their signatures vouching for the spirit of this letter and affixing their 'mark' against each name.

With the Compliments of the Season and the wish that the coming year will be one of the utmost success for you personally,

Yours faithfully,

J. M. A. Cameron, *Superintendent Engineer* (*North*)
Vincent A. M. Bulow, *Asst. Superintendent Engineer* (*North*)
R. M. Owen, *Asst. Superintendent Engineer* (*North*)

(followed by fifty-one other signatures)

10 DIGRESSIONS

To paraphrase a childhood memory of Sir Walter Scott:

> We weave a tangled web, no less,
> When first we practise to digress.

The risk of such an outcome must be taken, because certain important factors cannot be given sufficient prominence in the main stream of this narrative.

First Digression

Students used to be taught that engineering is a branch of economics and that 'an engineer can do for twopence what any fool can do for a shilling'. This technique has recently been given the special name of 'value analysis', which seems a pity – for engineering itself is the art of giving the best value at the lowest cost. Sir Frank Gill (already mentioned in these pages) constantly stressed the importance of engineering economics in a series of IEE papers from 1917 onwards.[58, 59, 60] The concept of 'discounted cash flow' had not then been given a name, but it already formed the basis of engineering decisions.

From the start this consideration was prominent in the minds of those BBC engineers who had responsibility for design and planning and for the placing of contracts. However, the largest item in the annual budget of a broadcasting service is not the amortisation of capital expenditure, but the cost of staff. Many of the engineering developments described in later chapters were directed towards savings in the cost of operating staff by handing over to machines the more uninteresting jobs formerly done by people.

In design and planning it is often relatively easy to find the cheapest way of achieving a desired end; it is more difficult to decide what the end should be. As Charles Curran, the present Director-General of the BBC, has put it; 'The teleological approach attaches first importance to the purpose of what is being done.' In broadcasting, it is often difficult to decide what purposes should be pursued, because it is necessary to strike a balance between what the programme production departments would like to have and what the Engineering Division can provide at reasonable cost. It has been a source of strength to the BBC that, apart from a few periods in its history, there has always been close co-operation between the two sides. In the BBC, the Management has usually given due weight to technical considerations; this may seem a platitude, but it is by no means universally true of all broadcasting organisations.

It would not be right to claim that cost and value have always been well matched. Producers, particularly in television, have from time to time asked for, and been given, technical facilities that they would not have considered justified if they had known how much they would cost in money and effort. Attempts to remedy this weakness have recently led to the application of 'total costing' to individual programmes.

Second Digression

Engineering is also a branch of applied mathematics. Many of the most far-reaching developments and extensions to knowledge that have been made during these fifty years have been based on, or at least supported by, mathematical analysis. The achievements of BBC engineers in research and development have required a great deal of painstaking calculations and sometimes real mathematical insight. The BBC has employed very few mathematicians as such, but every engineer must have a basic understanding of mathematical principles.

Many technical papers, and nearly all research reports, abound in mathematical formulae. This book contains almost none; it is, at least to that extent, an inadequate tribute to those whose labours it attempts to describe.

Third Digression

Nowadays engineering tends to become more and more a branch of psychology. It has always been so to some extent, for most of the progress described herein resulted from team-work and could not have been achieved unless, with a few exceptions, those concerned had known how to get the best out of their staff and how to co-operate with their colleagues.

While the engineering staff of the BBC remained very small, personnel management could be done by senior engineers, mostly in an informal way. So long as people wanted to give their best and were encouraged to do so, there were no great problems. Many leaders unconsciously followed the maxim *Virtus laudata crescit*, even if they had not been to Berkhamsted School. Moreover, they knew all their staff personally, so that the massive machinery evolved by the modern science of management was not necessary.

A few years ago the following sentence appeared in one of the glossy magazines devoted to that science: 'There is less satisfaction in trying to be loyal to an organisation than in being loyal to a leader.' This is certainly not true of the BBC. Those who have spent most of their lives in it, have certainly found satisfaction in loyalty to a succession of leaders, but leaders come and go. The spirit of the organisation commands enduring loyalty from those who are in sympathy with it. Though buffeted by external forces, and occasionally by internal dissensions, it continues to survive. The quotation might be rephrased: 'There is satisfaction in being loyal to an organisation that has a worth-while objective and is loyal to its staff.'

Nevertheless, it is people who create an organisation and keep it in being. One ought therefore to describe the people whose work figures in these pages, their personalities and the kind of atmosphere they created. Alas, this is beyond the powers of the author, who, being an engineer, is by definition interested in ideas rather than people. Some tentative observations may nevertheless be made.

The first generation of BBC engineers was necessarily drawn mainly from industry and most of them were of an essentially practical turn of mind, though this was often coupled with vision and sometimes with an almost mystical insight. An outstanding example of this was H. L. Kirke, for many years Head of Research. He distrusted theories and always insisted on trying out every new idea under practical conditions. As a trouble-shooter he had a remarkable gift; faced with something that did not work he would put his finger unerringly on the source of the trouble, apparently without any of the painstaking sifting of evidence and the discarding of successive hypotheses that his colleagues would have found indispensable in like case.

As the BBC grew, specialisation inevitably became more marked and engineers tended to fall into fairly well-defined groups: the specialists who were responsible for research, planning and installation, civil engineering, and the provision of equipment; maintenance engineers who kept the operational equipment in working order and often carried out extensions and alterations to it; operating staff who were responsible for the day-to-day running of the whole broadcasting system, including transmitters, studios and communications; and engineers performing various necessary services such as information, personnel administration, and liaison work.

All these groups were headed by people well-qualified in their own spheres, and those in the first group tended to include a proportion of engineers and physicists with an academic outlook, though it had necessarily to be directed mainly to practical ends. When the External Services and the Television Service were introduced in the 1930s, and later when they were greatly expanded, the fact that this nucleus of specialist engineers was already in being and available to serve the whole of the BBC greatly strengthened its technical resources.

The engineers in the other three groups kept the service going and these pages do less than justice to their importance, simply because a record of progress must be concerned with discontinuities rather than with continuous functions.

It is naturally at the top that personalities count for most. Mention has already been made of the ebullience and enthusiasm of Peter Eckersley, the BBC's first Chief Engineer, which certainly infected his staff. His successor, Noel Ashbridge, was cast in a different mould – reticent, shrewd, realistic to the point of pessimism, and with a kindly smile that belied his sometimes trenchant remarks. Harold Bishop, different again, never forgot his early training as a mechanical engineer or lost his interest in the careers of young engineers or in the welfare of older ones who had fallen on hard times. Francis (Charles) McLean saw his objectives clearly and pursued them with single-minded purposefulness – yet he was always ready to hear the other man's point of view. James Redmond made his mark in the exciting field of television and has brought a note of freshness, relaxed and forward-looking, to the leadership of the Engineering Division.

This chapter closes with the end of the lifetime of the British Broadcasting Company. It had established the new medium on a firm basis and in every field of its activity it had found ways of solving entirely unprecedented problems. On the engineering side it had established low-power transmitters serving most of the population, the first high-power long-wave transmitter planned exclusively for broadcasting, studio centres equipped to produce a wide range of programmes, methods of simultaneous broadcasting, equipment for outside broadcasts, and effective means of checking the technical quality of the output. It had laid the foundations for some of the major technical achievements that were to follow, and it had set professional standards over the whole field of broadcasting engineering.

CHAPTER III

The British Broadcasting Corporation: The Early Years: 1927–39

I   THE CORPORATION TAKES OVER

During 1925 the future of broadcasting in this country had to be reconsidered, because the Company's licence was due to expire on 31 December 1926. In July 1925 the Government set up a committee under the chairmanship of the Earl of Crawford and Balcarres, which reported early in 1926. It warmly commended the Company for its achievements in establishing a broadcasting service, but proposed that it should be wound up and that it should be replaced by a public authority, so as to ensure that the policy of public service and impartiality initiated by the Company should be continued.

The Company, in the short space of just over four years, had created a viable broadcasting service with over two million licence holders (in 1927 there were about 6½ million radio sets in the whole world). Broadcasting had established itself as a medium of communication and as an art-form, and the technology had already made a spectacular advance. The 'Big Six' companies had borne the major part of the financial risk and with little direct financial reward, but they and other manufacturers had benefited by the demand for receivers and for the equipment used by the BBC itself.

It was, however, time for British broadcasting to be put on a basis that would be clearly seen to be independent of both commercial and political pressures.

The Corporation's first Charter came into force on 1 January 1927. It was to last for ten years and it placed the BBC in the charge of a Board of Governors. It was made clear that they should be responsible for the day-to-day control of the affairs of the Corporation, so that BBC programmes would be independent of Government control, although ultimate powers were reserved to Parliament. The transmitting stations were to be operated under a licence from the Postmaster General.

Reith was translated from being Managing Director of the Company to being the Chief Executive of the Corporation with the title of Director-General; he received a knighthood on 1 January 1927. Eckersley remained Chief Engineer. The transition from Company to Corporation passed smoothly and, from the point of view of listeners, almost unnoticed. On the engineering side, the principal effect was that the way was clear for the Regional Scheme of programme distribution to go ahead.

The Governors were to be appointed by the King in Council and were to be 'persons of judgment and independence, who would inspire public confidence by having no interests to promote other than the public service.'[1] The Charter remained in force until 1937 when it was replaced by a new one following the main provisions of the old, but making express provision for the Empire Service and the Television Service.

2 TRANSMITTERS AND RECEPTION: THE REGIONAL SCHEME

The foundations of future technical policy had been laid before the Company gave place to the Corporation and preliminary steps towards a scheme that would give listeners a choice of programmes had already been taken, notably the decision to establish an experimental high-power medium-wave transmitter (5GB) at Daventry (in addition to the existing long-wave transmitter), which had been approved by the Post Office in 1926. It was estimated that it would cost £10,000 and that the running costs would be about £3000 pa.

The design of this 50-kW transmitter, to which reference has already been made in the previous chapter, was completed by the BBC team under B. N. MacLarty in little more than six months – a remarkable achievement since no medium-wave transmitter of such high power had been built before.

The drive was provided by an oscillating valve circuit tuned by means of a vario-meter and fed through a separator stage. The modulator stages were prototypes for those to be embodied in the design of the Regional transmitters. A sub-modulator was resistance-capacity coupled to the modulator. The Heising system of modulation was used and the output of the modulated amplifier excited an intermediate amplifier. This had a single CAM 1 valve and for the first time a hose coil, mounted above the unit, was used in the water cooling system so as to provide sufficient insulation from earth. The final amplifier had six CAT 5 water-cooled valves, one of which was used as a spare. The output circuit comprised an inductance and a fixed air-spaced capaci-tor, which often flashed over on account of the intrusion of insects. Fine tuning of the output circuit was done by means of a variometer. A 45-kW dc motor-generator was installed for the ht supply, but before the station opened it was decided to in-crease its power and a 50-kW thermionic rectifier was operated in parallel with the output of the machine. The cooling water was discharged into a pond from a point above water level, and a wooden plank was provided for rescuing sheep that fell into the pond. A T aerial supported between two 325-ft tubular steel masts was provided. The transmitter was modified after about two years to a push-pull system conforming with the design adopted for the Regional transmitters.

Some difficult technical problems had to be overcome in the design, construction and testing of the transmitter, which was the first of its kind to be made in this country. The design of the final amplifier was particularly difficult because of the lack of instrumentation, and an unexpected trouble occurred because the natural resonance of the main smoothing circuits fell within the modulating frequency band.

One of the most serious difficulties was the 'Rocky Point' effect, which produced violent discharges within the valves of the final amplifier at random intervals. This effect, named after a transmitter in the USA where it was first observed (and also called 'flash arc'), was thought to be due to the release of occluded gas from the elec-

G

trode structure. At one time it became so serious at Daventry that it was thought that the station might have to be taken out of service. However, as a result of a similar experience at the Post Office station at Rugby, it was decided to reduce the eht voltage and also to replace the CAT 5 valves in the final amplifier by CAT 6 valves, which were less prone to the effect. These palliatives made some improvement, but the trouble was not completely cured until MacLarty inserted in the positive eht connection a CAR 2 rectifier valve, with its filament voltage adjusted until the valve would pass only just enough current for normal working. This proved to be a complete cure and made it possible to increase the eht voltage to normal and so to restore the full output power. Further investigation led to the design of a self-quenching circuit by H. L. Kirke and B. N. MacLarty, in which a resistance was introduced into the ht supply to each valve; this caused the eht voltage to collapse when there was a surge of current and reduced the duration of the flash arc so that its effect on the transmission was scarcely noticeable. This circuit was patented and afterwards widely used by broadcasting organisations.

During the testing of this transmitter, the BBC's first cathode-ray oscilloscope was used. The trace was so dim that a photographer's cloth had to be put over the observer's head. The life of the tube was only nine hours. For plotting linearity curves an Avometer was inserted in the anode circuit of the main amplifier. As the case was at 10 kV above earth potential a second engineer stood by to knock MacLarty's hand away if he were tempted to reach over the guard rail to tap the instrument.

The difficulties with Daventry 5GB having been resolved, a series of radiation tests started on 31 May 1927 on 325·1 m (920 kHz), the frequency then used by Bournemouth, and also on 491·8 m (610 kHz), then used by Birmingham. The first alternative programme for the Midlands started on 21 August 1927 from this transmitter, operating on 491·8 m (610 kHz) with an output power of 30 kW.

One of the masts used for long-wave transmissions by 5XX on the same site distorted the radiation pattern of the medium-wave aerial and reduced the signal strength in the direction of Birmingham, which was one of the most important places to be served. A new aerial for 5GB had to be installed a few days before the station opened. Despite these difficulties the new station was a success and such complaints as there were referred to the swamping effect of the strong signals from 5GB in nearby towns. It was at this station that the first fatality in the BBC occurred a few weeks after the station opened, when an engineer leaned over the guard rail to make an adjustment and touched a high-voltage conductor.[2]

At this time the nine main stations and a number of relay stations (together with the high-power long-wave transmitter at Daventry) brought about 80 per cent of the population within the range of the transmissions, even if simple cheap receivers were used. People who could afford the more expensive valve receivers and put up with the inconvenience of batteries could receive the programme beyond crystal-set range. Only one programme was available to listeners in any particular area, except that those who could receive the long-wave station as well as the local medium-wave station had a choice at those times when the local station was originating its own programme.

84

Daventry was the first station to have two transmitters and it showed that Eckersley's idea, conceived in 1924, to provide a dual-programme service throughout the country was feasible, although the first twin-transmitter station (at Brookmans Park) was not completed until 1929. Eckersley did not remain with the BBC long enough to see the completion of the Regional Scheme, but his vision and determination had established the technical foundations of sound broadcasting in this country on a firm basis.

The object of the Regional Scheme was to give every listener a choice of two programmes. A choice between random alternatives would merely double the available material, but a choice between *planned* alternatives would do far more. The needs of minorities could be met, and more scope could be given to programme builders for experimentation. (This concept was the basis, thirty-five years later, of the planning of the two television programmes BBC-1 and BBC-2.) Eckersley's idea of the Regional Scheme was, however, specifically to provide for 'national' and 'regional' programmes – the former being of interest to the whole country and the latter reflecting local culture. During the following years, the conflict between 'regionalisation' and 'centralisation' went through many vicissitudes, but the principle of choice remained inviolate.

The Regional Scheme had to be built around an allocation of only ten medium wavelengths and one long wavelength under the Prague Plan of 1929 (see Section 13 of this chapter). All the relay stations had to operate on the UK Common Wave of 288·5 m (1040 kHz), with the exception of Leeds, which used an International Common Wave. As the dual-programme Regional Scheme developed, the medium-wave assignments were used up and in 1933, when the National Programme transmitter at Washford was being built, no separate channel was available for it. This transmitter was therefore synchronised with the National Programme transmitter at Brookmans Park on 261·3 m (1148 kHz). (The shortage of wavelength was slightly eased in 1934 when an additional medium-wave channel became available to the BBC under the Lucerne Plan. The National and Regional transmitters at Droitwich, commissioned in October 1934 and February 1935 respectively, were to take over the wavelengths previously used by Daventry 5XX and 5GB. The remaining channel under the Lucerne Plan was taken up by the Lisnagarvey transmitter, which opened in March 1936. Increased use of groups of synchronised transmitters made it possible to fit into the available channels all the other stations that would be needed to complete the dual-programme coverage.)

The transmitters used in the Regional Scheme were of much higher output power (up to 100 kW) than had previously been used and the stations had to be sited in areas with relatively sparse population to avoid 'blanketing' many receivers with a high local field strength. The progress in receiver design described in the previous chapter had reduced, but not eliminated, this effect. Eckersley finally persuaded the industry of the rightness of his scheme, saying that 'the transmitter is to the receiver as environment is to the evolution of the species'.

It was evident that high-power stations would be more economical to run than a larger number of low-power stations giving the same coverage, especially as each station had to be staffed. Capital costs would also be lower, and the use of high-power would make the best use of the limited number of frequency channels available.

It was initially proposed to build five twin-wave stations to cover the following areas:

1   London and the Home Counties
2   Manchester and the Industrial North of England
3   Glasgow, Edinburgh and the Scottish Lowlands
4   South Wales and the West of England
5   Birmingham and the Midlands

The preliminary estimate of the cost of these stations, including the land, was £115,000 each, although the final estimate for Brookmans Park was £130,500. As about £0·5M was to be spent on the first four stations, and as the BBC administrators knew little of the technicalities involved, Reith thought that it would be advantageous to have an independent technical Committee to examine and report upon Eckersley's proposals. Accordingly, the BBC appointed the Eccles Committee in 1927, with the following membership:

Dr W. H. Eccles, FRS	Chairman
Prof. E. V. Appleton, FRS	University of London
Dr L. B. Turner	Cambridge University
R. T. B. Wynn	Technical Secretary (BBC)

The Eccles Committee endorsed Eckersley's Regional Scheme without suggesting any modifications, but in spite of this the Post Office withheld its approval saying that the permanent allocation of wavelengths for broadcasting purposes was the province of Telecommunications Administrations and, as there was to be a World Wireless Conference in 1927, its outcome must be awaited before approval could be given. The Post Office was also doubtful whether crystal sets would be capable of receiving a programme in the presence of another transmission of equal strength. Finally, on 20 April 1928, the Post Office gave its approval and the construction of the first of the permanent twin-transmitter stations was started at once.

It had been decided that this first station should be planned to give high-quality reception of two programmes in London and the south-eastern counties, with sufficient signal strength to permit inexpensive receiving equipment to be used. Much thought was given to the location of the site, which had to avoid areas subject to Government restrictions and at the same time to fulfil the following requirements:

1   to be within about fifteen miles of Oxford Street, so that the signal would be strong enough in central London to permit the continued use of existing receivers.
2   to be far enough from populated areas to avoid 'blanketing' a significant number of receivers.
3   to be far enough from the coast to avoid wasting a large part of the energy over the sea.
4   to be in an open position to avoid absorption of energy by neighbouring buildings.
5   to be accessible to a Post Office cable route.

The site finally chosen at Brookmans Park was thirty-six acres in extent and was about sixteen miles north of Charing Cross on one of the highest points in Hertfordshire – 414 ft AMSL. Work started in July 1928 and was expected to take about twelve months, but owing to the severe frost of early 1929 the first transmitter, carrying the London Regional programme, was not put into service until 21 October 1929. It used the wavelength of 356 m (842 kHz) assigned by the Prague Plan. On the same date the London 2LO transmitter at Selfridges was closed down.

This first twin-transmitter station served as the prototype for the next three Regional stations, whose buildings and layouts were modified only slightly to meet local technical and planning requirements. (Although the Droitwich transmitting station used the same general plan, extensive modifications were made to the internal design of the building there and to the arrangement of the plant within it.) The later single-transmitter stations at Lisnagarvey, Burghead, Stagshaw and Start Point again used the same basic building layout as was employed at the first of the Regional Stations, but with the building scaled down to accommodate the reduced amount of plant. The low-power medium-wave stations at Penmon, Redmoss and Clevedon had smaller buildings of a different design.

The power of the medium-wave transmitters to be used in the Regional Scheme was limited by the maximum (initially 50 kW, but increased to 100 kW by 1935) that could be achieved with the valves and power supplies then available, which was not far below the maximum power that can usefully be used in the absence of external interference for ground-wave coverage at night. The range corresponding to this is limited to about 100 miles by interaction between the sky wave and the ground wave; it can be achieved with powers in the region of 100 to 150 kW and cannot be exceeded by increasing the power of the transmitter beyond this.

Each of the two Marconi transmitters at Brookmans Park consisted of five units completely enclosed in an aluminium framework covered with enamelled steel panels to provide screening between the units. Low-level choke modulation was used, and the first unit comprised a master oscillator, a separator stage, sub-modulator and main modulator stages, and the modulated amplifier; the valves in this unit were air cooled. The second unit was a single-stage amplifier with two water-cooled valves in push-pull. The final amplifier was housed in two units, the two groups of valves being connected in push-pull. Another unit contained the rf output circuit and was connected directly to the feeders running from the transmitter building to the aerial transformer house. The doors of all the units were fitted with interlocks, except the one carrying rf currents only (it being thought at that time that high voltages at rf were not lethal). A control table for each of the two transmitters was placed in the middle of the transmitter hall. The design of these transmitters owed much to the development work done by B. N. MacLarty, on the experimental transmitter, 5GB.[3,4]

The circulating water for the valves in the power stages flowed by gravity from two tanks mounted on the roof of the building, through the jackets of the valves and then into two tanks in the crypt. It was then pumped through two banks of tubes over a concrete-lined pond outside the building and thence returned to the tanks on the roof. The banks of tubes were cooled by sprays of water, but the circulating system itself was entirely closed and filled with distilled water. This was the first use of an enclosed cooling system since the method was developed at the Daventry experimental station, 5GB.

Separate aerial systems were provided for the two programmes, each aerial being supported by two 200-ft self-supporting insulated lattice steel towers. An aerial transformer house was located beneath each aerial. Each of the two earth systems consisted of eighty copper wires radiating from the aerial transformer house in all directions and buried one foot below the surface of the ground.

It was decided to install diesel engines for the power supply rather than rely on the mains; this decision was made on the score of reliability (the national grid did not then exist) and running costs (at the prices then current). Power supply was accordingly derived from four diesel engines driving dc generators each giving an output of 234 kW. (The reason for generating dc rather than ac was that this permitted the use of a storage battery as a stand-by power source.) Three of the engines could run the two transmitters on full power, the fourth being spare. The exhaust gases from the engines were used to heat a boiler for space heating, but an ancillary oil-fired boiler was provided to give sufficient heat to prevent condensation in the equipment when the engines were not running.

A storage battery of about 2000 Ah capacity was provided for lighting and to run the station for a short time in an emergency. Fifteen motor-generator sets were housed in the machine room to convert the supply received from the power house at 200 V dc. Of these, three 160-kW machines generated dc for the anode supply at between 10 and 11 kV. High-power generators producing dc at this voltage were unique; their design presented novel problems, but was successfully achieved by C. E. Calverley of the English Electric Company. They were necessary because no rectifiers were available capable of producing dc at such high power from an ac source. These machines were enclosed in a steel grille, the doors of which were interlocked. Three other machines produced 1300 A at about 23 V for the filament supplies (except those for the master oscillator valve, which had a separate battery). Other machines provided anode supplies for the low-power stages of the transmitters and for grid bias. The main switchboard ran along the end of the transmitter hall.

Two separate control rooms were provided for the programme input equipment and line terminations, which were connected by four Post Office cable circuits to the studios at Savoy Hill. A small studio was provided for testing and emergency purposes.

The operating power of the transmitter working on 356 m was 45 kW and that of the one working on 261 m was 67·5 kW, the difference being an attempt to equalise the range of the two transmitters by using higher power on the less favourable wavelength.

Listeners over a wide area would receive stronger signals from the new station than they had had from the 2-kW transmitter at Selfridges. Others in Central London would receive a weaker signal and others again might be expected to have difficulties later, when the second transmitter at Brookmans Park was brought into service 4½ months after the first. It was therefore necessary to prepare the public in London and the Home Counties for possible difficulties in reception. The thoroughness with which this was done by R. T. B. Wynn, Head of the Technical Correspondence Section, resulted in the public reaction to the introduction of the new high-power station being almost entirely favourable.[5] The only complaints came from people living close to the transmitting station. Extensive tests were made before the second high-power transmitter, which was to carry the National programme, was brought into full service on 9 March 1930 on 261·3 m (1148 kHz). Again, there was practically no adverse criticism from listeners. (The BBC had gained experience from the unfortunate events of August 1927, when the Daventry 5GB medium-wave transmitter took over the service previously carried by the Birmingham 5IT transmitter. There had, at that time, been an outcry from listeners in Birmingham about the reduction in signal strength. Eckersley, supported by Reith, was not discouraged and he dealt effectively with the complaints in letters and in broadcast talks delivered in his inimitable style. Nevertheless, it was decided that in any future operations of this nature, a much more comprehensive public relations exercise would have to be mounted.)

The Brookmans Park station continued to radiate the Regional and National programmes from the original Marconi transmitters until the change-over to wartime operations on 1 September 1939. Technical changes at Brookmans Park during its first ten years' service were mainly concerned with improvements to the aerial and feeder systems, improved carrier-frequency control in readiness for the Lucerne Plan of 1934 and improvements to the synchronising arrangements for the National transmitter.[6] The station continued to operate from its own diesel generators until November 1939 when the public electricity supply was brought into the station for normal use, the diesel generators being retained as a stand-by power source.

The second of the regional transmitting stations was built on a 31-acre site at Moorside Edge, five miles to the west of Huddersfield, at a height of 1117 ft AMSL. The site was chosen after extensive tests had been made with a mobile transmitter to find a location where suitable land was obtainable and where intervening hills would not screen the large areas of Lancashire and Yorkshire that it was planned to serve. This transmitter was assigned the longest medium wavelength available to the BBC under the Prague Plan: 479 m (626 kHz). Since the effective range on medium wavelengths is greater the longer the wavelength, this channel was chosen to serve the widespread area representing what was to become the North Region. The design of the station followed closely that of Brookmans Park. However, experimental work carried out on the design of transmitting aerials, which had been started in 1928, had shown the advantages of a 0·5λ aerial, i.e. one with a vertical height equal to about half the operating wavelength.[7] The self-supporting towers at Brookmans Park – only 200 ft in height – had already been ordered by the time these aerial tests had been concluded, but the opportunity was taken to order 500-ft masts for Moorside Edge. Three stayed lattice masts were erected to support the regional transmitter T-aerial (between masts 2 and 3) and the national transmitter vertical aerial (between masts 1 and 2). Each mast was insulated at the base.[8]

The regional transmitter started service on 17 May 1931 and at the same time the

Manchester 2ZY transmitter and the relay transmitters at Liverpool, Stoke-on-Trent, Hull, Nottingham, Leeds, Bradford and Sheffield were all closed down. The second, national programme, transmitter at Moorside Edge, followed on 12 July 1931. This transmitter used the exclusive wavelength of 301·5 m (995 kHz). A particular feature of the regional transmitter aerial at this bleak and wind-swept site was the provision of de-icing arrangements, comprising a dc supply that could be connected to the aerial outside programme hours and passed through the aerial wires to melt any ice formation. Another unusual feature at this station was the erection of a water reservoir of 200,000 gallons capacity as a precaution against drought, such as had occurred in the area in 1929.

Power was supplied by four diesel generators having a total capacity of 936 kW at 230 V dc and it was not until June 1940 that a public electricity supply was brought into the station, the diesel generators being then retained as a reserve. (It was, by then, common practice to provide mains supply to BBC stations, if possible from two independent feeders, with diesel-generators in reserve. In general, the cost per kWh is now slightly higher when the generators are used.)

The third instalment of the Regional Scheme was a station to serve, primarily, Glasgow and Edinburgh and the densely populated Forth-Clyde belt, but it was hoped to include in its service area Dundee and much of the rural Scottish Lowlands. The selected site was at Westerglen, about 2½ miles to the south-west of Falkirk. Two 500-ft stayed, lattice masts were erected to support the T-aerial for the regional transmitter between them; an 'umbrella' aerial for the national transmitter was erected around one of the masts.[9] The regional transmitter came into service on a wavelength of 376·4 m (797 kHz) on 12 June 1932 and the satisfactory coverage it gave in Glasgow and Edinburgh, and also in Dundee, enabled the existing transmitters in those cities to be closed down. The national programme transmitter was brought into service on a wavelength of 288·5 m (1040 kHz) on the same date, sharing this channel with the Swansea, Plymouth and Bournemouth stations. At the same time, the Aberdeen transmitter was converted to a 'relay' station and the wavelength was changed to 214·3 m (1400 kHz) on 12 June 1932.

Technical innovations at Westerglen between 1932 and 1939 included the first tests using a common aerial for two high-power transmitters; this development was to have a far-reaching effect on the design of transmitting stations later. Improved synchronising equipment for the national transmitter was supplied and one of the first quartz crystal drives was installed at Westerglen in 1938.

The fourth regional station was planned to serve the populous areas of South Wales, Bristol and as much of the West of England as possible.

In order to take advantage of the low-attenuation path over the sea to the South Wales coastal towns it was decided to build the station on the southern shores of the Bristol Channel, not too far from Bristol. Several sites were investigated during the autumn of 1930 and the station was built at Washford Cross. Two 500-ft stayed lattice masts were erected to support the T and 'Umbrella' aerials for the regional and national programme transmitters respectively.[10] The West Regional Transmitter opened on 28 May 1933 on 309·9 m (968 kHz). Its satisfactory coverage of Cardiff and Swansea enabled the transmitters previously operating in those towns to be closed down, but parts of Devon, Cornwall and Dorset were not well served and the low-power stations at Plymouth and Bournemouth were retained. By the time the second transmitter at Washford was ready for service all the medium-wave channels allocated to the BBC under the Prague Plan had been used up and it was therefore necessary for the West National transmitter to be synchronised with the London National transmitter on 261·6 m (1148 kHz). Tuning-fork drives were provided at each station and tone was transmitted experimentally over a line from Brookmans Park, as the 'master' station, to control the drive at Washford. Tuning-fork filters and automatic facilities for changing over to a local tuning-fork were provided in case of line failure. This system worked fairly well, but needed a considerable amount of semi-specialised attention.

Thus, by the middle of 1933, the four main twin-transmitter stations of the Regional Scheme had been completed. The soundness of the design of the equipment can be judged from the fact that six of the eight transmitters, some now more than forty years old, are still available as stand-by transmitters.

In July 1937 it was decided to split the Welsh and West of England programmes, and from 4 July the Regional transmitter at Washford carried the Welsh Regional Programme from the Cardiff studios on 373·1 m (804 kHz), while the other carried the West of England programme from the Bristol studios on 285·7 m (1050 kHz). Listeners in the former national transmitter service area were able to obtain the national programme satisfactorily from the Droitwich long-wave transmitter on 1500 m (200 kHz). In fact, within the service area of Droitwich, the local national programme transmitters were needed only to serve urban areas where the level of electrical interference on the long wavelength was high.

The Washford station was notable for the gardens in the front of the building, which in summer used to attract visitors from the surrounding countryside in considerable numbers to the benefit of the 'Week's Good Cause', a collection box for which was provided in the entrance hall.

Although the coverage of the Daventry 5XX long-wave transmitter was satisfactory, bearing in mind the 25-kW power restriction there, thought was being given in the early 1930s to the building of a new high-power transmitter using the full 150 kW permitted to the United Kingdom on 200 kHz by the Lucerne Plan. (Daventry had opened on 187·5 kHz on 27 July 1925 and changed to 187 kHz on 3 July 1927 and to 193 kHz on 30 June 1929. It changed again on 15 January 1934 to the new frequency of 200 kHz, which has been used by the BBC ever since and now carries Radio 2 from Droitwich with a power of 400 kW. It is now maintained to an accuracy of $\pm$ 2:10^{11} and the transmissions are used in several countries to provide a reference frequency.) As it was not possible to obtain a second long-wave channel, the new station would have to replace Daventry. Search for a site to the west of Daventry was made in view of Government restrictions on power in the Daventry area. A site at Wychbold, near Droitwich, some sixteen miles to the south of Birmingham, was chosen after a series of tests, which started in 1932.

The high-power long-wave transmitter started to radiate the national programme on 1500 m (200 kHz) on 7 October 1934 using a T aerial suspended between two 700-ft stayed, lattice masts. These masts were, for the first time in the BBC, provided with electrically-operated lifts for maintenance purposes.[11] The transmitter was designed by the Marconi Company in close co-operation with the BBC engineers, MacLarty and Macnamara. Macnamara worked at Chelmsford as the technical liaison engineer throughout the design and construction period.

Several interesting problems arose during the design of this station. For example, it was necessary to produce a good response characteristic from the long-wave aerial, which had an asymmetrical impedance characteristic at the driving point. A transducer was designed by W. Proctor Wilson for insertion between the output of the transmitter and the transmission line and a substantially flat frequency response was obtained for modulating frequencies between 30 Hz and 8 kHz. There were to be six valves in the output stage; four working and two spare. It was necessary to use valves capable of dissipating about 120 kW, but none was available when the station was planned. This problem was solved by the Marconi-Osram Valve Company, which designed the type CAT 14 valve, requiring an anode potential of about 20 kV. It was decided to use series modulation in the penultimate rf stage of this transmitter; as this meant that the filament circuits were at a potential of 20 kV above earth, a new design of filament generator had to be produced for this stage to provide the necessary insulation from earth. A suitable eht supply was a further problem as it was required to give 30 A at 20 kV. The solution was found in a continuously-pumped, steel-tank, mercury arc rectifier installation.[12]

Teething troubles were experienced with the new design of high-voltage, mercury arc rectifier installation. The rectifiers were subject to 'backfires' and consequent tripping of the eht supply. At one stage, this trouble was so severe that a temporary thermionic rectifier was installed at Droitwich to power the transmitter while modifications were being made to the design of the mercury arc rectifiers.

Droitwich was the first of the regional stations to be supplied with ac power from its own prime movers. As the power requirements for this station were considerably greater than those of the earlier regional stations, the provision of a large capacity secondary battery as a stand-by power source would not have been economic and this gave freedom of choice between ac and dc power sources. Four six-cylinder diesel engines were installed, each driving an alternator having an output of 470 kW at 415 V, 3-phase, 50 Hz. Three of these alternators could supply the station at three-quarters full load, making the fourth diesel alternator set available for routine overhauls as required. The public electricity supply was brought into Droitwich in mid-1940, but the diesel alternators were used throughout the preceding six years to carry the full load of the station.

The Droitwich building was a departure from the design of the previous regional transmitter buildings in that the transmitter hall was constructed with two storeys. The water-cooled valves had to be supplied with cooling water through long hoses to give sufficient insulation against the unusually high anode voltage. The transmitter units were installed on the first floor with their hose coils mounted on the ground floor in the lower part of the units, which also housed the coils and capacitors associated with the anode circuits and the transducers. The ground floor also accom-modated the rotating machinery supplying the filament power, auxiliary ht and grid bias to both national and regional transmitters. All these machines were operated remotely from a large control desk on the first floor.

A 50-kW medium-wave transmitter was installed at Droitwich later and this came into service carrying the Midland Regional Programme on 17 February 1935, re-placing the Daventry 5GB transmitter. The Midland Regional transmitter used a directional aerial system suspended from triatics on one of the 700-ft masts and the radiation pattern was adjusted to increase the signal strength in the Birmingham area and in the North Midlands generally. This transmitter followed the design of the previous 50-kW transmitters, but with some improvements.

With the completion of the fifth regional station, at Droitwich, the first stage of the Regional Scheme had been implemented and attention was then given to improv-ing reception in the remaining areas of the United Kingdom where alternative pro-grammes were still not available. For example, although Northern Ireland was covered satisfactorily by the national programme transmitter at Droitwich, the coverage of the alternative regional programme was limited to that given by the low-power (1-kW) transmitter in Belfast. Many listeners in the Scottish Highlands could receive the national programme on long waves, but were unable to receive the regional transmitter at Westerglen, except during the hours of darkness – and even then the signal was subject to severe fading. The Aberdeen transmitter being of low power provided only a local service around that city. The next stage in the develop-ment of the Regional Scheme was to extend the coverage by providing alternative programme transmitters in these two areas, and an order for two 100-kW medium-wave transmitters was placed with the Marconi Company in mid-1935.

In Northern Ireland five sites were considered and one near Lisburn was chosen. The station, named Lisnagarvey, was some nine miles south-west of Belfast. The 100-kW medium-wave transmitter – the first to be built for the BBC – used series modulation in the penultimate rf stage.

It was at first intended that the two new 100-kW transmitters should be supplied with main anode power from steel-tank, mercury arc rectifiers, like those installed at Droitwich. However, owing to the initial troubles experienced with this plant, it was decided to use a high-voltage dc supply from machines for the next two stations, since this method had been tried and tested by experience. A modified design of eht motor generator was accordingly produced. The overall power conversion efficiency was similar to that obtained on the long-wave transmitter at Droitwich (about 20 per cent). Improved methods were used to protect the valves and eht supply from overloads; the anode current was cut off within 0·01 s of the incidence of an overload, and this restricted the instantaneous current in the armature of the eht generator to a value not exceeding twice the normal full-load current.

The physical layout of these transmitters was changed from the row of free-standing cubicles ('Bun Boxes') used at the earlier Regional stations, to a single enclosure, entry to which was made through a small number of interlocked doors. This provided a more economical and compact layout and a simpler interlock circuit with fewer potential fault points. The output from the transmitter was routed to the aerial matching circuits through a Marconi 5-in. concentric feeder and a pilot voltage was used to protect the feeder by cutting the transmitter output in case of damage to the aerial system.

At Lisnagarvey, the otherwise uninspiring appearance of the station was somewhat relieved by the design of the mast. This was the first BBC transmitting station to use an anti-fading aerial. It consisted of a 500-ft mast radiator in the form of two pyramids joined at their bases. This resulted in a cigar-shaped structure, which was supported by two sets of stays at the point of widest cross-section. At the top of the mast was a capacity ring mounted on a supporting mast, which could be raised or lowered to alter the electrical height of the whole mast. One advantage of this configuration was thought to be that, the voltage stresses being minimal at the mid-point, the design of the stay insulators would be eased. However, this type of mast was expensive to build and it was not repeated for the BBC.

Lisnagarvey was the first BBC transmitting station to take its power from the public electricity supply *ab initio*, and an interesting feature was the introduction of an electrode boiler for heating the building. This boiler was brought into use as soon as the transmitter had closed down for the night and was switched off when transmission started on the following morning. As its loading was similar to that of the transmitter it was possible to attain a 100 per cent load factor, which resulted in a very advantageous tariff. It is believed that this was the first night-storage heater of industrial size used in the United Kingdom. Lisnagarvey was opened on 20 March 1936 and on the same day the Belfast transmitter was closed down. Lisnagarvey radiated on 307·1 m (977 kHz), the carrier frequency being derived from a Marconi constant-frequency ('Parkin') drive, which ensured the degree of precision required under the Lucerne Plan.[13]

The second of the 100-kW medium-wave regional transmitting stations was installed on a twenty-acre site at Burghead on the southern shores of the Moray Firth about seven miles north of Elgin. This station was required to serve the coastal towns from Thurso to Fraserburgh, Inverness, and as many of the inland towns in the Scottish Highlands as possible. Lengthy pre-service tests took place to confirm the estimated coverage and these included observations of field strength made from a small boat in the Moray Firth – to the considerable discomfort of some of those concerned who lacked marine experience. Observations were also made to determine the interference pattern between the Burghead and Westerglen regional transmitters, which had to share the wavelength of 391·1 m (767 kHz); from the results, the operating powers of the two stations were determined. The 500-ft stayed mast radiator of lattice construction carried aircraft obstruction lights at five levels. This form of lighting gave an unusually festive appearance to the station by night and during severe gales there was an alarming visual indication of the relative movement between different parts of the structure. The transmitter was connected to the aerial matching network by a Marconi 5-in. concentric feeder with pilot voltage protection. The station was opened on 12 October 1936.

A new design of tuning-fork drive equipment was used at Burghead and Westerglen to synchronise the regional programme transmitters at these stations. This was produced by the Research and Transmitter Departments and was based on the experimental apparatus used for the medium-wave national programme transmitters. Standard Telephones and Cables manufactured this new drive equipment, which embodied 'Elinvar' tuning forks made by Muirhead & Co. (Elinvar is a nickel-chrome-steel alloy having an almost constant value of Young's modulus over a wide range of temperature and a much lower coefficient of thermal expansion than the mild steel previously used in making electrically-maintained tuning forks.) The long-term frequency stability of the mild steel forks, when enclosed in a temperature-controlled oven and associated with a valve maintaining circuit having closely regulated supply voltages, was of the order of $\pm\,20/10^6$. The long-term frequency stability of the Elinvar forks under the same operating conditions was at least one order better, *viz* $\pm\,2/10^6$.

Tone derived from the 'master' station tuning fork at a frequency of $1498\cdot05$ Hz was transmitted over a special line to the 'slave' station. However, the tone circuit was far from reliable and for several months it was necessary to operate a 'nursing' rota worked by specialist department engineers from London who spent two-week spells at Burghead and Westerglen dealing with the teething troubles on the new equipment and coping with numerous line faults. These engineers included D. B. Weigall (later Deputy Director of Engineering) and W. E. C. Varley (later Chief Engineer, Transmitters).

After the Welsh and West of England regional programme split in 1937 listeners in South Wales could receive the regional programme service satisfactorily, but those in North Wales had an unsatisfactory day-time service and no service after dark. It was therefore decided to build a station to serve Anglesey and the North Wales coastal area, making use of low-attenuation sea paths if possible. Several sites were investigated, including one at Great Orme's Head and one near Beaumaris, Anglesey; the latter was selected and the station named Penmon. The transmitter was an 8-kW medium-wave Marconi installation and was unique in that it employed series modulation in the final rf stage, with a CAM 3 valve modulating a CAT 6 in the modulated amplifier. It went into service on 1 February 1937 and shared the frequency of the Welsh Regional transmitter, 804 kHz. Tuning-fork drives, embodying forks with a low temperature co-efficient provided by H. W. Sullivan & Co., were supplied to both stations, Penmon being designated the 'slave' station. A reference tone at a frequency of 6732 Hz was transmitted over the programme circuit between Washford and Penmon, and many hours were spent in testing for mutual interaction between tone and programme during close-down hours. A test record entitled 'The Nightingale's Song of Morning Greeting' was found suitable for this purpose because some of the trills contained components at 6732 Hz.

In 1937 the development of quartz crystal oscillators for precision frequency control had reached a stage where stations in a synchronised group might work satisfactorily with independent oscillators. The Washford/Penmon group was chosen for trials of this method. Accordingly, two quartz bars maintained in oscillation at a frequency of $50\cdot25$ kHz were installed, one at each station, together with frequency multipliers, each consisting of four doubling stages. By making adjustments manually each hour at Penmon, it was found possible to maintain the carrier frequency synchronisation within 0·1 Hz. A visual display of the frequency difference was provided at Penmon using a heavily damped recording meter.[6]

Listeners in Northumberland, Durham, Westmorland and Cumberland were the next group to be given an alternative programme, as the North Regional transmitter at Moorside Edge did not provide them with a satisfactory service and the Newcastle transmitter had only a range of twenty miles or so. In 1935 and 1937, two 100-kW transmitters were ordered, this time from Standard Telephones and Cables Ltd., and they were earmarked for the north-east and south-west of England. By then a transmitter design of higher efficiency than before, had been produced by STC, using anode voltage modulation of the final stage; the modulation transformer was fed by a high-power audio amplifier operating in Class B. This permitted the rf output valves to operate in Class C at an efficiency of about 70 per cent, compared with the 30 per cent efficiency of the earlier transmitters modulated at low power. Negative feedback, which had been introduced by H. S. Black in the USA as a means of reducing distortion and noise, was applied for the first time to a high-power MF transmitter in this country.[14,15] The results obtained using this system were satisfactory, with a low distortion factor and good frequency response characteristic. The transmitters were so designed that, if the feedback system proved unacceptable, each transmitter could be operated with the modulator in Class A without feedback.

Stagshaw and, later, Start Point were the last of the high-power transmitting stations in the Regional Scheme to be provided with an eht supply derived from machines; at these two stations a novel feature was the mounting of the filament supply generator on an extension of the armature shaft of the main generator. Thus, the major transmitter supplies were all obtained from one rotating machine. The synchronous motor used to drive the generators was also used to improve the station power factor by adjustment of the excitation current.

The Stagshaw station was about sixteen miles west-north-west of Newcastle upon Tyne. A 450-ft stayed lattice mast radiator was erected and the station used the Lucerne Plan allocation of 267·4 m (1122 kHz). The output had to be restricted to 60 kW to meet international requirements and the station was opened for service on 19 October 1937, when it replaced the low-power (1-kW) transmitter at Newcastle.

As the Aberdeen area was in the interference zone between the Westerglen and Burghead transmitters, which used a common wavelength, the alternative programme was available in this area only from the low-power (0·3 kW) transmitter in the city. To improve the coverage, a new station called Redmoss was built three miles south of Aberdeen. A 250-ft stayed lattice mast radiator with a capacity top was provided. The STC transmitter had a nominal output of 10 kW, being a stock unit, but was operated at Redmoss at a reduced power of 3½ kW on a wavelength of 233·5 m (1285 kHz) shared by international agreement with Poland. Power was taken from the mains and no stand-by power supply was provided. The station started service on 9 September 1938, replacing the Aberdeen transmitter on that date.

Two solutions were considered to the problem of improving the poor reception of the regional programme by listeners in Devon, Cornwall and Dorset, one using high-power stations and the other a number of low-power transmitters. Extensive site tests were made in the area between January 1935 and April 1937, and it was finally decided to adopt the high-power solution. Sites for two stations were selected, one at Start Point in South Devon and the other near Clevedon in Somerset. Altogether twenty-three sites had to be investigated before the final selection was made. These two transmitting stations were in operation under pre-war conditions only from June to September 1939: they were both closed down on 1 September 1939 and were used for other services during the war, as described in a later chapter.

MAIN AND RELAY STATIONS UP TO 1 SEPTEMBER 1939

Station	Frequency (kHz)	Wavelength (m)	Power (kW)	Opening Date
Droitwich (National)	200	1500	150	Oct. 1934
Brookmans Park (National)	1149	261·1	40	Mar. 1930
Moorside Edge (National)	1149	261·1	40	July 1931
Westerglen (National)	1149	261·1	50	June 1932
Moorside Edge (North Regional)	668	449·1	70	May 1931
Stagshaw	1122	267·4	60	Oct. 1937
Westerglen (Scottish Regional)	767	391·1	70	June 1932
Burghead	767	391·1	60	Oct. 1936
Redmoss	1285	233·5	5	Sep. 1938
Washford (Welsh Regional)	804	373·1	70	May 1933*
Penmon	804	373·1	5	Feb. 1937
Brookmans Park (London Regional)	877	342·1	70	Oct. 1929
Lisnagarvey (N. Ireland Regional)	977	307·1	100	Mar. 1936
Droitwich (Midland Regional)	1013	296·2	70	Feb. 1935
Start Point (West of England Regional)	1050	285·7	100	June. 1939
Clevedon	1474	203·5	20	June 1939

* As West Regional Station.

The 100-kW medium-wave transmitter at Start Point was similar in design to the one installed at Stagshaw in 1937. The station was opened for service on 14 June 1939 and the West of England transmitter at Washford was closed on the same day to release its wavelength of 285·7 m (1050 kHz) for use at Start Point. The site was just north-west of the Start Point Lighthouse. The power supply was taken from the mains via two independent 11-kV feeders. A diesel alternator set was installed as a reserve power source with an output capacity of 400 kW at 440 V, 3-phase. The aerial system was designed to have a directional radiation pattern in order to avoid wasting power over the English Channel and to enhance the signal to the east and west. Two 450-ft stayed lattice masts were erected, one being used as a mast-radiator and the other as a parasitic reflector. Both masts were provided with a mast break insulator at the 310-ft level at which an inductance could be inserted to adjust the electrical length of the structure.

When the Start Point transmitter was brought into service, the low-power transmitters at Plymouth and Bournemouth were closed down, as the new transmitter gave adequate alternative programme coverage in those cities.

The site of the Clevedon transmitter is distinguished by being the lowest site in use by the BBC, its height being only 10 ft AMSL. (The war-time Ottringham station at 50 ft AMSL and the Penmon station at 50 ft AMSL were its nearest competitors in this respect.) The Clevedon transmitter was supplied by STC and had an output power of 20 kW. The aerial consisted of a 350-ft stayed lattice mast radiator with a capacity top, and the transmitter used a wavelength of 203·5 m (1474 kHz), which was an International Common Wave under the Lucerne Plan.

With the commissioning of the twelve transmitting stations of the Regional Scheme between 1929 and 1939, listeners in most parts of the country could receive two alternative programmes. The coverage of the Regional Programme was provided on medium waves only and that of the National Programme by the long-wave transmitter at Droitwich, supplemented by the medium-wave transmitters at Brookmans Park, Moorside Edge and Westerglen – which were retained to supplement the long-wave coverage in areas where electrical interference was troublesome on long waves.

Valves were important components in transmitters of all kinds; indeed it is hard to think of any technical development in broadcasting that has not depended either on thermionic valves or on semi-conductor devices. Such 'active' components are essential elements in the broadcasting chain from studio to loudspeaker and they have been developed by a highly specialised branch of the electronics industry. Valves have limited lives and their replacement accounts for an appreciable part of the running costs of high-power transmitters. Much attention was paid just before the war to methods of prolonging the lives of valves and increasing their efficiency. By 1939 filaments of pure metal (tungsten or tantalum) had given place, in small valves, to the more efficient oxide-coated and thoriated filaments, but pure metal still had to be used to withstand the high voltage-gradients to which large valves might be subjected.

In 1933 a Valve Section was formed in the Research Department to investigate valve problems in liaison with the manufacturers. H. S. Walker was the first head of the section and remained so until he retired in 1960. In 1938 the growing volume of work in acquiring, testing and storing valves necessitated a move from Nightingale Square, where the Research Department then was, to the White House, Motspur Park, adjoining the sports ground of the BBC Club; at the same time the section became part of the Transmitter Department. Purchases of large valves were controlled by reference to a series of 'Walker curves', which showed for each type the number that ought to be held in stock according to the number in use and their expected lives.

The BBC has been well served by British makers of transmitting valves (including

Marconi's, Mullard's, M–O Valve Co., STC and English Electric). Small valves, classed as 'receiving valves', cathode-ray tubes and camera tubes have been produced in bewildering variety and in great quantities by a number of makers and BBC engineers have co-operated in studying the problems that have arisen in matching their performance to the conditions of use.

The masts used at all the stations mentioned in this section were either stayed lattice masts or self-supporting towers. Towers can be used where the site is not large enough for stays. They require a greater weight of steel than stayed masts, but are cheaper for heights up to 150 ft. At most BBC stations, stayed lattice masts are used. If the mast itself constitutes a radiator, it must be insulated at the base. Towers have been used at some stations, the legs being insulated, if necessary, from earth. More recently tubular steel masts and concrete towers have come into use, even for very high structures; but the stayed lattice mast, where practicable, remains the cheapest form.

Considerable progress was made in 1928 on the formulation of the properties of transmitting aerials including the calculation of their effective height, radiation resistance and directivity.[16] The T aerial was commonly used at medium-wave stations and comparisons were made between the performance of a T aerial loaded with inductance to resonate at the wavelength of the transmission and that of a vertical aerial half-a-wavelength in height. It was found that at a distance of sixty-five miles the vertical aerial produced somewhat less fading. Experiments showed that whichever type of aerial was used, high masts were essential for maximum efficiency and optimum vertical directivity.

Advances in receiver design before the beginning of this period have been indicated in the previous chapter. The trends towards improved selectivity and increasing use of superheterodyne sets continued and there was progress in the design of band-pass filters and ganged tuning. Loudspeakers were now commonly built into the receiver. By 1933 automatic gain control had become established and 'quiet' agc circuits were introduced. Car receivers made their appearance at about this time. Both mains-operated and portable battery-operated receivers were available and by 1937 the 'all-wave receiver' had become popular. Towards the end of the period, push-button tuning was widely used.[17]

During this period a great deal of attention was paid to the problem of reducing interference from electrical apparatus, including domestic appliances.

In 1933 the Institution of Electrical Engineers set up a committee on 'Electrical Interference with Broadcasting', reconstituted in 1945 as the 'Committee on Radio Interference', to recommend what should be done to deal with it. A start had already been made on developing methods of measuring and suppressing interference. The continuation and extension of this work led to the production of a number of specifications produced by committees of the British Standards Institution, on which all the interested parties were represented. The first British Standard in this field was BS 505:1933 dealing with interference from traffic signals; BS 613:1935 dealt with components for suppressors; BS 727:1937 was concerned with interference-measuring apparatus, and BS 800:1937 prescribed limits of radio interference. Later a series

H

of Codes of Practice dealing with those aspects of electrical interference that could not be put into the form of British Standards was produced jointly by the BSI and the IEE. Compliance with these standards was voluntary, but they made information on the subject widely available and they paved the way for the statutory regulations that were to follow after the passing of the Wireless Telegraphy Act of 1949.

It had already become apparent that the matter would have to be taken up internationally, so that electrical apparatus complying with the limits of interference adopted in one country would satisfy the corresponding requirements in other countries. On 17 September 1931 the International Electrotechnical Commission, which is concerned with standardisation in the field of electrical engineering, decided in principle that a committee should be set up comprising representatives of a number of international organisations with the object of studying all aspects of electrical interference. The International Special Committee on Electrical Interference (CISPR), which had the status of a Special Committee of the IEC, was in fact established in 1933. It comprised delegates nominated by the National Committees of the IEC (which is itself a voluntary rather than a governmental organisation) and by members of the UIR, with representatives from other international organisations. It was enjoined to study the question from the technical point of view taking account of economic factors.

From the start the new committee was much concerned with the requirements of international commerce, that is to say with the interests of manufacturers wishing to export electrical apparatus, particularly domestic appliances. The interests of the broadcasters were naturally different; they wanted to protect their audience from interference and their object was to ensure that internationally agreed limits would give sufficient protection. The CISPR thus comprised the manufacturers of interfering apparatus on one side and the broadcasters on the other; with the PTT Administrations, which are responsible for maintaining order in the ether, holding the balance between them. As a result of action by the UIR, the part it played in the CISPR was considerably strengthened and from 1934 to 1939 the UIR acted as the permanent secretariat of the CISPR. BBC engineers took part, and continue to do so, in the work of the CISPR and its various specialised sub-committees. The interference limits it has proposed have been widely adopted in national specifications and have, broadly speaking, succeeded in keeping interference within reasonable bounds. Inevitably, there are circumstances in which electrical interference is still troublesome and indeed the CISPR recommendations do not aim higher than to ensure that when a type of appliance has been approved at least 80 per cent of individual appliances of that type will comply with the limit with at least 80 per cent confidence. Attention was also given, in this and other countries, to interference produced by power lines and by heavy electrical equipment, such as lifts, trolley-buses, and mercury-arc rectifiers. When television started, interference from the ignition systems of vehicles and from radio-frequency heating and medical equipment also came under scrutiny.[18]

The Technical Correspondence Section conducted a lively exchange of letters with listeners and from the middle of 1925 issued a fortnightly report to Engineers-in-

Charge. Extracts from correspondence between 1929 and 1934 ranged from elation to wistfulness:

'The striking of Big Ben came through as clear as a bell.'

'An outside aerial is impossible as the children will swing on it, being close to the school.'

'My mother spends all her time saying silly things down the loudspeaker. I am 12 . . . I have one summer frock and four partly made because she spends so much time over the wireless. She does not know I have written this, so please do not let her know or she will hit me.'

'Will you kindly tell me for what purpose the Greenwich Time Signal is broadcast? . . . it is an irritating little noise.'

'I have a lisense since four years, and have not yet heard nothink.'

'Since the change in wavelength there has been fading, which I think must be due to the engine not running level.'

Many letters were received appreciating the BBC's advice on reception problems. In those days some radio dealers made blunders such as using a gas-pipe as an earth connection, and the BBC's advice enabled listeners to put things right. The Technical Correspondence Section, under R. T. B. Wynn, showed a great deal of sympathy for the plight of individual listeners. A crippled lady living near the centre of London had been told that her crystal set was useless for receiving Brookmans Park; a BBC engineer visited her and five minutes work enabled her to get excellent reception.

'The British Wireless for the Blind Fund' was opened by a Christmas Day Appeal broadcast by Winston Churchill in 1929. BBC engineers designed special receivers for blind people, starting with a crystal set. By the beginning of 1934 £60,000 had been subscribed to the fund and 24,000 sets distributed, with the support of the industry. J. Underdown of the Engineering Information Department devoted much of his time to this work, in which the Department continues to participate. (By 1970 the fund had provided over 213,000 sets for registered blind persons.)

3   BUILDINGS

With the exception of the transmitting stations at Daventry and Bournemouth and the studio premises at Birmingham, the Company had had no premises specially designed for broadcasting, either for studies or for transmitting stations. The new Corporation took over on 1 January 1927 a number of premises that had been adapted from buildings designed for quite different purposes. Most of these buildings, though in good situations and pleasant enough in themselves, were architecturally undistinguished. One or two, notably the studio centre in Linenhall Street, Belfast, were really unsuitable for broadcasting.

The architecture of the buildings in which the early transmitting stations were installed was certainly not distinguished, because the main consideration in those days was to find a power station or factory with a high enough chimney to support the required aerial, and the transmitter was housed wherever space could be found near the chimney. At Daventry, however, the building for the long-wave transmitter (5XX) had been designed for the purpose and a building for the new experimental transmitter (5GB) had been completed just before the Corporation took over, though the transmitter itself had not yet been installed. It was a single-storey building about 70 ft long, with three offices at one end. The centre portion was the transmitter hall and the other end was the machine room.

By 1927 it had become clear that broadcasting was going to have a great future and expansion was already beginning to take place. The studios at Savoy Hill were being extended. The Regional Scheme for twin-transmitter stations with alternative programmes in each region had been accepted, and this, combined with the fact that it was now obvious that Savoy Hill would not be adequate for long, meant that a considerable building programme lay ahead. The Company had had no architect or civil engineer on its staff until 11 January 1926, when M. T. Tudsbery was appointed Civil Engineer, reporting to N. Ashbridge, the Assistant Chief Engineer. Much of Tudsbery's work at first was concerned with improving the Savoy Hill building, but was soon extended to include a search for a new Headquarters in London. In 1926 he was asked to look for a property within easy reach of Piccadilly Circus, which could be adapted for new and larger headquarters, or, alternatively, for a site on which to build. He was to take any steps he might consider necessary to bring to notice any sites or buildings that he felt might be suitable, but without disclosing that he was acting for the Company.

Upwards of twenty sites and buildings were inspected before a decision was reached. Among the more important was Dorchester House, an old Palladian-style building in Park Lane; this was very seriously considered as a result of Tudsbery's report on his inspection of the building – with its magnificent staircase of white marble and columns of pink granite, all beautifully proportioned – and its grounds. It was agreed that plans should be prepared for its conversion for broadcasting purposes, but the proposal was dropped because a site in Portland Place offered opportunities equal to those of Dorchester House at lower cost. Among the many other sites that were considered were Adelphi Terrace (part of the island site), Bush House, the Langham Hotel, the Russell Hotel, and the Philharmonic Hall in Great Portland Street (better known today as 'Brock House'). Some of these were occupied by the BBC during and just after the war.

Early in the spring of 1927 Tudsbery heard that a private house with garden, on a site at the corner of Portland Place and Langham Street, was for sale. The site comprised numbers 2, 4, 6 and 8 Portland Place. No. 8 was at one time called Foley House. (The original Foley House, a famous mansion built about the middle of the eighteenth century and owned by Lord Foley, stood on the site of the Langham. The corner house referred to here was called Foley House after the old mansion and was built about 1780 by James Wyatt, the architect, for his own residence.) At first the owner,

Lord Waring, wanted to dispose of the whole freehold of the site, but the BBC was not then able to purchase so large a freehold and, bearing in mind the very considerable cost of developing the site to suit the Corporation's particular requirements, the proposal was not pursued at that time.

In February, however, Tudsbery chanced to be told by a friend that Foley House was to be demolished for the development by a financial syndicate of high-class residential flats, and the agents said that their clients would be prepared instead to erect on the site a building to suit the Corporation's special needs. Details of the subsequent negotiations with the syndicate and an account of the building of Broadcasting House appeared in 1932 in the BBC publication, *Broadcasting House*. Surprising as it now seems, the BBC would agree to the acquisition of the site in 1928 only on condition that parts of the future premises were let. The building was to be planned for shops, with basements, on the ground and lower-ground floors, a garage, and a bank on the corner. The first and second floors were not to be taken over at once, but were to serve for later expansion.[19]

The BBC declared, and the syndicate accepted, that it would not be prepared to pay more than six shillings per foot of floor space, including corridors, but not including space for lifts and for heating- and ventilation-plant. In view of the unusually intricate nature of the undertaking, the syndicate also accepted that their architect, G. Val Myer, should work on the plans step by step with Tudsbery; the BBC welcomed this, as it would help to ensure that the building would meet their requirements for the arrangement and design of studios. A joint report presented by Val Myer and Tudsbery on 3 July 1928 contained the following passages:

'The guiding principle adopted has been to exploit to the utmost the peculiar advantages in shape and size of the site, and with this objective the offices and similar departments to which daylight is essential have been arranged around the whole exterior of the building. On the other hand, the studios and their suites to which insulation from external noise is the first need, have been grouped in a vast central tower of heavy brickwork, ventilated by artificial means and protected from the streets by the complete outer layer of offices . . . and insulated from the offices themselves by wide corridors and thick brick walls.'
'The building, as planned, will give all the accommodation required for the present needs of the Corporation besides leaving a reserve of more than twenty thousand feet of excellent office space on the first and second floors, which, together with the shops and bank on the ground and sub-ground floors (amounting to 14,425 ft), it is proposed to let off to other tenants.'

The second of these passages explains why some of the ground-floor windows of the present building are shaped for shop-fronts.

The formal agreement required the syndicate to develop the site at its own cost to the approval and satisfaction of the BBC's Civil Engineer, and that its architect should be directly associated with him in the development. Naturally there were some departures from the original plans. On learning of the project, the Ellerman Estate insisted that light to their properties on the west side of Langham Street should not be reduced and the mansard roof on the east side of the present building was the result. A notable success was achieved in getting an LCC Byelaw altered to permit the ventilation of all lavatories inside the brick core of the building by mechanical extract; the earlier byelaw would have compelled the use of a great number of vertical shafts, with 'natural' ventilation. This easing of the requirement released a great deal of floor space for studios and other purposes. It was decided that a water supply, independent of the Metropolitan Water Board, should be provided by sinking a borehole into the chalk that lies beneath the blue clay. In an attempt to ascertain for certain where the Bakerloo Tube lay in relation to the site before the boring operation began, Tudsbery visited the late Sir Harley Dalrymple Hay, the the engineer for the tube railway, but he was unable to say precisely where it was designed to be. By law, underground railways had, at that time, to avoid the building lines of properties along their course, but the curve of Portland Place would have brought the tube very close to the building site if not actually within it. Happily the borehole met with no obstruction and the well was completed. The rising mains in the building were so arranged that pumping equipment could be provided quickly to bring the borehole into use if the need arose. In fact the Metropolitan Water Board was able to provide an adequate supply of water on acceptable terms, and the well was never used.

A major difficulty that had to be overcome before building could start was the presence of the great London sewer that runs diagonally across the site. This sewer, laid about 1830, is of brick; being incapable of bearing any of the load of the building, it had to be encased, foot by foot, at great depth (about 35 ft), in a reinforced-concrete sheath before the retaining walls and foundations could be constructed above it.

One of the most striking features of the equipment of the building was the air-conditioning plant. Great importance was rightly attached to the design of this plant, not only to achieve an adequate supply of fresh air at the correct temperature and humidity, but also to eliminate noise that could be transmitted through the ventilation trunking from studio to studio. The importance attached to the latter point can be gauged from the specified limit for the loudness of sound introduced by the ventilation to the very low figure of 10 dB (presumably meaning 10 phons). The Carrier Engineering Co. Ltd was responsible for the installation, and they designed a form of sound-arrester, constructed of sound-absorbing material arranged to form a number of restricted passages in the ducts, in which the sound energy was dissipated in friction. The following figures give an idea of the size of the installation: there were 32 fans handling 614 tons of air per hour, 16 pumps delivering 641 tons of water per hour under pressure, 54 electric motors having a combined capacity of 504 hp, sheet steel ducting weighing 120 tons and 60 independent automatic controls. Steam was supplied for heating by two oil-fired return-tube boilers, each fired by two low-pressure burners and having a capacity of 6700 lb of steam per hour.[20] This air-conditioning plant was at that time a quite remarkable and unique installation.

A great deal of pioneer work had to be done to solve the problems of studio construction for broadcasting. Almost the only useful lesson that could be learnt from experience was that brick was the best material that could be used for a sound-proof building – and that resulted from the happy chance that Savoy Hill was built of brick and not with steel and stone. Much thought was given to the acoustic treatment of the studios, as will be seen in the next section.

To achieve the necessary sound insulation, it was necessary for the studios to be fitted with two sets of doors, with rubber inserts between the doors and the door-frames. It was also necessary to ensure that large objects, such as pianos, could be moved in and out of the studios. There is an apocryphal story that during the planning of Broadcasting House a 'mock-up' of a grand piano was made in plywood in the workshop, but that when it was completed it could not be moved out of the workshop.

Broadcasting House was completed and occupied as a rented building in 1932, but it was later purchased and the freehold of the site was transferred to the BBC on 16 July 1936. The transfer of the freehold contained the proviso that the carrying on of certain trades, businesses or callings was forbidden: namely, those of 'a meat slaughterman', 'a quasi-medical or quasi-surgical establishment' and 'a brothel or bagnio keeper'. These covenants have been scrupulously observed by the BBC to this day.

The Carrier Engineering Co. was the only firm able to give an unequivocal assurance that they would satisfy the requirements of the specification for the air-conditioning equipment. Tudsbery accordingly recommended that their tender, which was the highest, should be accepted; the Board decided to seek a second opinion by referring his specification and recommendation to an expert, Dr Oscar Faber, who was an eminent consulting engineer. Dr Faber dissented from Tudsbery's proposals and offered to call for new tenders on a specification prepared by himself. Tudsbery relates that he prepared a long report, disagreeing with the proposals of the expert and offering his resignation. He was then asked to confront the expert to argue his views in the presence of Reith himself, the Chief Engineer (Ashbridge) and Sir Gordon Nairn (one of the Governors). This meeting took place on Christmas Eve 1929, with Reith in the chair. Tudsbery's recommendations were accepted and the episode consolidated the reputation that he was already beginning to acquire.

The rest of the engineering architecture in this period was, with one exception, concerned with transmitting stations. The exception was Broadcasting House, Belfast, which, however, did not come into service until after the war had started, and will therefore be mentioned in a later chapter. Building work at other studio centres was confined to the adaptation of existing buildings.

Pioneer work was being done on the planning of transmitter buildings – an early example of the design of standardised buildings for specialist use. An outside architect was retained for consultation on the elevations of the buildings, but the rest of the planning was done by BBC engineers, who prepared all the specifications, working drawings and detail drawings, according to the equipment to be housed in them. The first architect to be commissioned in this way was L. Rome Guthrie, who designed the elevations of the Brookmans Park station, which was to set a pattern for the others. By agreement, the copyright in the elevation drawings was vested in the Corporation so that the BBC was free to use the design for its further stations

with whatever changes were necessary on account of size (for single, or dual, transmitters), locality and materials. The stations that followed this plan were: the four
twin-transmitter stations Brookmans Park, Moorside Edge, Westerglen and Washford, the four single-transmitter stations Lisnagarvey, Burghead, Stagshaw and
Start Point, and Droitwich with its high-power long-wave and high-power medium-
wave transmitters. The new stations were far larger than the old; the area at Brookmans Park was 20,500 sq. ft (for two transmitters), compared with about 725 sq. ft at
Selfridges.[21] In fact, they were larger than was strictly necessary for technical reasons
because Reith wanted them to symbolise the status of broadcasting as a part of the
national life. Nevertheless, some critics complained that the Burghead station was
'hardly worthy of its importance'.

The design of transmitting station buildings, however, was already changing
before the war, both because of the need for smaller, medium-power stations and
also because advances in design had reduced the size of the equipment. Three smaller
stations, Clevedon, Redmoss and Penmon, were built towards the end of this period,
and Bartley was commissioned during the early months of the war. These stations
had low ceilings (11 ft or slightly higher) as opposed to the very lofty ceilings of the
original 'Regional' type of building: they were designed to stress the horizontal lines
and were built either in brick with concrete mullions to the windows or cement-
rendered with brick piers between the windows.

Buildings for transmitting stations often presented special difficulties on account
of the wide range of sub-soils that occurs in different parts of the country and on
account of the exposed sites of some of the stations. Stagshaw was built on solid rock
only 7 in. below the surface. The advantage of a secure foundation was offset by the
high cost of blasting the rock to form the vault of the transmitter hall, which needed
an excavation 80 ft long, 65 ft wide and 9 ft 6 in. deep. At Moorside Edge, Burghead
and Start Point, the buildings were particularly exposed to storms and cavity walls
had to be used with a $4\frac{1}{2}$-in. external skin, separate from the main structural wall,
which was steel-framed and 9 in. thick. In some cases it was necessary to treat the
internal face of the outside wall with waterproofing material, or, as at Penmon and
Aberdeen, to coat it externally with cement rendering.[21]

In each case, the architect's responsibilities ended with the acceptance of his
drawings for the elevations and thereafter he was called in only when Tudsbery felt
that his advice and assistance on the elevations would be desirable. The tenders were
based on bills of quantities professionally prepared by the firm of Ainsley. All the
planning and preparatory work that had to be done within the BBC for Broadcasting
House, the buildings and masts for Brookmans Park, the renovation and alteration
of newly leased or purchased premises for studios in the provinces, and the day-to-
day alterations at Savoy Hill, was done in Tudsbery's two small offices at Savoy
Hill. The staff, besides Tudsbery himself, comprised at that time two architectural
draughtsmen, two clerks of works, and one secretary.

The move to Broadcasting House more than doubled the number of studios
available in London. There were 22 at Broadcasting House compared with nine at
Savoy Hill (plus Studio 10 – the largest in the country – which had been opened in

PRINCIPAL STUDIO PREMISES OF THE BBC: 1926 AND 1939

	1926	1939
LONDON	Savoy Hill, WC2	*Broadcasting House, W1
BIRMINGHAM	282 Broad Street	*Broadcasting House, 282 Broad Street
MANCHESTER	Orme Buildings, The Parsonage	*Broadcasting House, Piccadilly
GLASGOW	21 Blythswood Square	Broadcasting House, Queen Margaret Drive
CARDIFF	39 Park Place	*Broadcasting House, 38–40 Park Place
BELFAST	31 Linenhall Street	*31 Linenhall Street
ABERDEEN	15 Belmont Street	Broadcasting House, Beechgrove Terrace
NEWCASTLE	54 New Bridge Street	Broadcasting House, 54 New Bridge Street
BOURNEMOUTH	72 Holdenhurst Road	—
EDINBURGH	87 George Street	*Broadcasting House, 5 & 6 Queen Street
BRISTOL	—	*Broadcasting House, 21–5 White-ladies Road
LEEDS	Cabinet Chambers, Basinghall Street	Broadcasting House, Woodhouse Lane
BANGOR	—	Broadcasting House, Meirion Road
SWANSEA	Oxford Buildings, Oxford Street	Broadcasting House, 32 Alexandra Road
PLYMOUTH	Athenaeum Chambers	Athenaeum Chambers

* Regional Headquarters.

1930 at Big Tree Wharf, near Waterloo Bridge, and continued in use until 1935). Office accommodation was also improved by the move for many of the staff who had been poorly housed at Savoy Hill and various outlying premises, but for the next forty years the continued growth in activity produced constant pressure on office space and made it impossible to concentrate all the headquarters staff on one or two sites in London.

The table shows how the principal buildings occupied by the BBC as studio centres developed between 1926 and 1939. The largest outside London was Broadcasting House, Glasgow, which was opened on 18 November 1938. The Palladian-style buildings of Queen Margaret College were taken over and extended to house ten studios, two echo rooms, a control room, library, and offices. The existing buildings were solidly constructed of brick and well suited to their new purpose. Studio 1, occupying a rebuilt north wing, was large enough to take an orchestra of a hundred players. Intake and extract fans circulated air through the studios and there were three main air-conditioning plants giving control of temperature and humidity, but without refrigeration.[22]

107

The success of building work done by contractors depended very much on the personality and efficiency of the Clerks of Works appointed by the BBC. They knew exactly what was needed and they got it. For example, during the building of the station at Brookmans Park in 1929, the builders had put one of the plinths on which a machine was to be installed in the wrong position. The Clerk of Works, H. J. Franklin, insisted that it should be taken out and replaced. His firmness caused the builder to say with great feeling: 'You miserable old bastard'. This earned Franklin the title of 'M.O.B.', in which he took considerable pride.

4 STUDIO DEVELOPMENTS

During the first twelve years of the life of the Corporation, up to the outbreak of war in 1939, there was a tremendous expansion of studio facilities; not only did the number of studios increase but they had to cope with increased sophistication in the presentation and production of programmes. More studios were needed because of the expanded coverage and the increasing diversity of programmes, and, more particularly, because of the development of the Regional Scheme, which demanded two programmes for a large part of the day, and of the Empire Service. This expansion was accompanied by technical advances in studio acoustics, methods of presentation, amplifying equipment, balance and control, measuring equipment, programme monitoring, control room operations, microphones and the performance of lines.

The Corporation inherited from the Company a number of studios, which in general, were very heavily damped, for the reasons stated in the previous chapter. At first, only one microphone was provided and unless the studio was 'dead' artists at different distances were heard differently. The need for different acoustics for various types of programme came to be recognised, and gradually the drapes in studios became less, especially when better microphones became available. At Linenhall Street, Belfast, for instance, when the two upper floors were taken over an elaborate orchestral studio was built, with wooden panelling of Oregon pine, Ionic pilasters and large panels of carpet-felt about an inch thick covered with wallpaper. However, the main area of development in studio acoustics was Broadcasting House, London, to which almost all the London studio activities were transferred on 15 May 1932. The change in acoustics of the studios must have been very great. No. 3 studio at Savoy Hill, for example, had been 'acoustically oppressive, and damped the ardour of singers and speakers alike; in fact, speaking in it was almost like hearing a voice disembodied from one's self', and yet 'large orchestras used to be squashed into it, and at times a chorus and soloists would be added for the performance of operas.[23] Even at Savoy Hill there was some reduction in the heaviness of the drapes when it was realised that different kinds of programme and different sizes of studio demanded different reverberation times. BBC Research Engineers made many measurements on the acoustic properties of studios and concert halls, as they have continued to do through the years, and the knowledge gained from these tests was turned to good account in the design of the Broadcasting House studios, where an attempt was made to meet the special requirements of each type of programme. Dramatic productions were the most complex and ten of the twenty-two studios could be used either singly or in groups, the outputs being combined in a Dramatic Control Room under the direction of the producer. Provision was now made in many studios for the addition of artificial reverberation from echo rooms, for special effects and for inserts from gramophone records.[24]

One of the most important features of Broadcasting House was the Concert Hall, which for the first time provided the BBC with its own auditorium, suitable for orchestral music and with accommodation for an audience. The Concert Hall was provided with a pipe organ and was designed for eighty players and an audience of 524 people. It had its own announcing room, and also a listening room where the outputs of the six microphones could be mixed.

The aim in designing studios was that each should have a reverberation time slightly less than the optimum for direct listening in the studio, so that the added reverberation time of the listener's room would give a pleasing result. It was also thought that the effect of reverberation was enhanced when one listened to a mono-phonic broadcast, whereas the accepted values of optimum reverberation time had been determined by binaural listening in the room itself. The Concert Hall was designed to have a reverberation time of 2 s, while towards the other end of the scale a small Debates Studio, 8B, was constructed to have a reverberation time of $0 \cdot 6$ s. Two types of material were specified for the acoustic treatment of the Broadcasting House studios: ordinary building board and 'felt-and-wallpaper treatment'. The latter con-sisted of a layer of 1-in. hair felt applied to the wall surface and covered with one or more thicknesses of lining paper and a soft porous type of wallpaper for decoration.[25]

Though most of the studios in Broadcasting House were treated in accordance with the principles outlined above, some, intended for talks and dramatic produc-tions, were made acoustically 'dead' by covering the walls and ceiling with rock wool applied between battens to the wall surface to a thickness of several inches. The reason for this treatment in talks studios was that the listener's room would provide all the reverberation needed. In the case of drama it was desired to be able to use different degrees of reverberation at will. Several echo rooms were provided for this purpose, each comprising a room with bare walls, furnished with a loudspeaker and a microphone. The output could be superimposed on the programme at any desired strength, provided the reverberation time of the studio was low enough to give the minimum amount of 'echo' required. (The term 'echo' was commonly used, although the object was not to produce discrete echoes, but to achieve a smooth decay of sound with time.)

Sound insulation had to be provided against both external sounds and sounds arising within the building. The studios were well protected against external sound by the fact that they were located within the central brick tower, which was so massive that Blue Staffordshire bricks had to be used in the lower part to support the weight. Sounds could, however, be transmitted within the building, either as air-borne sound or by transmission through the structure itself. Structure-borne sound was reduced by the fact that the central tower contained no steel-work. Air-borne sound between one studio and another was reduced by taking care that studios with a high level of music were not adjacent to talks studios and by designing the internal walls to provide the maximum sound insulation. It had been found that a double wall with an air space between the two skins of brickwork provided considerably more attenuation than a single wall with the same thickness of brickwork. Special care was taken in the design of Studio BB where the walls separating the studio from the corridor and from the cubicle were formed of two skins of pumice concrete, each 3 in. thick, separated by an air space of 3 in. Unfortunately, the bonding between the two skins reduced the value of the double-wall construction and the air space had to be filled with Cabot's quilt. Later, it was found that the pumice walls were introducing structural resonance and the sound insulation had to be sacrificed to some extent by grouting the space with liquid cement. It later became necessary to provide two additional talks studios by using two adjacent rooms. The partition between them was made of 3-in. breeze, with a timber stud partition on each side, spaced about 1 ft from the partition. The timber stud partitions were covered on both sides with plywood and partly filled with rock wool.[26, 27] The transmission of sound in a vertical direction was reduced by the use of suspended ceilings.

At Broad Street in Birmingham, where the studios had been officially opened in January 1926, Studio 1 was hung with artificial silk on curtain runners and the ceiling panels were draped with curtains that could be pulled back by cords. This studio was very versatile, and it must have been one of the first to have variable acoustics. Being 48 ft by 40 ft it was claimed to be 'the largest and most up-to-date studio in Europe, providing programmes for the first experimental high-power medium wavelength transmitter under the Regional Scheme of distribution'.[28] The Studio 2 was similar to many elsewhere, being heavily carpeted in 1-in. hair felt, papered over in a Chinese pattern. The windows were heavily curtained and the ceiling was covered with building board. This studio was used for talks and chamber music groups, and was once used by the Prince of Wales, later King Edward VIII. Studio 3 was an effects studio and had a 'thunder sheet', a 'wind machine', a 'rain machine', a 'sea machine' and gramophones. (Birmingham, though in the middle of England, seems to have been deeply conscious of the power of the elements.)

Other Regional Studio centres were similar in size, generally having three or four studios, treated in a somewhat similar manner. There were smaller studio centres at the relay stations and later at regional sub-centres like Leeds, Newcastle and Bangor.

The main functions of the control rooms at the studio centres were to control the quality of the output and to connect it at the correct level to the line network. The development of new equipment for these purposes, first at Manchester and then in London, initiated a sustained deployment of engineering effort that has continued ever since. When the Corporation took over, it was already being realised that much more flexible control equipment was needed, so as to put an end to such announcements as: 'Just a few moments, please, while the orchestra takes its place.'

Up to 1928 all switching in BBC control rooms had been done by plugs and sockets and double-ended cords, but A. S. Attkins, who was head of the Lines Section, had come from the Post Office where the conversion of the telephone system to automatic working had begun. He worked out a scheme for automatic switching, and it was decided that the new studio premises at Piccadilly, Manchester, should be equipped on these lines. This was the first of the more modern Regional studio centres to be put into operation, and the switching of circuits in the SB system was transferred from Leeds to Manchester and incorporated into the automatic scheme. This scheme was based upon the use of uniselectors and two-motion final selectors, in conjunction with a manual switchboard similar to a normal Post Office telephone switchboard. The uniselectors were used to switch all programme sources and destinations, except OBs. Each uniselector was allotted to a particular destination, which might be the input to a control position or an outgoing SB circuit, the destination being connected to the wipers of the uniselector. All the sources were connected to the bank contacts and 'multipled' to all the other uniselectors. To perform the switching, a locking key corresponding to a particular destination was operated to prepare the appropriate circuits for the operation of the uniselector connected to that destination and to switch on the outgoing amplifier (directly-heated filaments made it unnecessary for the amplifier to be switched on in advance). A non-locking, or 'punching' key corresponding to the desired source was then depressed; this applied an earth to the appropriate bank contact in the uniselector and caused the latter to hunt in the manner of a telephone exchange line-finder until the wipers encountered the earthed contact, which brought them to rest. The source was thus connected to the destination. Release of the destination operating key restored everything to normal.

This elaborate arrangement was far more complicated than anything the BBC had ever handled before. Attkins was responsible for obtaining the Post-Office-type switchboard, the keys and the selectors, while the amplifiers and associated equipment were designed in the Development Section under H. L. Kirke and made in the workshops of the Equipment Engineer, F. M. Dimmock. Unfortunately, at about the time that the equipment was installed, Attkins had a serious breakdown in health (he left the BBC shortly afterwards), just when it was found that there were serious faults in the equipment. V. A. M. Bulow became head of the Lines Section for the time being, having been Assistant Superintendent Engineer (South), and a rescue operation was mounted with the help of staff from the Development Section. The situation was critical, because the BBC had to quit the former premises at The Parsonage, where the lease had expired and could not be extended. A temporary control room had to be set up to carry on the service while efforts were made to get the automatic equipment to work. The trouble was found and cured in the end, but a dialling facility that had been intended for the selection of OB sources by means of the two-motion selectors was never successful. This all took place in 1929 and, although there was trouble from time to time with the automatic equipment, it remained in service for many years. A fundamental defect in the system was that switching methods, well-tried and adequate for telephony, were taken over unmodified into a broadcasting system, where the requirements were much more severe.

As all the amplifiers for the new Manchester control room were manufactured by the BBC, the equipment began to take on the appearance that later became very familiar. There were, for example, 'A', 'B', 'C' and 'D' amplifiers mounted on open racks in a standard manner, as opposed to the varied methods of mounting that had grown up in London control room. The standard 'BBC grey' colour appears to have had its origin in the Manchester equipment. Hitherto all equipment had been painted black, and the Manchester amplifiers were to have been the same; but it was discovered that the Post Office-type uniselectors were going to be grey and the BBC changed to grey from that time onwards.

The power supplies for the amplifiers, ht, lt, and grid bias, as well as supplies for the operation of relays, were obtained from central batteries of accumulators. This was one reason for locating all the amplifiers (except, where necessary, microphone head amplifiers) in the control room rather than in the individual studios. The supply for relays was at 24 V, with the negative pole earthed. At Manchester, exceptionally, the relays operated at 50 V and the positive pole of the supply was earthed; these differences arose from the influence of Post Office practice in the design of this centre.

The new Manchester control room and one or two others were equipped with transmission measuring sets. These were modelled on well-tried telephone system practice and could measure gains or insertion losses on steady tone in terms of attenuator readings at any frequency up to 10,000 Hz by the substitution method. The tone source, TS/4, operated on the heterodyne principle; the outputs of two oscillators, each with a single LS5 valve, were fed to the grid of an LS5B valve. The output of the latter was fed in turn to an LS5 output valve and thence to the transmission measuring set proper. The correct output was set by means of a thermocouple and meter, which could be calibrated on direct current. The receiving part of the equipment was an amplifier-detector, AD/2, which comprised an amplifier followed by an anode-bend detector, in the anode circuit of which was a dc milliammeter. The set was remarkably precise; in measuring loss, a difference of $\frac{1}{4}$ dB was easily readable at a level of -55 dB. A difference of $\frac{1}{4}$ dB was also easily readable on gain measurements up to gains of 55 dB.

This control room also incorporated a new method of measuring the volume of the programme signal. 'Modulation meters' had been used in Savoy Hill control room since 1927, but the traditional method of setting levels when feeding the local transmitter was by means of a device known as a 'slide-back' and officially described as 'an apparatus for indicating in the control room of a broadcasting station the presence of grid current (and hence distortion) in the modulation system of the transmitter'.[29] The slide-back consisted of an input transformer coupled via a volume control to the grid of an LS5B valve with a galvanometer in series with the anode. The valve was biased to cut-off at the point, found by trial and error, where the transmitter just did not overmodulate. A more precise method of measuring programme volume, preferably on a direct-reading instrument, was needed especially if there was a long transmission line made up of several links in tandem. The 'Volume Indicator', used by telephone engineers, was introduced for this purpose. Essentially this was a valve detector in which the rectified current was measured by means of a dc galvanometer in the anode circuit. The secondary of the input transformer was tapped and was bridged across the grid and filament of the valve in parallel with a tapped resistance. The ten tappings of the transformer winding were designed to give 2 dB steps and the three resistance tappings, controlled by a three-position key, gave relative levels of 0, 16 and 30 dB. The grid bias was adjusted until the galvanometer indicated ten divisions, and the volume indicator was then connected across the transmission path and the level switches were adjusted until the galvanometer needle kicked up to the reference mark about once in every ten seconds: occasional larger deflections and more frequent smaller deflections were neglected. The sum of the two level-switch readings then indicated the volume level of the programme. Volume levels between −10 and + 40 dB could be read in steps of 2 dB. The time constant of the galvanometer and associated circuit was about one-fifth of a second, so that the reading would tend to indicate the mean power during this period of time. This was suitable for speech, where the average syllable lasts about one-fifth of a second, but had little meaning when applied to music.

Mention has been made in the previous chapter of the genesis of the techniques of 'balance and control', later called 'programme engineering', and later still 'programme operations'. Briefly, the need was to secure the right balance among performers in relation to the microphone and to control the volume of the output to keep it within the permissible limits. Balance had perforce to be done in the studio, but at this time control was performed in the central control room.

Although a separate Balance & Control Unit had been set up in London, the control of programmes in the Regions remained, in general, the responsibility of engineers. Engineers with some knowledge of music could control musical programmes; so also could programme-oriented people who had, or could be given, some basic understanding of the function and limitations of the broadcasting system. An example of the kind of situation to which the differences of opinion between engineering and programme staff could lead occurred in Belfast. In 1927 there was one studio, rectangular in shape, small and heavily draped and equipped with one Round-Sykes microphone. The engineers had determined that the best balance, in their opinion, was obtained by placing the microphone in the middle of the narrow side of the studio opposite the door, and they had adopted this as the standard arrangement. Each time there was to be an orchestral programme, however, the Musical Director moved the chairs and music stands so that the orchestra faced the long side of the studio. The EiC immediately had the chairs and stands altered back to the original arrangement. This happened again and again: nothing was said directly by either side, and this foolishness went on until a new studio was built.

The alternate marriage and divorce between Engineering and Programme Operations was to go through a further cycle, but at this period the parties were separated – at least in London. There were occasional complaints that in orchestral items the conductors' intentions were being neutralised by bad balance and control and there were also complaints from the engineers that the transmitters were under-modulated, so that their effective range was unnecessarily reduced. In November 1929 a suggestion that had been made by Eckersley in October 1928 was implemented by the appointment of a committee to consider the problem, the members being Filson

Young, as Chairman, A. B. Howe of Research Section and Stanton Jefferies of the Balance & Control Section. The only concrete result of the deliberations of this committee seems to have been the erection in 1929 of a special cubicle for control, using loudspeakers, in one of the offices near Studio 3 at Savoy Hill. This was known as 'Room 24 Musical Control'. Thenceforth until 1935 there were no further changes that affected the engineers, though the B & C section was split into two in 1932, separate sections being formed for Music and Drama. There was, however, still some friction between the balance and control experts, the producers and the engineers.

A further attempt to improve matters was made in 1935 in a series of discussions. The Director of Internal Administration suggested that balance was a function of *producing*, i.e. a programme function, and control was a function of *transmission*, i.e. an engineering function, and should be done by engineers or ex-orchestral players attached to Engineering Division. This proposition, although generally accepted in principle, ran into immediate opposition from the Music Department, who strongly opposed handing over 'control' to the engineers. It was therefore agreed that the programmes of the Music Department should be controlled, as well as balanced, by musicians, and that other music programmes of a lighter nature – Variety, etc. – should be controlled, like non-musical programmes, by the engineers. This untidy arrangement proved unsatisfactory, because:

(*a*) balance and control staff had no one in authority to whom to refer, so there were no common principles to work on, and there was therefore a marked divergence between the practices in Music Department and in Variety, (*b*) the lack of technical training of balance and control staff, and lack of proper liaison with engineering, resulted in misunderstandings and (*c*) the status of B & C officials was too indefinite.

Discussions went on all through 1935 and 1936, and the early part of 1937, but meanwhile other developments were taking place in the field of studio acoustics, which exercised a considerable influence on the result.

Dr F. W. Alexander, having developed the BBC version of the RCA ribbon microphone, was given the job of seeing that it was properly used in the studios, and soon found himself drawn into the balance and control controversy. There were complaints about the acoustics of the studios; lack of bass obsorption was the chief defect, strings sounded lifeless and woodwind 'had no bite'. Studio 1 at Maida Vale, for example, specially built for the symphony orchestra, had a reverberation time between 3 and 5 s in the bass and less than 1 s at the higher frequencies. A group was formed, consisting of A. B. Howe, John McLaren, and Alexander, to see what could be done. They soon found that the importance of bass-absorption in all the studios, whether in London or in the Regions, was crucial, and they carried out many experiments with Cabot's quilting, wood panelling, and other materials.

Another serious trouble in Broadcasting House was the fact that Studios BA, BB and the Concert Hall suffered from noise caused by tube trains rumbling underneath the building on their way between Oxford Circus and Regents Park. The sound insulation, too, within the building was barely sufficient, and despite the two intervening floors there was some interference between the Concert Hall and the basement studios.

Rex Haworth, whose early work in the BBC has already been mentioned, left in 1928 to join the film industry. While there he realised the desirability of reflecting surfaces in a studio. They imparted naturalness to speech, and life and richness to music. When he rejoined the BBC in 1933 as a balance and control assistant in the Music Productions section, he unobtrusively tried out some of his ideas in a Sunday-afternoon concert by the Theatre Orchestra in Studio BA (which subsequently became the Broadcasting House war-time control room). He had as much as possible of the acoustic treatment on the walls covered up by acoustic screens; these were movable panels, with sound-absorbing material on one side and painted wood on the other. On this occasion they were placed with the reflecting sides outwards. The concert took place and Haworth controlled it. The producers and conductors were struck by the brilliant acoustic. Haworth was given a black mark for using acoustic screens the wrong way round, but the object was achieved. Both Stanford Robinson, then Conductor of the Theatre Orchestra, and Gordon McConnel, one of the Senior Producers, favoured the new acoustic. Further developments took place along the same lines, despite some opposition from the traditionalists.

In 1934 Variety Department was formed under Eric Maschwitz and included both the Variety Orchestra and the Theatre Orchestra. Soon they moved into St George's Hall, and Haworth went with them in charge of balance. (St George's Hall, dear to the hearts of the older generation as the scene of Maskelyne's Theatre of Mysteries, was destroyed, with the adjoining Queen's Hall, during the war; Henry Wood House, now the headquarters of the Engineering Division, occupies part of the site.)

St George's Hall, though in effect a studio, was officially regarded as a permanent OB point. Various experiments and the gradual changing of the studio to suit the ideas of the Variety Department were carried out with a certain amount of subterfuge. For instance, carpets would be taken up and sent for cleaning, but not replaced; heavy wooden rostra were bought, ostensibly for the staging of one specific programme but left in place permanently. In short, everything was directed towards the introduction of more bare wood, and the success of the treatment can be gauged from the fact that a conductor from the German Broadcasting Service came over for the purpose of finding out how the St George's Hall shows were done. In 1937 John MacLaren was put in charge of the Acoustics Section of Research Department, and he and Haworth spent many hours on the stage of St George's Hall. This led to a renunciation of the use of building board and felt in studios and of carpets in music studios. Acoustic brightness had become respectable.

A dramatic control panel, with ten channels, had been installed at Savoy Hill in 1928. Broadcasting House was initially provided with two such panels. Later, a very large dramatic control panel was built, originally with the idea of controlling the multi-source programme to be mounted in connection with the King's Christmas Message in 1934. This had fifteen channels, and was so large that it had a 5-ft bench seat on a little trolley, so that the operator could ride quickly from one end to the other to reach the control knobs. The use of the dramatic control panel for dramatic

I

productions, however, had some disadvantages. It was technically very complicated; once it was set up on transmission, it was impossible to locate faults. The use of many studios on one production meant that staff were dispersed on three or more floors, and it was necessary to have 'studio managers' (in the theatre sense) to keep track of artists and to make sure, not only that they reacted to the right cue light but that they were in the right studio. There was no control of dynamic range on the dramatic control panel, so again there was the problem of the engineer in the control room neutralising the intentions of the dramatic control panel operator. Finally, the range of acoustics of the various studios was limited: Studio 6A was always recognisable as Studio 6A, whether it was acting as a baronial hall, a law-court or a drawing-room. The dramatic control panel was thus very extravagant in both studio space and staff. In 1933 a musical programme called *The Castle on the Hill* required two orchestras, a big singing and speaking cast and many effects. It needed a total of fifteen production staff. Some years later, however, when Variety Department had moved into St George's Hall, there was plenty of space and up to eight microphones could be used, and it was soon realised that a range of acoustics could be got by moving the microphones around the studio. To give these ideas a full-scale test, Val Gielgud was persuaded to produce *The Castle on the Hill* again, using only one studio and without any adaptation of the script. With the same two orchestras and almost the same cast the whole programme was done with seven production staff instead of fifteen. After that the Variety Department did not use dramatic control panels, but they continued to be used for drama and also for feature programmes, such as the famous *Scrapbook* series.

Dramatic control panels, or production panels, were nevertheless developed further during the next few years and an advanced model was installed at Glasgow in 1938. The circuitry was quite complex because the contributions from the various sources could be controlled both individually and in groups, echo could be superimposed on any channel, cue and return lights and talk-back circuits communicated with each source and the whole programme could be heard on a loudspeaker in each studio (except that when a studio was contributing to the programme, its own loudspeaker was automatically silenced).[30]

Variety Department created its own techniques using a single studio, several microphones, and reflecting surfaces. These techniques were frowned upon elsewhere but in 1936 an event occurred which gave the Variety Department an opportunity to disseminate their views. This was the formation of the Staff Training School, with Gerald Beadle as the first Director of Staff Training. At lectures the accepted method of balance and control was described by various people, and the unorthodox approach was put forward by Variety Department, which invited students to come to St George's Hall and look for themselves. This provoked the kind of controversy which, in these days, would be welcome as a way of opening up discussion amongst the students. It seems to have fanned the embers of the balance and control controversy anew, because a committee was set up by the Board of Management in June 1937 'to investigate the whole question of balance and control'. It consisted of Gerald Beadle, then West of England Regional Director (Chairman), R. T. B. Wynn, Senior

Superintendent Engineer, and Dr R. S. Thatcher, Deputy Director of Music. This committee reported on 23 December 1937, and their findings are summarised below:

i Balance and Control staff must possess technical knowledge, up to a definite engineering standard.

ii The separate functions of balance and control should be carried out by one person, or a team of people, not only in Music Department, as at the time, but also in the other departments. (A system of listening-room control was suggested to this end.)

iii All Balance and Control staff should be assembled into one department, called Programme Engineers, within Engineering Division, with one head responsible for all technical balance and control methods. He should have considerable musical and general artistic qualifications.

iv Assistants should specialise as much as possible, being attached not necessarily to a department as a whole, but possibly to a programme unit within a department.

This committee collected its evidence from twenty-seven people, including eight engineers. A comment by its Chairman in sending out his report reads: 'I hope you will agree that unanimity between an engineer and a musician is an achievement almost without precedent!'

The Report was accepted by the Control Board, and the responsibilities of Balance and Control in London were transferred to a new unit called Programme Engineering, in the Engineering Division, under Dr F. W. Alexander as Head of Programme Engineering, with A. W. Parish as Assistant Head. Studio Assistants, Producers' Assistants, and Junior Producers' Assistants engaged in balance and control work were transferred to the new unit. Pending the possible extension of this organisation to cover the Regions, HPE was to act as adviser and co-ordinator to Balance and Control staff in the Regions. Later, on 19 July 1939, Regional Balance and Control was also transferred to the Programme Engineering unit under Alexander.

Proper control demands the proper tools for carrying it out. While the developments in studio acoustics and the discussions on organisation were going on, there had also been developments in the methods of measuring programme volume. Reference has already been made to the use of a 'volume indicator' in the new control room at Manchester in 1929, but at Savoy Hill the 'slide-back' voltmeter was still used. It was supplemented by a milliammeter, which followed something between a linear and a square law. Its function was to prevent the embarrassment of not knowing exactly what the level was until the slide-back voltmeter indicated that full modulation had been reached. By 1932 when Broadcasting House began to operate, the first monitoring meter to be given the name 'programme meter' had been developed by Charles Holt-Smith of the Research Department, and was often known as the 'Smith meter'. This was the first appearance of the familiar black scale with white markings. It was not a true peak meter, nor did it indicate rms or mean values. Its characteristics resulted from the circuitry combined with the inertia of the measuring instrument itself.[31] The signal was applied to a rectifier consisting of a pair of push-pull diodes; each diode was, in fact, a pentode, the control and screen grids being held at fixed potentials. Each diode had an anode-current anode-voltage characteristic that turned over at the top, in the manner typical of a pentode. This meant that the scale of the meter closed up at the top and, being roughly logarithmic, it could be calibrated in dB. This meter was used in lining up transmitters in such a way that when line-up tone was sent and the meter read seven divisions, the transmitter was modulated to about one-third of its full modulation. Music programmes were controlled so that the deflection reached peaks of seven divisions, and this arbitrary rule ensured that the instantaneous peaks would not normally exceed the equivalent of 100 per cent modulation. This type of meter remained in use until the advent of the peak programme meter in 1938.

C. G. Mayo, who joined the BBC Research Department in the mid-thirties, was responsible for the development of the peak programme meter. During this work, experiments were carried out to determine whether it was necessary to use a full-wave rectifier, as it was feared that transient sounds might have asymmetrical waveforms which would make a half-wave rectifier inaccurate. In the event, it turned out that all the transient sounds that were produced during these tests were perfectly symmetrical; it was sustained sounds of speech and some musical instruments that exhibited asymmetry and made it necessary to use full-wave rectification. Another problem was that Mayo wanted to achieve an instrument in which the readings were almost independent of the ballistics of the indicating meter.

A series of experiments was carried out to determine the best time constants for the peak programme meter. It was thought at first that it should respond to the instantaneous peaks of programmes, so as to prevent the transmitters from exceeding 100 per cent modulation. A model programme meter was produced that would respond to a pulse lasting only about 1 ms. It was found, however, that the ear is tolerant of distortion lasting a few milliseconds and that a 'registration time' of 4 ms would be sufficient. The time for the meter to return to zero had to be a compromise between a rapid return, which was tiring to the eye, and a slow return, which made control difficult; it was decided that the meter should take between 2 and 3 s to drop back 26 dB. In the design that was finally adopted, the input was applied through a tapped transformer and a gain control to the grid of an amplifying stage, using an AC/HL valve. The output from this was applied to a full-wave rectifier comprising two diode valves with a phase-reversing transformer. The output from the rectifier was applied to a reservoir capacitor shunted by a resistance. The value of the capacitor determined the registration speed and the value of the resistor controlled the return speed. The final valve was an AC/VP2 with the actual meter in its anode circuit. This arrangement had a logarithmic characteristic; the meter required 1·5 mA at full scale and had a right-hand zero. The zero adjustment was made on a potentiometer in the screen-grid circuit, the voltage being stabilised by a neon tube. One of the problems was to find a meter that was sufficiently quick-acting and at the same time well damped. A meter of German origin was found suitable, but Ernest Turner and Company produced a satisfactory meter in this country, which became an essential feature of the BBC peak programme meter.[32] This programme meter and its successors continue to be used by the BBC; other broadcasting organisations also use instruments of this kind, but many still use those of the volume-indicator type.

The problem of measuring volume has still not been solved in an entirely satisfactory manner, because the requirements are incompatible. It is necessary that the measurements should give a good indication of the likelihood of over-modulating the transmitters and the BBC programme meter meets this need. It is, however, most desirable to have a visual indication of loudness, which is a more complex problem. It can be solved reasonably satisfactorily by using elaborate instruments, but the indications they give will not necessarily correspond with the need to protect the transmitters from over-modulation – although the use of limiters and volume compressors makes this a less critical requirement than it formerly was. Accurate measurement of loudness is not the end of the matter, because surveys have shown that listeners differ in the relative loudness they like, their choice being largely determined by whether they are listening with full attention or using the programme as a background. It is also affected by the level of ambient noise at the place of reception. Furthermore, the desired loudness for a particular type of programme heard in a particular environment varies according to whether the programme comprises speech following music or vice versa. A partial solution to this problem has been achieved by making arbitrary rules in conjunction with actual listening to a loud-speaker.[33, 34, 35, 36]

Another field in which development was rapid and extensive was that of microphones. At the time when the Corporation took over from the Company, the Reisz carbon-granule microphone was displacing the older Round-Sykes magnetophone, and by 1929 all but one of the Savoy Hill studios were fitted with Reisz microphones. The one not so fitted had a Western Electric 'condenser' (i.e. electrostatic) microphone, which had appeared in 1928 and was a great novelty. Because of its low output this microphone had to have a head amplifier enclosed in the same housing, which was bomb-shaped and about 1 ft long and 6 in. in diameter. This was used during the period 1931 to 1935, but its quality appears to have been no better than that of the Reisz microphone at its best. There was also an RCA condenser microphone mounted, with its amplifier, in a cubical box, and a 'slack-diaphragm' microphone designed by P. G. A. Voigt of the Bell Recording Company. Condenser microphones fell into disrepute during this period because they became noisy when moisture condensed in them; the head amplifiers also introduced noise, because low-noise valves were not then available.

The two outstanding microphones of this period were the STC type 4017 moving-coil microphone and the RCA ribbon microphone, from which the BBC ribbon microphone later descended. The STC moving-coil microphone was one of the first really scientifically designed microphones, and it continued in service for two decades. It had a rather narrow acceptance angle at the higher frequencies, which was a disadvantage for some purposes; but one great difficulty, which had hitherto impeded the design of moving-coil microphones, was avoided: the natural resonance of the

119

system was flattened out by means of acoustic filters. There was also a permanent magnet instead of the enormous electro-magnet of the previous moving-coil microphone, the Round-Sykes.

The RCA ribbon microphone had been demonstrated publicly for the first time at the May 1931 meeting of the Society of Motion Picture Engineers at Hollywood, and it immediately became popular in the film world, both because it gave freedom of movement on the set and because it had an insensitive side that could be turned towards the camera and thus assist in the suppression of camera noise. It was, however, very expensive: it cost £130, including the head amplifier. This did not matter much to the film studios, which would need them in twos or threes, but the BBC, even then, had to think in terms of much higher numbers. Ashbridge was impressed by the ribbon microphone and Alexander was given the job of developing a BBC version of the ribbon microphone, which was introduced in 1935. There was a risk of infringement of patents but, after many meetings with patent agents, it was decided that the BBC had a valid patent, taken out in Alexander's name, and as the prior patents were held by companies closely associated with Marconi's it seemed desirable to get Marconi's to make the microphones.

The BBC microphone (type A) differed from the RCA mainly in the design of the pole-pieces, which were made much thicker to increase the sensitivity. This lowered the critical frequency to about 4500 Hz and the resulting drop in the response above this frequency was counteracted by shaping the pole-pieces to provide a resonant cavity on each side of the ribbon. Thus, the RCA version behaved as a velocity, or pressure-gradient, microphone up to 9000 Hz, whereas the BBC-Marconi microphone behaved as a pressure microphone at frequencies above 4500 Hz. The permanent magnet of the type A ribbon microphone was made of cobalt steel and was in the form of a horseshoe. The introduction of improved magnetic material (aluminium-nickel-cobalt) permitted a smaller, circular, magnet to be used and this resulted in the Type B ribbon microphone, only about 4 in. in diameter, which was brought into service in 1937.[37]

The advent of the ribbon microphone was a great advance. Before its introduction, all microphones suffered from inferior directional characteristics; sound reflected from the walls was not reproduced with the same 'brilliance' as that coming from the front, and this tended to make the acoustic sound 'dead'. The ribbon microphone did not exhibit this drawback; its response was double-sided, and it did not respond to sounds coming in at 90° from the axis. This reduced the effect of reverberant sound, and artists could therefore work well away from the microphone. The double-sided property was exceedingly useful in drama, where two artists could face each other across the microphone, instead of being side by side, as with the Reisz or the moving-coil types. There were, at first, some objectionable resonances, which were dealt with in the period just after the beginning of the war. During the trial period in 1934, it was necessary to use a pre-amplifier in the individual studio control rooms, because the output from the microphone was so low that interference was caused by switching clicks and other noise from neighbouring circuits. The microphone leads from the studios to the control room 'A' amplifier were at that time run in comparatively thick cable, which was not balanced to earth; it was found that if a balanced input transformer was used on the 'A' amplifier and the microphone leads were run in 1-pair 10-lb cable, no pre-amplifier was necessary. This was a great advantage, because the cost of the pre-amplifier would have been more than that of the microphone. Marconi's were manufacturing the latter for £9, a price that, coupled with the performance of the microphone, influenced the decision to make a clean sweep and introduce ribbon microphones everywhere.

To meet the need for a small microphone for sports commentators, the Type B ribbon microphone could be mounted on a breastplate. This arrangement was used for a number of national sporting events, but its success depended to some extent on the chest measurements of the commentators; it worked well with George Allison, but not so well with others. It led, however, to an important development – that of the lip microphone. With a lip microphone held close to the mouth, extraneous noise is reduced; moreover, a ribbon microphone close to the source of sound exhibits excessive bass response, so that a bass-cut can be used to reduce extraneous noise to a very great extent – so much so, that commentators at a public event could stand shoulder-to-shoulder in the open air, perhaps talking different languages, and there was no longer any need to put them into individual booths. This microphone was developed by Alexander, in association with D. E. L. Shorter; two examples were made in 1938, and the lip microphone is still in use in a version resulting from improvements made by Research Department during the 1950s.

One other microphone deserves mention, since it was used in the first Marconi-EMI Television Studio at Alexandra Palace in 1936. This is the EMI moving-coil microphone, which was used in the recording studios of EMI in Abbey Road, and was bought in small quantities by the BBC. It looked rather like a pepper-box (it was called the 'pepper-duster'), being a small black microphone with a perforated, chromium-plated face. It had a very wide polar response; the resonance was not acoustically damped, but was removed by an electrical filter in the amplifier. This microphone worked very well, but the resonance peak had to be checked every few months and the angular response was also variable.

At the beginning of this period the A, B, C and D amplifiers mentioned in the previous chapter had already been introduced and the broadcasting chain from studio to transmitting station had taken the form typified by the layout of the equipment in Broadcasting House, London.[38]

With the opening of the new Manchester studio premises in 1929, the appearance of control rooms had already begun to take on a 'modern' look. The amplifiers were all mounted on bays remote from the actual control desks, and were closely associated with the relay switching equipment that controlled them. The desks were used for switching, volume control, cueing, telephony and supervisory purposes, whereas all testing, measurement and maintenance work was carried out in the apparatus area. Transmission measuring equipment was now provided, which could be connected over internal tie-lines to any amplifier, equaliser or line that had to be tested. The photograph of the new Manchester control room (Plate V) shows that the method of mounting the apparatus now resembled that used in a Post Office repeater station.

Unfortunately, the resemblance stopped short at the panel width dimension, which was standardised in the BBC as 22⅛ in. rather than the 19 in. (48 cm) used by many telephone administrations of the world. In the end, the BBC changed to the more generally used standard.

The apparatus room at Manchester, Piccadilly, was a kind of dress rehearsal for the new London control room in Broadcasting House. That control room, in fact, set the pattern for the design of those at studio centres and transmitting stations (both for line-termination and programme input equipment) throughout the rest of the period under review. Clean lines and an orderly arrangement of the apparatus had now been achieved, although, by modern standards, the waste of space inside the covers of the amplifiers and similar apparatus was enormous. The internal wiring, too, was carried out in a way very different from that of today. An example of the panel wiring is given in the photograph of the back of an 'A' amplifier (Plate XII). All the wiring was in stiff insulated wire, which was very neat but caused difficulties when alterations had to be carried out. The components included massive input and output transformers, and chokes. These components had interleaved windings because nobody had yet attempted to turn the leakage inductance of a transformer and its capacitance to good account, so as to preserve the flatness of the frequency characteristic by making them operate as a filter. Capacitors, too, were large, as the electrolytic type had not yet been introduced. There was no negative feedback and, although the valves were of the directly heated type, dc was used for the heaters.

Each control position in the Broadcasting House control room of 1932, and subsequently in the regional control rooms also, had either a two-channel or a four-channel fade unit, a main fader and a programme meter of the type described earlier. The switching to connect the desired source of programme to the main channel fader was done at this position.[39]

There were six 'transmission' control positions in Broadcasting House and eight similar 'rehearsal' control positions. Each was associated with the input of a 'B' amplifier and the switching to connect the desired source of programme to the main channel fader was done, via relays, by means of keys on the control desks. The relays were interconnected so as to prevent more than one source being connected at the same time to any input channel. In addition to these control positions, operated by engineers, there were four 'control cubicles' where important programmes could be controlled by Balance and Control staff in quiet conditions while listening to a loudspeaker.

Microphones of low impedance and high output could be connected directly to the central control room through a balanced and screened pair up to 1000 ft in length, provided that the sheath of the cable was earthed and that a step-up transformer with an earthed screen between the windings preceded the amplifier. High-impedance microphones, such as condenser microphones, needed a pre-amplifier adjacent to the microphone. The ht and lt supplies could both be derived from a feed at 100 V passed over the two wires that carried the output of the microphone. This method had the disadvantage that it unbalanced the microphone pair and a more complicated arrangement was used at OBs: the battery supplies for two microphones were fed through the microphone cables via the centre points of the terminating transformers, the ht being supplied through one microphone cable and the lt through the other. Attempts were also made to reduce the size of the microphone casing by including in it only the valve and the input circuit of the amplifier, the output circuit and its transformer being some distance away.[40]

Soon the efforts of H. B. Rantzen and others in the Lines Section resulted in standardised transmission-measuring equipment being developed and installed in all the studio control rooms in the country. The equipment included the Tone Source, TS/4, and the amplifier-detector, AD/2, which used directly heated valves. In 1935, however, the AD/2 began to be replaced by the AD/3, which had indirectly heated valves, all operating as amplifying stages and feeding a metal rectifier circuit to operate the meter. This, in turn, was replaced by the AD/4, using AC/SP3 and AC/2HL valves in a more modern circuit, in mid-1939.

Because of the great number of small valves used in amplifiers and other equipment, special equipment had to be developed for testing them. It was found that the most useful method of ensuring that a valve was efficient was to measure its mutual conductance. A testing set was developed for this purpose, with a number of different types of socket and facilities for applying the appropriate voltages to the many different types of valves then in use.[41]

In Broadcasting House, Glasgow (opened in November 1938) all programme switching was done by relays operated from a supervisory position in the control room. Pre-fade listening keys were provided to permit the operator to listen to a programme source before fading over to it. The equipment included the elaborate dramatic control panel previously mentioned. Power supplies were provided by a motor generator set producing dc, with a floating battery. Much attention was paid to the studio acoustics at this centre, Studios 2 and 3 having graduated treatment; this was a development of the earlier 'live-end, dead-end' technique, in which the sound absorption was concentrated in the part of the studio remote from the orchestra – in this case by the use of rock-wool panels 1 in. thick.[42]

An idea of far-reaching importance that emerged during the latter part of the period under review was that of continuity working. It arose partly from the need to obviate switching errors and partly from the requirements of balance and control. It had been agreed in 1934 that programmes organised by Music Department should be controlled as well as balanced by musicians, and the only place where this could be done was the control room, since there were no programme meters elsewhere. The control positions were manned by Assistant Maintenance Engineers (AMEs), who could not all be expected to have an adequate idea of the content or impact of the programmes they were dealing with. This was a cause of complaint from the programme side and the Engineering Division was blamed for mistakes in 'presentation'. A particularly unfortunate example occurred at the time of the death of King George V. After an announcement had been made that the King's life was drawing peacefully to its close, the AME on duty faded back into a Maida Vale studio where Henry Hall was conducting the dance orchestra. R. T. B. Wynn, as Senior Superintendent

Engineer, however, took the side of the AME because he thought it wrong that decisions of this sort should be an Engineering responsibility. The 'Woodrooffe incident' afforded a further demonstration of the inflexibility, from the presentation point of view, of the centralised control room. There was a Review of the Fleet, as part of the Coronation celebrations, for which lines and radio links had been tested and equalised, and the transmission channel tested. During the pre-transmission microphone test, it became obvious that the commentator might not treat the occasion with suitable gravity and Harman Grisewood, who was in charge of the presentation, was warned of this. The Presentation Section had only one office and one loudspeaker, so by the time that Grisewood had made quite sure that he was listening to the right programme, the actual transmission had begun to go on the air with the now historic remark about the fleet being 'all lit up'; the programme was faded out by the senior engineers, who were present for this important occasion, on their own responsibility. It was largely because of these two incidents that R. T. B. Wynn put forward the idea of a continuity system and C. H. Colborn was given the task of developing it in the Designs Section of Equipment Department.

Strangely enough, there was at first considerable opposition from some people on the programme side to this idea because of the difficulty of finding people who could both announce and make executive decisions – the very problem that needed to be resolved. There was also some opposition from the engineering side. For the moment, the idea was shelved, apart from continuing argument about it, and from the time of Munich onwards Engineering Division had very different and more urgent things to think about. Continuity working did not, in fact, come into use in the BBC until 1940, when it was introduced in the war-time control room at Abbey Wood, near Wood Norton, which had been taken over for the Overseas Service. Thereafter, continuity soon became a commonplace of broadcasting technique. Its essential feature was that all the items constituting a particular programme, or network, were routed through a central continuity suite in which the presentation of the whole programme was continuously under firm control. As Asa Briggs says, 'The system consisted essentially of two rooms separated by a glass panel and sound-insulated from each other. One was manned by a technical operator who was provided with technical facilities for selecting and mixing programmes and checking quality. The other was an announcing studio manned by the presentation announcer for the programme or network. The latter was responsible for making quick decisions about the running of the programme and for making stop-gap announcements.' The system 'was so efficient that it quickly became taken for granted, like so many of the achievements of the engineers.'[43]

The problem of standardising musical pitch is on the fringe of BBC Engineering and its history goes back a good deal farther. Early attempts to prescribe and maintain a standard of musical pitch were made around the year 1600 by Michael Praetorius, but with little success. In 1859 decrees were issued in France giving legal sanction to a standard known as 'diapason normal'. This was 435 Hz for the note A in the treble stave, and was derived from a tuning fork operating at a temperature of 15°C. This standard was accepted by several continental countries at a congress held in Vienna in 1885 and it then became known as Continental Pitch. The UK took no part in this congress, but had its own Philharmonic Pitch, which varied between 425 Hz in 1813 and 455 Hz in 1874. A long battle ensued between 'Continental Pitch' and the English 'Concert Pitch'. The Philharmonic Society attempted to secure uniformity by adopting a new Philharmonic Pitch in 1896. This was numerically the same as Continental Pitch, but was related to a temperature of 68°F (20°C).[44, 45]

By 1938 it became evident that something ought to be done to obtain international agreement on a standard of pitch and to persuade musicians and musical instrument makers to conform to it. Broadcasting itself had increased the need for the observance of a universal standard because broadcasts from one country could be heard in others and because musical programmes were often relayed from one country to another. Moreover, musicians (and particularly singers) have difficulty in performing with orchestras using a pitch different from that to which they are accustomed.

The situation had become extremely confused, because (1) the pitch of orchestras tended continually to rise in order to obtain a more brilliant effect, (2) the Philharmonic Pitch was related to temperature, and (3) the French language, usually regarded as extremely precise, unfortunately used the word 'diapason' both for 'musical pitch' and for 'tuning fork'. This last confusion apparently led to the assumption that the temperature of 15°C, which was that at which the tuning fork was required to be accurate, was the temperature at which the standard pitch had to be observed during a musical performance.

The reason for the attempt to relate the standard to the ambient temperature in the concert hall was that the pitch of different instruments varies in different ways with temperature. In television studios instruments can be affected by radiant heat from the lights as well as by the temperature of the surrounding air. The effect of changes in humidity may be even greater than that of changes in temperature.[46] However, it seems obvious that what matters is the pitch at which the instruments are actually played, regardless of the ambient conditions.

In order to clear up the confusion, the BSI, at the suggestion of the International Standards Association (now the ISO), convened a meeting in May 1938 at which a great many organisations concerned with music in this country, including the BBC, were represented. Agreement had almost been reached that the standard should be 439 Hz when it was suggested that it might be easier to generate a tuning note at 440 Hz than at 439 Hz by electronic means (439 being a prime number). This meeting was followed by an international conference held in Broadcasting House in May 1939 under the auspices of the ISA. It was agreed that the standard of pitch should be an absolute frequency, not related to temperature, and that it should be 440 Hz. This value was adopted by the conference and was specified in BS:880 (first published in December 1939 and revised in July 1949, November 1950 and February 1967); makers of orchestral wind instruments were enjoined to test them at 20°C, but the standard pitch was a fixed frequency.[44]

This standard was published in ISO Recommendation R16 in November 1955. This prescribed that the note A should be 440 Hz (without mention of temperature) and that apparatus used to assist in the tuning of instruments should have an accuracy of $\pm$ 0·5 Hz. Instruments should be capable of conforming with this standard at the temperature and other conditions specified by the manufacturer, who was recommended to use tuning devices with an accuracy of $\pm$ 0·25 Hz. But it is one thing to have a standard written down in the archives and quite another to ensure that it is widely known and observed throughout the musical world. The BBC itself has done its best to publicise the standard and most instruments now manufactured in this country are tuned to 440 Hz. The BBC Music Department encourages musicians to conform to the standard and a tuning note of 440 Hz has been radiated before the start of the Third Programme (now Radio 3) each day since the programme began on 29 September 1946. This tone was derived from the 1-MHz crystal-controlled oscillator that was used for producing line-up tone at 1000 Hz and had an accuracy better than 1:10⁶.[47] A tone derived from the same source was also used in studios to help orchestras to tune their instruments, but it was found that a simple transistorised oscillator giving a tone rich in harmonics was more practical for this purpose and could maintain an accuracy better than 1:10⁴, which is ample for the purpose. Nevertheless, many musicians still prefer the traditional sound of the oboe to that produced by an oscillator. By 1967 a tone at the standard frequency was being transmitted on all the domestic radio networks and included in some television trade test transmissions and this practice has continued to help musical instrument makers and instrumentalists to conform to the standard.

5 SHORT-WAVE BROADCASTING

Amateur radio experimenters did a great service to broadcasting by directing attention to the possibilities of short waves (i.e. those in the high frequency part of the spectrum between 3 and 30 MHz) for long-distance communication. They were undaunted by the accepted theory of that time, which insisted that radio waves travelled in straight lines and that short waves could not cover long distances. This theory appeared to agree with practice, because long waves had been found to have a considerably greater range than medium waves. The mechanism of long-distance propagation was imperfectly understood, although Oliver Heaviside had postulated the existence of ionised layers in the upper atmosphere capable of reflecting radio waves and the existence of these layers was demonstrated by Professor E. V. Appleton (later Sir Edward Appleton), who explored them in 1924.

Amateurs had been allowed to transmit on 440 m, but this wavelength was absorbed into the medium-wave band that was allocated to the first BBC stations. Other professional users valued the low-frequency and medium-frequency parts of the spectrum, but thought little of the higher frequencies. Thus it came about that amateurs were relegated to the short waves. They made full, and sometimes spectacular, use of the opportunity to exploit the potentialities of this despised part of the spectrum.

The Wireless Telegraphy Act 1904 provided for the use of wireless telegraphy for experimental purposes. Amateur stations were active before the First World War and by 1914 no fewer than 990 experimental call-signs had been issued.[48] Reference has already been made to the transatlantic tests on MF organised by amateurs in 1921. From 1923 onwards they achieved long-distance contacts on wavelengths below 100 m. As early as 1921 amateurs in the USA had spoken to each other over long distances within the North American continent on wavelengths around 200 m. The first two-way transatlantic telephony on short waves was achieved on 8 December 1923 by a British amateur, J. A. Partridge (2 KF), who later became EiC of the BBC Receiving Stations at Keston and Tatsfield; he used a wavelength of 100 m. On 19 October 1924, C. W. Goyder (2 SZ), then a 16-year-old schoolboy at Mill Hill (later a member of the BBC Research Department, and subsequently Chief Engineer of All India Radio), established the first two-way telephone conversation with New Zealand on short waves. J. H. Ridley (G5NN), who later became Head of Engineering Secretariat, was the first person in the UK to pick up an American broadcasting station (WJZ, 325 m) – on 27 November 1922 – and was among the first amateurs to communicate with New Zealand (29 October and 6 November 1924). Another British amateur, Gerald Marcuse of Caterham, Surrey, had the idea of broadcasting to the Empire after he had established regular contact on short waves with an amateur station in Bermuda, which had relayed the transmissions to other amateurs in the West Indies. Marcuse was given permission by the Post Office to transmit speech and music for two hours a day for a period of six months on 23 m and 33 m with a power not exceeding 1 kW. But the Postmaster General was careful to say that he held out no hope that a licence to transmit regular programmes to the Dominions and Colonies would be granted to anybody other than the BBC. Marcuse started his series of experimental transmissions to the British Empire on 11 September 1927 with a concert broadcast to Australia and he continued the transmissions almost daily until the end of August 1928.[49]

The activities of amateurs proved that long-distance broadcasting on short waves would be possible, but their efforts were largely hit-and-miss, because the properties of the ionosphere and the way in which they varied with the season of the year and with the sunspot cycle, were not yet known. A frequency that gave satisfactory transmission over a particular path in summer might be useless in winter and one that was satisfactory in summer in one year might be useless at the same season the next year. It naturally took a long time to work out a system of prediction that would enable the optimum frequency to be chosen for any path at any time of day at a particular season and at a particular point in the sunspot cycle. This was a good example of the way in which theory and practice must go along hand in hand if full reliance is to be placed on the result. Methods of ionospheric sounding that were developed much later made it possible to study the refractive properties of the ionosphere in detail, but even then it was not possible to determine the density at a height above the point at which it was a maximum, because any waves transmitted from the ground could not be reflected from a higher region. The height of maximum density is of the order of 300 km. It was not until 1962 that an ionospheric sounder carried by a satellite was able to give information about the properties of the upper part of the ionosphere.

The start of regular overseas broadcasting services on short waves can be traced to those from the USA in 1924 and from Eindhoven, Holland, in 1926. In the BBC one of Reith's ambitions had been to broadcast to the Empire from London and to encourage the setting up of broadcasting services in India and other Commonwealth countries.[50] As early as 1924 he had approached Government Departments on the subject, but there were difficult problems both technical and financial.[51] In May 1926 the Post Office gave the BBC permission to radiate an experimental short-wave telephony transmission from Daventry on a power not exceeding 20 kW in order to establish whether a link with the Dominions and Colonies was possible 'if such a course were found to be desirable'. At this time Eckersley was giving first priority to the development of the Regional Scheme described in Section 2 of this chapter, and he did not want an Empire Service to be thought of as 'an affair of stunts and surprises but rather as a regular and reliable service to overseas listeners'.[52] The establishment of such a service and the means for financing it were discussed at the Colonial Conference in May 1927 when Carpendale said that the BBC were 'alive to the developments and the necessity for experiments in short-wave broadcasting' for Empire listeners. At this conference, Eckersley said that he was concerned that the proposed service should not be started until 'the quality of short-wave broadcasting had improved' as he feared that fading, distortion and unreliability would give such a service a bad name from the start. He rebuked critics who accused him of 'going slow', saying 'it is not enviable to be in a position where one feels that one has to be – in the general interest – apparently reactionary'. The Under-Secretary of State for the Colonies pressed Eckersley at this conference to go ahead with the introduction of an Empire Service remarking that he had heard complaints from some listeners in the Empire that they could 'receive Philadelphia, but could never get Daventry or 2LO. Bournemouth they occasionally get but it is pretty bad.'[53] Considerable discussions took place concerning the means of financing an Empire Service and the point was made that the money received from the purchase of wireless licences in this country could hardly be used to assist in running an Empire Service from which listeners in this country would derive no direct benefit. Finally, Carpendale said that the BBC would be willing to go ahead with experimental transmissions and 'not say anything about paying yet'. Eckersley agreed to this and the Control Board confirmed this view on 24 May 1927.

Steps were taken to rent a short-wave telephony transmitter from the Marconi Company and experimental transmissions began with a broadcast of the Armistice Day Cenotaph Service on 11 November 1927. The transmitter, whose call-sign, G5SW, was soon to become as well known throughout the Empire as 2MT and 2LO were known in the United Kingdom, was assembled by the Marconi Company from a 'beam' telegraphy short-wave transmitter and a modulator unit previously used for experimental purposes. The aerial consisted of a Franklin 'uniform' type suspended between two 475-ft masts at Chelmsford. This aerial had a substantially non-directional radiation pattern and the transmission was vertically polarised. The wavelength used was, at first, 24 m (12·5 MHz) but this changed to 25·53 m (11·75 MHz) on 1 January 1928 to conform to the Washington Radio-telegraph Regulations. The power output of this transmitter was 8 to 10 kW and the transmitter was operated by the Marconi Company's staff. The programme material was wholly derived from the BBC's Home Programme, but a small studio was provided, manned by BBC engineers (F. X. J. Abrahams – later Armstrong – and E. J. Alway) who made the opening and closing announcements. There was a two-hour transmission every day.

The transmissions from G5SW proved to be very popular with overseas listeners, but reception reports soon indicated that it would be desirable to use a directional aerial, so as to increase the signal strength in the target area. Because the propagation conditions changed from hour to hour (owing, as was afterwards established, to the effect of ultra-violet radiation from the sun on the ionosphere), it was desirable to use two different frequencies in different wavebands simultaneously, so that the listener could choose the better of the two at any moment. Furthermore, the optimum propagation conditions for different parts of the world varied with the times of the day. It was thus established that the timing of transmissions for particular target areas and the frequencies to be used should be subject to seasonal changes and should also vary through the eleven-year sunspot cycle. These principles have been applied ever since, but with the advantage of much more detailed knowledge of the behaviour of the ionosphere, to short-wave broadcasting services throughout the world.

It was evident that short-wave broadcasting could not give a service of such high quality or of such consistent reliability as could be achieved in national transmissions on long and medium waves within the ground-wave service areas of such stations. The vagaries of the ionosphere introduced fading; in its worst form, differential fading – which varied over the side-band spectrum – this could result in poor quality. These troubles were particularly evident when the transmission path necessitated more than one hop between earth and ionosphere. Moreover, periods of abnormal solar activity could occasionally interrupt transmissions completely over a particular path. Nevertheless, the use of sufficient power with a directional transmitting aerial, the careful choice of frequencies according to propagation conditions, and the use of efficient receiving installations could give a service that was generally satisfactory for speech and even acceptable for music. Much was to be gained by the use of short-wave broadcasting for keeping people throughout the Empire in touch with the home country and the introduction of a short-wave service was stimulated by keen competition from other countries, particularly Germany and Italy, in the early 1930s.

Meanwhile, short-wave experiments were conducted by the Radio Corporation of America and the Marconi Company at the end of 1927, to investigate the possibility of transatlantic programme exchanges and to examine diversity reception techniques.[54] A receiving station was set up at Terling in Essex operated by staff seconded by the BBC – W. Proctor Wilson (later Head of Research Department) and H. V. Griffiths (later EiC Tatsfield). The G5SW transmitter was used in this country and a General Electric transmitter, 2XAD, at Schenectady, NY, in the USA.

By the end of 1928 the Marconi G5SW transmitter was becoming unreliable and there were many long breakdowns. This transmitter had been hurriedly assembled for short-term experimental transmissions and it was not suitable for use in a permanent service. The BBC had expended about £19,000 on the short-wave experiment between November 1927 and the beginning of 1929 and in mid-1929 a further approach was made to the Colonial Office to obtain funds to set up and run a permanent short-wave broadcasting service. By this time domestic broadcasting had started in Australia, Canada, New Zealand, South and East Africa, India, Ceylon, Singapore and Hong Kong, although not yet in the West Indies, Southern Rhodesia, Colonial Africa or in other parts of the Empire. It was pointed out by the BBC that in other countries in Europe and elsewhere, 'short-wave stations were springing up everywhere' and it was felt strongly that Britain should not stand aloof from this important development. The Colonial Secretary agreed with the BBC's view and its proposals were submitted to the Colonial Conference of June 1930. It was stated that at least two wavelengths would be needed if all parts of the Empire were to be reached under varying conditions of light and darkness, and it was proposed that an experimental station with a life of at least five years should be erected at Daventry to continue the short-wave transmission tests. If further experimental transmissions proved successful, a permanent station would radiate four regular daily programme transmissions as follows:

(i)   A 'Colonial' programme during the afternoon
(ii) A 'South African' programme at the time of the Home evening programmes; this would include a News Bulletin in Afrikaans
(iii) An 'Australian and New Zealand' programme in the morning, but outside Home broadcasting hours
(iv) A 'Canadian and West Indian' programme during the small hours each morning. (This was the first time that a night shift was envisaged.)

These proposals were accepted, in principle, at the Colonial Conference by the Post Office, but the Treasury requested that the matter be deferred until it could be discussed at the Dominions Conference to be held in November 1930. At this conference the Dominions were far from being as enthusiastic as the Colonies for the introduction of an Empire Service and it was suggested that the BBC should ask all broadcasting authorities throughout the Empire to make contributions towards the cost of the proposed service. The replies were unfavourable.[55]

Meanwhile, the unreliability of the G5SW transmitter was increasing and the country was in the midst of the economic depression. In the summer of 1931 the financial crisis came to a head and the Labour Government fell. The Chancellor of the Exchequer of the subsequent 'National' Government asked the BBC for a voluntary contribution to the Exchequer and Reith's offer of £200,000 in two instalments was accepted. As part of the agreement, the BBC said it would be willing 'to carry the cost of Empire broadcasting'. On 28 October 1931 the Board decided to proceed with a high-power short-wave Empire Service station and the BBC, in a press release dated 6 November 1931, announced its intention of going ahead alone with an Empire Service.

The first step was to replace the Chelmsford G5SW transmitter by a completely new station at Daventry; on 13 January 1932 the Board approved a sum of £50,000 for the erection of this station, which was to have two transmitters. Tenders were called for and the Board awarded the contract for the transmitters to Standard Telephones and Cables.

The Empire Service station at Daventry was accordingly equipped with two transmitters, modulated at low level, each capable of supplying a power output to the feeders of 10 to 15 kW, the higher power being available on the longest wavelengths, i.e. those in the 49-m band. It was arranged that either transmitter could work on any of the wavelengths assigned to Daventry at that time and could be connected to any of the aerials via a two-wire open feeder system.

A great deal of thought was given to the choice and arrangement of the aerials. It was decided to build a directional aerial for each of five zones centred on Australia, India, South Africa, West Africa and Canada. To cover the wide areas represented by these zones the aerials had to be designed to produce beams considerably wider than those used for commercial point-to-point services. The layout of the aerials on the site corresponded to the required directions of transmission and their size was dictated by the wavelengths likely to prove most suitable for the principal transmission paths. The group of aerial arrays directed to India, for example, had to include three separate aerials for the three different frequencies that might be suitable in the 17-, 25- and 32-m bands, whereas for serving Australia only a single array designed for the 25·6 m band was needed. This latter aerial was made reversible so that the beam could be directed to follow the great circle path in either direction. Various configurations could have been adopted for the aerial elements, but it was decided that each directional array should consist of a radiating curtain of vertical elements, each corresponding in length to slightly less than a half wavelength at its designed frequency. A similar pattern of elements was placed a quarter wavelength behind the main array to form a reflecting curtain. The number of elements was between one and four, depending on the beam width required. Each radiating element was fed at its centre by a two-wire feeder across a coil in series with the element. All the feeders from one array were brought to an impedance-matching transformer to which the main feeders from the transmitters were connected. There were also six omni-directional aerials, each comprising one radiating element without a reflector.

These aerials, being composed of vertical elements radiated vertically polarised waves. The aerials were supported by triatics carried by tubular steel masts 80 ft high. Up to twelve aerials could be connected to the transmitter building at any one time and these could be switched manually to either of the two transmitters.[56, 57]

The programme schedule was as follows:

Zone 1: Australasia (25·6 m)   0930 – 1130 GMT
Zone 2: India (17·25 and 32 m)   1430 – 1630 GMT
Zone 3: South Africa (14 and 32 m)   1800 – 2000 GMT
Zone 4: West Africa (32 and 48 m)   2030 – 2230 GMT
Zone 5: Canada (19, 32 and 48 m)   0100 – 0300 GMT

The Daventry short-wave transmitters started testing on 14 November 1932 and the programme service began on 19 December 1932. The Christmas Day broadcast by King George V in 1932 was radiated by the Empire station and this was the first time that this special broadcast had been transmitted to listeners outside this country.

The Empire station at Daventry represented a considerable advance on the single-wavelength experimental transmissions from G5SW at Chelmsford. The service had now grown to the point where directional transmissions were being made on two wavelengths simultaneously, the programme material was specially planned for Empire listeners, and the transmission times were selected to suit local listening conditions in the target areas.

Reception reports from listeners overseas showed that the transmissions were reasonably effective, but could be improved by changes in timing. A number of such changes, and additions to the transmission schedule, were made during 1933. In October of that year the daily transmissions were divided into five sesssions known as Transmission 1, Transmission 2, etc. Later, in 1935, an additional session was added for evening listening in Western Canada and early-morning listening in India. The format of the transmission schedule for programmes in English then remained substantially unchanged until September 1939. The gaps between transmissions were reduced to fifteen minutes, as it was now possible to change wavelengths within this period, after allowing for pre-transmission testing.

Early in 1933 it became clear from reports from listeners that the Daventry transmissions were not being received as well as might be expected and poor performance of the transmitting aerials appeared to be a likely cause. A series of experiments with different types of aerial was undertaken, the first step being to suspend simple horizontal dipoles from the 500-ft masts carrying the Daventry long-wave aerial and to compare their performance with that of the existing low vertical aerials.[57] The first test was made in May 1933 to compare directly a high horizontal $0 \cdot 5 \lambda$ dipole (10 wavelengths above the ground) dimensioned for an operating frequency of $11 \cdot 86$ MHz – with one of the low vertically polarised non-directional aerials. The results of this comparative test were quite definite and showed the high aerial to give a gain of 5 to 10 dB in the strength of the signals received in Buenos Aires and Bermuda. In December 1933 a high horizontal $0 \cdot 5 \lambda$ dipole dimensioned for $9 \cdot 7$ MHz was compared with a low vertical four-element aerial operating on the same wavelength and oriented on India. The high dipole was found to give equal strength signals in Ceylon, on the centre line of the directional transmission, although the theoretical gain of the four-element aerial was 9 dB above that of the non-directional dipole. At this time it was not known whether the superiority of the horizontal aerial was due to its polarisation or to its height above ground. Two 350-ft towers were next erected and from these further test aerials were suspended to determine the choice between horizontally and vertically polarised aerials and to discover the minimum mast height for optimum reception with a given transmitter power. These tests were made using a wavelength of 12 MHz and eleven different aerials were tested, two at a time, for comparison.

These tests took place between October 1934 and March 1935 and the conclusion reached was that horizontal aerials at Daventry were better than vertical, that it would be unnecessary to have more than four horizontal radiators stacked vertically at 0·5 λ intervals, and that the lowest aerial element should be not less than 1·0 λ above ground.

As a result of these tests a new aerial and feeder system was designed for Daventry, comprising twenty-five aerials, fourteen of which were provided with reversible reflectors. This aerial complex was designed to cover the six short-wave broadcasting wavebands and to work on the twelve wavelengths assigned to the BBC in these bands at that time.

It became clear that more than two transmitters would be needed to carry the service, particularly when it was required to obtain simultaneous world-wide coverage for a special broadcast. There was also a need to have another transmitter available for further aerial experiments; an opportunity for making them had arisen from the fact that the long-wave 5XX aerial had become redundant with the transfer of the National programme to Droitwich, thus releasing the space between the two original 500-ft masts for test aerials in the short-wave bands. The G5SW transmitter used at Chelmsford was refurbished and re-erected at Daventry as Sender 3. This transmitter had been modified to operate in several wavebands and its output power had been increased to 20 kW. It was commissioned on 19 May 1935. Later it was fitted with a Metropolitan Vickers demountable valve unit and the output power was increased to about 60 kW from April 1937. The Abdication Speech of King Edward VIII, with Reith's introduction, was radiated by Sender 3 and was picked up at the RCA receiving station at Riverhead in the USA and passed to the Columbia Broadcasting System, where it was recorded. This recording was used as a Christmas card by E. C. Cohan of CBS in that year (1937).

Meanwhile, in 1933, Hitler had seized power in Germany and that country was rapidly increasing its broadcasting coverage on short waves and was radiating propaganda material in particular to Africa and South America. Italy, Russia and the USA had also stepped up their short-wave coverage. The best the BBC could do at the time to meet this competition was to extend the Daventry installation; an additional 95 acres of land was acquired adjacent to the existing Daventry site to accommodate a new aerial system and to house additional transmitters. In February 1935 the Postmaster General approved the Daventry extension and the Board approved the estimate for the site and extension building on 25 September 1935. Three additional high-power short-wave transmitters were ordered in 1935 and 1936, two from STC and one from the Marconi Company, together with new masts, aerials and feeders. By the Coronation of King George VI on 12 May 1937, two of the high-power short-wave transmitters – those built by STC – had been commissioned, with an output power of 50 to 80 kW. These were designated Senders 4 and 5 and the work of installing and testing was speeded up by the assistance given by BBC senior engineers: Kirke, Wilson and MacLarty. The third new transmitter was not ready for the Coronation programmes and the service scheduled for it had to be carried on a temporary low-power transmitter, type SWB 11, having a power output of only 7½ kW. The new Marconi transmitter (Sender 6) came into service in April 1938. A fourth transmitter was supplied by STC; this was installed as Sender 7 and was commissioned in December 1940.

The overall efficiency of the high-power Marconi transmitter at a wavelength of 35·3 m was 27·6 per cent at full modulation. The rms noise was 54 dB below 100 per cent modulation. The corresponding figures for the STC transmitters were 37·5 per cent for overall efficiency and 65 dB for noise when the rf amplifier filaments were heated by dc. The frequency response of both types of transmitter was flat within ± 1 dB between 50 and 10,000 Hz.[57]

With the decision to provide a new aerial system at Daventry (each aerial covering a narrower area, but with stronger signals), the number of transmitters had to be reconsidered. Empire countries subtended an angle of about 320° at Daventry and assuming each aerial to cover an arc of about ± 18°, nine transmitters would be needed to cover them all simultaneously with one programme, assuming unidirectional transmission. In practice, seven transmitters would give adequate coverage of the scheduled day-to-day transmissions and thus with the original Empire station transmitters (Senders 1 and 2), the rebuilt G5SW transmitter (Sender 3) and the four new high-power transmitters (Senders 4–7 inclusive) sufficient transmitter facilities would be available.

The programme broadcast in the Empire Service had been in English, and it was not until 1937 that the efforts of Reith over several years to persuade the Government to allow broadcasts on short waves in foreign languages bore fruit. The Italian short-wave station at Bari had, since 1935, been broadcasting in Arabic and had 'established itself as a purveyor of inflammable propaganda'. On 29 October 1937 the Postmaster General announced in the House of Commons that the BBC would undertake broadcasts in certain foreign languages. This announcement was later clarified by the Chancellor of the Exchequer, who made it clear that the BBC had been invited to make foreign language broadcasts in Spanish and Portuguese for South America and in Arabic for the Middle East. This was to be done without detriment to the Empire Service and until the necessary new transmitters came into service, the foreign language broadcasts would have to be on a limited scale.

The Arabic Service was inaugurated on 3 January 1938 by the Emir Seif-El-Islam Hussein, son of the King of the Yemen. The Latin-American Service was opened on 14–15 March 1938 in the presence of diplomatic representatives. These foreign language broadcasts required yet a further extension of the transmitter and aerial facilities at Daventry: two more high-power short-wave transmitters were ordered from the Marconi Company and an extension to the new building was put in hand to house them. (These transmitters were designated Senders 8 and 9.) In view of the trend of international events at this time, the extension building was made large enough to house not only the two additional high-power transmitters ordered but a total of four transmitters of this type. The total transmitter complement at Daventry was finally brought up to eleven with the commissioning of Senders 8 and 9 in February 1939 and Senders 10 and 11 in June 1940.

The Marconi transmitters (Senders 8 to 11 inclusive) were of type SWB18 and were similar in design to Sender 6, except that, whereas Sender 6 used series modulation, Senders 8 to 11 were provided with orthodox Class B high-power modulators. The maximum unmodulated output power was 100 kW on wavelengths between 30 m and 80 m (10 MHz and 3·75 MHz) falling to 75 kW on 13·5 m (22 MHz).

Each aerial curtain was composed of either two or four vertical stacks of half-wave horizontal elements, with four elements in each stack. The horizontal elements were spaced half a wavelength apart in the vertical direction and the lowest one was usually either one or two wavelengths above the ground. The various types were designated by a reference of the form H4/4/1, where H meant horizontal, the first figure indicated the number of vertical stacks, the second figure the number of horizontal elements in each stack, and the last figure the height (in wavelengths) of the lowest element above the ground. If a reflector was provided, HR was substituted for H. The directivity was indicated by the power gain in the most favourable direction over that of a hypothetical aerial radiating uniformly in all directions; it amounted to 42 times for an aerial of type H2/4/1 and 185 times for an aerial of type HR4/4/2; the reflector was assumed to be 85 per cent efficient in the forward direction. The width of the lobe to the 6 dB points was $\pm$ 34° for an aerial with two stacks and $\pm$ 18° for an aerial with four stacks. The vertical projection angle of the main lobe varied with the height of the lowest element above ground, being 7·8° for a height of one wavelength and 5° for a height of two wavelengths. The connections of the vertical part of each feeder were reversed between each pair of horizontal elements and the one above, so as to maintain the correct phase relationship for the half-wavelength spacing.

The aerials were designed by F. D. Bolt (later Head of Transmitter Service Planning) and the working drawings were prepared by Marconi's. An innovation was the use of stayed masts rather than towers for supporting short-wave arrays. In addition to two 350-ft towers, there were at Daventry by 1939 two 500-ft masts and seven of heights between 150 ft and 325 ft for this purpose. The suggestion to use stayed masts came from Ashbridge, but there were fears that the stays would interfere with radiation from the HF arrays. MacLarty worked out a plan to reduce the screening effect as far as possible and this proved successful.

The masts for the arrays designed for the longer wavelengths were 325 ft high, to allow for the sag in the triatic from which the aerials were suspended. One 25-m and one 31-m aerial with reflectors could be supported between a pair of these masts spaced 650 ft apart. Counter-balance weights were used to prevent the tension in the halyards from exceeding 5 tons.

It was decided to use open-wire balanced feeders because they were simple and cheap to construct and easy to repair or re-erect, although this type of feeder is susceptible to lightning strikes and, in adverse weather conditions, can become unbalanced and is then apt to radiate. The alternative of using concentric tubes was not pursued, mainly because of the cost and the difficulty of switching. The feeder lines were supported on steel poles to give a minimum clearance above ground of 10 ft. Each feeder comprised four wires arranged on a square with 12-in. sides, and had a characteristic impedance of 550 ohms. Great care was taken to match the impedance of the feeder to that of the aerial so as to avoid standing waves; this was done by attaching earthed stubs to the feeder line at appropriate points to act as matching reactances. Where necessary the horizontal feeder between the vertical stacks constituting the aerial were provided with alternative tapping points to which the main feeder was connected, so as to alter the phase relationship between the vertical stacks and permit the beam to be slewed a few degrees either side of the centre line.

The feeders were connected through an open-air distribution frame; the outgoing feeder from each transmitter was brought to the centre point of what amounted to a manually operated rotary switch giving access to six fixed points on the transmitter side of the distribution frame; the movable connection could be transferred, when the transmitter was not powered, through hook-and-eye connections, to the appropriate fixed point. This gave each transmitter access to six different points on the incoming side of the distribution frame; semi-permanent cross-connections within the frame permitted any aerial feeder to be connected to any point on any of the switches. Thus, any transmitter had immediate access to any of the feeders that would be required so long as the transmission schedule remained unchanged.

There had been considerable opposition to the proposal to use open-air switches for aerial selection, but the idea was fundamentally simple and proved to be entirely practicable.

The power supplies were derived from motor generators, except for the filament-heating current for the modulators in the Marconi transmitters. The anode power supply for the high-power valves was obtained from continuously evacuated steel-tank mercury-vapour rectifiers similar to those used at the Droitwich long-wave station. Distilled water was used for valve cooling, circulating in a closed system. The heat was extracted from the cooling water by air-cooled radiators mounted outside the building.

The responsibility for the operation and maintenance of the transmitter for the Empire Service rested on the Superintendent Engineer, Transmitters, and their day-to-day working was in the hands of the Engineer-in-Charge. Daventry was the first transmitting station to have a post designated 'Aerial Engineer' (later, SME (Aerials)) the holder of which was a specialist in all practical aspects of aerial and feeder work, both electrical and mechanical. (This post has been held by, among others, F. D. Bolt, E. W. Hayes, later Head of Planning & Installation Department, and L. W. Turner, later Head of Engineering Information Department.) The work was complicated, because it was necessary to make a seasonal change in the transmission schedule four times a year, so as to permit the use of all the frequencies required for transmissions to each of the target areas during the following three months. This meant that the dimensions of many of the aerials had to be altered to suit the new frequencies. The aerial curtains had to be lowered for this to be done and when they had been raised again impedance measurements had to be made to ensure the correct match between the aerials and the feeders. It was at Daventry that the first short-wave impedance-measuring equipment (an impedance bridge of bridged-T configuration) was introduced in 1935. By putting measuring equipment of this kind into regular use by station staff, specialist effort was saved and the work of engineers engaged on routine transmitter duties was given additional technical interest.

To follow the transmission schedule, it was essential that the frequency changes that had to be made during the course of each day were effected quickly. These changes necessitated switching the aerial, changing the driving frequency, and changing the tuned circuits of the rf amplifiers. The radiated carrier frequencies had to be stable within $\pm 1:10^5$. In addition to the crystal drives there was an auxiliary valve oscillator capable of continuous adjustment.

In the Marconi transmitters the frequency changes in the first and second rf amplifier and in the final amplifier were effected by means of circuits mounted in trucks, one truck being provided for each of the four frequency channels on which each transmitter might be required to operate. In the low-power rf amplifiers separate pre-set circuits were provided for each of the four working wavelengths.

In the STC transmitters, which used Class B modulators, the modulation was applied to the anodes of both the final and penultimate rf amplifiers. The amplifiers were of the series-connected, or 'inverted', push-pull type. The grids of the main amplifier were earthed and the drive from the penultimate amplifier was applied between the filaments of the two valves. Since the penultimate amplifier supplied power into the main load, being in series with the main amplifier, it was necessary to modulate both amplifiers to obtain 100 per cent modulation and to avoid phase modulation of the output. The grids of the main amplifier, being earthed, formed a screen between the anode and filament. Both the penultimate and final amplifiers were designed to operate at the same anode dc potential, so that modulation could be applied to both from one set of modulators. Frequency changes were effected by means of circuits mounted on turntables in each of these amplifiers.

When new transmitters came into operation, measurements of the field strength and signal-to-noise ratio were made in several of the target areas, i.e. at Ottawa, Riverhead (New York), Buenos Aires, Salisbury (Southern Rhodesia) and Cairo. It was concluded that 'it is now only on rare occasions of exceptionally disturbed ionospheric conditions that it is impossible to receive the news bulletins from Daventry, on a reasonably good commercial receiver, in any part of the world at least once every 24 hours'.[57]

The frequencies used for short-wave transmissions at different times and seasons were very carefully planned by E. J. Alway, H. Wilkinson and T. W. Bennington in the Overseas & Engineering Information Department, under the guidance of L. W. Hayes. The planning was based partly on measurements of the critical frequency and virtual height of the E and F layers in the ionosphere made by government research stations in the USA and the UK and partly on regular reports received from listeners in various parts of the world. In this way a body of information was built up, which enabled the appropriate frequencies to be predicted with considerable accuracy for any time of the day and season of the year in relation to the eleven-year sun-spot cycle. The working frequencies had to be chosen to lie between an upper limit above which refraction would not occur and a lower limit below which there would be severe attenuation; these limits depended on the critical frequency of the operative layer in the ionosphere and also on the angle of incidence, which was calculated from the geometry of the path and depended on whether the target area was reached in one hop or two hops.[58, 59]

Thus before the outbreak of war, the BBC had developed an efficient short-wave service with world-wide coverage that had already created an attentive audience for programmes dedicated to the ideal of objective truth.

6 TELEVISION

Television had long presented a challenge to experimenters because of the exciting prospect of being able to see things happening at a distance and because of the inherent difficulty of translating a moving image into an electrical signal. The problem was a great deal more difficult than the corresponding one in sound. The ear is able to analyse a single-valued stimulus into its frequency components; the eye integrates sensations over a period of time and therefore cannot distinguish between light of different colours emanating from the same point in space, but on the other hand it has some millions of separate receptors that enable it to perceive the spatial distribution of light over the scene.

A monophonic sound, however complex, is a single-valued function; the sound of a whole orchestra can be represented by one signal varying in amplitude, but of limited bandwidth. A moving visual scene contains vastly more information; to produce an acceptable picture of it at a distance, it is necessary to transmit a complex signal containing sufficient information to determine the brightness (if not the colour) of the image at, at least, 250,000 different points at each moment of time (this number corresponding to the definition of a 405-line picture). There are two possible ways of tackling this problem. One is to provide, say, 250,000 separate communication channels. The other is to dissect the picture into a large number of elements and to scan them successively so as to form a signal that, at any moment of time, represents the brightness of the scene at one point only; in that case the decay time of the reproducing screen and the persistence of vision of the viewer must be relied upon to give the impression of a complete and continuous picture.

Both these approaches were tried in early experiments. At the sending end the sensing device could be a light-sensitive cell, e.g. of selenium, modulating an electric current. At the receiving end the signal could light a lamp. A system of picture telegraphy using a number of channels of this kind was proposed as early as 1875 by Carey in the USA, but the number of separate transmission paths required to give sufficient detail was clearly prohibitive. The other approach was exemplified in Leblanc's vibrating mirror (1880), Nipkow's spinning disc, pierced with a spiral of holes (1884), and Weiller's mirror drum (1889). The resolution obtainable with mechanical systems of this kind was limited by the inertia of the moving parts.

The suggestion that pointed the way to practicable television was made by A. A. Campbell-Swinton in 1908.[60] He postulated the use of an electronic method of scanning based on the employment of cathode-ray tubes at both the sending and

Sir Noel Ashbridge, Chief Engineer/Director of Technical Services, 1929–52

Top Round-Sykes microphone, 1923

Left Lip microphone L/2, 1953

Right Stereo microphone pair with amplifier, 1961

Opposite page Reisz, moving-coil and ribbon microphones in use in 1942

X

'B' amplifier, 1927

Amplifier wiring, 1932

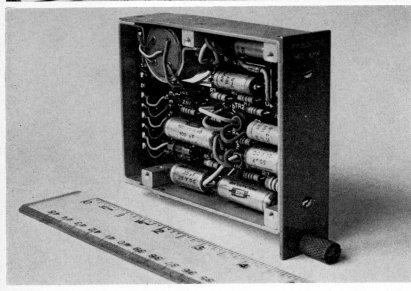
Transistorised microphone
amplifier, 1962

Portable line repeaters,
PER/2 and (in suitcase)
PER/3, 1938

OBA/8 amplifier equipment,
1939

Portable OB equipment, 1959

Crystal set, *c.* 1923

Valve receiver, 1923

Console television set with
mirror, 1938

LF, MF and VHF portable
set, 1972 (Photo: Roberts
Radio Co.)

Colour television set, 1972
(Photo: Decca Radio and
Television)

Wood Norton Hall, now the
Engineering Training Centre,
1939

'Feed-back' classroom at the
Engineering Training Centre,
1970

Television studio,
Engineering Training Centre,
1970

receiving ends of the system. (In this he had been partly anticipated by the Russian, Rosing, who built an experimental apparatus with a mirror drum at the sending end and a cathode-ray tube at the receiving end.) The cathode-ray tube itself had been introduced by Ferdinand Braun in 1897. It was the one practicable means of making electric impulses visible to the eye and is still one of the essential components of a television system, being the means of displaying the pictures in all receivers and picture monitors as well as an essential instrument for examining the television waveform.

Several years were to pass before Campbell-Swinton's concept could be realised in practice, but meanwhile the transmission of still pictures was being developed, stimulated by the introduction of the valve and of sensitive and quick-acting photo-cells. By the 1920s picture transmission by line or by radio was widely used for distributing news photographs. In transmitting a still picture, the problem of scanning could be solved by using a drum rotating after the manner of a phonograph cylinder, and the operation could take some minutes. (The BBC co-operated in experiments with the Fultograph in 1928; this was invented by Otto Fulton of Wireless Pictures Ltd. The transmissions were made from Daventry. The receiving equipment cost £22 and printed a picture 4 in. by 5 in.[61]) Television makes much tougher demands, because to reproduce a moving scene it is necessary to scan the whole of it repeatedly at least twenty-five times per second.

Despite the limitations of mechanical scanning, attempts were made in 1923 by J. L. Baird in England and Jenkins in America to transmit pictures composed of black and white elements, but no half-tones, by this means.[62] Baird pursued this line with dogged determination. He must be credited with having been the first to demonstrate real television, and even colour television, but his use of mechanical methods set a limit to his achievements, which fell short of the needs of television broadcasting. Nevertheless, he succeeded in drawing public attention to its potentialities.

Baird was the first to demonstrate television pictures with movement and with gradations of light intensity in 1926. He was tireless in his attempts to secure public recognition for his work and in July 1926 the BBC was persuaded to make some experimental broadcasts from its medium-wave transmitter in Oxford Street using his system. The Baird Company was subsequently licensed by the Post Office to operate its own transmitter (2TV) at Long Acre and also a transmitter located in Harrow (2TW). The licences restricted the output power to 0·25 kW and specified a frequency of 1·5 MHz (200 m). Reception tests were made in various parts of London.

The essence of the Baird system was the Nipkow disc, which was the scanning agent both at the sending and at the receiving end. It had thirty holes in it, arranged in a spiral, so as to scan vertically with an aspect ratio (width to height) of 3:7. At the transmitting end, a beam of light was projected through the holes in the disc on to the scene, so that the spot itself travelled over the scene in a series of thirty vertical lines. The light reflected from the scene was picked up on a photocell made by the General Electric Company (type CMG8) composed of caesium on silver oxide and filled with gas. The output from the photocell was fed to an amplifier specially designed to have a good response at low frequencies; the disc rotated at $12\frac{1}{2}$ revolutions per second, so that the output contained a strong component at $12 \cdot 5$ Hz. It was found impossible to avoid phase distortion in the amplifier at this frequency and this difficulty was mitigated rather by choosing appropriate subject matter than by improvements in the system. The picture had to be well broken up, without any large masses of the same tone. Backgrounds were designed to produce signals with components at frequencies that could easily be handled by the system.

At the receiving end the signals were amplified and fed to a neon tube with a flat surface about 3 in. by $1\frac{1}{2}$ in. The modulated light from this tube passed through a scanning disc, similar to the one at the sending end and running in synchronism with it, and was viewed through a magnifying lens. By modern standards the pictures were extremely crude, but people who saw television in this form for the first time were surprised to find that recognisable images were produced. The $12 \cdot 5$ Hz fllicker was very prominent, but those working and living with it got used to it. The synchronisation of the sending and receiving discs was performed by the black signal that occurred between frames. Mechanical blanking was deliberately inserted at the sending end in front of the scanning disc, so that there was a short interval between the end of one line and the beginning of the next, when a 'black' signal was sent. This signal was applied to a phonic wheel in the receiver, which kept the receiving disc in synchronism. This would have worked well enough if a black signal had occurred only at the end of each line in the way intended, but when there were black signals in the pictures along the lines, the phonic wheel motor would jump and go out of synchronism.

Baird was also working on a system of colour television and he demonstrated it on a large screen in 1928, using an elementary field-sequential method. He also attempted transatlantic television, as well as 'phonovision' – the recording of television on a gramophone record. Most of these ideas were dropped until better techniques became available several years later.

By 1929 Baird had achieved wide publicity, largely through the efforts on his behalf of Sydney Moseley, a journalist who had become a director of Baird's company. In the early part of 1929, in spite of the opposition of the BBC, the Postmaster General was persuaded that the BBC ought to take it up and make experimental transmissions. He called it a noteworthy scientific achievement, but stipulated that the transmissions should take place outside regular broadcasting hours.[63] The BBC was not pleased with this proposal, believing that there was no future in a system of such poor definition, and that better definition would need greater bandwidth. Since nobody knew how this could be achieved or how a public television service could be organised, the BBC was strongly opposed even to experimental transmissions – which would encourage people to buy receivers, only to have them left on their hands when the service was eventually abandoned.

In the end, after prolonged and sometimes rather acrimonious discussion between the BBC, the Post Office and the Television Development Company (Bairds), the Post Office engineers were sufficiently persuaded of the value of the Baird system to urge the BBC to allow one of its stations to be used for experiments. Since the 30-line system required a bandwidth of only 15 kHz, the pictures could be transmitted by a medium-wave sound broadcasting station.

The first transmissions, which began in August 1929, were originated at Baird's studio in Long Acre and sent by line to Savoy Hill, and from there to the transmitter on the roof of Selfridges. The object of the Baird Company was to produce pictures that would stir up interest and cause people to buy receivers, but it was difficult to produce anything like a 'programme', because of the limitations of the system in terms of noise, definition, and size of image. Only a head-and-shoulders view of a person could be shown. People appeared and sang songs or played the violin, or they would give talks or demonstrate simple things that could be done in close-up. T. H. Bridgewater, who had joined Baird's company in 1928 and later became Chief Engineer, Television, in the BBC, gave a talk about the deaf-and-dumb language, which could be done with two hands very close to the camera. This was before the start of the Regional Scheme with medium-wave twin-transmitters, so there was at first only one channel, and either sound or vision could be transmitted. A programme item was announced in sound; it was then switched off and the vision put on the line. It is hard to believe that an inaudible song from a visible singer could have had any programme value at all – the deaf-and-dumb language programme was a brilliant example of what *could* be done.

In March 1930 the second of the twin transmitters at Brookmans Park went into service and it became possible to transmit vision and sound simultaneously. Brookmans Park, however, is about 17 miles from the centre of London, and the lines were already in cable, so that there was a line transmission problem. The vision line had to be equalised to the then unheard-of upper limit of 15,000 Hz for the 30-line television transmissions. This was achieved, and on 30 March 1930 sound and vision were simultaneously transmitted for the first time. From then on, until 1932, the Baird Company originated regular, though experimental, programmes, which had to be broadcast after the radio programmes had closed late at night. 'We always had to wait for the Savoy Orpheans to close down,' Bridgewater recalls, 'which was about 12.15 am; in fact, I usually used to sleep in the studio, because I couldn't get home.' These transmissions went on until June 1932, when there was a two-month gap until the BBC took over the origination as well as the transmission of the programmes.

The transmissions were picked up at Marburg in Germany by Richard Theile, then a schoolboy but now Professor Theile, Director of the IRT, Munich. He had constructed a 30-line receiver and was probably the first overseas viewer of British television. He remembers that he worked under considerable difficulties, because his father insisted that he should go early to bed and he had to wake up at midnight to watch the programme.

The first television outside broadcast was of the Derby on 3 June 1931 – a feat that was repeated in the following year. Viewers saw about ten seconds of the just-recognisable horses flashing past the winning-post. This was done with a mirror-drum scanner set up in a van near the winning-post, and the signals were put on to a line and sent to Long Acre.

On 2 May 1932 Broadcasting House was opened and by this time the BBC, while still thinking that the system of 30-line television had no future, considered that it was at least desirable to establish a 30-line studio of its own so as to learn something about the principles of television production, however elementary. The first member of staff to be appointed to work in television was D. C. Birkinshaw (later Superintendent Engineer, Television); as a result of his work Bairds received an order for a set of 30-line studio equipment, which was soon installed in Studio BB, Broadcasting House. On 22 August 1932 the BBC took over the programme production side of the experimental transmissions from Bairds. This date really marks a watershed in television history, because it meant that the BBC became directly interested in producing television itself, rather than relaying programmes produced elsewhere. People who were to influence television in the future turned their attention to it; because they had to take the responsibility themselves, although they still disapproved of the system in principle, they found it interesting and many gradually became television-minded. Four programmes each of half an hour duration were radiated each week until 16 February 1934 when there was a ten-day interruption while a change-over was made to a new and larger studio that had been built at No. 16 Portland Place.

These developments generated the need for specialised staff, and T. H. Bridgewater and D. R. Campbell, both of Bairds, were invited to join the BBC and operate the equipment, much of which they had designed and made. Others from among the staff of the BBC were transferred to television and thus a body of knowledge on television principles began to be built up in the BBC. This proved of great use later, because working on 30-line television was like working on a scale model of what was to come later.

Meanwhile, television was arousing wide interest because of the realisation that the fast-developing science of electronics might be used to open the way to a high-definition system that could be of real value as a broadcasting medium. The Postmaster General (Sir Kingsley Wood) thought it advisable to set up an authoritative body to decide whether television was arriving at a state where it could be launched as a medium of public entertainment. Accordingly, in 1934, a committee was set up, with Lord Selsdon as chairman. The BBC members were N. Ashbridge, Chief Engineer, and Admiral Sir Charles Carpendale, Controller. The Committee, with the exception of Carpendale, visited America to see what was going on there, and found the Americans working on an electronic solution. They returned with the definite impression that television was going to come.

The main developments that were taking place on this side of the Atlantic were those of Baird and those of Electric & Musical Instruments Ltd (EMI), which had come into being as a result of the amalgamation of the Gramophone Company (HMV) and the Columbia Gramophone Company. About midsummer 1933 Birkinshaw left the 30-line team and handed over to Campbell, in order to work on a transmitter at Broadcasting House for the purpose of transmitting signals originated by the Baird Company, first on 60, then in turn on 90, 120 and finally 180 lines. This was a 3-kW 'ultra-short-wave' transmitter made by the Marconi Company for commercial telephony and the modulator had to be rebuilt to obtain the necessary bandwidth for the vision signals. This transmitter was used to send pictures from Baird film-scanning equipment installed in a neighbouring room.

The work of EMI was along electronic lines, and it was carried out by a brilliant team working under Isaac Shoenberg (later Sir Isaac Shoenberg), who had been a schoolfellow of Zworykin and Sarnoff in Russia. He persuaded the Board of EMI to devote money to research on television and he gathered around him A. D. Blumlein, P. W. Willans, G. E. Condliffe, C. O. Browne, J. D. McGee, E. L. C. White, and others. (Blumlein and Browne both lost their lives in an air accident during the war.) Shoenberg was remarkable, among other things, for his tremendous drive – which he communicated to his staff. He informed Ashbridge, about 1933, that he had mapped out a programme of development which would produce a system of television quite different from anything yet seen in this country. He wanted exactly twelve months for the project, and asked Ashbridge not to worry him for demonstrations, because they would be misleading. He agreed, however, to report progress once a month. The conversations continued, accompanied by pressure from the Press, which thought that the BBC was overlooking television developments. Eventually, Shoenberg agreed that, although his system was not yet right, he would give a demonstration. Ashbridge and Kirke came away from it much impressed, and Ashbridge told Reith that television had 'now come all right' on the EMI basis. He suggested giving it another month or so before giving information and a demonstration to the programme people. The demonstration of 405-line television, using electronic scanning, was duly given and those responsible for BBC programmes were enormously impressed – so much so that they were impatient to start television broadcasting 'tomorrow or Saturday at the latest'. This demonstration proved to be the genesis of a practical system of television in this country.

On 14 January 1935 the Selsdon Committee made its report, saying that the time had come to launch an experimental high-definition television service, that the BBC should undertake the first transmissions and that it should start with one station in London. One thing that the Committee could not decide, however, was what system should be used. Bairds were now offering a system with 240 lines, but EMI were offering 405 lines – a courageous and brilliant move at a time when it was very doubtful whether even 240 lines could be achieved. Since the Committee was unable to make a firm decision, it recommended that both systems should be used side by side in competition.[64]

As a result of these decisions, the Baird 30-line transmissions were closed down in the summer of 1935. Some of the 30-line receivers in use at that time used a Nipkow disc for scanning and others a mirror drum; a number were made up by enthusiasts from kits of parts. It is impossible to say how many were actually in use, but the number could hardly have exceeded 2500.

All attention was then given to the preparation of part of Alexandra Palace for the installation of both the EMI 405-line system and the Baird 240-line system. The work was entrusted to a small group headed by T. C. Macnamara, later to become Chief Engineer of ATV. Other members of this group were P. A. T. Bevan (later Chief Engineer of the ITA) and Hexel Lewis (later Broadcasting Manager of Marconi's).

By April 1936 Birkinshaw had been appointed the first Engineer-in-Charge of the Alexandra Palace television station, with two Senior Maintenance Engineers, T. H. Bridgewater and D. R. Campbell on the studio side, and two others, H. W. Baker and H. F. Bowden on the transmitter side.

Contracts were placed with Baird Television Limited and with the Marconi–EMI Television Company Ltd for the equipment required for their respective systems. The latter company had been formed in 1934 by a fusion of the television interests of the Marconi Company and EMI, since a complete television system would require the development of new techniques both for the studio equipment and for the transmitters and aerial. Marconi's provided the vision transmitter for the EMI transmissions, while EMI produced the modulator and the 405-line studio equipment. Bairds produced the vision transmitter and the studio equipment for their own system and Marconi's supplied the sound transmitter and the aerials for both systems. All this equipment was installed at Alexandra Palace.

The essence of the EMI system was the Emitron camera. Attempts to put the ideas of Campbell Swinton into practice by developing electronic scanning had been made by several experimenters, and A. C. Cossor Ltd and Scophony Ltd were experimenting with such systems in this country. In the USA Dr Zworykin had introduced his iconoscope in 1923; it consisted of a photo-electric mosaic having millions of small silver globules sensitised by caesium. An image of the scene to be televised was thrown by a lens on to this photo-sensitive surface, which was deposited on a sheet of mica coated on the other side with metal. A cathode-ray gun focused a stream of electrons to form a spot on the screen, which was swept over it in a series of lines. The electron beam discharged the small capacitors forming the mosaic and their discharge constituted the picture content of the television signal. The instantaneous amplitude of the signal current thus depended on the amount of light falling on each element in the mosaic.

The camera developed by the EMI team was the Emitron, which used the charge-storage principle of the iconoscope, in which the scene was focused on to the target area of the mosaic. Since the geometry of the tube required the scanning beam to attack the target at an angle, the width of the line scan had to increase gradually as the beam travelled down the target. The Emitron camera was later superseded by the Super Emitron (image iconoscope), the CPS Emitron (orthicon) and the image-orthicon, but in the early days the difficulties inherent in the Emitron had to be offset as far as possible by extreme care in the adjustment of the scanning circuits, so as to reduce geometrical distortion and shading. The shading distortion in the form of 'tilt and bend' gave a great deal of trouble; the small control room at Alexandra Palace, which had to be kept darkened to allow the pictures to be seen on monitors, contained a series of apparatus bays at each of which an engineer sat to operate the controls. To allow each of these engineers to see the monitor screen they sat on stools of graduated heights.

One of the most ingenious and successful products of the EMI team was the design of the television waveform, as it was originated and transmitted. Apart from the synchronising pulses needed in any system of television, the waveform introduced interlaced scanning in a manner that would lead to the simplest electronic design of both the transmitter and the receiver. It also included tolerances that would obviate difficulties in scanning certain types of picture, and it was well adapted to transmission over paths that would introduce a certain amount of distortion. This waveform, though an entirely novel concept at the time, proved most successful and has remained in use, with minor changes, in the 405-line service to this day.

Eckersley had seen clearly that television would require a wide bandwidth and that this could not be achieved in any of the existing broadcasting bands. Television would have to be broadcast on what were then called 'ultra short waves' and Eckersley thought that these would have too short a range to be practicable. He later confessed that this was a wrong forecast.[65] The range of a modern high-power television station on VHF (the modern term for ultra short waves) is often in the region of seventy miles and even on the higher UHF frequencies a range of about forty miles can be achieved.

A whole series of fundamental problems arose from the wide bandwidth necessary to transmit the 405-line signal. Whereas sound broadcasting needed a bandwidth of only some 10 kHz, television needed 3 MHz for the vision signal. New techniques had to be developed for handling such a wide bandwidth in radio links, cables, transmitters and aerials. Furthermore, the synchronising pulses had to be transmitted with accurate timing and without spurious modulation.

The new EiC at Alexandra Palace had to select some staff, being careful to explain to those interested that they might be approaching a dead end, but on the other hand might be helping to develop one of the most successful technologies of this era. There was an enormous amount to be learnt about high-definition television, especially about the way in which EMI were tackling it. The Emitron camera was different from anything any of the team had ever worked with before, since it represented electronic as opposed to mechanical television. One of Birkinshaw's main tasks was the instruction of his staff in the new techniques and in the way the various circuits functioned, and it was at this point that a somewhat tense situation began to develop. Much of the equipment provided by the two companies was so new that it had not yet been patented, and it was therefore imperative that the secrets of one company should not escape to the other. In the event there were no leaks by way of the BBC staff; indeed there seem to have been no leaks at all. The situation did, however, create a difficulty: the companies were unwilling to tell the BBC staff how the equipment was designed and how it worked. Yet it was obvious that the staff would have to learn about the equipment, and Birkinshaw set himself the task of learning for himself, by experiment and by talking to the designers. In what came to be known as the 'Black Book' he described in detail every circuit in Alexandra Palace. When the Second World War came, and many BBC staff went to work in radar, the book was in frequent demand in the Services, because of the basic information on electronics that it contained.

A demonstration of the Baird system on 240 lines, 25 frames per second, took place on 19 May 1936. It consisted of the reproduction of a film by one of two 35-mm telecine machines. The definition and gradation of the picture were reported to be very good, the blacks were good and 25-Hz flicker was noticeable only when there were large white areas in the picture; but the line structure was quite apparent. The optical system consisted of a 60-A carbon arc as the light source, a shutter, a water-cooled film gate, two Zeiss objectives focusing the film image on to the scanning disc aperture, and a lens and photocell followed by the vision amplifier chain. The scanning disc rotated at 6000 rpm in an evacuated chamber; it was about 20 in. in diameter and had sixty scanning apertures arranged in a circle. As each hole represented a line, four revolutions of the disc scanned one frame. The film motion was continuous; this avoided some of the problems associated with the more usual intermittent motion and it also provided the field scan. Below the picture scanning apertures, on an inner circle on the disc, were sixty slits, which, through a separate optical system, generated line synchronising pulses. The picture apertures in the scanning disc were hexagonal, spaced 0·0035 in. between flats. If a speck of dust got into one of these apertures, a black line would appear in the picture. To rectify such a fault, it was necessary to stop the projector, reduce the scanning disc chamber to atmospheric pressure, open the chamber housing (by removing many hexagonal nuts), extract the disc, locate the blocked hole, remove the foreign matter, and then reassemble and re-evacuate the whole apparatus. This process could take anything between 30 and 45 minutes, when done by expert mechanics. This telecine equipment, although producing good pictures, would have been difficult to maintain in regular service, and this was not the only trouble from which it suffered. It was clear to many of the BBC engineers, before the public service started, that Baird's men were fighting a losing battle from the start. The Baird engineers worked very hard and produced some excellent equipment, but it suffered from the defects inherent in a mechanical system and the electrical parts of it did not have the sophistication which marked the activities of their competitors. When they made their system work, it seemed to be always with a struggle. The two systems, however, were gradually brought to a fit state to be put on the air; a starting date for the service was planned for November 1936, but there was a request for a few days' transmission in August for the Radio Show. This was carried out under higher pressure than ever, with all the difficulties to be expected when careful planning is upset by a last-minute anticipation of the target date.

After the Radio Show the service closed down again until 2 November 1936, when 'the world's first regular public service of high-definition television programmes was launched'.[66] The validity of this claim has been challenged, notably on account of a statement made in a BBC publication of more than a year before, in which the opening words read: 'Herr Eugen Hadamovsky, Director-General of the German Broadcasting Service, opened the world's first regular high-definition television service on Friday, 22 March' (1935).[67] It all depends on what one means by 'high definition'; the German system of 1935 used 180 lines, whereas in 1936 BBC Television had alternately 240 and 405 lines. The difference between pictures composed of 240 lines and those with 180 lines is not very marked, but 405 lines represented a real advance. The line structure on this standard was not sufficiently noticeable to detract seriously from viewers' enjoyment of the programmes. It should be noted also that the Baird system had twenty-five pictures per second, scanned sequentially, whereas the EMI system used interlaced scanning with fifty fields per second, so that although there were still only twenty-five complete pictures per second, flicker was much less noticeable. In short the 405-line system constituted a viable public service for the first time. The choice of 405 for the number of lines in a complete picture resulted from several considerations: the number had to be odd to facilitate interlacing and it had to be the product of a number of simple factors (e.g. $5 \times 3 \times 3 \times 3$) to facilitate generation of the waveform. Furthermore, the number of lines depended on the video bandwidth available, since it was desirable that the vertical resolution should be roughly the same as the horizontal resolution. It may be thought that the Marconi-EMI team were creating difficulties for themselves by adopting interlacing, since their new and untried 405-line system was already extremely complex. In fact, interlacing turned out to be fairly easy to achieve and it made a worthwhile reduction in flicker.

At the double opening ceremony performed by the Postmaster General, Major G. C. Tryon, Bairds went first because they had been selected by a coin tossed by Lord Selsdon at the suggestion of Ashbridge. Sir Henry Greer, Chairman of Bairds, was televised during the opening transmission of the Baird system, which lasted half an hour.[68] Unfortunately apparently through a mere oversight, Mr Baird himself had not been invited to join the group in the studio and he was naturally hurt by this slight. During the next half-hour Sir Alfred Clark, Chairman of EMI, appeared on the screen.

Thereafter, programmes were transmitted on each system in alternate weeks and the competition had started in earnest. Receivers had to be capable of being switched from 240 lines 25 fields (sequential) to 405 lines 50 fields (interlaced). Receiver manufacturers succeeded in meeting this requirement, which was a foretaste of the problem they would have to meet in 1964 when BBC-2 started, using 625 lines 50 fields (interlaced), while BBC-1 and the ITA programme were still transmitted on 405 lines 50 fields (interlaced). When the Industry drew attention to the difficulties of making dual-standard receivers on the latter occasion, the BBC was able to remind them that they had solved a similar problem nearly thirty years before.

The origination of programmes on the Baird system took place in a studio at Alexandra Palace, of 70 ft by 30 ft floor area and about 23 ft high. In this studio one camera was placed near the side wall, bolted to the floor and quite immobile. This took a picture of the scene on film, which was immediately developed, fixed and very briefly washed. While still wet, the film was put into the disc scanning device already described, in which the television signals were generated. The most rapid processing methods were used, and the operation took 64 seconds; this intermediate film system was the only way of transmitting a large studio scene on the Baird system. The camera was a $17 \cdot 5$-mm Vinten film camera using 35-mm film installed in a glazed enclosure so as to prevent pick-up of camera noise by the studio microphone. The fact that the camera could not follow the artists was a serious limitation, because the movement of artists had to be subservient to the camera rather than vice versa. Furthermore, there was only one camera and even at that time it could be seen that several would

L

be necessary for a production. Technically the process was subject to the most serious hazards. The system of rapid processing was unreliable; since the film had to be televised while wet, it was passed through a gate filled with water through which the scanning beam was passed, and often a bubble would form in the gate and dance over the picture. On more than one occasion the storage tanks were drained of water because of the enormous demand of the system; on such occasions the transmission had to come to a premature end. The variable density sound recording system combined with rapid film processing produced very poor sound quality and sprocket noise.

It was possible to televise live scenes directly by the Baird system, but only by using a moving spot of light as in the old 30-line system. For the purpose of small scenes and interviews, Bairds provided a second, spotlight, studio from which announcements were also made. This studio had to be maintained in darkness, and a large disc, illuminated by a powerful arc, scanned the artist with a travelling beam. Announcers had to make up with bluish-green lipstick on account of the excessive red-sensitivity of the caesium photo-electric cells, which were used with secondary-emission multipliers. The picture was very noisy and, on account of the special make-up requirements of this studio, it was not possible to interchange people quickly between one studio and the other. The best part of the Baird system was the telecine, and for a time their film transmissions, even though they were only on 240 lines, were considered to be superior to those of EMI. This was mainly because of the 'tilt-and-bend' distortion associated with EMI film transmissions, which could not be corrected quickly enough to cope with movement in the scene.

The EMI studio presented a quite different aspect and conformed much more closely to operational needs. There were three all-electronic cameras (a good deal lighter than the cameras of today) on very light 'run-trucks', as they were called, which could easily be moved around the studio. Strangely enough, these cameras started off with a serious disadvantage which, in view of the far-sighted design of the rest of the equipment, is difficult to understand. There was no proper means of focusing them; the only way in which one could see whether the picture was in focus was to open the side of the camera and look through a small port-hole at the target of the Emitron tube itself. This was not good enough for studio operations, and it was not long before an optical viewfinder, ganged with the main lens, was fitted. The scene inside the EMI studio was much as one might see it today; the three cameras were moved in accordance with the plan of the production, close-ups and long shots could be taken and fading between the various cameras could be done, though it took $2\frac{1}{2}$ seconds. At first, cutting was not possible because of electronic complications, but, on the plea of the producers, this problem was overcome and quick fading and cutting between cameras could be done, as at the present day. The EMI studio thus provided much greater scope for studio productions than the Baird studio, and the EMI system could be applied to outside broadcasts.

The competition between the two systems ceased when the Television Advisory Committee, which had been set up on the recommendation of the Selsdon Committee, decided at the end of January 1937 to recommend the abandonment of the

148

Baird system. Accordingly, from 8 February 1937 the transmissions from the London Television Station were wholly on the EMI system on 405 lines.

In retrospect, it is obvious that there was no point in making the trial of the two systems, except to prove beyond all question that the final choice was the right one. Already in 1934 everything had pointed to the eventual triumph of EMI. In January of that year, Ashbridge and Kirke saw an EMI demonstration at Hayes, and Ashbridge reported that it was 'far and away a greater achievement than anything I have ever seen in television'.[69] The arguments, claims and counter-claims have been set out at length by Asa Briggs.[70] Baird and Sydney Moseley had brought such pressure to bear on the Government, the Post Office and the BBC that the Selsdon Committee had little choice but to recommend that the Baird system should be given an opportunity to prove itself in service. The impression that had been made on the then Prime Minister, Ramsay MacDonald, can be gauged from the account given by Sir Henry Greer of the Prime Minister's visit to a Baird demonstration in Film House, Wardour Street, London, on 12 March 1934: 'Last week the Prime Minister came to view this miracle . . . He was aghast. So stunned was he by the marvel which had been shown to him that he spoke in alternate admiration and fear – admiration for the genius that had created it, fear that mankind might not be wise to use it for its good.[71] Yet the engineers concerned, both in the Post Office and in the BBC, were convinced that the EMI system was much the superior.

After 8 February 1937, when the service was exclusively on the EMI system, attention began to be devoted to the problem of outside broadcasts. The first OBs were done by simply taking a camera out into the grounds of Alexandra Palace on the end of 1000 ft of cable from the control room; it was found possible to apply the necessary correction, electrically, for this length of cable. In February 1937 a local OB was done from the concert hall of Alexandra Palace. This was the annual North London Boxing Championship, which on that occasion was attended by many hundreds of spectators. A scaffold-tube platform was designed and built, and slung some 10 ft above the audience so as to get a good view of the ring. A standard Emitron camera was installed on the platform. About 30 kW of lighting was provided over the ring, but, because of the time factor and lack of experience, no protection had been provided under the lamps, which were fitted in eight units each of eight 500-W lamps. One minute before the contestants entered the ring, one of the bulbs dropped out of its holder and fell on to the floor, luckily not breaking. It was retrieved, and the boxers entered the ring, but the BBC engineers had an anxious time, praying for an early knockout before another lamp fell, perhaps to be intercepted by a straight right. Fortunately, there was no more trouble, and the event was such a success that it was repeated in the following year – but with proper protection for the lamps.

Had it not been for an approaching event of the greatest national importance, and indeed international interest, the development of television OBs would no doubt have started with some simple outside events and worked up to something bigger. But the Coronation of King George VI was imminent, and the BBC decided to televise what was possible of the event, which took place on 12 May 1937. Permission could not be obtained to put television cameras in Westminster Abbey, but it was decided to try to transmit the scene at Apsley Gate, Hyde Park Corner, using three cameras. Early in the year EMI were asked to build a set of studio equipment into a large van and to find a way of getting the signal from Apsley Gate to Alexandra Palace. The van had to be very large, because it was not possible, in the time available, to change the layout of the studio equipment so as to make it more convenient for mobile use and the van had to be constructed with both sides hinged top and bottom, opening upwards and downwards like flaps to give access to the back of the equipment. C. O. Browne and his team at EMI made a strenuous effort to have the mobile unit ready in time. There was no possibility of making extensive tests on the equipment or of training BBC staff in its use. It was therefore operated by the EMI team on Coronation Day. It behaved well until the procession was heard approaching, when all three cameras failed. Browne coolly appraised the situation, realised that there was only a small section of the equipment that was common to all three channels, located the fault, and corrected it before the procession came into view.

The procession was to come from Hyde Park and go through the archway, and the three cameras were disposed one on each side of the arch, and one on top. The three cameramen on this historic occasion, which gave a tremendous impetus to the development of television, were J. L. Bliss, R. J. C. Price and Harry Tong. Scarcely less important, in its long-term effects, than the ability to pick up television signals at an OB point was the method of carrying these signals to the transmitter. This aspect again illustrates the foresight of Shoenberg and his team of engineers at EMI. He had realised that this sort of event would take place, that radio link transmission would be difficult, that a cable was the best answer, and that the Post Office had no experience of transmitting television signals. He therefore set his own research team to work on the design of a television cable with terminal equipment which would transmit video signals over the 7 or 8 miles from Hyde Park Corner to Alexandra Palace. This was done, and when the eight miles of cable, manufactured by Siemens Bros, had been coiled up in the EMI Laboratories at Hayes, the Television Advisory Committee was invited to come and see the pictures before and after being passed through the cable and its terminal equipment. The demonstration showed that there was no appreciable loss of quality. The cable was pulled into ducts by the Post Office and became their property, rented by the BBC. This was not only the first high-definition television transmission over a line more than a thousand yards long but also the first over a cable circuit. If such a cable had been available two years earlier, the television transmitter and the studios might not have been put into the same building.

The cable was of the twin or balanced-pair type, with two 0·080-in. diameter conductors each located centrally within a tube of paper insulation. This tube had an external diameter of 0·91 in., and the conductor was centrally located by crimping it into a roughly sinusoidal shape, successive crimps lying in planes at right-angles to each other. Two tubes, each with its one crimped conductor inside, were twisted together and had copper screening laid round them, the whole being covered in a lead sheath.[72] Over the frequency range between 10 Hz and 3 MHz, the attenuation varied between 0·036 and 8 dB/mile, the velocity of propagation varied between 18,000 and 180,000 miles per second, and the characteristic impedance between 3000 and 190 ohms.

This type of cable could be used in lengths of up to 8 miles, after which it was necessary to insert an amplifier. The length from Broadcasting House to Alexandra Palace was 7·25 miles; Broadcasting House thus became a very convenient 'repeater point' for OB transmissions into Alexandra Palace.

On the day of the Coronation, BBC engineers went to the site at Apsley Gate at about 2 am, as the enormous crowds that were expected could have prevented them reaching the site any later. The weather was against them, and it had rained by the time of the procession. None of them had ever done an outside production before, and no producer was attached to the event at all. Gerald Cock, the Director of Television, came down to the rehearsal the day before and on the morning of Coronation Day. He seemed to know everybody and was able to persuade police officials to keep the crowds away from the camera positions so that the view was not obstructed. Apart from this help, Bridgewater, who was the engineer in charge of the operation, looked after the production side himself. The weather deteriorated to the point where news-film cameras had to stop turning, but the BBC went on transmitting excellent pictures, including a close-up of the State Coach as it passed through the gates of Hyde Park. These pictures were transmitted over the balanced-pair cable, though there was also a stand-by radio link, ordered from EMI and operating on about 60 MHz with an output power of about 1 kW. This required a mast carrying a directional aerial pointing approximately towards Alexandra Palace over a nearly optical path.

The Remembrance Day Service at the Cenotaph on 11 November 1937 was the occasion of the first use of the Super-Emitron camera (see Chapter V, Section 5). The first broadcast of the Derby on high-definition television took place on 24 May 1939.

From 1937 onwards OBs expanded and became a very popular feature of television programmes. This was made possible by the extension of the balanced-pair cable to strategic points in the West End: Hyde Park Corner, Victoria Station, Buckingham Palace, Whitehall and the Albert Hall. This worked very well for events on the cable route, but it was soon realised that it was too restrictive. The cable was on one side of Whitehall and it was impossible to make contact with it if the OB was on the other side. An early requirement for a television OB was from one of the theatres in Shaftesbury Avenue, where the cable ran down the middle. Application was made to the Post Office for an extension on ordinary paper-insulated cable, from the middle of the road into the theatre. The Post Office wanted to use crimped cable for the extension, but the cost and delay made it impracticable. This led to the development, in Lines Department, of a system for putting television signals on ordinary paper-insulated cable over short lengths as extensions to the crimped cable. The Post Office representatives said that cables designed for telephony were totally unsuitable for transmitting the wide range of frequencies required for television transmissions, but that if the BBC cared to spend effort and money to develop a method of using such cables, the Post Office would help as far as they possibly could. Most of the junction cables in and around London and other big cities were non-loaded and therefore theoretically had an infinite frequency range; the only difficulty was that, as the frequency range increased, the distance over which signals could be transmitted without amplification was severely reduced. However, during the next two years, much work was done on the development of such a system, and the outcome was so successful that about 100 OBs were done in this way, lengths of existing telephone cable serving as extensions to the balanced-pair crimped-conductor cable. This work was done, under the guidance of Dr A. R. A. Rendall, and the first live OB over a telephone cable was from the Paris Cinema. This was quite successful, although the equipment was neither robust enough nor in the right form for carrying out regular broadcasts; developments continued and a portable television repeater was designed for use when the distance was more than one mile.

Balanced equalisers of the 'bridged-T' constant-resistance type were developed for use on telephone cables in conjunction with phase-correcting lattice networks. The attenuation-frequency characteristics of circuits in telephone cable were measured by a substitution method, using a tuned detector in conjunction with a variable attenuator. The phase characteristics were determined by calculation from impedance measurements made with the far end of the circuit alternately open-circuited and short-circuited. [73, 74]

By 1939 plans were afoot for extending the balanced-pair cable to other places, but the war intervened and when it was over and television started once again, the Post Office exercised their right to provide all such circuits themselves. There was a time when the Post Office's 'main concern was the jealous preservation of its monopolistic powers'; these words might seem harsh were they not quoted from the Post Office Electrical Engineering Journal. [75]

Outside broadcasts were also done by radio link. A frequency of 64 MHz was used and at first the receiving aerial was mounted on top of the Alexandra Palace mast, but pick-up from the transmitting aerials caused interference on the OB pictures and eventually a site was found at Swain's Lane, Highgate, which proved satisfactory as a receiving point and gave access to the balanced-pair cable. A wooden tower, 150 ft high, carried the receiving aerial. Wood was preferred to metal as being less likely to re-radiate interference, but the tower failed after a few years and was replaced by a steel structure. At the OB end of the radio link a $1\frac{1}{4}$-kW transmitter was used, mounted in a vehicle. This was used in June 1937 for the Tennis Championships from Wimbledon, using an aerial array supported by two tripod masts 30 ft high. The use of open-wire feeders for a high transmitting aerial presented difficulties, but in 1938 a flexible lightweight cable was produced by co-operation between the BBC and the Telegraph Construction & Maintenance Company. This permitted the use of an 80-ft fire-escape to support the aerial, which enabled it to be erected in about five minutes. [76]

Meanwhile, development was also proceeding apace in the studios. The staff were finding out that television was not merely pointing a camera at an artist; it was necessary to develop the same flexibility and sophistication and the same artistic standard of production as were already being applied in the world of film. The tendency to expand was evident from very early days. Productions, which at first used perhaps one third of a studio, filled the whole of a studio and two studios were coupled together for the ambitious programmes, such as 'Hassan'. There were also developments in organisation. The BBC Management wanted each member of the staff to have a wide range of activities so as to give the widest scope for promotion, but it soon became evident that some specialisation was essential. The duties of studio staff were very different from those of transmitter staff and within the studios themselves work on cameras, lighting, and control-room equipment required different skills. It soon became necessary also to differentiate between operational duties and maintenance, especially as the equipment was so novel and complicated that its maintenance required specialist knowledge.

A routine was established for setting the equipment to work each morning. Tests were first made using 'black level and syncs' only, followed by 'grey level and syncs', and finally by 'artificial bars', which produced a black cross on a white background. Artificial bars were transmitted for two one-hour periods each morning separated by an hour of film transmission, mainly for the benefit of receiver manufacturers, dealers, and servicemen. Test cards were used for lining up the cameras and while this was being done the sound circuits were tested.

The central control room provided the master timing pulses for the studio control rooms and also contained a sound-mixing desk and a vision-mixing desk. If it was necessary to switch to an OB source, the picture was momentarily faded down to black while the synchronising signals from the new source of programme were substituted for those from the central control room. Some maintenance work was done in the lunch-hour, when there was no transmission. One of the telecine equipments was used for captions.[77]

The transmitters at Alexandra Palace presented many new problems. A carrier frequency in the region of 40 to 50 MHz was indicated if adequate sideband response was to be achieved without introducing severe difficulties in design. Although no international allocations had yet been made at frequencies above 30 MHz, the Post Office allocated a band of frequencies from $40 \cdot 5$ MHz to $52 \cdot 5$ MHz for television broadcasting in the United Kingdom and the Television Advisory Committee recommended that the London station should radiate vision on 45 MHz ($6 \cdot 7$ m). The sound component could have been radiated in any of the broadcasting wavebands, but for simplicity in receiver design it was desirable that it should be on a frequency close to the vision carrier frequency and $41 \cdot 5$ MHz ($7 \cdot 2$ m) was chosen.

The choice of the band $40 \cdot 5$ to $52 \cdot 5$ MHz, which later became part of Band I – still in use for 405-line television – was dictated by the fact that it was thought that the video-frequency band would extend to about $1 \cdot 5$ MHz for the Baird 240-line system and to about 2 MHz for the EMI 405-line system. To ensure adequate response at the upper sideband frequencies, it was desirable that the ratio of the carrier frequency to the highest modulating frequency should not be much less than 20:1. The separation of $3 \cdot 5$ MHz between the vision and sound carriers was thought to be sufficient to avoid interference between the sidebands of the two signals and it was small enough to permit a single receiving aerial to be used for both vision and sound, and also to avoid encroaching on channels that would be required for future stations. Double sideband transmission was used for both vision and sound, though later stations radiated only a vestigial upper sideband of the vision transmission, so as to economise in spectrum space.

The choice of a site for the London Television Station raised a number of problems. As the studios were to be on the same site as the transmitters, the station must not be too far from the centre of London so that artists could easily get there. (Nowadays it is usual for transmitting stations to be remote from the studio centres, mainly because the best transmitting sites are seldom convenient of access for artists.) The centre of London itself was ruled out because it was low-lying and it would be impossible to build a high mast there; furthermore, a considerable amount of space would be needed for the studios and this would be expensive in the central area. Since propagation in this band (then known as the ultra-short-wave band) was not effective far beyond the horizon, a high site was essential. Sites in Hampstead and Highgate were too expensive and there were restrictions on building a high mast. The Crystal Palace would have been suitable, but was thought to be too far to the south to give optimum coverage in the Home Counties; also, it was at that time occupied by Bairds. (The erp that could be produced at that time was limited to 34 kW; when it later became possible to use an erp of 200 kW, giving a considerably greater range, the move to the Crystal Palace was made – in 1956.) The choice fell on Alexandra Palace, which was 306 ft AMSL, where there was plenty of space in the existing building and where permission could be obtained for a 300-ft mast. This elevation, with a vision erp of 34 kW, gave an effective range of some twenty-five miles in all directions.

Because of the major differences between the 240-line and 405-line signals, it was necessary to use separate vision transmitters for the Baird and EMI systems. Each of these provided an output of 17 kW at peak white, so that the average power was about the same as that of the sound transmitter, which had an unmodulated carrier power of 3 kW. The vision transmitter for the Baird system was installed on the ground floor below the Baird studio. It comprised a master oscillator, an intermediate amplifier, a final amplifier, a 'conditioner', a synchronising modulator, and a vision modulator. The master oscillator produced an output of 100 W at 45 MHz by multiplying and amplifying the output of a temperature-controlled crystal oscillator operating at 1·406 MHz. The intermediate amplifier comprised a pair of Metropolitan Vickers de-mountable tetrodes, one of which constituted a spare. The synchronising signals were applied to the grid circuit of this amplifier. The final amplifier was similar to the intermediate amplifier and the picture signals were applied to its grid circuit. The conditioner was needed to prepare the de-mountable valves for service by driving off the last traces of occluded gas after the valves had been evacuated. The synchronising and vision modulators were four-stage and seven-stage vision frequency amplifiers respectively. Filament supplies were obtained from motor generators delivering 200 A at 25 V. The anode and screen supplies were also produced by motor generators, the supply to the anode of the final amplifier being 40 kW at 10 kV. The control desk was provided with an oscilloscope for examining the radiated waveform.[78]

The de-mountable valves were continuously evacuated by two oil condensation pumps and a rotary pump. The required degree of vacuum was maintained automatically. The valves were water-cooled and the system was protected by water-flow relays.

The Marconi-EMI vision transmitter was quite different. The carrier frequency was derived from a drive unit with an output frequency of 22·5 MHz, followed by a frequency-doubling stage in the transmitter itself. There followed six stages of amplification. Mixed vision and synchronising signals were applied to the modulator, which comprised four stages of amplification. The first two and the last two had dc coupling, but between the second and third stages the dc component was lost and it had to be restored subsequently. Grid modulation was effected in the sixth amplifier. The eht supply was obtained from a motor alternator set giving 50 kW at 500 V, 500 Hz. Valve rectifiers were used for the earlier stages, but a mercury-pool rectifier was used for the fourth stage. Generators were provided for the dc filament supply to the final stage. The generator for the last stage had to be insulated from earth as the filament was at a high potential. The eht supply for the output stage at 6000 V was obtained from a hot-cathode mercury-vapour valve rectifier. A supply at 4500 V was similarly obtained for the third, fourth and fifth stages of the final amplifier. As in the Baird transmitter, a cathode-ray oscilloscope was provided on the control desk, so that the waveform of the picture and synchronising signals could be examined at the output of each stage of the modulator and also at the output of the modulated amplifier. A sequence starting-switch was provided to prevent damage to the transmitter from the application of power supplies in the wrong order, and all the equipment was protected by interlocks and water-flow monitoring devices.

The Marconi sound transmitter used with both television systems was designed to work on any frequency between 35 and 50 MHz with an output power of 3 kW at 90 per cent peak modulation. The carrier frequency was derived from a master oscillator and doubler, followed by five amplifying stages. Modulation was effected at the anodes of the fifth amplifier. The main eht supply at 6000 V was obtained from a hot-cathode mercury-vapour rectifier and the high-power valves were water-cooled.

Separate aerials were used for the sound and vision signals, the upper of the two aerial systems being used for vision. The upper part of the mast was octagonal and each aerial consisted of eight end-fed dipoles uniformly spaced around the mast. An energised dipole was mounted behind each of the radiating dipoles to act as a reflector. Each dipole comprised three wires at the corners of a triangle with a 15-in. base and all eight aerials and reflectors were connected in parallel, with concentric networks to make the necessary impedance transformations. The main feeder was of the concentric type and a special network was needed to match it to the balanced aerial system. Care was taken to minimise reflections in the feeder by inserting compensators into it at intervals. The sound aerial was similar to the vision aerial, except that the dimensions were appropriate to the lower frequency and the elaborate arrangements for maintaining the impedance constant over a wide band were not necessary for sound. The feeder used for the sound aerial was similar to that for vision.

Progress in the design of receivers was essential to the development of television. The first receivers had used mechanical scanning as did the first picture-originating equipment, but by 1936 it had become apparent that a high-definition television service depended as much on the availability of the cathode-ray tube to produce the display in the receiver as on the camera pick-up tube to originate the pictures. Cathode-ray tubes had already been incorporated in receivers when the BBC Television Service started in 1936. Because of its narrow deflection angle the tube had to be very long to produce a picture of acceptable size and this fact, together with the large number of other bulky components that had to be accommodated on a number of separate chassis, made the television receiver a very substantial piece of furniture. Some sets had the tube mounted vertically so that the pictures could be viewed through a mirror housed in the lid of the receiver, which was tilted at an angle of 45°. During this period, cathode-ray tubes used electrostatic deflection. The high voltage required for the eht supply was obtained by using a mains transformer and a rectifier; this method required cumbersome components and presented some risk of dangerous electric shock.

Home construction of television sets presented a much greater challenge to amateur enthusiasts than had the construction of radio receivers in the early days of broadcasting. Nevertheless, constructional details of a television receiver were given in *Wireless World* as early as 2 June 1937. It was of the trf type with three rf stages, a diode detector and one video stage.[79] Just before the war a 9-in. picture tube was introduced, which reduced the cost of the cheapest television receivers on the market. At about the same time there was a change from electrostatic to magnetic deflection and focusing.

As in radio receivers, the use of the superheterodyne principle became common in television receivers at an early stage, and this later assisted the development of multi-channel receivers. Since 1922 the BBC and the receiver industry had been mutually inter-dependent, as the BBC depended for its licence income on the availability of efficient and reliable receivers at a reasonable price, while the receiver industry depended on the BBC to attract its customers. This inter-dependence had continued and received a new impetus with the start of television in 1936.

The effective range of the Alexandra Palace station proved to be greater than had been predicted and its coverage embraced 25 per cent of the population of the whole of the United Kingdom. By August 1939, 23,000 television receivers had been sold to the public and it was expected that the number would rise to 80,000 by the end of the year. This forecast was not to be realised until nearly seven years later, because the Television Service had to be closed down when it was clear that war was imminent. There were several reasons why television could not continue in war-time, the over-riding one being that the frequencies were needed for radar. Instructions were given to the EiC by telephone at 10.00 hours on 1 September to close the service at noon on that day. The last words broadcast before the break of $6\frac{3}{4}$ years were from Mickey Mouse: 'I tink I go home'.

7   THE SIMULTANEOUS BROADCASTING SYSTEM

The Lines Section in 1927 was headed by A. S. Attkins who, however, left after a breakdown in health in 1928, when V. A. M. Bulow became for a time acting head of the section. In the same year, H. B. Rantzen of Standard Telephones and Cables was recruited to the Lines Section and before long became its head. The performance of the lines, which were still being taken over from the Post Office temporarily when required, has been described as 'appalling'. This was mainly because of poor equalisation of the loss-frequency characteristics and irregularities in them produced by reflections at the terminals. Rantzen approached Eckersley, declaring that the only way to get lines engineering going in the BBC and to improve the bad quality over the SB lines was to spend about £500 on test equipment and add a few more staff to the section. This proposal was accepted and a start was made on line testing, the building of equipment with which to do it, and a study of methods of equalisation. The line network, such as it was, consisted of overhead lines linking a large number of stations. A certain amount of switching was done remotely by connecting dc to the centre points of line repeating coils; this appreciably increased the noise on the lines, but in those days the increase was hardly noticed.

The problem of improving the quality of transmission on the lines was a formidable one because there were so many aspects to be tackled. The most important was the need for equalisation, but there was also the need to persuade the Post Office to offer more uniformly constructed lines; as late as 1929 there were thirteen changes in the type of construction in the programme circuit feeding the 5GB regional transmitter at Daventry. Each change represented a discontinuity in the characteristic impedance of the line and therefore introduced reflections, which, in turn, caused irregularities in the frequency response of the circuit. This state of affairs resulted from the fact that the lines had been designed for telephony; it was too much to expect that they would satisfy the more exacting requirements of programme transmission, which imply some approach to fidelity – as distinct from mere intelligibility. There were many other transmission problems; interference from Post Office carrier telephone systems had to be eliminated by the insertion of suitable filters in the music circuits.

Of hardly less importance than the problem of equalisation was the provision of suitable equipment for measuring the performance of the lines in order to keep them up to standard. Until 1928, when an amplifier-detector was designed, the only instruments for measuring the level of a steady tone were the thermocouple and the valve voltmeter. The thermocouple was slow and tedious to use because of its thermal inertia; it was also expensive and inclined to burn out when a frequency run was being done on an unequalised line with large and unpredictable variations in the measured characteristic. The valve voltmeter was free of these defects, but the readings still had to be converted into decibels to make them practically useful. The amplifier-detector, in association with the oscillators that were designed during this period, made line-testing much quicker and easier. The amplifier-detector could also be used to measure line noise. For this purpose it was often preceded by a weighting network designed to correspond with the frequency-response characteristic of the ear; a performance specification for such a network had been internationally agreed in the CCIF.

Testing equipment was installed permanently at the principal centres, but when line tests had to be made elsewhere a large amount of heavy and cumbersome portable equipment had to be brought, together with the batteries required to operate it.

Attempts were made before the war to provide automatic means for testing the frequency of lines, because conventional methods necessitated taking a number of individual readings and plotting a graph of the response over the whole audio-frequency band. An attempt was made by F. A. Peachey to produce an audio-frequency oscillator that could be driven through the frequency range by a motor working in synchronism with a level recorder at the far end of the line. As heterodyne oscillators were not yet available, it was difficult to achieve the required range of frequencies extending over seven or eight octaves. This was, however, accomplished by using a variable capacitor with extremely long curved plates and driving the vanes of the capacitor through a cam, the contour of which could be pre-set so that the combined effect produced a logarithmic relationship between frequency and angular displacement.

The simplest equaliser comprised essentially a damped tuned circuit connected in parallel with the line. The loss introduced by an equaliser of this type depended on the impedance of the line to which it was connected and was therefore unpredictable. The early work on constant-resistance equalisers in the BBC was based on investigations done in the Bell Laboratories in America. The 'Sullivan' equaliser, previously introduced by A. S. Attkins, had a 'Z' configuration as described in Chapter II, Section 4. The output terminals of the equaliser were connected to the input of the line amplifier, the impedance of which was standardised at 600 ohms and was non-reactive. Even so, the loss introduced by the equaliser was unpredictable, because its input impedance depended on the values of the components in it. It occurred to the engineers of the Lines Section that a simple rearrangement would convert the Sullivan equaliser into a constant-resistance one and that the values of resistance, inductance and capacitance already available in the box would be suitable for this. It was merely necessary to reverse one arm of the equaliser, so that both the capacitative elements were on the line side, one connected to each leg of the line, and the inductive element was connected directly across the input of the amplifier. Then if R_0 is the input resistance of the amplifier, if the total impedance in the series arms of of the equaliser is equivalent to Z_1 in parallel with R_0 and if the impedance in the shunt arm is Z_2, it is merely necessary to make $Z_1 Z_2$ equal to $R_0{}^2$. The input impedance is then equal to the terminating impedance R_0 at all frequencies and the insertion loss of the equaliser at any frequency is independent of the characteristics of the line to which it is connected and is therefore predictable. This was to prove extremely valuable and the introduction of constant-resistance equalisers was an event of far-reaching importance in BBC lines engineering.

By taking measurements of the attenuation-frequency characteristic of the equaliser at every possible setting, a family of curves was obtained; these were plotted on a transparent mask, with an index mark at 100 Hz. The frequency characteristic of the line, without any equaliser, was plotted on graph paper with a logarithmic frequency scale. The mask was then placed over the graph, and the component values required to give the best fit were read off from the mask. This method was extended to a whole range of networks, which could be coupled up to give almost any desired frequency characteristic. It is the basis of methods still in use today, not only in the BBC but also elsewhere. Towards the end of the 1930s the Post Office adopted similar methods.[80]

The theory of transmission lines and iterative networks was somewhat specialised and it was necessary to impart an understanding of the behaviour of the lines and of methods of testing them to the staff at all the stations. An extensive series of data was provided on the attenuation-frequency characteristics of different gauges of non-loaded underground cable circuits and on the expected performance of two new types of loaded cable circuits that were to be provided for the Regional Scheme. Notes on filter design, and a summary of the way in which records of the performance of the SB system were to be kept, were also distributed. The Engineers-in-Charge also received copies of the Lines Section reports on the equalisation of any of the lines in which they were interested. The need for this attempt at keeping staff informed was exemplified by the extremely poor quality radiated by some of the relay stations. Rantzen visited one of these stations and found that all the available equalisers had been connected in parallel across the line that was being used for programme transmission – evidently on the assumption that one cannot have too much of a good thing.

All this work needed staff, and when Rantzen became Head of the Lines Section, with the title of 'Lines Engineer', he began to build up the section by engaging engineers with a knowledge of line transmission. Several of these came, then and later, from Standard Telephones and Cables and the International Standard Electric Corporation.

These engineers recruited from the communications field had to adapt themselves to a world that was different in many ways from that in which they had grown up. In the BBC line communication was subsidiary to the techniques of radio broadcasting and those techniques were themselves ancillary to the production of programmes. Moreover, those who had been accustomed to dealing with fully engineered systems found themselves faced with a miscellany of lines rented from the Post Office, in the planning and design of which they had played no part. This situation demanded a great deal of adaptation and improvisation and often led to results that were far from satisfying the professional consciences of those concerned. A further difficulty they faced was that the technology of line transmission, based on the theory of iterative networks, was already fully developed and used a language different from that of the radio engineers who now surrounded them.

With the coming of the Regional Plan and the increase in broadcasting hours, lines had to be rented permanently instead of being taken over from the Post Office when required. Thus, a permanent SB network was established, comprising both programme lines and control lines.

The distributing centres, or repeater stations, at Leeds and Gloucester have been mentioned in the previous chapter. Gloucester had, in addition to programme amplifiers, a two-wire telephone repeater or 'two-way repeater', as it was called in the BBC. These repeaters were inserted in long control lines to reduce the overall loss. They gave more trouble, in proportion to their importance, than almost any other equipment used by the BBC. This was partly because they employed techniques with which the staff were unfamiliar and partly because they were required to work in conditions that were inherently difficult. This type of repeater depended on the use of balancing networks, which simulated the impedance of the lines on both sides of the repeater. The balancing networks were designed to give the best possible match over the whole frequency range and the gain at which oscillation occurred (the 'singing point') could be calculated from the amount of impedance mis-match on either side. If the balance was poor in any part of the frequency range, the repeater was apt to 'sing' and the gain had to be reduced until the singing stopped. Repeaters of this kind worked well when they were permanently connected between lines having smooth impedance-frequency characteristics, because the balancing networks could be designed to simulate the impedance of the lines fairly closely. With open-wire lines on both sides, it was possible to use a gain of about 20 dB and with loaded cables gains of up to 30 dB were possible. In BBC conditions, however, the repeaters had to be used with a variety of lines, whose impedance-frequency characteristics were often highly irregular, owing to the inhomogeneity of the line construction, and were apt to change from time to time; moreover, the repeater sometimes had to work directly into a local subscriber's line, the impedance of which was variable and uncertain. The best that could be done was to provide a network giving a rough impedance match in average conditions; the gain had then to be adjusted so that the repeater just did not sing and it might or might not be sufficient to be worth while.

Up to 1931 open-wire lines were used for programme transmission. By that time a considerable part of the Post Office network of long-distance telephone lines had been transferred to underground cables. The London-Glasgow telephone cable was already in operation in 1926.[81] To achieve the low attenuation required for long-distance telephone circuits, loading coils were inserted at intervals of 2000 yards. For telephony, two types of circuit were commonly used, one with a cut-off frequency at about 2800 Hz and another, used for long-distance four-wire circuits, with a cut-off frequency at about 4800 Hz. The latter could be used for programme transmission, although the upper audio frequencies were lost and the levels of noise and of crosstalk from other circuits did not satisfy the exacting requirements of broadcasting. The idea of incorporating a screen of metal tape into a cable to separate some of the circuits from others had already been introduced in the Paris–Strasbourg cable, which was brought into service in 1926, but this was for the purpose of reducing interference from telegraph circuits into telephone circuits; it was not until 1931 that circuits specially designed for programme transmission came into use in the United Kingdom.

Special circuits for broadcasting transmission were introduced in some Continental countries (e.g. Denmark) in 1927–8; these achieved the required frequency range by the use of continuous loading in which the inductance of the circuit was increased by wrapping a magnetic material around the conductors (Krarup loading).[82,83]

The report of the Plenary Session of the CCI held in June 1928 already looked forward to the provision of circuits specially designed for broadcast transmission, stating that 'in long-distance cables of the types specified by the CCI, when specially loaded circuits have been reserved for the relaying of broadcasting transmission, it would be possible, both economically and technically, to prescribe for these circuits a cut-off frequency of approximately 10,000 periods per second'.[84]

In the United Kingdom the first cable to include circuits specially designed for programme transmission was between London and Birmingham. Four pairs in the centre of the cable were each separately screened and they were loaded with coils of lower inductance than those used for telephony, so as to raise the upper frequency limit to 8000 Hz, but at the expense of an increase in attenuation. During 1931 these circuits were provided by the Post Office for use by the BBC; during that year circuits of this type were available from London to Leeds and Manchester, as well as from London to Birmingham. Extensions from Leeds to Newcastle and Edinburgh followed in 1932. These screened pairs were of the gauge corresponding to 40 lb per mile (1·27 mm) and were loaded with 15 mH coils at intervals of 2000 yards, with repeaters spaced at about 50 miles. They represented a major improvement in the performance of the SB system, since they could be equalised up to at least 7500 Hz (often 8000 Hz) and, when in proper order, were almost free from noise and crosstalk. They were also much more reliable than open-wire lines.[85,86]

The reliability of the SB system in February 1931, when many open-wire lines were still in use, was such that there were about sixty faults per hundred hours of programme transmitted over the lines. With the introduction of cable circuits the number of faults began to diminish. It was recorded in 1932 that:

'At present many of the lines which the BBC uses are overhead, but the Post Office has an ambitious scheme on hand whereby all lines in the next few years will be carried underground. . . . In the old days underground cables were useless for broadcasting because they had a bad "cut-off". Intelligible speech was all very well, because the lack of frequencies was not very noticeable; but they were hopeless for music. With all the new underground cables there is a repeater station every 40 or 50 miles. There is a rather complicated network of condensers, chokes and resistances in a filter circuit, which keep the tone right.'[87]

There was considerable public interest in these developments. An anonymous author reported that one of the questions he asked on a visit to Savoy Hill was:

'There is still a popular belief that landlines cut off the bass. Is there any truth in this?'

The answer from the SB Engineer was somewhat oblique:

'There is very little difference in quality at the studio end of the amplifiers and at the end of a long SB line. On the latest buried cables we find, on checking up the telephone lines by a howling oscillator, that a level response is now attainable between

50 and 8000 cycles, on a fairly short run. The cut-off does not occur before 7000 cycles, even on a long SB line (buried) from, say, London to Leeds.'[88]

With the growth of the SB system to meet the requirements of the Regional Scheme, the lines engineers became more extended in their efforts to 'keep the tone right' and as a consequence there were more increases in staff. A lines engineer based in Manchester was appointed to serve the North and Scottish Regions and later another was posted to Bristol. Up to the outbreak of war in 1939 it was necessary to do all the checks on the SB system after the close-down of the programmes, which meant that most of the work was done in the middle of the night, in order to get the circuits corrected and handed back in time for the first transmission next day. Lines engineers were not always popular guests at the hotels where they stayed, because of their habit of coming in at about 3 am.

The activities of BBC engineers were sometimes a sore trial to the Post Office. The power-handling capacity of some of the early amplifiers must have permitted the sending of very high levels to line, with evil effects on the neighbouring telephone lines, especially in the open-wire era. In 1930 the Post Office requested the BBC to limit the sending level to 3 to 4 mW, though the method of measurement was not specified and the quantity to be measured was not defined (whether maximum or average power or some other parameter). As volume indicators were still in use in the BBC, the BBC interpreted the requirement to mean that the maximum reading on an instrument indicating the power over about 1/5 s should not exceed 4 mW into a 600-ohm line. This corresponded to a reading of -4 on the volume indicator, and control rooms were asked to work to a maximum reading of -6. Later, the Post Office allowed a maximum level of 5 mW.

The lines to Daventry were particularly important, since it was here that the first tests on the prototype high-power medium-wave transmitter for the Regional Scheme were carried out. It was unfortunate, therefore, that there was crosstalk on the circuits from London that fed 5XX and 5GB with their different programmes. Although the lines were suspected, it was found that the amount of crosstalk arising from them was very small, but there were some unsatisfactory level relationships in the London control room. This incident led to a discussion about quality and line-terminating arrangements generally, including remedies for line noise, such as earthing or not earthing the mid-points of repeating coils. The use of repeating coils, even on programme circuits, seems to have been rather haphazard at first, but in 1930 it was agreed that they should be put in permanently. By the beginning of 1932, the Daventry circuits were transferred to cable, but the new 15-mH loading was not yet available on this route. The two music lines were loaded with 44-mH coils and the frequency range transmitted extended from 50 to 4500 Hz, though in April 1933 it was extended to 5000 Hz, with a variable 'tip-up' of 6, 8 or 10 dB, chosen at will by moving a flexible lead.

During this period there were some changes in line routings. Up to 1932 Gloucester was still feeding Swansea, Plymouth and Birmingham, but Bournemouth had a direct line from London. With the opening of the studio premises in Whiteladies

Road, Bristol, on 18 September 1934, Bristol became the headquarters of the new West Region and the repeater station at Gloucester was given up.

By the middle of 1934 all SB circuits were in underground cable and were permanently rented. The change to cable circuits made it necessary to use equalisers of greater complexity than the simple five-element type derived from the 'Sullivan' equaliser, which could give a maximum slope of only 6 dB per octave. It was necessary to add further sections, sometimes containing resonant arms, but because the equaliser sections were now all of the constant-resistance type the insertion loss of each section could be predicted.

Up to the outbreak of war in 1939 programme lines were rented at a rate of £12 pa per mile; this was the so-called 'tariff E', and was 50 per cent higher than the rate for a telephone private wire. The higher tariff covered not only the extended frequency range obtainable on a music circuit but also a certain amount of 'special' treatment in the maintenance, such as the use of distinguishing markings on fuse-mountings and U-link sockets in Post Office telephone exchanges to avoid the accidental breaking-down of the circuits during operations on neighbouring wires.

The Post Office equalised each repeater section, but the BBC had to insert an equaliser at the receiving end to deal with the frequency response of the 'local ends' at each terminal and with any cumulative deficiencies in the equalising of the repeater sections. The overall response tended to have a dip or a step in the middle of the frequency range and a considerably more complex constant-resistance equaliser (EP/2) was designed to equalise the upper and lower frequencies and those in the middle of the audio range independently. Multi-element equalisers and methods of designing them thus became more and more sophisticated.[89]

In 1936 the Chief Engineer wrote to the Engineer-in-Chief of the Post Office (then Sir Stanley Angwin) in glowing terms about the lightly loaded circuits and expressed the hope that they would come into service on every route when the initial term of five years for the rental of existing circuits ended. The Engineer-in-Chief replied that, as long-distance telephony circuits were being provided in carrier-systems in the future, the Post Office were 'examining methods of providing music circuits in these new circumstances'. They envisaged the use of the frequency band below the carrier-frequency spectrum on the physical pairs of 24-channel carrier telephone systems, the lowest frequency required by the telephone system being 12 kHz. Such a circuit was, in fact, taken over during the early months of the war.

With the introduction of loaded cables for programme transmission, the question of phase distortion had to be considered. On the longer circuits, such as those from London to Scotland, the effects of phase distortion on transients were occasionally noticeable. The transmission time over some of these circuits probably exceeded the limits fixed by the CCIF in 1936: 70 ms at 50 Hz and 10 ms at 6400 Hz. However, it was not considered that the distortion was sufficiently serious to justify the installation of expensive phase-correcting networks.

In many of these activities the Post Office, as the sole agency authorised to provide lines for all communication purposes, naturally played a large part. Generally speaking, when engineers on each side were dealing with one another, they found

M

that they spoke the same language and relations were cordial – as they have been ever since. Post Office engineers would always help to the best of their ability, often going 'beyond the rule-book' in order to provide some special facility. There were, however, many troubles on the lines, even after most of them had been put into cables. The Post Office staff, being accustomed to providing a telephone service, did not always seem to appreciate the impact that a line fault could have on a programme for which the audience might run into millions. Their main preoccupation was, necessarily, with communication services rendered to the general public, and at the beginning it was difficult for their staff in the stations up and down the country to master the very different requirements of programme circuits. The state of affairs changed during the war, when there were many occasions on which all kinds of services were provided with great speed and with minimum formality, often without written confirmation until long after. By 1938 the average number of faults on the line network had already been reduced to less than one per hundred hours of transmission.[90]

In 1936 there seems to have been the first suggestion, from the Post Office side, that it might be a good thing to eliminate the sending and receiving repeaters on Post Office premises at the terminal offices of the circuits and substitute amplifiers and equalisation at BBC centres. This suggestion was adopted and the policy has been maintained ever since.

Among the miscellaneous activities to which a considerable amount of attention was devoted just before the war was the use of tone for synchronising transmitters. To enable transmitters to radiate on the same carrier frequency, the carriers had to be almost identical in frequency; otherwise serious deterioration in reception would occur over wide areas. At that time the drive equipment was not sufficiently precise to enable the transmitters to run independently. It was therefore decided to try to link them by sending a tone over rented telephone lines and to multiply the frequency of this tone by a factor of 2^{10} at the far end of the line to produce the carrier frequency for the local transmitter. Unfortunately the phase stability of the lines was inadequate and this introduced a new and highly undesirable feature into the programmes, the so-called 'door-bangs'. When the phase on the line suddenly shifted, the carrier frequency shifted a great deal more because of the multiplication of frequency, and quite a loud bang was heard by all listeners to those transmissions, particularly those on the edge of the service area of any one station. A considerable improvement was made by using a tuning fork as a filter to reduce the 'door-bangs' and to provide momentary continuity of the drive if there was a break in the line.

Arrangements were also made for a local tuning fork (of which the frequency was accurately maintained by manual adjustment and later by automatic means), to be switched rapidly into circuit if the incoming tone failed. It was later decided to transmit the tone over the music circuits; these were much more stable than telephone lines and their use would avoid the cost of renting lines exclusively for transmitting the tone. A great deal of work was done to cut a narrow notch in the frequency band of the music circuit in which a tone at a high audio-frequency could be transmitted. Equipment was installed for the synchronisation of various groups of transmitters and experiments were made; a satisfactory degree of synchronisation was achieved, but another difficulty arose. The tone intermodulated with the music and caused a certain roughness in some programmes. Attempts were made to mitigate this effect, but by that time sufficiently accurate drive equipment became available to enable the stations to work independently.

Although programme transmission demanded the most attention, since the business of the BBC was to broadcast programmes, steps had to be taken to fulfil the demand, both from Engineering and from Administration Departments, for better telephone communication between Head Office and the studio centres and transmitting stations. Trunk calls were expensive, and attempts were made to exploit more efficiently the existing control lines rented on a permanent basis between control rooms in the SB system. These were intended for passing service messages about the programmes or about technical matters, and for use when clearing technical faults and when testing the programme lines. Many of the messages concerning these matters were short, but they were almost always urgent. The control lines were lightly loaded, in terms of actual duration of use, and there was plenty of line time available for other purposes. By 1935 it was becoming a common practice to leave control lines connected through to PBX switchboards at each end of the line; a voice-frequency receiving device sensitive to a continuous tone of 700 Hz was bridged across the line between the control room and the PBX switchboard, so that it would respond to such a tone sent from a distant PBX. Tone at this frequency would not affect the normal control room 17-Hz ringing relay, nor would the 17-Hz ringing current affect a distant 700-Hz receiver. In the first 'Ring Receive Panel' (RR/1), the tuned circuit at the input was not effective enough as a guard against voltages of other frequencies operating the device, and there was a considerable amount of trouble from this cause. Moreover, speech components at frequencies near 700 Hz could also cause false operation of the panel, and it was soon realised that what was needed was something that would inhibit the panel when there was a 700-Hz component in the presence of other frequencies. A problem of a different kind was that there were frequent complaints from the switchboard operators that the line would be taken without warning by the control room for urgent messages. To remedy some of these difficulties the Ring Receive Panel circuit was modified to include a negative dc feedback element, which would be active in the presence of frequencies not around 700 Hz, but overborne by the positive feedback circuit when only 700 Hz was present.

The control-line system was composed of individual links between adjacent BBC centres and it became more and more necessary to have telephonic communication between distant stations. Attempts were made to link up control lines in tandem, but the overall losses were often so high that communication over the whole circuit was practically impossible unless means could be found for inserting gain somewhere in the circuit. The two-wire repeater previously mentioned had been designed in the BBC, but was not a great success. When Dr A. R. A. Rendall (later Head of Designs Department) joined the BBC, he realised that the problem of designing networks to simulate the line impedance at all frequencies within the transmitted bandwidth would be greatly eased if the bandwidth were reduced. Perhaps BBC engineers had

had exaggerated ideas about the bandwidth needed for telephony, because they had long been accustomed to the transmission of music. The repeater was improved on these lines and it was decided to test the feasibility of installing cord-circuit repeaters in several control rooms. Impedance-frequency runs were made on the control lines and many of them had smooth enough characteristics to permit gains up to 10 dB to be given by the repeater: on some circuits a gain of only about 3 or 4 dB could be hoped for. Some repeaters were put in, though not in cord-circuits and some worthwhile improvements were achieved; but the repeaters were regarded as a nuisance by the engineers, who had to adjust the gain according to which particular two lines were being interconnected. They tended to leave the gain of the repeater permanently set to suit the worst combination of control lines. It was proposed to provide for the automatic insertion of the repeaters by switching from the sleeves of the cord-circuits and for the adjustment of the gain by means of attenuator pads as required; indeed it was intended to give the PBX operators a similar facility to enable them to insert the repeaters themselves when required. This plan was never carried out, because the war was imminent. In a sense, this was fortunate because developments in the line network during the war, notably the introduction of carrier phantom circuits as programme circuits, made it possible for a far better communication system to be developed after the war.

One may ask why, in view of the unsatisfactory state of inter-office telephonic communication and the need to economise in trunk calls, no use was made of teleprinters or any other form of telegraphy, especially as there was hardly a station where there were no former wireless operators. This was suggested in 1938, but was rejected because it was thought that the improvement over existing facilities would not justify the operational complications.

One of the less successful attempts, though an interesting one, to improve telephonic communication was the installation of a 'voice-operated' repeater in the Newcastle control room. This was a two-wire repeater which had been developed by STC for use in situations where it was difficult to obtain a good impedance balance. It used the same principles as a relay-operated echo-suppressor. The idea was that the speech of the person talking operated a switch in the repeater which gave him a through path, and he could go on talking until the other party interrupted. Conversely, when the other party was talking he held the line in the same way. In this way the repeater gain was suppressed in the direction in which transmission was not taking place, so that 'singing' could not occur. In this particular case, the repeater was not a success. Although the operating time of the relays was very short (probably not more than 10 ms), there was nevertheless some clipping of the initial syllables of words, which proved disconcerting to the listening party. Another difficulty was ambient noise in the rooms where the telephones were located; the main purpose of putting this repeater into the Newcastle control room was to enable Stagshaw to talk to Head Office in London, but Stagshaw was a transmitting station and the high ambient noise there was sufficient to hold the line against the attempts of the London speaker to break in. Such problems illustrate the fact that in some ways telephone transmission is more difficult than programme transmission, because

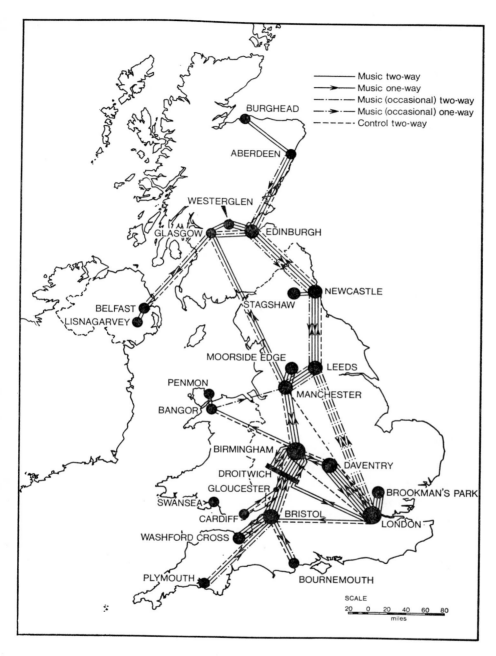

SB Line Network (1938)

of the need to transmit simultaneously in both directions. The war brought to an end for the time being nearly all these adventures in telephone communication but they had nevertheless provided the engineers concerned with much useful experience in the problems peculiar to the BBC system, and this was turned to good account later.

The extent of the SB system near the beginning of the period under review may be compared with that near the end of it. The lines that were available in 1927 were all open-wire lines and were taken over only when required for programme purposes, which was normally from 5.30 pm. This network was required to feed one main programme plus the new alternative programme then being broadcast experimentally from the 5GB transmitter at Daventry. All the other transmitting stations and relay stations were the same as they were when the Corporation took them over from the Company. By June 1938 the SB system had reached the stage shown on p. 167. The Regional Scheme had by then been put into operation; Bristol had become the headquarters of the West Region, Gloucester BBC Repeater Station had been given up, the long-wave station had been moved to Droitwich, the Empire Service had been instituted at Daventry, and the west-coast route had been taken over between Manchester and Glasgow. Most of the lines were permanently rented and they were in underground cables; the SB network comprised 4000 miles of programme circuits and 2200 miles of control lines.[90]

During this period several controversies reached an international level. One concerned the question whether the equaliser should be inserted at the sending end or the receiving end of the line. If it were put at the sending end there would be some degree of 'pre-emphasis', which could be useful if the line noise was predominantly at the upper end of the frequency range. On the other hand, this practice could result in excessive crosstalk to other circuits and the overloading of repeaters, because the input power could be excessive at the higher frequencies. It was much more convenient to put the equaliser at the receiving end, where it could be adjusted during frequency-response tests by the engineer making the measurements.

Another dispute, which occasioned long discussions in the CCIF and the UIR, concerned the choice between the 'constant voltage' and 'constant EMF' methods of measurement. In the constant voltage method, the output of the oscillator at the sending end was adjusted so that the voltage across the line input, when measured by an amplifier-detector, was constant at all frequencies. In the constant EMF method, the oscillator had a constant known output impedance and its EMF was constant at all frequencies. The constant voltage method had the advantage that the measurement at the line input could be made easily with an amplifier-detector and the result was independent of the peculiarities of the oscillator, but the oscillator output had to be constantly adjusted. With improvements in the design of oscillators, the constant EMF method won the day.

Still another controversy concerned the unit of attenuation. For some years the recognised unit had been the 'mile of standard cable'. This was based on the attenuation of a defined type of cable circuit at 800 Hz. Unfortunately, the American MSC differed from the English MSC by just over 2 per cent. Efforts to find a more scientific unit resulted in two conflicting proposals:

168

1 The βl unit, subsequently known as the Neper.
2 The transmission unit (TU), subsequently named the decibel (dB).

The number of units representing a given power ratio was $\frac{1}{2} \log_e P_1/P_2$ Nepers or $10 \log_{10} P_1/P_2$ decibels. The name βl unit derived from the fact that the propagation constant of a cable circuit was expressed as $\beta + j\alpha$ per unit of length (although, to add to the confusion, it was sometimes expressed as $\alpha + j\beta$). Conversion tables had to be used showing the relationship between TUs, βl units, American MSCs, English MSCs, and the corresponding power ratios and current ratios.

The abbreviation for decibel used in the BBC was originally dB, but for a long period db was preferred, and the choice finally settled on dB in the 1960s. In such matters the BBC tries to conform with BSI recommendations, which are in turn co-ordinated with IEC recommendations.

8 OUTSIDE BROADCASTS

Like almost everything else, outside broadcasting was expanding when the Corporation took over from the Company in 1927, though the possibilities were still restricted by the limited facilities available in the Post Office line network; the great expansion of their underground cable system had not yet begun. Moreover, as in the SB system, the absence of proper equalising methods and the lack of understanding at that time of the principles of line transmission meant that the quality of OB transmissions received over any but very short distances was very poor. It was, in fact, difficult to make any quantitative assessment of the performance of a line because the only measuring instruments were thermocouples and valve voltmeters.

Reference has already been made to the building up of a group of staff with knowledge of the ways in which the available lines could be used for programme transmission, and their activities were encouraged by the attitude of Gerald Cock, later to be the first Director of Television, who was head of the OB department. He believed in the value of immediate, live broadcasts, as opposed to recorded material that was already 'dead'. As a result of this attitude, the OB Department pressed more and more strongly for immediate access to all important events. This meant that the studio side of the Operations and Maintenance Department and the Lines Section had to build up an organisation prepared to go anywhere at any time to rig up microphones and amplifiers and to take over, test and equalise the lines put at their disposal by the Post Office. Close contact was established very soon between the OB Department and the Lines Section with the object of expanding as quickly and as cheaply as possible the range from which OBs could be taken. At the end of the 1920s only a few hundred lines were available for OBs over the whole country, but by 1939 it was possible to broadcast from any of about 10,000 OB points, through one or other of the studio centres. In the year 1939 there were about 5000 sound OBs.

Until 1927 the BBC was not permitted to give running commentaries on sporting events, because of objections by the Press. Broadcasts of such events were limited to

169

such things as the sound of horses' hooves coming round Tattenham Corner on Derby Day.[91] In January 1927, however, the BBC was given freedom to broadcast running commentaries and eye-witness accounts.[92] The first broadcast of an event actually in progress was a commentary on the England versus Wales rugby match at Twickenham at the beginning of January. At sporting events generally, it was necessary to insulate the commentator from the public; a specification was issued for a commentators' hut made in sections and lined with sound-absorbing material and with a wide glass panel in front. The hut was about 6 ft by 5 ft and, though reasonably comfortable during the rugger season, could become uncomfortably hot during the tennis championships at Wimbledon.

It was not always easy to set up a commentators' hut: in Glasgow, where its first use was at the Rangers' ground at Ibrox Park, the hut sections had to be hauled up into the Press Box, which was nothing more than a large area at the top of the main stand. The hut cut out most of the noise from the crowd, so that to create 'atmosphere' it was necessary to provide a separate microphone for it. At a Rugby Union match a Reisz microphone, used for the effects, was slung from one of the stanchions supporting the roof of the stand. The microphone cable was armoured and the armouring was earthed to the stanchion – probably not very effectively. The amplifier used on this occasion was of a new BBC design incorporating a 'tone' circuit, the main effect of which was to alter the frequency range of the amplifiers when capacitors were plugged in. During testing for this OB, very strong Morse signals were picked up by the amplifier, but were eliminated by altering the tone circuit. Later designs, however, omitted this refinement.

One of the most impressive OBs of the pre-war period was the first broadcast of the Oxford and Cambridge Boat Race in 1927. To permit a commentary to be given from the launch *Magician* following the race, it was necessary to develop a mobile radio link. A transmitter was built at Savoy Hill by the Development Section to a circuit developed by H. L. Kirke. It was authorised to operate on a wavelength of 120 m and caused trouble while it was being tested because the rf was rectified by metalwork in the building and the modulation was induced into the telephone lines, making telephone conversations impossible. Two receiving points were set up for the radio link, one at the house of Mr Kenyon Secretan at Castelnau, Barnes – about a hundred yards or so on the Barnes side of Hammersmith Bridge – and the other at the Radio Communication Company's works in High Street, Barnes. The operation was not without practical difficulties; on going to see the preparations on the previous day, the Chief Engineer had to be carried pick-a-back to the launch by a waterman because the tide was out and the mud was exposed. Nevertheless, the broadcast was successful and became an annual event.

Apart from London, the Region that was most active in producing OBs was the North Region. There was a large OB unit of thirty staff in Manchester, and any kind of broadcast could be done without assistance from other areas. The opening of the Mersey Tunnel by King George V was an example of this. Technical requirements had to be subordinate to the King's desire that the microphone should not be seen; a Reisz microphone was mounted underneath a hole in the top of the table at which he was to stand and the hole was disguised with gold braid. The acoustics were still further jeopardised when the King placed a page of his speech over the microphone.

Improvisation found even greater scope in outside broadcasts than in more static areas of BBC work. At a broadcast of Henry Hall's dance band in the Gleneagles Hotel, crystal dishes were borrowed from the hotel's dining-room to augment the sound produced by the small orchestra. In sartorial matters, however, improvisation was taboo: OB engineers had to wear dinner jackets at evening functions.

In 1932 Broadcasting House, London, had become the headquarters and the main studio centre, and it was then possible for King George V's Christmas Message to be the climax of a 'Round-the-Empire' Christmas Day programme, contributions from different parts of the world being mixed on the new dramatic control panel. This introduced the idea of 'Royal' transmissions, in which special precautions were taken to avoid breakdown. For the broadcasts from Sandringham, which were to continue for many years afterwards, there were two or three lines on different routes, each repeatered at two or three intermediate points. If there were three routes, all three were tested through to the control room the day before the transmission; the two better routes were selected on the morning of the Royal broadcast and extended to the dc panel. The better of these two routes was then used for the start of the broadcast, with the other one available on the dc panel so that the producer could 'roll over' to it if need be. These precautions were essential because the open-wire lines were susceptible to storm damage and, at this time of the year, to loss of insulation caused by fog deposit on the insulators. These troubles could crop up without warning, but they never prevented the broadcast from being carried out.

Another OB of considerable importance as well as technical difficulty was the *Everyman* play from the church at Marazion near The Lizard in Cornwall. This went on for some years during the thirties, and had to be repeatered at two or three points in Cornwall on its way to Plymouth, where it entered the cable system. This OB was sometimes particularly difficult because in the early days of its history the lines from Marazion to Plymouth were entirely on open wire. The two lines were identical, so that if the programme line failed for any reason the control line could be used for the programme. On one occasion both lines were entirely satisfactory until one minute before the broadcast was to begin, when they both went completely dead. As there was then no means of communication between the church and the outside world, nothing could be done. A few seconds before the starting time both lines miraculously came good, and there was no further trouble. It was suspected that there had been sabotage by members of an ultra-protestant organisation against what they considered were the popish practices going on in the church, but it was subsequently found that the pole route carrying the local circuits also carried the telephone line to the vicarage. One of the wires of this telephone line had broken and wrapped itself round the other two pairs; a fortunate gust of wind at the right moment restored both circuits, thus simultaneously clearing the fault and the low-church party.

This was the era of 'great events', which it was the duty and pride of the BBC to bring live to the people. Even if the BBC had been appropriately equipped, recordings would not have been acceptable – the commentator had to be *there* and the listener had to hear what was happening, not what had already happened a few hours ago. Apart from the Christmas broadcasts of King George V already referred to, one of the early royal occasions was the wedding, on 29 November 1934, of Prince George, Duke of Kent, and Princess Marina of Greece in Westminster Abbey. The ceremony was broadcast throughout the world; J. H. Holmes remembers hearing it clearly in Bucharest.

One of the first, probably the first, funeral OB that the BBC broadcast was that of Lord Carson in St Anne's Cathedral, Belfast, on 26 October 1935. Not only was it broadcast nation-wide, but loudspeakers carried the ceremony to the crowd outside the Cathedral. The BBC had already shown itself capable of handling great occasions with efficiency and dignity, and although the arrangements had to be made in a hurry, they were successful. The OB was carried out entirely by engineers – there was no time for the programme people to bring their stop-watches to bear on it and to demand complicated refinements. A screen was built for the mixers by the west door of the Cathedral, and there was no compromise about the position of the microphones; they had now become a part of life and must be accepted, not hidden away. There was even a microphone over the grave, and 'ashes to ashes, dust to dust' could clearly be heard, with the shovelling of the gravel. The only recorded complaint was that the BBC engineers were not suitably dressed for the occasion.

The BBC was soon to have more experience of organising funeral broadcasts. In the following month, on 25 November 1935, there was the funeral of Admiral of the Fleet Earl Jellicoe in St Paul's Cathedral; on 28 January 1936 there was the funeral of King George V; on 16 March, that of Admiral of the Fleet Earl Beatty in St Paul's Cathedral; on 19 May, that of Field-Marshal Viscount Allenby in Westminster Abbey.

Royal events were many during these years. The Silver Jubilee of King George V and Queen Mary had taken place in 1935, and there were separate reviews, during the summer, of the Fleet, the Army and the Royal Air Force. The King died in January of the following year, and there were all the customary Accession Proclamations for King Edward VIII. At the end of the year, there was the Abdication of the new King, and the Proclamations of his successor, King George VI. The most complicated OB of the period was naturally the Coronation on 12 May 1937. It must have strained the resources of the BBC almost to their limit, especially as some of the available effort had to be diverted to the televising of the procession at Apsley Gate, Hyde Park. The technical arrangements were described in detail by R. T. B. Wynn in *World Radio* at the time.[93, 94]

In addition to the great events, however, the BBC OB engineers of the time were able to take their microphones and OB amplifiers to an enormous variety of places of less spectacular, but no less real, interest: a youth hostel at Ludlow, a lambing-pen on the Wiltshire downs, a midnight bowling match at Thurso, the Eton Wall Game, a London sewer, a gipsy encampment, the Royal Mint, fly-fishing, village cricket, a haunted house, Cruft's Dog Show, a diver under Waterloo Bridge, and the maiden voyage of the *Queen Mary*.

The very large number of OBs that were done annually required a great deal of equipment and the deployment of much skill and enterprise by the OB engineering teams in all the Regions, aided on the communications side by the OB section of the Lines Department and by lines engineers in the Regions. In those days the Post Office did not undertake to insert amplifiers in the lines from the OB points to the studio centres; the BBC Lines Department had to order the necessary lines from the Post Office (sometimes after much discussion about their availability and suitability, permissible times for testing, etc.) and to ensure that the transmission levels along the lines were within the limits that would permit satisfactory quality and freedom from noise. If necessary portable repeaters, incorporating equalisers, had to be taken (either by train or in the Lines Engineer's car) to a Post Office exchange or repeater station along the route. Much pride was taken in reliability and the lines equipment was always sent out in duplicate: two repeaters, two lt batteries, two ht batteries, the only exceptions being the portable telephone set and, before it was incorporated into the repeater itself, the 'line volume meter' – an early programme meter in portable battery-operated form. The earlier forms of the portable repeater were housed in teak boxes of stout construction, and the ht batteries, each of 200 V, were also strongly crated. A portable equaliser-repeater, PER/2, was in use from about 1930 until it was superseded in 1938 by the PER/3. The PER/2 employed triodes, two of which were indirectly heated, and had a simple constant-resistance equaliser, the series arm of which consisted of a capacitor in parallel with a resistor. The PER/3 was more ambitious, and contained three variable equalisers in an 'equaliser unit', the different sections of which could be brought into operation by the removal of insulating plugs from a series of jacks. Three directly-heated valves were used in the 'amplifier unit', and a fourth operated a built-in peak programme meter which, by means of another jack used as a switch, was made to serve also as a feed meter. A 'line change-over unit' formed the third section of the repeater, and contained various jacks, keys and terminals to enable rapid interchanges of line to be made and to provide for connecting the telephone and the check phones.[95] The whole repeater was mounted in a fibre box and, although it was, in flexibility and facilities, an un-doubted advance on the previous repeater, it nevertheless had its drawbacks; the case, though light, was somewhat pliable and caused wiring faults, and the jacks that served to switch the various equaliser settings suffered from bad contacts at times, no doubt through being normally open, i.e. with an insulating plug inserted.

By far the greater proportion of OBs were fed by line into the appropriate studio centre. Occasionally, where this was not possible, the Post Office would permit the BBC to use a radio link of its own. Permission had to be sought on each occasion. Sometimes, too, a Post Office radio circuit would be used, as for the opening by Walter Elliott of the telephone link from the Outer Hebrides to the mainland in the late 1930s. The route for this was through a BBC repeater at Tobermory on the Island of Mull, which was the terminal of the radio link, a line to Oban, where there was another BBC repeater, and a line from Oban to Glasgow.

Comprehensive line tests had to be made from each OB point to the studio centre and much heavy and bulky equipment with accumulators for the filament supplies and dry batteries for the ht supplies had to be taken to the OB point. Naturally the transport of the apparatus by car to remote parts of the country resulted in wiring faults, so a repair outfit had to be taken as well. Line testing included the origination of variable-frequency test tone at a standard level at the OB end of a line, and for this purpose various designs of portable audio-frequency oscillator were produced by Lines Department during the period under review. Some of them were of the heterodyne type.[96] In addition to taking loss-frequency characteristics on each section of line between amplifiers and working out appropriate settings of the variable equalisers at the repeater points and the terminal control room, it was necessary to make noise measurements, and dc tests of the insulation, loop resistance and resistance unbalance. Line noise could be troublesome and much effort was sometimes spent in locating the source of it, although the dc tests sometimes gave a good indication. It was not always easy to persuade the Post Office to take steps to reduce the noise sufficiently to satisfy the BBC's requirements, which were more severe than those of their other customers. A particularly troublesome source of noise was the teleprinter system operated by the Post Office, and it was often extremely difficult to find the offending circuit, which might be transmitting only intermittently.

Many OBs were done on open-wire lines, especially in the early part of this period, though in the neighbourhood of a BBC centre in a town or city the circuits were usually underground, probably in either 40-lb (1·27 mm) or 20-lb (0·89 mm) 'bunched pairs'. Bunched pairs, indeed, were a great stand-by in the provision of lines for OBs. The Post Office telephone system had developed very greatly during the early thirties, and much of it used loaded pairs in cables. The loaded pairs had a sharp cut-off at about 3000 Hz and therefore could not be used for programme transmission. The cables were laid up in 'quads', or groups of four wires, and these quads could be formed in two ways. In the 'multiple-twin' construction, two twisted pairs were in turn twisted around one another to form the quad; a 'phantom' circuit could be derived from the two pairs and was also loaded. In the 'star-quad' cable, the four wires were twisted continuously in one spiral. The advantage of the star-quad was that it took up much less room in the cable than the older multiple-twin quad, but phantom circuits were not used on it by the Post Office because of the high attenuation resulting from the high mutual capacitance between conductors. The BBC could, however, make good use of phantom circuits on the star-quads, because they were not loaded and therefore had no cut-off frequency and could be equalised to cover the whole frequency range needed for programme transmission. They were put at the BBC's disposal by the Post Office by simply bunching the two wires of each pair together and treating each of the pairs as one leg of the line to be extended to the BBC. The bunching had the effect of cancelling out the inductance of the loading-coils in the side circuits almost entirely, although there were some routes where the balance of the windings of the loading-coils was not exact and some residual inductance was left; this tended to lower the upper frequency limit of the transmission. The range achievable by, for example, a 20-lb bunched pair circuit without a repeater was about 15 miles, depending upon the amount of noise on the line.[97]

At the OB point the essential equipment, apart from the microphones, was an amplifier of sufficient gain to raise the low-level output from the microphone to a suitable value for sending to line. Other components included mixers, monitoring facilities and telephones. The microphones used for OBs in the early days of the Corporation's existence were of the same type as those used in the studios, and it is apparent from many contemporary photographs that the Reisz carbon microphone was a familiar part of the outside broadcast scene up to at least the mid-thirties. When the BBC version of the RCA ribbon microphone was introduced, however, it quickly displaced the Reisz even at OB points. The type B ribbon microphone, introduced in 1937, in which aluminium-nickel-cobalt was used for the magnet instead of cobalt-steel, was smaller and more convenient for OBs.[98, 99]

The first amplifiers used for OBs were the Western Electric type 8A and a small two-valve Western Electric loudspeaker amplifier. The former was used for the first OB, from Covent Garden, on 8 January 1923. Special OB amplifiers, types 1 and 1 A, were introduced, the latter giving a choice of input impedance. In 1936 the staff in Belfast designed two OB amplifiers of their own, called BE/1 and BE/2. The latter had properly decoupled stages, giving a gain of 90 dB with an output at a level of + 20 dB. These amplifiers were frowned upon because they were non-standard, but they appear to have worked very well. Modified designs succeeded one another rapidly, and it was always necessary to compromise between portability and versatility. At the end of the twenties the Marconi type GA2 had, in its final form, three 2-V directly heated valves with transformers at the input and output, and resistance-capacitance intervalve coupling. The valves had an extraordinarily inflated appearance because, to reduce microphony, the glass envelope of the valve itself was enclosed in an outer glass envelope, rubber packing being inserted between the two. This amplifier weighed 19 lb; terminals were provided for the microphone and a fade unit, and there was a 6-V supply terminal wired directly to another terminal on the input side of the panel to provide feed current for a Reisz microphone. The fade unit was a variable resistance connected in parallel with the primary of the input transformer of the amplifier. Other types of amplifier soon followed, each type of studio amplifier being designated by a letter to denote its purpose, and a number to signify a change in design, while OB amplifiers were numbered with a digit to denote purpose and a letter to signify change in design. The type 6 amplifier of about 1928 had four stages. The gain was 76 dB, the input and output impedance were 253 ohms and 106 ohms respectively and the amplifier could deliver a maximum output level of +4 dB. The type 1A OB amplifier was also a four-stage amplifier; it had resistance-capacitance coupling and there was a microphone equaliser between the first and second stages; this could be cut in or out by means of a key. With the equaliser cut out, the gain into 600 ohms was approximately 76 dB; the input impedance was 330 ohms and the output impedance 250 ohms. The type 1B amplifier, designed in 1935 for use with the ribbon microphone, also had four stages, giving a gain of 96 dB at 1 kHz. This amplifier seems to have had a rising frequency characteristic, and when a Reisz microphone was used a silk covering had to be placed over it to compensate for this. From now on, output impedances were low; in the 1B amplifier the input impedance was 300 ohms and the output impedance 80–85 ohms. Both these amplifiers had total ht feeds of about 28 mA. The type 5B amplifier introduced in 1936/7

175

was a modification of an earlier type 5 dating back to 1927/8, the circuit being similar to that of type 1B; it had an input impedance of 250 ohms and an output impedance of 114 ohms, with a gain of 89 dB. The type 5B weighed 50 lb, as compared with 37 lb for type 1B.

By the mid-thirties there was a need for OB amplifier equipment to be standardised and modernised. Operations at OB points were hampered by the cumbersome equipment, with the massive boxes of batteries needed to supply several stages of triode valves. To improve the overall frequency response, lines engineers specified that a 50-ohm shunt should be bridged across the line at the sending end, while still requiring a sending level of + 4 dB to line. This meant that there were occasions when other amplifiers, normally non-portable, had to be taken out as well, with still more, and larger, batteries to achieve the specified output level. It was decided that a standard OB amplifier should be designed as successor to all the different types then in use. Engineers of Research Department visited OB sites and talked to OB engineers about the requirements, so that they could appreciate the practical conditions of operation and the shortcomings of existing equipment. A number of meetings were held between the Research Department and Designs Section and the specification for the new amplifier was issued in July 1934. The result was the OBA/7, which was intended to operate either from batteries or from an engine-driven generator. It was not a success. The specification turned out to be unrealistic in important respects; for instance, although it included thirteen different requirements, it did not place any limitations on weight or size. Moreover, it was based on a distrust of mains supplies, although by that time such supplies were available at most OB sites.

In 1935 R. T. B. Wynn was appointed Senior Superintendent Engineer and thus became head of operations and maintenance. He immediately realised that a new approach was needed and he succeeded in getting the OBA/7 written-off after a very short life and wrote a specification for a new OB amplifier (OBA/8) himself. It was required to be mains-driven, but with facilities for switching over to batteries (of which there need be only one set), and for volume control at the OB point. Hitherto, the control of the dynamic range of OBs had been done at the studio centre, although it is now obvious that, since the object of the control is to keep the volume between the upper limit that can be handled without distortion and the lower limit required to maintain a satisfactory signal-to-noise ratio, the control should be effected as early as possible in the transmission chain and certainly before the OB line. However, the staff at the studio centres were skilled in effecting the control and were accustomed to performing this function for all programmes originated in their territory, whether from the studios or from OBs. The decision to transfer the control to the OB point thus represented a break with tradition, but was fully justified on technical grounds.

Meanwhile, H. L. Kirke, Head of the Research Department, had made up his mind that some work ought to be done on the fundamentals of amplifier design. A. E. Barrett, who was already in charge of the microphone and recording sections of Research Department, was given the task of setting up an audio amplifier section. Work was started on circuit techniques, but was not at first directly related to the

OBA/8. The Research Department set about the design of a new series of transformers, including a 30:1 input transformer, a study of the AC/SP3 valve (which became available in 1938), and the design of a special negative feedback circuit. These and other advances in design made it possible to produce an amplifier with only two stages that fulfilled the specification for the OBA/8, and they were in fact applied to it.

The design of the OBA/8 was greatly facilitated by the appearance of the AC/SP3 valve, which was a high-gain pentode developed by the Cosmos Lamp Works specially for the BBC. It was doubtful whether it would be available in sufficient quantities and H. S. Walker, Head of Valve Section, took the initiative in committing the BBC to buy 600 of the new valves before a price had been agreed through the proper channels. This unauthorised action naturally provoked criticism, but it had far-reaching consequences that proved to be of great value. The OBA/8 was a great success, not only for its original purpose but for equipping war-time control rooms and for dealing with many emergencies that arose during the war.

The circuit design was done by Research Department and the production engineering by Equipment Department. Apart from the use of pentodes instead of triodes, the amplifier had several novel features including the use of the same type of valve throughout (so that spares of only one type need be carried) and, when operating on mains supply, the use of ac for all the valve heaters (even in the first stage, which worked directly from the microphone output). Resistance-capacity coupling was used between the two stages, with transformers at the input and output.[100, 101] An important advantage was that the OBA/8 amplifier weighed only 35 lb compared with 62 lb for the OBA/7. The first set was completed by Equipment Department in the spring of 1938. Forty sets were ordered, at about £270 per set, and by May 1939 thirty-three were in service. Some OBA/8 equipments are still in use, thirty-four years after the first was commissioned.

The total gain of the amplifier was 97 dB, but this was reduced to 91 dB by the use of negative feedback to reduce linearity distortion. The equipment incorporated an equaliser to offset the slight fall in response of the ribbon microphone at the upper audio frequencies. Without the equaliser the gain was constant within $\pm$ 0.5 dB from 30 Hz to 10 kHz when working into a load of 75 ohms. Great care was taken to ensure that the equipment would be easily portable and easily stacked for transport; the components were chosen so as to reduce weight and the chassis, the front panels and the screening covers were all of aluminium. The input impedance was 300 ohms, the output impedance 75 ohms, and the maximum output power + 14 dB with reference to 1 mW. The harmonic distortion was about 1 per cent at peak output and the noise level 54 dB below peak output. The amplifiers and mains units were duplicated to guard against breakdown and the complete equipment for an OB also comprised a four-channel mixer, a loudspeaker unit containing its own amplifier, lt and ht batteries, a programme meter and a communication unit for operating the cue lights. A pre-amplifier was also designed for use when the operator had to work in a position remote from the main amplifier. This was provided with a volume control and a programme meter; it had a gain of 30 dB between the mixer and the main amplifier. The equipment could be mounted on a rack when required, the connections being brought out to a row of contacts at the rear so as to facilitate the removal of a unit for inspection or repair.

As there were occasions when only one line was available from an OB point for both programme and control purposes, the Lines Department designed a small portable carrier system to permit telephone communication over the circuit without affecting the programme signal. A set of splitting filters divided the available frequency range at 6000 Hz, and the lower part was used for the programme, the portion above 6000 Hz being set apart for communication purposes. Communication had to take place in 'simplex' fashion, one direction at a time, and was effected on one sideband of the carrier. This equipment could be used on non-repeatered open-wire lines or on short lengths of cable.

9 RECORDING

Recording was a relatively late starter among broadcasting techniques. This was not for want of enterprise on the part of the BBC, nor was it due to any lack of incentive; the reason was simply that no really practical recording equipment was available until 1930. The making of gramophone records was already an established industry, but the process was complicated and altogether unsuitable for use in the BBC, where it was essential that the recording should be available for playback almost immediately after it had been made. As early as 1925 the BBC had followed up Stille's invention of the magnetic recorder. In 1927 Reith told the Board that close touch was being kept with developments in the recording field. This was said in the context of Empire broadcasting – the experimental transmissions from 5SW Chelmsford were to start that year. Certainly the need above all others that spurred the BBC to introduce sound recording was the launching of the Empire Service, with its programmes largely derived from the national and regional output and repeated to each time zone in turn.

When it did finally emerge at the beginning of the 1930s recording in the BBC developed along three distinct lines – the Blattnerphone (and its successor the Marconi-Stille system), direct disc recording and the Philips-Miller system. In the account that follows, these three strands will be followed through to the outbreak of war.

The origins of the Blattnerphone go back to the beginning of the century when Valdemar Poulsen demonstrated his Telegraphone at the Paris Universal Exhibition of 1900.[102] It was a device for recording telegraphy transmissions, the signals being impressed in magnetic form on a steel wire. Many years were to elapse, however, before Poulsen's invention could be developed to the point where it could record speech satisfactorily. When this development eventually came about, in 1924, it took the form of an office dictating machine, developed by a German engineer, Dr Stille, and produced by the Vox Gramophone Company.[103] Stille developed an improved electromagnetic system which reduced distortion. The BBC heard of this machine, and in 1925 Bishop and Hayes went over to Berlin for a demonstration;

but the fidelity of the recording was disappointing, falling far short of the standard needed for broadcasting.

Not long afterwards, however, Louis Blattner, a German who had settled in England at the beginning of the century, took up Stille's inventions, and a company was formed to develop and market them. Towards the end of 1929 Ashbridge and Carpendale visited the Blattner studios at Elstree and witnessed a demonstration of one of their machines. By this time steel tape had replaced wire as the recording medium. Ashbridge was sufficiently impressed to recommend a thorough investigation of its potentialities. Negotiations with Louis Blattner and Wilfred Dawson, chairman of British Blattnerphone (Stille System) Ltd, culminated in the BBC getting an option for a year's trial at a royalty of £500.

A machine was installed at Avenue House in September 1930 for tests. It was used on 12 November for recording and reproducing King George V's speech at the opening of the India Round Table Conference in London. The results were reported as good for speech, but not for music. However, despite this reservation the performance of the trial machine was sufficiently encouraging for the BBC to negotiate a five-year rental agreement with the British Blattnerphone Company in January 1931. The rental for one machine was to be £500 for the first year, and £1000 a year thereafter, plus £250 a year for each additional machine.

In May 1931 the Blattnerphone was removed from Avenue House and installed in Room 66 at Savoy Hill for service. Although the quality was not really satisfactory for reproducing music, the machine had potentialities for rehearsal purposes, since any recording could be reproduced, after rewinding, as soon as it had been made.

The Blattnerphone was moved into Broadcasting House in March 1932, and a second machine was mounted alongside it on the seventh floor, so that recordings of unlimited length could be made. This installation went into action unexpectedly early on 23 May. It was still being completed, and one machine had been wired up, when shortly before the nine o'clock news the senior control room engineer telephoned to say that Amelia Earhart was in the studio after her solo flight across the Atlantic, and asked whether she could be recorded. The engineers took a chance, ran the machine up, and it worked. The recording subsequently featured in H. L. Fletcher's composite programme *Pieces of Tape*.

Both these original machines were of German manufacture. They used steel tape 6 mm wide and 0·08 mm thick, spooled in lengths of a little over a mile, which at a speed of 5 ft/s gave a playing time of 20 minutes. A full spool weighed 21 lb. The drive was from a dc motor, the speed of which had to be regulated by watching a stroboscope and manipulating a sliding rheostat.[104] The steel tape was drawn vertically through the recording, reproducing and wiping heads.

In September 1932 a third machine was installed in Broadcaasting House. Like its predecessors it was made in Germany, but it differed markedly from them. The tape width was only 3-mm, the playing time was increased to 32 minutes to accommodate a half-hour programme, and the drive was by an ac motor. Research Department carried out extensive tests on this machine. They concluded that mechanically it showed a considerable improvement over the 6-mm dc machines, although uneven

N

tape speed was a serious defect. Once they had established an optimum width for the pole-pieces, the technical quality was probably better than anything that had gone before, although the improved results could be achieved only by critical adjustments of the recording and reproducing heads and their pole-pieces.

A second 3-mm ac machine, ordered in November 1932, was delivered in February the following year. This was the first machine to be designed (by von Heising of the British Blattnerphone Company) and built in England. Unlike the earlier machines it was mounted on a bench instead of being free-standing. Another new departure was that it had two ac motors, one for the constant-speed tape drive and the other for the spools. The new machine was better engineered and much less liable to mechanical breakdown than its predecessors, but it was noisy and its speed constancy was not as good as that of the original machine.

Thus, at the beginning of 1933, the BBC had four Blattnerphones altogether – two of the original German 6-mm dc machines, one German 3-mm ac machine, and one 3-mm von Heising machine. But the 6-mm machines were by then worn out and unfit for transmission; indeed, the only reason for retaining them was to complete the transfer of 6-mm recordings to pressings. The 3-mm machines were kept going only at the cost of a great deal of maintenance work. There were serious difficulties over replacements and spares, particularly for the pole-pieces. As a result, programme bookings had to be curtailed. Despite this, the demands made on the equipment were heavy and the recording engineers were hard pressed to meet them, a state of affairs which no doubt accounted for such disasters as the inadvertent washing out of the Canadian contribution to the 1932 Christmas Day programme.

In March 1933 events took an unexpected turn, when the Marconi Company purchased the Blattnerphone rights and offered to let the BBC buy the four rented machines for £4500. As part of the deal, Dawson undertook to incorporate in these machines any improvement devised by Marconi's in their development programme, or, if that were not practicable, to replace them by a new design of machine free of charge. The BBC offered £4500, less £875 already paid as rent, on the understanding that British Blattnerphone would replace all four with machines of new and improved design from Marconi's as quickly as possible. At this point, however, there was a hitch. Machines of an entirely new design, with all the improvements the BBC wanted, could not be delivered in under nine months. A way out of this dilemma was eventually found by the BBC agreeing in September 1933 to hire three machines of the von Heising type at £100 each, to tide over the period until the four machines of entirely fresh design were ready.

The first of the temporary machines was delivered in November, and all three were installed in Broadcasting House by January 1934. The only way in which they differed significantly from the von Heising design was that they had five heads on the central pillar instead of three. Experience had shown that the pole-pieces were easily damaged if there was any discontinuity in the tape. Spare recording and reproducing heads were therefore added, so that an immediate change-over could be made if one of the heads was put out of action.

By 1934 it had become obvious that recording was outgrowing its accommodation in Broadcasting House. First thoughts were that it might be transferred to St George's Hall, but this proved unsuitable and the choice eventually fell on the studio centre at Maida Vale. In November the three Marconi Blattnerphones and the von Heising machine were removed from Broadcasting House and installed there.

Meanwhile, discussions had been going on with Marconi's about the four machines of entirely new design. Among the improvements called for were a faster run-up to make change-over easier, a direct motor drive to reduce speed variations, quieter running, and high-speed rewind. The direct drive would not of itself have eliminated speed variations altogether, but Marconi's isolated the constant-speed drive from the spools interposing a tape reservoir on each side of the drive. The size of the tape loops in the reservoirs controlled the two motors driving the delivery and take-up spools, and the loops were kept within the required limits by means of thyratrons operated by contact between the tape and a conductor in the reservoir through relays controlling resistance in the motor circuit. This was a very successful feature of the design.

This was a good example of team-work, Marconi's being responsible for the mechanical design and the BBC Research Department for the electronics, on the understanding that all developments were to be agreed upon by both parties. In these machines the tape was transported horizontally through the double-pole wiping, recording and reproducing heads, the recording and reproducing heads being in duplicate. During the development work, a great deal came to be known about the magnetic recording process, the effects of using different amounts of dc bias, and the design and arrangement of the pole-pieces. Wiping was done by a double-pole head carrying dc so as to magnetise the tape fully.[103]

After some delays the first of the new Marconi-Stille machines was delivered to Maida Vale in March 1935. In response to an earnest plea from the BBC, Marconi's managed to complete two more in time for King George V's Jubilee on 16 May. The fourth machine arrived in July, and an additional pair, ordered in June, were delivered in September, bringing the total complement at Maida Vale to six. They were grouped in pairs to give three channels, each channel occupying two rooms, one for the machines and apparatus and the other for monitoring. The BBC designed and built all the amplifiers for these recording channels. The installation broke new ground in that it was the first to be powered from the mains rather than from secondary batteries. Metal rectifiers provided the low-tension supplies, and mercury-vapour rectifiers the high-tension. Two engineers were assigned to operate each channel.

The Marconi-Stille machines with their more sophisticated design surmounted many of the mechanical difficulties that had beset the earlier models. They quickly established a good record for reliability. In a year's running, during which they totalled 1957 hours of reproduction, the percentage breakdown time was only 0·33 per cent, and none of this was due to the machine itself – most of it was attributable to tapes breaking at the joints, and the remainder to amplifier or electrical faults.[103] They were also capable of higher standards of technical quality: the frequency response was within $\pm$ 2 dB between 100 and 6000 Hz, and ultimately a signal-to-noise ratio of 35 dB or better could be attained. Despite these advances, the machines did not prove an immediate panacea for all the difficulties that had gone before. Inevitably there were teething troubles and occasional disasters, which provoked severe criticism from the programme people. But there was favourable comment as well. A significant improvement (10 dB) in the signal-to-noise ratio was achieved towards the end of 1935 by adopting a single pole-piece for reproduction and by modifying the frequency characteristic, and this may have had something to do with Roger Eckersley's comments in January 1936: 'I would like, as a constant listener to the Blattnerphone, to tell you how enormously I think the quality has improved during the last few months. I listened to a programme last Thursday, which might well have been coming direct for all the difference the extra mechanism made.'

Most of the steel tapes were obtained from the Uddeholms Company of Sweden through British Blattnerphone, but a few came direct from Sandvik Charcoal Steels in Sweden. Several attempts to find a British supplier were made, but they all failed, not surprisingly as the manufacturing process was complicated and the demand was small. The tape was 3-mm wide and 0·08-mm thick, and was rolled in lengths of about 1000 m. Three lengths were then silver-soldered together and wound on a spool to give a playing time of thirty-two minutes. (A full spool weighed 25 lb.) The tape and the spool cost about £21, so that the cost per minute for a single playing worked out at just under 15 shillings (75p). However, a tape would stand up to at least thirty playings, and considerably more if it had not been cut for editing. When this was taken into account, the cost was nearer sixpence (2½p) a minute. Tapes could be edited, but this was rather laborious, each joint having to be soldered or welded. Nevertheless, as early as 1932, the composite programme entitled *Pieces of Tape* was compiled from several tapes recorded in the course of the year. Another example of an edited tape was *Stars in their Courses* produced in 1933, and featuring Dame Irene Vanbrugh, Fay Compton, Sir Frank Benson, and Matheson Lang.[104]

As the Marconi-Stille machines were commissioned during 1935, the Blattnerphones were gradually taken out of service and returned to the makers – except one of the German machines which was retained for research work, at a cost of £5, and transferred to Nightingale Square. There it remained until September 1939, when as a last resort in the emergency it was hurriedly shipped to Wood Norton, where it was got going in the nick of time to record Neville Chamberlain's speech on the declaration of war. It came through the war unscathed, and now, as the sole surviving Blattnerphone, has a place of honour in the BBC's engineering collection.

Despite its occasionally erratic behaviour and the injuries inflicted by the sharp edges of the tape, the Blattnerphone has a secure place in the annals of BBC recording, since for nearly four years it was its sole means of recording programmes. The Empire Service, with its need to broadcast the same programme to each zone in turn, could hardly have kept going without it. By 1934 twenty tapes a week were being recorded, edited and reproduced for the Empire Service, enough to keep the machines busy for up to seventeen hours every day.

Before the end of the Blattnerphone era, the day of direct disc recording had begun to dawn. Before this, the BBC had looked to the Gramophone Company to make any records it needed to provide copies of a programme or to preserve it for posterity. One of the first programmes to be so recorded was the opening of the London Naval Conference in the House of Lords by King George V on 21 January 1930. The making of pressings from recordings on wax was expensive, costing nearly £50 per hour. Moreover, it took a long time. The King's speech at the Naval Conference could not be repeated in the nine o'clock news that evening, although it had taken place ten hours earlier and dispatch riders were standing by to rush the recording to Broadcasting House at the first possible moment. Even when the processing sequence was curtailed, which was possible if only a few copies were needed, it took at least twelve hours from start to finish. Another difficulty was frequent uncertainty about the precise moment to start recording, with the risk of clipping the start of the programme.

In 1933 the British Homophone Company introduced a soft-wax system and a quicker method of processing. Moreover, their recordings could be played back immediately to assess whether they were worth using or not. The soft disc was destroyed in the process, but this did not matter because more than one would be cut in the first place.

Quite extensive use was made by the BBC of commercial recordings made by the Gramophone Company and British Homophone. In 1934 – the last year before the BBC had its own disc recording system – over 600 waxes were cut. Of these about half were processed, and more than 4000 pressings were made.

All these disc recording systems, like the MSS system about to be described, used lateral displacements of the cutter head to produce horizontal corrugations in a spiral groove, the pitch of the groove being determined by a worm drive. There was, however, a great deal of discussion about the possibilities of hill-and-dale recording, in which the displacements of the cutter head were vertical. A system of this kind had been patented by the Western Electric Company. It was capable of giving good quality, but the reproducing pick-up was fragile and the recording had to be soft, which meant that pressings had to be made. The method was not therefore suitable at that time for direct disc recording. One argument in favour of hill-and-dale was that the groove walls were less likely to break down during periods of heavy modulation, so that more grooves to the inch were possible. An important reason against its use in the BBC was that it was not compatible with commercial gramophone records. The hill-and-dale method did not come into its own until much later when stereophony demanded both vertical and lateral movements of the cutter.

Meanwhile, another development of great significance had begun. About 1930 a musician and dance band leader, Cecil Watts, became convinced that there would be a good market for a high-quality recording system. He had sufficient faith in his idea and enough confidence in himself to take the risk of setting up in business on his own to manufacture recording equipment. Soon afterwards, he started the Marguerite Sound Studios in Charing Cross Road (Marguerite was a family name, which was thought to be lucky), which in 1933 became the MSS Recording Company. Watts had had no formal engineering training, but he was endowed with two qualities that more

183

than made up for this: mechanical ingenuity and perseverance. He hit on the idea of a metal-based lacquer-coated disc, and this was to prove an important development. The particular virtue of the lacquer disc was that it was soft enough for a stylus to cut, yet hard enough to withstand wear by the pick-up during reproduction. Playback directly after recording thus became possible, and this gave rise to the term direct disc recording. Its importance to the BBC can be appreciated only by comparing it with the older method of making pressings. In the latter, the original recording was cut on wax, which was then electroplated to make a 'master'. A 'mother' was then derived from the 'master' by a second electroplating process. One or more 'stampers' or 'working matrices' were derived from the 'mother', again by electrolytic deposition; the stamper was thus a negative of the original recording. Finally, a number of pressings could be made from each stamper. In the early gramophone records the pressings were made of shellac copal and a mineral filler. Later, thermoplastic materials, such as vinyl, were used. Shellac pressings produced a considerable amount of background noise or 'needle scratch'; the later materials were less noisy and also permitted a greater number of grooves per inch, which made long-playing records possible. Pressings were much used in the BBC, both as commercial gramophone records and as specially made recordings of BBC programmes – either recorded by a gramophone company from the live transmission or by handing over a direct recorded disc to the company for processing. (If only a small number of pressings were required they could be obtained direct from the master, which was then called a 'master stamper'; this method of 'half-processing' considerably reduced the time required to produce the pressings.)

The great advantage of this method was that full processing could produce any number of copies indistinguishable from ordinary gramophone records and that each copy could be played many times. The disadvantages were the high cost and the time taken, even if this was shortened by half-processing. What the BBC required for most of its recording work was a cheap method of producing recordings quickly. The need for many copies and for repeated playing arose much less frequently. Magnetic recording fulfilled the latter need in part and was later to be widely used, but in this period it was cumbersome and it did not lend itself easily to the making of copies.

By the early 1930s Marguerite Sound Studios were taking on all kinds of recording commissions, such as advertisements for Radio Luxembourg. The first approach from the BBC came in the autumn of 1933, and so began what was to prove a long and fruitful association between the BBC and the MSS Recording Company.

An experimental MSS recorder was obtained on loan by Research Department for tests. Another machine was installed in Broadcasting House shortly afterwards, and in April 1934 this was supplemented by the one from Research Department to make a complete channel. A. E. Barrett of the Research Department, aided by J. W. Godfrey, a founder member of the technical recording section, proceeded to carry out extensive side-by-side trials of the Watts machine and a Neumann recorder from Germany. The Neumann was fully developed, whereas the Watts machine was still at the prototype stage. Despite the handicap, the Watts machine was at least the equal of the Neumann and so carried the day.[104] It was first used for programmes at the beginning of April, and by the middle of May over a hundred programme recordings had been made.

The success of the experimental machines led to an order for four machines of a new design. The cost was not to exceed £75 each, including servicing. The cutter heads, which were adapted from the 'Blue Spot' loudspeaker unit, were to be hired at £12 a year rather than bought outright, because Watts was continually making improvements to the design and so preferred not to sell them. One pair of machines was destined for Maida Vale and the other for mobile use. Among the design features that the BBC specified were alternative speeds of 78 and 60 rpm (the experimental machines operated at 80 rpm until July 1934 when they were changed to 78 rpm), a 16-in. turntable, at least 100 grooves to the inch, and no belts of any description to be used. The speed of 60 rpm was a legacy from commercial recording practice where it was used to save cost as well as gain more playing time. Some means for substituting $33\frac{1}{3}$ rpm for the 60 rpm speed was also called for. In the event it was found that the gear trains did not readily lend themselves to this speed exactly, and $33\frac{2}{3}$ rpm was accepted by the BBC instead.

In May there was an anxious moment when it appeared that the project might have to be abandoned because the Watts cellulose-nitrate disc might infringe a patent by Dr Robert Pollak Rudin of Vienna. To some extent the issue turned on whether or not the material for coating the disc was colloidal in nature. A patent search was instituted, and an earlier patent by John Edward Thornton of Jersey was discovered, which anticipated many of Rudin's claims. In the light of this, the patent agents advised the BBC that Rudin's patent could safely be ignored and that there would be little risk in using the Watts process.

Cecil Watts manufactured the lacquer discs himself at his factory under the arches of Kew Bridge. The manufacture of the recording machines, on the other hand, he put into the hands of B. J. Lynes Ltd, a firm of experimental engineers in Euston Road. They handed over the four machines to Equipment Department at the beginning of December 1934, although Research Department had received a prototype for tests before this. The first Maida Vale channel, with its pair of MSS machines and amplifier equipment designed and built by the BBC, was commissioned on 17 June 1935.

Meanwhile, in December 1934, an allotment of £7600 was approved by the Board for the expansion of recording, notably by increasing the Maida Vale installation to three channels, each with two machines. At the beginning of 1935 it was learnt that Watts was making radical alterations in design on the next generation of recorders, and the BBC was apprehensive about the delay that this would entail. A sample machine was handed over to Research Department for evaluation at the beginning of April 1935. Despite the earlier ukase, the turntable was belt-driven from an induction motor, which gave less noise and vibration than the synchronous motor previously used. The design was a great improvement on previous models, although various modifications were required. In September 1935 an order was placed for four machines, at a cost of just under £200 each. They were delivered in December, so that from 1936 onwards three disc recording channels were available at Maida Vale.

The Watts lacquer discs came in two sizes, 12-in. and 13-in., giving playing times of $4\frac{1}{2}$ and 5 minutes at 100 grooves to the inch, the pitch the BBC had standardised. At first they were cut from inside to outside, the reverse of ordinary gramophone records, the idea being that wear on the needle and cutter would be compensated by increasing cutting speed. This method also had the advantage that the swarf automatically collected at the centre of the disc. As many recordings were brief and required a cut of only an inch or so, these advantages were more apparent than real, and there was a risk of confusion between gramophone records and Watts pressings. After brushes had been fitted to all the recording machines to cope with the swarf, the change to outside-to-inside recording was made on 27 April 1937.

Originally the discs cost two shillings (10p) for the 12-in. size and three shillings (15p) for the 13-in. Expenditure on them was quite heavy – £900 for 6500 discs in 1935, rising to over £2500 in the following year and £3000 in 1937. By 1939 consumption was running at the rate of 25,000 discs a year. If a recording was of sufficient importance to be kept permanently, pressings were made from it by arrangement with the Decca Company.

A recurring difficulty during these early days was the uneven quality of the discs. In some batches, for example, the lacquer would become hard and powdery, and this resulted in excessive surface noise. Another besetting problem was the deterioration of recordings while in store. Research Department solved this problem by giving the disc a coating of vaseline after recording, thus protecting the grooves from the air. This technique, which also made it possible to play a disc up to fifty times, was adopted at the end of 1937. Variations in the lacquer coating became a serious problem, because foreign matter in the coating could wreck the recording cutter, and there was a high rejection rate. Faced with this predicament, the BBC sought the advice of a consulting chemist, Dr Yarsley. Fortunately, he was able to put his finger on the trouble and set Watts on the right track, after which there was a real improvement in the quality of the discs.

In October 1938 the MSS Company launched a new kind of disc, called the 'Supercut'. It was claimed to be unbreakable, and to have a long playing life and an absolutely silent surface. The 12-in. side (single-sided) cost two shillings and threepence (11p), and the 13-in. three shillings and ninepence (19p). Lubrication with a very light machine oil before and after cutting was recommended, in order to increase the number of playings the disc would withstand. Both Research Department and the Technical Recording Section were very favourably impressed by the Supercut disc, the surface noise being far lower than on the ordinary type.

A friendly relationship rapidly grew up between the BBC's engineers and Cecil Watts, who was an engaging character and won the affection and respect of everyone who came in contact with him. He readily lent recorders to the Research Department for test without charge; in return, A. E. Barrett and H. Davies contributed handsomely to improving the performance and reliability of the machines. Davies, for instance, eliminated vibrations that were causing patterning on the discs by devising a flexible coupling made of two rubber discs riveted together at the rims. This was so successful that it became a standard feature on all MSS recorders. Watts himself was very sensible of the help he had received from the BBC. In November 1935 he wrote: 'With regard to the valuable research and assistance given by all departments of the BBC in the perfecting of our recording system, we find it difficult to express our thanks for the co-operation so freely given . . .'

By present-day standards, the MSS recorder was crude; every recording engineer of that era will recall the Watts coupling made out of flexible curtain rod and rubber tubing, and the cutter head dangling on a piece of string and bobbing up and down like a dinghy in a choppy sea. Nevertheless, these machines successfully recorded countless programmes, including the Coronation ceremony of 1937 which ran for three hours and was recorded in triplicate without a single hitch.[104]

There were two schools of thought on the question of reproducing Watts discs. The operational side considered it essential to be able to play them on the same reproducers as ordinary gramophone records. Research Department, always seeking for the best possible performance, demonstrated that the classical constant-velocity characteristic for recording was not the optimum choice and that a constant-acceleration characteristic would be much better; but recordings made to this prescription would be incompatible with gramophone records and another set of reproducers would have to be specially designed for Watts discs. This would not have been impossible, because recording operations were centralised at that time and the reproducers could have been associated with the recording channels as they were for tape and film operations. The whole system could then have been engineered to attain optimum performance without any of the restraints implicit in compatibility with gramophone records, but operational requirements were paramount and the decision went in favour of a compatible system.

This problem having been resolved, another immediately took its place. It arose from the fact that Watts discs imposed more drag on the reproducer turntable than gramophone records. The variable-speed induction motors in use at that time were not strong enough, their lack of torque giving rise to speed variations and juddering. Synchronous motors, with their invariable speed, were not acceptable to the programme people. Improvements to the induction motors eventually made them satisfactory for 78 rpm recordings, but the difficulty with 60 rpm recordings remained. It was decided to dispense with 60 rpm direct recordings, except for those intended for processing; and 33⅓ rpm direct recordings had proved a failure. In June 1935 it was therefore agreed that future MSS recorders need cater only for 78 rpm recordings.

A twin-turntable desk specifically designed for reproducing Watts discs and gramophone records was produced in 1935. Known at the time as the Watts desk, and later as the TD/7, it was installed in operational areas such as studio listening rooms. It was fitted with a parallel-tracking arm with a vernier adjustment for precise groove location, which had been devised by J. E. Lock of the Designs Section. The groove-locating mechanism was capable of an extraordinary degree of precision. A classic example of this was the recording of the Proclamation of the Accession of

King George VI. The Garter King at Arms stammered over the phrase 'our rightful liege Lord', but when the disc was reproduced it was possible to cut out the stammer and to reproduce the speech as it had been intended.[105] Asa Briggs says that this story cannot be traced in the archives, but the present author remembers the recording very clearly. An improved version of the groove-locating device, designed by Davies, superseded this original design in 1937. Two types of needle-armature pick-up were current in the BBC at that time: the Burndept, which had been designed by J. H. Ridley, later Head of Engineering Secretariat, and the BTH. The TD/7 desks had BTH pick-ups; there was a suggestion that an EMI design should be used, this came to nothing at the time, mainly because it made groove location more difficult.

The most elaborate reproducing installation of the period was the recorded programmes mixer on the fourth floor of Broadcasting House, which was completed in August 1935. This was for synthesising any number of recordings to make a composite programme. The equipment consisted of three TD/7 desks, accommodating up to six discs at a time, and a mixer panel with means for lowering the pick-ups by remote control. To enable the editor to locate in advance the passages he wanted to use, a dial in the mixer room showed the number of grooves cut by the recording head as it moved across the disc. Thus the groove number relating to any particular sentence or word in the recording could be noted and then located on the disc.

The need for a mobile recording unit began to emerge as early as 1932. In September of that year H. L. Fletcher made a proposal for a transportable Blattnerphone to make a weekly topical programme for the Empire service. His idea was that events should be 'bottled day by day and uncorked when required'. As time went on, this idea gathered force, winning support beyond the confines of the Empire Service, but the creation of some form of organisation to deal with recorded programmes was still in the air at that time, and it was felt that until this had taken shape the question of mobile recordings was best left in abeyance.

The subject was revived early the following year. By that time, opinion had moved strongly in favour of disc recording, because it would be cheaper than tape and the equipment more compact. Approval to equip a recording van was given in August 1934. Talks Department were impatient to have it as soon as possible, and so it was decided to make do with a makeshift installation, using a pair of MSS recorders originally destined for Maida Vale. The cost was estimated at £1200, including £300 for a 30-cwt Morris van. Benches were fitted along each side to take the equipment, which was powered from 24-V accumulators charged by a generator driven by the engine.

The first van, M53, was first used for recording part of Laurence Gilliam's feature programme *Gale Warning* on 6 March 1935 at Battersea power station. The *Wireless World* referred to the mobile recording unit as the 'BBC's Flying Squad'. In reality there was nothing very dashing about M53; Marsland Gander of the *Daily Telegraph* saw it as a cross between a Green Line bus and a plain van. The *Sunday Referee* pointed out that the BBC, usually so go-ahead, had lagged behind the Germans who had had recording vans for a long time. Nevertheless, the original van broke new ground with its visits to faraway places like the Hebrides and Sark (the gear had to be off-loaded for this assignment) and its coverage of the last voyage of the old RMS *Mauretania*.

The M53 had a crew of three – two engineers and a driver. A number of modifications were found necessary during the first few months' operation, among them means for recording in duplicate, better monitoring arrangements, and talk-back between the microphone point and the van. By October 1935 the van was a proved success, having taken part in nearly a hundred programmes, in the course of which seven hundred discs had been cut.

Meanwhile an earlier proposal for equipping the Regions with recording vans had been shelved, on the grounds that experience must first be gained with the London van. However, in June 1935 it was decided to proceed with two more vans, one to be shared between Scotland and North Region, and the other between the Midland and West Regions. The main improvements required were the provision of a small studio within the vehicle, more compact layout of the equipment (which could be achieved by rack-mounting much of it), and better insulation against heat and cold. At the same time, the users stipulated that the weight must, if possible, be kept within the limit permitted for a speed of 30 mph, and that the vehicle should not be materially bigger than M53. These requirements were conflicting and the new vans turned out to be a good deal bigger, and heavier, than M53. The choice fell on a Thorneycroft chassis, as used for London's buses. This was a ponderous vehicle, over 23 ft long, as against 17 ft or so for M53, and weighing very nearly seven tons when loaded; it was therefore restricted to a maximum speed of 20 mph. The Regions were not enthusiastic about the prospect of using a unit of this size. West Region took alarm at the probability that the van would not be able to negotiate unclassified roads, and pointed out that there were 2000 miles of these in Cornwall and Devon alone. Wales, similarly, reckoned that it would be unable to cope with many of the narrow hilly roads in the remoter parts, and that the low speed would seriously limit the number of recordings they could make. Scotland were equally dubious; the vans would be completely ruled out for the Highlands and Islands, which were precisely the areas they wanted to tap. Nevertheless, the proposal went ahead.

While T39 and 30, as the new vans were coded, were being fitted out in the early part of 1936, the programme policy that had brought them into being was changed. The main justification for allocating two vans to the Regions was that they would be able to contribute topical material to the news bulletins. This promise had not been borne out in practice, for News hardly used the original van at all: most of its time was spent on feature programmes for Laurence Gilliam and Felix Felton. It was finally decided that both vans should be based on London, though they were expected to spend up to two months at a time collecting material in one or other of the Regions. This decision in turn gave rise to misgivings that there might not be enough work to keep all three vans busy, for Talks Department, which had been in the forefront of the lobby for mobile recordings, never made use of it either.

As the Regions were going to be concerned with recording, it was necessary for them to have their own reproducing equipment. So in the course of 1936 banks of TD/7 desks were installed at each of the main Regional centres and at Glasgow and Newcastle.

The two new vehicles were ready for service in September 1936. Each was divided into three compartments – driving cab, apparatus room, and studio. A glass observation turret giving an uninterrupted view all round and above the vehicle topped the studio. It was also possible to use the roof, which had been specially strengthened with this in mind, as a vantage point for commentaries. Two sets of recording machines and amplifiers were fitted, enabling programmes of any length to be handled. The recording machines were supported on hydraulic mounts, so that they could be levelled, and were driven by dc motors, the speed of which was controlled manually against the frequency of a tuning fork. The whole installation was powered by a 100-V battery. This could be charged from a 2-kW generator driven by the engine or from the mains through a rectifier. The recording amplifiers had a gain of 120 dB and an average power output of 8 W.[106]

During the next three years up to the outbreak of war, T29 and 30 travelled all over the country gathering material, almost exclusively for feature programmes.[107] In October 1937 one unit was transferred to Manchester to cover Scotland and the North of England, so as to eliminate the long journeys between London and the North.

The original suggestion for a truly mobile recording unit in the form of a car instead of a van came from L. F. Lewis in June 1936. But the times were not propitious. The BBC was going through one of its phases of financial stringency, and preparations for the Coronation, already beginning to loom, were taking up all the time of the Designs Section. However, two events conspired to bring this idea to the fore again. By 1937 the first recording van, M53, had reached an advanced state of dilapidation. With the introduction of the two big vans, M53 had been turned over more and more to recording topical events around London. News Department had thus acquired a taste for recorded items and were making more and more use of them in their bulletins. They wanted a recording car exclusively for News, pointing out that what was needed was something fast and adaptable, unfettered by the regulations that circumscribed the van driver's turns of duty. This had been particularly frustrating during the Fenland floods in 1937, when over and over again Richard Dimbleby had found the van held up at Ely with no driver to take it out.

An outline specification for a recording car was approved and the design work was entrusted to Research Department, with some assistance from Designs Section. They completed two sets of equipment, each made up of a recording machine, amplifier, and supply unit, all working from a 12-V battery. The amplifier consisted of the newly designed OBA/8 with an extra power stage added. The recording machines were modified commercial units, fitted with Neumann cutter heads, dc motor drive, and piezo-electric pick-ups. The car chosen was a Chrysler, American cars being the only ones able to accommodate three people in front. The recording equipment was normally placed on the back seat, but it could easily be taken out and used elsewhere. The car made its maiden trip to Europe in September 1938, at the time of Munich, spending a fortnight or so in Germany, with spells at Godesberg and Hamburg.

Because of its novelty, the first recording car, C88, attracted considerable controversy. The second set of equipment was supposed to be held in reserve at Maida Vale, so that a faulty unit could be replaced immediately and the car kept on the road. But the programme people, faced with conflicting assignments, pressed the reserve set into service.

On 9 March 1939 a telegram was received at Broadcasting House to the effect that C88 had met with disaster on the return journey near Boulogne. While rounding a bend one of the back wheels had come off, and the car had gone through some alarming contortions before finally coming to rest. The occupants were lucky to escape with their lives. The cause was put down to overloading and uneven distribution of the weight coupled with excessive speeds. As a result of this experience, the Chrysler was replaced temporarily by a 14-hp and finally by a 21-hp Wolseley.

In 1939 the equipment was augmented from two sets to four, so that by the outbreak of war the BBC had two completely self-sufficient sets of light recording equipment ready for action.

Although by 1934 the Blattnerphone was fairly well established and a tentative start had been made with Watts discs, Engineering Division continued to cast around for other systems that showed any signs of promise. In August tenders were invited from British Acoustic, BTH, Technical and Research Processes, and Western Electric for film recording and reproducing equipment. Almost simultaneously Laurence Gilliam heard of a new kind of film recording developed by Philips, which had the great advantage that the recording could be played back immediately without any processing. This was the Philips-Miller system. A variable-width track was cut with a sapphire in a thin opaque layer on the film, the recording being reproduced by means of a photo-electric cell, in the same way as a variable-area photographic track. The film was coated with a layer of gelatine to which was applied a fine skin, about three microns thick, of black mercuric sulphide, The cutter was V-shaped, the apex angle being 174°. The modulation thus appeared as a symmetrical push-pull transparent track down the centre of the opaque film.[108] Each equipment consisted of two combined recording and reproducing machines placed side by side in a single unit to form a complete channel capable of continuous recording and reproduction. In the first experimental method the film was perforated and driven by sprockets. This caused flutter, which was avoided on subsequent models by the use of non-sprocketed film.[109]

The idea of combining a mechanical method of recording a sound-track with an optical method of reproduction can be traced back to some experiments made by Hymmen in 1891 at Iserlohn, near Essen. He used a paper strip coated with a black layer into which a lateral groove was cut. In 1930 Berthon proposed a method in which a lateral cut was made along the centre of a thin black film, so as to leave a variable-width sound-track on the edge of each half of the film when it was split down the middle. Berthon developed a machine in collaboration with Nublat and it was marketed in Europe under that name. The results were not considered good

191

enough for use by the film industry, but in 1931 J. A. Miller of Flushing, NY, devised the Millerfilm system, which was the basis of the Philips-Miller equipment. Miller used a cutter that moved vertically instead of laterally, so that it produced a variable-width track by removing the black surface so as to leave a transparent track. By making the cutter in the form of a wedge with an obtuse angle, a considerable amount of mechanical amplification was achieved and this proved to be the secret of the success of Miller's system. In 1932 the Philips research laboratory at Eindhoven reached agreement with him on the use of his patents and carried out further development work. [110, 111, 112]

As soon as this system was brought to its attention, the Engineering Division took prompt action. By the end of November 1934 a set of experimental equipment had been installed at Nightingale Square for trials, and a preliminary quotation was obtained from Philips in January 1935. The equipment was priced at £4500 and the film at 1·3d (0·54p) a foot. The film ran at 32 cm/s and so would have cost about £20 an hour. There followed several months of negotiation, and, in August, Philips submitted a fresh offer. This was on the basis that the equipment should be rented, rather than bought outright, the rental being £650 a year on the first machine and slightly less than this for each additional machine. The film was now priced at 0·4d (0·17p) per foot, corresponding to £7 an hour, its width having been reduced from 17·5 mm to 7 mm. Additionally, a royalty of 0·5d (0·21p) per receiving licence was proposed. This quotation was unacceptable to the BBC, and, after some bargaining, agreement was reached in February 1936 for a six months' trial of a machine at Maida Vale, for which the BBC would pay £1000.

The results of acceptance tests, made at Eindhoven at the end of March were very encouraging. The performance figures quoted in the tender were:

The overall amplitude-frequency characteristic: within $\pm$ 2·5 dB between 50 and 7000 Hz and within $\pm$ 6 dB between 30 and 8000 Hz with reference to the amplitude at 1000 Hz.

Total distortion at 30 per cent modulation: 3·2 per cent at 60 Hz, 3·5 per cent at 1000 Hz, and 6·0 per cent at 4000 Hz.

Noise: at least 50 dB below the output level at full modulation.

The equipment was shipped from Holland at the end of April, installed in Room 21, Maida Vale during May, and formally taken over on 1 June.

Arrangements were made to record a series of sample programmes chosen to reveal the technical performance of the system and also its value to the programme people. At the outset the trial ran into trouble, much of which was due to imperfections in the film itself. Unless the film was absolutely uniform in thickness, a spurious modulation of the sound-track resulted, and the opaque layer had to be wafer-thin – otherwise the sound track would have a grey border, which generated distortion. These setbacks culminated in a breakdown on transmission, and the equipment had to be taken out of service to avoid the risk of another fiasco and to give the engineers a chance to put the defects right. By October 1936 this had been done, and the equipment was opened to programme bookings once more. As four months of the original

192

trial period had been lost, Philips conceded that the six-month trial should be deemed to have started on 1 October.

The Philips-Miller equipment then gave excellent results, but there were doubts about the wisdom of using it extensively because of the cost. For the Empire Service, it was doubtful whether the improvement in quality was of much value because it would be masked by the vagaries of short-wave reception. Furthermore, there was a deep conviction that a wrapped-up system (tape or film) could never replace disc recording, because with such systems it was impossible to pick out a particular point in the recording instantly as could be done with a disc. This attitude of mind resulted from the practice of picking out items from a disc recording during actual transmission – a process in which the operators had become expert. The trend has since been in the other direction, because tapes can be edited before transmission.

However, the engineers claimed that they could match with film the expertise in editing that the Recorded Programmes staff had acquired with discs. Also the Philips-Miller system was far cheaper than processed discs for making a permanent record. It also scored in terms of performance and reliability, so that by using it the BBC could take upon itself the sole responsibility for recording programmes of outstanding importance. These considerations led to the start of negotiations for a new contract with Philips.

Meanwhile, Philips had proposed that running costs should be reduced by recording on twin-tracks and by reducing the film speed from 32 to 20 cm/s. These modifications reduced the running costs to under £2·50 an hour. Two sets of equipment were hired, one at a charge of £800 pa, plus a royalty of £1250, and the other at a lower rental as a standby. The use of twin tracks proved satisfactory and the first of the new machines was taken into service on 28 March 1938.

It was decided that recordings for which the highest quality was essential should be made at 32 cm/s, but that other recordings would be made at 20 cm/s. The lower speed resulted in some loss of response at frequencies from 4kHz upwards. Both tracks were to be used, but to allow for the possibility of subsequent editing there had to be an interval of 4 to 6 weeks between the recording of the first and second tracks.

During this period the cutters for disc recording were of steel. The use of specially cut sapphires for this, with the need for skilled lapidaries to grind them, was not introduced by the BBC until 1941. Sapphire cutters were, however, used in the Philips-Miller system.

For the remaining two years of the 1930s the Philips-Miller was unsurpassed. It was used in preference to discs and tapes when high quality was essential and when it was necessary to retain the recording permanently. But for subsequent improvements in magnetic recording, the Philips-Miller system might well have remained the best recording system to this day.

The BBC had to wait until after the war for the dramatic improvements in magnetic tape recording resulting from the use of plastic tape and supersonic bias. The writer saw a demonstration of the 'Magnetophon' in Berlin before the war. It was then using paper tape impregnated with iron dust, but the tape frequently broke and the system would clearly have no application in broadcasting until this problem had been resolved. A magnetic tape with a cellulose acetate base was first produced in Germany in 1934, but it was not applied to broadcasting on a significant scale until some years later, as will be seen in Chapter V, Section 7.

10 TATSFIELD RECEIVING STATION

The new Receiving Station at Tatsfield mentioned in the previous chapter was opened in September 1929. It comprised a main building with a receiver room, a frequency-measurement room, an office and a garage, with a second smaller building intended to house batteries and power plant. The public electricity supply mains became available unexpectedly early, before the smaller building was completed, so that the latter was not required for its original purpose and it was used as a canteen and later as a store. No piped water supply was available and rain-water was directed from the roof of the main building to storage tanks under the garage floor. The station was commissioned on 8 August 1929 and took over the work previously done at Keston. J. A. Partridge and L. G. Shuttleworth were transferred from Keston to Tatsfield and were joined there by E. L. Payne making an initial staff of three.

The chosen site proved to be an excellent one. Although less than twenty miles from the centre of London, it was relatively free from electrical interference and efforts to keep it so were successful thanks to the co-operation of the Post Office, the electricity supply authorities and neighbouring landowners.

In 1933 an additional building was erected on the site for the use of Research Department staff. It was in this building in 1937 and onwards that the development of precise frequency-control equipment for transmitting stations took place. This work was a joint effort by staff of Transmitter Department and Research Department. The availability of frequency measuring facilities at Tatsfield made it an ideal location for this work and, in spite of pessimistic forecasts, no interference was caused to the routine work of Tatsfield.

In 1935 additional land was leased on the northern boundary of the site extending the total area to 40 acres. On the additional land, two horizontal rhombic aerials were erected and in the same year the main building was extended and additional equipment installed. In 1937 a further small addition was made to the main building to provide additional office and workshop accommodation.

During this period the main activities at Tatsfield were:

(i)   Frequency measurement on long, medium and short waves;
(ii)   Relaying programmes (rebroadcasting) from European and USA stations;
(iii) Technical monitoring of BBC transmissions;
(iv)   Direction-finding and field strength measurement.

The type 81 heterodyne wavemeter for the medium waveband was transferred to Tatsfield from Keston in 1929, and in 1930 a 1-kHz electrically maintained tuning fork, supplied by H. W. Sullivan & Co., was installed. This sub-standard of frequency embodied thermal control of the tuning fork assembly and its output was used with multivibrator harmonic generators to calibrate the heterodyne wavemeters. The accuracy of measurement was thus improved to 1 or 2 parts in 10^4. Later in 1930 a short-wave wavemeter (H. W. Sullivan type 833) was provided for measurement in the range 3 to 30 MHz. In 1932 a Sullivan-Griffiths sub-standard heterodyne wavemeter was obtained for long- and medium-wave measurements and this improved the measurement accuracy to 5 parts in 10^5.

In 1933 a significant advance was made in frequency measurement with the installation of a Marconi type 482C equipment. This had a specified accuracy of 1 part in 10^5, but experienced operators, using a high precision tone source for low frequency interpolation, could measure frequencies with an accuracy of 1 part in 10^6. This Marconi equipment was based on a crystal-controlled oscillator operating on 250 kHz and using a quartz crystal in the form of a cube suspended in a cradle of fishing line between two air gaps. This was an early attempt to introduce mechanical constraint on the position of the quartz in its holder to overcome vibrational instability. In 1934 a variometer-type AF oscillator was installed for operation in the narrow range 860–1180 Hz for low-frequency interpolation and using this with the type 482C equipment an accuracy of 5 parts in 10^7 was obtained. During the period 1929–39 the sub-standards of frequency at Tatsfield were checked daily against the time signals from the Post Office station at Rugby, GBR. In 1939 a Post Office crystal-controlled oscillator operating on a frequency of 1 MHz was obtained. This oscillator used a type 6A quartz crystal in which the plate was clamped at its nodal points and was contained in an evacuated holder enclosed in a two-stage constant-temperature oven.[6] The accuracy of the Marconi equipment using this Post Office oscillator as a source was increased to 1 part in 10^7.

These improvements in accuracy were made possible largely through advances in the science of crystallography, which led to a greater understanding of piezoelectric effects and made it possible to cut quartz crystals in such a way as to improve the frequency stability and reduce the effects of temperature changes. The Post Office developed methods of grinding crystals that enabled the thickness, and hence the natural frequency, to be adjusted to a high degree of accuracy. Arrangements were made for the Post Office to supply the crystals required by the BBC, both for frequency measurement and for the frequency control of transmitters.

For relaying programmes from abroad, particularly on short waves, it was necessary to take special steps to obtain the best possible quality of reception, to overcome the effects of fading and to reduce interference from unwanted stations. These requirements made it necessary to use highly directional receiving aerials and to operate receivers in diversity – that is to say, to use two or three receivers receiving the same programme, either from two or more stations using different frequencies (frequency diversity) or by receiving the same station at two or more points on the same receiving site (space diversity). The object of both these techniques was to reduce the effect of fading by selecting at any moment the strongest of the available signals. Means were developed for doing this automatically by inter-connecting the agc circuits of the receivers, so that the receiver momentarily contributing the strongest signal suppressed the output from the others.

Four programme-relaying receivers were initially installed at Tatsfield. These were designed and built in the Research Department and each receiver filled a standard apparatus rack. It consisted of one radio-frequency stage, oscillator and mixer stages, and a three-stage tuned intermediate-frequency amplifier. A fifth bay carried the terminations, diversity mixing facilities and agc units. The routine operation of this relaying receiver occupied the attention of three men: one on diversity mixing, one on the af controls and one making frequency changes. It was usual to operate the receivers in three wavebands to obtain the best results, changing from dual to triple diversity repeatedly during a relay of only half an hour's duration. These receivers were later modified by Murphy Radio Ltd, to include custom-built 'front ends' and standard Murphy receivers for the intermediate-frequency stages. During the later 1930s other receivers (National HRO and Hallicrafter) were added to the Tatsfield plant. In 1938 a Cossor type 137T television receiver was provided for monitoring the Alexandra Palace television transmissions.

The aerials installed at Tatsfield in 1929 were mainly domestic types, but a Marconi 'Franklin' short-wave array for 19 m (15 MHz) was also erected. This was supported by two 110-ft steel tubular masts and was used for short-wave relays from the USA early in 1930. In 1935, when additional land had been made available, two horizontal rhombic aerials were erected. These were oriented on a bearing of 288°ETN and had a designed frequency of 15 MHz and tilt angles of $14 \cdot 5°$ and $23 \cdot 5°$. In 1935 two more horizontal rhombic aerials were erected on the same bearing, but having tilt angles of 18° and 20°. All these rhombic aerials were supported from wooden poles and their design was based on information published by E. Bruce and others.[113] The aerials were connected to the receiver room by means of coaxial transmission lines and were matched to these lines using transformers mounted at the mast-head. The first pair of rhombic aerials were, and are, most effective for reception of stations in the USA. In 1938 the Franklin array was dismantled and replaced by two inverted-V aerials oriented at 060°/240° and 120° ETN respectively.

From its inception, Tatsfield has been responsible for checking BBC transmissions at frequent intervals for quality, modulation depth, freedom from interference and accuracy of carrier frequency (to ensure that it is at least within internationally agreed tolerances) and, in the case of short-wave transmissions, to ensure that the correct programme is being radiated according to the operational schedule. With the start of the BBC's foreign-language broadcasts in 1938, monitoring for content of foreign programmes was introduced at Tatsfield,[114] but the accommodation was soon found to be too limited as the staff needed for this work increased in numbers with the increasing international tension. This language monitoring activity was therefore transferred in the first instance to Wood Norton. At the outbreak of war, half the Tatsfield staff went to Wood Norton to form the nucleus of an emergency Technical Monitoring Unit, but the remainder stayed at Tatsfield (except for a short period from July to November 1944) throughout the war years.

A Marconi-Bellini-Tosi direction finder capable of operating in the 150–1500 kHz range was installed in the early 1930s and was in constant use for locating sources of interference and identifying foreign stations. In 1939 Tatsfield acquired a Marconi type TME/18 field-strength measuring equipment for use in the long-, medium- and short-wave bands.

In the decade preceding the war, the Tatsfield staff also made special observations for Commonwealth and foreign broadcasting authorities, reports on a wide range of receivers offered for test, observations on propagation (particularly in the short-wave bands) and observations on special test transmissions by BBC stations. Throughout the 1930s the Tatsfield staff, who seldom moved away from this work to take up other posts, acquired increasing expertise in station identification, programme relaying and frequency measuring techniques. This led to a considerable store of information on the operating characteristics of broadcasting stations throughout the world and from 1934 included details of jamming signals which then began to be radiated by German and Russian stations. This knowledge proved invaluable during the war years as a complement to the information provided by language monitors when evaluating the effect of BBC transmissions to enemy and occupied countries.

The first Engineer-in-Charge of Tatsfield was J. A. Partridge, who was replaced on 19 June 1933 by H. V. Griffiths on the latter's return from taking part in a series of Marconi-RCA experiments in diversity reception at Terling, Essex. The number of staff at Tatsfield in 1929 was three, increasing to eight in 1936 and to twenty by September 1939. By that time Tatsfield had fully established itself as the BBC's Argus of the ether. The staff were enthusiastic and took pride in the exacting precision of their work. In trapping 'sounds and sweet airs' from remote parts of the earth they came nearer to the true spirit of Ariel than anybody else in the BBC.

The equipment and operation of the Tatsfield station have been described in more detail elsewhere.[115-118] Tatsfield is the oldest established of the dozen or so measuring stations that now exist in Europe. It was followed in 1929 by one in Italy at Sesto Calende (later transferred to Monza) and later by stations in Switzerland (1940) Portugal (1941), France (1944), Germany (1947) and Finland (1947), all operated by the broadcasting organisations in those countries.[119] Stations of this kind also exist in Eastern Europe and in other parts of the world.

The first international monitoring station for broadcasting was established in Brussels in 1929 by the International Broadcasting Union, to supervise the occupation of the long- and medium-wave bands under the Prague Plan. The station was taken over by the European Broadcasting Union in 1950 and moved from Brussels to a new site at Jurbise, near Mons, in 1953. The EBU monitoring station collaborates closely with monitoring stations belonging to EBU Members and produces regular lists of radio and television stations in the European Broadcasting Area in the long-wave, medium-wave, VHF and UHF bands.

11 ORGANISATION, STAFFING AND TRAINING

The transition from Company to Corporation as 1926 faded into 1927 brought no immediate changes in the engineering organisation. Head Office staff were still all

197

under one roof at Savoy Hill, but 1927 was to be the last year for which this would be so. The first engineers to feel the effects of the general expansion then in progress were those in the Research and Development Sections. They inhabited the attics of Savoy Hill, where conditions were already cramped; H. L. Kirke, for instance, shared a small office with his assistant, L. W. Hayes, and his secretary. As further growth at Savoy Hill was out of the question, the BBC started to look for new premises. The choice fell on Avenue House, a roomy Victorian house in King's Avenue, Clapham, originally the official home of the Governor of Brixton jail. This, complete with the splendid heraldic beasts flanking the entrance, was taken over and the work of adapting it was put in hand. Towards the end of 1927 the Research and Development Sections moved in. The Lines Engineer, with his assistants, stayed behind at Savoy Hill, later moving to Cecil Chambers in the Strand, which were taken over in September 1928, and L. W. Hayes also stayed behind to take up the new post of Foreign Liaison Engineer.

In February 1929 MacLarty left the Development Section to become Installation Engineer, in charge of a new unit set up to grapple with the Regional Scheme, then just beginning to get into its stride. A. S. Attkins resigned, and his place as Lines Engineer was filled temporarily by V. A. M. Bulow, and later by H. B. Rantzen. A. G. D. West and both his assistants left, and this brought the Research Section to an end.

These events were overshadowed by a traumatic experience in the life of the Engineering Division. In May 1929 Eckersley was asked to resign because he was, to use his own words, 'about to become what is called the 'guilty party' in an action for divorce'.[120] He afterwards said that he 'felt unable to continue to serve an organisation which attempted to usurp the functions of my conscience in a matter which I believed only concerned my private life' (op. cit.). However, a man of such extrovert personality could hardly prevent his private life from colouring his public image. He left the BBC on 30 September. Ashbridge succeeded him as Chief Engineer on 1 October, and Bishop became Assistant Chief Engineer in his stead. The post of Senior Superintendent Engineer than lapsed until P. A. Florence took it up again in 1933.

In April 1930 the Development Section was renamed Research Department, with Kirke assuming the title 'Senior Research Engineer'. A year later the Designs Section of the Department, with its test room and drawing office, was transferred to Equipment Department under F. M. Dimmock, the Equipment Engineer. During 1932 the Head Office staff moved into Broadcasting House from Savoy Hill, and were joined by the Lines Section from Cecil Chambers. At the end of 1932 the Research Department moved from Avenue House to new premises in Nightingale Lane, Clapham, and in 1934 they made a further move to Nightingale Square, Clapham. This was a gaunt-looking building in Victorian Gothic style, which had been built in 1858 for a Belgian religious order and used as a convent for aged nuns. Though ugly, it was commodious – there were thirty-six rooms including the chapel – and three acres of ground went with it.

The knighthood conferred on Noel Ashbridge in 1935 was widely acclaimed throughout the Engineering Division as a recognition of the great contribution he had made to the development of broadcasting and of the status of engineering in the BBC. This precedent was to be followed in 1955 when Harold Bishop received his knighthood, and again in 1967 when the same dignity was accorded to Francis McLean.

A major change in the organisation of the staff responsible for the operation and maintenance of the transmitting stations and studio centres was made in 1935. Up to that time there had been a geographical dichotomy, all the studio centres and transmitting stations in the north of England and in Scotland and Northern Ireland being grouped under the Superintendent Engineer (North), while those in the south and west of England and in Wales reported to the Superintendent Engineer (South). This arrangement enabled the Superintendent Engineers to keep in touch with the stations and centres for which they were responsible, with a minimum of travelling, but it became apparent that the problem of running a studio centre was very different from that of running a transmitting station and that some specialisation was desirable.

At the beginning of 1935 the responsibilities of the two Superintendent Engineer posts were changed, one being placed in charge of all the studio centre, OB units, recording units and Education Engineers, while the other was to look after all transmitting stations. The idea of grouping the transmitting stations under one head proved sound and has remained in force to the present day. The corresponding organisation on the studio side has since been split between the Radio, Television and External Services and these three groups are still responsible to the head of the Engineering Division for professional standards, though they now form part of their respective programme directorates.

On 21 May 1935 an incident occurred that had far-reaching effects. A meeting of the BBC Club was held in the Concert Hall at Broadcasting House with Reith in the chair. It was during the depression, when there was severe unemployment. The normally friendly, if somewhat stiff, atmosphere of such meetings was suddenly dispelled when Reith proposed that the BBC Club should do something to help the unemployed; as Tyneside was one of the worst-hit areas, he suggested that the Club should establish a centre in Gateshead for this purpose. There was considerable support for this proposal, and a centre, known as 'BBC House', was later established in Gateshead to provide occupation and recreation for unemployed men and women. It was supported by voluntary contributions from BBC staff. Before the end of the discussion, however, a member of the workshop staff at Avenue House rose at the back of the hall and said: 'We are asked to adopt a scheme to assist the unemployed. But there are people working in the BBC who are very little better off than the unemployed. They should be attended to first. I know I am prejudicing myself by saying this.'[121]

Four other workshop staff spoke to the same effect and a mechanic from Nightingale Square complained that manual staff were prevented from joining the pension scheme. These protests caused a considerable stir and were reported in the *Daily Worker* under the headlines: 'Sensational Revolt at the BBC. Bombshell

199

for Sir John Reith. Exclusive Story of Inside Uproar. Engineers at 7d per hour.'

This incident, whatever the grounds for complaint may have been, clearly showed that lines of communication between management and staff needed strengthening. One direct result was that an investigation into rates of pay was made in the following month and a revised pay scale was adopted for manual staff. It was also decided to set up a post with specific responsibility for all staff matters in the Engineering Division. This post was originally entitled 'Engineering Establishment Officer' and the Superintendent Engineers and heads of departments were instructed to deal with that officer 'on all matters connected with the engagement, dismissal, transfer, personal services or welfare of staff'. The first holder of the post was P. A. Florence who took up his duties on 1 October 1935 and was aided by Col. F. W. Home, a retired officer of the Royal Marines, as Engineering Staff Liaison Officer. It was Col. Home's job to provide a line of communication with all members of the Engineering staff and to advise them on their conditions of work and general welfare; it was part of his duties to travel to all the centres throughout the country where engineers were employed. These measures no doubt effected a considerable improvement in staff relations and they incidentally prevented a repetition of what had been described as 'the highly regrettable incident' in the Concert Hall. (Col. Home later joined the Overseas & Engineering Information Department, where he was noted for his facility in composing disarming letters to listeners in an elegant style. One angry letter he received displayed a certain freedom in the use of four-letter words. Home replied, giving straightforward technical advice on the point at issue, and asking his correspondent to be good enough to bear in mind in future that his letters might be read by a lady secretary. So touched was the listener by this reply that he sent a present of a large box of cigarettes by return of post.)

The BBC had always striven to be a good employer. From the earliest days it had a Medical Officer and from 1932 a surgery at Broadcasting House and a cafeteria restaurant open 24 hours a day. The BBC Club founded during the days of the Company received a stimulus with the opening of the sports ground at Motspur Park in 1929. A provident fund, started in 1925, was replaced in 1931 by a staff pension scheme,[122] an important feature of which was that on voluntary resignation staff received not only their own contributions, with interest, but also an equal sum (though without interest) from the BBC. The engineers participated in these advantages and there were few signs of discontent until the incident mentioned above. There had, however, been a Press campaign in 1934, which attacked the BBC for, among other things, its staffing policy. This led to a memorial being signed by 800 members of the staff expressing disgust at the allegations and affirming their loyalty to the BBC.

The Ullswater Committee that was set up to advise the Government on the future of the BBC and the renewal of its Charter reported in February 1936.[123] The BBC had informed the Committee that under the existing system staff had every opportunity to make their views known and that a more official procedure would be almost unworkable and would bring with it a loss of the personal touch. In the course of the parliamentary debates that followed the publication of the report, the Postmaster

General nevertheless announced that there would be reforms in staffing arrangements and that a staff association would be set up.

The BBC had never sought to prevent members of its staff from joining Trade Unions, but it did not normally, at that time, take part in collective bargaining. In 1935 a further inquiry was made to find out whether the staff wanted a staff association. In the Engineering Division the responsibility for conducting this inquiry among the O. & M. staff rested on R. T. B. Wynn, as Senior Superintendent Engineer. He visited every station and centre and held meetings of the engineers. These were arranged so that people on both of the two shifts then being worked could attend. Great care was taken not to influence the staff one way or the other; as Wynn put it in his own words, 'the BBC cares no more whether you have a staff association and wish to join that than if you join the local tennis club.' At the end of each meeting, after questions had been answered, a secret ballot was held. These ballots included all engineers in the operations and maintenance departments, with the exception of 2 to 3 per cent who were absent. The vote was overwhelmingly against a staff association and it was clear that the engineers had more faith in the BBC Management of that time than in a system of collective bargaining, though some thought that an association might be necessary in the future if there were changes in the management team.

An important development in staff relations was the appointment of W. St J. Pym as Director of Staff Administration in November 1936. He reported that there seemed to be little incentive for a staff association, though one or two Trade Unions had asked for right of access and organisation in the Engineering Division.[124] A committee, presided over by Sir James Rae of the Treasury, reported in 1938 in favour of setting up joint councils to provide for staff representation. By this time the climate of opinion among the staff had swung towards this view, and when the matter was put to the vote 77·7 per cent of the staff voting expressed themselves in favour of joint councils;[125] of 922 engineers eligible to vote, 788 did so (85·3 per cent) and of these 610 (77·3 per cent) were in favour of joint councils (almost the same proportion as in the staff as a whole). The practical result of this move did not emerge until after the outbreak of war.

The organisation of the Engineering Division underwent a further transformation on 1 October 1935. At the same time the BBC as a whole was reorganised in four divisions: programme, engineering, administration and public relations. To preserve uniformity among the divisional heads the Chief Engineer's title was changed to that of Controller (Engineering) – though he continued to use his old title for external purposes when convenient. The post of Engineering Establishment Officer came under the Director of Staff Administration in the Administration Division.

Further changes resulted from this reorganisation. When P. A. Florence became Engineering Establishment Officer, R. T. B. Wynn left the Engineering Information Department to take up the post of Senior Superintendent Engineer. Engineering Information was combined with Empire & Foreign Liaison work to form the Overseas & Engineering Information Department under L. W. Hayes, which also took over the responsibility for the Tatsfield receiving station. Hayes retained his

ORGANISATION OF ENGINEERING DIVISION: 1935

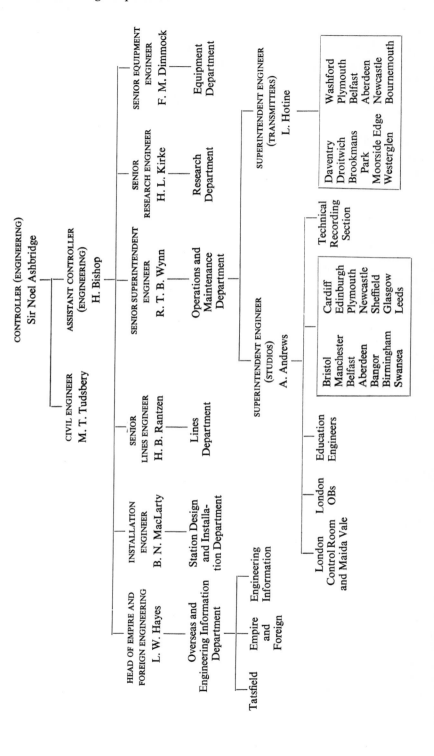

CONTROLLER (ENGINEERING)
Sir Noel Ashbridge

ASSISTANT CONTROLLER
(ENGINEERING)
H. Bishop

CIVIL ENGINEER
M. T. Tudsbery

HEAD OF EMPIRE AND
FOREIGN ENGINEERING
L. W. Hayes

Overseas and
Engineering Information
Department

Tatsfield

Empire
and
Foreign

Engineering
Information

INSTALLATION
ENGINEER
B. N. MacLarty

Station Design
and Installa-
tion Department

SENIOR
LINES ENGINEER
H. B. Rantzen

Lines
Department

SENIOR SUPERINTENDENT
ENGINEER
R. T. B. Wynn

Operations and
Maintenance
Department

SUPERINTENDENT ENGINEER
(STUDIOS)
A. Andrews

London
Control Room
and Maida Vale

London
OBs

Education
Engineers

Bristol
Manchester
Belfast
Aberdeen
Bangor
Birmingham
Swansea

Cardiff
Edinburgh
Plymouth
Newcastle
Sheffield
Glasgow
Leeds

Technical
Recording
Section

SENIOR
RESEARCH ENGINEER
H. L. Kirke

Research
Department

SENIOR EQUIPMENT
ENGINEER
F. M. Dimmock

Equipment
Department

SUPERINTENDENT ENGINEER
(TRANSMITTERS)
L. Hotine

Daventry
Droitwich
Brookmans
Park
Moorside Edge
Westerglen

Washford
Plymouth
Belfast
Aberdeen
Newcastle
Bournemouth

202

interest in the development of the Empire Service and his continued study of propagation conditions resulted in a great advance in mthods of determining the optimum frequencies and aerials for transmission to all the target areas.

There were further changes of organisation in 1936, also some changes in designation: the young men who had been classified since about 1929 as 'Improvers' became Junior Maintenance Engineers, Assistant Maintenance Engineers became Maintenance Engineers, and Supervisory Engineers became Senior Maintenance Engineers – a process of escalation not uncommon and not unnatural in an expanding organisation. By this time pressure on the limited office accommodation in Broadcasting House was increasing and the Station Design and Installation Department moved to 103 Great Portland Street.

The practice of writing annual confidential reports on individual members of the staff was in force as early as 1926, though the most junior grades (boys, engineers' assistants and improvers) apparently did not qualify at that time. An extant copy of a report dated March 1926 on an Assistant Maintenance Engineer at one of the smaller stations, typed on a blank sheet of paper reads as follows: '(a) Excellent, (b) None, (c) Excellent, but young, (d) In due course. Length of service: 17 months. Present salary: £104. Proposed salary: £200 (on promotion from "boy").' The letters evidently refer to conduct, qualifications, performance during the year, and fitness for promotion respectively. As the candidate was still designated as a 'boy' his youth could hardly be held against him in judging his performance.

In 1927 printed report forms were introduced on which similar information was given, with the addition of the date and amount of the last increment. In 1937 a new form appeared providing space for more detailed observation by the head of department or Superintendent Engineer and for comments by the Chief Engineer or Assistant Chief Engineer. Annual interviews were made part of the regular reporting procedure in 1947. (These arrangements have continued ever since, and those responsible for writing and counter-signing reports have been given detailed guidance on the points that should be brought out and on those that ought, in fairness to the person reported upon, to be brought to his attention during the interview.) Annual increments, though seldom withheld, had to be earned and recommendations for them had to be approved by the Assistant Controller (Engineering); exceptionally good work could be rewarded by a double, or even a treble, increment.

In the 1920s salary levels were naturally modest by present-day standards. Engineers' Assistants (aged 16 and upwards) started at £0·75 per week rising to £2·00 a week by the time they were 21 when, if their record was satisfactory, they were promoted to the grade of 'Improver'. The Improver could expect to rise from £3·50 a week by £0·25 each year to £4·25. In the middle of the 1930s Assistant Maintenance Engineers earned £235 pa increasing to a maximum of £340 pa. When the grade of Senior Maintenance Engineer was introduced in 1936, the salary started at £350 pa and rose to something over £400 pa.

Allowances for absence from base while on duty varied between £0·62½ to £1·55 for an absence of 24 hours, according to grade. Because of the risks of air travel, staff were not in any circumstances to be compelled to fly against their will and if they did agree to take to the air the BBC insured their lives in the sum of £10,000.

Efforts were made as early as 1929 to encourage recruitment to the Engineering Division. University students were given the opportunity to spend a part of the long vacation working in the BBC. In 1933 a student apprenticeship scheme was started to attract graduates by giving them attachments to all the engineering departments over a period of two years. The last batch of student apprentices joined in 1937 and during the six years in which the scheme was operated, a total of 31 student apprentices passed through it. Of these only 13 stayed with the BBC for a substantial length of time and of these three retired early. Of those who remained, one achieved the rank of Deputy Director of Engineering and one that of Superintendent Engineer. The scheme provided an excellent insight into BBC engineering over a broad field. Yet its success in preparing people to fill the top posts in the Engineering Division was limited, no doubt partly because the selection had to be done before the men had had an opportunity to prove themselves in a career and partly because they found themselves in competition with engineers who had previous experience in industry – a major advantage for many responsible posts in BBC engineering. On the other hand the wastage represented by BBC student apprentices who found work elsewhere was offset by recruits who had passed through similar schemes in industry and the Services, so that there was probably a net gain to the profession as a whole. Under later arrangements numbers of 'direct entry' engineers were recruited, many of them from the universities. They were given training courses and attachments, which to some extent took the place of the student apprenticeship. (A two-year Graduate Apprenticeship was started in 1953 – see Chapter V, Section 11.)

To set these observations in perspective, it is necessary to indicate the actual numbers of staff of the Engineering Division during this period. In January 1927 the total was about 300; by October 1935 it had increased to 800 and by the beginning of 1938 to over 1200. At the outbreak of war in September 1939 there were then over 1600 staff in the Engineering Division. These figures include professional engineers, technicians, workshop staff, draughtsmen, and clerical and secretarial staff.

Television, when it started at Alexandra Palace in November 1935, was not organised as a separate unit, but was fitted into the existing structure. Thus, both the Superintendent Engineers – (Studios) and (Transmitters) – had responsibility for Alexandra Palace. And the television OB unit, when it came into being the following year, was made a section of London OBs.

The BBC has been greatly strengthened at various times in its history by the recruitment of people from the Services. This was particularly true when demobilisation was at its height at the time of the Geddes Axe in the early days and again after the Second World War and after the various cuts in the personnel of the Services that have occurred since. Many of these recruits had had distinguished war-time careers and they were all accustomed to work in an organised and loyal team. Those who had technical qualifications were particularly welcome in the Engineering Division, wherever they could be taken on without seriously prejudicing the prospects of established members of the staff.

Sea-going wireless operators also provided an important source of recruitment.

A high proportion of the staff, particularly in the operations and maintenance departments, were drawn from their ranks. During this period only a few of the engineers were professionally qualified, but most of them, particularly those recruited from the Services and the Merchant Navy, were extremely well disciplined. Many of the recruits from these sources combined judgment with reliability and several rose to highly responsible positions.

Engineers at remote stations sometimes had to deal with emergencies that not only threatened the continuity of the broadcasting service but could be extremely dangerous. Gale damage to masts could create alarming conditions until a specialist firm could be called in to make permanent repairs. Help or advice from Head Office could be called upon, but until it arrived the Engineer-in-Charge must have felt very much 'on his own'.

Relations between the man on the spot and the central authority could become strained, and a 'we and they' attitude was inclined to develop. 'Head Office' had to introduce rules of general application and the dividing line between good administration and bureaucracy was thin. E. F. Wheeler, the first EiC at Moorside Edge, struck a blow for freedom in the early 1930s; there was a rule that soft soap must be ordered through official channels, but Wheeler insisted on buying it locally at a lower price. He was eventually allowed to do so, provided that no purchase exceeded £1 – one of the few occasions in the BBC when 'soft soap' cut any ice.

The BBC was unique in employing people with an extremely wide range of abilities, background and outlook. A certain acerbity grew up between the engineers and the 'programme people', though on the whole their relationship was good-natured. The engineers rightly or wrongly thought that the programme production staff had no understanding of their problems and regarded engineers as Philistines intruding into the civilised world, wielding oil-cans and blow-lamps. Both sides tended to over-play their own expertise. At that time balance and control was done by programme staff and the engineers felt that, since it required a practical understanding of the capabilities and limitations of the equipment, it ought to be entrusted to them.

Liaison between engineering and programme staff was not always as close as it should have been. The need for better understanding between them was brought to a head by an incident that occurred in 1935. The engineers had placed a ribbon microphone in a studio that was to be used for a drama production. The programme staff, finding that the Reisz microphone to which they were accustomed had suddenly been replaced by one of a new and revolutionary type, were very much upset – understandably so, as they had been given no opportunity to appreciate the characteristics of the new microphone and the changes in their own techniques that it would require. To prevent this kind of thing and to provide an opportunity for the engineers to draw attention to proposed technical changes and to invite comments on them, a liaison committee was set up with R. T. B. Wynn as Chairman. All the programme departments were represented on it as well as F. W. Alexander, the Head of Programme Engineering, and it succeeded in promoting mutual understanding and constructive consultation.

12   ENGINEERING FINANCE

Over the twelve years from 1927 to 1939 the BBC's income mounted steadily year by year. From just under a million pounds in 1927 it had risen to nearly four million by 1938. Capital expenditure also followed a rising trend, though the variations from year to year were much more erratic, varying between £10,000 in 1927 and £928,000 in 1931, with an average of £352,000 over the twelve years. Most of the capital expenditure represented engineering costs for building work, masts and equipment. (In the year ended 31 March 1969, the BBC's capital expenditure amounted to over eleven million pounds, for most of which the Engineering Division was responsible.)

The Corporation followed the methods for dealing with expenditure that had been set up by the Company. Reith crystallised the arrangements for sanctioning expenditure in the following statement dated 4 January 1927: 'Requisitions for material and expenditure of all kinds have first to be authorised by the Head of Department concerned and are then dealt with in the Chief Accountant's Department and passed by him after consultation, if necessary, with the Head of the Department and after reference, if necessary to the Director-General, Admiral Carpendale or Mr Goldsmith.'

The BBC Handbook for 1929 throws a little more light on how these matters were dealt with:

'From these indications of what broadcasting involves financially, it will be realised that it is no easy matter to regulate expenditure to the best advantage. This can be done only by the most careful planning and the strictest control throughout. A system of financial control at Head Office has been evolved to meet these conditions. The income for the year can be fairly accurately estimated. Estimates of expenditure are also drawn up, taking into account all fixed charges and commitments, and programme and engineering requirements. Allocations are then made in accordance with these figures, and actual expenditure is carefully compared with the estimates at frequent intervals. The same principle is carried out with regard to particular items of expenditure; the estimated cost is submitted for approval beforehand, and is checked with the actual cost. The kinds and extent of expenditure to which the principle of approval in advance cannot apply are reduced to a minimum, and all transactions are scrutinised in detail. This strict control is not, however, allowed to stifle initiative.'[126]

The last pious words sounded somewhat hollow during the several periods of financial stringency to which the BBC was later subjected.

For the first few years of the Corporation's life, the Regional Scheme made the greatest demands on capital expenditure, and its progress shows how the system worked. The Governors were given an outline of the scheme in a report by Reith at the beginning of 1927. The cost had been at least roughly estimated, for Reith was able to say that provision had been made in the financial estimates for the next five years for the necessary borrowing, and for the payment of interest and the establishment of a sinking fund. In July this report was followed by an outline estimate 'on a liberal basis' for a twin-wave station, together with an expenditure forecast at two-monthly intervals from October 1927 to June 1928, assuming that two stations would go ahead simultaneously. In January 1928 another outline estimate was put forward; the cost had risen from £115,000 to £130,500 for one station, mainly on account of increased provision for building work.

By the date of the second estimate, some of the tenders had already been received. On the same day that the Board approved the estimate, they also accepted Ruston & Hornsby's tender of £11,827 for the diesel engines. In the succeeding months tenders for the other main items were accepted and by September 1928 all the orders had been placed.

The financing of the next two stations, North Regional and Scottish Regional, between 1929 and 1931, was dealt with in much the same way. In 1932 the Board's approval to financial allotments for specific schemes first begins to figure regularly in the minutes of its meetings. In January an allotment of £200,000 was agreed upon for the transfer of Daventry 5XX and 5GB to a new site, and another of £50,000 for the construction of the Empire station at Daventry. Acceptance of tenders followed quickly after the allotment of funds for a new project, and occasionally preceded it so as to avoid delay in the placing of the major contracts on which progress depended. This was thirty years before the introduction of critical path analysis, but the principles were already acted upon.

By no means all the schemes that came before the Board were large ones. Quite modest projects went through the same procedure, such as the new receiving station at Tatsfield (£2600), the sinking of an artesian well on the Broadcasting House site (£700), and accommodation for recording at Maida Vale (£3500). Parkinson's laws had not been formulated then either.

Although the Finance Division was responsible for keeping the accounts and for keeping close watch on the BBC's finances, it was necessary for the Controller (Engineering) to satisfy himself that money allocated to engineering projects was well spent and was kept within the approved allotments. This responsibility he delegated to the Assistant Controller (in accordance with a rough demarcation of duties by which the Controller looked outwards and the Assistant Controller looked inwards), who prepared a forecast of engineering expenditure in outline each year by methods that were simple and direct, but sufficiently accurate for the purpose. The process was aided by the fact that prices were then relatively stable; indeed, the cost of some equipment had dropped slightly between September 1928 and January 1932. It was necessary, as each major contract was authorised, to ensure that it came within the amount of money allocated to the project, and keeping track of 'commitments' became one of the responsibilities of M. J. L. Pulling when he was appointed Assistant to the Assistant Controller (Engineering) in July 1937. He kept a 'Scheme Book' with a page for each major scheme. It gave brief details about each scheme, the amount of money allocated to it and the major sums committed against it under contracts and large purchase orders. In this way it was possible to ensure that no commitments were entered into unless money was available in the scheme allotment.

This rudimentary system had to be considerably elaborated during the war years, and subsequently, with the increasing number of projects and the increasing need to keep a close watch on expenditure.

13   INTERNATIONAL RELATIONS

Following the formation of the UIR in March 1925 and the implementation of the Geneva Wavelength Plan in 1926, there was a succession of international conferences on the allocation of frequency channels to broadcasting stations. This matter was, and is, of vital interest to the BBC because space in the radio frequency spectrum is a scarce commodity, essential to its existence.

In the autumn of 1927 an International Radiocommunications Conference was held in Washington, DC, and this was the first such conference to be held for fifteen years. Preparatory work for it was done by the Technical Committee of the International Broadcasting Union (UIR) during a meeting of European Wireless Engineers held in Brussels in January 1927, when experts from twenty-two countries attended, including for the first time representatives from the USSR. The proposals drafted at this meeting were accepted by the delegates from eleven countries and were tabled by the UIR delegation at Washington. Here, for the first time at an international conference, an examination was made of the wavebands allocated to the various services, including broadcasting. It was realised that in partitioning the radio-frequency spectrum it is first necessary to allocate bands of frequencies to the various radio services and subsequently to assign channels to individual stations. The first step must embrace the whole world, or at least a large part of it; the second may be done on a more restricted geographical basis.

The Washington Conference was attended by 400 delegates representing 76 states and 40 private companies. The BBC was represented by Vice-Admiral Sir Charles Carpendale and Capt. P. P. Eckersley. In spite of all the efforts by the broadcasting organisations represented at Washington, broadcasting suffered some reduction in the medium-wave band to 445–200 m (675–1500 kHz). Broadcasting on long waves was allotted the band 1875–1314 m (160–228 kHz). Six bands of frequencies were allocated for the first time to short-wave broadcasting, as follows:

6000 – 6150 kHz (49 metre band)	15,100 – 15,350 kHz (19 metre band)
9500 – 9600 kHz (31 metre band)	17,750 – 17,800 kHz (17 metre band)
11,700 – 11,900 kHz (25 metre band)	21,450 – 21,550 kHz (14 metre band)

The channel separation in each of these short-wave bands was set at 50 kHz; this wide separation represented, by modern standards, a highly inefficient use of the spectrum, but was dictated mainly by the poor frequency stability of superheterodyne receivers.

The broadcasters were far from happy with the spectrum space allotted to them in the long-wave and medium-wave bands. Siffer Lemoine, Chief Engineer of the Swedish Telegraph Administration, put forward some proposals in an attempt to establish the number of channels to which each country in Europe ought to be entitled.[127] He suggested that the number of channels for each country should be proportioned to an arbitrary factor representing its area as a percentage of the total area of Europe (excluding Russia and Turkey), plus half its population, also expressed as a percentage. Further, since the lower frequencies give better coverage than the higher, the value of each channel should be expressed by a 'wavelength equivalent', based on the cube root of the reciprocal of the frequency in MHz. The sum of the wavelength equivalents of the channels allotted to each country, expressed as percentages, should be in proportion to the factors corresponding to the area and population.

This early attempt to evolve a rational, though idealised, basis for the allocation of channels was to be subject to modifications to allow for 'special requirements' such as those arising from unfavourable geographical conditions and the existence of multi-lingual countries. Lemoine underestimated the importance of the 'special requirements' and the practical difficulty of taking away any part of the spectrum already allocated to an established service, or an individual channel already in use for broadcasting. He suggested that the polygonal method of planning, in which high-power co-channel transmitters are spaced at optimum distances from each other (a method still in use for theoretical planning, though hardly achieved in practice), should be replaced by the assignment of groups of adjacent channels to each country, so that interference would come mainly from stations in the same country as the wanted station and thus be under the control of that country. This idea was never put into practice; it might have had some administrative advantages, but would have made very inefficient use of the channels available to Europe as a whole.

With the restriction of the medium-wave band and the increasing number of new stations proposed in Europe, it was obvious that there would have to be a new assignment of channels within the band. A European Conference of Wireless Engineers was therefore convened in Brussels to produce a new European Wavelength Plan. (The atmosphere of the conferences of this period was caught, with a wealth of personal detail, by P. P. Eckersley.[128]) The Brussels Plan was implemented on 15 January 1928. Its main features were a reduction in channel separation above 300 m (below 1 MHz) from 10 kHz to 9 kHz, the redesignation of most of the channels above 250 m (below 1200 kHz) as exclusive wavelengths, and the assignment for the first time of channels in the long-wave band. The BBC assignments in the Brussels Plan are listed on p. 210; they comprised one long-wave and 16 medium-wave channels, plus the use of an 'International Common Wave'.

At the time of the implementation of the Brussels Plan, the UIR set up an improved frequency measuring station. Previously, the only method of maintaining some degree of control over the accuracy of the carrier frequencies of European broadcasting stations had been to issue to broadcasting authorities a number of wavemeters designed and manufactured by the UIR in Brussels. In the early part of 1927 it became clear that daily supervision of transmitter carrier frequencies was absolutely necessary for the proper functioning of the European broadcasting network. Raymond Braillard and Prof. E. Divoire set about constructing improved frequency-

BBC ASSIGNMENTS UNDER THE BRUSSELS PLAN (IMPLEMENTED ON 15 JANUARY 1928) AND THE PRAGUE PLAN (IMPLEMENTED ON 30 JUNE 1929)

Station	Brussels (kHz)	Prague (kHz)	Station	Brussels (kHz)	Prague (kHz)
Aberdeen	600	995	Hull	1020	1040
Belfast	980	1238	Leeds	1080	1500
Daventry 5GB	610	752	Bradford	1190	1040
Bournemouth	920	1040	Liverpool	1010	1040
Cardiff	850	968	Nottingham	1090	—
Glasgow	740	797	Plymouth	750*	1040
London	830	842	Sheffield	1100	1040
Manchester	780	626	Stoke-on-Trent	1020	1040
Newcastle	960	1148	Swansea	1020	1040
Dundee	1020	1040	Daventry 5XX	187	193
Edinburgh	1040	1040			

* International Common Wave.

measuring apparatus, which, after a period of use in the laboratories of the University of Brussels, was installed in the garage of Braillard's house at 54 Avenue Beau Séjour, Brussels.[129] This location was fairly free from electrical interference and was thus suitable for long-distance reception for frequency-measuring purposes. The UIR entrusted Braillard and Divoire with the operation of this checking station, the objects being:

(i)   to measure the carrier frequency of each European broadcasting transmitter once in each 24-hour period;
(ii) to intervene rapidly (using telegrams direct to the station, with copies to the operating Authority) when any out-of-tolerance operation was observed;
(iii) to maintain the accuracy of the checking centre equipment to an order better than that of the most stable transmitter to be measured;
(iv) To publish, in graphical form, the results of all frequency measurements made at the checking station, thus stimulating an atmosphere of competition amongst broadcasting authorities in this sphere.

These functions are still performed by the EBU, at its measuring station at Jurbise in Belgium, though with some reduction in the frequency with which all the stations in the long-wave and medium-wave bands are observed.

Certain Administrations did not fall in with the Brussels Plan and in an attempt to improve a steadily worsening situation, the UIR proposed that a further European Wavelength Conference should be held in Prague in mid-1929. This Conference differed fundamentally from its predecessors, since it was a governmental conference comprising representatives of the European Telegraph Administrations, whereas the previous conferences organised by the UIR had had no official status, being concerned to enable broadcasting organisations to reach agreement among themselves. The change was unwelcome to some of the representatives of broadcasting, notably P. P. Eckersley; among Members of the UIR agreement between engineers could be rapidly translated into action, but against this advantage the Union had no power to enforce its decisions. It was beginning to be appreciated that space in the spectrum was a valuable national asset and that responsibility for enforcing international agreements on the assignment of frequencies must rest with the appropriate government agency in each country.

The Prague Conference met in April 1929 and general agreement was reached on a more complete and effective wavelength plan. The Prague Plan was implemented on 30 June 1929. The Administrations undertook to keep to the wavelengths assigned to their countries and to be subject to the control of the Brussels checking station, which thus became officially recognised. The Prague Plan was based on the previous Brussels Plan, but the 9-kHz channel separation was extended to wavelengths below 300 m (above 1 MHz) in order to accommodate more channels in the band available. The Prague Plan provided for 200 medium-wave stations having an aggregate power of 420 kW. The BBC assignments in this Plan are listed on p. 210; they include one long-wave channel and ten medium-wave channels, of which two were International Common Waves and one a UK Common Wave. The Plan did not in general assign frequencies to individual stations, but only to countries. The assignments to the UK for the use of the BBC were somewhat less favourable than those in the previous Brussels Plan, both in terms of the number of channels and in their effectiveness; this was inevitable because other countries were becoming more active in broadcasting and there was keen competition to secure as many channels as possible. Channels near the low-frequency end of the medium-wave band were particularly coveted because, other things being equal, they gave a greater range than those at the high-frequency end. At the date of implementation, the BBC made several agreed alterations within its allocations as follows: Daventry 5GB took over 626 kHz from Manchester; Manchester took over 797 kHz from Glasgow, and Glasgow took over 752 kHz from Daventry 5GB. In accordance with the Prague Plan, Daventry 5XX (long-wave transmitter) changed its frequency to 193 kHz (1554·4 m) on 30 June 1929. The Plan assigned no fewer than ten channels as International Common Waves, on which low-power stations in any country could work. Another point of interest about the Plan was that provision was made for certain stations in the USSR to work on frequencies differing by 4·5 kHz from those used in Western Europe – a stratagem since widely adopted in the short-wave bands to increase the maximum number of stations that can be accommodated without intolerable interference.

The state of development that broadcasting had reached at this time (1929) can be judged from the fact that there were 189 radio transmitters in Europe and about 1000 in the whole world. The League of Nations already had its own short-wave service, broadcasting from Kootwijk in the Netherlands (later from Geneva). The first live programme exchanges between Europe and America took place in that year. The Graf Zeppelin kept in touch with radio stations during its voyage round the world and the Byrd expedition to the South Pole reported on the reception of European stations in Antarctica. The Turkish Government was using broadcasting to promote the use of the Latin alphabet, and Radio Moscow broadcast a programme in Esperanto to mark the fifth anniversary of the death of Lenin. A station in Holland owned by a commercial company was broadcasting daily on short waves for Europeans overseas.[130]

The increasing number of new stations in Europe and a general increase in power soon necessitated modifications to the Prague Plan and the UIR prepared proposals for discussion at the Madrid Conference arranged for September 1932. At this Conference, telegraphy, telephony and broadcasting users of the radio-frequency spectrum were represented. Delegates from eighty Administrations attended and eighty-five representatives from broadcasting authorities took part. The medium-wave broadcasting band was extended by 41 kHz and it was agreed that a new wavelength plan should be prepared for consideration at a Conference to be held in Switzerland in 1933. This further conference was held in Lucerne during the six weeks commencing 15 May 1933 and produced a plan; this received some measure of agreement, but a number of Administrations refused to sign the draft and of those that did, a number made reservations. There was some friction between participating Administrations; for example, the French raised objections to L. W. Hayes being a member of the Technical Committee[131] (presumably because he was a broadcaster and not a government official).

At the time of the Lucerne Conference there were 275 stations either operating or under construction in Europe with an aggregate power of 4300 kW and a maximum individual power of 500 kW. The Lucerne Plan was implemented on 15 January 1934 and an intensive frequency-measuring campaign was mounted by the UIR in association with national measuring stations. The latter were responsible for ensuring that the stations in their own countries were adjusted to their new frequencies before final measurements were made by the Brussels Control Centre; the latter reported its results in broadcast messages, using a number of European long-wave transmitters, including Daventry 5XX. An interesting account of the events of the night of 14–15 January 1934 is given in an article in *World Radio* of the time.[132] Under the Lucerne Plan, the BBC obtained the use of one long-wave channel, nine medium-wave 'exclusive' channels, one National Common Wave and two International Common Waves. The BBC long-wave channel was changed to 200 kHz (1500 m) and this frequency has been retained by the BBC for 38 years throughout the vicissitudes of the Second World War and the Copenhagen Conference of 1948. It is especially useful as a sub-standard of frequency, and the uses to which it has been put since 1945 will be described in later chapters. The BBC assignments under the Lucerne Plan are listed on p. 213, but a number of modifications were made to the use of the channels between January 1934 and September 1939.

By 1936 the Brussels Control Centre had improved the accuracy of its frequency measurements to 1 part in 10^6 and in August 1936 a Company was formed (Société Immobilière du Centre de Contrôle Technique de l'UIR – SICUIR) of which the sole shareholders were the broadcasting authorities of twenty-three different countries. The object of the company was to build a permanent Control Centre in

Brussels to replace Braillard's original checking station. Work started in May 1937 at 32 avenue Albert Lancaster, Uccle, Brussels, and the equipment was installed in March 1938. The new centre was officially inaugurated on 15 November 1938 and its frequency measuring accuracy was of the order of 1 part in 10^8.

BBC ASSIGNMENTS UNDER THE LUCERNE PLAN (IMPLEMENTED ON 15 JANUARY 1934)

Station	Frequency (kHz)	Station	Frequency (kHz)
Moorside Edge Regional	668	Belfast	1122
Midland Regional (5GB)	767	London National	1149
Westerglen Regional	804	Washford National	1149
London Regional	877	Aberdeen	1348
Washford Regional	977	Newcastle	1429
Moorside Edge National	1013	Plymouth	1474
Bournemouth	1050	Daventry ⎱ 5XX	200
Westerglen National	1050	Droitwich ⎰	

A Plenary Conference of the CCIR was held in Bucharest in June 1937 and here the requirements of short-wave broadcasting were considered in detail and the need for a World Plan for short-wave broadcasting allocations was stressed. The number of short-wave broadcasting transmitters in the world had increased from 131 in May 1936 to 245 in October 1937 and they were still steadily increasing in number and power. In order to make more effective use of the available short-wave bands it was urged that there should be closer frequency tolerances for short-wave transmitters. It was agreed that the Madrid Regulations of 1932 were in need of revision and a conference was called in Heliopolis, Cairo, which worked from 1 February to 8 April 1938. This conference produced a compromise agreement on the allocation of wave-bands for broadcasting as follows:

(i)   the long-wave band was retained unchanged at 150–300 kHz;
(ii) the derogation bands (within which certain broadcasting stations were permitted to work, provided they did not interfere with the services to which the bands were allocated) remained unchanged;
(iii) the upper limit of the MF band was extended from 1500 to 1560 kHz;
(iv) three new bands were allocated for 'tropical' broadcasting, each 200 kHz wide;
(v)   the bands between 6000 and 2500 kHz were extended by a total of 500 kHz;
(vi) in the band 25–200 MHz, allocations were made for the first time for television and sound-broadcasting;
(vii) a new HF broadcasting band from 25·6–26·6 MHz was added.

(By mid-1939, the BBC had received nineteen assignments in the short-wave broadcasting bands.)

The Cairo Conference requested the UIR to report on the scope for sharing HF channels, with or without time-sharing, and the Swiss Administration was requested to convene a conference to produce a new plan for the long- and medium-wave bands for Europe, since these bands had already become overcrowded within two years of the implementation of the Lucerne Plan.

The UIR held a meeting in Brussels in November 1938 to construct a draft plan and it was soon apparent that the main difficulty in Europe was that the number of long- and medium-wave transmitters had increased from 123 in 1926 to 463 in 1939 – an increase of 275 per cent – whilst the bandwidth allocated to broadcasting had been increased by only 8·5 per cent. Further, the aggregate power of the transmitters had increased during the same period from 112 kW to 11,750 kW. Also, whereas in 1926 each 'exclusive' wavelength was used by a station having an average power of 1 kW, by 1939 each of the so-called exclusive channels was being used by an average of four stations each having an average power of 25 kW.

The Swiss Conference was held in Montreux during the seven weeks ending 15 April 1939. The implementation date chosen for the Plan was 4 March 1940 and its main features were:

(i)   an extension of the long-wave band to 156·5–300 kHz;
(ii) the retention of the 9-kHz separation in the medium-wave band, 550–1560 kHz, but with increased use of synchronised networks for national purposes.

Owing to the outbreak of war in September 1939, involving many of the signatories to the Montreux Plan, it was not possible to implement the Plan in March 1940 as proposed. In the event, most European countries, belligerent and non-belligerent, adhered to their Lucerne Plan assignments throughout the war years and up to the implementation of the Copenhagen Plan in 1950. At a meeting held in Lausanne on 15 February 1940 it was decided that the work of the Brussels Control Centre should continue for the time being, but that plans should be made to move the equipment to Geneva during May 1940. In March 1941 the BBC temporarily suspended its collaboration with the UIR.

International relations were particularly important in the field of frequency usage, because propagation in the LF, MF and HF bands could extend beyond national frontiers and cause mutual interference between stations in different countries. International co-operation extended into many other fields, and technical questions of common interest to broadcasting organisations were being discussed in the CCIR, the CCIF, and the Technical Committee of the UIR. Many of these questions concerned the international exchange of programmes over cable circuits and over radio-telephone channels, both types of facility being provided by the Telecommunications Administrations. By 1939 programmes were being taken live from almost every country in Europe and circuits from as far afield as Warsaw and Prague were capable of giving reasonably good quality. Two-way relays were undertaken from time to time; these necessitated precautions to prevent howl-back, the incoming programme line being connected to headphones in the studio, while the studio output was fed to the outgoing music line, and both the incoming and outgoing contributions were mixed before transmission over the BBC network.

In April 1930 L. W. Hayes visited Leipzig with Stanton Jeffries to arrange for a relay of Bach's St Matthew Passion from the Thomaskirche. A particularly adventurous programme was *Christmas Over Europe* in 1938. This included live contributions from Lyons, Berlin, Prague, Rome and Stockholm, all of which were connected by music lines to London, and also a contribution from Athens that had to be recorded – the discs being sent to London in advance. As each contribution had to start on a word cue, telephone circuits were ordered from London to each of the contributing centres, so that the whole programme could be heard at each of them. Control lines were also ordered from each point to London. The circuits from Stockholm, Berlin and Prague were switched in Berlin and fed to London via Brussels; those from Lyons and Rome came on separate circuits to London via Paris. All the circuits were ordered half an hour in advance to enable the circuits to be tested and the levels to be adjusted.[133]

Relays from the USA and Canada increased rapidly between 1935 and 1938 and included the memorable series of commentaries by Raymond Gram Swing in 1935; Alistair Cooke was already familiar to BBC listeners in 1936. These relays were taken over the public radio-telephone service, the performance of which was satisfactory for speech. Rebroadcasts of programmes from distant countries were also made by direct reception of short-wave transmissions at the BBC Receiving Station at Tatsfield.

14 PREPARATIONS FOR WAR

One of the earliest references to the role of broadcasting in time of war appears in Reith's diary in September 1933, when Sir Maurice Hankey told him that he thought a series of BBC talks should be given to prepare the public for the action they should take during air raids.[134] In August 1934 Reith appointed N. Ashbridge, M. T. Tudsbery and Col. F. W. Home to deal with questions of Defence, Civil Disturbance and Air Raids as they might affect the BBC, and in May 1935 the Government set up a Broadcasting Committee to consider the general policy to be followed in respect of broadcasting in time of war. This Committee reported on 31 December 1935.[135]

As the shadow of war lengthened, discussions took place between Reith and Sir Maurice Hankey, General Sir John Dill, Director of Military Operations and Intelligence at the War Office, and Wing Commander E. J. Hodsoll of the Home Office Air Raid Precautions Department. These discussions were characterised by 'complete understanding and confidence' from the start,[136] and they included the general policy on the use of the BBC in time of war, the physical protection of the BBC against hostile air attack, and the protection of the BBC against sabotage.

Hodsoll's view was that the second and third of these matters were the province of the BBC itself and Reith immediately initiated a series of inquiries which led to the preparation of a BBC 'Memorandum on Protection against Air Attack' (undated).[137]

Colonel Home visited all BBC regional studio centres and transmitting stations during 1935 and made recommendations for the provision of security fencing, the installation of steel shutters to buildings, and other protective measures. On 11 March 1936 the Board approved a sum of £50,000 to implement his recommendations.

Broadcasting in war-time would clearly make heavy demands on the Engineering Division, and during the latter part of 1935, Bishop had begun to draft a report on the technical operations of the BBC in war-time. This task was rendered difficult by the lack of a solution at that time to a basic technical problem, which held the key to any war-time transmitter distribution scheme. This related to the use enemy aircraft might make of broadcast transmissions as an aid to navigation when approaching this country. Any proposal that denied navigational aid to the enemy should, if at all possible, provide an adequate service to listeners at home however bad conditions might become. Flight trials had taken place as early as 1928 to determine the magnitude of direction-finding errors that might be expected by day and by night when using transmitters operating on a common wavelength as radio beacons. The trials were made using BBC low-power relay stations and the information obtained formed the basis for the proposals put forward by the BBC from 1936 onwards for a secure system of war-time broadcasting. As these proposals required the use of high-power transmitters, new flight trials took place using the London and West national transmitters operating on 1149 kHz. The results obtained, supported by calculations, indicated that reliable navigational aid could be denied to an aircraft attempting to take bearings on a synchronised group of transmitters until it flew within about twenty-five miles of one of them, provided that the transmitters were accurately synchronised and that the transmitter powers were suitably proportioned.

From January 1936 Ashbridge and Bishop were members of a technical subcommittee of the Imperial Defence Committee, which sought to finalise the BBC's war-time transmitter arrangements. The Air Ministry would have liked to close down broadcasting altogether in war-time because the transmissions could assist enemy aircraft, but the Home Office wanted broadcasting to continue as a means of communicating with, and reassuring, the public.[138] Finally, as will be seen, the Air Ministry's objections were overcome. Research Department engineers produced field-strength contour maps for various schemes, based on synchronisation to within 0·05 Hz and assuming a 'safe' field-strength ratio of 4:1. After some of these schemes had been turned down by the Air Ministry, one was accepted embodying two groups of synchronised transmitters, each group consisting of four high-power transmitters; Fighter Command was to be authorised to close down one or two transmitters in each group if enemy aircraft were plotted within about twenty-five miles of them. If it became necessary to close down a third transmitter, owing to increasing enemy activity, it was accepted that the complete group would be closed down. This scheme had the advantage from the broadcasting point of view that listeners had a chance of receiving a signal from other stations in the group, particularly at night time, if their 'local' transmitter was closed down by Fighter Command. The technical subcommittee accepted this proposal in July 1938 but preparations had been put in hand several months before so that there should be a minimum of delay in installing equipment.

Unfortunately, the Air Ministry would not permit the Droitwich high-power long-wave transmitter with its nation-wide coverage to be used for war-time broadcasting because there were no other high-power long-wave broadcast transmitters in the country suitably located to act as 'spoilers', i.e. to prevent its use as a radio beacon. It was accepted, however, that this transmitter could be used exceptionally for the radiation of urgent navigational warnings issued by the Admiralty.

Between October 1937 and September 1938 a BBC committee on broadcasting in war-time met nine times, with Ashbridge present on each occasion. Sub-committees were formed to work out the logistics of staffing under war-time conditions and to divide the staff into those who would be needed to operate and maintain war-time broadcasting and those who would not be required and who would be encouraged to find war-time service that the BBC could approve.[139] The latter staff were designated Category C and, as might be expected, the number of Engineering Division staff falling into this category was a small proportion of the total number of staff in the Division – about 12 per cent. The sub-committee also dealt with the protection of key points against air attack, the provision of emergency supplies, the acquisition of sites outside the London area and the equipping of them as emergency studio centres, and the erection of blast walls and gas-proof shelters to protect the staff. By September 1939 the plans for evacuation and dispersal of staff were well advanced.

Reith left the BBC on 30 June 1938 and was replaced some ten days later by F. W. Ogilvie. By this time the BBC's preparations for war were fully under way and no modifications to policy in this respect resulted from the change in Chief Executive. The preparations were intensified as the international situation deteriorated and by the time of the Munich crisis in September 1938 arrangements were complete for the operation of two groups of synchronised transmitters radiating a single programme and subject to being closed down on the instructions of Fighter Command. A mobile reserve transmitter of 2 kW output power was also available for operation in either of the two groups as a replacement for a transmitter which might be damaged by air attack. The Munich crisis served as a dress rehearsal for the change to war-time arrangements, which were to come into full operation a year later. The intervening period allowed time for consolidating the temporary, but workable, installations at transmitting stations and for preparing studio and recording facilities outside the London area.

Each of the eight high-power transmitters was provided with a high-precision radio-frequency drive to replace the temporary equipment hurriedly installed in the summer of 1938. Means were provided for the 'slave' transmitters in each group to compare their carrier frequencies with that of the 'master' station of the group by radio pick-up, thus obviating the need for line links for this purpose. In order to reduce the likelihood of enemy monitoring stations obtaining a 'DF fix' on the master station of a group when it was radiating alone for frequency-checking purposes, it was planned that such radiation should be for a few minutes only at random times each day and would take place only if Fighter Command confirmed that there was no enemy air activity reported in the vicinity of the UK.

A series of very stable transmitter drives was produced and each variation in design, of which there were some fifty during the war years, received a 'CP–' coding. The temporary pre-Munich drives were coded 'CP–1' and the consolidated version was coded 'CP–2'. On the same apparatus bay as the 'CP–2' drive was installed a second equipment coded 'CP–3' and overtly referred to as the wave-change drive for 1940. This equipment was, however, used as a reserve for the main war-time equipment after being rebuilt during the first three months of the war and housed in a secure location in another part of each transmitting station. The synchronising equipment used at this time has been fully described.[6, 140] The success of the synchronising scheme was due in no small part to the excellence of the quartz crystals provided by the Post Office Research Station at Dollis Hill. The BBC engineers received full co-operation from the Post Office engineers engaged in the production of the crystals and they were invariably delivered in time to permit the BBC to keep its target dates.

The two initial synchronised transmitter groups were as follows, the first-named in each group being the 'master' station:

Group A (668 kHz)	*Group B (767 kHz)*
Moorside Edge (Northern Regional)	Westerglen (Scottish Regional)
Droitwich (Midland Regional)	Burghead
Washford (Welsh Regional)	Lisnagarvey
Brookmans Park (London Regional)	Stagshaw

Apart from the provision of synchronising apparatus, five of these transmitters had to be adjusted to their war-time frequencies – the remaining three transmitters were not required to change – and information had to be given to the Engineers-in-Charge to ensure a trouble-free changeover when the time came. During the preliminary wave-change tests, arrangements were made to radiate from more than one station on the frequency being used with the idea of confusing an enemy monitoring station that might be attempting to discover the locations of transmitters operating on BBC channels. The many precautions taken to confuse enemy intelligence agencies interested in the BBC's activities may now seem unnecessary, but in the years immediately preceding the war there was a strong feeling that the enemy would attempt to disrupt broadcasting at the start of hostilities by attacking transmitting stations and studio centres or by intensive jamming. In the event, this did not happen.

The realisation in September 1938 that the menace of Hitler's Germany might have to be resisted by force of arms gave new impetus to the planning work of the BBC's Defence Committee. The following account stems largely from notes written by Ralph Wade who, as Director of Office Accommodation before the war, was closely concerned with preparations for the evacuation of London premises if enemy bombardment made this necessary. It was the idea of evacuation that sprang to the forefront as a result of the events of Munich; there seems to have been an assumption that, whereas German aircraft would attack London, cities such as Bristol and even Glasgow would be immune.

After the 1938 crisis it was suggested that it might be wise to send to the country various records and possibly a part of the Accounts Department in the event of war. There were clearly engineering implications in such plans, and when the search for suitable 'country' premises began, it was a trio consisting of H. Bishop, M. T. Tudsbery and Ralph Wade, which, during the autumn and early winter of 1938–9 made excursions over various parts of the Home Counties to the north and north-west of London to look for suitable premises. During these trips the worsening international situation and the general national attitude towards the evacuation of London helped to expand the original plan into one of much greater scope and caused the net to be thrown much further afield, until it reached Toddington in Gloucestershire, where the group found what was until then the most likely property. By this time, however, other factors had begun to influence the search. There were thoughts of possible emergency studio accommodation and of finding a suitable location for a monitoring service, for both of which adequate communications would be essential. When the agents (Knight, Frank & Rutley) mentioned Wood Norton Hall, a detour was made to inspect it. It seemed to fulfil the requirements, including the important one of adequate Post Office lines, and thus it came about that in the spring of 1939 the BBC became the owners of Wood Norton Hall, which had been once the home of the Duke of Orleans and later a preparatory school.

The mansion could be described in estate agents' language as a commodious residence of period charm standing in its own spacious grounds and private woodlands. It was (and is, despite the ravages of a fire that occurred during the war) an attractive building with fine wood panelling in the principal rooms and with a remarkable proliferation of fleur-de-lis – particularly in the bathroom. It is approached through magnificent gates, which came to be known as the 'Golden Gates', and a winding drive leading up to the eminence on which the main building stands. An important feature from the practical point of view was that there was plenty of room for the erection of temporary buildings and also of a monitoring hut remote from possible sources of electrical interference.

Almost immediately on the acquisition of Wood Norton, W. Bruce Purslow was transferred there as Engineer-in-Charge. He took up his duties there on Easter Monday 1939. (Mussolini had invaded Albania on Good Friday.) Everything was done in strict secrecy. As a part of the precautions, the purchase of Wood Norton had been carried out in the name of F. L. Hetley, one of the BBC's Legal Assistants, who, while walking round the grounds one day, found himself challenged by Purslow who, quite properly, insisted on everyone showing his pass. Hetley was able to say, with some pride, 'Oh, it's all right, I'm only the owner.'

The efforts to maintain complete secrecy on the purpose for which Wood Norton was to be used were assisted by rumours that circulated locally and were not denied by BBC staff. Among the more colourful of these was one that Wood Norton was being prepared as a home for the Duke and Duchess of Windsor, and another that the Emperor of Abyssinia was to settle there. It seemed that the secret had been kept

219

until a BBC engineer, H. Sarney, reported that he had visited the Berlin Radio Exhibition in the spring of 1939 and had there met a German acquaintance who claimed to know all about Wood Norton and actually produced photographs of it.

The existing buildings at Wood Norton included not only the mansion itself but houses nearby, which retained their original names and subsequently became known to generations of students of the Engineering Training Centre as the Steward's House, and Mrs Smith's Cottage. A number of temporary buildings were put up by the BBC during the development of Wood Norton as an emergency studio centre and later as a training centre. The studio that was hurriedly set up in 1939 had old-fashioned OB equipment, the new OBA/8 amplifier being not yet generally available. A temporary control room was installed in the pantry of the Steward's House, with the OB amplifiers mounted on the original shelves. This pantry was about 12 ft by 8 ft and its small size proved to be a disadvantage when a soda-acid type fire extinguisher was accidentally discharged while the room was occupied by a visiting party that included the Vice-Chairman of the Board of Governors and the Director-General.

In the last few days before the outbreak of war the temporary control room in the Steward's House was being supplemented by the installation of a more permanent and better-equipped one in the main building. This work was done with great urgency because of the rapid deterioration of the national situation, and within a few days of the outbreak of war half a dozen studios were ready for use at Wood Norton. A monitoring station had been established on the top of Tunnel Hill, within the grounds, and a fully-equipped workshop had been provided. Two Post Office teleprinter channels had been installed for transmitting monitored material to London and Post Office lines had been installed by two alternative routes for communication with the main network and with the telephone exchange. Cables had also been put in by the Post Office on the estate itself to inter-connect the various buildings and huts. The lines terminated at a distribution frame in a small room, which also contained a manual PBX with two operators' positions and capacity for 100 extensions. Plans were also made for the distribution of News Agency services by teleprinter to Wood Norton when required, but these plans had not been carried out when war broke out.

By the summer of 1939 it was realised that, although there would be only a single programme for home listeners in war-time, this would have to include not only news but other ingredients of a balanced programme to entertain the people, maintain their interest, and keep them in good heart. This made it necessary to provide other dispersal centres in addition to Wood Norton and arrangements were made to set up such centres in Bristol, Bangor (North Wales) and Bedford for the various programme departments. The OBA/8 amplifier and its associated equipment began to come off the production line in appreciable quantities about this time and it proved to be one of the most valuable technical assets the BBC possessed. It was versatile, it could be either mains-driven or battery-operated, and it had its own four-channel mixer and built-in programme meter. It was therefore well suited to many emergency purposes and was widely used in war-time control rooms and emergency OB premises.

Preparations for war also included the rapid expansion of broadcasting in foreign languages. News Bulletins in French, German and Italian were radiated by the medium-wave national transmitters for short periods each day, displacing the normal programme in English. The additional short-wave transmitters mentioned in Section 5 of this chapter increased the complement of operational transmitters at Daventry to eight and by September 1939 thirty aerial arrays were available for broadcasting in the short-wave bands.

The preparations also included the provision of a 'War Book', which was compiled by M. J. L. Pulling ready for issue in August 1939. It gave detailed instructions on what was to be done in all foreseeable circumstances when an executive message was received to put the war-time plans into operation. These included changes in wavelength of some of the medium-wave stations, the closing of others, the start of the single national programme, the closure of the Television Service, and the re-scheduling of the Empire Service. These arrangements were protected by a number of security checks and code words. A preliminary warning message from the Home Office would result in the long-wave transmitter and the London, North, and West National medium-wave transmitters on 1149 kHz being switched to London to take announcements telling listeners on which wavelengths they should listen when the change to war-time conditions had been effected. Similar arrangements were made for informing short-wave listeners of the changes in the Empire Service schedule. The Engineers-in-Charge of all transmitting stations had already received sealed instructions telling them what to do when the executive message was received, the time allowed to effect the transition from peace-time to war-time frequencies being two hours.

Engineering preparations for war did not end with installations in the United Kingdom. In 1938 the Air Ministry began to press the French Ministry of Aviation to introduce transmitter synchronising in France, because efforts to deny navigational aid to the enemy would be partly nullified if the French continued to operate their broadcasting transmitters on exclusive wavelengths – particularly those in Northern France. As no agreement had been reached by August 1939, a delegation from the Air Ministry and the BBC then went to Paris to urge the importance of introducing a synchronised transmitter scheme as soon as war was declared. After much discussion, the French accepted the British proposals and, to assist them in putting them into effect without delay, the BBC manufactured three synchronising equipments (CP–6) for installation at French stations. The installation of this apparatus was done by G. G. Gouriet (later Chief Engineer, Research & Development) and Norman D'Arcy of the Research Department under the direction of W. Proctor Wilson, then a Squadron Leader in the RAF. The installations were completed just before the fall of France in June 1940, but the failure of the French authorities to close down or synchronise the Fécamp transmitter in Normandy somewhat reduced their effectiveness.

The Irish Republic maintained its neutrality throughout the war, which was officially known there as 'The Emergency'. Since 1925, when plans were being made for a broadcasting service in Ireland, the BBC and the British Post Office had given constant help and advice to the Irish broadcasting service and this has been hand-somely acknowledged by Maurice Gorham.[141] During the war Ireland suffered very severe shortages and it was almost impossible to obtain supplies of equipment. In January 1941 the BBC made a 2-kW medium-wave transmitter available to Radio Eireann to replace the original Dublin transmitter (2RN), which had been in operation since 1926.

The 100-kW transmitter at Athlone on 565 kHz constituted a radio beacon that would have been valuable to enemy aircraft approaching the United Kingdom from the south-west. The BBC accordingly installed synchronising equipment at Clevedon, Penmon and Redmoss, so that these stations could be synchronised with Athlone on the outbreak of war. Later, in October 1940, three stations in Ireland (Athlone, Dublin and Cork) were synchronised on the Athlone frequency.

At this time there were substantial developments in the monitoring of foreign stations for programme content. Monitoring of news bulletins from foreign stations had been started by the Foreign Office during the war between Italy and Abyssinia in 1935, and in March 1939 plans were made to set up several monitoring stations capable of receiving foreign programmes twenty-four hours a day. An alternative scheme was to provide selected experts with short-wave receivers for use in their own homes. When Wood Norton became available a small monitoring unit was estab-lished there. The equipment included a number of National HRO receivers with simple aerials and a long-wire Beverage aerial directed towards Germany. Frame aerials were also provided to assist in reducing interference.

CHAPTER IV

The War Years: 1939–45

I STUDIOS FOR THE RADIO SERVICES

On 1 September 1939 the BBC was already on a war footing. On that day the television service closed down, the radio services for home listeners were reduced to one, changes were made in the external services, outside broadcasts almost ceased, and plans for the dispersal of staff were put into effect. The BBC periodical *World-Radio*, often quoted in the earlier chapters of this book, ceased publication with the issue of that date.

At 11 am on 3 September 1939 the Prime Minister (Neville Chamberlain) announced in a broadcast that Britain was at war with Germany. The single programme for home listeners was being distributed from a war-time control room, which had just been set up in a small room adjacent to the balcony of Studio BA in Broadcasting House. (The normal control room was on the eighth floor in an exposed position under the mansard roof and could not be used during air raids.) The PBX had been moved to the balcony of Studio BA. Wood Norton had assumed the functions of a reserve studio centre for the Home Programme, with W. B. Purslow as Engineer-in-Charge. Work had been going on there during the spring and early summer to create both an emergency headquarters and a monitoring centre. In August, when war was at last seen to be inevitable and might come within days, a supreme effort was made to extend the facilities at Wood Norton. Earlier in the year three small studios had been set up in the 'Steward's House', and connected to a makeshift control room in the same building. Before the end of August a more permanent control room was being installed in the main building and more studios were being prepared to bring the total up to six. OBA/8 amplifiers and other equipment were on order, but were not scheduled for delivery for some months. Events would not wait for the usual procedures of making drawings and specifications, but on 25 August 1939 an engineer in Equipment Department (L. G. Smith) had undertaken to move some mains-operated OBA/8 equipment from the Training School in Duchess Street and re-install it 'in a secret place' within a month. Most of the manual staff had been dispersed and most of those who were left were either unfit or unskilled. Many of the engineers had also been dispersed to various places by that time. Smith commandeered a large pantechnicon from the garage at Avenue House, Clapham, and with a charge-hand and a good wireman who were working in Broadcasting House, started the same afternoon to dismantle the equipment; with the help of another engineer, a gardener and a handyman, they had assembled it ready for collection early the next day. They set off in the morning, arriving at Wood Norton after lunch on Saturday, 26 August, and for the next week worked almost day and night on the installation of the equipment to form the new control room in the main building. By the following Tuesday week, 5 September, two days after the war had started, the new control room was ready for operation with temporary equipment despite the fact that lt rectifiers and two transformers had had to be installed in the cellar and heavy lead-covered 7/·036-in. twin filament-supply cables had had to be run from each rectifier to each amplifier. All the ht leads were of single lead-covered cable, and 1-pr/10-lb lead-covered cable was used for all the programme circuits. The main control position was formed from a large microphone-decoupling box turned on its side, with the old six-channel dramatic control unit from Duchess Street mounted on top of it.

From 6 September 1939 the studios at Wood Norton were in frequent use for Music Productions, Schools Programmes, Features and Drama, these departments having moved to Wood Norton during the first few days of the war.

More equipment gradually became available, and some three months later the rack-mounted amplifiers that had originally been ordered began to arrive – so that by the beginning of 1940 Wood Norton had become one of the largest broadcasting centres in Europe, with an output averaging 1300 programme items per week, or about 835 hours of broadcasting.

The preparations that had been made for the movement of staff began to be put into effect eight days before Germany invaded Poland – ten days before Britain declared war on Germany. Ralph Wade, the Director of Office Administration, was to take an advance party from London to Evesham, on 24 August 1939. Buses were ordered, collected their passengers and set off. Wade started simultaneously in his own car with his secretary and a typist, fortified with £100 in notes in case of need. This gave rise to the legend that Wade started with £100 and two girls and arrived with £2 and a hundred girls. Owing to magneto trouble the buses did not arrive until the early hours of the following morning, by which time Wade had broken the news to the people of Evesham that they would have to stay awake half the night to receive into their homes a host of unwelcome strangers. J. H. Holmes (later Head of Lines Department) had earlier been designated as Lines Engineer at Wood Norton and had gone there on 23 August to make some tests on the SB lines. At the railway station he was handed a message telling him to stay at Wood Norton until further orders – which did not come until almost three years later.

The people of Evesham, essentially an agricultural community, found themselves faced with a new and strange experience. They were called upon to take in an alien population, many of whom were foreigners employed in the Monitoring Service, who spoke strange languages and came from different backgrounds. In the words of S. G. Williams, who was in charge of the administrative arrangements for the Monitoring Service, 'it seems remarkable that the people of Evesham responded so well to what must have been a traumatic experience for them'. The military authorities in the area viewed the presence of so many foreigners with considerable suspicion and had to be persuaded that they were carrying out an important war-time duty.

The staff at Wood Norton had not long to wait for their initiation into war-time conditions. Immediately after the Prime Minister's message on 3 September, the air-raid sirens sounded in many places; but not at Wood Norton, where the outbreak of war was heralded by the playing of the 'Teddy Bears' Picnic' through loudspeakers. This was a prearranged air-raid signal, and the staff carried out their instructions and took shelter in the woods. As, through an oversight, no 'All Clear' signal had been prearranged, their stay in the woods was prolonged indefinitely.

At first conditions at Wood Norton were far from easy. The gravel paths that traversed the estate became a sea of mud in wet weather and the stream of messengers carrying recording cylinders between the main building and the monitoring station at the top of the hill had a long walk through tangled woods up a steep hill difficult to negotiate in icy weather. The cellars were damp and thousands of envelopes became stuck down prematurely. There were compensations. The staff treated the whole thing as a great adventure and, as Wade has recounted, the canteen manageress, Miss E. M. V. Lawrence, produced wonderful meals in the adapted cowshed that was then used as the restaurant. A particular menace was the ornamental fountain on the lawn in front of the main building. It caused several misadventures in the blackout, and the pleasure of watching the goldfish in the day-time was offset by the discomfort of falling into the water at night. Approval to demolish the fountain was long in coming and, according to Wade, plans were made to eliminate it 'by mistake'. It was finally demolished with official approval. At least once a car remained bogged down in the woods for some days before a tractor could be spared to salvage it. There were at Wood Norton a hundred or so bicycles, one or two lightweight motorcycles, an old Austin car and a shooting-brake; if anybody wanted transport between Wood Norton and the town of Evesham he took whatever vehicle was available and drove it from Wood Norton into Evesham, leaving it in the courtyard of the Northwick Hotel. If anybody wanted to come back, he went to the courtyard of the hotel, took whatever vehicle might be there and drove it back to Wood Norton. It was not long before order was brought into the use of transport, and two double-decker buses were acquired; these were old LGOC solid-tyred buses, purchased before the war for emergency use.

When the time came to wire up the Wood Norton control room (after the initial hurried installation had been completed) 1-pr/10-lb lead-covered cable was scarce, and to connect the distribution frame to the jack-field a length of 38-pair quadded cable was used. From that day on multicore cable was used increasingly in the Wood Norton installation and elsewhere.

Wood Norton was the first of many war-time studio premises to be equipped with the new OBA/8 amplifier and its associated MX/18 four-channel mixer. Also associated with it were two new trap-valve amplifiers. (A trap-valve amplifier was simply an amplifier with a high-impedance input, several of which could be paralleled across the output of the main amplifier to feed individual distribution lines without risk of interaction between them.) The TV/17 had one input and four outputs, and the TV/18 had two inputs, each of which had two outputs (input 1 fed outputs 1 and 2, input 2 fed outputs 3 and 4). There was considerable confusion about the labelling of all these inputs and outputs on jack-fields, especially as the diagram referred to inputs 1 and 2, while the labels on the amplifiers referred to inputs A and B – one of those little contretemps that can occur even in peace-time.

The provision of communications for Wood Norton was, in itself, a major undertaking. The initial installation for office telephones, which had been put in before the war, was limited to a hundred extensions provided in connection with two positions of a Post Office switchboard, powered from Leclanché cells. These cells produced unpleasant fumes and the whole installation was seen, almost immediately, to be too small for the rate at which it was likely that Wood Norton would expand; already on 29 September, that is, less than one month after occupation, a meeting was held with the Post Office to decide on the location of an extended PBX switchboard.

The few programme circuits that were in regular use were those that formerly ran through Stratford-on-Avon on one of the direct routes between London and Birmingham, but could be diverted to Evesham and thence to Wood Norton. There were also two open-wire lines to Droitwich that were intended for emergency purposes. As an extra precaution, in case normal telephonic communication broke down three trunk subscribers' circuits to the Birmingham trunk exchange were rented.

The equipment at Wood Norton for the Monitoring Service will be described in section 7 of this chapter, but it is convenient to mention here the communication facilities that were provided for this service. The direction of the service remained in London in Scott's Hotel, adjoining Broadcasting House, and, from the beginning of the war, the unit at Wood Norton needed a teleprinter channel to communicate the monitored material to London. This channel, provided by the Post Office, caused a great deal of trouble at the beginning, and joint efforts to keep it working marked the beginning of years of friendly and fruitful co-operation between the BBC engineers at Wood Norton and those from many different sections of the Post Office in the North Midlands area. Tribute must be paid to A. G. Cook, who was Acting Telephone Manager. He was a blunt, stern man who, once a need became apparent to him, would let nothing stand in the way of fulfilling it. Wood Norton was also fortunate in having one of the local Post Office staff, Maurice Hughes, to look after the maintenance of their equipment; BBC engineers were often saved from having to turn out in the middle of the night to deal with a 'BBC fault' by the fact that Hughes was on the premises and dealt with it, and vice versa.

The expansion of the Monitoring Service into new wooden huts on the Wood Norton estate meant the provision of more and more communication facilities. Soon there were two teleprinter channels to London and even these were so fully occupied that an automatic tape perforator and an automatic transmitter had to be provided to increase the capacity of the lines. It proved hard to persuade the Monitoring Service to accept this method of working and the staff found the actual operation difficult. There were, however, a few operators who could use the system successfully, and in the end it settled down.

The PBX had to be extended by the installation of four new positions, which made it necessary to extend the existing switchroom while the two existing boards, heavily loaded, were kept in service. In 1940 the stable yard adjoining the canteen was roofed over to provide a much larger restaurant, which has remained in use for more than thirty years. By this time most of the monitoring activities had been transferred from the top of the hill to huts near the main building and the total staff at Wood Norton then exceeded a thousand. Several outlying premises had also been taken over, including Park Hall, Salford Priors, which was intended for the Accounts Department and was finally occupied by the Registry when it moved from Bristol. The Equipment Department occupied Hampton House where workshops, stores and garages were set up. The planning of a camp at Park Hall, to provide sleeping accommodation, was undertaken by the Building Department. It was partially erected, using pre-fabricated reinforced concrete sections, but was never completed.

The arrival of the Latin-American, Spanish, Portuguese, Indian and Near East Departments at Wood Norton and Abbey Manor in September 1940 meant that further news agency teleprinters had to be provided, in addition to those already installed in the Steward's House for Home News in case the latter had to be evacuated from London. The number of news agency services to be accommodated also increased: Press Association had two and British United Press, the Exchange Telegraph and Reuters one each. These five services shared a four-channel voice-frequency Post Office carrier telegraph system via Birmingham, and a metallic circuit from London. The receiving terminal of the carrier system was installed in the Wood Norton main building, and the Post Office was responsible for its maintenance. The Post Office were also responsible for the maintenance of the BUP teleprinter, but Lines Department took over the maintenance of all the other agency teleprinters, J. S. Norwell being the expert in this field. This was something entirely new in the BBC and started a proliferation, both during the war and afterwards, of teleprinter and associated apparatus in the internal communications system.

Many other communication facilities were put into Wood Norton, including 'private wires' (for telephony) to Government Departments and various key points. As in London, there was a private wire to Fighter Command, so that in the event of Wood Norton having to take over the control of programmes, Fighter Command would still be able to exercise immediate control over the BBC transmitters. There was also a facility for the diversion of this line to the emergency Fighter Command Headquarters – two belts and two pairs of braces. Similar double-banked emergency telephone connections were provided to other key points. Some of these emergency lines terminated at Abbey Manor, about a mile from Wood Norton, where the emergency offices of the BBC Direction were to be.

Abbey Manor, the home of the local squire, had been taken over as an evacuation centre for Empire News – the 'Red' Network – when enemy air attacks on Britain were intensified in the summer of 1940. This placed still heavier demands on facilities for communication at a time when there was a shortage of all kinds of line plant, owing mainly to the presence in the Midlands of an increasing number of airfields and service camps with higher priority than the BBC.

There were finally at least seventeen cables, ranging in size from four pairs to 152 pairs at Wood Norton. Those coming in from outside were rented from the Post Office, which also supplied and installed those within the estate itself.

Abbey Manor was the scene of the first introduction of continuity working. The

Q

idea of using such a system at Abbey Manor originated with T. W. Chalmers, who was in charge of programme operations there. The possibilities of some such way of working had been discussed before the war, as mentioned in the previous chapter, but had never been put into practice. R. T. B. Wynn was a strong champion of this system and the plan was discussed with W. B. Purslow (a colourful personality, described by Chalmers as an 'unorthodox engineer') who was then, as EiC Wood Norton, responsible for the technical operations at Abbey Manor. J. A. G. Mitchell supervised the formation of a continuity suite to take the output from the three studios, for distribution over the network via Wood Norton. A presentation assistant sat alongside the engineer who was doing the mixing, fading and communication.

Almost at the peak of activity of the Wood Norton complex came the great fire. On the evening of 4 September 1940, everything was going on as usual – the EiC, for once, had gone off on time, the AEiC was still in his office at about 6 pm signing a few memoranda, the Lines Engineer was in the control room testing an OB circuit from Bourton-on-the-Water – when the AEiC, R. C. Patrick, noticed smoke blowing past the office window. He ran out of the office and up to the top floor, seizing a fire-extinguisher on the way. When he got to where the smoke was densest he found the foreman to the building contractors, Higgs & Hill. The seat of the fire appeared to be in the attic, and the foreman knew a place where the floor of the attic could be breached (the trap-door was by then unapproachable because of dense smoke). Patrick managed to hoist him up and he shouted that there was nothing that could be done with fire extinguishers. Meanwhile, the SME in charge of the control room had sent for the Evesham, Pershore and Worcester fire brigades. They arrived very promptly, but had to run their pipes right down to the river because, owing to the very dry summer, there was no water in the compound. The flames were finally got under control at about 1 am the next morning. The engineers were successful in getting all the valuable equipment out of the control room, though, fortunately, this room remained undamaged. Broadcasting was not interrupted; an orchestral broadcast under the direction of Stanford Robinson had to be cancelled, but by about 2 am the following morning, Wood Norton was able to give a tape reproduction of it via the emergency control room in the Steward's House, to which the circuits had been plugged through as soon as it was possible to regain access to the main control room – then about a foot under water. There was no lack of volunteers to salvage records, office furniture, filing cabinets, typewriters, and even teleprinters, and within about three-quarters of an hour almost everything of any value was saved from the fire and the water. The extent of the damage – apart from the drenching of the whole building with water – was confined to the roof and a few rooms directly beneath it. Within a very short time a temporary roof was put up, all the equipment was re-installed and, although the number of available rooms was now reduced, Wood Norton went back to normal. Several of the Post Office circuits were put out of action, but were quickly restored by means of 'interruption cable'.

The cause of the fire was never definitely known. The most likely explanation seems to have been that sunlight coming through a glass skylight had ignited a beam. There was much concern in London, as well as at Wood Norton, lest the fire should act as a beacon for enemy aircraft, which were known to be in the vicinity of Wood Norton. But a number of heath fires had broken out on the Malvern Hills and it was these that attracted the attention of the enemy bombers.

In the summer of 1941 a BBC carrier telephone system was installed, working over two programme circuits, one in each direction, between London and Wood Norton. (A system of this kind had already been tried out experimentally between London and Bristol.) These programme circuits were an outgoing circuit used for dispatching programmes from Wood Norton for the network, and an incoming one for receiving contributions. The telephone circuits provided by the carrier system could be used when the lines were not needed for programme transmission. This was a notable milestone, because it led after the war to a complete revolution of the internal communication system of the BBC. The equipment provided two telephone channels, one in the lower half of the frequency band on the physical circuit and the other a single side-band suppressed carrier channel in the upper half of the band. Later, a teleprinter circuit was added as a London–Wood Norton inter-office teleprinter channel.

Owing to the devastation in London caused by heavy air raids in 1941, plans were made for crash evacuation, and emergency studios were constructed on the lawn at Wood Norton. A Lines Department hut, too, was built on the lawn adjacent to these studios, and was planned to house various items of communication equipment, carrier systems and test gear. These huts, with their associated communication cables, were ready by April 1942.

In spite of all these plans to cope with a deteriorating situation, activity at Wood Norton began to wane during the latter part of 1941. By 1 April 1943, when the Monitoring Service moved to Caversham, Wood Norton had reverted to little more than the potential evacuation centre that it had been in 1939.

The war created a pressing need for more studios at other centres too. Features and Drama moved on from Wood Norton to Manchester in November 1939. At Bristol, designated as the evacuation centre for the Music Department, a hall in the centre of the city was taken over and converted for use by the Symphony Orchestra, which played there for about a year until bombing became too heavy. Almost immediately after the outbreak of the war there arrived a large number of people from Light Music, Entertainment, Listener Research, Administration, and others. In April 1940 Schools Programmes, which had been at Wood Norton, also came to Bristol. A great effort therefore had to be made to find premises that could quickly be converted into studios. Bristol, being a centre of non-conformity, had a large number of church halls, mostly built in the Victorian era of stone with lean-to timbered roofs and wooden floors; it was found that these, with very little alteration, apart from hanging up Cabot's quilting, could be used. It was necessary to install a control room in each of these premises and to find OB-type amplifiers and mixers for them. One of the Bristol SMEs, G. T. Myers, renowned for his great girth and as a spectacular swimmer and diver, entered into this work of conversion with tremendous enthusiasm. One of the church halls consisted of two large rooms, one above the other; the

229

ceiling height made them unsuitable as studios individually, so the floor between them was removed and they were made into one large studio.

When the bombing in Bristol increased, Light Entertainment was transferred to the Winter Gardens, Weston-super-Mare, where more church halls were taken over, and some hotels. They stayed for some years until new accommodation was found for them in Bangor, North Wales. The Symphony Orchestra went to Bedford towards the end of 1941.

An important feature of the war-time broadcasting arrangements in Bristol was the Clifton Rocks Railway Tunnel. This was a funicular railway tunnel built about a hundred years before through the solid rock from the river up to Clifton, about 400 ft higher up. When the enemy bombing became very intense in the winter of 1940–1, this tunnel was taken over and seven studios were formed in tiers up the steep surface of the subterranean rocks, each being a self-contained unit with an emergency power supply and its own store of food and water. There were also several transmitters, including a medium-wave one that served as the Bristol 'Group H' transmitter. There was also a recording studio, but there seem to have been no live broadcasts from the tunnel.[1]

On one of Queen Mary's visits to Bristol, she wished to see the broadcasting arrangements, including those in the Clifton Rocks Tunnel. Attempts by the EiC to dissuade her from climbing several hundreds of steps through the dripping rock were unsuccessful and the stamina of those accompanying her was sorely tried.

During the 'phoney' war period people, understandably, became dissatisfied with the emergency accommodation provided for them. No doubt they felt that, as there appeared to be no emergency there was no need for them to be so far removed from their normal personal and professional background. This showed itself especially at Wood Norton. First the Drama Department went off to Manchester, where a temporary studio had to be erected for them in the theatre below the Public Library. The Schools Department did not like Wood Norton and went to Bristol, to be followed later by the part of the Music Department that was at Wood Norton. This meant finding more and more studio accommodation in Bristol; fortunately the number of church halls seemed to be limitless, but when Bristol became untenable as a production headquarters further dispersion became inevitable. At one time there were three groups of the Variety Department in separate places (Bristol, Weston-super-Mare and Bangor), but the whole of Variety was eventually moved to Bangor. This again led to a great search for church halls; two theatres, most of the church halls and a cinema in the North Wales district were taken over. During the period of the German-Russian campaign in 1942, and the lull in the bombing of this country, most of the cinemas and theatres in London had reopened and Variety Department could not get the artists to go as far afield as Bangor. They then moved back to London, leaving only a unit in Bangor. This meant again converting halls, notably the two in Bond Street known as the Aeolian Halls. Drama Department were in the same difficulty through not being able to get their artists to go to Manchester, and they, too, gradually filtered back to London and used the large Maida Vale studios. Other conversions in London were the Paris Cinema, the Monseigneur Cinema and the

Criterion Theatre. When the flying bomb (V1) and rocket (V2) attacks began, no further attempt was made to disperse departments; each carried on as best it could in one or other of these studios.

The emergency control room near the gallery of Studio BA in Broadcasting House, London, was only about 15 ft by 20 ft and, even with the reduced programme commitments at the beginning of the war, it soon became intolerably cramped. After about a year it was decided to convert Studio BA itself into a war-time control room. This was the occasion to introduce 'continuity', which had already proved a success at Abbey Manor, into the working of the Broadcasting House studios. Continuity cubicles, each consisting of a control point and a place for the announcer, were constructed in Studio BA; at first there were only two, one for the 'Home' and one for the 'Forces' programme (which was introduced in 1940), but continuity had now become an essential part of the broadcasting chain and has remained so ever since.

In 1941, when the LF Section of Equipment Department was transferred to the Station Design and Installation Department, C. H. Colborn and H. D. Ellis of that department were asked to design simplified studio equipment for war-time control rooms. Supplies of the AC/SP3 valve were coming in and mains-operated amplifiers were designed around it; a small mains unit, the MU/16, was also produced in large numbers to give supplies of 6 V ac and 300 V smoothed dc. These units were freely used in the construction of the war-time control room in Broadcasting House, as well as trap-valve amplifiers of the types mentioned in connection with Wood Norton. There were, however, extreme difficulties caused by the war-time shortage of components and materials. Relay and lamp-signalling on control lines was abandoned and the simpler drop-indicator was used for calling. Standard jack-strips, each consisting of a row of twenty jacks mounted on a narrow wooden panel, were used to build up whatever jack-fields were necessary. Switching operations were performed by means of double-ended cords, with the result that there was an apparently inextricable cat's-cradle of connecting cords, and switching was always fraught with some danger to programmes on neighbouring cords.

Inside the control room was a table for the Senior Maintenance Engineer and a small glass-fronted cabin for the Senior Control Room Engineer. Two rows of line-termination bays were used for switching SB lines and those connecting other London Studios with Broadcasting House. Next came rows of amplifier bays, including ac test bays towards the rear, and right at the back there was a distribution frame where cables were terminated, and other bays containing U-link panels connected with the Post Office main distribution frame on the Lower Ground Floor. These U-link panels marked the frontier of the Post Office's responsibility. On the right-hand side of the control room was a row of positions equipped with OBA/8 amplifiers, which were used for programmes for recording and for those in transit through Broadcasting House. In the gallery there were more bays containing all the OB positions, connected by separate link cables to the Post Office main distribution frame and comprising transmission test equipment, variable equalisers, etc.

Asa Briggs refers to the 500-lb bomb that exploded inside Broadcasting House on 15 October and the land-mine that descended in the middle of Portland Place on

8 December 1940.[2] The bomb killed seven people and caused extensive damage, but the fact that the building as a whole withstood the explosion testified to its great strength. Bruce Belfrage, reading the nine o'clock news, continued as if nothing had happened. Even more serious damage was done by the land-mine; Asa Briggs mentions the 'superb job' done by BBC engineers in restoring the equipment and wiring afterwards. The present author has vivid memories of the land-mine. When it drifted down on a parachute, a fire warden on the roof reported by telephone that something had just passed him so close that he could almost have caught it. Immediately afterwards the building was rocked by the explosion and the Security Officer below responded: 'Butter fingers!' The fire produced a great deal of acrid smoke from smouldering building-board inside the air ducts. The quantity of water discharged in fighting the fire made the staircases like waterfalls. The canteen staff continued to dispense tea, the invigorating effects of which were somewhat chilled by water dripping from pendant lights on to the tables, though the lights did not go out. An engineer, L. D. Macgregor, who was on the pavement in Portland Place when the bomb exploded in the centre of the road, has described how the alternate waves of compression and rarefaction pulled him back and forth across the pavement and how he saw masonry falling around him in absolute silence. His eardrums were pierced by the blast, but he afterwards regained his hearing. He doubtless owed his life to the fact that the main force of the explosion went upwards and passed over him.

During the war, engineers, like other staff, took their turn in fire-watching and fire-fighting. Many of those whose duties permitted it joined BBC contingents of the Home Guard. At one time, sleeping accommodation had to be provided for about four hundred members of the staff each night. Mattresses were laid in the Concert Hall and in the inner corridors in Broadcasting House, in the Paris Cinema, in the Criterion Theatre, and in the basement of Scott's Hotel.

The studio centre in Belfast was in rather a different position from the other studio centres during the war. In the mid-1930s the BBC had taken over some land adjacent to the old Linenhall Street premises, the mid-nineteenth-century linen-mill previously mentioned. Plans were prepared for a new building and for demolishing the old buildings on the site. Building work was started, but unfortunately was not finished when the war began, so the new centre was not occupied until the spring of 1941. The PBX installation had been got ready, but on the morning of a heavy air raid, when the Post Office were understandably otherwise engaged, the EiC (J. B. Basébé) changed over the PBX system himself, and the new building was then taken over. As at some other BBC centres, the EiC commanded the Home Guard, and was in charge of defence. In addition, in Belfast, Basébé took over a good many of the Regional Executive's duties, including the move to the new building, black-out, furnishings, etc. A temporary war-time control room was formed in the new studios with OB equipment, but the studios themselves had no more elaborate treatment than carpet-felt hung on the bare brick walls.

Special regulations applied to travel to and from N. Ireland. Basébé and his wife wanted to go to Scotland to visit some relations and attend to other matters. He succeeded in getting a permit for himself, but his wife's was refused, so he quoted

Article 36 of Magna Carta, which prohibits exile without trial, and she got hers.

Because of the effects of the 'blitz' in 1940–41 it was decided to provide a secure refuge in London, so that news and information services in particular could continue to be provided from London even if Broadcasting House were destroyed. It was to be a surface-built heavily-reinforced concrete structure, or 'stronghold', to give protection against 500-lb bombs. The Civil Engineer, M. T. Tudsbery, kept a clear account of the planning and construction of this massive building, and the following points are taken from his record. The contract for the building was placed on 15 December 1941, and the work was completed in November 1942. It was a single-storey structure on the corner of Duchess Street and Hallam Street, on the site where it had been intended before the war to build an extension to Broadcasting House. It was so planned that it could later be incorporated into the Broadcasting House extension, and this has since been done. Accommodation was provided for four news studios, a small manual telephone switchboard, a control room, and a diesel engine room, all served from a central corridor. In anticipation of the additional weight of the super-structure that would be erected after the war, it was decided to drive 58 piles of the 'cored' type, each about 22 in. in diameter and capable of carrying a working load of 85 tons. The base-slab and side walls were 5 ft thick and heavily reinforced; the roof-slab was of similar construction, 5 ft 8 in. thick. In the summer of 1942 additional protection was given to the roof by a further 3 ft 10 in. of concrete in the form of 4¾-ton concrete blocks cast *in situ* and laid on builders' felt for convenience of breaking-out at a later date – two lifting eyes were cast in each block for this purpose. A total of 10,000 tons of concrete was used, the packing of which around the closely-spaced steel reinforcement was assisted by pneumatic vibrators. The stronghold was made self-contained and sealed against gas attack by the installation of mechanical ventilation with a gas filtration unit; there were thick reinforced concrete shields to protect the ventilation intakes and extracts against the mischance of a bomb entering them. Much thought was given to the future, despite the grim circumstances in which the stronghold was constructed. An internal staircase was provided at the west end of the central corridor to give access to the future sub-basement of the extension to Broadcasting House.

Finally, there was a large complex of studios at Bedford during the last four years of the war. When Bristol ceased to be a desirable headquarters for the Music and Variety Departments, and the latter moved to Bangor, a new home was sought for Music Department in the Midlands. Bedford was finally selected, there being reasonable line communications with London; furthermore, Bedford Town Council was co-operative in offering a number of premises suitable for studios, control room and offices. These included the Bunyan Hall Schoolrooms (taken over in June 1941 to provide three studios and the main control room), Castle Billiard Hall, Co-Partners' Hall, St Paul's Mission Hall, sundry hotels, the Corn Exchange, Bedford School Hall, and Trinity Chapel in St Paul's Church, though the last three were treated as OB points.

Planning had been practically completed by April 1941, and in June R. Haworth was transferred to Bedford as Engineer-in-Charge. The first programme, the Daily

Service, went on the air on 28 July, less than half an hour after the programme lines had been handed over. The installation was carried out with remarkable speed, under the direction of the redoubtable G. T. Myers already mentioned, by widespread use of the OBA/8 equipment. The BBC was fortunate in finding a number of reasonably good studios in the Bedford area, because they had to accommodate the Symphony and Theatre Orchestras, the BBC Chorus, the Theatre Chorus, and the Religious Broadcasting Department as well as vocal and piano recitals.

The Corn Exchange was used as a studio, although it was still functioning as a corn exchange and also as a dance hall, a canteen, and an entertainment centre for the Forces (for whom the BBC sometimes provided a Sunday-afternoon concert). It was used mainly by the Symphony Orchestra, and the technical equipment in the hall had to be stowed out of sight when not in use. Acoustically, the Corn Exchange was difficult. At first, Cabot's quilting strips were applied to three walls, but over a period of two years this was gradually removed until there was no treatment at all except the black-out curtains. The quality achieved was highly praised by musical listeners and in the technical press; it was the result of an unorthodox microphone set-up, consisting of two ribbon microphones about 10 ft apart on the same suspension wire at a distance of about 8 ft from the edge of the platform, angled so that between them they included the whole of the front row of strings. The angle of tilt was critical, and the two microphones were connected in parallel. This gave good internal balance with crisp definition, but the quality was aggressively 'hard' and there was far too little reverberation. This deficiency was corrected by introducing an 'atmosphere' microphone above the balcony at the other end of the hall, with the insensitive side directed towards the platform, so that it responded only to the reverberant sound. The microphone mixture was critical and varied with the size of the audience. On a Sunday afternoon when the hall was packed with troops wearing thick battle dress, the atmosphere microphone had to be fully faded up and the orchestral pair cut back slightly; but with a normal audience, more lightly clad, the orchestral pair had to be fully up and the atmosphere microphone cut back. The Gramophone Company were impressed with the quality from the Corn Exchange and made a number of recordings from there, including one of Holst's *The Planets*, with Sir Adrian Boult and the Symphony Orchestra, which won an award as the best recording of the year. It was recorded again, with remarkable success, at St Hilda's, Maida Vale, on equipment using the new type 'D' cutter-heads, which had just been developed by Research Department.

One of the Bedford studios, at the St Paul's Mission, was noteworthy because it was provided with adjustable acoustic treatment. Large hinged shutters were placed on the walls and ceiling, which could present either reflecting or absorbent surfaces according to the acoustic effect required. In this studio an experiment was carried out that was to influence the design of post-war music studios. After more than two years of effort, no cure had been found for poor definition in the lower register, which sometimes made it impossible to distinguish what notes were being played by the basses and the timpani. In the end, it was realised that, as these particular instruments were played while in direct contact with the top of a rostrum, the mechanical vibration from the instrument would be transmitted to the rostrum, and from the rostrum to the floor. The latter was of wood-on-joist, so that it, too, was free to vibrate at its own resonant frequencies. Haworth, who had encountered similar trouble at St George's Hall some years earlier, decided to cut a number of holes in the studio floor and to build up brick piers from the concrete foundations, locating the piers so that each leg of the rostrum affected should rest on the bricks and thus be isolated from the studio floor. Some 24 piers were needed, but the cure was complete and the expense was justified. Whenever possible, music studios now have solid floors.

The Trinity Chapel of St Paul's Church was known as Studio 6 and was the home of the Daily Service and other religious broadcasts. There were two problems to be faced here: mixing and balance. There was no suitable room in visual contact with the chapel that could be used as a control cubicle, so OBA/8 gear had to be arranged on an office table in the chapel itself, and moving-coil headphones were used for monitoring – the table was disguised with a polished oak surround and a lockable lid. Strangely enough the nearly empty chapel was acoustically dead, because of a vast blue carpet, covering the entire floor area, and long black-out curtains. The carpet had come from Bristol, and was known as 'Queen Mary's Carpet'. Queen Mary always took an interest in what was going on in Bristol and had objected to the sight of wiring scattered over the floor of the chapel in Bristol Cathedral that was used for religious broadcasting. This was felt to justify the purchase of carpet to conceal the wires, and 'Queen Mary's Carpet' later came to Bedford. Several different microphones were tried without success. Finally an STC 4021 microphone (the 'apple and biscuit') was chosen; it was one of a batch that was regarded as sub-standard by the manufacturers and they had sold it to the BBC on condition that it would not be used for actual broadcasting, but merely for talk-back. It therefore had to be disguised by a cover of blue silk matching the carpet, and so remained until the end of the war.

Another hall from which the Gramophone Company made several recordings in 1945 before the BBC left Bedford was the Bedford School Hall. This too created acoustic problems, which were successfully solved, and the Alexander Nevsky productions, an outstanding programme series of the time, were done there.

There was generous provision for OBs at Bedford, and many were done from churches and outside halls in the area. Public concerts by the Symphony Orchestra from Cambridge and Luton were regular features, and occasionally broadcasts from airfields were done for the US networks, NBC and CBS. In view of all this OB activity, and the amount of heavy rigging work required in several of the studios, there were no women operators at Bedford throughout the life of the centre.

Religious Broadcasting Department had a reputation for making arrangements for broadcasts without enquiring about the availability of lines. This, on one occasion, caused the AEiC to remark with feeling to the Rev. Cyril Taylor: 'I know that a belief in miracles is one of the requirements of your post, old boy, but you're stretching it too bloody far!'

An OB, which turned into an investigation of bass absorption, was done from the office of the Cambridge Group H transmitter. A series of talks was to be given by

Professor Dodds, who could not come to Bedford for the purpose, and pronounced room resonances had to be eliminated before the room could be used as a studio. Two panels of linoleum, each 6 ft by 3 ft, were fixed to frames of 3-in. by 3-in. timber, which were screwed to the ceiling and one wall. Some cotton wool was loosely nailed to the frames in the 3-in. space between the linoleum and the wall. These panels proved remarkably effective.

The same method was used to cure the boom in the Bedford Continuity Studio, and its success caused Haworth to have six transportable 6-ft by 3-ft membrane units built. When these were measured by Research Department at the end of 1945, they were found to have an absorption coefficient of about 0·80 over a frequency range of 60–200 Hz; these results provided an impetus for further investigation of membrane absorbers.

When the war in Europe was seen to be coming to an end, it was arranged that the first programme from Bedford after the announcement of peace would be a Service of Thanksgiving from an RAF Camp at Cardington. To be ready to go on the air at very short notice (only thirty minutes could be guaranteed) microphones and OB gear were installed in a lockable steel cupboard well in advance, and a Technical Assistant was sent to sleep in camp for a week (well looked after in the Sergeants' Mess). The service was attended by a number of airmen from different countries, including three coach-loads from US airfields.

The drift back to London started immediately after VE-day, and, when the time came to close down, the Bedford centre was dismantled by its own staff. Nothing was wasted and practically nothing was lost. Even 24 studio doors were salvaged, and when the handles and finger plates had been removed the doors were provided with feet, thick felt was stuck to one side, and they were sent to London for use as acoustic screens.

2 TRANSMITTERS FOR THE RADIO SERVICES

Instructions to close down the Television Service were given at 1000 hrs on 1 September 1939 at the end of the advertised morning transmission on that day and television accordingly ceased at 1210 hrs. But the sound broadcasting service, far from closing down, became an essential part of the national life, though truncated and adapted to war-time conditions. At 1855 hrs on 1 September the Senior Control Room Engineer in London received a warning message and immediately closed down all the medium-wave transmitters with the exception of the London, North and Scottish National transmitters operating on 1149 kHz, which, together with the Droitwich National transmitter on 200 kHz, proceeded to broadcast announcements interspersed with recorded music. These announcements told listeners for the first time which medium wavelengths they should try for best reception of the BBC's single war-time programme. The announcements continued until the two synchronised groups, each of four transmitters, were ready to take the war-time service on 668 kHz (449·1 m) and 767 kHz (391·1 m). Five of these eight transmitters had to be changed from their peace-time frequencies, but both groups were ready for service well within the time allowed in the introductory phase of the plan. It was decided to start the war-time service at 2015 hrs on 1 September and at this time the Droitwich long-wave transmitter and the three medium-wave National transmitters were closed down.

A press notice was issued and a telegram was dispatched for display in Post Offices throughout the country giving the wavelengths and times of transmission of the Home Service, as the single programme was now called.[3]

The carrier frequencies of the transmitters in the two groups were compared at 0810 hrs on 2 September and no adjustments were found to be necessary. The carrier of the master station of each group was picked up at each of the slave stations on a commercial receiver modified for the purpose; the slave stations were closed down for 30 seconds while the comparison was being made. It was repeated each day at a different time to limit the amount of information given to enemy monitoring stations about the location of the master stations, but as soon as the necessary equipment could be provided frequency checking was done by means of a reference tone transmitted by line.

The change to war-time working was made without a hitch, thanks to the care and foresight that had been put into the preparatory work and also to the respite following the Munich crisis, which had allowed many of the engineering arrangements hastily prepared in September 1938 to be consolidated.

The plans for closing down individual transmitters under orders from Fighter Command have been described in chapter III, section 14. It was essential that the operative messages for closing individual transmitters should be received promptly, even at the most remote stations. This made it necessary for the control line network to be maintained to a high standard of reliability. Despite the fact that the messages from London to the transmitting stations had to be relayed by word of mouth at various points in the network, the normal time for the acknowledgment to be received in London was between 60 and 70 seconds, although the route mileage to a remote station such as Burghead and back was about 1000. One of the Senior Control Room Engineers hit on the idea of sending the messages over the control lines in Morse code by keying a 1000-Hz tone; this reduced the time to less than a minute. To guard against the failure of a control circuit, it was arranged that, if a transmitter had to be closed, the programme circuit would be cut and the station staff would interpret the loss of the programme for more than three minutes as an instruction to close the transmitter. This system had the advantage that accidental failure of a programme circuit would cause the transmitter to cut its carrier so that its listeners could receive weak signals from distant transmitters in the same synchronised group. Engineers at the control room duty positions at transmitting stations were provided with switches to enable them to close down a transmitter immediately upon receipt of a message to do so.

The application of these rules could be effectively maintained throughout the war only by constant alertness and rigid discipline among the operational staff; this was in fact maintained, assisted by a competitive spirit that developed among the transmitting stations. A heavy responsibility rested on the Senior Control Room Engineer (SCRE) on duty in the control room at Broadcasting House. The engineers entrusted with this duty established themselves as the immediate point of reference in the complex, and sometimes unforeseen, circumstances that arose during the war. If all but one of the transmitters in a synchronised group was closed down by Fighter Command, it was the SCRE's duty to close down the remaining transmitter, so that no station would radiate alone. The closing of transmitters under this procedure reached its peak in 1940; during that year the SCRE transmitted no fewer than 8591 messages for the closing of transmitters and a similar number for their reopening. This activity continued, on a reduced scale, until the end of March 1945.

The efficacy of the transmitter synchronising arrangements in denying navigational aid to the enemy, while still providing listeners in this country with an acceptable quality of service, was later proved during the interrogation of prisoners of war and by the fact that Italy used a similar method as soon as she entered the war and Germany introduced it after some two years of hostilities.[4]

From the point of view of listeners in this country they worked satisfactorily, although there were inevitably times when listeners had to rely on weak signals from distant stations because the local transmitter had been closed down. There was, in the London control room, a large board carrying coloured discs to indicate which transmitters had been closed; on one or two occasions, the whole of the board had changed to red, though only briefly, indicating that every medium-wave transmitter was 'off the air'.

The initial scheme, using two synchronised groups of transmitters radiating the single Home Service from 0700 to 0015 hrs daily, did not remain static for long. The idea of an alternative programme was aired during the first few weeks of war-time broadcasting, but the Air Ministry was adamant that only one programme should be broadcast as originally planned. Before long, however, the provision of an alternative programme became linked with the need to entertain the British Expeditionary Force in France during the unforeseen 'phoney' war. Although the BBC Home Service was heard by the Forces in France, particularly during the news bulletins, there was a good deal of listening for entertainment to Radio International at Fécamp in Normandy operating on 1415 kHz. At this time the Air Ministry were trying to persuade the French authorities to close down the Fécamp transmitter and to set up a group of synchronised transmitters in Northern France. Thus the need for an acceptable alternative to the Home Service was becoming increasingly urgent.

During October 1939 Research Department engineers under H. L. Kirke carried out a number of experiments at the Start Point transmitting station using a horizontally polarised medium-wave transmission. The object was to determine whether a broadcasting service could be provided without the necessity for setting up a group of synchronised transmitters whilst at the same time denying navigational aid to the enemy. The first tests were made on a frequency of 1474 kHz and were followed by others on 877 kHz using pulse modulation. For these tests, a horizontal dipole was erected between the two 500-ft masts at Start Point and this was fed by means of a double 'sausage' type feeder. This arrangement proved to be successful and Ashbridge was able to inform the Air Ministry in November 1939 that horizontally polarised transmissions were reasonably secure by day and by night against use by the enemy for direction-finding. The Air Ministry accepted a proposal that a second programme should be broadcast by this method. Service trials started immediately, the Home Service being radiated from Start Point from 19 December 1939. What was termed an 'experimental' programme, incorporating excerpts from the Home Service, replaced the test transmissions on 7 January 1940 between 1800 and 0015 hrs daily, the period being extended to 1100–2300 hrs from 18 February 1940. Until 15 September 1940 this programme, by then known as 'The Forces' Programme', was radiated by Start Point only, on 877 kHz. From that date it was also radiated by a group of synchronised transmitters operating on 804 kHz from 1100 to 2000 hrs daily and from Start Point on 877 kHz from 1800 hrs to close-down.

To improve the coverage in those areas where the medium-wave synchronised transmitters were not well received, and to act as an emergency distribution facility if the line network suffered major disruption, the Home Service was transmitted from a newly installed high-power short-wave transmitter at Start Point (Sender 22) from 20 January 1940 on 6075 kHz. The Forces' Programme was also radiated on a short-wave channel (6150 kHz) using Sender 3 at Daventry in the first instance, and from 20 November 1941 a newly installed high-power short-wave transmitter at Lisnagarvey, Sender 51.

To provide against the loss of the important control circuits used for the transmission of Fighter Command instructions to transmitting stations, a network of low-power short-wave telegraph transmitters was set up to work on 7260 kHz. Commercially manufactured transmitters were installed at the main transmitting stations, at studio centres, at Valve Section (Motspur Park, Surrey) and at the Research Department (Nightingale Square, Balham). Although there was a nucleus of operating staff, composed of ex-seagoing telegraphists in Engineering Division who were capable of operating such a network efficiently, it became necessary to train a number of other staff in the Morse code and operating procedures. In a surprisingly short time many of the trainees were able to send and receive at 10–15 wpm. Training exercises were arranged in order to keep the network in a state of readiness, and a code was devised based on the use of passages selected from *New Every Morning* – a book of prayer used for the daily religious service, which was readily available.

Throughout the war some of the senior engineers based on Broadcasting House, London, served on a rota of 'Senior Duty Engineers'. Each of them was on watch for 24 hours at a time to receive instructions from Fighter Command and see that they were carried out, to deal with any emergencies requiring action by Engineering Division, and to inform the Controller (Engineering) of any important developments.

With the intensification of enemy air attack in the autumn of 1940, the reception of the Home Service became increasingly unsatisfactory during air raids when Fighter Command closed down several of the high-power synchronised transmitters in the same group at the same time. The threat of invasion was a very real one at this time, and the need arose for some means by which Regional Commissioners could speak to the people in their Regions, if they were cut off from the central government.

DETAILS OF GROUP H TRANSMITTING STATIONS
1474 kHz (203·5 m), 0·05 — 1·0 kW

No.	Station Name	Type of Location	Service Date	Closed Down
1	Belfast	Studio premises	1.11.40	14.8.43
2	Cardiff	Studio premises	1.11.40	14.8.43
3	Edinburgh	Studio premises	1.11.40	14.8.43
4	Glasgow	Studio premises	1.11.40	14.8.43
5	Leeds	Studio premises	1.11.40	14.8.43
6	Bristol	(i) Studio premises	1.11.40	13.9.41
		(ii) Clifton Rocks Tunnel	14.9.41	28.7.45
7	Manchester	Studio premises	1.11.40	14.8.43
8	Newcastle	Studio premises	1.11.40	14.8.43
9	London	Swains Lane Tel. OB Reception point	1.11.40	14.8.43
10	Birmingham	Studio premises	1.11.40	14.8.43
11	Plymouth	Studio premises	15.1.41	28.7.45
12	Nottingham	Hosiery Dyers' Plant	15.1.41	28.7.45
13	Stoke-on-Trent	Minton's China Works	16.1.41	28.7.45
14	Liverpool	Biscuit Factory	16.1.41	28.7.45
15	Aberdeen	(i) Studio premises	21.1.41	26.10.44
		(ii) Redmoss, open site	27.10.44	28.7.45
16	Hull	Oil jetty	8.3.41	12.10.44
17	Brighton	Garage	24.3.41	28.7.45
18	Tunbridge Wells	Laundry	22.4.41	28.7.45
19	Reading	(i) Restaurant Buildings	5.5.41	10.2.43*
		(ii) Seedsmen's Grounds	22.2.43	28.7.45
20	Cambridge	(i) Room in Shire Hall	20.5.41	29.6.43
		(ii) Building in Shire Hall grounds	30.6.43	14.8.43
21	Dundee	Jute factory	12.6.41	28.7.45
22	Ipswich	Swimming Baths	14.6.41	28.7.45
23	Lincoln	Asylum	26.6.41	28.7.45
24	Ayr	Carpet works	18.6.41	28.7.45
25	Leicester	(i) Mortuary	27.6.41	26.4.43
		(ii) University Buildings	27.4.43	28.7.45
26	Hastings	Garage	27.6.41	28.7.45
27	Sheffield	School	28.6.41	14.8.43
28	Gillingham	Shoe factory (Jezreel's Tower)	5.7.41	14.8.43
29	Wrexham	Leather works	11.7.41	28.7.45
30	Aberdare	Brickworks	20.7.41	28.7.45
31	Barrow	Brickworks	5.8.41	28.7.45
32	Redruth	(i) Garage	8.9.41	19.2.44
		(ii) Lannar Hill, open site	20.2.44	28.7.45
33	Blackburn	Mill	15.9.41	14.8.43
34	York	The Yorkshire Museum	19.9.41	14.8.43
35	Worcester	Brickworks	19.9.41	14.8.43
36	Middlesbrough	Institute for the Blind	21.9.41	10.10.44
37	Torquay	Brickworks	24.9.41	28.7.45
38	Swansea	Brickworks	25.9.41	14.8.43

* Destroyed

No.	Station Name	Type of Location	Service Date	Closed Down
39	Northampton	Water Tower	26.9.41	14.8.43
40	Peterborough	Laundry	10.10.41	28.7.45
41	Shrewsbury	Castle	25.10.41	14.8.43
42	Exeter	Coach-house	26.10.41	28.7.45
43	Swindon	Open site	30.10.41	28.7.45
44	Carlisle	Mill	3.11.41	9.10.44
45	Moorside Edge	Transmitting Station	13.11.41	28.7.45
46	Whitehaven	Brickworks	15.12.41	28.7.45
47	Inverness	Mill	7.1.42	14.8.43
48	Oxford	Water Tower	5.1.42	28.7.45
49	Folkestone	School	22.1.42	28.7.45
50	Ramsgate	Water works	24.1.42	9.9.44
51	Taunton	Sewage Disposal Works	30.1.42	14.8.43
52	Blackpool	Swimming Baths	24.2.42	28.7.45
53	Guildford	Open site	24.2.42	28.7.45
54	Gloucester	Reservoir	24.2.42	14.8.43
55	Weymouth	Laundry	3.3.42	28.7.45
56	Scarborough	Poor Law Institution	10.3.42	12.10.44
57	Doncaster	Engineering Works	20.3.42	14.8.43
58	Bournemouth	Refuse Destructor	23.3.42	14.8.43
59	Hitchin	Water tower	2.4.42	14.8.43
60	Fareham	Open site	7.12.42	28.7.45
61	Norwich	Sweet Factory	5.10.44	28.7.45

A partial solution to this latter problem was provided by the installation at the main studio centres of low-power Air Ministry transmitters, type T77, but wider coverage was required. The solution to both problems was to install a large group of low-power synchronised transmitters in towns having a population of 50,000 or over. Some sixty transmitters were contemplated, each having an output power in the region of 50–100 W and operating on 1474 kHz. The Air Ministry agreed that, provided these transmitters were accurately synchronised and would close down on a local Air Raid Warning 'RED', they could be freed from Fighter Command control. It was specified that these transmitters would also have to close down if local gunfire was heard, even if no air raid warning had been received.[5]

It was clear that the BBC's peace-time standards of installation, apart from safety precautions, would have to go by the board if these stations were to be made available at the rate required. The first consideration in finding a site was to obtain adequate accommodation adjacent to a structure capable of supporting a transmitting aerial, however rudimentary in design. Most of the sites were at locations where there was an existing chimney or tall building and very few of the stations had conventional mast-supported aerials. The table lists these Group H stations, as they were called. In September 1941 as many as eight stations were commissioned in one month. For the first ten installations, which were completed by November 1940, a number of

241

RCA type 1E transmitters were used, but at later stations a variety of equipment had to be pressed into service, including a simple 100-W transmitter designed by the BBC.

Except for the stations at Fareham and Norwich, all 61 stations in the group had been commissioned by April 1942. The staffing of these stations on a three-shift basis posed a severe recruitment problem and the general pattern was to appoint a Maintenance Engineer as the Engineer-in-Charge with a staff of Technical Assistants (Female) and Youths (Transmitters).

When the supply of commercially manufactured transmitters for Group H dried up, efforts were made to persuade firms in the Midlands to produce a batch of transmitters based on a prototype made by Research Department; this was a low-power short-wave transmitter adapted to work on medium waves. No firm could be found to deliver the quantity needed in the time available and it was decided to design a transmitter, *ab initio*, and have it built either in the BBC workshops or at a number of factories in the Midlands. The design was based on an rf output valve, STC type 4212E, which was available in good quantities; this was series-modulated by type AL60 valves. (This valve was a pentode developed by Mullards during the war and was extremely versatile, since it could handle 25 W of power at audio-frequencies and could also work at frequencies up to 2 MHz.) Series modulation had the great advantage that no large iron-cored components were required in the modulation chain. The transmitter, designated type SMT-100, cost about £200 and the initial batch were made in the BBC workshops at Hampton House, near Evesham. Wherever possible, wood was used to replace metal, then in very short supply, and components were obtained from a variety of sources without regard to the standardisation of spares. Later batches of these transmitters were made by Strattons of Birmingham, who produced the rf sections, and by Wodens of Wolverhampton, who built the modulator sections.

This was a period of rapid development in the technique of frequency-control of transmitters. Independent crystal oscillators of simple design had been introduced in 1938 for use at synchronised transmitters. The crystals were of the bar type and were mounted in evacuated glass envelopes. In 1939 an improved battery-operated crystal drive was developed using GPO type 6A crystals. These were AT-cut plates with an improved temperature coefficient. The square quartz plates were rigidly supported by steel pins inserted into indentations in the edges of the plates at vibration nodes. The electrodes were air-spaced from the quartz plate, the lower one being of stainless steel and the upper consisting of a gold-sputtered area on the glass cover plate. In the original type 6A holder, a small manometer tube was inserted under the cover plate to permit any change of pressure in the evacuated holder to be observed. As no such changes were observed, and as the mercury vapour attacked the gold electrode, the manometer was omitted from the next design, type 6B.

The drive equipment was notable as being the first apparatus used in the BBC with demountable panels to permit rapid replacement in case of breakdown, the electrical connections being completed automatically when the panel was inserted into the apparatus rack. For the Group H stations the provision of a simple mains-operated drive was undertaken by the staff of the Superintendent Engineer, Transmitters. With the help of the Research Department workshops and outside contractors, these were produced to meet the target dates for the stations which averaged four per month. This equipment, type CP-17B, embodied a small constant-temperature oven to house a single GPO type 6B quartz crystal in its evacuated holder. The engineers at the GPO Research Station at Dollis Hill co-operated whole-heartedly in producing precision quartz crystals to meet the target dates. The quartz plates were cut for an operating frequency of 737 kHz, because plates cut for a fundamental frequency of 1474 kHz – the carrier frequency – were too thin for stable mounting in the well-tried type 6B holder. A frequency-doubler was provided as part of the design. This relatively cheap and simple apparatus was able to maintain the carrier frequencies of the group within $\pm$0·1 Hz for several weeks at a time in normal ambient temperatures; this corresponds to a long-term stability of $\pm$7 parts in 10^8.

The final stage in the war-time development was represented by the type CP-17E equipment, also mains-operated and using the GPO type 6B crystal, but incorporating frequency converters which, in association with a wide-band amplifier, enabled output frequencies between 140 and 1600 kHz to be derived from crystals with fundamental frequencies between 600 and 1200 kHz.

It was also necessary to design reliable and cheap apparatus to permit the comparison and adjustment of the carrier frequencies. The method used at the beginning of the war for the synchronised groups, using radio pick-up for the comparison, was replaced in January 1940 by a new system developed jointly by the Transmitter and Research Departments. A reference tone at an audio frequency was transmitted by line from the main station to the slave stations. It was derived from the carrier frequency of the master station by means of frequency dividers of the multi-vibrator type; frequency multipliers with five stages were used at the slave stations in conjunction with 'crystal beat indicators' and recording milliammeters. Transmission of the reference tone over long lines made frequency comparison difficult, because of amplitude and phase variations. Moreover, when the number of synchronised groups was increased to nine in 1944, tones at nine different frequencies had to be identified and distributed over the network during the short time each night when the programme lines were not required for programme transmission. A new technique was therefore developed in 1942 in which the frequency difference was displayed on a cathode-ray tube, or alternatively was shown in graphical form on the chart of a recording meter with a highly damped movement. This new apparatus became available late in 1943. It required only one reference tone, at 1 kHz, to be distributed to all LF and MF stations (all their carrier frequencies being integral multiples of 1 kHz). At each station the reference tone was applied to a pulse generator producing pulses about 0·5µs long. These were applied to produce the vertical deflection in a cathode-ray tube, the horizontal deflection of which was derived from a stepped waveform locked to the frequency of the slave station. The trace remained stationary when accurate synchronism with one of the harmonics of the reference tone was achieved. Even if the pulse was broadened by phase fluctuations in the line, there was no difficulty in making the frequency adjustments. The standard reference tone was derived from a generator in Broadcasting House, London, with a long-term stability within ±2 parts in 10^8. (The generator produced outputs at various other frequencies for different purposes, including $0 \cdot 1$ kHz for checking the speed of gramophone turntables, and $0 \cdot 44$ kHz for the standard musical pitch.)

In 1946 the transmitters were provided with receivers tuned to 200 kHz with frequency dividers producing an output of 1 kHz. This could be used instead of the reference tone from London, thus obviating the need for line-transmitted tone altogether. The carrier of the Droitwich transmitter provided an accurate reference frequency at 200 kHz.[6] As these successive stages of development did not obviate the need for manual adjustment of the carrier frequencies, experiments were made in performing the adjustment automatically, but this was rendered unnecessary by further improvements in the stability of crystal drives.

The reference tone system used for the high-power synchronised groups could not be applied to the large number of transmitters in Group H, because of the shortage of materials during the war. An attempt was therefore made, with the approval of the Air Ministry, to make short test transmissions on low power at a frequency of $147 \cdot 4$ kHz using a transmitter at Daventry that had formerly been used for the 'Air Met.' service. It was hoped that a sufficiently strong signal would be obtainable at all Group H stations to permit a simple oscilloscope display to be produced for frequency comparison purposes. Unfortunately, the aerial efficiency at Daventry was very low and sufficient effort could not be spared to pursue this line of development. Instead, frequency measurements were made at Tatsfield on six selected stations each night, radiating in sequence to a time schedule. Corrections were sent over the telephone network, using a code to avoid errors in communicating signs and numerals, and the stations made corrections when necessary using a calibration chart.

Enemy action resulted in damage and destruction at several of the low-power stations, although none occurred at the high-power stations. The most serious case was the destruction of the Birmingham (Adderley Park) low-power station during a heavy raid on Birmingham on the night of 19 November 1940. This transmitter was a 'spoiler' for the European Service on 804 kHz and was located in the grounds of a biscuit factory. Unfortunately, the three BBC staff on duty at the transmitting station were killed outright. The service was restored on the following day using a low-power transmitter installed in the studio centre at Broad Street, Birmingham. Damage also occurred during the so-called Baedeker raids on cathedral cities in April and May 1942. The York transmitter lost its mast during a raid on 28 April, but was back in service the following morning reporting the event laconically by internal memorandum. The Exeter transmitter sent a service message on 3 May reporting the loss of power, lines and roof, but little time was lost in restoring the service. The Norwich transmitter, installed in the grounds of the Caley Chocolate factory, was damaged when the factory was 'blitzed' on 28 April. The aerial system was brought down, but the plant was relatively undamaged and the service was restored at 2000 hrs on the same day. There was a second raid with incendiary bombs two days later when power and lines were lost. Service was restored on 2 May, the delay being due to the loss of control lines. (This transmitter was then on 668 kHz, but later joined Group

244

DISTRIBUTION PLAN 1C (IMPLEMENTED 2 MARCH 1941)

Northern Group:	767 kHz	Home Service	(Group N)
Burghead T.1	50 kW		
Westerglen T.1	50 kW		
Stagshaw T.1	50 kW		
Lisnagarvey T.1	50 kW		
Daventry (ex-5XX)	30 kW		
Fraserburgh	1 kW	(Masking transmitter)	
Penmon	4 kW		
Redmoss	1 kW		
Southern Group:	668 kHz	Home Service	(Group S)
Brookmans Park T.1	50 kW		
Washford T.1	50 kW		
Droitwich (5GB)	50 kW		
Moorside Edge T.1	50 kW		
Bartley T.1	10 kW		
Norwich T.1	0·5 kW		
London Swains Lane	5 kW	Reserve for Brookmans Park and used temporarily during aerial work there starting 4.3.41	
Forces Group:	877 kHz	Forces Programme	(Group F1)
Westerglan T.2	50 kW		
Moorside Edge T.2	50 kW		
Brookmans Park T.2	50 kW		
Washford T.2	50 kW		
Droitwich T.2	2 kW		
Stagshaw T.2	2 kW		
Burghead T.2	2 kW	Joined group 3.9.41	
Redmoss T.2	2 kW	Joined group 17.3.41	
Group H:	1474 kHz	Home Service	(Group H)
Stations Nos. 1–15 inclusive as in Table I			

H). On 10 February 1943 the Reading Group H station was destroyed during a night raid, but fortunately the staff had sought shelter and were uninjured. A temporary service was restored during the evening of the following day, using a mobile transmitter. A new site was found near Reading where a replacement transmitter was installed in a large gazebo in the grounds of Sutton's Seeds Ltd and took over the service on 22 February 1943.

From the start of war-time broadcasting on 1 September 1939, strenuous efforts were made to improve the coverage for listeners in the United Kingdom and, apart from the introduction of Group H, a new distribution plan (known as Plan 1C) was implemented on 2 March 1941. (Details are given in the table.) Between that date and 8 May 1945 (VE-DAY) a number of changes were made in the synchronised groups, either to improve the coverage or to provide better 'masking' in some areas to meet Air Ministry requirements. As the war progressed, transmitter equipment became available from various sources such as new manufacture in this country, diverted export orders, and the USA (under the 'Lease-Lend' arrangements). Much of the new plant was used to expand the coverage of the Overseas Services, but some of the lower power transmitters – up to 10 kW output – were used to reinforce the coverage of the Home and Forces Programmes.

Friendly relations between the BBC and the Air Ministry were maintained throughout the war period. In 1941 enemy air activity over the United Kingdom decreased, and Ashbridge was able to persuade the Air Ministry to allow broadcasting on long waves to be resumed. A group of long-wave transmitters was accordingly formed to carry the European Service, as described in section 4 of this chapter. It was later agreed that higher power could be used at some of the medium-wave stations. The better coverage so obtained and the virtual disappearance of the invasion threat enabled a number of the Group H stations to be closed down. On 14 August 1943 twenty-four were closed and a further six were closed during September and October 1943. These closures had the advantage that they released operating staff for transfer to the rapidly developing short-wave services. Group H was finally closed down when the Post-War Interim Distribution Plan was implemented on 29 July 1945.

With the invincible optimism of those days, the post-war arrangements were being given some consideration as early as June 1941, when it was decided to make provision for all high-power medium-wave transmitters to operate at short notice on any wavelength between 200 and 550 m (1500–505 kHz). Orders were placed for a number of absorption-type wavemeters – having an accuracy of about 5 parts in 10^5 – to assist in the setting up of those transmitters not already provided with variable-frequency drives of good stability. The absorption wavemeters were converted into heterodyne meters with improved accuracy. The end of the war was, however, a long way off and it was not until early in 1945 that the Post-War Distribution Plan was prepared. This envisaged an interim condition, starting on VE-DAY-plus-three-months and remaining in force for about nine months. The Final Plan was then to be implemented. The proposals provided for three programmes, initially known as the 'A', 'B' and 'C' programmes and later renamed the Home, Light and Third Programmes. It was estimated that the post-war plan would provide day-time coverage of the following percentages of the population of the whole country:

Programme 'A'	Interim	96·4%	Final	97·1%
Programme 'B'	Interim	93·7%	Final	94·4%
Programme 'C'	Interim and Final			47·0%

The date of implementation of the Interim Plan was brought forward to 29 July 1945 for Programmes 'A' and 'B', but was delayed until 29 September 1946 for Programme 'C'. Details of this plan are given on p. 247. The arrangements for Programmes 'A' and 'B' were implemented as planned, but there were major changes in the distribution scheme for Programme 'C', which will be described later.

POST-WAR DISTRIBUTION SCHEMES: INTERIM AND FINAL

Station	Frequency kHz	*Interim* Power (kW)	*Final* Power (kW)
Programme 'A'			
Moorside Edge	668	60 (T1)	200 (T3)
Westerglen	767	60 (T1)	200 (T3)
Burghead	767	60 (T1)	100 (T1)
Redmoss	767	2 (T2)	10 (T2)
Washford	804	60 (T1)	60 (T1)
Penmon	804	10 (T1)	10 (T1)
Brookmans Park	877	140 (T3)	140 (T3)
Droitwich	1013	60 (T1)	200 (T5)
Norwich	1013	1 (T1)	1 (T1)
Start Point	1050	120 (T1)	120 (T1)
Stagshaw	1122	120 (T1)	120 (T1)
Lisnagarvey	1122	100 (T1)	100 (T1)
Londonderry	1122	1 (T1)	1 (T1)
Clevedon	1474	20 (T1)	20 (T1)
Bartley	1474	10 (T1)	10 (T1)
Programme 'B'			
Droitwich	200	200 (5XX)	400 (high-power medium-wave converted)
Brookmans Park	1149	60 (T1)	As for Interim
Moorside Edge	1149	60 (T1)	As for Interim
Westerglen	1149	60 (T2)	As for Interim
Lisnagarvey	1149	10 (T2)	As for Interim
Stagshaw	1149	10 (T2)	As for Interim
Burghead	1149	20 (T2)	As for Interim
Redruth	1149	2 (T2)	As for Interim
Redmoss	1149	2 (T2)	As for Interim
Londonderry	1149	1 (T2)	As for Interim
Programme 'C'			
Brookmans Park	977	60 (T2)	As for Interim
Moorside Edge	977	60 (T2)	As for Interim
Westerglen	977	60 (T1)	As for Interim
Washford	977	60 (T2)	As for Interim
Stagshaw	977	10 (T3)	As for Interim
Lisnagarvey	977	10 (T3)	As for Interim
Birmingham	International Common Wave 10 kW (New Station)		

3 STUDIOS FOR THE EXTERNAL SERVICES

Wood Norton was intended as a reserve headquarters for the domestic broadcasting services, but several Overseas Departments broadcast from there during the early part of the war. In September 1940 the Latin-American, Spanish, Portuguese, Indian and Near East Services moved from London to Wood Norton and Abbey Manor. (By June 1942 they had all departed, leaving Wood Norton to revert entirely to its original function.) The headquarters of the Overseas Service, including Radio Newsreel and Presentation, was at Abbey Manor. The direction of the European Service was still done from Broadcasting House until the autumn of 1940 when bombing necessitated a move to Bedford College, which was taken over at short notice. The Latin-American and Near East Services operated from Wood Norton.

Expansion of the External Services was so rapid that additional studio centres were needed during the early stages of the war; some units were accommodated in Broadcasting House, Maida Vale, and Bush House, but during 1940 and early 1941 enemy bombing raids were causing damage and acute problems of accommodation for all these services. Nevertheless, in December 1940, the Ministry of Information pressed for the return of the Overseas staff who had been dispersed to Wood Norton and for the concentration of all the Overseas Services in London. Simultaneously they were asking for the output to be trebled. These demands gave rise to a proposal that a site should be found which could accommodate three buildings, each with complete safety accommodation. The scheme finally put forward for the expansion of the output would have required capital expenditure of roughly £5,000,000, of which about half was for transmitters and half for a concentrated studio centre at Aldenham. The high cost of the proposed studio centre was due to the need to build, rather than rent, the accommodation and to the need to provide living accommodation for as many as 6500 staff on or near the site.

Soon, however, there were misgivings. By 11 February 1942 it was reported that:

(*a*) the shortages of building labour and materials were making drastic curtailment of building projects inevitable
(*b*) further calls for military service were causing increased difficulties in recruitment
(*c*) and travel restrictions were making the selection and immigration of staff from overseas (essential to the project) a piecemeal and long-term process.

A 'partial plan' was proposed, comprising two programme service buildings and one engineering building, with a total staff of around 1800. Plans for constructing living accommodation were given up in favour of an attempt to billet the staff in the Aldenham area. This plan, too, was soon whittled down, and on 19 June 1942 estimates for the 'Aldenham Main Scheme' were called for, in terms of one general-purpose building, planned to deal with a maximum of six programmes, with four continuity studios, two general purpose studios, four rehearsal studios, recording channels and working accommodation for 580 persons. This reduced scheme was finally approved in December 1942, and some work was begun, but on 17 February 1943 doubts were expressed about the advisability of proceeding with it, and it was abandoned in favour of several smaller schemes to provide the required accommodation.

Meanwhile, the Overseas Services had to go on. The BBC had begun to acquire accommodation in Bush House in September 1940, when it had taken over, at first for OB programmes, a studio of the J. Walter Thompson organisation. By the end of October 1940 it had been agreed that Bush House was to serve as an emergency news centre, but in January 1941 it was decided to move the European Service there. Requisitioned areas on the lower ground and basement floors of the south-east wing were formed into studios and the European Service moved in on 17 March 1941 from Maida Vale. The Spanish and Portuguese units came to Bush House from Wood Norton in March 1942. There were at first four studios, but these were immediately found inadequate and, by the end of the war, there were fifteen studios.

Every important language of Europe was broadcast from Bush House, except Russian. The various languages were divided into three 'networks': one for Western and Central Europe, one for Eastern and South-Eastern Europe, and the third for Scandinavian and the Iberian Peninsula. The reason for grouping the Scandinavian with the Spanish and Portuguese Services was that the target areas were approximately 180° away from one another, so that both could be served by a single aerial radiating in either of two opposite directions.

In common with other war-time studios, those at Bush House were acoustically treated in a makeshift way. Some were treated with acoustic tiles and were satisfactory for intelligible speech, which was the main objective. Two were very primitive, their acoustic treatment consisting of strips of thick felt hung over rails.

A new studio suite, installed in April 1942, contained a 'Continuity Studio', from which linking announcements and interlude material could be interpolated into the programme. Continuity working had already proved its value at Abbey Manor and at Broadcasting House. At Bush House, however, the continuity studio could not be used in the same way, because the language difficulty made it impossible for a Presentation Assistant to maintain the continuity of the service at a point remote from the main studios. The studio control cubicles were later designated 'Continuity Rooms', but by then the method of working was that each language transmission occupied a period of exactly quarter-hour, half-hour or possibly one-hour and the programme was cut off at the end of the allotted time whether it was finished or not, so that the start and finish of each programme was synchronised with the changes at the transmitting station. There was a 'censor key' in every studio suite, and a censor was present at every transmission, though the occasions on which he used his key seem to have been extremely rare.

The control room was in the basement, and because it was underground it was supposed to be a security area, but in fact the ceiling was level with the pavement in the Strand. In 1944 all the studios were below ground level, except two on the ground floor. The latter were designated 'safety areas', not 'security areas'; the instructions were that they should be evacuated if there was an 'imminent danger' warning. This instruction was ignored, but it was repeated so often, with threatened penalties, that one evening the senior engineer on duty evacuated the studios concerned.

The following day, without structural alterations, they became a 'security area'.

The control room equipment at Bush House, as at the other war-time premises, was based on the OBA/8 amplifier. For feeding programme to line there was also a single-stage amplifier built in 'do-it-yourself' style on a plywood base. In those days safety precautions were less thoroughly codified and less strictly observed than they are today and several people received quite severe shocks from these amplifiers. All the connections were made by means of standard double-ended Post Office type cords, and by the end of a day the various boards where the connections were made resembled rather untidy knitting; to remove a cord, it was necessary to trace it carefully to see where it led. Mistakes were inevitable, but they were surprisingly few. The performance of the equipment was good and it was also reliable; if it did go wrong, only makeshift repairs could be made by the available staff.

Bush House thus became the war-time studio centre of the European part of the Overseas Services, but in the meantime the World Service News was urgently requiring a centre in the London area. It was proposed to accommodate this group at Aldenham House, which the War Office consented to release to the BBC. Vacant possession was obtained on 1 October 1941, and the fact that Engineering Division had been able to do some planning before that date enabled the work to proceed immediately, with the result that Empire News, News Talks and Presentation were able to move from Abbey Manor to Aldenham on 27 and 28 December 1941. Their stay was short, and the implementation of other plans enabled them to move on the night of 30–31 May 1942 to 200 Oxford Street. The Latin-American and Near-East Services moved to Aldenham from Wood Norton on 18–19 June 1942.

Aldenham House, now the home of the Haberdashers' Aske's School, was described as 'a lovely old country house, set in a large park' – Aldenham Park. It was well placed for communications and it had the advantage of being in a fairly large community, where billets could be found for the staff. The control room was in one of the beautifully proportioned reception rooms of the house, with a corniced ceiling. It was fitted with equipment similar to that in the other war-time studio centres, with the exception that there was a semi-automatic switching system for rapidly changing the connections between the sources of programme and the outgoing lines at the end of each quarter-hour period, in accordance with the distribution requirements. The number of programmes and the number of networks into which they were assembled were increasing to such an extent that cross-plugging on a jackfield was no longer practicable. It was not easy to get automatic devices, such as relays or uniselectors, and one of the important requirements of design work at that time was to avoid the use of any components that were difficult to obtain. A change-over system using two jackfields was therefore devised. In principle, one jackfield would be plugged up according to the network requirements; this was the transmission jackfield. During the quarter-hour while this transmission was taking place, the second jackfield would be plugged up according to the requirements for the next quarter-hour period, and when the clock indicated the exact moment a button would be pressed to cause relays to operate and change over from one jackfield to the other. Then the first jackfield would be replugged for the third quarter-hour, and so on. This arrangement was much less greedy for relays than a fully automatic system and it went into service on 17–18 May 1943. Aldenham, in fact, acted as the switching centre for all the overseas programmes, there being lines on several routes between Aldenham and Broadcasting House, Bush House, and 200 Oxford Street, so that if an emergency occurred on any one route, the programmes would still be reasonably sure of getting to Aldenham.

There were four studios at Aldenham at the beginning. It was not as large as other overseas programme centres, but it soon began to expand. The Turkish News Unit from Maida Vale moved into Aldenham on 24–25 June 1942, shortly after the arrival of the Latin-American and Near-East Sections; by October there was a demand for a new studio, and work was put in hand for an extension to the building to cope with this and other requirements.

The third major studio centre for the Overseas Services was 200 Oxford Street. This building, which had been the East Block of Peter Robinson's store, was requisitioned in June 1941 and the planning of a broadcasting centre there began almost immediately. The installation in 'PR Building', as it was at first called, was a large and urgent job and the small installation group, which had Aldenham and Bush House to deal with as well, was strengthened and became part of the Station Design & Installation Department, the forerunner of the later Studio & Transmitter Planning and Installation Departments. Planning these major war-time studio centres was a very different matter from planning a pre-war studio centre. Before the war, all installations had been designed as individual layouts; each desk, each apparatus bay, was drawn very carefully with all its details, even down to tag numbers on the connection blocks at the bottom of the bay. Every studio was different. In war-time, many materials and components became very scarce and rigid standardisation was necessary. Ideas introduced into one project could often be applied in another, such as the use of multi-core cable for inter-bay wiring and the design of cubicle desks. Before the war these desks had been designed to present a pleasant physical appearance. In war-time, however, there was no time for architectural design, and the studio desks at 200 Oxford Street were made from office tables faced with plywood. A standard OBA/8 amplifier was placed on the top, with a five-way key-switch unit and a standard MX/18 mixer. The mixer was tilted on a piece of wood so that the cue keys could be placed under the front panel. These keys were wired to an elementary terminal block. A porcelain-based copper knife-switch (common in earlier days in domestic installations for shorting the aerial to earth in a thunderstorm) was fitted inside the desk to terminate an emergency line to control room so that the microphone could be switched through direct if the amplifier failed.

In addition to the cubicle desks, standard apparatus bays were also designed. There was, for example, a control position bay carrying the main APM/1 (Amplifier Programme Meter, a rack-mounted version of the OBA/8 amplifier), a row of twenty studio signalling keys, a small telephone communication panel, and a programme meter panel. There was also a trap-valve amplifier bay and a standard jack-field bay was introduced. This had a number of rows of jacks, some wired in 'Listen/Line' formation, i.e. with a jack for listening purposes wired across the line jack. Other jacks were wired in the 'Listen/Line/Apparatus' formation, so that the line

251

was normally connected to the amplifier, with a listening jack in parallel, but plugging into the line disconnected the amplifier from it and plugging into the apparatus jack disconnected the line from the amplifier. This arrangement, which came into general use at studio centres and transmitting stations, provided the maximum facilities for monitoring across the line and for checking whether a fault was on the amplifier side or on the line side of the jacks. The system gave rise to a number of faults on its own account through poor contact within the break-jacks. There were also jacks with one input connected to ten outputs in parallel. The jackfields were wired up in multi-core cable in the workshop; when installed they were connected to a distribution frame. The inter-connections between the input and output sides of this frame were made in 'jumper' wiring and could be varied to suit changing requirements. A drawing of a typical talks studio suite layout showed all the power points, red, white and green lights, buzzers, talks desks, cubicle desks and TD/7 gramophone desks; this could be given, whenever a talks studio was wanted, to the staff responsible for building and wiring, or to contractors.

The control room and studios at 200 Oxford Street were in the basement, and much heavy steel reinforcement was applied to the floor and ceiling of the ground floor; concrete was used in the basement and the lower ground floor to stop flooding and also to give some protection to the studios and control room from any missile that might fall down the lift-shaft. Installation was begun in December 1941, and during May and June of the following year a gradual cut-over took place. It had been intended that the accommodation above ground level should be duplicated below ground level for use during air-raids. In fact, the accommodation above ground was occupied more often than the 'security' accommodation below. The offices had to be planned on an austere basis, with short partitions and mostly without direct access to outside windows. Despite these limitations, 200 Oxford Street provided sufficient studios and other accommodation for what had by then become a large operation. On the night of 30–31 May 1942 the Overseas Services were transferred from Aldenham. Radio Newsreel arrived from Abbey Manor at the same time and occupied one of the mixer suites from which many of the great stories of the war, either in recorded form or live, were broadcast to the world. The Indian Section came from Abbey Manor in June 1942. There were at first nine studios, of which the cubicles of two were equipped for multi-channel mixer work. One of the continuity suites was the source of the Green Network, which provided a World Service for most of the twenty-four hours. The continuity suite for the Red Network served mainly Australasia and the American Continent. Two other networks, Purple and Brown, served particular areas with special programmes.

Just as the noise from the Bakerloo Tube could be heard in the basement studios of Broadcasting House when it was opened in 1932, so the noise of the underground trains on the Central London Line could be heard in some of the studios at 200 Oxford Street, which were about 50 ft below ground level. It was, in fact, possible to distinguish the arrival and departure of the trains, and the opening and closing of their doors. One of the many overseas visitors who came to visit Bush House after the war claimed that he had been able to identify a particular studio when listening 5000 miles away by the sound of the underground trains – and he was right.

There was an obligation on all staff in possession of secret papers to destroy them in the event of an invasion. This would have been facilitated at 200 Oxford Street by the fact that in the cubicle of Studio 1 there was a large manhole cover; when removed this revealed another cover which, when removed in turn, revealed a waterfall still further down. This was the River Fleet from Hampstead, finding its way down to the Thames; in the words of the Engineer-in-Charge, W. Furze Mills, 'We hoped that our papers would be lost in the swirling waters beneath Fleet Street.'

When a large part of the Overseas Service moved to 200 Oxford Street, the Latin-American Service and the Arabic Service moved from Evesham to Aldenham. These moves considerably eased the social problems of dealing with the staff, because it was less necessary for the BBC to concern itself with their personal activities than when they were in the much smaller community of Evesham. There was, however, still a problem of billeting and the inducement to householders to take in unsought guests was only the standard billeting fee of one guinea per week (for bed, breakfast and evening meal) and the feeling that they were contributing to the war effort. There were occasions when incompatibility between the residents and the billetees had to be resolved by transfers, but there were few, if any, occasions when there was serious trouble.

The growth of the External Services during this period had been spectacular. From the eight transmitters available at the outbreak of war, the number had increased to 37 by 1943. The peak of activity was reached in May 1944 when 111 hours of programme was broadcast in 46 languages each day.

Among the recollections of the war years there figure many distinguished visitors from allied countries who broadcast to their own people from BBC studios, among them Queen Wilhelmina, Prince Bernhard and Professor Gerbrandy of the Netherlands, King Haakon of Norway, King Peter of Yugoslavia, General Sikorski of Poland, and Jan Masaryk of Czechoslovakia.

4 TRANSMITTERS FOR THE EXTERNAL SERVICES

In 1939 the Overseas Service was strengthened by the building of four more high-power short-wave transmitters and the service could reach all the other continents. It was, however, vitally necessary to broadcast to Europe and the problem was a different one. Only the longer short-wave bands could be used effectively for transmission over relatively short distances and only a minority of listeners in Europe had short-wave receivers. Long waves were not available and the range of medium-wave transmissions was limited, especially with the limited power then available. Moreover, the amount of money provided by the Treasury as a grant-in-aid for the Overseas and European Services did not permit any large-scale expansion. News bulletins in French, German and Italian had been started at the time of Munich; they displaced the domestic programmes on some of the medium wavelengths. The consolidated European Service was started in August 1939,[7] but the resources were limited.

At the beginning of the war the term 'Overseas Service' had replaced 'Empire Service' and the Overseas and European Services together constituted the External Services. When the plans were put into effect, the frequency of 1149 kHz was used during the hours of darkness for European Service transmissions. At first, three 50-kW 'Regional' transmitters – at Brookmans Park, Moorside Edge and Westerglen – were synchronised on this frequency, but on 7 October 1939 the Droitwich long-wave transmitter, which had by then been converted for medium-wave operation with its output power increased to 200 kW, joined the 1149-kHz group. A transmitter at Washford was added to the group on 5 November 1939.

The successful experiments with horizontal polarisation at Start Point led to the erection of a horizontal dipole aerial at Droitwich for the 1149 kHz transmissions; this was brought into use on 17 February 1940 with the Droitwich 1149 kHz transmitter radiating alone during darkness. On the same date an additional medium-wave outlet was provided for the European Service with the introduction of a synchronised group operating on 804 kHz. This consisted initially of the three 'Regional' transmitters at Brookmans Park, Moorside Edge and Westerglen that had been used earlier on 1149 kHz.

When France fell in June 1940 there was an urgent need to increase the power of the existing European Service transmissions and to carry them on more wavelengths in order to circumvent the increase in jamming by the enemy. This problem was not made easier by the enemy's use for domestic broadcasts in the occupied countries of the transmitters they acquired as they advanced westwards.

In October 1940 a third medium-wave outlet was added to the European Service using the Start Point transmitter operating on 1050 kHz. The power output of this transmitter had been increased to 180 kW at the expense of some increase in distortion, which was unimportant as the programme consisted mainly of speech. The Start Point transmitter used a horizontally polarised aerial and radiated only during darkness. (The reason for using horizontal polarisation was simply that a single station with horizontal polarisation could not be used as a beacon by enemy aircraft as could a single transmitter with vertical polarisation. However, the polarisation also has an effect on propagation. A vertical aerial radiates more strongly at low angles to the horizontal, whereas a horizontal aerial radiates more strongly at high angles. Also the loss that occurs at the point of reflection in the ionosphere is greater for horizontal than for vertical polarisation in temperate latitudes. Thus, a horizontal aerial in the European area produced a lower field strength at distances greater than 1000 km and for this reason the use of horizontal polarisation has been reconsidered quite recently as a means of reducing interference between distant stations.)

Additional high-power transmitters were installed at existing stations as soon as the plant could be obtained. The first was installed at Brookmans Park in an extension to the original building. It was a 140-kW unit manufactured by STC for Lithuania just before the war. A similar installation at Moorside Edge used a Marconi 150-kW transmitter. These new high-power medium-wave transmitters were brought into service on 2 March 1941 synchronised on 804 kHz together with the former long-wave transmitter at Droitwich.

The most ambitious project attempted in this period was the installation of a transmitter at Droitwich with, for those days, the exceptionally high output power of 400 kW on medium waves. There was neither the time nor the man-power available to design a single transmitter of this advanced type and it was therefore decided to install two 150-kW transmitters then under construction by the Marconi Company and to attempt to operate them in parallel. For the Droitwich installation their output power was increased to 200 kW, at the cost of a slight increase in distortion, and circuits were designed for the parallel operation of the two transmitter units. This was an innovation that was to have far-reaching use in later years.[5, 8] The new transmitter, which was installed in a separate two-storey building of austere construction on the main site, became known as 'Droitwich HPMW'. On 12 February 1951 it took over the European Service transmissions on 1149 kHz, using horizontal polarisation and operating on a 'sliding schedule' from 15 minutes after sunset until 15 minutes before sunrise. The transmitter units had been designed for quick wave-changing – a facility not previously available on medium-wave transmitters. MacLarty was in charge of the planning and he devised a high voltage dc current-transformer to give a remote indication of the current in circuits at a high potential above earth. It operated through the saturation effect of superimposing dc magnetisation on ac. The circuits for paralleling transmitters were worked out by P. A. T. Bevan (later Chief Engineer of the ITA) and included means for ensuring correct load-sharing between the transmitter units, for protection against over-load and for ensuring that if a fault developed in one unit it automatically suppressed the drive to the others. There were some difficulties in preventing instability of the individual transmitter units, but none in paralleling them. The aerial was supported between the two existing 700-ft masts and consisted of two horizontal half-wave dipoles, spaced by a quarter-wavelength in the vertical direction and driven in phase. From 16 November 1941 the upper dipole, with its vertical transmission line, was used as a T-aerial for radiating simultaneously the long-wave European Service on 200 kHz. The dipoles were replaced by a mast radiator on 19 December 1943.

There was cross-talk between the European Service transmissions on 1149 kHz, the Home Service on 767 kHz, and the Forces Programme on 1013 kHz, which were all broadcast from Droitwich. The trouble was overcome by installing acceptor circuits in parallel with the input end of the feeder from the HPMW transmitter; one of these was tuned to 767 kHz and the other to 1013 kHz, and both were associated with rejector circuits tuned to 1149 kHz. These prevented currents from the Home and Forces transmitters that were induced in the European Service aerial from reaching the anodes of the modulated amplifier of the HPMW transmitter, where the intermodulation was found to be occurring.

A long-wave European group was then made up by using the Droitwich 5XX transmitter, converted back again to long-wave operation, the old Daventry 5XX transmitter with an output power of 30 kW, and a newly installed 15 kW STC transmitter in the extension building at Brookmans Park. This long-wave group was intended only as a temporary expedient, because a site was being sought in the east of England for a very high-power transmitting station, whose signals would be radiated over a sea-path to North Germany. It was estimated that such a station would give a consistent field strength on long waves in Berlin of about 2 mV/m. Various sites were investigated with the aid of a low-power transmitter to measure the ground conductivity. A 94-acre site was finally acquired at Ottringham, near Spurn Head, in the East Riding of Yorkshire, and the Air Ministry agreed to its use for a high-power station.

The Ottringham station (known as OSE5), built at the beginning of 1943, was capable of radiating a maximum power of 800 kW on either long or medium waves and this station was, at the time, the most powerful broadcasting station in the world. Four 200 kW Marconi transmitters were installed, each in its own heavily protected building, and the transmitters were driven and fed with programme from a fifth building. The transmitter outputs were combined in a sixth building, while a seventh housed three 740-bhp diesel alternator sets for use in case of failure of the public electricity supply. The Ottringham station was designed to operate on either 200 kW, 400 kW, 600 kW or 800 kW and to radiate up to four separate programmes simultaneously.[5] Test transmissions began on 22 January 1943 and the station came into service on 12 February 1943, with an output power of 600 kW on 200 kHz. It had been hoped to operate the station some ten months earlier with a single 200-kW transmitter, but a number of setbacks occurred, the most serious of which was the collapse of two of the 500-ft masts in August 1942 while they were being erected. The delay was particularly disappointing to BBC engineers, because at that time a 500-kW medium-wave station was being built (independently of the BBC) at a site near Crowborough, Sussex, for the Political Warfare Executive. This transmitter, which consisted of three 170-kW units connected in series, had been purchased in the USA and was installed underground at a site prepared with the assistance of Canadian Forces personnel. The BBC obtained partial use of the station from 8 November 1942, when it radiated the European Service on 804 kHz. Synchronising equipment had been provided by the BBC to maintain the carrier frequency stability within the required limits when the transmitter was operating in a BBC group. At other times this transmitter, known colloquially as 'Aspidistra', was used by PWE for 'black' broadcasting.[9,10]

The fourth transmitter unit at Ottringham was used to reinforce the Home Service in the East Riding and North Lincolnshire, operating with an output power reduced to 30 kW on the Northern group frequency of 767 kHz. Although built above ground and on the east coast this large station never suffered air attack.

At the end of hostilities in Europe in May 1945 the long- and medium-wave transmitters in use for the European Service were:

Ottringham (OSE5)	600 kW	200 kHz Blue and Grey Networks
Droitwich (HPMW)	400 kW	1149 kHz Blue, Yellow and Grey Networks
Start Point	100 kW	1050 kHz Blue, Yellow and Grey Networks
Brookmans Park	140 kW	804 kHz Blue, Yellow and Grey Networks
alternating with		
Crowborough (Aspidistra)	500 kW	804 kHz Blue, Yellow and Grey Networks

While every effort was being made to increase the signal strength of the BBC's transmissions on long and medium waves directed to Germany and the occupied countries in Europe, it was realised that these transmissions were very susceptible to jamming from transmitters of quite low power located near the point of reception. On the other hand, short-wave transmissions could not only reach countries beyond effective range on long and medium waves, but were also less susceptible to jamming. This was because short-wave transmissions, being dependent on refraction from the ionosphere, exhibit a 'skip' effect, so that signals from a distant broadcasting station may be received more strongly than those from a nearer jamming transmitter.

At the beginning of the war, the BBC had only eight short-wave transmitters (Senders 1–6, 8 and 9), all at Daventry. Three of these were of relatively low power.[11] Two additional Marconi high-power transmitters (Senders 10 and 11) were under construction at Daventry when war was declared and these were commissioned in mid-June 1940. An eleventh transmitter, Sender 7, supplied by STC, was commissioned in December 1940. It was considered undesirable for all the BBC's short-wave facilities to be concentrated at one location and early in 1940 it had been decided to convert the Start Point medium-wave transmitter so that it could be used on short waves by day – when it was designated Sender 21 – and on medium waves, horizontally polarised, at night carrying the Forces Programme. At that time, a high-power short-wave transmitter (type SWB 18) was being manufactured by the Marconi Company for a foreign government and this was acquired and installed at Start Point as Sender 22. A skeleton aerial system was provided, so that the station could act as a limited replacement for Daventry if the latter station was put out of action. Sender 22 came into service on 20 January 1940 carrying the Home Service on short waves and the European Service (Norwegian) at set periods. From 19 September 1940 this transmitter carried the European Service exclusively throughout the war years.

To provide yet another site for short-wave transmissions, the medium-wave transmitter at the Clevedon station, near Bristol, was converted to short-wave operation with an output power of 15 kW and came into service in September 1940, radiating the European Service.

Thus, by the end of 1940 the BBC had fourteen short-wave transmitters operating from three separate sites. While this 'first-aid' development programme was being put into effect, a completely new high-power short-wave station was being planned. A 189-acre site was acquired in November 1939 on Rampisham Down, near Maiden Newton, Dorset, and the station, known as OSE3, was equipped with four Marconi, type SWB 18, 100-kW short-wave transmitters (Senders 31 to 34). The transmitter halls, each containing a pair of these transmitters, were separated by heavy blast walls. A comprehensive aerial system was installed consisting of 29 arrays supported between 15 masts of heights varying between 100 ft and 325 ft. Full world coverage was given by this aerial system, although the transmissions were primarily intended for areas outside Europe. This was the first of the BBC's short-wave stations to be provided with 4-wire transmission lines, following tests made at Daventry, and a remotely controlled switching tower for connecting any transmitter output to any aerial array.[12] The switching tower proved successful, but as it was in the open air there was at first some difficulty on account of the formation of ice on the tracks; this was prevented by installing soil-heating cable and this practice was followed in later installations of a similar kind. To give complete flexibility in the choice of operating frequencies, variable-frequency drives were designed by the Drive Section of Transmitter Department. Many technical difficulties had to be overcome in the design of this precision equipment and the limited availability of components in war-time necessitated some compromises.[13]

OSE3 was provided with an emergency power supply consisting of two 750-bhp diesel alternator sets. The diesel engines, which had been designed for railway locomotives abroad, were equipped with battery starting facilities instead of the compressed-air starting arrangements that were conventional for diesel engines of this size. The station came into service on 16 February 1941 and during May of that year a number of tests were carried out using a captive balloon to measure the performance of the horizontal dipole arrays and to determine the effect of the contour of the ground close to the station on their vertical radiation pattern.[14] Similar tests were also made at Daventry.

On 20 November 1941 further insurance was effected against the disruption of the BBC's overseas services by the commissioning at the Lisnagarvey medium-wave transmitting station in Northern Ireland of a Marconi, type SWB 18, 100-kW short-wave transmitter (Sender 51). At first this new transmitter was used to radiate the Forces Programme on 6140 kHz, but from 7 November 1942 it carried the Overseas and European Services.

During 1941 work was started on the provision of a Central Drive Room at Daventry to house fifteen variable-frequency drives of the new design to replace the hotch-potch of drives that had accumulated at Daventry since Empire Broadcasting started in 1932.

In 1942 an additional facility was commissioned at Daventry, when Sender 7 was brought into service as a double-channel transmitter with a common modulator.

In the same year the question of synchronising the carrier frequencies of short-wave transmitters located at different sites was first raised by L. W. Hayes; methods of doing this were investigated, but it was not until frequency synthesisers became commercially available some years later that it became a normal operational procedure.

In January 1943 the possibility of constructing a short-wave station to relay programmes from the United Kingdom to the USA and Canada by a southerly route, clear of the propagation vagaries of the auroral zone, was being considered. It was tentatively proposed to set up a relay station in the Caribbean area; in August 1945 a survey was made in the West Indies, but the project was deferred.

Early in 1941 consideration had been given to a much more ambitious development. It had become clear that the demands of the Overseas Service could be met only by a major expansion of short-wave facilities. It was decided to build eighteen more high-power transmitters at three separate sites. One station was to be used mainly for services beyond Europe, one for the European Service, and the third to serve Europe by day and more remote target areas by night.

In 1943 two large short-wave stations were opened at Skelton, near Penrith, Cumberland, and a third high-power station at Woofferton, near Ludlow, Shropshire. It proved extremely difficult to find suitable sites for these stations, but eventually a 320-acre site was acquired at Skelton large enough to accommodate two stations, placed at opposite ends of the site and separated by about one mile from each other. At Woofferton, a 183-acre site was obtained, although this had the disadvantage that the water table was abnormally high. The buildings for these three stations were not of bomb-proof construction, but heavy blast walls separated pairs of transmitters and emergency control and drive rooms were provided remote from the main control and drive room areas.

Skelton was the largest short-wave transmitting complex in the world at that time, comprising twelve 100-kW transmitters – six supplied by the Marconi Company (type SWB 18) and six by STC (type CS8).[5] The latter were capable of operating as six double-channel 70-kW transmitters, each pair of channels having a common modulator. The two separate aerial systems at Skelton consisted of a total of 51 arrays supported by 31 masts ranging in height from 200 ft to 325 ft. The Marconi-equipped station was known as OSE8 (opened 15 April 1943) and the one equipped by STC as OSE9 (opened June–November 1943). Each was provided with three stand-by diesel alternators. These emergency power supplies were capable of operating six transmitters at a reduced output power of 50 kW at OSE8 and five channels with an output power of 60 kW at OSE9.

The Marconi transmitters at Skelton were similar to those installed at Rampisham, but the design had been simplified to save materials and factory labour, and the overall size had been reduced without sacrificing performance. The design of the STC transmitters followed that of the similar transmitters installed at Daventry, but had been simplified wherever possible.

The eht supplies for the Skelton transmitters were obtained from steel-tank mercury-arc rectifiers.[15] Only one rectifier and one filament machine was provided for each transmitter, and they were connected directly to the units without any intermediate switchgear. The valve-cooling system employed air-blast radiators as heat exchangers and the output of these was used for space heating in the buildings, no other form of heating being provided.

The station at Woofferton, known as OSE10, was equipped with 50-kW transmitters supplied by RCA. These transmitters were the only ones available at this time and in any case the use of existing designs of Marconi or STC transmitters, which required crypts to house the valve-cooling plant, was ruled out by the high water-table at this site. The supply of the transmitters from the USA for this station caused some anxiety and by January 1943 only one had arrived, but the remaining five were delivered in time for the station to be opened on 17 October 1943. These transmitters were of the high-power, Class B, anode-modulated type, but were not designed for rapid wave-changing. At the expense of a considerable amount of maintenance work by the station staff, the operational schedules were maintained in spite of this limita-

S

tion. (Modifications to the wave-changing arrangements were made by the EiC and his staff after the war.)

When the radio-frequency sections were removed from two of the transmitters in 1944 for another purpose, a new design of amplifier was introduced. This was a BBC idea, due to B. N. MacLarty and his staff, and employed screen-grid valves. Single-sided, unbalanced tuning circuits were employed in the first and second rf stages, tuning being by means of continuously variable inductances and fixed capacitors. The final rf stage was tuned in a conventional manner using variable capacitors and fixed inductors. The usual insulating hoses for supplying valve-cooling water to the anode jackets were replaced by lengths of polythene tubing, thus saving space and cost.

The Woofferton station was provided with an aerial system with twenty-six arrays for world coverage. These arrays were supported between fifteen stayed, lattice masts of heights ranging between 150 ft and 325 ft. The power supply for the station was usually taken from the public supply mains, but three 750-bhp diesel alternator sets were installed for emergency purposes. The engines were super-charged and to-gether were capable of carrying the full load of the station.

This considerable expansion in the number of short-wave transmitters necessitated the production of some fifty variable-frequency drives and, as no suitable equipment was available commercially, design work was started immediately by the Drive Section of Transmitter Department. This work was done at Tatsfield, where frequency-measuring facilities with a high order of accuracy existed; a fully screened test room and workshop were constructed to accommodate additional staff and plant. The new equipment, type VFO/4, was based on experience with earlier types and, by using outside contractors for the manufacture of sub-assemblies, a pro-duction rate of five complete drives per month was achieved.

The staffing of these additional short-wave transmitting stations presented a prob-lem, but the closure of a number of the low-power Group H stations between August and October 1943 had released a number of trained staff for employment at the new short-wave stations. The remaining staff required were recruited from out-side the BBC and were given training.

Thus, by November 1943, the BBC was operating forty-three separate short-wave transmissions simultaneously, radiating not only its own External Services, but also 'America Calling Europe' relayed direct from New York. This complement of short-wave transmitters was used throughout the remaining years of the war, modifications and additions being made from time to time to the aerial systems.

The various Overseas Station Extensions were designated as follows:

OSE1	Daventry	Senders 4–7A & B
OSE2	Daventry	Senders 8–11
OSE3	Rampisham	Senders 31–34
OSE4	Start Point	Sender 22
OSE5	Ottringham	(Medium-wave and long-wave)
OSE6	Droitwich	(Medium-wave)

OSE7	Lisnagarvey	Sender 51
OSE8/9	Skelton	Senders 61–66 and 71A & B to 76A & B
OSE10	Woofferton	Senders 81–86

These designations were used until 1969, when they were dropped in favour of the station names.

5 THE LINE NETWORK

When BBC operations were placed on a war footing on 1 September 1939 the two major effects on the line system were that outside broadcasts almost ceased and that there was only one domestic radio programme to be transmitted. The reason for the reduction to one domestic programme has already been explained; the disappearance of outside broadcasts was due mainly to the fact that the Post Office line system became congested by the demands of the Services for communication facilities of all sorts. In comparison with the Services, the BBC did not enjoy high priority; furthermore, the Post Office insisted that those few OBs that were possible should be done only after 7 pm on weekdays and after 2 pm on Saturdays, and the same restriction applied to the necessary period of line-testing in advance of an OB. It is fair to say, however, that OBs would have been curtailed in any case as part of the changes in the balance of programmes that formed part of the BBC's plans for war-time.[16]

Reorganisation of the staff of the Lines Department was necessary, because some who were in category 'C' had joined the armed forces, and it was now necessary to cope with a different set of conditions. Alternative routeings and emergency circuits had to be planned against the time when enemy air raids would dislocate the service. The period of the so-called 'phoney war' – nearly a year – gave time to establish special arrangements with the Post Office for fault reporting, and to carry out an extensive rearrangement of the network. More circuits had to be ordered, and sheets showing 'War-time SB Routings' had to be kept continuously up to date. These sheets in the end included almost every line in the whole system, even small local circuits that might be pressed into use in emergency. It was at about this time that the Post Office brought into use a new and more systematic scheme of line numbering, which has persisted until the present day. Every rented private wire had the prefix PW, and a number indicating the renter and the type of line. Thus, lines in the 12,000 series were BBC private wires; if the 'hundreds' digit was 1 or 5 the line was suitable for sound programmes; if the 'hundreds' digit was 0 the line was for speech; if it was 7 the line was a teleprinter channel, and so on. If the line was entirely local to one particular telephone area further letters appeared in the prefix: PW/NM numbers referred to lines in the North Midlands area, in which Wood Norton was situated. The programme and speech circuits correspond to Tariff 'E' and Tariff 'D' circuits respectively, but as soon as war broke out the Post Office applied a 25 per cent surcharge, and Tariffs 'E' and 'D' went up to £15 and £10 per mile per annum respectively. Emergency circuits were also planned in large numbers by the Post Office.

Normally such a circuit did not exist as a separate entity, but was made up from one or more portions of existing private wires, the prefix PW being replaced by EC. It was important to remember that when an EC circuit was formed, one or more private wires probably ceased to exist.

A great deal of work had to be done on the testing and equalisation of so many emergency circuits, and equaliser components were not always easy to obtain at this time. The variable resistors in the pre-war equalisers were no longer obtainable, being of German origin, and inductors wound on permalloy dust cores were scarce. In 1942 after the arrival of F. J. Stringer in Lines Department, determined efforts were made to safeguard the supply of components and to get the construction of equalisers properly organised.

After a time, outside broadcasting began to revive, and an alternative programme, the Forces Programme, went on the air on 7 January 1940. Wood Norton was now part of the network, not only acting as a studio centre but also as a receiving centre for OBs in the same way as other SB centres throughout the country.

Two other major developments necessitated a great expansion in the network. One was the provision of a large number of small 'Group H' transmitting stations to radiate the Home programme. The other was the expansion of the Overseas Services, with large transmitting stations at Skelton, Rampisham, Woofferton and Ottringham, and an increase in the number of transmitters at Daventry. The new stations at Skelton, Woofferton and Rampisham each had to be fed with three programmes from London and thus added thousands of circuit-miles to the SB system. Efforts were made to put the new circuits on routes already in use for the domestic services, through intermediate BBC control rooms, so as to achieve as much interchangeability of circuits as possible.

During the bombing of London in 1940 the former Scott's Hotel, into which Lines Department had moved before the war with all their equipment, was destroyed – fortunately without loss of life. Most of the equipment, and valuable archives belonging to other departments, were lost. The Lines Engineers installed what they had left in the gallery of studio BA in Broadcasting House, just above the war-time control room. All the circuits went through the gallery via a set of U-links under the eye of a Home Guard armed with a loaded double-barrelled gun. He took his duties seriously and insisted on seeing the pass of anybody who went down the ladder to the control room and wanted to get back to the gallery. Access was further restricted by a great iron door on the lower ground floor leading to the gallery. The communications room containing carrier equipment for telephony and telegraphy circuits was on the lower ground floor and a small room near the control room housed the teleprinters and inter-office communications. (The first BBC inter-office teleprinter, rented from the Post Office, had been on a circuit to Bristol; later another worked on a BBC-derived channel in the carrier system between London and Wood Norton.)

A small photographic darkroom on the first floor of Broadcasting House, inside the tower, was turned into a test-room with a transmission measuring set and other equipment. From here the work of maintaining the network was continued as well as could be managed. To maintain the supply of equalisers, a series of inductors was made up as required by winding the appropriate number of turns on a small 'Gecalloy' core. Sets of these coils were included in a number of 'patch-boxes', containing also buzzer-operated test bridges, for field use. These were sent into the Regions, so that the local Lines Engineers could build their own equalisers without being dependent upon London. The coils were made to within ± 2 per cent of a range of inductance values proceeding in steps of $\sqrt[4]{2}$. All masks and calculating tables were based on this range of coil values. This was an important step in rationalising the supply of equalisers, and thousands of coils of the standard values have been made since this system was inaugurated.

Precautions were taken so that, if bombing attacks interrupted communications between the various overseas studios and their respective transmitters, emergency measures could be taken immediately – if possible without having to wait for action by the Post Office, which in any case was likely to be hard pressed in such circumstances. Overseas broadcasting was being done from Bush House, 200 Oxford Street, and Aldenham, and many of the circuits passed out of London towards the West, through Egham or Uxbridge. At these two places certain circuits were diverted into premises for which the BBC assumed responsibility, so that circuits from Aldenham could be routed westwards without having to pass through London. At Uxbridge there was a small room with amplifying and test equipment, which could, in emergency, also be used as a studio. At Egham the layout was more ambitious; there were two huts of Post Office pattern on concrete bases, one of which contained a diesel generating set for emergency power supply.

Another such switching centre, taking in a wide sector of the SB network and handling domestic as well as overseas circuits, was at Salisbury. The circuits were those feeding Bartley, Rampisham, Bristol and the other West Country transmitting stations; all these circuits could be diverted via Salisbury because of the triangulation between these places and Salisbury and London. The switching centre was established in the Post Office repeater station at Harlem, and comprised a control room and switching point and an office, part of which could be used as an emergency studio.

There was little routine work at Salisbury and the engineers there took part in the development of a technique of far-reaching importance in the maintenance of transmission quality on long SB circuits. They observed the change of equalisation needed on the four sub-carrier circuits between London and Salisbury as the temperature varied. G. Stannard (later Chief Engineer, Communications), who made these observations, was at Salisbury from August 1941 until May 1942, so that the results showed the nature of the variations in each season of the year. These results proved valuable when the carrier phantom circuits, that were beginning to be offered by the Post Office, showed the same tendencies as the sub-carrier circuits. A theoretical exercise was carried out, which showed that it was necessary to take into account not only the resistance and capacitance changes but also those of inductance and leakance. The next stage was to design a 'temperature equaliser', the characteristic of which could be changed to follow, in steps of 2 dB, the change of attenuation-frequency characteristic with temperature. Tables and formulae were devised to enable the characteristic measured at any time of the year to be normalised for a temperature of 0°C. From this, a basic equaliser could be constructed and a standard temperature equaliser added. The latter could then be adjusted in steps in accordance with seasonal temperature changes. This technique was a considerable advance on earlier methods of temperature-correction, which had merely varied the gain of repeaters to compensate for changes in the attenuation of open-wire lines.

For these adjustments it was necessary to know the temperature at cable depth (2 ft 6 in.); this was ascertained by measuring daily the loop resistance of a long un-repeated section of line and comparing the average temperature over that distance, calculated from the change of resistance, with Meteorological Office measurements taken at depths of 1 ft and 4 ft at some point in the vicinity of the cable route. In this way any jump in the temperature due to a cable fault could be detected, and it was found that a sufficiently accurate measure of cable temperature throughout the system could be obtained by taking observations at Glasgow, Manchester, Birmingham, Bristol and London. Cable temperature bridges were made for this purpose and were permanently connected to the cable pair to be tested in such a way that the temperature measurement could be made without interfering with any programme the circuit might be carrying.

Besides Salisbury, Egham and Uxbridge, other emergency switching centres were set up at Northampton, Leicester and Carlisle (at the Group H transmitting stations), and also at Falfield near Bristol, Penketh near Manchester, Mount Vernon near Glasgow, Newbattle Terrace near Edinburgh, and Ponteland near Newcastle-upon-Tyne.

The proliferation of munitions factories in 1940 led to a great increase in OBs, and a number of famous programmes began at about this time, such as *Workers' Playtime* and *Music While You Work*. These often came from airfields and other remote locations, and the provision and testing of the lines were often difficult. Some of the programmes were broadcast round about midnight, for the night shift, and were transmitted in the BBC Overseas Service. New weapons featured in broadcasts as soon as they came off the secret list. OBs were done, for example, from gun ranges on Salisbury Plain and from the South Downs behind Newhaven. The latter was a multi-point OB; there was a microphone near the gun itself, from which the commands of the officer in charge and the firing of the gun were heard; at another point the whistle of the shell passing overhead was picked up, and from a third point listeners could hear the explosion of the shell as it hit the ground. These effects were fed back by line from the three points to a central mixing point, with equalisation for each. The lines to the outlying points were run out by Army Signals, in close co-operation with BBC engineers, in 'Don 8' cable (one strand of copper surrounded by seven strands of iron wire). At first, the firing of the gun put the moving-coil microphone out of action, but by moving the latter much further away – as much as a quarter of a mile – satisfactory results were obtained. Many OBs, too, were done from the Dover area when aerial 'dog-fights' were going on in the Channel; these aroused great interest among the Americans, who had only just come into the war.

During 1943 the American Armed Forces Radio Service was developed to provide entertainment for members of the US Services,[32] and in July of that year the first stations of the American Forces Network were established in the United Kingdom, using studios at Carlos Place, London, and transmitters located at or near American bases. The transmissions were on 1402 and 1420 kHz and could be received by some 10 per cent of British listeners. They appealed to some younger listeners in much the same way as the 'pirate' stations were to do in 1964. The circuits for this network were lined up and serviced by the BBC Lines Department. There were particularly big installations at the American Bomber Command HQ and at various airfields in East Anglia, but generally there was one transmitter serving three or four airfields in the locality. The network extended into Scotland and into the West Country, the programme being originated in the West End of London. At some camps there was a public-address system rather than a radio transmitter. At a later stage there was also a Canadian Forces' Programme, on a much smaller scale, with a studio centre in London and transmitters serving small areas in the southern part of the country around Hindhead and Aldershot. The American Forces network had forty or fifty stations; the Canadian about half a dozen.

In May 1943 the BBC 'War Reporting Unit' was officially launched and as time went on became active in many theatres of war.[17] At home, in the period just before D-Day, there was a feeling that invasion of the Continent would soon take place, but naturally no hint of where or when. Communication facilities would be needed to handle the programme material coming from the War Correspondents, and the Lines Engineers did their best to cover the coast from Great Yarmouth to Plymouth with installations consisting of local ends from suitable points into the appropriate exchange. Unfortunately, about three months before D-Day, it was learned from the Post Office that trunk circuits would not be available because of the tremendous build-up of traffic; the reception points therefore had to be limited to BBC transmitting stations where, by the use of private wires in the reverse direction, the material could be got back to London. When D-Day came, Fareham Group H station was used with considerable success. This was between Southampton and Portsmouth, which was the main departure area, and a circuit was used from there to Bartley and thence back to London to feed the material into the programmes.

Another development in the technique of outside broadcasting was the introduction, during the last year of the war, of the 'split-band' system of transmission. A demand arose for OBs from places where it was out of the question to provide any of the types of line that could be used, as they stood, for broadcasting. A new method was developed for using two telephone circuits to provide the wider frequency band required for broadcast transmission. The lower half of the frequency band was transmitted on one telephone circuit, and the upper half of the music band over the other after it had been shifted into a position in the frequency spectrum low enough to be carried by a speech circuit. At the receiving end the upper music frequencies were re-established in their original position in the spectrum and combined with the lower music frequencies arriving on the other speech circuit. A system of this sort was used for a Christmas Day broadcast from Londonderry in 1944. Another applied a frequency shift to the lower band also, to bring it within the range of a standard international telephone circuit (300 to 3200 Hz): this was hurriedly constructed after the liberation of Paris and enabled many programmes to be taken from there that otherwise would not have been acceptable.

It was often necessary to introduce an intermediate repeater on long OB lines; the PER/3 portable equaliser-repeater had been introduced just before the war for the purpose and the PER/4 mains-operated version was coming into use when the war broke out. This consisted of two identical amplifiers in a box, each with its own mains unit, and was designed for use at Post Office telephone exchanges. Each amplifier had a pre-set equaliser and a variable attenuator; the repeater would be switched on by the local Post Office man and if one unit became faulty, he had merely to change over the connecting cords. When the SB system was damaged by enemy action, the PER/4 turned out to be a most useful piece of equipment. During the raids on Liverpool some damage was done to the Post Office installations in the area, and PER/4 repeaters were put in on some of the Birmingham-Manchester circuits and left for some months while the Post Office repaired their own installations. Thus, three invaluable BBC-designed equipments all became available at the time they were most needed: the OBA/8, the PER/3 and the PER/4.

Alongside the large developments in SB and OB facilities, techniques had to be introduced in a field new to the BBC: that of inter-office telephony and teleprinter working. Teleprinter channels had to be provided to convey a digest of monitored material to London; much of this material, containing important news items, sometimes picked up from enemy sources, was extremely urgent. The original four news agencies, Reuters, Press Association, Exchange Telegraph, and Central News, were supplemented now by the Associated Press and the British United Press, and these were all required at Wood Norton with, in addition, two channels from the Ministry of Information for 'handouts'. Since Wood Norton was remote from any of the centres where news agency material was available the BBC had to make its own arrangements to get it there. A number of teleprinters and associated voice-frequency equipment had been ordered for Wood Norton just before the war. In late 1940 a second set of news agency machines was provided at Wood Norton to serve the needs of the various overseas departments that then arrived there. All the channels were maintained by the Post Office, except the teleprinters connected to Reuters, Exchange Telegraph and Press Association, which were maintained, by agreement with these companies, by Lines Department staff.

On the telephony side war-time conditions made it necessary to abandon the use of relatively short links connected together by cord-circuit repeaters. There were, however, a number of routes in the SB system where there were one or more 'contribution' or 'reserve' programme circuits, which were idle during substantial periods each day. Pairs of these were made into four-wire circuits by fitting a hybrid coil at each end to permit two-way transmission. Such a combination formed an excellent low-loss telephone circuit, and a voice-frequency ringer panel was installed at each end. Since each leg of such a four-wire circuit was a programme circuit, the frequency band was wide enough to accommodate two speech channels, when fitted with suitable modulators, demodulators, and filters. Such a carrier system was designed for use between London and Bristol, but the results were poor because there was not enough bandwidth. Soon, however, a better system was designed, using ring modulators with suppressed carrier, and installed to work between London and Bristol. This system had a normal voice circuit using the lower part of the band; above this came a telegraph circuit working at about 2500 Hz, and above that again there was a suppressed-carrier voice channel with a carrier frequency of about 5000 Hz. The successful operation of this system led to a further system between London and Wood Norton, providing two voice channels (one 'physical' and one carrier) and one teleprinter channel.

The telegraph channels on these systems used a converter of BBC design at the receiving end. It derived from the incoming tone pulses (which were in the standard five-unit code) the 'mark' and 'space' pulses needed to operate the teleprinter magnet. As no telegraph distortion-measuring apparatus was available during the war, nobody knew how much distortion there was, but the converter gave very good service for a long time. These carrier telephone and telegraph systems were the precursors of many that were embodied in the post-war communications plan. Two more carrier systems were put in during the war, another '1 + 1' system (one physical and one carrier circuit) from London to Leeds, and a '1 + 2' system in 1944 between London and Wood Norton. One of the channels of the London–Leeds system was extended to Manchester on a 'two-band' carrier system to give a low-loss London–Manchester PBX channel. The two-band method was adapted from a pre-war German system called 'Zweiband', in which a non-repeatered line of sufficient bandwidth (say, 6 kHz) could carry transmission in one direction on the physical circuit using half the total bandwidth, while transmission in the other direction was on one sideband of a suppressed-carrier channel using the upper half of the band. The two channels were combined into a low-loss telephone channel by means of four-wire terminating sets at the ends, with vf ringer panels. (This system was, in a sense, the reverse of the 'split band' method of programme transmission previously mentioned.) The Leeds–Manchester two-band system was operated on a reserve two-way music circuit, at times when it was not required for programme. Similar systems were later put into operation between Glasgow and Edinburgh, and between Birmingham and Daventry.

Among the more bizarre 'by-product' channels that were devised during the war was a teleprinter circuit between London and Manchester, which operated on dc phantoms on two separate routes as far as Birmingham; from there onwards it operated on a tone system.

The widespread developments in 1943 led to the setting-up of a complete telegraph network with five key points: Broadcasting House, 200 Oxford Street, Aldenham, Wood Norton and Caversham (which was to be the new monitoring centre). The telegraph network was to carry news agency services to all five key points, monitored material from Caversham to London, and miscellaneous material from London to Caversham.

The security requirement was met by arranging the routes in a kind of 'ring main', so that in the event of a breakdown on any one route all, or nearly all, the services could be rerouted the other way round the ring. The network consisted of five Post

Office 4-channel voice frequency telegraph systems and one 12-channel system (Aldenham–Wood Norton). At Broadcasting House and 200 Oxford Street there were two complete sets of telegraph relays fed by the news agencies. Outputs from each of these were fed to each of the other two London premises, so that there were always two sources of the material.

The Monitoring Service needed two teleprinter channels to pass their traffic from Caversham to London, where it had to be distributed to various out-stations, mainly Government offices. To effect this distribution, the Post Office provided two telegraph 'broadcast switchboards' in London for selecting the particular out-stations to which any message was to be directed. The switchboards had to be set up manually and this duty, which involved manning day and night, fell to the lot of the Lines Department duty engineers, who strongly protested that their skills were being wasted on this task. This protest led to one of the first cases to be taken up by the embryo War-time Staff Association. It was settled amicably in the end, by the installation of a remote-selection system controlled from Caversham over slow-speed voice-frequency channels. The Post Office provided the switching equipment for selecting the different combinations of out-station required, while the BBC undertook the transmission of the switching signals. These were transmitted, at 250 Hz for one channel and 300 Hz for the other, on the Tariff 'E' 2-wire line between Caversham and London carrying the Post Office vf system, and were well below the part of the frequency band occupied by the vf telegraph signals. H. B. Rantzen has claimed that this was probably the first method of operating a teleprinter 'broadcast board' remotely over vf circuits. The system was rather slow in operation and there were some operating troubles, because the teleprinter operators were not used to working 'blind', i.e. the circuits were one-way and the production of a local copy on their teleprinters did not guarantee that the signals were arriving at their destination. Neon lamps were provided, which flashed when the teleprinter signals were actually going to line, and the operators then became confident that what they were typing was in fact going out. This method did not show whether there was a line fault preventing the signals from reaching London and, in the end, it was necessary to have a loop system by which the local copy was received after going to London and back. This caused a further crisis among the teleprinter operators (generally referred to at that time as 'teleprincesses'), because the local copy appeared a split-second later by the return loop from London; this threw them out of correct typing rhythm and reduced some of them to tears – not unnaturally because a delay of a fraction of a second between utterance and perception can cause symptoms of hysteria (as can easily be shown by making a speech while listening to a delayed recording of it). Finally, however, the operators became used to the system.

All this experience was turned to good account in the planning of the post-war communications network,[18] which started soon after D-Day. The first discussions on the subject led to the following conclusions:

(*a*) the Regions would spring to life again as they were before the war;
(*b*) there would be a need for far more communication facilities than ever before;

(c) much of this communication could be done by teleprinter, in spite of the rejection of this method of communication before the war by those responsible for administration. Many people had now become used to the teleprinter as a means of communication, and it was thought that if they could be persuaded to go on using it in peace-time, a really good and rapid telephone service could be given, because the telephone lines would not be loaded with material that could wait a few hours before being transmitted and delivered to the recipient;

and (d) the inclusion of engineering control lines in the planning of the network would make it desirable to consider whether it would be economic to include telephone circuits in 3-channel carrier systems, with the possibility of deriving, in addition, a sufficient number of teleprinter channels to handle the expected traffic.

Some bold assumptions had to be made about the extent of the post-war traffic. Plans were made for an Engineering Teleprinter Network to be formed by including one channel, on an 'omnibus' basis, along each of the routes that were contemplated for the carrier systems. There were so many routine service messages that had to be passed laboriously from one station to the next through the system, that it seemed better to use an omnibus teleprinter channel; this would provide a written record, save engineers' time at the intermediate stations and leave the telephone control lines free for more urgent traffic.

The Post Office had developed 12-channel telephone systems using pairs in non-loaded repeatered cables, with separate cables for each direction of transmission. The telephone channels were fitted into a band 48 kHz wide between 12 and 60 kHz. The part of the band below 12 kHz was not used, because, if more channels were required, it was cheaper to extend the range upwards rather than downwards, so as to yield a wide band with repeaters covering only a few octaves. The lower part of the band might have been used for programme transmission, but it was found more economical to derive phantom circuits from the pairs in the carrier telephone cables. (They were given the curious name of 'carrier phantoms', although they were derived from the physical circuits.) Each one-way phantom circuit was obtained from two pairs, by using centre taps on the secondary windings of the repeating coils at the sending end and on the primary windings of the repeating coils at the receiving end. Each of the carrier telephone repeaters throughout the length of the circuit had to be bridged in a similar manner and repeaters had to be inserted in the phantom circuits. During the war, the Post Office began to offer such phantom circuits for programme transmission. The BBC also used them for telephony by devising its own carrier system providing one physical circuit and two carrier channels, each about 2300 kHz wide and all in one direction, on each phantom circuit. Two phantom circuits in opposite directions had to be used for two-way communication. To check whether the intelligibility of speech on such channels would be adequate, a long series of tests was carried out to evaluate the effects of the various parameters of a telephone circuit. The method used was that of 'Immediate Appreciation', which had been developed

269

by W. H. Grinsted of Siemens Brothers and was the most up to date at the time. The result of these tests was somewhat surprising: the arbitrary objective of 90 per cent immediate appreciation could be achieved for 90 per cent of calls on channels with a cut-off frequency of 2300 Hz, provided the overall loss did not exceed 15 dB.

The main features of the post-war carrier systems had thus been settled, though plans for them had to wait until Regional broadcasting started again and it was possible to make the necessary traffic studies and to agree on the grade of service to be given.

6 RECORDING

On the outbreak of war the BBC could muster only eight static recording channels (each comprising two machines, and capable of continuous recording). They were concentrated at Maida Vale and made up as follows: three disc (MSS), three tape (Marconi-Stille) and two film (Philips-Miller). For the first year or so it was a case of 'make do and mend': getting the most out of the equipment available, dispersing it for greater security, and adding to it where possible by buying or leasing anything suitable that was to be had in this country. The fact that the importance of recording in war-time had not been appreciated much earlier was no doubt due to the persistence of the idea that recorded news items and documentaries had less validity than live material. Events were to prove that recordings made in the front line could have a dramatic impact far greater than a live news item composed far from the heat of battle.

The sole precaution that had been taken before the war was to prepare for recording at Wood Norton by putting in a set of amplifiers for a tape channel. In October 1939 it was decided to complete this installation by buying a pair of Marconi-Stille machines at a cost of £2000; by March 1940 this channel was working. In the meantime much of the equipment that had been concentrated at Maida Vale was dispersed, and the three available recording vans were given a predominantly static role. As a result of these steps, static recording had been placed on a more secure footing by March 1940, with resources as follows:

Wood Norton	2 tape channels
	3 disc channels (including the two vans T29 and T30)
	1 film channel (Philips-Miller)
Maida Vale	1 tape channel
	2 disc channels
	1 film channel (Philips-Miller)
Broadcasting House	1 tape channel
Bristol	1 disc channel (M53 van)

The excellent results that had been obtained from the Philips-Miller equipment, the first of which had been installed in 1936, made it desirable to acquire more of these machines. It so happened that J. Walter Thompson & Co. had a pair of rented

Philips-Miller film channels at their Ariel Studios at Bush House and another pair at the Scala Theatre. These had been used largely for making recordings for commercial radio stations in Europe, and this need ceased in war-time. The company offered to release these equipments and the BBC opened negotiations in July 1940 to hire them from Philips-Ciné-Sonor. One of the channels from Bush House was installed at Maida Vale and one at Wood Norton. These machines were installed by the end of August 1940, after having been modified to work at 20 cm/s as well as 32 cm/s. (The lower speed gave somewhat inferior quality, but was widely used in order to conserve scarce supplies of film; this lower speed was abandoned later when deliveries of film from the USA were assured.) One of the channels from the Scala Theatre was installed at Bristol in November 1940; for greater security this was moved into the Clifton Rocks Tunnel in July 1941. The other was sent to Maida Vale and moved to Bangor in 1941.

There was also a modest increase in disc recording facilities. Two MSS recorders were bought and, after being modified to work at $33\frac{1}{3}$ rpm, were installed at Maida Vale. There was, however, considerable anxiety about the security of the recording installations during the air-raids in the summer of 1940. The accommodation at Maida Vale gave almost no protection either to the engineers or to the equipment. The staff working after dark ran considerable risks, and it was decided to move the equipment below ground, except for one of the film channels, which was transferred to Broadcasting House and installed in an area on the ground floor where it was protected by steel shutters. (Ironically, this was the only recording channel in London that was damaged by air attack; it was severely damaged by the land-mine that exploded in Portland Place on 8 December 1940, but was made serviceable again within a few weeks and transferred to Manchester for use by Features and Drama in August 1941.)

No such protective measures were taken at Wood Norton, where the recording equipment was in wooden huts and in lorries. The risk of bomb damage there was regarded as fairly slight, and did not justify the diversion of men and materials to the major work that would have been required. There was, nevertheless, considerable concern about the security of the recording facilities, because Philips-Miller equipment had been completely unobtainable since the invasion of the Netherlands, Marconi-Stille equipment could not be obtained in less than a year and the capacity of the MSS Company to make disc recording machines was limited.

By the summer of 1941 six film channels were available – two at Wood Norton, and one each at Maida Vale, Bangor, Bristol and Manchester. Those at Bristol and Manchester were used to record the final rehearsal of all major productions, so that if an air-raid put a stop to the performance during transmission the recording could be substituted. The number of tape channels remained constant at four throughout the war (two at Wood Norton and one each at Maida Vale and Broadcasting House, London). In 1942 consideration was given to ordering further tape channels, but by then a large number of disc recording equipments had been ordered from the USA.

Towards the end of 1940 it became clear that there would have to be a big expansion of recording to keep pace with the impending increases in output, notably in the

Overseas and European Services. The resources were already strained by the need to record programmes during the day, so as to minimize the effects of air-raids at night and the risk of radiating the sound of gunfire, and also because many programmes had to be pre-recorded for censoring. A Recording Services Committee was set up, with representatives of the Engineering, Programme and Administration Divisions; M. J. L. Pulling represented the Engineering Division. It was decided that since Philips-Miller film equipment was unobtainable and supplies of magnetic tape from Sweden could not be guaranteed, attention should be concentrated on the disc system. A speed of $33\frac{1}{3}$ rpm was preferred as this permitted a 15-minute programme to be recorded on one side of a $17\frac{1}{4}$-in. disc with 120 grooves per inch. No British equipment operating at this speed was available, but both EMI and MSS could supply direct-recording discs – though not yet of consistently high quality.

Negotiations started in 1941, to obtain disc-recording equipment from the USA. Two Presto dual-turntable $33\frac{1}{3}/78$ rpm recording units and two reproducers were ordered at the beginning of February. One set was lost at sea, but the other got through safely at the beginning of May and was installed at Bush House. In March an RCA channel with two reproducers was ordered. It too went into Bush House, where it was commissioned at the end of October, after Research Department had carried out several modifications to fit it for BBC operation.

In July 1941 the Board authorised the purchase of twenty-five more Presto recording channels and fifty reproducers for £41,250. The order was placed in October. All but two recording and reproducing channels of this consignment arrived safely, during the period March to August 1942. The first twelve channels were allocated to: Oxford Street (4), Bush House (2, bringing the total up to 4), Bedford College, Aldenham, Glasgow, Bristol (to replace the M53 van), Manchester, and Research Department. Five of these channels were working by June 1942.

After a good deal of heart-searching, a scheme for another twenty-five Presto recording channels at a cost of £30,000 was put forward and approved by the Board in August 1942. Nobody wanted to buy more of this equipment than was likely to be needed, especially as a new recorder was being developed by the BBC Research Department. On the other hand, the BBC would be running a serious risk if it withheld the order, because it was not known when the BBC-designed equipment would start to come off the production line. Subsequently the order was modified to ten Presto and ten Gates channels, though in the event fifteen Prestos were delivered and the order for Gates recording channels was cancelled.

The Presto channels were obtained under Lease/Lend. There was little scope for choice in these circumstances, but A. E. Barrett inspected the equipment in the USA before it was despatched and accepted it as the best that could be obtained. The Presto equipment had to be modified for use in the BBC. This work was done by the Research Department and so many equipments had to be dealt with that the whole of the transmitter laboratory had to be diverted to this purpose. Even so, the equipment had certain shortcomings, but it saw the BBC through the war and without it the recording services would have been in desperate straits. With its aid, the BBC had, by 1945, amassed nearly forty channels of static recording equipment.

Meanwhile, there had been progress in the development of mobile recording units. In August 1939 the BBC's mobile recording fleet comprised one van and two large lorries fitted with MSS equipment, and two Wolseley saloon cars fitted with single-turntable transportable equipment of BBC design. About a week before the outbreak of war one of the cars was shipped over to France and garaged in Paris in readiness. The other was based on London, where it was at the disposal of the News Department. The van and the lorries, as we have already seen, were immediately turned over to a static role.

During September 1939 two more sets of the transportable equipment were forthcoming and these were installed at Queen Margaret College, Glasgow, where it was felt they would be reasonably safe. At the end of the month, when BBC Correspondents were seconded to the British Expeditionary Force, H. Sarney accompanied by Richard Dimbleby and Rex Howarth (of Recorded Programmes) collected the car in Paris and moved up with it to Lord Gort's headquarters at Arras. The duplicate set of equipment was taken out of the News car and sent out to them as a stand-by. To replace this, A. E. Barrett, in the space of three days, lashed up a fifth set based on an MSS recording machine belonging to the Research Department. This makeshift equipment was put into a Ford shooting brake and handed over to News Department in October 1939.

The winter of 1939–40 was bitterly cold, and it was a tough time for the recording unit in France. The electrolyte in the batteries froze and frost patterns were apt to form on the discs, which made it extremely difficult to cut good records. On occasions Sarney took the discs to bed with him so that they would be in good condition the next day. This was the period of the 'phoney-war', and the team was hard put to it to find any war-like material to record. For the most part they had to be content with ENSA concerts, quizzes in which the soldiers competed with their relations at home, and occasional church services. Many of these programmes were relayed to London by line from the French PTT repeater station at Lille.

During May the car moved up to Brussels and then back by way of Lille to Amiens. When the Germans invaded France it was only by the skin of his teeth that Sarney got out of Amiens with the car and one set of equipment (the other had to be abandoned). He made for Boulogne. There was no chance of getting the car home and so it was dropped in the dock, but the equipment was shipped safely back to England.

In the spring of 1940, L. F. Lewis, with Charles Gardner, had taken another set of equipment over to France and installed it in a car which he bought in Paris. They joined up with the RAF Advanced Air Striking Force near Rheims. It was in one of their dispatches that listeners heard for the first time the sound of bombs dropping. When France fell, Lewis managed to get himself and some of the equipment home by air from Calais.

The mobile recording equipment that was available at the beginning of the war had been assembled from various units to meet the immediate demand. There was a need for equipment specifically designed for mobile use. Accordingly, in the summer of 1939, Research Department undertook the design of the Type C recorder, which was to be manufactured jointly by the Research and Equipment Departments at a cost of £400 per set. Much ingenuity went into the design of this equipment, which proved highly successful and was able to withstand arduous journeys on bumpy roads and in the air; it also stood up extremely well to the shocks of war and to the heat and all-pervading sand of the North Africa campaign.

The Type C equipment was in three units: the recording machine, the amplifier (based on the OBA/8 with a power stage added), and the supply unit with its rotary converter for the ht supply. It worked from two 6-V accumulators in series, which gave a playing time of six hours, and it weighed about 450 lb in total. The discs had a diameter of 12 in., which at 78 rpm gave a recording of $4\frac{1}{2}$ minutes. The recording head was of BBC design (type A). It used the moving-iron principle, with grease damping. To keep down the size, weight and power consumption of the whole equipment, it was important that the recording head should be highly sensitive. This was achieved at the expense of the bandwidth, which was restricted to about 60 to 6000 Hz, the frequency of mechanical resonance being about 4500 Hz. The recording head was mounted on a tubular arm, pivoted at its centre of gravity and with a counterbalance weight at the opposite end. This arrangement reduced variations in the depth of cut resulting from vibration.

The turntable was driven by a 12-V dc motor, carrying a rubber-covered roller. The traverse mechanism was driven by a belt from the under-side of the turntable shaft, and the groove pitch was adjustable between 100 and 125 grooves per inch. A swarf-collecting brush was actuated by an eccentric disc-clamping boss; when the machine was used for reproduction, the brush unit was replaced by the reproducing head and arm. The turntable speed could be adjusted by means of a variable resistance in series with the field winding of the motor and the correct speed was indicated by a stroboscope. As the equipment was battery-operated, the stroboscope had to be illuminated by a neon lamp fed from an oscillator with good frequency stability. The recording amplifier was adapted from existing BBC amplifiers and incorporated a programme meter.

Six sets of Type C equipment were ordered in November 1939 and a further six in December 1940. (Further orders were placed in subsequent years, and by 1944 more than fifty sets had been made.)

Meanwhile, the MSS Company had produced a portable recorder; but after a comparison of its merits with those of the BBC Type C recorder it was decided that the higher cost of the latter was fully justified and the orders for it were confirmed. The possibilities of reducing the weight and cost were considered in May 1940, before the second batch was produced, but only minor modifications were made to the design.

In September 1941 a set of Presto portable equipment was ordered, and this arrived at the beginning of 1942. It was a twin-turntable design, mains-operated. It cut 16-in. discs with a choice of $33\frac{1}{3}$ and 78 rpm speeds, though in practice the $33\frac{1}{3}$ rpm was never used. Six more sets were ordered in November 1942 and saw some service, but the brunt of mobile recording in the field was borne by the BBC's Type C recorder, which was preferred on account of its reliability and robustness – both vital for war-time operations.

After the withdrawal from Europe in June 1940, the recording cars were engaged on reporting in this country. By that time, cars were based on Glasgow and Manchester as well as London. They contributed some spectacular broadcasts during the Battle of Britain, one of the most memorable being Charles Gardner's account of the battle in the Straits of Dover on 14 July 1940. These assignments were hazardous, not least for the engineer shut up in the car with the recording gear. H. L. Fletcher commented on 20 August 1940: 'Robin Duff's recent commentary at Dover with the light car was made under difficult circumstances, all three of them (the team) being machine-gunned.' He asked that, if names were mentioned in any broadcast in which recordings of this kind were used, they should always include those of everyone in the team, including the engineer. He also drew attention to the great risks that were being taken both of casualties among the staff and of damage to scarce equipment.

The success of the Type C portable recorder, coupled with the difficulties of obtaining satisfactory equipment from the USA, naturally led to the idea that the BBC might develop its own static disc recording equipment. This idea crystallised in February 1942 when it was decided that the design work should go ahead and that twenty-five sets of equipment should be built. M. J. L. Pulling prepared a specification of the requirements and in July 1942 it was decided that Research Department should proceed with the design of a first model. H. Davies was to be in charge of this work. The equipment was referred to as the Type D recorder. An allotment of £4000 was approved in October 1943 for two channels to be made by Research Department. The first model was given preliminary operational tests in February 1944. Further progress was delayed by the flying bomb attacks in that year, which made it necessary for the recording section of Research Department to move to Bagley Croft near Oxford. The first complete channel was installed on the lower ground floor in Broadcasting House and, after demonstrations and a service trial, it was handed over for full service on 23 April 1945.

The Type D recorder had two turntable speeds, 78 and $33\frac{1}{3}$ rpm, and two directions of traverse. The groove pitch was adjustable between 95 and 130 grooves per inch and discs up to $17\frac{1}{2}$ in. in diameter could be cut. Correction circuits were provided to give a range of frequency characteristics and radius compensation. Each channel comprised two recording machines and a separate control desk. The recording machine, which could also be used for reproduction, consisted of sub-assemblies for the turntable, traverse, main drive and scrolling units, all of which were on a cast-iron bedplate elastically mounted on a massive pedestal composed of cast-iron frames connected together by steel tubes and covered by a sheet-steel casing. The turntable with its detachable top-plate weighed 79 lb. The turntable shaft ran in bronze bearings and its weight was supported by a single ball, the journals and bearing being submersed in oil. The main driving motor ($\frac{1}{8}$-hp three-phase 1500 rpm) was mounted vertically and connected by an elastic coupling to a vertical layshaft, which was coupled by an idler wheel to a large friction wheel mounted on the same shaft as the turntable. The motor was suspended from elastic mountings, but as these were less effective at the lower frequencies a pair of vibration absorbers was provided, each consisting of a weight on the end of a steel rod; these were designed to resonate at the rotational frequency of the motor, i.e. 25 Hz. The traverse unit was of the parallel-motion type with

T

two widely-spaced slide-rods and a lead-screw with 32 threads per inch. The lead-screw was driven through a spring-loaded friction disc engaging with a sleeve on a vertical shaft driven by a belt from a pulley on the turntable shaft.

The recording head (BBC type B), which was carried on an arm pivoted at its centre of gravity, was of the moving-iron type with Ticonal magnets. The amplitude of the cutter was a linear function of the input up to a level 8 dB above normal and the frequency characteristic conformed to the required shape from 60 to 10,000 Hz, with a tolerance of ± 2 dB at the upper limit of frequency.

A suction system was used for the removal of swarf, in conjunction with a jet of air blown across the disc to drive the swarf towards the centre. Radius-compensation circuits were used to increase the response of the recording amplifier at the upper frequencies as the cutting speed fell towards the centre of the disc. [19, 20]

One of the major problems during the war was maintaining stocks of all the day-to-day things that a recording service must have in quantity in order to keep going – films, tapes, discs and cutters. The original source of Philips-Miller film was the Gevaert factory in Antwerp, and supplies ceased in May 1940 when the Germans occupied the Low Countries. Eastman Kodak succeeded in producing this highly-specialised type of film in the USA and by the autumn of 1940 a small consignment had reached this country and was subjected to tests. The main shortcoming was a variation in the thickness of the film, which gave rise to increased background noise, a trouble to which the early Gevaert film had also been prone. The BBC placed an order at the end of the year for 3000 reels, but with the proviso that up to 50 per cent of the reels could be rejected if they fell below a reasonable standard.

By the end of February 1941 stocks had fallen to barely six weeks' supply, and on 1 March news was received that the first consignment of 1000 reels had been lost at sea. Steps were taken immediately to reduce film recording to an absolute minimum, so as to conserve stocks. Slow-speed operation (20 cm/s) was already fairly general, and as a further economy measure a second track was cut on used film. Fortunately, three consignments of film arrived early in May. From then on supplies came in steadily and there was no further worry on that score. Indeed, by August 1941 the situation was felt to be secure enough to go back to normal recording speed (32 cm/s) as part of a drive to achieve a substantial improvement in technical quality. There was also a gradual improvement in the film from Eastman Kodak, and by 1943 it was as good as the pre-war Gevaert film.

The supply of sapphire cutters for Philips-Miller machines was also difficult. In the early part of the war America was the main source of supply, but by 1943 Philips-Ciné-Sonor had succeeded in manufacturing good quality sapphires in the United Kingdom, with considerable help from the BBC.

Before the war the 3-mm steel tape for Marconi-Stille recordings came from the Uddeholms Company in Sweden. In August 1940, when there seemed to be no prospect of getting any more supplies from this source, the BBC's total stock was 340 reels, each of half an hour's duration. Unlike the Philips-Miller equipment, the Marconi-Stille system could use the tapes over and over again, so that, provided there was good discipline in not retaining recordings longer than was necessary, stocks of tape could be spun out almost indefinitely. Nevertheless, the arrival of eighty reels of new tape in April 1942 was a most welcome windfall.

For its 78 rpm disc recordings, lasting $4\frac{1}{2}$ minutes, the BBC had used steel cutters, but these were not satisfactory for cutting $33\frac{1}{3}$ rpm recordings with a duration of 15 minutes, which started in 1941. Something much harder and more durable was needed, and development of sapphire-tipped styli was begun. The problem was to produce the styli in sufficient quantity and of the right quality. It was found during manufacture that the stylus was prone to chip just when grinding was approaching completion. However, a chance meeting between Pulling and Sir Clifford Patterson, who was in charge of the GEC Research Laboratories at Wembley, led to the solution of this difficulty. The GEC had been set a similar problem in making dies for wire-drawing, and had found that the grading of the diamond dust used for the grinding process was crucial – the right particle size had to be determined and then maintained with great precision. F. H. Dart and S. R. Lance armed with this advice developed means for producing sapphire-tipped styli with great success,[21] and from then on there was no difficulty in keeping up supplies of the right quality.

Disc consumption increased spectacularly as the war went on, reaching 7000 a week at the peak, compared with 500 a week in 1939. There was a constant battle to maintain supplies; aluminium, the preferred base material for the discs, was scarce and other materials, such as glass and zinc, though unsatisfactory, had to be used. Aluminium discs could be stripped after use and recoated with lacquer, but even so the demand far outpaced the supply. There were only two suppliers, the MSS Recording Company and EMI. The MSS Company entered into an agreement by which the company came under the control of the Post Office from the summer of 1941. This worked to the BBC's advantage, for the additional capital that the Post Office could infuse into the company and the priorities they could get for machinery and building all helped towards an increase in output. EMI started supplying discs in 1941. In January 1942 they set about providing factory space and equipment to enable them to raise their output to 1500 discs a week against a guaranteed BBC order of 80,000 discs a year. Their new plant came into production early in 1943.

As the Allies' fortunes began to improve, attention was increasingly focused on plans for the Second Front. As early as January 1943 the Treasury had approved a blanket estimate totalling £100,000 for what was at that stage termed 'Front-Line Reporting'. During the summer the concept of a War Reporting Unit was firmly established, and plans began to take shape. By the autumn of 1943 it had been decided to fit out twenty-four mobile recording units for this venture. Each unit was to consist of a Humber military ambulance with four-wheel drive, fitted to take the Type C equipment, backed up by a utility vehicle to serve as a tender. By November 1943 six of these vehicles were fully equipped and standing by, and another three had already been sent out to join the campaign in Italy. A few of them had two sets of recording equipment, the Type C being supplemented by one of the Presto mains-driven twin-turntable channels.

As D-Day approached, five Humber trucks were allocated to Stewart Macpherson (south of the Thames), to Kent Stevenson (north of the Thames), and to Howard

Marshall, Chester Wilmot and Colin Wills, who were to be the first BBC Correspondents to cross to France. In addition, Type C equipment was put aboard a warship and a merchant ship, and two sets were turned over to Robin Duff and Robert Dunnet, who were with the United States forces. By 23 June 1944 one truck with Chester Wilmot was on its way to France and two more were waiting to cross. Thereafter there was a steady build-up, and by the beginning of September seven units were operating in France and two in Italy. At the beginning of 1945 the War Reporting Unit had nine units on the western front (two of them equipped with jeeps and trailers for the equipment), two in the Mediterranean theatre, and one in South-East Asia.

It was appreciated quite early that if the war correspondents were to be able to keep pace with the Allies' advance they must have a really portable recorder that they could carry and operate themselves. J. B. Clark, Controller (Overseas), had pointed out in October 1942 that a small portable recording machine would be essential for the 'proper reporting of future operations'.[35] With this in mind, a few American wire recorders were ordered from Heller and General Electric in the summer of 1943. However, by October none had been received. By this time the News people were getting anxious. Howard Marshall wrote to Bishop in October, stressing that the portable recorder was the key to successful war reporting and pointing out that the Americans and Canadians were using them and thus gaining an advantage over the BBC. He thought it was vital that a truly portable recorder should be available for news reporting in general and asked that high priority should be given to its development. Bishop explained that the development of a really portable recorder would take at least six months, and then only at the expense of other equally important work. He then went on to outline the prospects for the BBC's midget disc recorder; Pulling had arranged in 1943 for its development, in collaboration with the MSS Company. By September six were being made up by the MSS Company, one of which had already been subjected to a user's test with a fair degree of success. In the autumn one of these recorders was turned over to Research Department for them to produce an improved version. In the remarkably short space of three months, W. J. Lloyd and D. E. L. Shorter had produced a prototype. Bishop considered that the design had been very well thought out; Ashbridge was impressed with it and so were the commentators in the WRU.

The midget disc recorder, or 'Riverside Portable', accommodated double-sided 10-in. discs, which gave just under three minutes of recording time per side.[22] Its turntable was driven by a double-spring gramophone motor. The recording head was a modified crystal pick-up. To make it as simple as possible to operate, there was only one control, which did everything – removing the brake on the motor, switching on the amplifier, and lowering the recording head on to the disc. A flickering neon lamp indicated when the level was right for recording, and another warning light showed when there was only fifteen seconds of recording time left. The amplifier incorporated a limiter to spare the war correspondent the distraction of adjusting the gain. The midget recorder weighed 35 lb complete with its batteries. The original prototype had a steel case; but all the production models had wooden cases, for these proved quite strong enough and also reduced the weight by 6 lb. Power consumption was very economical – 0·3 A at 3 V and between 8 and 12 mA at 100 V, derived from dry batteries housed in a light metal cassette. About forty discs could be recorded before the batteries needed changing.

These portable recorders were first introduced to the war correspondents during a week-end session at Wood Norton to which, under Howard Marshall, as many of them as could be mustered were summoned. One of their number was John Glyn Jones, who had been a radio producer. He was asked to christen one of the Riverside Portables. Without a moment's hesitation, he conjured up a scene in which Mr Faraday from Britain, Dr Ohm from Germany, Signor Volta from Italy and Dr Ampére from France were all simultaneously present on the dais to pay honour to this latest manifestation of the advance of electrical science. Each of these characters in turn mounted the rostrum and spoke – the foreigners in appropriate broken English – in eloquent and glowing terms.

In the light of events it was indeed fortunate that Pulling had taken the initiative and set in motion the development of the midget disc recorder. Towards the end of 1943 Frank Gillard had tried out an American General Electric wire recorder in Italy. There were a few shortcomings, but it had, he thought, the makings of an ideal instrument. But, despite great efforts by A. E. Barrett in America, there were serious delays in delivery of the American wire recorders, and when they did arrive they did not come up to the required standard. Thus, it was left to the BBC's midget disc recorder to save the day. By D-Day, eleven were available. Two were allocated to war correspondents with the Navy, four to those with the Army, and three to those with the RAF. One had been demonstrated to General (shortly afterwards Field-Marshal) Montgomery a few weeks before D-Day and he expressed much interest in it.

By 9 June 1944 eight of the Research Department's improved version of the midget recorder (Mk II) had been delivered and the number in service in the field had gone up to eleven. Even in this short space of time they had proved their worth, both in this country and in Normandy.

By the end of September 1944, forty-eight midget disc recorders had been made, including the original six manufactured by the MSS Company. Of these, twenty were in the field with war correspondents. At the end of 1944, Equipment Department began another run of 24, thus bringing the total number made up to 72. Losses were fairly light – five in all, including No. 122, on which Stanley Maxted recorded his memorable report from Arnhem in September 1944.

Recording played a major part in war reporting, which also made heavy demands on other technical resources as described in section 9 of this chapter.

7   PROGRAMME MONITORING AND TECHNICAL MONITORING

Regular monitoring in this country of programmes broadcast by foreign stations had its origins during the winter of 1935 at the time of the Italo-Abyssinian War when monitoring of news bulletins in English was started by the Foreign Office. Monitoring of Arabic broadcasts from Italian stations followed in 1937, and programmes directed to South America from Germany were monitored for four or five nights each week late in 1938. In March 1939 an 'enemy propaganda' organisation was set up under Sir Campbell Stuart with A. P. Ryan acting as the BBC's liaison officer.[23]

The initial proposals for war-time monitoring envisaged the setting-up of a number of stations like the BBC's Receiving Station at Tatsfield, Surrey, and the distribution of short-wave receivers to members of the BBC staff for use in their homes.

Meanwhile, in June 1938, selected news bulletins in English from Paris, Berlin, Rome, Prague, New York, Pittsburgh and Tokyo were being monitored regularly by the BBC in London and at Tatsfield. In April 1939 it was decided to create a Monitoring Unit, staffed throughout the twenty-four hours, and the Ministry of Information was asked to finance it. When this plea proved unsuccessful, the BBC purchased, out of its own funds, a wooden hut, six receivers and material for simple aerials for the sum of £810 in the hope of recovering this outlay from the Ministry later on.[24] The embryo Monitoring Unit moved to the BBC's emergency premises at Wood Norton, near Evesham, shortly before the outbreak of war, leaving only a few special monitors and liaison staff in London. Under the direction of W. Proctor Wilson of the Research Department, the hut and aerials were erected on Tunnel Hill at Wood Norton and the first receivers were installed. The Monitoring Service then began its task of listening throughout the twenty-four hours to all forms of broadcast transmissions from abroad whether by spoken word, in Morse telegraphy, or by auto-printers such as the Hellschreiber.

At first the direction of the Monitoring Service remained in Scott's Hotel, adjoining Broadcasting House, London, but a large number of monitors went to Wood Norton, where several huts had been built for them to work in. The monitoring staff, most of whom were foreigners, had to be billeted in the neighbourhood. The problem of assimilating them into the local population has already been mentioned in section 1 of this chapter. They also had to be provided with adequate physical conditions for their work, and the technical facilities required for it. Although the monitors moved to Wood Norton, the Information Unit (which picked out the information that would be required by Government Departments and the BBC news services), and the report writers (who prepared daily summaries of the monitored material), remained in London.

When Broadcasting House was bombed on 15 October 1940, and four members of the Monitoring Service were killed,[2] it was decided to concentrate the whole of the Monitoring Service, including the Information Unit and the report writers, at Wood Norton. The monitors worked in the main building at Wood Norton and in the huts, although the receivers were installed on Tunnel Hill, some 300 ft above the mean level of the surrounding countryside.

S. G. Williams, who was Monitoring Service Executive, has remarked on the skill with which the monitors and the engineers built up a totally new activity, for which there had been no previous experience of any kind. The staff was made up of people drawn from diverse activities in the BBC and built into a team to operate the Monitoring Service.

The equipment installed on Tunnel Hill was at first planned to be operated exclusively by Engineering Divison staff, who would record the monitored material. The initial facilities comprised one T-aerial, two Beverage aerials directed towards Germany and Italy, a set of Bellini-Tosi crossed loops with a radiogoniometer, fourteen all-wave communication receivers, six office-type recording machines and a set of frequency-measuring equipment. (The first recorders were Dictaphones and Ediphones, which required an acoustic input, but these were later superseded by Telediphones, which could be connected to a line or to the output of a receiver.) A simple open-wire distribution system permitted any one of twelve of the receivers to be connected to any of the three aerials, whilst the remaining two receivers were used with the radiogoniometer for direction-finding purposes and with frequency-measuring equipment. It was arranged that the output of the monitoring receivers could be connected to the recording machines and also passed to language monitors working in the main building at the foot of the hill. Communication facilities were provided on private wires from Wood Norton to the interested departments in London and in other dispersal areas; teleprinter equipment was installed, so that important and urgent information could be 'flashed' to special consumers.

The news bulletins or other material to be monitored were intercepted and recorded by the engineers and the wax cylinders were carried by hand down the hill to the monitors, who used them when checking their notes made from the 'live' material. The wax cylinders were shaved after use and returned by hand to the Interception Hut at the top of the hill for reuse. Although these simple arrangements worked satisfactorily for the first few months of the war, it was not long before the increasing demands of the consumer departments drew attention to the limitations of the system; the aerial and receiver facilities were inadequate and the delay between the time of receiving an important piece of information and the 'flashing' of it to the consumers was too great. At the same time the language monitors expressed an understandable desire to operate their own receivers and there was a shortage of experienced interception engineers. Tatsfield was the only source of such engineers and half of its staff had already been sent to Wood Norton on the outbreak of war. It was evident that the Monitoring Service would have to be replanned so that the language monitors controlled their own receivers for the reception of relatively strong signals, while the weaker signals would be intercepted by engineers equipped with communication receivers and directional aerial systems. Each monitor would be able to select either the output of his own receiver – a high-quality domestic type of set – or the output of the communication receiver operated by the engineers on Tunnel Hill. It was desirable that the aerials for the monitor's receivers should be remote from the electrically noisy buildings and from this grew the idea of an 'amplified aerial system'.

This system comprised wide-band radio-frequency amplifiers installed in the receiver hut with their outputs connected by buried coaxial cables to simple resistive distribution networks in the monitoring rooms some 600 yards away. The monitors' receivers were then fed directly from these networks using coaxial cable connections. Up to sixty receivers were fed by this means from the aerials on the hill and a supervisory position was installed in the monitoring area where the output of any monitor's receiver or that of any of the communication receivers could be observed. Each monitor was provided with relay switching facilities which enabled him to select a recording machine at any time.

Simultaneously with these improvements in the monitoring rooms, the technical facilities in the engineering area were improved with the addition of more receivers mounted on racks. The frequency-measuring facilities were also improved and additional aerials erected. The final aerial installation at Wood Norton for the Monitoring Service comprised the following:

Twenty-five vertical wire aerials suspended from triatics between three 80-ft steel masts;
Two inverted-V arrays for 9–17 MHz, one directed on Moscow and the other on New York;
One 6-MHz dipole aerial for reception from the USA and Europe;
Ten Beverage aerials oriented on: Tokyo (short path) on a bearing of 033°, Moscow (and the USSR generally) on 065°, Germany, Central Europe and the Far East on 086°, South-Eastern Europe on 110°, the Balkans, Italy, the Near East and India on 120°, France, Spain and N. Africa on 183°, Tokyo (long path) on 213° and North and South America on 290°.

All these aerials were connected to a coaxial distribution panel from which they could be connected to the inputs of the wideband amplifiers. Rejector circuits were included in the amplifiers used on long and medium waves to suppress intermodulation products caused by the very strong signals received at Wood Norton from the Droitwich transmitters, some thirteen miles distant. (At this time, Droitwich was radiating 400 kW on 1149 kHz, 150 kW on 200 kHz, 50 kW on 767 kHz and 2 kW on 1013 kHz). The resistive distribution networks in the monitoring area gave an attenuation of about 27 dB between the coaxial feed cable and any receiver input, so that there was an attenuation of about 55 dB between receiver input circuits connected to the same distribution point. This helped to overcome the nuisance of local oscillator pick-up between the monitors' receivers.[25]

These improved facilities met the needs of the Monitoring Service during the early part of the war and permitted it to undertake additional tasks such as the monitoring of BBC transmissions to watch for interpolations by the enemy. In June 1940 a War Office Monitoring Group was transferred to Wood Norton where it was known as the 'Y' Unit, the BBC's Monitoring Service being known as the 'M' Unit.

With the extension of the war and the increase in the number of transmissions to be monitored, it became necessary once again to replan the monitoring organisation. It was not possible to expand further at Wood Norton without encroaching on accommodation required for other broadcasting purposes and there were obvious advantages to be gained in merging the Wood Norton and London monitoring staff. At the same time it was desired to improve communications (telephone, telegraph, road and rail) between the Monitoring Service and London, while retaining adequate communications with Wood Norton and other dispersal areas. Technically it was desirable to find a site where the field strength of BBC transmissions was much lower than at Wood Norton and also to avoid interference from power lines, which was troublesome at Wood Norton. Finally, the site selected had to be relatively safe from air attack. Taking all these considerations into account it was thought that a site in the Reading area of Berkshire would meet most of the requirements. After a preliminary search, a site at Caversham Park some two miles north of Reading was chosen for reception tests, which were carried out in July 1941. These tests covered all the frequency bands then in use for broadcasting and were made in representative weather conditions. Simultaneously, reception tests and measurements were made at Wood Norton for comparing the two locations. The radio noise levels at Caversham, although not ideal, were considerably better than those at Wood Norton. No other likely site could be found in the area and the only enemy air activity in the locality up to that time had been one or two minor incidents to the south of Reading. (Later, an incident occurred much nearer to Caversham with the destruction of the Reading Group H transmitter.)

It was therefore decided to establish the main body of the Monitoring Service at Caversham and, since the centre itself would inevitably create electrical noise, a search was made for a second site in the area, as free as possible of electrical interference, for receiving weak signals. A suitable site for this was found at Crowsley Park, Oxfordshire, about $3\frac{1}{2}$ miles north of Caversham, and an engineering interception station was set up there, with an extensive directional aerial system.

The idea of moving to Caversham had been notified to the staff concerned in August 1941, but Treasury approval for the move was not given until April 1942 and it was carried out in March and April 1943. The staff difficulties arising from the change of location have been described by Asa Briggs.[26] From the technical point of view it was an immediate success, many stations that were unreadable at Wood Norton being easily received at Crowsley, if not at Caversham.

In August 1939 the staff of the Monitoring Service had numbered fifty. The total number of staff employed at Caversham increased to nearly 1000, of whom some 650 were engaged directly in the operation of the service. At the peak period of its war-time activity, 1·25 million words were being monitored each twenty-four hours, of which 300,000 words were transcribed and 100,000 words were distributed to consumers in a daily digest. In addition, 24,000 words were 'flashed' daily over the teleprinter circuits.[27]

A fresh look had to be taken at the engineering problems when the installations at Caversham and Crowsley Park were planned. The technical developments were in two main directions. First, there was the design of an improved 'amplified aerial system'. The system used at Wood Norton did not cover all the wavebands satisfactorily and there was trouble from intermodulation products arising from strong BBC signals there. For Caversham and Crowsley it was decided to use octave amplifiers, with means for combining their outputs. The reason for this decision was that intermodulation between strong signals could be much reduced, and the design of coupling units simplified, if the bandwidth of each amplifier was limited, by means of filters, to a frequency ratio of 2:1. This not only reduced the number of interfering

283

signals present in each amplifier, but also eliminated all harmonics of the signals passing through each amplifier. The whole of the frequency spectrum occupied by the normal broadcasting bands between 0·5 and 27 MHz could be covered by eight such amplifiers. As the amplifiers had to be located near the aerial system, while the receivers were in the main building some distance away, the cost of providing a separate coaxial cable for each amplifier would have been excessive. Paralleling the outputs of all the amplifiers would not have been satisfactory and it was decided to divide the eight amplifiers into three groups, those in each group having pass bands separated by at least two octaves. The number of coaxial cables required to carry the outputs of eight amplifiers was thus reduced to three.

Secondly, an improved design of distribution network was developed using a new wideband transformer designed by C. G. Mayo of Research Department. This transformer covered the band of frequencies between 100 kHz ahd 27 MHz with an insertion loss of only about 4 dB. The transformer-coupled distribution network introduced only about half the attenuation of the previous resistive network thus giving a welcome enhancement of the signal at the input of the monitors' receivers.[25]

Two separate amplified aerial systems were installed at Caversham for the 'M' and 'Y' Units, each capable of feeding up to sixty receivers. The system for the 'Y' unit was provided with an additional amplifier to cover the band from 15–100 kHz. The first aerial systems at Caversham were simple long-wire, semi-vertical (i.e. sloping) aerials for all the octave bands with an inverted-L aerial for the 15–100 kHz band. Subsequently, the aerials for frequencies above 4 MHz were replaced by horizontal-V omni-directional aerials. These had an included angle of 90° and the length of each arm was half a wavelength at the mid-band frequency of the octave for which the aerial was designed. The height above ground was half a wavelength at 5·7 MHz. Each arm was composed of a six-wire cage to reduce the impedance to about 500 ohms. The gain of these aerials, known also as quadrant aerials, over a simple semi-vertical aerial was 5·5 dB in the 16–27 MHz band rising to 8·2 dB in the 4–8 MHz band. The aerial field comprised ten acres of flat land and the main aerial system was supported by six 100 ft tubular steel masts arranged in a rectangle.

The interception station at Crowsley was equipped with forty rack-mounted communications receivers and the aerial system comprised five rhombic aerials, twelve Beverage aerials, and about thirty omni-directional aerials. Here also octave amplifiers were used. The outputs from the receivers were sent over a multi-pair cable to the main building at Caversham and distributed to the various monitoring points there. The monitors had the option of using their individual receivers or of listening to the output of the receivers at Crowsley. A Bellini-Tosi crossed-loop aerial was also available at Crowsley for picking out particularly difficult signals by setting the minimum in the direction of an unwanted transmission.

The equipment initially installed at Caversham and Crowsley Park was varied in type and origin and most of it was replaced after the war with British-made equipment specially suited to the operational requirements of the Monitoring Service.

Although the Tatsfield Receiving Station was used for language monitoring from 1938 to the beginning of the war, its principal use has always been for technical monitoring and related work. With the large increase in the number of transmitters used for the Home and Overseas Services as the war progressed, the checking of carrier frequencies and the monitoring of transmissions to ensure that the correct programme was being radiated necessitated an expansion of staff and accommodation at Tatsfield. In 1941 the main building was extended, almost doubling the original floor area, and six listening cubicles were provided in an extension. BBC short-wave transmissions were checked in five of these and all the BBC's long- and medium-wave transmissions in the sixth. An additional frequency-measuring equipment was installed – the Marconi type TME/2 – which was the precursor of the later synthe-siser equipment. It had a locked decade system and a stroboscopic display which was invaluable for observing carrier frequency drift. The frequency sub-standards at Tatsfield were improved throughout the war and in 1945 the frequency measurement accuracy was of the order of 1 part in 10^8.

Throughout the war, Tatsfield provided an 'on-demand' frequency measurement service to the Transmitter Department staff, who were working on the development production and testing of variable-frequency drive equipment in a separate building at Tatsfield. Tatsfield also provided a service to transmitting station staff by assisting them to maintain accurate carrier frequency synchronisation after interruptions to the station's electricity supply or faults in the drive equipment. The speed and reliability of the frequency-measuring service was largely due to the example set by the then Engineer-in-Charge, H. V. Griffiths. A healthy spirit of competition soon developed between the staff at transmitting stations and those at Tatsfield in the field of precision frequency control.

During the war broadcasting stations on both sides adopted various measures to deny navigational aid to enemy aircraft and Tatsfield was able to provide information on the location of enemy transmitters; this was of considerable value to the BBC and to the Services. Broadcast announcements intentionally gave no information concerning the siting of transmitters in use and some announcements were definitely misleading. For example, the broadcasts by William Joyce ('Lord Haw Haw') were stated to be from Bremen, but in fact came sometimes from Osterloog, near Norden (some eighty miles from Bremen) and sometimes from the Lopik transmitter in the Netherlands (some 200 miles from Bremen). By observing minute changes in carrier frequency when the transmitters were changed over and by using their Adcock direction-finding equipment, Tatsfield staff were able to distinguish between the two transmitters.

The Tatsfield staff also made a special study of jamming signals and became skilled in identifying their types and origins, and even in decoding the identification signals used by the enemy for his own purposes. The first intentional jamming of broadcast transmissions recorded by Tatsfield was that by Germany against Russia, with Russia retaliating, in 1934. This was followed by Italian jamming of Abyssinian broadcasts in 1937 and of the BBC's Arabic transmissions in 1938. After the war had started there was a rapid increase in jamming by the enemy and Tatsfield's work on identification assisted in the BBC's efforts to devise means to circumvent this nuisance.

Another important contribution made by Tatsfield was the checking of BBC Overseas Service transmissions to ensure that the correct programme was radiated on each frequency. Some forty-two different languages were being used by the Overseas Services and few of these languages could be recognised by the transmitter staff; the fact that errors were seldom made was due in no small part to the constant watch maintained at Tatsfield. Assistance was also given in identifying and reporting intermodulation products and harmonics radiated from multi-transmitter sites.

Propagation conditions over selected paths were continuously observed at Tatsfield to facilitate the choice of the optimum frequency for transmitting overseas over any path at a particular time. Warnings of ionospheric disturbances were given to Engineering Division and Programme Departments to permit alternative arrangements to be made for transmission and also for the reception of relays.

During the war years additional aerials were provided at Tatsfield, including inverted-V aerials erected from 100-ft self-supporting towers, which replaced the 110-ft stayed masts brought down when Tatsfield suffered an air attack in 1940. On this occasion two oil bombs were dropped on the site followed by one 500-lb high-explosive bomb and another that exploded some three hours after impact. Fortunately, there were no serious injuries to the staff on this occasion and the building suffered only broken windows and roof damage. In 1943 a Beverage aerial was erected for reception from North Africa of the two-way channel used by War Correspondents through the French PTT transmitters THA-1 and THA-2 at Algiers. Bi-square aerials (bi-directional aerials comprising eight half-wave elements arranged in two squares in vertical planes about $\frac{1}{8}$-wavelength apart) were erected for a 17-MHz circuit from India and a 9·5 MHz circuit from Australia, as well as a 17-MHz curtain array for improved reception of signals from the USA. In 1945 a wideband amplifier system similar to that provided for Caversham was installed at Tatsfield.

Tatsfield was the first British user of the RCA type AR.88 receiver, which was later used extensively by the British Forces before it became a standard issue to the US Signal Corps. The first of these receivers to arrive in the United Kingdom was brought in by the Royal Navy after a first attempt to fly one in had failed with the crashing of the bomber carrying it.

In July 1944 the Air Ministry instructed the BBC to evacuate the Tatsfield site on account of the acute danger from V1 Flying Bombs. The entire staff and all the equipment, except the aerials, the aerial termination bay and the batteries, were removed in three days to Crowsley Park and with the co-operation of EiC Caversham the normal services provided by Tatsfield were maintained throughout the move. The staff and equipment returned to Tatsfield in November 1944.

The radio relay work at Tatsfield increased very considerably during the war years and a special contribution in this field was the reception of most of the despatches carried by BBC mobile transmitters from War Correspondents working in the Mediterranean and, later, the European war zones. Temporary aerials were erected for this task to obtain maximum directivity, which was needed on account of the low power of the transmitters.

The number of staff on the Tatsfield establishment in 1939 was twenty and this increased to seventh-two by the end of the war in Europe in 1945. These numbers include those working on interception duties at Wood Norton and, later, at Crowsley Park.

8 CONTRIBUTIONS TO THE WAR EFFORT

In addition to its job of maintaining and expanding BBC facilities and adapting them to war-time conditions, the Engineering Division placed its special knowledge at the disposal of the Services and other organisations. Much of the assistance that was given was informal and unrecorded. Many engineering staff were seconded to, or recruited by, the Services and direct assistance was given to them on a number of projects to which broadcasting techniques were applicable.

The arrangements for synchronising medium-wave transmitters to avoid giving navigational aid to enemy aircraft have already been described. An excursion by BBC engineers outside the broadcasting field was in connection with the development of misleading beacons, later known as Meacons. The enemy used a navigational system in which dots were heard if the aircraft was on one side of the correct course and dashes when it was on the other side; the dots and dashes merged into a constant note if it was on course. The Meacon intercepted the transmission of either the dots or the dashes and reradiated them, thus giving a false indication on the equipment in the aircraft. The Meacon was a 1 kW MF transmitter mounted in a motor-coach, the power being supplied by a battery-driven generator in another coach. The receiver that picked up the enemy's navigational signals had to be at least a mile away from the Meacon, so as to give at least 40 dB protection against the retransmitted signals. The BBC provided radio links operating on about 6 MHz to feed Meacons with the intercepted signals.[28]

The RAF operated a chain of radar stations, which depended for their effectiveness on being locked to the frequency of the public electricity supply. In case this ceased to be available at one or more of the stations, it was decided to distribute a reference tone to them. This was derived from precision oscillators supplied by the GPO and the monitoring equipment was developed by the BBC. A first batch of twenty-five of these equipments was delivered to the RAF on 10 March 1942. A by-product of this work was of permanent value to the BBC, the Drive Section having been provided with a well-equipped building to facilitate their work on the project.

When the Television Service was closed down on 1 September 1939, the transmitters at Alexandra Palace were placed on a care-and-maintenance basis and T. H. Bridgewater (later Chief Engineer, Television) was appointed the 'technical care-taker'. All remained quiet at Alexandra Palace until 23 May 1940 when the BBC was requested to bring the vision transmitter back into use modulated with 'artificial bars'. It had been observed that enemy tank formations had been using frequencies in the vision band of the Alexandra Palace transmissions for communication purposes and, the threat of invasion being a very real one at that time, it was decided to prepare to jam such communications. H. W. Baker (later Senior Superintendent

Engineer, Television) was sent very early one morning to get the transmitter on the air. When Bridgewater came on duty later that morning, he could hardly believe his eyes to see the activity on his ostensibly 'cocooned' station. Fortunately enemy tanks never crossed the Channel and this particular counter-measure never had to be used.

The first hint of a possible use for the Alexandra Palace sound transmitter came on 7 January 1941 with a request to prepare the transmitter for operation on a carrier frequency of 42·5 MHz with facilities to adjust its frequency within a band 100 kHz on either side of this frequency. A Marconi variable-frequency drive was transferred from Brookmans Park and frequency multipliers were designed and built by the Drive Section. The transmitter first radiated for a short test on 15 January 1941 and arrangements were made for it to be switched on when the monitoring station installed in the Television OB premises at Swain's Lane, Highgate, observed a signal being transmitted by an enemy aircraft for ranging purposes. Tones of various frequencies were available as modulation and the Swain's Lane operator could steer the carrier frequency of the Alexandra Palace transmitter to zero beat with the aircraft carrier frequency. The object was to disable the navigational system developed by the Luftwaffe and known to them as 'Y-Gerät'. On 4 February 1941 during an air raid on London the expected signals were heard on 42 and 47 MHz. The Alexandra Palace transmitter radiated immediately and it was soon obvious that the effect of this counter-measure upon the 'Y-Gerät' system was going to be catastrophic. A second jamming transmitter was erected by the RAF on Beacon Hill, near Salisbury, and with only these two 'DOMINO' stations operating, it was found that during eighty-nine sorties using the 'Y-Gerät' system, during the first two weeks of March 1941, bombs were dropped by only eighteen of them.[29]

From May 1941 onwards German attacks on this country diminished, but on 11 August 1941 the BBC received another request for an Alexandra Palace transmitter – this time the vision transmitter – to radiate jamming signals. The frequency band specified was from 30–38 MHz and the transmission was required as a counter to transmitters expected to be used by German paratroops dropped over the south of England. An oscillator providing three crystal-controlled carrier frequencies was provided by the Research Department with means for modulating them by subcarriers to produce a band of interference 4 MHz wide. Although this equipment does not appear to have been used operationally, it occasioned much intensive effort by Research Department engineers and members of the Transmitter Department, as depicted by W. C. Pafford's cartoon. (Plate XXIV.)

An intimation of the possible use of BBC facilities for the GEE system of navigational aids for the RAF came when two senior members of the GPO Research Station staff visited Daventry on 11 April 1941 to discuss methods of obtaining accurate pulse repetition frequencies for a VHF transmitter to be installed at Daventry. Shortly afterwards the BBC was requested to provide the required facilities at Daventry and to design a suitable aerial. The Daventry GEE station became the master station of the Eastern Chain and it was fortunate that the staff at Daventry included a number of ex-Alexandra Palace engineers, under D. C. Birkinshaw, the Engineer-in-Charge. These people had a good knowledge of pulse techniques and relished the job of working on pulse transmissions again, so that the Daventry GEE station earned a reputation for its reliability. Two high precision oscillators and phasing equipment were provided by the Drive Section for the RAF monitoring station in May 1942.[30]

Early in 1942 the RAF requested the BBC to provide transmissions to aid homeward-bound bombers after raids over enemy territory. High-power long- and medium-wave transmitters were used without masking and with low-level modulation for identification. These transmissions were code-named 'WASHTUB'. The Droitwich 200-kHz transmitter was first used in this way to assist our aircraft returning from the first 1000-bomber raid over Cologne on 30 May 1942. This operation was called 'WASHTUB 1' and later Start Point was used with vertical polarisation on 1050 kHz and was called 'WASHTUB 2'.

A quite different facility code-named 'DARTBOARD' was used to confuse enemy night fighters attacking RAF bombers over enemy targets. At the start of the 'DARTBOARD' operations it had been deduced that the German 'Anne Marie' Forces broadcasting station at Stuttgart was being used in a crude fashion to indicate to German night fighters the general position of the RAF bomber 'stream'. For example if waltzes were played this indicated the Munich area, church music indicated Munster, jazz music meant Berlin, and so on. When the attackers had left, the march 'Old Comrades' was played and the station then resumed its normal programme pattern. This effort to assist their night fighter crews resulted from the havoc wrought to the normal night fighter control system by an operation code-named 'CORONA' during which spurious instructions were broadcast on the German night fighter control frequencies in the 3–6 MHz band using GPO, Cable & Wireless and BBC short-wave transmitters. 'DARTBOARD' created a strong jamming signal on the broadcasting frequencies in the medium-wave band being used for enemy fighter communications. In December 1943 the Droitwich high-power medium-wave transmitter was used and between December 1944 and January 1945 the Moorside Edge high-power transmitter. At the latter station keyed tones of various frequencies were radiated to confuse the Morse code instructions that were being used by German medium-wave stations. The Moorside Edge transmitter was also modified to permit fairly rapid wave-changing to counter the attempts of the enemy fighter controllers to find a clear space in the medium-wave band and to use a number of channels simultaneously to overcome the jamming. Preparations were made to use one of the Group Y1/Y2 50-kW transmitters at Moorside Edge in addition to the high-power transmitter at that station, and early in 1945 further DARTBOARD operations were planned using the Foreign Office 'Aspidistra' transmitter at Crowborough on 695 kHz and one of the Ottringham (OSE5) transmitters on 832 kHz. These latter plans were not implemented although all the necessary preparatory work was completed. A mobile form of DARTBOARD was designed by the BBC Research Department in the form of a 1-kW medium-wave transmitter for installation in a Liberator aircraft. To reduce weight by keeping down the size of the ht smoothing components, a power supply at 300 Hz was used. Special attention had to be given to the design of air-spaced components, because the aircraft had to fly at

20,000 ft and was not pressurised. Satisfactory trial flights were made, but the transmitter was never used in its intended role and was later returned to the BBC and converted for use as a pulse transmitter.

At Daventry, a 1-kW transmitter had been used from February 1935 to August 1939 to radiate the Meteorological Office's 'Air-Met.' service for civil aviation on 250 kHz. During the war it was used for communications and as a navigational beacon. The Drive Section was asked to design and install a variable-frequency drive for this transmitter to cover the frequency band from 280 to 380 kHz and to provide a fixed frequency of 151 kHz for the beacon transmission. The resetting accuracy requested was 1 part in 15,000 and the frequency stability was to be of the same order. This was a useful excercise in the development of a variable-frequency drive and it led directly to the improved type VFO/3 equipment designed for the Rampisham (OSE3) station. The 'Air-Met.' service was reopened on 7 June 1946 on 245 kHz using an RCA Type 10E transmitter. On 1 June 1949 the frequency was changed to 248 kHz, but the service had to be closed down on 14 March 1950, as no channel was available for it under the Copenhagen Plan.

In January 1945 the former 5XX transmitter at Daventry, which had been used in the Overseas Service long-wave group until December 1944, was transferred to an Air Ministry service on 530 kHz, using keyed Morse transmission, until the end of hostilities in Europe.

Among the miscellaneous projects on which the BBC gave advice was the provision of mobile long-wave transmitters for use by Regional Commissioners if their areas became cut off from the central government as a result of invasion. Another was the setting-up of a video circuit over a cable pair, using the equipment that had been developed by the BBC before the war, to operate a plan position indicator for gunnery control. The understanding of frequency control, which BBC engineers had developed, was applied to a number of problems in communications and also to timing devices. Advice was also given on electronic means of analysing the vibrations of propulsion machinery on ships.

In August 1941 the 'Mocking Voice' posed a problem that gave considerable entertainment to the engineers concerned. The Germans themselves were the first to suffer from this nuisance when Russian transmissions were superimposed on those of Deutschlandsender during intervals in the programme by a high-power station working on the same frequency. The Germans countered this by altering their carrier frequency by about 1 kHz whenever the spurious speech was present, so as to produce a heterodyne note intended to drown the interfering remarks. In October an Italian station attempted a similar kind of interference with the BBC Forces Programme on 877 kHz. A number of methods of combatting this were considered, including a cyclical variation in the carrier frequencies of BBC stations, and varying the carrier frequency in steps by manual control. The method that was actually used was to pick up the interfering signal at Tatsfield, transmit it by line to Broadcasting House and put it through a speech inverter. The output from the speech inverter was automatically radiated by the transmitters in the 877 kHz group whenever the Mocking Voice appeared. Shortly after this idea was adopted the nuisance ceased.

Advice on the setting up of synchronised groups of broadcasting stations was given in 1942 to Australia and New Zealand, and also, in close co-operation with the Air Ministry, to the USA.

In September 1943 the advance of the British and American troops in North Africa led to the recovery of a number of broadcasting stations. L. W. Hayes undertook a mission to North Africa to make recommendations on their use and a 'United Nations Radio' service was set up. W. E. C. Varley was seconded to direct this work and the BBC supplied OBA/8 amplifiers and other equipment, which was of considerable interest to the Americans, who were not accustomed to the peak programme meter or to studio equipment with such a low noise level.

The assistance given to the American and Canadian Forces Networks in the UK has been mentioned in section 5 of this chapter. In October 1943, the Americans proposed to create a new 'station' called A.B.S.I.E. (American Broadcasting Station in Europe) for the purpose of broadcasting to the population of Europe at the critical moment in support of the Second Front. A.B.S.I.E. used both medium- and short-wave BBC transmissions, the programme being designated the 'Stripes Network' for internal identification. On 30 April 1944, the first programmes were broadcast in eighteen languages and the BBC was expected to provide 1 to $1\frac{1}{2}$ hours of the $8\frac{1}{2}$ hours of programme material radiated each day.[31] On the engineering side, apart from the provision of facilities from the BBC's battery of short-wave transmitters, a reciprocal aid operation took place to provide for the medium-wave transmission. The Americans provided six RCA type 50-E 50-kW transmitters and six low-power masking transmitters, while the BBC arranged for the construction of buildings for them at Moorside Edge, Westerglen and Rampisham, and erected the necessary mast radiators. The 50-kW transmitters were installed in pairs in rather austere buildings and the RCA (type 250K) 250-W masking transmitters were installed in existing premises at Start Point, Bartley and at Alexandra Palace. The BBC provided the synchronising equipment for all these transmitters, which operated in two groups, one on 977 kHz and the other on 1122 kHz. These groups (Y1 and Y2) continued in operation until American Independence Day, 4 July 1945.

During 1943, and the early part of 1944, the Engineering Division had to prepare facilities that were to come into operation as soon as the allied armies had landed in North-West Europe. These facilities included those for the War Reporting Unit described in the next section and also studios, lines, and transmitters for the programme that was to be broadcast by Supreme Headquarters Allied Expeditionary Force (SHAEF) from D-Day plus 1 (7 June 1944) until 28 July 1945.[32] The medium-wave transmitter at Start Point was withdrawn from its hybrid MF/LF operation on 24 May 1944 and was set up on a frequency of 583 kHz for the SHAEF programme. The use of a propagation path substantially over sea to the French and Belgian coasts and the Netherlands, together with the use of one of the lowest frequencies in the medium-wave band, ensured good reception of this programme throughout the area of military operations. SHAEF also requested facilities for a special programme on behalf of Headquarters, Airborne Troops, to be radiated in the Orange Network of the European Service immediately before the landings on

U

D-Day. The rescheduling of BBC short-wave transmissions at short notice, to be-come effective directly the executive message was received, required meticulous planning. The handling of the communiqué that would announce the first landings, to be followed by a special message to the peoples of Europe from General Eisen-hower, had to be planned in absolute secrecy; despite this handicap, the technical arrangements worked without a hitch.

The Psychological Warfare Division of SHAEF was concerned with policies and propaganda designed to demoralise the enemy.[33] In April 1944 F. C. McLean (later Sir Francis McLean, Director of Engineering) was seconded to PWD/SHAEF with four other engineers, whose main task was to rehabilitate the broadcasting facilities in the liberated areas as the armies advanced, and to provide mobile radio units through which the military authorities could distribute information and instructions to the civilian population. Depending on the thoroughness with which the enemy had destroyed the equipment, the team had to repair it or replace it with mobile studios and transmitters sent from the United Kingdom. Public-address systems were also provided to help the military authorities to establish normal conditions in the liberated territories. The team arrived in Paris ten days after the liberation of the city and, having previously worked there with the ITT subsidiary Le Matériel Téléphonique, McLean was soon able to organise broadcasting facilities there. He was joined by other engineers from the United Nations Radio organisation in North Africa and directed the reorganisation of the Belgian broadcasting system when Brussels was liberated on 5 September 1944.

One of the stations that were liberated was Radio Luxembourg, which was almost undamaged, and operated under the control of PWD/SHAEF from September 1944. Asa Briggs notes (quoting E. Barnouw, quoting 'Yank' 11.5.45) that an engineer of Radio Luxembourg had encouraged the Germans to shoot holes in the transmitting valves to divert them from more ambitious schemes of destruction. After liberation he dug up a set of valves that he had buried four years earlier.[34]

Throughout the war and for some years afterwards, a rigid control was exercised by the Ministry of Supply over the consumption of strategic materials, such as steel and timber. Liaison was established between the Engineering Secretariat and the Ministry to keep the BBC's requirements to a minimum and to ensure that permits were obtained quickly for essential purchases. The construction of masts in particular made heavy demands on supplies of steel. An elaborate procedure was also needed to obtain supplies of equipment from the USA under the Lease-Lend agreement.

A notable non-event among the BBC's contributions to the war effort was that at no time was there any attempt to jam foreign broadcasts. Although the enemy in-dulged freely in the jamming of BBC programmes, there was no retaliation from this country. The policy on this point was reaffirmed in 1940 by the Government, which agreed when Ashbridge pointed out that jamming could not be effective over large areas and that it was better to use BBC transmitters to broadcast on as many channels as possible, rather than divert some of them to jamming. It was also considered that British listeners able to hear both sides would be in no doubt where the truth lay.

9 THE WAR REPORTING UNIT

One of the most outstanding contributions to the BBC's broadcasts on D-Day and the many broadcasts that followed was the intensive effort by several departments of the Engineering Division to provide and operate the facilities required by the War Reporting Unit. The co-ordination of the technical arrangements was in the hands of L. Hotine, Senior Superintendent Engineer, assisted by M. J. L. Pulling, Superintendent Engineer (Recording) who organised the provision of equipment for the BBC staff in the field.

As early as August 1942, before SHAEF was established, the Director of Outside Broadcasts, Michael Standing, had suggested the use of 'actuality recordings' when the Second Front opened up instead of official dispatches and eye-witness accounts. The development of portable recorders for this purpose has been described in section 6 of this chapter; it was also necessary to establish a communications system, now to be described, to bring the programme material to London and to maintain contact with the War Correspondents in the field.

A study was made of the lessons to be learnt from the American landings in North Africa (Operation Torch: 8 November 1942); in that case the Americans were in exclusive control of outward transmission facilities, having taken over the Algiers short-wave station at Eucalyptus and appointed military supervisory staff to direct the work of the local operators. The short-wave transmitters (THA-1 and THA-2) employed high gain aerials and were used extensively by the Americans to carry voice-casts, dispatches and telephoned material from North Africa (and later from Sicily) to the USA. BBC War Correspondents in North Africa found themselves short of equipment and transport, although some technical assistance was provided by the small British component in the United Nations Radio organisation in Algiers and limited use was made of the Algiers short-wave transmitters for sending material to London.[35]

It was evident from experience in the North African and Italian campaigns that the introduction of non-military units into the fighting area, using their own communication transmitters, would require careful handling when the invasion in North-West Europe took place. In the United Kingdom, as part of the preparations for the Second Front, the idea of a 'Radio Commando Unit' was taking shape and a pioneering exercise for BBC Reporters – Operation Spartan – was planned in co-operation with the Army. This exercise took place in March 1943 when commentators and engineers were attached to the opposing armies in a mock battle and the whole operation was made as realistic as possible. The results of this exercise were most impressive, and it was agreed that the BBC should be given the fullest co-operation from all three Services during the forthcoming invasion of Europe.[36, 37]

The BBC's next step was to form a 'Front Line Reporting Unit', which, in May 1943, was renamed the 'War Reporting Unit', S. J. de Lotbinière being given the task of selecting commentators for it. In November 1943, Howard Marshall was appointed Director of the War Reporting Unit (DWR), with Malcolm Frost as his deputy. It was decided that the organisation of the Unit should transcend departmental boundaries and that it would be responsible for controlling all radio reporting from the fronts as they opened up.

It was realised that the demand for news and eye-witness reports on D-Day would be insatiable and that every phase of the departure of the invasion forces from the United Kingdom would have to be covered in speech and sound recordings. It was also foreseen that one of the main difficulties would be the establishment of a suitable communications link across the English Channel during the first battle for the beach-heads.[38] The Engineering Division lost no time in setting about the task of providing the technical equipment needed, although at this period of the war most of the material was extremely scarce. The transmitters had to be obtained either from the USA, with the attendant transport risks, or from the Services, who were naturally reluctant to part with radio equipment of any sort. In September 1943 H. Bishop and B. N. MacLarty produced a statement about the availability of transmitters and R. T. B. Wynn tackled the task of staffing the technical facilities. In addition to creating the teams required for North-West Europe, it was necessary to consider setting up a team for Italy, because of the inadequacy of facilities there for sending despatches to London; the British situation compared unfavourably with that of the Americans for whom the US Signal Corps were operating a high-power point-to-point circuit from Naples, and later from Rome, to the USA.

A complete list of Recording and Transmitter Engineers who were seconded to the WRU is given in 'War Report'.[39] Although there were many precedents for accrediting War Correspondents, the accrediting of civilian engineers met with considerable opposition and they were eventually designated 'Engineer Correspondents'.

On 28 September 1943 it was decided to unify the War Reporting Unit and its staff, who up to that time had remained on the establishments of their parent departments; they were now seconded to the WRU Establishment under directions issued by the Director-General on 1 November 1943. It was decided that two teams should be set up for operations in North-West Europe, one for Italy, one for prospective operations in India, and one in the Balkans. Estimates were prepared for the additional equipment required and a start was made in recruiting the staff.

By February 1944 the work of crating the 5-kW, type AVT22A, short-wave transmitter, previously installed in the Stronghold at Broadcasting House, had been completed; the crates were stored in two 3-ton trucks in the Equipment Department garage in South London, but were later moved to Bletchington, to avoid air raid damage, before being sent overseas.

At the end of February 1944 consideration was being given to the provision of lines between towns on the south and south-east coasts and London to carry dispatches during the early stages of the landings before cross-Channel radio-communication could be provided. As it was most unlikely that lines would be available 'on demand' from southern coastal areas at such a time, it was decided to use existing music circuits between certain Group H transmitters and London, reversing them when they were needed to carry incoming material to London. Accordingly a list of suitable stations was prepared covering the entire southern coastline of England, viz.:

Norwich	Folkestone	Weymouth
Ipswich	Hastings	Exeter
Gillingham	Brighton	Torquay
Tunbridge Wells	Fareham	Start Point
Ramsgate	Bartley	Plymouth
	Redruth	

It was accepted that for the period of reading a dispatch and for a short time before and afterwards, the station concerned would have to take its programme from a re-broadcast receiver or, failing that, to close down. It was intended to provide all these stations with high-grade microphones and disc reproducers, but in fact only Fareham, Brighton and Bournemouth were so equipped.

By April 1944 a number of transmitters had been made ready for dispatch overseas and others were being modified for sending programme material. One was a 250-W MF and HF STC transmitter, type HS1, which had been modified and mounted in a Bedford truck, two were 5-kW RCA HF transmitters, four were $7\frac{1}{2}$-kW RCA HF transmitters modified to take British valves, two were 2-kW Marconi SWB8 telegraph transmitters, for which new modulators were designed and built in the BBC, and one was a 1-kW MF transmitter that had been produced for airborne use. One of the 5-kW HF transmitters was sent to Naples where, after some delay, it arrived on 23 June 1944. No power supply unit was sent, as it was hoped that either a mains supply or a power unit would be available locally. The transmitter was transported in crates to a site six miles from Rome, which had previously been used by the Italian Army as a receiving station. There were some difficulties in finding a suitable power unit and in setting the transmitter to work, but the first transmissions took place on 8 August 1944 using 7585, 9830 and 14485 kHz according to the time of day. The studio was at the transmitter site, but was later moved into the city. A rhombic aerial was used for the transmitter and the transmissions were picked up at Tatsfield.

In addition to the transmitters needed for sending the dispatches to London, it was necessary to provide for telegraphic communication with the units in the field. A Harvey transmitter, which had been modified for the purpose, was installed in a cubicle on the balcony of the war-time control room in the basement of Broadcasting House, and frequencies of 1500, 3376 and 5555 kHz were allocated to it. In addition, an RCA type 1E transmitter was installed in the senior engineers' duty room to work on 1500 kHz. It could be keyed either from the duty room or from the communications cubicle.

An important part in these preparations was an operational exercise, which was carried out, in close secrecy, to test the arrangements for war reporting. Everything was carried out under realistic conditions from the origination of material from remote points at Plymouth, Fareham and Guildford to the final dubbing of the discs after security censorship. Minor improvements in the arrangements were made following an analysis of the results made on 2 June 1944.

The deployment of the transmitters overseas was not without incident. The 250-W transmitter was sent first, because the more powerful sets were not ready. It had been modified to work on either of the three WRU frequencies and could either be keyed or modulated by speech. Although the weight of the equipment had been scaled down as far as possible, the Marshalling Officer rejected the vehicle outright, because of insufficient ground clearance and the lack of four-wheel drive. It was claimed that the Bedford truck was unsuitable for driving off the ramp of a landing craft on to a beach. Fortunately, the Ministry of Supply and the War Office both offered to supply a suitable 3-ton truck with four-wheel drive at short notice. To be on the safe side, both these offers were accepted and both vehicles were delivered. One already had a 15-kVA diesel-alternator set installed in it and this unexpected gift was accepted with alacrity. The transmitter was sent to Droitwich where it arrived at 0100 hours on 27 May 1944 and teams of engineers and mechanics worked round the clock until the equipment had been installed in the vehicle, tested at 0500 hours on 29 May, and dispatched to the marshalling area for embarkation.

On 1 June 1944 the Senior Duty Engineers' watch was tightened up so that one was available in Broadcasting House throughout the twenty-four hours until 'such time as forthcoming events materialise'. (The Senior Duty Engineers' rota was maintained throughout the war to provide a focal point for all emergencies requiring action by engineers and to supervise the operation and the control of transmitters by Fighter Command mentioned in Section 2 of this chapter. They were sometimes called upon to deal with emergencies outside their professional field. Early in the war the author once encountered H. G. Wells walking along a corridor on the third floor of Broadcasting House long after midnight. A hasty search among recollections of Anne Veronica and Mr Lewisham failed to produce any appropriate topic of conversation, but the great man cut short the encounter by gruffly demanding where, for God's sake, he could get a drink. In those days, such a demand was entirely beyond the resources of the Engineering Division to fulfil, but fortunately the Duty Officer was well prepared to meet it. During the most critical periods of the war several of the senior members of the Division, plus the Senior Duty Engineer, slept in the duty room, which had formerly been Echo Room 1 in the basement of Broadcasting House. The room was sparsely furnished and a large part of it was occupied by the communication transmitter. At night it was dimly lit and movement in it was restricted by a large loudspeaker cabinet and the feet of L. W. Hayes, which projected some inches beyond the end of his bed. It gave an impression of security, which was probably illusory as it was only a few feet from the pavement of Portland Place. The gloom that descended upon it from time to time was relieved by an innovation, hitherto undreamed of in the BBC, which before the end of the war permitted drinks to be sold in the nearby canteen. Distinguished visitors from the world outside occasionally dispelled the claustrophobia; they included Alistair Cooke, John Gunter, Ed Murrow, Sir John Anderson and BBC engineers returning from service abroad.)

Rome fell to the Allied Armies on 4 June 1944, but this event was eclipsed two days later by the long-awaited news of the allied landings in Normandy on D-Day (6 June). The news was first monitored by the BBC at Caversham where an announcement was heard on the German Radio at 0700 hours as well as on the Hellschreiber

Service. Sefton Delmer records that a news 'flash' from a German station was picked up even earlier – 0450 hours – by 'Soldatensender Calais' (a 'black' broadcasting station on the English side of the Channel) and broadcast from that station.[40] The BBC announced the news at 0800 hours in advance of the official communiqué, which was broadcast at 0930 hours in the Home, Overseas and Forces programmes. The communiqué was followed by a message from General Eisenhower read in the BBC services by John Snagge and in the A.B.S.I.E. programme by an American, Col. Dupuy.

A congratulatory message on the 'faultless handling' of the D-Day arrangements was received by Engineering Division from W. S. Paley, the Chief of PWD/SHAEF.

At 0600 hours on D-Day plus 1 the signature tune 'Oranges and Lemons' heralded the start of the SHAEF programme radiated by Start Point.

The 250-W transmitter had a rough trip across the Channel on 17 June in the tail-end of the gale that had raged in the Channel throughout the second week after D-Day. The landing craft carrying the transmitter vehicle was beached at Arromanches and the truck was disembarked down the ramp into some four feet of water, thus vindicating the Marshalling Officer's decision to refuse the Bedford truck. The transmitter (call-sign MCO) arrived just in time; for the gale that had disrupted cross-channel surface transport made it necessary for the Army type 399 transmitter, through which some of the early BBC dispatches had been sent, to be reserved exclusively for military traffic. The first message from MCO was received at Broadcasting House on 18 June and the first dispatches followed immediately. The studio at first consisted of a tent, but this was soon replaced by improved accommodation in a fourteenth-century castle at Creully, near Bayeux.[41] As the armies advanced, however, it became clear that some form of mobile studio would be necessary, so that the correspondents would not have to return to base to send off their dispatches and voice-casts. On 22 June E. L. Lycett was seconded to WRU and given the task of rehabilitating studio facilities for BBC correspondents as towns became liberated during the advance. The first transmissions from MCO were on 1500 kHz, but on 23 June clearance was obtained for this transmitter to use the two WRU HF channels in the military area.

On 28 July the first 5-kW transmitter (MCP) arrived at the 'Mulberry' harbour and was installed at Le Marais, five miles north-west of Bayeux. This transmitter used the two HF channels to provide a high-quality link through Tatsfield. In the meantime the 250-W transmitter moved up the coast with the Army, remaining within its restricted range for working to receiving points on the south coast.

The first 7½-kW transmitter (MCN) landed at the harbour on 1 September 1944 just as the rapid advance towards Paris and Brussels was under way. Unfortunately this transmitter did not have the mobility needed to keep up with the armies, but it arrived in Brussels on 4–5 September and moved on to Eindhoven on 5 October. During its stay in Brussels, many modifications were made to the equipment and to the aerial system to improve their mobility; these changes proved a godsend during the final stages of the campaign.

The 5-kW transmitter was moved from Le Marais to Paris and re-installed at

Pontoise, where it remained until February 1945. The 250-W transmitter was moving with the Canadian Army along the coast, being at Dieppe on 3 September, Dixmude on 20 September, near Ghent on 27 September, near Antwerp on 11 October, and in Brussels on 12 October.

On 22 January 1945 it was decided to send the second $7\frac{1}{2}$-kW transmitter and this arrived in Brussels on 12 February. It took over the call-sign, MCP, of the 5-kW Pontoise transmitter (which had by then been returned to England), and was allocated to the 12th US Army Group at Namur. It stayed with the Americans through the Ardennes offensive and on to Cologne and Berlin. There it remained until it was required to cover the Nuremberg Trials, after which it was handed over to the British Forces Network.

The transmitters MCO and MCN went forward with the 1945 Spring advance, leap-frogging over each other to achieve maximum mobility, and crossed the Rhine near Wesel on 23 March 1945. They continued on to Luneburg, arriving on 30 April. After the signing of the surrender on 4 May 1945 these two transmitters returned to the UK. The $7\frac{1}{2}$-kW transmitter was taken out of its vehicle and re-installed at Wood Norton where it is still in use for training.

The last broadcast of the long series of 'War Report' programmes took place on 5 May 1945. The engineers were anxious to return to their BBC work in the UK and it was decided that VE-Day would be the signal to start disbanding the unit; the Traffic Office in Broadcasting House was closed down at midnight on 31 May 1945, and the staff returned to their original departments.

10 ORGANISATION, STAFFING, TRAINING AND FINANCE

Despite the general upheaval of the war, 1939 to 1945 was a period of relative stability in the organisation of the Engineering Division. The most important moves took place in 1943. When Sir Cecil Graves retired because of ill-health, the new Director-General, R. W. Foot, chose Sir Noel Ashbridge as his Deputy Director-General. Ashbridge was to concern himself with the business side of the Corporation's work, but at the same time he was to continue as the Corporation's chief adviser on engineering matters. H. Bishop succeeded Ashbridge as Controller (Engineering), with R. T. B. Wynn as Assistant Controller (Engineering). This reshuffle took place on 1 September 1943. A week later, L. Hotine took over from Wynn as Senior Superintendent Engineer, and E. F. Wheeler replaced him as Superintendent Engineer (Transmitters).

In the course of the war two new departments were created. In January 1941 a new department in the Operations and Maintenance Group was set up specifically for recording, with M. J. L. Pulling as its Superintendent Engineer. (On the programme side, H. L. Fletcher became Recorded Programmes Director, and was replaced in 1944 by Brian George.)

When Pulling became Superintendent Engineer, Recording, E. L. E. Pawley took his place as Assistant to A.C.(E). Keeping track of engineering expenditure and the preparation of estimates had always been one of the tasks of this office. When more stringent methods of financial control were introduced by Foot in 1942 this part of the work became more onerous, and to cope with it a new department (the Engineering Secretariat) was eventually set up in January 1943. Pawley became the first head of this department, with E. C. Drewe as assistant head. It was responsible for liaison with the Ministry of Supply to obtain permits for the purchase of controlled materials (steel, timber etc.) and for the ordering of equipment from the USA under Lease/Lend. It also administered BBC patents (in conjunction with the Patent Agents) and technical suggestions.

Foot's reorganisation of the Corporation into five operational divisions in 1942 did not affect engineering, except that Engineering Establishment Officer (P. A. Florence) and his department moved from Administration into the Engineering division.

In 1941 C. H. Colborn's L. F. Section was transferred from Equipment Department to the Station Design & Installation Department under B. N. MacLarty. Rather belatedly, recognition was given to this change in October 1944 when the title SDID was altered to DID (Design & Installation Department), to take account of the fact that the department was as actively engaged on studio work as it was on transmitting station installations.

During the war there was no wholesale dispersal of engineering departments. SDID did move, however, at short notice to huts on the Droitwich transmitter site on 18 September 1940 when the blitz on London was at its height. They remained there until the end of the war. In October 1940 Ashbridge suggested that premises somewhere between Daventry and Banbury should be found for the Research Department in case things got so bad that they had to move out of London. In the event the choice fell on a house at Hinksey, just outside Oxford, called Bagley Croft. The Board approved the purchase of this (at £10,500) at the end of October. There was a momentary set-back when it was discovered that the Ministry of Health had already ear-marked it for their purposes, but this was overcome and the house was bought. It lay fallow for nearly four years, apart from some workshop activity. But its acquisition was not in vain, for on 18 June 1944 the Research Department headquarters at Nightingale Square suffered a near-miss, with minor damage to the workshops, and the Field-strength Section left the same evening for Bagley Croft, where they were joined soon after by the Radio and Recording Sections.

One of the besetting problems of the war was to find enough people to man the transmitters and studio centres. This resulted from the unprecedented expansion of broadcasting just at the time when experienced engineers had been lost in large numbers to the Services. Between September 1939 and the beginning of 1942 the number of transmitters went up from 24 to 90, and transmitter-hours increased fivefold. Over the same period, the number of languages in which the BBC broadcast was stepped up from 9 to 40, with a corresponding increase in programme output from 44 to 230 hours a week. In addition, the Forces Programme and the Home Service were on the air for greatly extended periods each day.

At the beginning of the war the Government conceded that BBC engineering staff over twenty-three years old should be exempt from military service. Accordingly everyone in the Division between nineteen, the minimum age for call-up, and twenty-three was released. In addition, some fifty experienced engineers above the age of twenty-three were transferred at the request of the Air Ministry to undertake special wireless work. By March 1941 nearly 400 had left to serve in the Forces. In June 1942, when the expansion programme was at its height, Ashbridge noted that the Corporation had lost over 30 per cent of its experienced pre-war engineers. At that time there were 417 peace-time engineers in the Forces, 90 in the Royal Navy, 3 in the Royal Marines, 150 in the Army, and 174 in the RAF. By the end of the war over 500 of the pre-war engineering staff had been released to the Forces.

Another worry was the liability of junior engineers for military service on reaching the age of nineteen. To begin with the Ministry of Labour did not exercise their right to call them up, but towards the end of 1941 the Ministry decided that this *de facto* deferment could no longer be granted. The result was that a hundred young engineers were under the threat of call-up in November 1941. As they had been taken on between the ages of seventeen and eighteen and needed at least six months to shake down, the Corporation at best would have had only eighteen months' useful service from them if this happened. An appeal against the Ministry's decision was rejected, although some small concessions were made.

Faced with these losses of experienced pre-war engineers, and of junior engineers just when they were becoming really useful, the BBC had to cast its net wider in recruiting staff. As early as November 1940 C. H. G. Millis, the Vice-Chairman, had asked whether there was any objection to employing women to make up for the shortage of men. Ashbridge took the line that while there was no objection in principle, there were certain difficulties; for instance, they would be unsuitable for life at transmitting stations. The subject was not, however, allowed to lapse. In the following January the Board expressed the opinion that greater use should be made of women to replace men called to military service.

On 26 March, Ashbridge, Wynn, and Florence, agreed on the appointment of women operators at studio centres and in technical recording, but not for the time being at transmitters. A proposal by Florence that only a small number – twenty was suggested – between the ages of twenty-one and thirty-five should be recruited initially at a starting wage of £3·25/£3·50 a week was accepted, and advertisements appeared in the London and provincial papers and in *The Listener* at the beginning of June. The first batch of seven women operators joined on 30 June. They went first to the engineering training school, where they took the A & B courses, and were appointed to stations on 11 August, three going to London Control Room, and three to Technical Recording. The next batch of twenty-one finished their training on 23 August. Most of these went to the Regions.

In the meantime, the ban on appointments to transmitting stations was rescinded, though with the proviso that for the time being women operators should work only in the control rooms. Even this restriction was waived in September. Later on, at the beginning of 1942, plans were put in hand for having four women operators on Group H transmitters. They were to work in pairs, on their own, taking over two out of the three shifts. In March two girls were working a shift by themselves at each of the stations at Brighton, Fraserburgh, and Torquay. By the end of 1942 there were women operators on shift work at twenty-seven of the Group H stations. But they were forbidden to open up the transmitter or attempt to rectify faults. If there was a breakdown, they had to summon help from the EiC or one of the other male staff. This ban on doing repairs did not apply to men who had no more experience or training than the girl operators; the girls, not unnaturally, resented this discrimination. Moreover, it inevitably prolonged breakdown times, because faults had to wait for the EiC or his deputy to clear them. It was then ruled that no distinction should be made between men and women operators, but attention was drawn to the fatal accident (the second in the BBC's history) to R. W. Angell that had occurred at Brookmans Park the year before. The ruling was suspended, and it was not until May 1943, when a clean bill of health was given by the consulting engineers, Highfield & Roger Smith, on the BBC's safety measures at transmitters, that it was agreed that women operators could do simple maintenance work without supervision.

There must have been some uneasiness about how the old hands would react to the startling innovation of women in what had always been a man's world. In July 1941, just before the first batch was launched into operations and maintenance work, Wynn wrote in these terms to the Superintendent Engineers:

'In the course of the next fortnight or so, the first of the women operators will take up their duties in control rooms and on recording channels. I most sincerely hope that Es-i-C, Assistant Es-i-C, SMEs and regular MEs will give the women a fair run for their money. . . . Many of these girls are married women who have taken on this job to help out a national service as part of their own personal war effort. That they are dead keen and will try very hard is quite obvious from their behaviour at the school and it would be a most unfortunate thing if our regular staff did not accept them in the spirit in which they have come to us.'

But the women quickly earned golden opinions. J. W. Godfrey, who was the B-course instructor on recording, summed up his impression of the first three courses as follows:

'I think we need have no apprehension about the maintaining of a good recording service even should a large proportion of the male staff be called away. There is generally an exceptional keenness on the part of the women operators and they are anxious to learn faster than facilities allow.'

Pulling took up this theme in a memorandum to Wynn:

'I think we have every reason to be satisfied with the performance of these girls to date and, provided their interest in the job is maintained, there seems to be no reason why the experiment should not prove a success. My own impression, based on what I have seen of these girls both during their B course and subsequently, is that provided we keep them strictly to operational work there is no reason whatever why they should not fulfil an extremely useful job.'

301

And Bishop, writing in the 1945 *Year Book*, had this to say of them:

'It has been particularly noteworthy how women operators with no previous technical experience whatever have absorbed the intricacies of broadcasting and have become, within a few months, useful members of the staff.'

But this reaction was not universal. The BBC, like any big organisation, had its share of reactionaries who did not favour the idea of women invading what had always been a man's preserve. A few of the Engineers-in-Charge did not really trust the women on their stations, and sought to limit their activities as much as possible, relegating them to such tasks as control room operations. One EiC complained to Wynn that he could not employ them on work inside the transmitter unit because their clothes got caught up in the components. In the next breath, he was complaining about women wearing trousers on his station; he had forbidden them to do so except on the night shift – in contravention of the official line that there was no objection to trousers provided that 'they were of a reasonably quiet colour'. As late as 1943, E. F. Wheeler was constrained to write to all his Engineers-in-Charge at main transmitting stations:

'It has recently become very evident that some Es-i-C are restricting the activities of the women TAs and this is seriously retarding their progress. . . . This is just nonsense. Our experience is that women can do just as good a job of work as the male TAs, and at a recent examination for promotion to TA1, 80 per cent of the women were able to operate their station throughout, including the engine room . . . If women are to gain promotion they must be given the same opportunities as the male TAs for learning and doing jobs. It follows therefore that women are not to be relegated to such places as control rooms.'

From 1941 onwards there was a steady increase in the number of women operators. At the end of the year they were 400 strong. In June 1942 there were 450 of them, rising to 500 in December. At that time they made up one quarter of the Operations and Maintenance complement. By the end of 1943 their numbers had reached 600. In the course of the war over 800 women operators were recruited and passed through the engineering training school. A count in the summer of 1971 revealed that a quarter of a century later there were still seventeen survivors of the war-time women staff in engineering operations.

In April 1943 to make up for the loss of junior male engineers called up for the Forces at the age of nineteen, it was decided to bring in a number of what were called 'Youths in Training'. These were boys not older than sixteen, of school-certificate standard – good secondary school types. They became eligible for promotion after six months. In 1944 this period was reduced to two months. With the arrival of these youngsters on the stations, the Engineering Division found itself truly *in loco parentis* for the first time, as witnessed by a memorandum written by Florence in May 1943:

'We have a definite responsibility for the welfare and conduct of all juveniles and staff under age. We must assume moral responsibility to the parents for their protection and well-being while they are in the Corporation's service. I should be glad if Es-i-C would take a personal interest in all the youthful personnel attached to their command. They should ensure that they are accommodated in suitable billets and with people who have a proper appreciation of their needs.'

R. M. Gibson, who was one of the senior engineers at Bush House, has given a glimpse of what it was like to run a big control room largely staffed with women and adolescents:

'As in other places in the BBC, the staff at Bush House mostly consisted of women who had had varying occupations before joining the BBC. We had a children's nanny, a millinery buyer, two or three school-teachers, and at least one model. The remainder of the staff were mostly boys between school-leaving and military call-up age, or younger men, who for one reason or another were not acceptable to the Services. We worked four shifts, and if there were two reasonably good engineers on any shift, one was quite lucky. With that kind of staff, there were some difficulties. The boys expected to do no more than two or three years in the job, and so it was not a career prospect. Ordinary discipline, civilian as opposed to military, was rather difficult to enforce because the boys knew perfectly well that if they went we should have difficulty in getting anybody else. With very few exceptions the women were really excellent. They were most conscientious. I remember one woman who was on night shift when her flat was virtually demolished by a bomb during the day. The only sign of this was that when she reported for duty on the night shift she was very dirty, and arrangements had to be made for her to have a bath so that she could continue with her work.'

The idea of some form of engineering training school certainly goes back as far as 1935. In September of that year, Ashbridge, having as he said 'twelve student apprentices studying for two years before absorption in our staff, two Indians for two years before returning to their country, and one Iraqi student for six months', outlined the possibility to the Control Board. But the proposal was not pursued until 1937, when it was revived in a different form by Purslow, who was then the Engineer-in-Charge at the Staff Training Department; that department was responsible for the training of programme and administrative staff, and gave them some insight into the technical background to their activities, but it had nothing to do with the training of engineers. Purslow suggested a two-week refresher course for engineers at the staff training school during its summer vacation, to give them, as he said 'an opportunity of seeing and gaining information about various branches of the Corporation's Engineering Departments'. He had in mind particularly engineers in the provinces, who might never have seen a television picture or a tape recording machine. His suggested curriculum consisted mainly of talks by senior engineers, with visits to Droitwich, Alexandra Palace, the Research Department at Nightingale Square, and so on. The reaction of the Director of Staff Training at the time was that the proposal bristled with administrative difficulties, and after some exchange of correspondence it petered out.

303

The initiative that eventually brought the engineering training school into being came from F. C. Brooker. In London control room at the beginning of the war he realised that many of the new recruits were out of their depth, and were really more of hindrance than a help. Brooker gathered two or three of the newcomers together at odd moments, usually in one of the studios, to teach them something of the rudiments of broadcasting. Encouraged by the results, he took his educational campaign a step further by writing up some notes, with diagrams, on the broadcasting chain and providing a copy for each shift.

In February 1941 Brooker expounded his views to Florence on the need for a training scheme and on the form he thought it should take. He left with Florence a summary of his lectures for new recruits who had little or no familiarity with electricity or radio. It dealt with the nature of sound, its conversion to electric signals, the decibel notation, the equipment and lines constituting the broadcasting chain and procedures for switching and control. Florence was impressed, and wrote to Wynn: 'There is, in my view, every reason for a training scheme to be developed, because there is no doubt in my mind that if we can attract a large number of suitable youths and later, inevitably, suitable women, we shall be obliged to spend a certain amount of time in giving preliminary training if they are to be made effective in the quickest possible time.'

Wynn's reaction was enthusiastic, and things moved quickly from then on. By April Florence was able to outline a training scheme consisting of an intensive two-week 'A' course in London, covering the whole spectrum of broadcasting from microphone to transmitting aerial, with some explanation of the engineering organisation. After that the trainees were to go to London control room, Maida Vale, or Daventry for four to six weeks of practical training in studio and control-room work, recording, or transmitters. This was termed the 'B' course. Florence recommended that the scheme should get under way on 19 May and that the aim should be to have fifty trainees going through the 'A' course, and subsequently the 'B' course, at a time.

By this time, D. H. Schaschke, one of the senior maintenance engineers at Birmingham, had been appointed as Instructor. Later he became EiC of the Engineering Training School. The original 'B' course instructors were C. Smith at London control room, J. W. Godfrey on recording, and R. C. Harman at Daventry.

The school opened on 19 May 1941 at Delaware Road, Maida Vale, with a two-week 'A' course, and thereafter there was a steady succession of courses. Soon afterwards, in July, Brooker was appointed Assistant Instructor. He thought that much of the teaching was over the heads of the trainees, and so he made it his business to explain to them, before every lecture, what they would be hearing about, and he used the question and answer session after the lecture to inculcate some of the fundamentals of broadcasting. By September there was concern about the size of classes, which had gone as high as seventy-nine, whereas fifty was reckoned to be the optimum size. Florence was asked to guarantee a ceiling of fifty for the future. There was also pressure for the men and women to be separated into different classes throughout their training, but this proved to be impracticable. By the end of the year, the 'A' course had been found to be too rushed and it was extended to three weeks. In order to maintain the flow of trainees, the numbers on the 'A' course had perforce to go up again from fifty to seventy-five, and this meant that a bigger lecture room was essential. As a result the school moved to more spacious premises at St Hilda's, Maida Vale.

In March 1942 it reopened at St Hilda's, after a brief recess, with a modified prospectus. By this time the recruitment rate had tailed off, and so it became possible to give more time for training. The 'A' course was lengthened to four weeks, much of which was taken up by lectures by Brooker and Schaschke on the fundamental principles of electricity and the elements of broadcasting. At the same time the duration of the 'B' course was increased to eight weeks. There was an examination at the end of the twelve weeks – a *viva voce* to test the trainee's general knowledge of the broadcasting chain, and a written paper on his 'B' course subject, either control rooms, recording, or transmitters. Those who failed the examination were discharged. Refresher courses were also started at this time for temporary staff who had joined before the training school came into being and for more senior people, including Engineers-in-Charge; occasional special courses were also given for announcers and other programme staff.

During 1942 the school was provided with a modest laboratory for practical work. The installation included a standard control position, a bay on which various types of amplifier could be mounted, wired, and 'repaired', a TD/7 gramophone desk, a 'bread-board' transmitter, and equipment for demonstrating various kinds of distortion. The facilities were expanded as time went on, the aim being to have examples of types of equipment that were in operational use and to demonstrate fundamental electrical phenomena.

Altogether over 2500 trainees, 800 of them women, went through the Engineering Training School in the four years of its war-time existence. Of these, 650 were subsequently lost to the Forces as they became eligible for call-up.

Soon after joining the training school, Brooker suggested that he should compile a text-book for the trainees. By February 1942 a draft had been completed. It was decided that the book should be published and that L. W. Hayes should edit it and see it through the proof stages; the style was to be 'cheerful, but not too flippant, along the lines of Silvanus P. Thompson's *Calculus Made Easy*.' By October 1942, 2500 copies had been printed. Experience on the first 'A' course on which it was used showed that the training manual had proved to be what was wanted, both in the ground it covered and the way in which it explained things. It was to become the foundation stone on which future 'A' courses rested.

During 1942 the idea of providing some instruction at selected stations began to gather force. The idea was to make it as easy as possible for those who wanted to learn to do so; for by that time promotion examinations had been instituted for each rung of the ladder in Operations and Maintenance, and those who wanted to get on had to study. Early in 1943 staff were appointed to the new job of 'On-station Instructor' at eleven stations (Broadcasting House/Maida Vale, 200 Oxford Street/Bush House, Wood Norton, Manchester, London Recording, Daventry, Rampisham,

Skelton, Droitwich, Ottringham, Glasgow/Edinburgh). As people could not be released from shift-work to attend classes, they had to attend in their free time. The scheme consequently rested entirely on a voluntary response and it was regarded very much as an experiment, with the possibility that it might be a complete failure.

The instructors were given considerable freedom in their methods of working, though they had to keep in mind the examinations that their students would have to take. In April a survey was made to find out how the scheme was progressing. In general, the results were disappointing; at some stations the trainees refused to attend lectures in their own time and at others the Engineers-in-Charge were either over-zealous, and interfered too much, or unenthusiastic in their support of the instructor. A turning-point was reached in August 1943 when a meeting of all the instructors was held at which they discussed the scheme with Wynn and Florence. By that time they were able to report that it was working much better; so much so that by the end of the year a further four instructors were appointed to Bristol/Cardiff, Moorside Edge, Woofferton, and Programme Engineering.

In April 1944 the Engineering Division was suddenly faced with the prospect of having to release between 250 and 300 juniors to the Forces by the end of June. The training school had been turning out about 120 trainees each quarter, but this output could not be expanded quickly enough to make good such big losses. To meet this emergency, seven of the station instructors (at Bristol, Glasgow, Manchester, Droitwich, Rampisham, Ottringham, Skelton) were taken off their normal duties to give courses to new recruits in control-room and transmitter work. In this way an extra hundred trainees were put through courses by the end of June, and the crisis was surmounted.

Before the war technical instructions dealing with BBC equipment and its operation, were written by J. C. Bradford of the Overseas & Engineering Information Department. On the outbreak of war instruction-writing lapsed, and it was not until the end of November 1942 that it was resumed. It was then put under the wing of the training school, with J. W. Godfrey in charge of this work.

In October 1940 formal recognition was given to the BBC Staff (War-time) Association, with H. Lynton Fletcher as its first chairman. The newly formed Association was open to all staff, including engineers, but it was not long before a rival began to emerge. In November two engineers at Wood Norton, J. C. Bradford and W. T. Milsom (both of whom had played a major part in the formation of the War-time Staff Association), sent out a letter to engineers at every transmitting station, studio centre, and engineering department, propounding the view that in negotiations with Management, engineers should be represented by engineers rather than by others. The letter proposed that, if enough support was forthcoming, a separate association would be set up exclusively for engineers. Before sending out their letter, Bradford and Milsom had canvassed opinion among their colleagues at Wood Norton; the results had been reassuring, for out of forty-seven people they had approached no fewer than forty-four had welcomed their proposal.

By February thirty-seven of the forty-five stations and departments circularised had sent in returns, with an aggregate of 612 signatures in favour. The percentage in favour was estimated to be 61, but after allowing for the probability that it had not been possible to approach more than 80 per cent of the staff, the measure of support was reckoned to be 76 per cent. Armed with this response, Bradford and Milsom proceeded to set up national and regional committees for an Association of BBC Engineers.

The War-time Staff Association did not suffer these moves in silence. In April they issued a memorandum discouraging engineers from supporting the rival association, pointing out that they were already providing for their representation and had 500 members in Engineering Division. The Corporation did not at the outset welcome the idea of a second staff association. In an open memorandum countering the Staff Association's claims, the Wood Norton committee had stated that 'from the indications they had already received from high authorities in Engineering and Administration they were confident of getting full recognition and every encouragement'. W. St. J. Pym, as Director of Staff Administration, considered this statement misleading; his department had no wish to deal with more than one Association – and so far as he was aware the originators had been given no encouragement.

Despite the hostility of the Staff Association and the discouragement of the Management, the plans for forming an Association of BBC Engineers went steadily ahead. In June the Secretary, Milsom, was able to write to Staff Administration telling them that an association had been organised, that the first meeting of its central committee had been held (on 11 June 1941), and that a membership of 620 had been achieved, with more enrolments still to come in. The aim of the Association was, he said, 'to provide a fully responsible and properly elected organisation for the representation of all BBC engineers', and he went on to ask for formal recognition by the Corporation. This was eventually given in October 1941.

Although Bradford and Milsom played a prominent part in launching the Association of BBC Engineers, its chief architect and mentor was Purslow, at that time Engineer-in-Charge at Wood Norton. Because of this he was the obvious choice for Chairman, and, indeed, he was anxious to take on the chairmanship in order to see the Association get started along the right lines, rather than (as he said) 'become a vehicle for agitation and discontent'. But there were difficulties. Pym was opposed to the idea of Purslow becoming chairman, on the grounds that it would not be compatible with the managerial responsibilities he might have to exercise as EiC Wood Norton. In the event Purslow did take on the chairmanship, but with the proviso that he would relinquish it as soon as he had steered the Association through the initial stages and it had received official recognition. Accordingly, at a meeting of the central committee in November 1941 Purslow tendered his resignation. The committee, however, refused to accept it and he continued as Chairman until July 1942, when J. Wardley Smith became Chairman. By 1945 the membership stood at 1400, and in addition a number of Youths in Training had been admitted to honorary membership. Of the 1400 members, 600 were monthly-paid staff; included among them were Es-i-C and assistants to Superintendent Engineers.

Towards the end of the war feelings had changed, and on 25 March 1945 a joint meeting was held between the War-time Staff Association and the Association of

BBC Engineers to discuss the possibility of amalgamation. The meeting resolved unanimously that the creation of a new, single, organisation to represent all staff was possible and desirable, and a joint committee was set up to go into this. The Engineering representatives on this committee included J. A. J. Cooper, then Chairman of the Association of BBC Engineers. Finally, on 23 June 1945, a special meeting of delegates of both associations was held in the Concert Hall at Broadcasting House. As a recent ballot had shown an overwhelming vote in favour of a single system of representation, the meeting resolved to form a Staff Association open to all members of the Association of BBC Engineers and the BBC Staff (War-time) Association, and any other members of BBC staff qualified to join. So began the organisation that finally became the Association of Broadcasting Staff.

A feature of war-time operations was the co-operation between engineers and programme and administrative staff that was fostered by inter-divisional committees such as the Studio & Equipment Committee. Their interests were by no means always identical, and it frequently fell to the engineers to tell the programme people that they could not have what they wanted. Nevertheless, effective co-operation was established and the exigencies of the time were met by sensible compromises.

The total number of staff in the Engineering Division rose during the war from 1674 at the beginning of October 1939 to a peak of 3733 (plus 449 who were serving in the Forces) at the end of March 1945.

During the war there was close liaison between the BBC and the Ministry of Information on programme policy (not without moments of strain, as recorded by Asa Briggs).[42] On the financial side the BBC was dependent on a Parliamentary vote and to scrutiny by the Treasury of its estimates and expenditure. Naturally in war-time the Engineering Division often had to put emergency arrangements in hand without any possibility of accurate estimating in advance and in 1941 there were complaints from the Treasury about over-spending – though only a fraction of it was on engineering. Fortunately the BBC's finances were under the management of T. Lochhead as Controller (Finance), a clear-sighted accountant with a gift for expounding the techniques of financial control in a way that secured the whole-hearted co-operation of the Engineering Division.

In 1941 Lochhead wrote a paper on the subject and in the following year the system of control was tightened up; it took the same basic shape as it has followed ever since. The budget for capital expenditure was broken down into individual schemes, each marked with the expected date of authorisation and the estimated expenditure in each future year. There were also 'Bulk Allotments' for small capital items under various headings. This system checked the risk of over-spending, but it inevitably led to the opposite. In war-time, especially, projects were often delayed by all kinds of difficulties, so that the expenditure against them was deferred and the budget figure for any one year was under-spent, while developments that might have been undertaken had had to be deferred to keep the estimates within the budget.

Control of running costs was based on 'annual rates' under a number of account headings. The authorised annual rate against each heading obeyed Newton's first law of motion: it remained unchanged from year to year unless it was varied by an approved increase or decrease. At that time rising costs were a minor factor, and the annual revenue expenditure corresponded fairly accurately with the total of the annual rates. Engineering running costs included the rental of SB and communication circuits and the cost of staff, power, lighting and heating for all BBC premises, plant maintenance and transport.

A booklet was prepared by the Engineering Secretariat describing the financial procedure as it affected the Engineering Division. The procedure for estimating and for circulating details of approved schemes was tidied up by the use of standard forms and the flow of paper for requisitioning equipment and components was streamlined in co-operation with the Engineering Accountant (then a member of Finance Division). Large individual items of expenditure were usually covered by contracts negotiated by one or other of the specialist departments; smaller items were the subject of requisitions originated by the department responsible for the project. These requisitions went through a chain of authorisations and finally resulted either in an order on BBC stores or in a purchase order on an outside supplier. Then, as now, limits were laid down, defining the authority of Heads of Departments, Controllers, Heads of Divisions, and the Director-General for approving estimates and also for authorising contracts and requisitions placed against those estimates. A record of capital commitments kept by the Engineering Secretariat was reconciled from time to time with the actual expenditure recorded by Finance Division, after allowing for outstanding commitments. This system enabled a continuous control to be exercised over capital expenditure by the Engineering Division, which, apart from the purchase of buildings, furniture and fittings, constituted almost the whole of the BBC's capital costs.

II RESEARCH AND DEVELOPMENT

When the war started there was naturally a marked shift of emphasis in the activities of the Research Department. Effort was concentrated on the immediate and practical problems of broadcasting under war-time conditions, and most of the more theoretical and fundamental work was put on one side 'for the duration'.

The number of reports issued by a research organisation are not a true measure of the nature or quantity of its output, but they give some indication of what has been done. The total number of reports issued by the Research Department fell from 29 in 1938 to 10 in 1941, but rose again to 35 in 1943. In 1938 the predominant topics were field-strength measurement and recording, whereas in 1942 recording was top of the list, and in 1945 receivers and methods of measurement preponderated. Work on mathematics virtually ceased during most of the war period, and little was done on acoustics – rough and ready methods based on previous experience had to suffice.

At the outset, Research Department suffered the loss of some of its senior people to the Forces. W. Proctor Wilson was seconded to France at the end of August, becoming Liaison Officer in Paris in January 1940. In 1943 a batch of senior people left to join TRE at Malvern, among them E. K. Sandeman and C. G. Mayo. Despite these serious losses, the department, under the inspiring leadership of H. L. Kirke, made a solid contribution to wartime developments. It was responsible for the design of a variety of new equipment to meet war-time needs, and it also played a major consultative role, investigating and advising on a whole range of immediate problems.

Recording was a prolific field of endeavour. Altogether three designs of disc recording equipment were produced in the space of five years (see section 6 of this chapter): the Type C transportable equipment (1940) which was the mainstay of the mobile units in every theatre of war; the midget disc recorder (1944) for the war correspondents to operate themselves, which was produced in six weeks for D-Day; and the Type D recorder (1945), a high-fidelity recorder for studio centres and transcription work.

Early in the war the expansion of short-wave broadcasting created a demand for better rf measuring equipment to ease the task of lining up feeders and aerials at transmitting stations. To meet this need, Research Department developed a number of impedance and admittance bridges with their associated oscillators and detectors; H. L. Kirke took this as the subject for his Chairman's Address to the Radio Section of the IEE in the autumn of 1944.[43]

Another major design project was the development of amplified aerial systems for the monitoring service, first at Evesham and later at Caversham (see section 7 of this chapter). Wide-band amplifiers covering the spectrum 100 kHz to 27 MHz were produced for feeding up to sixty receivers from a common aerial system. A key component in these systems was the rf transformer for the distribution circuits, which covered the entire frequency range from 100 kHz up to 27 MHz with an insertion loss of only 4 dB.[25]

Other achievements by the Research Department that deserve mention are: limiter amplifiers enabling the average modulation of transmitters to be raised while protecting them against over-modulation, a monitor for indicating depth of modulation, a standing-wave indicator for short-wave stations, a total harmonic analyser, and improvements in the design of the BBC ribbon microphone to give it a better frequency response and make it less susceptible to electrical interference.

Much effort was devoted to aerial problems. Elaborate tests were carried out to determine the performance of the horizontal dipole arrays used at the short-wave stations, under various conditions[14] and the possibilities of dual-frequency aerial arrays were examined. Towards the end of the war work was started on the design of mast radiators with low angles of propagation for high-power medium-wave stations.

Throughout the war, there were frequent highly-specialised problems to be solved some of which have been mentioned elsewhere in this chapter; the resulting developments included the following:

High-accuracy crystal-drive equipment for the medium-wave synchronised groups of transmitters, having a frequency stability of $\pm$ 1 part in 10^7. This equipment incorporated a series-tuned Colpitts circuit devised by G. G. Gouriet.[6]

A system of frequency comparison for stations in synchronised groups, which was impervious to amplitude and phase variations of the reference tone received by line from the master station. Towards the end of the war this system was further improved by being adapted to use, as a reference signal, a 1-kHz tone fed by line from Broadcasting House, London. This reference tone had a nominal stability of $\pm$ 2 parts in 10^8.[6]

Precision variable-frequency drive equipment for the short-wave stations. This gave continuous coverage from 140 kHz to 22·4 MHz, with a re-setting accuracy of 50 parts in 10^6.[13]

The operation of high-power medium-wave transmitters in parallel into a common aerial. This was first achieved at Droitwich in 1941, and culminated in the construction of the 4 × 200-kW station at Ottringham in 1943.[8]

A four-wire feeder and an aerial/feeder switching system for short-wave stations installed first at Rampisham and subsequently at Skelton and Woofferton.[12]

The method of programme presentation and handling known as 'continuity working'.[44]

Compensation for the effects of temperature variation on the characteristics of Post Office circuits carrying programmes, introduced in 1944.[45]

The split-band system for outside broadcasts from places where the Post Office lines were not suitable for conventional methods, introduced in 1944.[5]

An interesting patent case arose in 1943 out of H. B. Rantzen's invention of a method of superimposing identification signals on programme circuits, by inserting a modulated tone in a notch within the audio-frequency band. The level of the tone was so low as to be practically inaudible to listeners, but it could be extracted by a selective amplifier at the transmitting stations. The Patent Office refused the application on the ground that the invention did not result in a manufactured product. The BBC appealed to the Patents Tribunal; Mr Justice Evershed decided that an electrical oscillation could be regarded as a manufactured product and the patent was granted (No. 587,447).

12 THE TELEVISION COMMITTEE, 1943

We have already remarked on the optimism with which plans for broadcasting in peace-time were being considered long before the end of the war. A notable example of this was the setting-up of the Television Committee in September 1943 to consider plans for the restoration and development of television after the war. The decision to set up the Committee was made by Sir John Anderson, then Lord President of the Council, and the members were nominated in September 1943, although the Government made no announcement on the subject until 18 January 1944. Sir Maurice

Hankey, later Lord Hankey, was Chairman of the Committee and it included Sir Stanley Angwin, Engineer-in-Chief of the Post Office, Sir Edward Appleton of the Department of Scientific and Industrial Research, Sir Raymond Birchall, Deputy Director-General of the Post Office, Professor J. D. (later Sir John) Cockcroft of the Air Defence and Research Establishment, R. J. P. Harvey of the Treasury, with the Director-General (at first R. W. Foot and later W. J. Haley) and the Deputy Director-General (Sir Noel Ashbridge) of the BBC.

The Committee held its first meeting on 26 October 1943, and its thirty-first and final meeting on 29 December 1944. In the course of its deliberations numerous witnesses were called, including Isaac Shoenberg of EMI, John Logie Baird, J. Arthur Rank, Gerald Cock and H. L. Kirke of the BBC, and representatives of the GEC, STC, and Scophony Ltd. T. C. Macnamara of the BBC attended all but two of the meetings in the capacity of a technical witness.

The crucial point upon which the Committee had to pronounce was the line standard on which the services should reopen after the war. In reaching their conclusion on this question, the main considerations that they had to take into account were:

(i) The widely held belief, which the Committee shared, that television had a part to play in the cinema, and the need therefore to develop a new system with a higher standard of definition approaching that of the cinema, preferably of the order of 1000 lines.

(ii) The fact that the pre-war system could be got going again at Alexander Palace in about a year, so long as key staff in the Services and Government establishments could be released promptly, whereas the development of an improved system with higher definition would take between five and seven years.

(iii) The fact that the pre-war system had given good results and its potentialities had still not been fully exploited. In particular, receivers had not kept pace with the standards of performance attained at the transmitting end.

(iv) The thought that to wait five or more years for an improved system, with no television at all in the meantime, would seriously retard commercial development and also lead to the complete dispersal of the nucleus of highly skilled people who had put television on the map before the war.

The Committee concluded that the right course would be to reopen the service from Alexandra Palace on the original 405-line standard, and they recommended that this should be done as soon as possible after the end of the war. They went on to recommend that the service should be extended to six of the most populous areas outside London soon after Alexandra Palace had been reinstated. The extension of the service should be planned on the assumption that it would be on the 405-line standard, but this should be kept under review.

The six areas to be served were not specified in the report, but it is clear from the minutes that the Committee had the following transmitter sites in mind: Birmingham, Manchester, Sheffield, Falkirk, Cardiff, and Durham (or possibly Belfast). This was two more than the Television Advisory Committee of 1938 had recom-

mended – Birmingham, Huddersfield, Falkirk and Bristol. The BBC's view, represented by Ashbridge, was that it would not be possible to give a satisfactory service
to the industrial areas of both Lancashire and Yorkshire from a single station on the
Yorkshire Moors, the coverage of which would be partly wasted on the sparsely
populated area of the Pennines. The BBC recommendation that two separate high-
power stations should be provided in the Manchester and Sheffield areas was not
followed and a single station at Holme Moss was provided for the whole area. The
BBC view was vindicated much later when the Band III station at Winter Hill was
opened in 1964 to reinforce the service of BBC-1 on 405 lines in Lancashire and
Cheshire, and a station at Belmont (also in Band III) was opened in 1966 to serve
Lincoln and the south-eastern part of Yorkshire. These later changes were made
partly because the Holme Moss station gave a barely adequate service in Band I over
the whole area and also because of the demand for partially separate programmes for
Lancashire and Yorkshire. Another reason was that the ITA, set up in 1955, had to
use channels in Band III, in which the coverage attainable from a single station was
less than in Band I. They also required different programmes for the two parts of the
area.

In parallel with these developments the Committee recommended that vigorous
research work on a radically improved system of television should begin as soon as
staff could be made available. They agreed that the aim should be to approach the
standard of the cinema and felt that definition should eventually be of the order of
1000 lines and that the introduction of colour and stereoscopic effects should be
considered.[46]

The Committee spent some time discussing various ways of organising television
research. One idea was that the big firms should be persuaded to pool their resources
and form a research association under the wing of DSIR. Against this, it was doubtful
whether such a consortium would lead to the development of a practicable system
and there was one firm, Electric and Musical Industries, that was predominant in
the television field and controlled many of the essential patents. These latter views
prevailed and the Committee confined itself to a compromise on research, calling
for co-operation between all the interests concerned and some co-ordination by an
Advisory Committee, the appointment of which they recommended.

The Committee's report was published in March 1945, and the Government gave
its approval to the main recommendations in October 1945. It caused remarkably
little stir. *The Times* devoted half a column to a résumé of the recommendations,
backed up by a rather inconclusive third leader.[47] *Electronic Engineering* had a leader
on the subject, but ventured no decisive opinion on the proposals.[48] There were
mentions in *Electrical Trading* and the *Electrical Times*. The *Wireless World*, on the
other hand, was more forthcoming. Their leader in the May issue had this to say:

'There is much that is admirable in the Report, but we think it fails to take into
account the psychological reactions of the average viewer, on whose attitude will
ultimately depend the success or failure of British television. In particular, he has
heard so much of war-time developments that he is unlikely to be more than luke-

warm towards the restarted pre-war system, especially when there is a promise of "better television round the corner."

'. . . *Wireless World* inclines more strongly than ever to the view that a new start should be made with a standard of definition involving no radical departure from well-tried technique, either in transmission or receiver design. But within that limitation, definition should be the highest that can be achieved. Let us concentrate on that without too many "1000 lines" distractions.'[49]

R. W. Hallows in the same issue was an even sterner critic. He wrote:

'. . . What is the point of extending the 405-line system to the provinces if something better is to be introduced at no distant date? Is not the spending of a million and a half of good money on such a scheme something very like sheer waste? Why should people in the provinces rush to buy 405-line television receivers when the millions in the London service area would not do so? Even though they have the assurance that the 405-line transmissions will be continued for years after the arrival of the improved system, will there be any real inducement to people to buy such sets? I think not, for very few are content to have something that is notoriously second best. My own belief is that, were the money spent and the six extensions made, the result would be a ghastly flop . . . From almost every point of view then it behoves us to cease as soon as may be from flogging the almost dead horse of 405-line television and to put our money on an altogether better and very much alive animal, which will prove a winner, surely.'

Despite these adverse views, the Committee's main recommendation was put into effect and the service was restarted on 405 lines in 1946. Addressing the Institution of Electrical Engineers on 8 October 1953, eight years after the Television Committee's report, Sir Harold Bishop said:

'In the light of development since that time there is no doubt that this was the right decision (to reopen on 405 lines). It would have been undesirable and unnecessary to delay the re-opening until an improved system had been developed and brought into service. In the past seven years great improvements have been made in picture quality by the development of improved camera tubes, by better use of the available bandwidth, and by the development of improved receivers. A system employing a greater number of lines would have needed a wider bandwidth to convey the information, and would have required more channels for national coverage than are available in the band 41 to 68 MHz. Incidentally, all pre-war receivers would have been made unserviceable without considerable change, and it would have been more expensive to distribute the programme by line or radio link.'[50]

Meanwhile, many of the 20,000 to 25,000 receivers that had been in the hands of the public immediately before the war had suffered from lack of use, from damp, and in many cases from enemy action. It is doubtful how many of them survived to be used again when the service was resumed in 1946.

The decision to reopen the service on the pre-war standard of 405 lines has since been criticised on the ground that if it had been reopened on 625 lines, a great deal of trouble would have been avoided later when the transition to 625 lines was finally made. This is hardly fair, because the 625-line system was not standardised until July 1950, when a sub-group of CCIR Study Group XI met in Geneva under the chairmanship of Dr W. Gerber of Switzerland. (One advantage of choosing 625 lines was that the line frequency of a 625-line 50-field signal was almost the same as that of the American 525-line 60-field signal. This, incidentally, enabled American receivers to be used in Europe during the early stages of the introduction of the 625-line service.) This standard came to be known as the 'CCIR Standard', although it was only one of several recognised by the CCIR; it was also referred to as the 'Gerber Standard'. It was brought into use in several European countries between 1950 and 1954.[51] To wait for it would have meant denying television to British viewers for at least a further four years. The public mood immediately after the war demanded reassurances that peace had really returned, despite the rigours of rationing, and the resumption of BBC Television helped to meet this need. The 405-line service yielded pictures that were entirely acceptable to the public and it was to continue without a rival in this country until the 625-line service was opened in 1964; it still provides a valuable service to those parts of the country that have not yet been reached by the 625-line services on UHF.

CHAPTER V

Post-War Reconstruction: 1946–55

I STUDIOS AND OUTSIDE BROADCASTS: RADIO SERVICES

The pattern of peace-time broadcasting was already being planned before the end of the war. It was evident that conditions would never be the same as they had been before September 1939. Not only had many technical advances been made during the war, a number of which had had to remain unpublished for security reasons, but the different needs of war-time listeners and the ever-present possibility of air-raids had caused new methods of presenting programmes to be developed, with the result that many techniques in use before the war had been forsaken and some of them would never return.

The BBC–Marconi ribbon microphone (type A) had been in use throughout the war, but had been modified in two ways. The original springy aluminium ribbon, which had objectionable resonances, was abandoned in favour of very thin beaten aluminium foil (type AX). When studios were formed in the basement of 200 Oxford Street in 1942 it was found that ribbon microphones could not be used in some of them because of a 1200-Hz whistle, apparently produced by the magnetic field set up by commutator ripple from the rotary converters supplying dc to the conductor rails in the Central London Tube; this was eliminated by altering the wiring inside the microphone to make it magnetically balanced – this modification was retained permanently in the type AXB of 1943. Just after the war some ribbon microphones were converted to Ticonal magnets to give increased sensitivity, but it was not possible to use the new material to the best advantage without a redesign of the structure.[1, 2]

The redesign produced the type AXBT of 1944. All these variants of the type A ribbon microphone were rather cumbersome; the demand for a smaller and lighter microphone was met by the type B ribbon, also called the PGS, microphone. It was much smaller than the type AXBT and only one-third of the weight.[3] It was manufactured by STC to the BBC design and became available just in time for the Coronation of 1953. These microphones have been very widely used, especially in studios. They were pressure-gradient microphones; that is to say, the ribbon was open to acoustic pressure both at front and back, so that the microphone operated by virtue of the difference in pressure between the two sides, rather than the pressure at the front only.[4] One advantage of this was that the ribbon microphone was bi-directional its polar sensitivity characteristic in the horizontal plane being in the form of a figure-8 (though with some variation at the high frequencies). This characteristic made it particularly useful for drama and discussions.

For commentaries at sporting events it was essential to have a microphone that could be held close to the face and be insensitive to extraneous sounds. The lip microphone mentioned in the previous chapter had been evolved in 1937. An improved version produced in 1951, the L2, was then the only 'noise-cancelling' microphone of its kind in the world.[3, 5] As it was held so that the ribbon was only 6 cm from the mouth, the sound waves attacking the ribbon were almost spherical and the pressure gradient at low frequencies was excessive. The resulting accentuation of these frequencies was equalised, partly by the insertion of silk gauze screens on either side of the ribbon, which also reduced the effect of wind, and partly by an electrical network inside the case. Since sound waves caused by extraneous sources are almost planar, their low-frequency components (which are the most troublesome) were largely eliminated.

A number of lip microphones, type LP1, were made during the war by Marconi's. some of the type LP2 were made by the BBC and others by STC.

Several other types of microphone, having different directional properties, were also used – including moving-coil and piezo-electric types.

Condenser (or, more accurately, electrostatic) microphones had been introduced in the early 1930s and their shortcomings have been mentioned in Chapter III, Section 4. Improvements in their design were made just before the war, particularly in Germany. In its simplest form, the electrostatic microphone consisted of a flat metal back-plate and a diaphragm (either of thin metal or of plastic material coated with gold) spaced a short distance from the back-plate. A polarising voltage was applied between the diaphragm and the back-plate and the variations in the capacitance between them produced variations in voltage, which constituted the output of the microphone. The response corresponded with the sound pressure and was therefore omni-directional. In another form, the back-plate was pierced with holes so that the diaphragm responded to the pressure gradient rather than the sound pressure; the response pattern was then in the form of a figure 8, i.e. bi-directional. An ingenious variant devised by von Braunmühl and Weber in 1935 had a cardioid response pattern and was therefore uni-directional. This microphone was similar to the pressure gradient type, but had a second diaphragm at the back. The electrical connections were taken between the central electrode and the front diaphragm, the rear diaphragm being electrically inoperative. The pressure gradient vibrated both diaphragms in the same phase, and therefore did not compress the air in the intervening space, whereas sound pressure applied equally to both diaphragms caused them to vibrate in opposite senses and compressed and expanded the intervening air. The operative diaphragm therefore responded both to sound pressure and to pressure gradient and the result was a cardioid response.[6]

It was then realised that if electrical outputs were derived from both diaphragms and were added or subtracted in various proportions, a variable response pattern could be obtained by varying the setting of a potentiometer in the external electrical circuit. In this way the directional pattern could be chosen at will to be a cardioid, a circle or a figure 8.[7] This principle was adopted in the type C12 microphone developed by the AKG Company in Vienna about 1949. These developments widened the scope of the electrostatic microphone, though the ribbon microphone continued to be used extensively, especially in studios used for drama, talks and presentation.

The war had acted as a stimulus to the development of new ideas in programme presentation and in studio design. Before the war the practice had been to use particular studios for particular classes of programme, and even to use a number of studios for different episodes in a dramatic production. On the technical side the equipment for the studios was, as far as possible, centralised in a single control room. When the war came the difficulty of providing studio accommodation in areas safe from bombing resulted in the same studios being used for many types of programme and also in several microphones being used in different parts of a single studio, where previously several studios would have been employed. This pointed the way to an increase in the efficiency of utilisation of the studios. During the early part of the war the only studio equipment available for new installations was the OBA/8 and this was in use on a wide scale. Thus, the technical and physical limitations imposed by the war indicated the line of development that was to be followed afterwards. The 'general purpose studio' had come to stay and the self-contained studio unit, made possible by the use of equipment that was mains-operated and no longer dependent on central batteries, had shown great advantages; for instance, rehearsals no longer needed any operational intervention from the control room engineers. The self-contained studio also facilitated the introduction of continuity working, which had been shelved when war broke out, but had been adopted before the end of the war in the External Services, the Home Services and the Forces Programme.[8, 9]

The many different kinds of building that the BBC had been compelled to use during the war had afforded opportunities for observing the different acoustic effects resulting from different types of construction and had necessitated some experimentation. The results contributed, after the war, to the evolution of new methods of studio design. The pre-war studios were much in need of improvement; as an expedient Cabot's quilting had been hung on the walls and sometimes on the ceilings of studios in London and in the Regions. The austerity of the times, however, and the restrictions on capital expenditure, which persisted until almost the end of the period under review, resulted in very little money being available for the renovation or rebuilding of studios until the early 1950s. A good deal was done, but it had to be done simply and cheaply. As an example, the walls of the Belfast studios, the fabric of which had been hurriedly completed in 1939–40, were still bare brick in 1945, with hangings of carpet felt. On the recommendation of J. McLaren of Building Department, it was decided to form a dado up to about 6 ft from the floor of the studio, covered with linoleum, and to treat the rest of the wall with hessian backed with rock-wool damping. This interim treatment was applied to all the studios except the concert hall. When it became essential to use the concert hall for the Northern Ireland Light Orchestra, acoustic boxes of various dimensions were made locally and mounted on the walls. These boxes were Helmholtz resonators which absorbed sound at frequencies around their resonant frequencies. Such boxes had been used for obtaining absorption at low frequencies in the studios of All-India Radio by C. W. Goyder (formerly of the BBC Research Department). Their design was developed

318

during the years following the end of the war. The dimensions of the boxes were adjusted to suit the resonant frequency required. In the original form they were made of wood, about 5 ft by 2 ft and about 1 ft 6 in. deep. They were lined with building-board and the front was covered with perforated asbestos tiles with a pad of glass silk immediately behind the tiles. The space behind the glass silk was divided up by cardboard partitions into sections about 8 in. square.[10] Later it was found that plaster boxes were more easily mounted on the walls of the studio and the interior was divided by internal partitions; circular holes in the front of the unit communicated with the cavities. It was found most effective to arrange the acoustic boxes in line arrays, a number of them being applied to the walls until the required effect was obtained.[11]

Membrane sound absorbers were also developed. These consisted of a wooden framework covered by a membrane of bitumen roofing felt. A blanket of rock wool might be hung behind the membrane and a protective cover was put in front of it; this also served as an acoustic filter.[12]

There were important advances in the application of acoustics to the design of studios during this period. The main problems to be overcome were lack of sufficient sound insulation, which permitted extraneous sounds to reach the microphone, excessive reverberation at the lower frequencies, and coloration. A number of developments helped to solve these problems. In the first place the application of transmission line theory to acoustics led to greater understanding of the problem. Secondly, a great deal of work was done, much of it in the BBC Research Department, on measurements of sound absorbing materials and resonant absorbers. Thirdly, the methods of measuring the acoustics of studios led to improved correlation between the measured results and the aesthetic effects.

In specially designed buildings the problem of sound insulation could largely be solved by appropriate planning, that is by arranging for studios to be well separated from other studios or rooms in which loud sounds might occur. Improvements in insulation could also be made by the use of floating floors and by placing partitions on resilient mountings, so as to avoid the direct transmission of sound through them. The excessive reverberation in the bass could be overcome by the use of appropriate acoustic treatment, such as resonant panelling and mineral wool on the walls, lath and plaster ceilings and boarded floors. In general there was a move to the more extensive use of sound reflecting surfaces, as typified by the wooden floors. It had long been recognised that disagreeable echoes could be produced by the natural modes of vibration of the air in the room at frequencies depending on its dimensions – the so-called 'Eigentones'. The dimensions of studios were therefore important and it was generally found that the lowest common multiple of the three dimensions should be as high as possible. These resonances could also be reduced by making the walls non-parallel and by breaking up the surfaces of walls and ceilings by coffering or by making them in a saw-tooth shape.

By 1947 it had been realised that the traditional methods of measuring reverberation time were insufficient. The practice had been to use a pulse of sound, produced by a loudspeaker in the studio, and to measure the time for the intensity of the sound to decay by 60 dB. To avoid standing-wave effects a warble tone was used, in which the frequency was varied cyclically about the mean frequency some five times per second. Thus, a curve of reverberation time against frequency was produced, but this gave no indication of the way in which the sound decayed at a particular frequency. It was therefore necessary to develop special techniques to determine the shape of the decay curve. One of the objects of these studies was to find out why two studios with apparently identical reverberation characteristics might differ widely in their acoustic properties. If a pulse of sound at a single frequency was used instead of a warble tone, and the results were examined on a cathode-ray oscillograph, it was possible to see how the sound decayed with time. This method was used to study the acoustics of the Philharmonic Hall in Liverpool and St Andrew's Grand Hall in Glasgow, both of which were known to have excellent acoustics. The result showed at least partial correlation between the results of the measurements and the acoustics of the two halls as determined by subjective appreciation.[13]

An improved method of investigating the acoustic properties of studios was developed in the early 1950s. This used a display in the form of a 'pulsed glide' in which a photographic record was made of the decay of sound pressure, the film being moved continuously so as to show a succession of traces with gradually increasing frequency of the tone. The pulsed glide brought to light any abnormalities in the rate of decay at any frequency.[14] A further development of this method used phase-coherent detection and correlation methods, in which the microphone output was modulated by the exciting frequency before being applied to the cathode-ray oscillograph. When applied to small studios this proved to be a useful method of diagnosing colorations and of identifying the various modes of vibration of reverberant sound.[15]

The first studio to be re-treated after the war, using the results of the researches that had been made up to that time, was Studio 1 at Maida Vale, which was used by the Symphony Orchestra. A considerable improvement resulted and gradually other studios in London and in the Regions were brought up to date by the application of the new techniques. By about 1955 most of the existing studios had been re-treated. One result of the investigations was to establish that, in spite of the difficulty of obtaining concordant aesthetic judgments, the fine tone quality and clear definition of the best of the traditional halls was at that time unsurpassed in any of the modern ones. Some of the principles that had recently been adopted by the designers of concert halls had to be abandoned one by one and it was established that the important features were the provision of adequate scattering of sound, no deliberate reinforcement of the direct sound, ample height, and appropriate reverberation time. The results caused the BBC to avoid the use of fan-shaped studios and also of reflectors and concave ceilings in the design of new studios. In large studios and concert halls, added absorption is necessary only at low and medium frequencies; at the higher frequencies the absorption of sound by the air and by the audience is usually more than is desirable. Great attention was paid to securing good diffusion of sound. Studio 1 at Maida Vale, with its rectangular diffusers is a good example of the application of this principle, though the result still left something to be desired and were the subject of further study in 1970 using an acoustic scale-model.

In the post-war period of austerity, many of the jobs of renovating studios in the Regions had to be left to local enterprise. The main difficulty then was, as in the early days of broadcasting, to ensure that common standards and common practices were adopted, while not inhibiting the enthusiasm of local staff; this was the task of D. B. Weigall (later Deputy Director of Engineering).

As early as 1943–4 some thought was being given, notably by H. D. Ellis of Equipment Department, to the kind of studio equipment that would be needed in the post-war era. With the experience that had already been gained of working with the OBA/8 amplifier and its associated apparatus, the requirements for the post-war design soon crystallised into the following:

(*a*) the studio to be a self-contained unit,
(*b*) the facilities to be as comprehensive and flexible as possible consistent with economy,
(*c*) the design to provide standard frameworks to which alternative control arrangements could be fitted to suit various sizes or types of studio as required,
(*d*) adequate spare apparatus to be provided to ensure continuity of the programme in the event of failure in the equipment,
(*e*) simplicity and comfort in operation, and
(*f*) convenience of maintenance.

The equipment in which these ideas were incorporated became known as the type 'A' equipment. An important difference between this and the pre-war system was that whereas before the war the level of programme in transit from studio to control room was of the order of −70 dB with reference to zero programme volume (at which the peak programme meter indicated frequent excursions to 8 dB above the reading corresponding to zero level of steady tone, i.e. 1 mW in 600 ohms or 0·77 V), the type 'A' equipment, following the OBA/8 system, produced an output at zero volume. The equipment consisted of two main items, the control desk and the apparatus cabinet. The control desk was designed with one end quite unobstructed, so that more than one person could sit at it (e.g. the programme engineer and the producer), and its three apparatus panels were arranged to swing forward to give access for maintenance. The left-hand panel carried purely technical controls, the central panel carried all the important mixing and control knobs and the right-hand panel carried such controls as the 'talk-back' microphone operating key, which the producer might wish to reach. The carcass of the desk was designed in three pieces to be bolted together, and the dimensions were carefully determined, both for comfort (desk height 2 ft 4 in. to allow the forearm to be comfortably supported when operating the controls on the centre panel) and to allow an uninterrupted view into the studio (overall height of desk not to exceed 3 ft 3 in.). The electrical equipment, apart from the controls on the desk, was housed in a separate lockable steel cabinet; this could be installed in an area used by non-technical personnel and it could be equipped in advance and transported to site after building operations, with their unavoidable dust and disarray, had ceased. To save space, the equipment was mounted on shelves, which could be pulled forward for access like the drawers of a filing cabinet. The electrical circuit of the equipment was designed so that a single type of amplifier unit could be used throughout, except for the monitoring amplifier which had to have a special circuit. The amplifier unit was specially designed and, because of the large number required, it had to be cheap to produce; it had a single stage giving a maximum voltage gain of 50 dB adjustable in 10-dB steps, and all its external connections were carried on a single plug, so that it took only a few moments to remove this plug, slide out a faulty unit and replace it with a new one. If an amplifier became faulty during a programme, a spare could immediately be switched into circuit by a relay controlled from the desk; the operation of these change-over facilities was so silent that if a good amplifier was replaced by another it was virtually impossible to detect the change. The first model of this equipment went into Studio 8A Broadcasting House and was handed over to the Engineer-in-Charge on 11 December 1944; its performance was carefully watched and tested by the Station Design & Installation Department for some time afterwards.[8] For some years, however, most studios continued to operate with the OBA/8 equipment, which had given such excellent service since 1939, and the replacement with the type 'A' equipment was not completed until the 1950s.

The type 'A' equipment was the first mains-operated equipment to be specially designed for use in BBC studios; the OBA/8 equipment, designed primarily for OBs, had been capable of operating from the mains and had been so used in studios since it began to be installed in them in 1939.

By 1950 there was a need for news reports and interviews from parts of the country where there was no BBC studio centre. The need was economically met by installing simple studios with equipment that could be operated by an experienced broadcaster without engineers in attendance. The first of these was opened in the Guildhall at Southampton on 15 August 1950. The broadcaster had to operate only one switch to bring the equipment and studio lights into operation, and another to change to another microphone and a spare amplifier in case of a fault. Lines to Bristol were booked when required. This studio made it possible to interview personages disembarking from transatlantic liners without having to send engineers and equipment from Bristol to Southampton.

During this period, the Research Department became interested in the development of means of artificial reverberation. The early echo rooms gave crude results and were used mainly to achieve dramatic effects, but later the technique was refined by the use of acoustically treated auxiliary studios instead of bare-walled echo rooms. After the war, when television started again, the demand for some form of artificial reverberation was intensified because the acoustics of a television studio were frequently rather 'dead'. Moreover, reverberation rooms are expensive and take up valuable space. From 1949 onwards, Research Department carried out many experiments on alternative methods of producing artificial reverberation. One was to use acoustic delay tubes through which sound was propagated and picked up by microphones. One of the most spectacular devices of this kind consisted of 150 ft of $1\frac{1}{2}$ in.-diameter tube in a coil, with moving-coil microphones let into it at intervals. This line of approach, however, soon led to the conclusion that the standard of perform-

322

ance required could be obtained only with bulky and elaborate equipment, and attention was turned to the possibilities of magnetic recording devices as delay elements. An artificial reverberation unit, making use of a multi-track recording system to simulate the effect of a multitude of reproducing heads, while requiring the physical presence of only a fraction of that number of heads, was designed and built and went into regular operation on television transmissions in July 1952; others later went into limited use in the Radio Services and in the Transcription Service. It was found to be advantageous to supplement the delay system by the equivalent of a reverberation chamber having a relatively short reverberation time – an ultrasonic reverberation tank; the greater part of the signal spectrum was translated to ultrasonic frequencies and transmitted as a pressure wave through water in the tank. Equipment incorporating this device, as an addition to one of the magnetic-recording units mentioned above, went into experimental service in April 1954.[16] The complexity of this system was due to the need to obtain a smooth decay of sound and to avoid discrete echoes. Shortly after the period under review, the reverberation plate was developed and also other methods using springs.

The principle of continuity working had been introduced during the war in both Radio and the Overseas Services. The only important change after the war was that in the Home Service the single continuity suite in London was supplemented by a number of such suites in the Regions, which were now able to assemble their own programmes. Special operating practices had to be developed for the smooth working of all the continuity suites involved in the Home Service as a whole. For example, if a Region was originating an item that was simultaneously broadcast by all the Home Service transmitters, the master continuity suite was the one at the Regional Centre originating the item; that suite would handle all enquiries, concerning the running of the programme, from the other continuity suites taking it. The continuity announcer in any of the other Regions, however, could, if he wished, break away from the programme at any time and broadcast whatever he pleased, provided the network had been set up in such a way that this did not embarrass other Regions. The Light and Third programmes were still presented from their respective continuity suites in London, wherever the contributions might originate, since these programmes were always broadcast by the same network of transmitters. The practice of routing signals within a studio centre at zero level made it easy to bring to the control position in the continuity room all the programme sources that might be required, with minimum risk of noise or crosstalk. This was still the era of OBA/8 equipment in the continuity suites and they were generally equipped with four-channel mixers. The means of connection were still by standard Post Office plugs, flexible cords and jacks.[9]

The adoption of continuity working and the introduction of the type 'A' studio equipment, already mentioned, changed the appearance of control rooms. For a given level of activity, the amount of operational work to be carried out in the control room itself was materially reduced, and the only switching operations left were those of making incoming programmes available to the appropriate continuity suite, routing the output from the continuity suite to the proper destinations, passing contributions in transit from one centre to another or for recording, and re-routeing programmes in the event of a fault on the line network. However, the level of activity continued to increase, so that in the larger centres the use of plugs and jacks for source selection and for connecting communication circuits between sources and destinations was becoming too unwieldy and prone to error. Accordingly, it was decided, as early as 1947, to use selectors as in automatic telephone-switching equipment, which would be capable of connecting sixteen inputs simultaneously to any one of fifty outlets. In this way not only the required programme source but also the associated telephone and signalling facilities could be selected. The selectors would be operated by the continuity suite staff to select the required programme source, but in control rooms, where other switching operations had also to be performed, it was decided to set up 'miscellaneous switching positions'. On these a number of 'link circuits' would be provided, one end of each terminating on a bank of destination selectors and the other on the wipers of a bank of source selectors. Any switching operation would then consist of choosing a particular link and connecting this by dialling, both to the source required and to the destination. In any particular control room the number of links needed would depend on the peak traffic, but would be only a fraction of the total number of destinations, so that a considerable economy of switching equipment could be looked for. Unfortunately, in the climate of economic austerity which prevailed for so many years after the war, these ideas could not be implemented, and the London control room had to remain in a tangle of plugs and cords until the late 1950s.[17]

Outside broadcasting in the radio services revived quickly after the war, when restrictions were removed and sporting and other activities of interest for broadcasting were resumed. The OBA/8 equipment, which had had a splendid record of service for fourteen years in control rooms all over the country was still the mainstay of OBs. At the beginning of the 1950s, however, a need was felt for new OB equipment giving improved facilities. A new design was undertaken by Designs Department, which resulted in the development of the OBA/9. It was designed to the following general specification and was introduced in 1952:

(*a*) The technical performance to be similar to that of the OBA/8 with improvements wherever possible.

(*b*) the size and weight of the individual units to be a minimum without sacrifice of reliability and robustness.

(*c*) all main units to stack together and be clamped to form a rigid assembly for easy transport and operation without dismantling.

(*d*) subsidiary items used on all OBs – microphone cable, cue-lights, telephones, comprehensive switching facilities, etc. – to form part of the assembly wherever possible.

(*e*) equipment to be readily demountable for transport, for operation at awkward locations or for building up more elaborate systems for complicated broadcasts.

The equipment, consisting of six units of five different types, was mounted on a trolley, on the back of which were three drums each containing 150 ft of screened microphone cable. Apart from this assembly there were a portable loudspeaker and a box for spares of the same length as the rest of the equipment so that they could be carried on the trolley for transport. The amplifier, of 90 dB maximum gain, had three resistance-capacitance coupled stages and the gain control had thirty-eight steps of 2 dB each, with two larger steps to an 'off' position. The single potentiometer was arranged so that it simultaneously increased the negative feedback over the first two valves and introduced attenuation between the second and third valves, so as to reduce the gain. The output stage of the amplifier could be converted into an oscillator to give a test frequency of 1100 Hz for line-up purposes at normal testing level.[18]

No mention has yet been made of the most important development in the whole field of electronics during this period: the invention of the transistor in the USA by Shockley, Bardeen and Brattain in 1948. The design of equipment using transistors instead of valves on a wide scale did not take place until the second half of the 1950s and therefore belongs to the next chapter.

2 TRANSMITTERS AND RECEPTION: RADIO SERVICES

The development of the radio transmitter network between VE Day in 1945 and the end of 1955 can be subdivided into two phases. First, there was the rearrangement and augmentation of existing long- and medium-wave transmitters to provide substantially national coverage for the Home and Light programmes, followed shortly afterwards by the introduction of the Third Programme on medium waves with more limited coverage. During this period, transmitters of higher power and greater overall efficiency replaced some of the old plant which had been in continuous service since the inception of the Regional Scheme in 1929. Secondly, in 1950 the Copenhagen Plan was implemented; it was the first European Plan for the reallocation of long- and medium-waves to be put into effect since the Lucerne Plan of 1933, which had been implemented in 1934. The new Plan necessitated an intensive programme of work on modifying transmitters for the new channels, which had to be done without affecting transmission on the frequencies in use until the change-over date. Other developments to be followed up in this section include (1) the introduction of semi-attended and unattended transmitters, which led to substantial savings in the capital and running costs of the stations, (2) the design of automatic monitoring and switching apparatus to free skilled staff from the unrewarding duty of listening for long periods to detect technical blemishes in the programmes, and (3) the introduction of sound broadcasting on VHF in 1955. The first two of these trends met with some opposition based on traditional BBC perfectionism, but a realistic attitude won the day and led to the widespread use of the new methods – without which the continued expansion of sound and television coverage would not have been economically possible.

The interim arrangements mentioned in the previous chapter for the use of the existing long- and medium-wave transmitters in the immediately post-war period were introduced for the Home and Light Programmes on 29 July 1945. As shown in

HOME AND LIGHT PROGRAMME TRANSMITTERS FROM 29 JULY 1945

Station	Frequency (kHz)	Power (kW)	Programme
Home Service			
Moorside Edge	668	60	Northern Home Service
Westerglen	767	60	Scottish Home Service
Burghead	767	60	Scottish Home Service
Redmoss	767	2·5	Scottish Home Service
Washford	804	60	Welsh Home Service
Penmon	804	10	Welsh Home Service
Brookmans Park	877	140	Basic Home Service
Droitwich	1013	60	Midland Home Service
Norwich	1013	1	Midland Home Service
Start Point	977	120	West of England Home Service
Stagshaw	1050	120	N. England/N. Ireland Home Service
Lisnagarvey	1050	100	N. England/N. Ireland Home Service
Londonderry	1050	0·25	N. England/N. Ireland Home Service
Clevedon*	1384	20	West of England Home Service
Bartley*	1384	10	West of England Home Service
Light Programme			
Droitwich	200	200	
Brookmans Park	1149	60†	
Moorside Edge	1149	60†	
Westerglen	1149	60†	
Lisnagarvey	1149	10	
Stagshaw	1149	10	
Burghead	1149	20†	
Redruth	1149	2	
Redmoss	1149	2	
Londonderry	1149	0·25	

* From 29 September 1946.
† Directional aerial.

the table, the frequencies and powers used followed closely the original plan. The Third Programme, which was to operate from 1800–2400 hours daily, could not start until 29 September 1946, because of the difficulty of obtaining a suitable frequency.

The policy decision to start the Third Programme gave rise to misgivings on the technical side because of the limited coverage that could be achieved in the medium-wave band with the channels that were, or were likely to be, available. Partial coverage would have been possible on 977 kHz as originally planned, but this frequency was needed for the European Service from Ottringham. A search was made to find another medium frequency that was relatively free from interference from foreign stations and sufficiently near the low-frequency end of the band to give reasonably good coverage. The choice fell on 583 kHz, which had previously been used by a station in Latvia under the Lucerne Plan of 1934. Its use was authorised for a high-power transmitter at Droitwich, to be supplemented by a synchronised group of low-power transmitters operating on 1474 kHz.

During the latter part of 1945, the question of operating some of these low-power Third Programme transmitters without staff on site was being pursued; the first stations selected for this treatment were those at Newcastle, Leeds, Glasgow and Edinburgh. These stations were to be remotely switched and monitored from the nearby studio premises, where staff were available to deal with major faults. It was decided to use existing transmitters installed in the studio premises at Newcastle, Leeds and Glasgow while sites were being found for permanent unattended transmitters. At Edinburgh, a manned mobile transmitter was used temporarily. The Third Programme was scheduled to start on 5 May 1946, using Droitwich (150 kW) on 583 kHz and fifteen low-power transmitters on 1474 kHz. Owing to delays in obtaining agreement to the use of 583 kHz, the start of the programme was deferred until 29 September 1946. Early in that month, a disturbing event occurred: the USSR announced that the frequency of 583 kHz was about to be used by a high-power station in Latvia. It was decided that if severe night-time interference from the Latvian station reduced the effective coverage of Droitwich to a thirty-mile radius, thus reaching only Birmingham and a small part of the Midland Region, its nominal power would be reduced and additional ex-Group H stations would be brought into service on 1474 kHz at Sheffield, Moorside Edge, Manchester, Liverpool, Bristol and Cardiff to be followed by others at Doncaster, Gillingham, Leicester, Nottingham, Aberdare, Stoke-on-Trent and Swansea. The coverage of the Greater London area was to be provided by a 5-kW or 7½-kW transmitter to be installed at the Royal Military Academy at Woolwich, but this proposal was abandoned in favour of a 2 kW transmitter at Nightingale Square operating on 1474 kHz.

On 15 September 1946 only a fortnight before the scheduled starting date for the Third Programme, the Latvian station started radiating. It was decided to bring some, but not all, of the projected low-power stations into service as shown on p. 328, to reduce the power of Droitwich on 583 kHz to 40 kW, and to steer the Droitwich carrier frequency as nearly as possible to that of the Latvian station, which appeared to have good short-term carrier frequency stability, although the accuracy was poor. A variable-frequency drive of the latest BBC design – type VFO/4 – was installed at Droitwich, together with a high-stability crystal oscillator operating on precisely 583 kHz. A direct-reading frequency meter was provided and the required offset, as determined at Tatsfield, was then obtained by manual adjustment at Droitwich. Strenuous efforts were made to find means of improving the coverage particularly in the London area. None of the alternative schemes was adopted, but the frequency difference between Droitwich and the Latvian station was kept as small as possible, although large variations in the Latvian frequency during the closing months of 1946 made this difficult. The problem finally disappeared when, in June 1947 the interference ceased and Droitwich reverted to normal operation (150 kW on 583 kHz). The Third Programme then reached between 60 and 70 per cent of the population on medium waves at night.

THIRD PROGRAMME TRANSMITTERS FROM 29 SEPTEMBER 1946

Station	Frequency (kHz)	Power (kW)	
Droitwich	583	40	Increased to 150 kW June 1947
Belfast	1474	0·1	Increased to 0·25 kW on 20.5.48
Bournemouth	1474	0·25	
Brighton	1474	0·1	Increased to 1 kW from new site from 21.11.48
Bristol	1474	0·1	Closed down 14.3.50
Cardiff	1474	1	Closed down 14.3.53
Dundee	1474	0·25	
Edinburgh	1474	0·25	Mobile. Replaced by 2 kW from new site 10.3.48
Fareham	1474	1	
Glasgow	1474	1	Replaced by 2 kW from new site 12.12.49
Hull	1474	0·25	Closed down 14.3.53
Leeds	1474	1	Replaced by 1 kW from new site 1.12.47
Liverpool	1474	0·25	Transferred to new site 23.12.49
Manchester	1474	1	Closed down 1.9.51
Middlesbrough	1474	0·25	Transferred to Stockton 2.7.48
Moorside Edge	1474	0·25	Closed down 18.11.47
Newcastle	1474	1	Replaced by 2 kW at Wrekenton 15.3.50
London (Nightingale Square)	1474	2	
Plymouth	1474	1	
Preston	1474	0·25	Replaced by 1 kW in new building 15.7.48
Sheffield	1474	0·1	Replaced by 1 kW at new site 6.6.50
Redmoss	1474	2	

A difficulty arose as soon as the London 2 kW transmitter started transmitting from Nightingale Square. There was an immediate storm of complaint from Post Office telephone subscribers in the neighbourhood, whose conversations were accompanied by a strong background of the programme. The local Post Office engineers installed suppressors, which cleared the trouble.

With so many problems arising at this time it was a cruel stroke of fate that during the severe winter in the early part of 1947 the overloading of the CEGB plant led to a request to the BBC to restrict its power intake from the public electricity supply. The first victim among the Radio Services was the Third Programme which was closed down completely from 10 February 1947 until 26 February 1947. The Home and Light Programmes suffered less, but were closed down at 2300 hours daily. During this severe weather, the Moorside Edge station suffered damage to its Home and Light Programme aerial systems and these services had to be transferred to a station on an adjacent site that had formerly been used for the ABSIE programme. The patience of the engineers at Moorside Edge was further taxed when the electricity supply feeder to the station failed and the transmitters had to be powered continuously from the stand-by diesel generators. Fuel tankers could not reach the station and, by the time fuel reserves had fallen to a few days' supply, it was necessary to man-handle fuel oil in drums from the nearest accessible road in atrocious weather conditions. The station staff rose to the occasion and no programme time was lost during this emergency.

The first unattended dual-transmitter station was opened at Farnley, four miles south-west of Leeds, on 1 December 1947, carrying the Third Programme. The design adopted at this and a number of other stations was based on the use of duplicate 1-kW or 2-kW transmitters, remotely controlled from a nearby studio centre. A calibrated receiver was installed at the studio centre to check the power radiated by the transmitter, the quality of the radiated programme and the depth of modulation. Alarms were provided to indicate failure of the mains supply or of the temperature of the oven containing the crystal-controlled oscillator. Two programme lines were provided between the studio centre and the transmitting station and one line for communication. The second programme line was normally used for sending the programme, as radiated, back to the studio centre for comparison with the programme sent to the transmitter. A dc signalling system, superimposed on the programme lines, was used for the remote control of the transmitters and for operating the alarms. It was intended that the remote-control and monitoring arrangements should be capable of operating over distances up to ten miles. As this was the first exercise in remote control, the design naturally erred on the side of caution and some redundant features were omitted in later developments.[19]

Other remotely controlled low-power transmitters were commissioned at Edinburgh, Glasgow and Newcastle on 10 March 1948, 12 December 1949 and 15 March 1950 respectively. A new site was found near Shoreham-by-Sea, Sussex, to provide coverage of Brighton, Hove and Worthing, replacing the inefficient ex-Group 'H' transmitter in Brighton. At the new station, a manned 1-kW Western Electric Doherty-type transmitter went into service on 21 November 1948. This transmitter was replaced in October 1949 by a prototype multi-unit transmitter manufactured by Wayne Kerr Laboratories in conjunction with the Planning & Installation Department. The concept of a multi-unit transmitter arose out of the desire to reduce the amount of idle installed plant, and thus the size and cost of the transmitter build-building, without any sacrifice of reliability. It was known at this time that for navigational systems the Decca Company employed transmitters consisting of ten separate unmodulated rf amplifiers with their outputs in parallel. Wayne Kerr Laboratories produced a broadcasting transmitter based on this idea and embodying ten 150-W units, each consisting of a power supply, a modulator and a modulated amplifier. These units were mounted in a single framework and driven from duplicated rf and af sources. They were connected to a common output circuit and it was arranged that a faulty unit would be disconnected automatically from the output circuit without disturbing the performance of the remaining units. Up to five units could be disconnected before the transmitter shut down completely.[20] In practice these low-power units were found to be too small to permit the use of orthodox methods of transmitter design and the ten-unit scheme was abandoned. Experience with the prototype had indicated that the choice of transmitter arrangement lay between two or three units in parallel and a larger unit with a similar one as a stand-by.[21] It was decided to adopt the former arrangement using bridged-T output combining networks which permitted each transmitter unit to have its own automatic monitoring devices. It was found that three units represented the best compromise between reliability and complexity for a 2-kW output. A multi-unit transmitter of this type was developed by the Marconi Company, initially for the BBC.[22]

The work of preventive maintenance and fault clearance on the first of the unattended stations was done by engineers at nearby studio centres, as it was thought that it could be fitted in with their other duties. It was found, however, that an improvement in the breakdown record of these stations could be achieved by using staff specialising in work of this kind. In January 1951 two teams – each consisting of two engineers – were formed, one based at the Stagshaw transmitting station near Hexham, Northumberland, and responsible for the Glasgow, Edinburgh and Newcastle transmitters and the other based at Moorside Edge, near Huddersfield, and responsible for the transmitters at Leeds and, later, Wrexham. Each team was provided with an estate car and, when the number of unattended stations increased, a third team was based at the Bartley station near Southampton to be responsible for stations in the South of England and in South Wales. Each team carried test instruments and tools, and also a simple field-strength meter to make checks at points where Research Department had already made accurate field-strength measurements. Thus, during routine journeys, a watch was kept on the radiation performance of stations, so as to relieve Research Department of this task.[21] At the base stations, equipment was provided to enable faulty units brought back from unattended stations to be examined and power-tested if necessary. Each unattended station was visited at intervals of four to six weeks or when a major fault developed, which the resident technician could not clear without assistance. These resident technicians, or 'Technical Assistants in Attendance', were engaged on full-time contracts, but were required to visit the local transmitter only for an hour each day, five days a week. At other times they were expected to keep a general watch at home on the output of their stations during transmission hours, using a receiver specially modified to sound an alarm if the local transmitter failed. Each station was also provided with a telephone indicator panel to give a coded reply when the station number was dialled or when a call was connected by a telephone operator. The code indicated various normal and abnormal operating conditions and an informed caller could then decide what action to take.[21] The Post Office was most helpful in making provision for the fact that there was normally nobody at the called station to answer an operator.

Many of the resident technicians were retired members of Engineering Division staff and, in return for a technically interesting job and some addition to their pensions, they performed a useful service at a time when the development of unattended transmitter operation was going through its initial phase.

The increasing use of unattended stations necessitated the development of automatic monitoring equipment for checking their performance and that of the lines feeding them. Equipment was provided to detect a break in the carrier, but for stations serving large communities something more sophisticated was required that would either sound an alarm at a main station or switch in reserve equipment if the quality of the output fell below the required standard. Ideally, the monitoring equipment had to respond to the same defects as would attract the attention of a human observer. In some ways the problem was more difficult than the corresponding one in television. The television waveform could incorporate special test signals in the intervals between active lines, whereas the sound signal was continuous. Also, because the ear is tolerant of small differences in the time of arrival of the components comprising a sound, the signal arriving at the end of a long line could be very different from the signal applied to the input, even if no audible distortion were present. The solution adopted was to compare the signals at two points in the chain after they had been processed in such a way that any substantial difference between the two processed signals would indicate a serious fault. This could be done in two ways: if the outgoing and incoming signals were both available at the same point, the processing and comparison could be done at that point, but if only one of the two signals was available, the corresponding processed version had to be transmitted over a line to a point where the other signal was present.

The design of automatic monitoring equipment in the BBC was started in 1947 and the first equipment of this kind to be used in broadcasting was produced by H. B. Rantzen, F. A. Peachey, and C. Gunn-Russell of the Designs Department.[20, 23, 24]

The original comparison monitor (the Automatic Monitor Minor) was suitable for use over local equipment or short lines. It gave an alarm if the weighted signal-to-noise ratio was less than 40 dB or if there was a significant change in programme level. To avoid unnecessary alarms caused by momentary clicks, an 'integration alarm panel' was used that would respond only to a continuous fault or a succession of momentary faults. The Automatic Monitor Major was developed for use over long links. The processed signal was transmitted on a carrier at 7 or 8 kHz superimposed on the programme link being monitored. These monitors made it possible to release staff from the unrewarding task of continuously monitoring programmes, so as to free them for more active work.

It was decided in August 1945, as part of the final scheme of transmitter distribution, to place orders for two high-power transmitters of modern design to replace the old Regional transmitters at Westerglen and Washford, carrying the Scottish and Welsh Home Service respectively. The Westerglen transmitter took the Scottish Home Service on 767 kHz from 10 December 1949, and the new transmitter at Washford came into service on 15 March 1950 using the Copenhagen Plan frequency of 881 kHz. The new high-power transmitters were supplied by STC. Each consisted of two separate 100-kW units. High-power Class B modulation was used and the eht supply was derived from English Electric Company pumpless mercury-arc rectifiers. A departure from traditional BBC practice was that, to simplify staffing, the switching of the transmitters was done in the adjacent control room, or at the transmitter units themselves, rather than at a transmitter control desk installed in the transmitter hall.

A new site was acquired at Postwick, five miles east of Norwich, for a new medium-power medium-wave transmitter to improve the Midland Home Service in that part of East Anglia. The Postwick station went into service on 1013 kHz on 19 June 1949.

In June 1947 a problem arose in carrying out maintenance work on the mast radiators at Burghead, Lisnagarvey and Stagshaw; this had not been possible since the masts were erected in 1936–7 because no alternative aerial system was available at these stations. It was decided to purchase two 300-ft stayed masts and to erect one of them on leased land adjacent to each station while the maintenance work was in progress. A simple earth system was ploughed in and a small prefabricated aerial tuning hut was provided. A six-wire transmission line was erected to feed the temporary mast radiator and the output power of the transmitter was reduced to 50 kW to suit the stay insulators of the temporary masts. These structures were not designed to withstand severe weather conditions and their use was restricted to the summer months. These two temporary masts were used successfully during maintenance work at the three stations mentioned and at other stations from time to time.

Also in June 1947 it was decided to install limiting amplifiers at all transmitters of output power greater than 10 kW to permit a higher mean level of modulation to be used, so as to combat the increasing interference from foreign stations on the medium-wave channels and to improve the signal-to-noise ratio on the long-wave channel. The simplest form of limiter merely clips off the peaks of the modulation and thus introduces severe distortion. The limiting amplifiers designed by the BBC, type LIM/1 and LIM/2, were more sophisticated: they were variable-gain amplifiers, which limited the maximum level of modulation to slightly less than 100 per cent by automatically varying the gain according to the peak level of the programmes. The gain was reduced rapidly, but restored slowly. The limiting amplifiers therefore acted, over a part of the working range, as volume compressors. When set to give '0 dB compression', the limiter operated only on occasional peaks to prevent over-modulation; if it was set to give '6 dB compression', it operated frequently and permitted the line-up level to be increased to that corresponding to 80 per cent rather than 40 per cent modulation.

In the decade 1945–55 the design of high-power transmitters was aimed at improving their overall efficiency and particular attention was given to the modulation equipment. Before the war, experimental work had been carried out by Research Department on the Chireix, Doherty and other high-efficiency modulation systems. The object was to improve the power-conversion efficiency of transmitters, while avoiding the use of large and costly components. In the classical 'high-power Class B' modulation system the average anode current of the modulator varied with the depth of modulation, so that the average power consumed was less than the peak power. But this system needed a large af transformer, a large choke and a large capacitor. Various suggestions were made to overcome this problem. In the Fortescue system,[25] there were two banks of valves in the final amplifier, one carrying unmodulated rf and the other giving an rf output proportional to the modulation and working in Class B. The two outputs were combined in an impedance-inverting network. In the

332

Chireix system,[26] the modulated rf was applied to the grids of two banks of valves operating in push-pull, while lightly modulated rf was applied to the grids in parallel, so as to produce two phase-modulated outputs that could be combined to produce an amplitude-modulated output.

In the Doherty system,[27] there were two banks of valves in the final stage both carrying modulated rf, but so arranged that one bank limited severely during one half of the modulation cycle, while the other made up the deficiency. This system was used in the low-power (1 kW) Western Electric transmitters installed at Brighton and at Fareham for the Third Programme. The system was also used in the high-power (50 kW) transmitters designed in the late 1960s by the BBC Transmitter Department for semi-attended operation at Start Point and other stations. The Chireix system was used in some high-power stations abroad, but not in the BBC.

On 10 April 1947 a new method came on the scene, when a full-scale trial was mounted at Brookmans Park by the Marconi Company of their 'ampliphase' system. Its object was to permit a high-efficiency transmitter to be designed without a costly and bulky modulator chain. It was based on the use of phase modulation within the transmitter, although the output was amplitude-modulated. Two separate chains of rf amplifiers operating in Class C were used, their outputs being combined with a phase difference of about 150° between them, so that the input to the load was the vector difference of the outputs of the two chains. The rf excitation for the two chains was derived from a single source through a phase-splitting circuit, and the excitation voltages were phase-modulated by the audio-frequency input; the resultant of the two phase-modulated carriers was thus modulated in amplitude. The system was capable of giving an efficiency corresponding to that of Class C amplification throughout the modulation cycle and, with suitably designed output coupling circuits and proper adjustments, the distortion at the output was relatively low.

There were some initial difficulties in applying the new technique at Brookmans Park, partly because the eht generators were not designed to cope with the load presented by the transmitter, which varied with the modulation. Eventually a production model of a 60-kW medium-wave 'ampliphase' transmitter was completed and this was used by the BBC for an extended field trial at Daventry carrying the Third Programme on 647 kHz from the date of the implementation of the Copenhagen Plan (15 March 1950) until the high-power Third Programme transmitter took over the service at Daventry on 8 April 1951. During the field trial the ampliphase transmitter gave satisfactory operational results and it was remarkably small for the output power obtained. After a short period as a stand-by for the high-power transmitter, the ampliphase transmitter was removed from Daventry and the BBC did not require any new high-power transmitters until some years later; the system was, however, widely used elsewhere.

The assignment of long and medium wavelengths in the European Broadcasting Area was undertaken by the Montreux Conference held in April 1939, which followed the ITU Radio Conference held in Cairo in 1938. The Montreux Plan was to be implemented on 4 March 1940, but the war intervened and its introduction was postponed 'until circumstances permitted'.[28] Throughout the war years most of the broadcasting authorities in Europe continued to operate in broad accordance with the Lucerne Plan of 1933. In the post-war period, broadcasting was becoming an increasingly important element in the life of most European peoples and many new transmitters were brought into service. The ensuing congestion was made worse by the fact that many of the new transmitters were of high power as a result of technical developments that had occurred during the war. A new wavelength plan for Europe was therefore essential and a conference was held in Copenhagen in 1948, which produced a new plan, for implementation on 15 March 1950. In this plan, the BBC was allocated one long-wave channel (200 kHz) and eleven medium-wave channels, together with the use of two international common frequencies (only one of which was taken up immediately) for its radio services. The work of preparing transmitters for the changes in wavelength was carried out on all existing transmitters by staff of the Transmitter Department with practical experience of rf bridging techniques. The cost of components for the wave-changes was fortunately not excessive as a considerable stock of capacitors and inductors had been accumulated during the war to cope with the many frequency changes that were then required. A special problem arose at Lisnagarvey where, under the Copenhagen Plan, the two transmitters were to have a carrier frequency separation of only 5 per cent with an output power ratio of 10:1. The Planning & Installation Department prepared all new transmitters for the change and were responsible for converting the high-power medium-wave transmitter at Droitwich (400 kW) for operation on 200 kHz carrying the Light Programme.

Under the Copenhagen Plan, the BBC was required to operate eleven groups of synchronised transmitters in the radio services and the transmitter drive equipment evolved during the war, types CP 17E and CP 17B, was employed extensively. To meet the complex requirements of 'pre-Copenhagen' and 'post Copenhagen' channels, a new design of crystal drive was developed (type COU–4), which has continued to be used for medium-wave transmitters up to the present time. It is of interest to note that the tuning fork drive equipment used in the mid- and late-1930s occupied four apparatus racks 9 ft high and in 1937 each set of equipment cost about £3000. The Type COU–4 drive equipment occupied only 4½ in. of rack space and, in 1960, cost only £150. Its frequency stability and accuracy were some fifty times better than those of the early tuning-fork equipment.[29, 30]

In 1945, as mentioned in the previous chapter, an improved method of checking carrier frequencies had been developed; it avoided the need for a tone at a different frequency for each synchronised group of transmitters by using a single reference tone at 1 kHz for all transmitters having carrier frequencies that were an exact number of kilohertz. At first this reference tone was generated in Broadcasting House, which was a convenient point for inserting the tone into the SB network outside programme hours, but in 1946 a further development enabled any station within the range of the Droitwich long-wave transmitter to receive it on a tuned radio-frequency receiver and, after the modulation had been removed, to drive a frequency-divider chain to produce a 1-kHz reference tone from the carrier frequency of 200 kHz. Increasing use was made of the Droitwich 200-kHz transmission for

STATIONS COMMISSIONED TO IMPROVE MEDIUM-WAVE COVERAGE: 1946–54

Station	Programme	Frequency (kHz)	Service Date
Hastings	West of England Home	1457	16.9.51
Brighton*	West of England Home	1457	16.9.51
Ramsgate	Basic Home	1484	16.9.51
Barrow	Northern Home	1484	7.10.51
Scarborough	N.E./N. Ireland Home	1151	11.11.51
Londonderry	N.E./N. Ireland Home	1151	11.11.51
Folkestone*	West of England Home	1457	23.12.51
Barnstaple*	West of England Home	1457	9.3.52
Towyn*	Welsh Home	881	14.2.53
Dumfries*	Scottish Home	809	24.2.53
Redruth	West of England Home	1457	18.10.53
Bexhill*	West of England Home	1457	8.11.53 (replaced Hastings)
Cromer*	Northern Home	692	26.12.53
Swansea	Third	1546	19.12.54
Whitehaven	Northern Home	692	7.10.51
Wrexham	Welsh Home	804	17.2.46
Plymouth	Light	1149	17.2.46
Newcastle	Light	1214	15.3.50
Exeter	Third	1474	26.2.47

* New station.

frequency standardisation, not only by the BBC but also by industry and broadcasting authorities overseas and this led to special attention being given to the maintenance of the frequency within close limits. By 1955 the long-term stability and accuracy of the drive had been improved to the point where the frequency was kept within $\pm 1/10^8$ of the nominal value. Later the accuracy of the frequency was increased by two orders of magnitude.

Although the Copenhagen Plan was at first fairly successful a great deal of interference soon developed mainly because the Plan was not adhered to by all the countries concerned and was not even accepted by some of them, including the occupying powers in Germany. In an attempt to improve reception of BBC programmes at night it was decided to use additional low-power stations for the Home Service and the Light and Third Programmes to reinforce the coverage in the fringe areas. Between September 1951 and the end of 1954 nineteen new or existing stations were brought into the networks, as shown above. Wherever possible, use was made of the automatic monitoring and control techniques mentioned earlier in this section; the stations were staffed initially by Technical Assistants in Attendance, but later became fully unattended.

The most important station to be planned for unattended operation was the high-power Third Programme transmitter at Daventry, which embodied a number of new features. It was installed in the original 5XX building at Daventry and was required to radiate the maximum power permitted under the Copenhagen Plan on 647 kHz, 150 kW. It was to operate with minimum attention by staff, who were normally engaged on other duties at the short-wave station some 150 m away. To ensure reliability under these conditions, it was decided to operate two transmitters in parallel and to provide air cooling for the large valves, ac heating for their filaments and an eht supply derived from an arc rectifier of new design. Since the transmitters had a high output power, the circuit employed to combine their outputs included automatically-controlled rf contactors so that in the event of a fault in one transmitter unit the combining circuit could be by-passed and the full power of the remaining transmitter unit would be applied to the aerial feeder. Earlier designs of high-power transmitters used much ancillary equipment, which itself needed a considerable amount of attention by staff; transmitters with water-cooled valves needed crypts, cooling ponds, and areas for pumps and pipework, which added substantially to the cost. In the new Daventry transmitter it was decided to use Class B modulation at high level as this system was thought to be the best for unattended operation and its performance was equal to that of other systems at that time. The large valves were cooled by air at low pressure circulated by a large industrial-type blower. The eht supply was derived from six type AR 61 Excitrons; these were glass-enclosed, mercury-pool, grid-controlled, half-wave rectifiers and were reliable and easy to replace. Air-cooled triodes for the modulator and rf stages were developed, with thoriated tungsten filaments suitable for ac heating. The overall efficiency of the transmitter was about 45 per cent. The installation was designed and manufactured by the Marconi Company and the BBC provided the automatic monitoring and switching arrangements and the duplicated rf drive equipment, with provision for automatic change-over.[22]

To achieve as large a service area as possible, using 150 kW on 647 kHz, it was decided to erect an anti-fading aerial, which had to be at a remote location so that its radiation characteristics would not be impaired by the presence of the many masts in use for short-wave services on the Daventry site. The mast radiator was erected at Dodford, about $1\frac{1}{2}$ miles from the Daventry station at Borough Hill. The Dodford site was as flat an area as could be found within a reasonable distance of Daventry. A conventional type of mast radiator was designed with a height of 732 ft ($0\cdot48\lambda$), but provision was made for double-feeding. A break insulator was inserted at a height of 470 ft ($0\cdot31\lambda$) and a capacity top increased the effective height by 56 ft to $0\cdot52\lambda$. Two aerial-coupling networks installed in a building at the base of the mast provided either double-feeding or base-feeding as required. During the design stages, extensive work was carried out by Research Department using small-scale model aerials working on a frequency of 400 MHz.[31] The object of feeding the mast radiator at two points was to concentrate the radiation at low angles so as to reduce the sky-wave and increase the ground-wave, and thus increase the primary service area. In practice, the improvement was found not to justify the complication in the feeding arrangement, because the night-time service area was limited more severely by interference from other stations than by the range at which the sky-wave interfered with the ground-wave (i.e. the non-fading range). The presence of a break insulator in the mast structure threatened the security of the mast because failure could lead to its collapse. (In 1955 it was decided to remove the break insulator and connect the two parts of the mast together so that it could be used as a conventional base-fed mast radiator.)

The transmission line from Borough Hill to Dodford was about 2400 m long and consisted of a 12-wire unbalanced open-wire line having 8 outer and 4 inner conductors. The line was supported on poles 5·5 m high, spaced at intervals of 46 m. The power loss introduced by the transmission line was about 0·35 dB, i.e. about 12 kW. Control and monitoring circuits were provided in a multi-core cable carried by a catenary along the route of the transmission line.

The Daventry 150-kW Third Programme transmitter was fully staffed during the running-in period from 8 April 1951 to 13 January 1952, after which it was operated by remote control and was treated as an unattended station.

The serious interference on medium waves after dark was the main factor leading to the rapid development of sound broadcasting on VHF in the immediate post-war years. In West Germany the lack of adequate medium-wave assignments accentuated the need for this development. The BBC decided just before the end of the war to carry out field trials to ascertain the propagation characteristics of the VHF band; VHF/FM transmissions had taken place in the USA before the war in the 40–50MHz band, but little information was available on which to base plans for broadcasting at frequencies in this part of the spectrum.

It was thought that the VHF band would be much less susceptible to interference from other stations than the LF and MF bands (not only because the VHF band was less congested, but also because long-distance propagation at VHF is normally weak). It would also be more resistant to most forms of electrical interference. Furthermore, the use of frequency-modulation (in which the instantaneous frequency of the carrier wave varies with the modulation) rather than amplitude modulation (in which the amplitude of the carrier varies with the modulation) was expected to give greater immunity from interference of all kinds. These expectations were borne out in practice.

The idea of frequency modulation was not new; it dated back to 1902. But its potentialities for broadcasting could not be realised until the exploitation of the frequency bands above 30 MHz permitted the radiation of a band-width considerably greater than the maximum audio-frequency to be transmitted.

The first of the BBC's field trials took place in the 45 MHz band; two 1-kW transmitters, built by Research Department, were installed at Alexandra Palace and Bagley Croft, near Oxford. One of these was later moved to the Moorside Edge transmitting station for propagation tests in hilly country. Special receivers were built to Research Department specifications and were used by a group of technical and non-technical observers. The next tests were aimed at comparing the relative merits of amplitude and frequency modulation. A VHF/FM transmitter at Alexandra Palace radiated the Home Service during the evenings on 46·3 MHz, while the television sound transmitter there radiated the same programme using amplitude modulation on 41·5 MHz. As there was a possibility that a higher frequency band might be allocated for sound broadcasting, two additional transmitters were built to operate in the 88–95 MHz band. In 1945 one of these was installed at Alexandra Palace for field trials in the London area and the other was sent to Bagley Croft for more detailed tests before being sent to Moorside Edge.

Propagation tests in both frequency bands were made using horizontal and vertical polarisation; the nature and extent of fading were observed at various distances from the transmitter, and the signal-to-noise ratio was measured in the various reception conditions. The results were compared using (*a*) amplitude modulation, (*b*) amplitude modulation with a limiter in the receiver, and (*c*) frequency modulation. It was concluded that the use of the VHF band would relieve the increasing congestion on medium waves; that the use of VHF/FM would extend the area of high-quality reception; that a reasonable number of VHF stations could provide national coverage of the United Kingdom; and that the cost of VHF/FM receivers would not be excessive when production increased to the expected level. It was recommended that the technical parameters should be as follows: maximum frequency deviation 75 kHz; pre-emphasis 50μs; carrier frequency spacing 200 kHz (400 kHz for stations serving the same geographical area).[32]

The results of the early field tests by Research Department were so promising, in spite of the low power used, that it was decided to build a high-power station capable of carrying out full-scale tests; it was to have two transmitters of 20-kW output power using a slotted cylindrical aerial system which increased the effective radiated power to 120 kW for each transmission. The outputs from the two transmitters were passed to a combining filter and the combined output radiated from a common aerial; this aerial was in two halves, each with its own feeder, so that transmission could continue on half the aerial if the other half or its feeder failed. Slot aerials of this type proved successful for use within the frequency range for which they were designed, although there have been isolated difficulties at exposed sites caused by sleet covering the slots. Slot aerials have also been used for television transmission.[33,34]

A site was acquired near Wrotham, Kent, early in 1949 at a height of 220 m AMSL and the station was ready for the first test transmissions in May 1950. One of the transmitters used frequency modulation and transmitted on 91·4 MHz and the other used amplitude modulation and radiated on 93·5 MHz. The aerial system was mounted on a 150-m mast with its centre at 115 m above the ground.

Horizontal polarisation was found to be somewhat less susceptible to ignition interference and to distortion caused by multi-path propagation than vertical polarisation. It also eased the problem of designing high-gain transmitting aerials. Nearly all other countries decided to use horizontal polarisation, although there has recently been a move towards vertical or slant polarisation to provide improved reception on car radios and portable sets. Horizontal polarisation was therefore assumed in planning national coverage of the Home, Light and Third Programmes on VHF/FM.[35] The plan was submitted to the Government in 1951, but there were still national restrictions on capital expenditure and the project demanded substantial investment by the industry in developing and producing new equipment for the transmitting stations and new receivers for the public, as well as expenditure by the BBC in setting up the new network and by listeners in buying new receivers. The Government did not therefore authorise the scheme at once, but gave approval in principle to a start being made in 1953.

The results of the long series of trials using the high-power transmitters at Wrotham led the BBC to recommend that FM should be used for the VHF service. The Television Advisory Committee accepted this recommendation in December 1953, and on 10 February 1954 the Government decided accordingly. It is now generally accepted that the decision to use FM rather than AM was the right one and this system has been adopted for radio transmissions in Band II by broadcasting organisations all over the world. Nevertheless, there are still some who contend that AM would have been preferable because it requires much less bandwidth (a commodity now scarce, even in the VHF bands) for each transmitter, though a greater number of transmitters to give the same coverage.

In FM the amplitude of the carrier is constant and the intelligence is conveyed by variations in its frequency. The receiver incorporates a limiter, which makes it insensitive to changes in amplitude. Provided the received field strength is above a certain minimum value, the audio-frequency output is independent of it and fading merely causes a change in the level of interference and noise. The advantages of FM stemmed mainly from the fact that the modulated carrier could spread over a wide band; though this made it impracticable for use in the LF and MF bands, it was well suited to one of the VHF bands. Provided the signal was strong enough to operate the limiter, FM was about 25 dB less susceptible to receiver noise than AM and was also much less susceptible to interference from other stations and from electrical machinery and domestic appliances; it was also resistant to ignition interference, though this was not always entirely eliminated. FM transmitters were cheaper than AM, because the output stage had only to cope with the carrier amplitude, whereas in an AM transmitter the peak power is four times the carrier power. The improved signal-to-noise ratio with FM made it possible to transmit programmes with a greater dynamic range; this was important, since the VHF network was intended to give a high-quality service. FM also permitted the use of pre-emphasis in the transmission, and corresponding de-emphasis in the receiver, so as to permit relatively higher levels of modulation at the upper audio frequencies (this can also be done with AM, but the resulting noise suppression is greater with FM).[32]

Experience has shown that the use of FM in Band II permits a substantially higher grade of service than is normally available from LF and MF transmissions, with almost complete immunity from interference within the prescribed service areas of the stations (i.e. where the field strength exceeds 48 dB μ V/m). At VHF, multi-path propagation may occur as a result of reflections from hills or tall buildings, but this can usually be reduced by using a directional receiving aerial suitably oriented. (An incidental advantage of horizontal polarisation is that even a single dipole has some degree of directivity.)

In July 1954 the BBC was authorised to start work on the first of the new VHF stations and on 2 May 1955 the Wrotham station opened the first regular VHF/FM

x

PLAN FOR NATIONAL VHF COVERAGE (1954)

Station	Frequencies (MHz)			erp (kW)	Site Height (ft AMSL)	Aerial Height (ft AGL)
	Light	Third	Home			
Stage I						
Wrotham	89·1	91·3	93·5	120	720	406
Pontop Pike	88·5	90·7	92·9	60	1000	296
Divis	90·1	92·3	94·5	60	1200	262
Meldrum	88·7	90·9	93·1	60	800	290
Wenvoe	88·9	—	92·1 West 94·3 Welsh	120	420	647
Norwich	89·7	91·9	94·1	120	230	332
North Hessary Tor	88·1	90·3	92·5	60	1675	538
Sutton Coldfield	88·3	90·5	92·7	120	555	647
Holme Moss	89·3	91·5	93·7	120	1720	647
Blaen Plwyf	88·7	90·9	93·1	60	565	332
Stage II						
Rowridge	88·5	90·7	92·9	60	450	296
Kirk o'Shotts	89·9	92·1	94·3	120	910	647
Sandale	88·1	90·3	92·5 Scot. 94·7 North	120	1220	332
Anglesey	89·6	91·8	94·0	60	500	500
Corwen	—	—	94·9	1	1840	250
Rosemarkie	89·3	91·5	93·7	6	680	302
Stage III (tentative)						
Les Platons				2		
Dover				1		
Isle of Man				1		
S.W. Scotland (Ayr)				2		
Galashiels				5		
Londonderry				1		
Central Berks.				5		
Hayle (Cornwall)				2		
Brechin (E. Central Scotland)				1		
E. Lincs.				5		
Mendips				120		

transmission of the Home, Light and Third Programmes serving the London area and South-east England. The method of obtaining the frequency-modulated carrier at Wrotham was devised by W. S. Mortley of the Marconi Company and known as 'FMQ',[36] although the BBC's FM test transmitter had used a method devised by G. G. Gouriet of the Research Department.

The BBC's plan for VHF broadcasting of the domestic services was arranged in three stages and these are listed above. All the stations were to transmit the Home, Light and Third Programmes and most of them, apart from Wrotham, were to be on the same sites as television stations and to use the same masts. This co-siting policy permitted economies in capital cost and also facilitated maintenance and unattended operation. The development of the plan falls mainly into the next period, but the following VHF/FM stations were introduced into service before the end of 1955:

Wrotham	120 kW erp	Home, Light, Third	2 May 1955
Penmon	1 kW erp	Welsh Home Service	2 Oct. 1955
(temporary station)			
Pontop Pike	60 kW erp	Home, Light, Third	20 Dec. 1955

The design of towers and masts for transmitting stations became firmly established by 1951 and the results were presented to a Joint Engineering Conference in that year.[37] All BBC towers and masts were designed, constructed, and erected by specialist contractors (notably British Insulated Callender's Construction Co., Marconi's and J. L. Eve Construction Co., and in earlier days the Radio Communication Co., and C. F. Elwell.) to specifications of detailed requirements prepared by the BBC's Civil Engineer, M. T. Tudsbery and his staff. The specifications concentrated upon factors of safety and wind loads. The factors of safety followed normal civil engineering practice and the wind loads were based on extreme weather conditions that were known to have been experienced in this country. Wind pressures were taken to apply to 1·5 times the net projected area of lattice structures and to 0·6 times the projected area of circular tubular sections. Alternatively, masts were permitted to be designed so that at maximum stress the combined loads should be those resulting from a factor of safety of 2·5 applied to the elastic limit for tension. The maximum deflection was not permitted to exceed 1 per cent of the height. These design data have held the field for a quarter of a century.

The design of mast-radiators presented special problems because the structure must be insulated from earth by inserting insulators in the stays and also at the base of the mast itself. The foot of the mast terminated in a steel disc and the top of the base insulator carried a similar disc; a steel ball 3 in. in diameter was partially embedded in each disc to locate the mast precisely. The opposing faces of the two discs were machined to a slight curvature so as to permit the mast to deviate slightly from the vertical.[38] The base insulator was subjected to a compressive load equivalent to the weight of the steelwork plus the vertical component of the tension in all the stays; the total load for a 700-ft mast could amount to more than 200 tons.

A broadcasting system does not end at the transmitting aerial: the costliest part of the system is in the homes of listeners and the most intractable part lies between the transmitting aerial and the receiving aerial. It is therefore appropriate here to mention trends in the design of receivers and some of the problems of reception.

The first post-war Radio Exhibition in 1947 illustrated the improvement in the design and manufacture of receivers that had taken place and the reduction in size that had resulted from 'miniaturisation'. There was increasing interest in refinements of design that were introduced to satisfy enthusiasts for 'hi-fi' (high-fidelity).[39] There was also a substantial growth in the number of homes equipped for radio reception: the number of licences increased from 9·71 million in 1945 to 13·98 million in 1955.

In 1950 33⅓-rpm records made their appearance on the domestic market under the name 'LP' (long-playing) and tape recorders for home use started to become popular in 1951. By 1954 printed circuits were widely used in receivers and ferrite rod aerials for portable sets. By the end of 1955 transistors had replaced valves in the audio-frequency stages of receivers and were beginning to be used also in the rf and if stages.

The trend towards smaller and lighter sets led to a marked increase in the use of portable receivers; there was less interest in large console receivers and radio-gramophones and consequently in the use of outside aerials. The BBC network of medium-wave transmitters had been planned on the assumption that efficient out-door aerials would be used – sensitive to broadcast signals, but beyond strong inter-fering fields produced by domestic appliances and wiring. Such aerials could be pro-vided with screened down-leads, and a simple vertical aerial could then be reasonably effective in discriminating against electrical interference.

Car radios began to become popular soon after the war, and the number of licences for them increased from 95,456 in 1951 (when the car radio licence was introduced) to 267,794 in 1955.

The increasing popularity of portable sets and the expectation of the public that they would work in any conditions accentuated the problem of dealing with electrical interference and was one of the reasons leading to the use of increased transmitter power by many stations in Europe. This in turn led to increased interference after dark and seriously restricted the effective night-time service areas of BBC medium-wave stations.

The VHF/FM network, starting with the opening of the station at Wrotham in 1955, offered a means of escape from this problem, since reception in Band II was almost immune from interference from foreign stations and also to interference from electrical apparatus, except the ignition systems of motor vehicles. VHF/FM re-ceivers differed from those used for reception in the LF, MF and HF bands, in that they had to cover a higher range of carrier frequencies (between 88·5 and 100 MHz), and they incorporated some additional components: a limiter, a discriminator to recover the modulation from the FM signal, and a de-emphasis circuit. It was important that the combination of limiter and discriminator should suppress any amplitude modulation that might be produced by distortion in the earlier stages of the receiver, or by interference or multi-path propagation, and could result in distor-tion and interference in the output. It was evident that if receivers were placed on the market that did not include adequate AM suppression, the high quality inherent in the VHF/FM transmission would not be available to listeners. The BBC encour-aged the receiver industry to pay attention to this point. Most modern VHF/FM receivers employ a type of discriminator called a 'ratio detector', which itself pro-vides a certain degree of AM suppression, but requires a limiter to give satisfactory results. The de-emphasis circuit was required to reduce the response at the higher audio frequencies, so as to compensate for the pre-emphasis introduced in the transmitter and thus to reduce the effect of noise in the upper part of the audio spectrum.

In order to take full advantage of the virtues of the FM system, listeners were advised to use high-performance receivers and also, in general, to use outdoor aerials, though in many places good results could be obtained with portable sets using telescopic aerials. According to the field strength available at the receiving site, an outside aerial could be either a single horizontal dipole, with a screened feeder, or a multi-element array giving a substantial gain in the direction of the wanted signal and minimum sensitivity in other directions. With portable sets, standing-wave patterns within a building might make it necessary to choose with care the position of the receiver in the room.

Despite the advantages offered by the VHF/FM transmissions, the public was slow to acquire VHF receivers and the proportion of listeners able to receive the VHF/FM transmissions was still only about 30 per cent after the service had been operating for ten years. This was no doubt because a high proportion of the population was concentrated in areas that were still reasonably well served on long and medium waves and because of the increasing popularity of small portable sets and car receivers; at first few of these were equipped for VHF and then only at substantially higher cost. However, in recent years, inexpensive portable VHF receivers have become available.

The problem of interference caused by electrical machinery and domestic appliances was tackled during this period, both on national and international levels. A great deal of work had been done by the industry and others before the war, and was continued during this period, on the design of suppressors to reduce interference in the frequency bands allocated to sound broadcasting, and later also in those allocated to television. One of the problems was to make the suppressor small enough for incorporation within the housing of small appliances, such as electric drills, containing commutator motors. This problem caused a great deal of difficulty in the early stages, but has since been largely solved by the use of miniature components.

In practice the degree of suppression that can be used depends not only on the cost of suppressors in relation to the selling price of the appliance and on the practicability of incorporating the suppressor in it, but also on the overriding requirement that the suppressor must not detract from the safety of the appliance in normal use. The assessment of the effect of limits could be done only on a statistical basis and in relation to the minimum field strength of the broadcast signal that could be regarded as providing a satisfactory service in the absence of interference – i.e. the field strength to be protected. Moreover, it is not usually practicable to test every appliance that is manufactured, but only a random sample. The limits that were adopted in many countries, either for voluntary or for statutory application, were intended to be such that when a type has been approved at least 80 per cent of the appliances of that type will comply with the limit with at least 80 per cent confidence.

At the start of the studies on the design of suppressors a great deal of attention had been given to interference produced by power lines and by relatively heavy electrical equipment such as lifts, trolley buses, and mercury-arc rectifiers. Domestic appliances such as vacuum cleaners, fans and refrigerators also came under scrutiny and, with the start of television, interference from the ignition systems of vehicles also had to be dealt with.[40] The results of these studies were incorporated in the pre-war series of British Standards mentioned in Chapter III Section 2. After the war other specifications followed and general guidance was given in British Standard Code of Practice CP 1006:1955. At first the application of the limits and methods specified in the British Standards was entirely voluntary. But it was soon felt, in this and other countries, that legal sanctions would have to be applied to the suppression of interference from some of the worst sources, if only to protect manufacturers who observed the requirements voluntarily from unfair competition by others who did not.

The Wireless Telegraphy Act of 1949 empowered the Postmaster General to make regulations for the control of interference and there followed a series of Statutory Instruments dealing with Ignition Apparatus (1952), Electric Motors (1955), Refrigerators (1955), and Electro-medical Equipment (1963). In some cases, the regulations applied to manufacturers, in others to users, and sometimes to both. They prescribed penalties for those who persisted in contravening the regulations after having received a warning in statutory form. In fact, no prosecution under any of these regulations has been brought, up to the time of writing, but they have nevertheless had a substantial effect in reducing interference, and in making manufacturers and users aware of the problem. The number of complaints dealt with by the Post Office fell by 28 per cent between 1960 and 1969, although the number of receivers and the number of electrical appliances in use had substantially increased during that period. One reason for the decrease was no doubt that, almost everybody being by then a listener and a viewer, it was in his own interest not to use unsuppressed appliances, which would interfere with his own reception as well as his neighbours'.

It was also necessary to deal with interference produced by the oscillators of super-heterodyne receivers, both radio and television. In the earliest radio receivers of this kind, the intermediate frequency had been in the region of 100 to 160 kHz, and the frequency of the local oscillator might be within the MF broadcasting band. In the 1930s a higher intermediate frequency, between 450 and 490 kHz, had gradually come into general use, but interference could still be caused by harmonics of the oscillator frequency. Recommendations for the permissible level of interference of this kind and also on the measures to be taken to reduce the susceptibility of receivers to electrical interference were given in BS 905 first published in 1940 and subsequently revised.[41]

The Post Office had always been responsible for locating sources of interference, for determining whether any relevant regulations had been complied with, and for persuading the users to take the necessary steps to reduce the interference. With the setting up of the Ministry of Posts & Telecommunications, and the establishment of the Post Office as a public corporation in 1969, the Ministry acts as the regulatory body and is also responsible for development work on measuring equipment and suppressors, while the Post Office investigates complaints on behalf of the Ministry. Such complaints are often received by the BBC's Engineering Division, which directs them to the Post Office, and also scrutinises the trend of the statistics in relation to the coverage of BBC stations. The Engineering Information Department also advises listeners and viewers on the use of efficient receivers and aerials to minimise the effect of interference.[42]

It was also necessary to deal with the problem of electrical interference at the international level, to facilitate the exchange of information, and to unify the standards adopted in different countries so as to facilitate the export and import of electrical appliances. This was the function of the CISPR (already mentioned in Chapter III Section 2), which was reconstituted as a committee of the IEC, but with other international organisations participating and with power to issue its own recommendations. With the dissolution of the UIR and the formation in 1950 of the EBU, the latter took part in the work of the CISPR. The broadcasters have continued to complain that manufacturing interests are given too much weight,[43] although it is arguable that it is more important for manufacturers to agree on limits that they can accept as economically practicable (even if the universal application of those limits would not abolish interference completely) than that limits considered satisfactory by the broadcasters should be set down on paper without any real hope that manufacturers would, or could, comply with them. These opposing views have confronted each other from 1933 until the present day and the result has been that the limits recommended by the CISPR, which have been widely adopted in national specifications, have kept the interference within bounds, though a certain percentage of listeners and viewers continue to be troubled by it from time to time.

The CISPR has succeeded in establishing international standards for measuring equipment and for the conditions of measurement and has exchanged a great deal of information on methods of suppression. Both aspects of the problem proved complicated. Methods of measurement had not only to give readings roughly corresponding with the subjective effect of interference of various types, whether continuous or impulsive or a mixture of both, but the position of the appliance under test and the connections to it had to approximate to the conditions in which it would actually be used. Reasonably satisfactory solutions of these problems were reached for most forms of interference with sound broadcasting, but the evolution of methods of measurement applicable to television has still not reached the stage where objective readings can be relied upon to correspond accurately with the subjective effect. BBC engineers have naturally taken part in the national and international studies of this subject.

3 STUDIOS FOR THE EXTERNAL SERVICES

At the end of the war the control room for the External Services at Bush House was still in the basement of the south-east wing, just above what had been at one time intended as a swimming pool, but had never been used for that purpose. The equipment was (as in most war-time studios) of the OBA/8 type, and the studios were mainly small studios for news and talks, mostly on the lower ground floor of the same wing of the building. There was one large studio in the north-west wing that was used as a general purpose studio for music and drama.

Until nearly the end of the period under review Bush House was concerned almost exclusively with the European Services, which were handled by four continuity positions. The four positions had associated studios, but continuity working in the full sense was not possible because of the language difficulty; there would be a sequence of different languages, few of which could be understood by those responsible for the switching and routing of the programmes. The practice of dividing up the programmes into exact quarter-hour periods, and switching over to the next combination of sources and destinations at the end of each period, had arisen during the war; it was continued and has persisted ever since with the addition of automated and more efficient methods of switching at the quarter-hour points.

All the External Services were grouped in Networks of which there were ten in 1947, each denoted by a colour. Each network was directed to particular target areas and comprised the languages (thirty-seven in all) appropriate to those areas; programmes in Spanish to Latin-America, for instance, constituted the Pink Network, while those in Spanish, Portuguese and Scandinavian languages for the Iberian Peninsula and Scandinavia formed the Grey Network. Each Network was carried by the transmitters assigned to it at different times of the day, and routed over the line network accordingly.

To connect the appropriate network programmes to the various chains at Bush House there had been an 'A' and 'B' switching scheme, where one set of conditions was changed by means of relays to another set that had already been established during the previous period. This scheme was in use until 1951, when the first of several more sophisticated switching systems was installed. This was suggested by R. H. Bullen and employed two rotating drums, each covering a twelve-hour period in quarter-hour intervals. Slides with combinations of segments corresponding to the required configurations were inserted into the drums. A Maltese-cross mechanism rotated the drum by one segment at a time and pushed a rotating arm forward against the segments of the slides that had been inserted; this arm in turn pressed against relay contacts, which closed in a pre-set sequence according to the slides that had been inserted. This device was exhibited at the Festival of Britain in 1951 and subsequently installed at Bush House, where it remained in service on one transmission chain until it was superseded by more advanced switching equipment in the late 1950s.

Studio operations continued after the war at Aldenham and at 200 Oxford Street, and the studios remained simple in conception, being required, as hitherto, almost entirely for talks, current affairs, and news. Shrinkage of the services, however, was gradually taking place during the ten years after the war, and in the early fifties the BBC began to move towards a concentration of all External Services at Bush House, though this object was not achieved until 1956. In May 1952, however, Aldenham was closed down as a programme production centre (though the premises remained as a training centre for Air Raid Precautions for some time afterwards), and the services that had been operated from there moved to Bush House and Oxford Street, mainly to the latter.

The simple studios used in the External Services were in general equipped with one or two talks tables and employed ribbon microphones, first the AXBT and later the 4038-C (the Standard Telephones and Cables version of the BBC-designed PGS ribbon microphone). Other equipment was based on the developments that have been described in section 1 of this chapter in connection with the Radio Services.

In addition to the programmes produced by the BBC, two programme services of the 'Voice of America' were relayed, starting in 1948. These consisted of material picked up at the Tatsfield receiving station and fed by line to Bush House, there to be mixed with local announcements and passed to the transmitters at Woofferton.

The ten years after the war were a period of consolidation for the External Services and of some retrenchment. The country was passing through a period of austerity and it was only after 1955 that any great changes took place.

4 TRANSMITTERS FOR THE EXTERNAL SERVICES

With the end of the war, the External Services were beset by difficulties. There was considerable pressure to make drastic economies in them. Severe intentional jamming by the USSR on short waves began in 1949, and to counter it the transmitters had to be used in uneconomic ways. Several of the long- and medium-wave transmitters that had been used for the External Services had to be returned to their peace-time use in the Domestic Services. The Copenhagen Wavelength Plan implemented in 1950 allocated only one long-wave channel to the United Kingdom and this was required primarily for the Light Programme.

On the other hand two medium-wave channels (1295 and 1340 kHz) towards the higher frequency end of the medium-wave band were available for use by the External Services and medium-wave relaying transmitters in Europe were leased to extend the coverage. Another favourable factor was that increased understanding of the behaviour of the ionosphere resulted in improved methods of forecasting optimum frequencies for HF broadcasting and a global interchange of information on this subject was developed during this period, the Department of Scientific and Industrial Research being the UK authority in this field.

At Daventry, the original 15-kW STC transmitters, which were installed in 1932 to initiate the Empire Service, continued in use together with the high-power STC transmitters (Senders 4, 5, 7A, 7B) and the high-power Marconi transmitters (Senders 6, 8, 9, 10, 11). Power reductions had to be made between 10 February 1947 and 21 March 1949 when all high-power transmitters at BBC short-wave stations were adjusted for a maximum output power of 50 kW. This was done mainly to save money, but also, during the early part of the period, to save power at a time when the generating capacity of the national electricity supply system was under severe strain.

At Rampisham, the four Marconi high-power transmitters (Senders 31 to 34) continued in service, but with power restrictions as at Daventry. The 50-kW medium-wave transmitters that had been used to radiate the ABSIE programme, as described in the previous chapter, were transferred to the European Service on 4 July 1945 until they closed down on 29 July 1945 (1122 kHz) and 29 September 1946 (977 kHz).

At Skelton the six Marconi high-power transmitters (Senders 61 to 66), and the six double-channel STC high-power transmitters (Senders 71A/B to 76A/B) continued to radiate External Services programmes throughout the period, with power reductions as at Daventry.

At Woofferton the transmitters had been removed during the final stages of the war for use by the Services for counter-measure work. The station was completely closed down from 28 August 1944 until October/November of that year. During that time four of the 50-kW RCA transmitters (Senders 83 to 86) were returned by the Services and reconditioned. Sender 81 with its BBC-designed HF stages returned to service in May 1946 and the five Senders continued to carry External Services programmes until the station was again closed down on 26 June 1948 for economic reasons. The frequent changes in the use made of Woofferton and the irregular periods of close-down of the station did nothing to improve the morale of the station staff, who had to be transferred frequently to other stations when their own was out of use.

On 18 July 1948 the station was reopened, Phoenix-like, financed this time by the 'Voice of America' (VOA). Five of the six senders radiated two VOA programmes – *Blue Stars* and *Grey Stars* – on a single-shift basis between 1400 hours and 2200 hours GMT daily. The programmes were received at Tatsfield and routed to Woofferton through the Bush House studios. On 11 July 1949, with the intensification of the jamming of BBC and VOA transmissions by the USSR, Woofferton started to carry BBC Russian programmes in addition to the eight-hour VOA Schedule and this pattern of working continued throughout the rest of the period.

At Start Point the 100-kW medium-wave transmitter that had been converted for alternative MF and HF operation carried the European Service on 1050 kHz during darkness and on frequencies in the 49-m and 41-m bands during daylight hours. This mode of operation continued until 25 May 1944, when the transmitter was converted back to its original MF condition in readiness for use by the Domestic Services from 29 July 1945. The high-power short-wave transmitter (Sender 22) was closed down at the end of 1945 and put 'under dust sheets'.

At Lisnagarvey the 100-kW short-wave transmitter carried the External Service programmes until it was closed down on 26 May 1946 and put under care and maintenance.

At Clevedon the converted medium-wave transmitter radiated European Service programmes on frequencies in the 25-m and 41-m bands until it was closed down on 2 June 1945 for conversion back to medium-wave operation in the Domestic Services.

Although some of the war-time transmitter facilities used by External Services were being closed down, expansion was being considered in other areas. Two major developments were contemplated during the years 1945 to 1955 with the object of improving reception by relaying the HF signals at strategically placed stations.

The first, which derived from a decision at the Commonwealth Broadcasting Conference held in London in February 1945, was the establishment of a relay station in the Caribbean area to overcome reception difficulties in Canada and the USA, which resulted from propagation disturbances when the transmitted signal passed through the Auroral Zone. A southerly route via the West Indies offered advantages in this respect. Such a relay station could also improve reception in Australia and New Zealand; instead of a compromise frequency for the entire 13,000-mile circuit, it would have been possible to use the optimum frequency for the UK-West Indies path and the optimum frequency for the West Indies-Australasia path. It was estimated that the period of usefulness of the UK-Australasian transmissions would be increased by this method from some six to twenty hours per day. Accordingly, a broadcast survey in the Caribbean area was carried out by A. E. Barrett of the Research Department between August and October 1945. He was at the time attached to the British Purchasing Commission in Washington and made his report in February 1946.

A search was made in the area of Georgetown, British Guiana (now Guyana) and suitable sites were found for the transmitting station and receiving stations and for the headquarters buildings. It was borne in mind that the station might serve not only as a relay station for the BBC but also as a Caribbean broadcasting station to serve Jamaica, British Honduras and the Bahamas using a 50-kW HF transmitter, and Trinidad and the Leeward and Windward Islands using a 20-kW HF transmitter.

The project would have cost some £2·5 million, and it was deferred indefinitely because of the financial stringency of the time.

Experience gained with the pre-war Empire Service had shown that it was not possible to obtain satisfactory global coverage from a single transmitting site and as early as 1937 a proposal was being discussed for relaying BBC programmes from an HF transmitter located in the Far East. On the outbreak of war, it was decided to construct a relay station at Jurong on Singapore Island. Unfortunately, the Marconi 100-kW HF transmitter dispatched to Singapore was sunk *en route* by enemy action and an RCA replacement transmitter arrived without its power transformers. The installation work was in the hands of the Diplomatic Wireless Service of the Foreign Office and much of the transmitter installation and the erection of simple aerials had been completed by Christmas 1941, but the Japanese advance through Malaya and the surrender of Singapore on 18 February 1942 put an end to this project before the new transmitter could be put into service.

At the end of 1945 the British Far Eastern Broadcasting Service (BFEBS) recommenced its activities still under the auspices of the Foreign Office but relaying BBC programmes and using staff seconded from the BBC. The transmitter facilities available at that time were four 7½-kW HF transmitters at Jurong. Plans to install high-power transmitters there were not implemented because the siting of the new Singapore Airport made the erection of masts of the required height at Jurong unacceptable. A search was therefore made for a replacement site in Malaya. F. C. McLean made a preliminary visit in July 1946, and H. Bishop went with him and Wing-Cdr Jowers of the Foreign Office and inspected several sites in July 1947. A suitable one was finally obtained at Tebrau, in Johore, comprising 450 acres of jungle with small areas of cultivated rubber. There were no access roads and the Japanese had left behind some bomb and ammunition dumps. Plans were drawn up for a building to contain two Marconi type SWB18 100-kW HF transmitters and four Marconi type SWB11 7½-kW transmitters. Twenty aerials of the BBC 'HRR' type were proposed with a two-tier switching tower of the design used at Rampisham, Skelton and Woofferton. The station was designed to be completely self-contained, to have its own diesel alternator power supply and to include living accommodation for both ex-patriate and indigenous staff. Recreational facilities were also planned. The reception of programmes for reradiation by the Far Eastern Relay Station was to be done at a separate receiving station.

W. B. Purslow was seconded to the Foreign Office in July 1946 to assist in the rehabilitation of BFEBS and was based in Singapore. C. Lawson Reece was appointed Controller, BFEBS, and Purslow became Chief Engineer. Purslow left Singapore in July 1948 and after a short gap was replaced by E. W. Hayes whose main responsibility was to commission the Tebrau transmitting station with the minimum of delay. Control of BFEBS was handed over by the Foreign Office to the BBC, and, after some delays, the installation of plant started in mid-1950. C. G. Rumsan visited Tebrau towards the end of 1950 to commission the three diesel engines coupled to 400-kW alternators. There were the usual difficulties of working some 9000 miles from base, but the first of the high-power transmitters was ready for service by Christmas 1950 and the second was commissioned in January 1951.

This was the largest transmitter construction project carried out by the BBC since the building of Skelton and Woofferton in 1943 and it was the first BBC transmitting station to be completely self-contained. Senior members of the locally recruited staff were brought to the UK for technical training, and many of them obtained a pass in the BBC's Grade C Examination.

During the building of the new station, use was made of the Radio Ceylon (previously Radio SEAC) station using one 100-kW HF transmitter and one 7½-kW HF transmitter from April 1949 until the end of 1950.

During the period treated in this chapter, the use of long- and medium-wave transmitters in the UK for the Overseas Services was restricted; the 400-kW transmitter at Droitwich, which had radiated the European Service on 1149 kHz, had been closed down on 29 July 1945 to release the frequency for the Light Programme. The long-wave transmitter (5XX) carried the European Service, outside the hours occupied by the Light Programme, from 15 February 1953, when Ottringham closed down.

Until 29 July 1945, when the peace-time broadcasting plan was implemented, Ottringham continued to radiate on 200 kHz, but on that date relinquished this channel to Droitwich (5XX). After much discussion, a new frequency was found for Ottringham, 250 kHz, but with the power restricted to 400 kW. Trouble was caused by the second harmonic of this frequency coinciding with the marine distress frequency and on 16 September 1945 Ottringham was changed to 271 kHz, pending attempts to reduce the second harmonic output of the 250 kHz transmission to acceptable levels. Finally a more suitable channel was found – 167 kHz – although it was necessary to accept a power restriction of 200 kW. This frequency was used until the Copenhagen Plan came into effect on 15 March 1950. Ottringham then broadcast the European Service on 200 kHz outside domestic broadcasting hours. It also contributed to the medium-wave transmissions of the European Service from 6 July 1945 to 20 September 1946, using 977 kHz (100 kW) and from 29 June 1947 to 1 March 1949 provided a one-day-a-week maintenance relief for the Crowborough transmitter on 1122 kHz. From 15 March 1950 onwards Ottringham carried the European Service on 1295 kHz. This unique station was closed down on 15 February 1953, to the regret of the many engineers who had been associated with its planning and operation, because neither channels nor funds were available for it to continue in service. The plant was removed and the land and buildings were disposed of.

The BBC continued to hire the high-power medium-wave transmitter at Crowborough operated by DWS throughout the 1945–55 period. In May 1945 the European Service was being radiated by this transmitter on 804 kHz for twenty hours daily, but from 29 July 1945 Crowborough took over 1222 kHz until the implementation of the Copenhagen Plan. The Crowborough transmitter then took the second of the available medium-wave channels (1340 kHz). The coverage of the European Service on the two medium-wave channels was not satisfactory by day; to offset this, on 22 October 1950, Crowborough started to use the Third Programme frequency of 647 kHz outside the hours of that programme, which were then from 1700 to 2300 hours GMT. This gave much improved day-time coverage.

To improve the coverage of the European Service on medium waves in north-west Germany and Berlin, it was proposed to use the 120-kW Telefunken transmitter located at Osterloog, near Norden. The Germans had erected this station during the war to broadcast the voice of 'Lord Haw Haw' for the benefit of British listeners. It relied on propagation over the sea path to the UK and used a directional aerial system with two 492-ft mast radiators and eight 394-ft reflector masts. W. E. C. Varley visited Norden in August 1946 to assess the usefulness of the station for External Services with the aerial system modified to provide maximum gain on a bearing of 110° ETN. It was hired from the Allied Control Commission Germany and on 1 September 1946 it began to radiate German programmes in the European Service on 658 kHz and continued to do so until 15 March 1950 when the channel ceased to be available under the Copenhagen Plan. Norden took over 1295 kHz when Ottringham was taken out of service on 15 February 1953 and it continued to use this channel until 1 April 1962 when the hiring of Norden was terminated because of the need for economy.

In Berlin, a Siemens 1-kW (later 10-kW) VHF FM transmitter was used to radiate German programmes in the European Service for listeners in the Greater Berlin area on a frequency of 89·5 MHz. On 1 July 1953 this frequency was changed to 87·6 MHz to fit in with the West German frequency plan for the Berlin area. The FM transmitter was at first programmed by direct pick-up of BBC HF transmissions from Skelton, but after about two months a line from the UK to Berlin via Hanover became available and this was used in preference to the radio pick-up.

Also in Berlin, from 19 August 1953, the European Service was rebroadcast on a 5-kW MF transmitter of NWDR on 1295 kHz in synchronism with the Norden transmission. The synchronising equipment was provided by the BBC. On 1 June

1954 the control of this transmitter passed to 'Sender Freies Berlin' and when the Norden operation closed down in 1962, the Berlin MF transmitter was synchronised with Crowborough on 1295 kHz.

A 75-kW Telefunken MF transmitter at Dobl in Austria was visited by A. N. Thomas in 1948 to assess its suitability for radiating European Service programmes to Central and South-East Europe. The station was hired to radiate BBC transmissions on 886 kHz from 30 August 1948. In accordance with the Copenhagen Plan the frequency was changed to 1025 kHz from 15 March 1950, but its use by the External Services was discontinued on 20 April 1955. The programme was received direct from Skelton, but during the winter months, when reception was unsatisfactory, a line feed was provided.

During this period, technical developments at External Services transmitting stations included the following:

(*a*) the improvement of HF aerial arrays and impedance matching techniques;

(*b*) the provision of equipment to permit transmitter synchronisation on high frequencies of stations at widely separated sites;

(*c*) the extension of the standard-frequency transmission service and the improvement of its accuracy and stability;

(*d*) the suppression of harmonic radiation from HF transmitters causing interference to the reception of television signals in Band I. (This type of interference restricted the use of certain frequencies, particularly those in the 15-MHz band, until suppressors were developed and installed at Daventry and elsewhere.)

(*e*) automatic programme switching and sequential monitoring equipment, developed by Designs Department for use at HF transmitting stations and first installed at Skelton;[44, 45]

(*f*) peak clipping, introduced at Skelton on 3 October 1951 on certain programmes. Langevin peak-clipping amplifiers were provided by the USIS and were adjusted to clip at 95 per cent modulation depth. (These devices also embodied frequency shaping to improve the intelligibility of speech in the presence of interference and a low-pass filter to reduce radiation of the high audio-frequency distortion components produced by clipping. The Langevin peak clippers were removed in the mid-1960s and replaced by BBC Type LIM/6 limiting amplifiers set for 16 dB compression and with frequency shaping added.)

(*g*) the operation of HF transmitters in parallel, using transmission lines in a bridge configuration. (This method was developed at Daventry in 1954 working into a redesigned HRR/4/4 array. Later, paralleling of HF transmitters was effected by driving each transmitter into one half of an array in a similar manner to the technique used at VHF/FM stations.)

(*h*) improvements to the type VFO/4 variable frequency drives and synthesisers.

(*i*) various tactical methods of scheduling transmitters, which were introduced during the period of USSR jamming.

An important event during this period was the setting up, in 1952, of the Drogheda Committee.[46] Its terms of reference included the assessment of the value – actual and potential – of the External Services of the BBC in the wider context of the Overseas Information Services of the United Kingdom. This Committee, chaired by the Earl of Drogheda met sixty-seven times and made, among others, the following recommendations affecting the development of transmitter facilities for the External Services:

(a) Two additional high-power transmitters should be installed forthwith at the Far Eastern Relay Station and a second shift should be manned at that station.
(b) Every effort should be made to get local stations in the Far East to rebroadcast BBC programmes. This, the Committee thought, would become easier if the signal strength was increased.
(c) There should be an improvement of transmitter coverage and the leasing of relay facilities in Europe.

The committee quoted the BBC's own assessment of the effectiveness of the External Services, as follows:

'Though the BBC's transmitters in the United Kingdom are still among the most efficient and powerful in the world, and the associated equipment such as aerials, etc., have, until now, been technically equal or superior to those used by comparable organisations, they can no longer be considered fully effective when they are the only means of reaching the audience. The reason for this is the ever-increasing congestion and chaotic conditions in the short-wave bands, which have now made it difficult, if not impossible, to provide by direct transmission a worth-while signal in many parts of the world. By 1938 short-wave broadcasting was in its infancy; very few countries employed this means for external broadcasting and almost no country employed it for its domestic services . . . Since that time, however, the output of international short-wave broadcasts has increased by more than ten times. Another development which has led to the overloading of the short-wave bands has been the use of short waves for the internal or domestic services of many countries. In the view of the BBC the various International Wavelength Conferences held under the auspices of the ITU failed to allocate adequate wavelengths for long-distance short-wave broadcasting and hence the BBC's External Services have suffered severely . . .'

The Committee concluded that through lack of money the BBC had been left a long way behind in the new development of high-power medium-wave outlets near to the target area, as used by the USA and the USSR, and that the first priority for broadcasting must be a large-scale programme of capital development designed to put the BBC's External Services on a proper technical footing. The capital cost of bringing the technical installations of the BBC up to modern standards of efficiency was estimated at an average of £500,000 each year for five or ten years.[46]

In the event it was decided to spend the limited amount of money available on improving the installations at the older stations in the UK, leaving the extension of the Far Eastern Relay Station until later. These developments belong to the next chapter.

5 TELEVISION STUDIOS AND OBS

The reawakening of television after the war was not from a deep sleep, but rather from a dream-filled state of suspension. Numbers of the pre-war television staff from Alexandra Palace had been released to the Services where, with their knowledge of electronics and pulse techniques, they were in demand for the development of the new science of radar. The 'know-how' of television was thus kept in practice, and this helped to offset the effects of the interval of nearly six years, which had put the BBC behind the United States in television development.

As a result of the work of the Hankey Committee described in the previous chapter the BBC knew, when the war came to an end, what it was going to do about television. The service was to reopen on the same standards as before, and the immediate target was to get it going again in time for the Victory Parade in June 1946. Those who had been engaged in television before the war had never lost sight of their objectives and more than a year before the end of the war the pre-war Director of Television, Gerald Cock, visited Aldenham House to find out whether it would be suitable for the main studio centre. He found that, although it had undoubted advantages, the 45-minute journey from London ruled it out.

The immediate task was to rehabilitate the studios and transmitters at Alexandra Palace and the first move was to assemble the staff with which to do it. A new post of Superintendent Engineer Television was created, and D. C. Birkinshaw was appointed to it on 21 November 1945. Birkinshaw recalls what a moving experience it was to meet again members of his pre-war staff and to listen to their experiences. 'All these men,' he says, 'had thought continuously of their work before the war on the television service and were mad keen to get back again.' H. W. Baker was appointed Engineer-in-Charge, Alexandra Palace, on 15 November 1945. Before the war, television OBs had been placed under the EiC of London Sound OBs, but were now separated under T. H. Bridgewater, as EiC Television OBs.

The two studios had not been tested for years and the central control room, the apparatus room, the receivers at Swain's Lane and the line termination room had all remained unused during the war. The studio equipment was in a sorry state. Nearly all the electrolytic capacitors had to be replaced, as well as many of the resistors, which were of the wire-wound, non-inductive, close-tolerance type. Nevertheless, trade test transmissions with electrically generated patterns (artificial bars) and 400-Hz test tone were started on 1 February 1946 and the studio equipment gradually became available for testing in March and April; some production exercises were started in May. The first television test card, test card 'A', was produced during the testing period early in 1946, to facilitate the testing of camera channels for frequency response, non-linearity, aspect ratio, streaking and gradation. The frequency response was indicated by the resolution of frequency gratings on the card, from 0·5 to 3 MHz; this method saved a great deal of time compared with the measurement of response, and test patterns came into universal use.

The OB vans, or Mobile Control Rooms (MCRs), had been completely dismantled, the equipment having been ruthlessly torn out during the war because the vans were needed for other purposes. The Station Design & Installation Department had an enormous task to perform in a very short time to get all the racks of camera equipment reinstalled and wired, but the first MCR and the first mobile transmitter were ready for the opening day.

The Television Service was re-opened by the Postmaster General at 7 pm on 7 June 1946. Mickey Mouse had had the last word on pre-war television, but the first post-war programme after the opening ceremony struck a loftier note – it was a harp recital. The first OB was the Victory Parade on the following day.

The BBC Television Service was thus the first in Europe to reopen after the war. Hamburg followed with an experimental service in 1950. (Television in Germany had not closed on the outbreak of war: a programme for the troops was started in 1940 and the Hamburg station started to relay programmes from Berlin in 1941 – the same year as the first commercial station was licensed in the USA. The Berlin transmitter was destroyed by bombing in 1943.)[47]

The two pre-war studios and two OB units (the second one was restored to service in November 1946) could not suffice for long. Although television was in competition with essential projects having priority in claiming the resources of the nation – such as repairing the physical damage of the war to houses and factories – it was evident that the BBC would have to extend the coverage of television to the Regions, and planning to this end was begun. The programme staff was gradually re-assembled, and the development of programme techniques began to be resumed. The Emitron camera was still used, but soon the need for better cameras was felt, and a new kind of camera tube was being developed by EMI, known as the CPS (cathode potential stabilised) Emitron. It was first used in November 1947 for the wedding of Princess Elizabeth.

The first year of post-war television was remarkable for the success with which the service was re-established and also for a 'non-event': having reopened eight months previously, the service was shut down completely for the month of February 1947. This was because the demand for power all over the country had out-stripped the generating capacity and serious power cuts were taking place; it was thought that every service that could be spared should be cut out during the cold month of February (the winter of 1946/7 was particularly severe). In spite of this set-back, by the end of the year 1947 there were 30,000 viewers. The question of standards had still not been finally decided, but on 24 August 1948 the PMG announced that the existing 405-line system would be used for the transmissions from the projected new regional station at Sutton Coldfield, and would continue to be used at Alexandra Palace 'for a number of years'. The BBC had already announced, on 4 June 1947, the acquisition of a site for the first regional transmitting station, and the way was now clear, subject to the restrictions on capital expenditure still prevailing, for the erection of further stations to give national coverage.

The new CPS Emitron camera went into regular use on 29 July 1948, starting with the Olympic Games at Wembley. This camera was characterised by tonal gradation far better than that of the standard Emitron, although some people maintained that its definition and crispness were not as good. It suffered from 'peeling-off', which occurred when an excessive peak of light caused a white patch to spread momentarily over the whole of the screen. The first experimental cameras were therefore not suitable for outside work, where there could be no control of the range of lighting, and they could not cope with high-contrast scenes. The BBC nevertheless placed an order with EMI in January 1948 for a mobile control room (MCR) with CPS Emitron camera equipment, to be available for the Olympic Games in July 1948. Meanwhile the CPS Emitron had been 'tamed' and it was able to accept high-contrast scenes without becoming unstable; it performed well at Wembley, Particularly on the indoor swimming events. Later, it was used for several OBs, including football and boxing. (The equipment from this mobile unit was afterwards transferred to the Lime Grove studios.) The CPS Emitron was eventually superseded completely by the image orthicon camera.

One of the more important developments in the cameras of the immediate post-war era was the introduction in 1949 of the 'zoom' lens, now indispensable. Until then, to change the angle of view one had to change the lens; turrets were developed for television cameras, similar to those used for many years on film cameras, by means of which one of three or four lenses of different focal lengths could be placed in front of the camera tube. This had two disadvantages: the number of different focal lengths was severely limited and in productions that could have been handled by one camera, it was necessary to have two, the second being used to cover the moment when the turret of the first was being rotated. A zoom lens had been developed by Siemens in Germany during the war for 16-mm film cameras; the magnification could be continuously varied and the image remained in focus. It was suggested to W. Watson & Sons Ltd., of Barnet, the microscope makers, that they might be interested in the manufacture of such lenses for television cameras. As a result the original Watson 2:1 zoom lens was developed and brought into action on an OB from the Albert Hall on 9 February 1949. It was used on a camera called the 'photicon', based on an extension of the iconoscope principle, forming part of a new OB unit that had been purchased from Pye's of Cambridge. The photicon employed the same principle as the EMI 'Super-Emitron'.

At this point it is necessary to review briefly the development of camera tubes. Zworykin had produced his iconoscope in the USA in 1923 and Farnsworth, working independently in the USA, had invented his image-dissector. In all the practicable forms of camera, the essential element was an electron gun in which electrons produced by a cathode were focused by an electron-optical system into a fine beam and deflected so as to scan the target line by line. In the iconoscope, of which the standard Emitron was an example, an optical image of the scene was formed on a mosaic of particles of a photo-emissive material deposited on a mica plate. The electron beam scanned the mosaic and the liberated electrons were collected by a metal film (the 'signal plate') on the back of the mica plate and applied to an external amplifier. The number of electrons emitted from each point on the mosaic depended on the intensity of light at that point and the electron beam, in the course of scanning, restored the electron charge on each particle of the mosaic so that the current passing round the external circuit between the signal plate, the amplifier input, and the final anode of the electron gun constituted a single-valued time function corresponding to the spatial distribution of light in the image. The signal plate was opaque to light, so that the electron beam had to be directed at it from the same side as the light falling on it. The geometry of the tube, and the correction circuits used with it, were complicated because the electron beam was directed obliquely at the mosaic and yet had to maintain a rectangular scan.

The next step was the image iconoscope, or Super-Emitron, in which the optical image was formed on a photo-cathode consisting of a transparent plate with a photo-emissive surface on the side away from the light. The electrons liberated from this surface were focused on a target, which was scanned by the electron gun; the secondary electrons built up a charge, which was collected by the signal plate and restored periodically by the electron gun. As the photo-cathode produced a great number of secondary electrons, the sensitivity of the image iconoscope was ten to twenty times as great as that of the iconoscope. This, together with the fact that the mosaic was smaller, permitted the use of much smaller lenses.

In the orthicon, typified by the CPS Emitron, the signal plate itself was transparent, so that the mosaic could be scanned from behind and the electron beam could strike the target at right angles. The high velocity beam used in the earlier tubes had caused secondary electrons to be emitted from the target, which reduced the sensitivity and produced spurious signals. In the CPS Emitron the beam was at low velocity and the target, when not illuminated, was at the same potential as the cathode of the electron gun – hence the term 'cathode potential stabilised' (CPS).

In the image orthicon the geometrical arrangement of the tube was similar to that of the CPS Emitron, but it included a photo-cathode as in the image iconoscope and also an electron multiplier. The sensitivity was therefore further increased. The electron multiplier comprised a series of surfaces emitting more secondary electrons to augment the main beam. It thus acted as an amplifier, but without introducing so much noise as a valve amplifier. The first image orthicons had a tube 3 in. in diameter, but were succeeded by those with $4\frac{1}{2}$-in. tubes giving better resolution and signal-to-noise ratio.

Although the vidicon camera did not appear until some time later, it is convenient to mention it here. It employed the photo-conductive principle rather than the photo-emissive effects on which the other tubes depended. The tube was very small, being only 1 in. or less in diameter, and 6 in. long. The target consisted of a layer of photo-conductive material on a transparent signal plate. The conductivity from front to back was affected by the light falling on the signal plate, so that the voltage at the surface of each element rose above the potential of the cathode of the electron gun. The scanning beam restored the voltage to that of the cathode and so sent a pulse of current through an external circuit connected to the signal plate. (The vidicon used antimony trisulphide as the photo-conductive material; in the 1960s improved results were obtained with lead oxide, as in the Plumbicon.)

An important property of both camera tubes and picture tubes is the transfer characteristic, i.e. the relationship between the brightness of the scene and the amplitude of the signal or between the amplitude of the signal and the brightness of the picture. Assuming that this relationship can be represented by a power law, it can be expressed as the ratio of the logarithm of the output to that of the input and is known as 'gamma'. Its value may not be constant over the operating range of the tube, in which case the average 'gamma' may be taken as the average slope of the transfer characteristic when the input and output are both plotted on logarithmic scales.

The gamma of the picture tubes used in early television receivers was taken to be about $2 \cdot 5$, although modern shadow-mask colour tubes have a gamma of about $2 \cdot 8$. The gamma of the early camera tubes was assumed to be unity and it was necessary to use non-linear correcting circuits to reduce the value to $0 \cdot 4$, so as to achieve an overall gamma of unity; the transfer characteristic of the whole system from scene to viewer would then be linear. (Modern photo-conductive tubes as used in colour cameras have a gamma of about $0 \cdot 95$.)

Apart from the gamma correction the early camera tubes needed correction circuits to counteract geometrical distortion of the picture and also the various forms of shading resulting from the method of scanning used in the camera tube. The camera control unit had therefore not only to control the power supplies to the camera and the necessary timing pulses, but also to apply the corrections, some of which in the early days had to be adjusted frequently.[48, 49]

Before the war television outside broadcasting was developing and there was an incentive to continue this development as soon as possible after the war had ended. The two mobile control rooms covered the OB requirements for a few years, but there were difficulties in accommodating them and maintenance work had to be done in the open air at Alexandra Palace, often in severe weather. (The sides of the van had to be opened for maintenance work to be done by staff standing on the bottom half of the door with the top half raised to give them some protection from the rain.) The only accommodation that could be found was the old Palace of Industry on the 1924 British Empire Exhibition site at Wembley, with no facilities at all: no heating and not even lavatories that worked. It was so cold in that vast area that the only way to keep the staff warm was to put tents into the building and electric heaters into the tents. After the end of the Olympic Games of 1948, for which another exhibition building, the Palace of Arts, had been taken over, the Television OB Department were able to move into a happier environment, with a proper working base for their equipment and vehicles.

A great amount of engineering effort went into the planning of studios to accommodate the rapidly expanding service, beginning in 1947 after a year of post-war operation. It was then decided that there were two separate requirements for studio expansion, long-term and short-term. The building of a purpose-built television headquarters was clearly part of the long-term plan, but in the meantime a small working party, with H. W. Baker (then Acting Superintendent Engineer, Television) as chairman, set about exploring the possibilities of a short-term plan. Areas that were considered and planned in respect of building work as far as the cost-magnitude estimating stage, were the Concert Hall at Alexandra Palace, the King George V Suite at the Athenaeum, Muswell Hill (formerly a cinema), the Westminster Ice Rink and the Highbury Film Studios. All these proved too expensive for temporary accommodation.

Finally, the Rank Film Studios at Lime Grove were taken over in November 1949; planning for their conversion to television studios was started in January 1950 by a Television Studio Development Committee under the chairmanship of M. J. L. Pulling, who had been appointed Senior Superintendent Engineer, Television Broadcasting (SSETel.B) on 1 November 1949. There were five studios, ranging in size from 3000 sq. ft to 10,000 sq. ft, but the largest studio had to be reserved for a scenery store and 'marshalling yard' for scenery going in and out of the four remaining studios.

The development of Lime Grove was done in three stages. Stage 1 was Studio D, which was converted as an additional studio for Children's Television, and opened on 21 May 1950. It was equipped with three CPS Emitron cameras, which had been used by the Television OB Department for the Olympic Games in 1948. Stage 2 was the equipping of one large studio, Studio G, for light entertainment programmes, and the smallest one, Studio H, for talks programmes. Studio G, which opened on 23 December 1950 with a Christmas Gala programme, was a trial ground for ventilation and air-conditioning plant, with refrigeration, on the scale which would be required in the large studios of the future Television Centre. It was a costly experiment, but a ten-hour test in hot August weather and with 300 kW of studio lighting gave a most satisfactory result and similar plant was later installed at the Television Centre. Studio H, which went into service in February 1952, enabled Studio B at Alexandra Palace to be closed down. In the final stage Studio E came into service on 21 August 1953 with four working camera channels using Marconi $4\frac{1}{2}$-in. image orthicon tubes. At this stage Studio D was taken out of service for alterations and improvements and, when it returned to service in March 1954, Studio A at Alexandra Palace was closed down. (The two pioneer studios, A and B, at Alexandra Palance were later re-equipped and used by Television News from 1954 to 1969.) The planning followed lines that later became general: a presentation suite was provided from which linking announcements could be made in vision and the nucleus of the technical operations was a central control room, associated with a central apparatus room. The selection, switching and supervision of the sequence of programmes was carried out in the central control room, while the central apparatus room contained two rows of bays carrying pulse generators, mixers, distribution amplifiers, line amplifiers and the terminating equipment for Post Office cables. When these areas came into service in 1953, the central control room at Alexandra Palace was closed down and all programmes were passed through the one at Lime Grove to the network. The large amount of equipment concentrated in the new central control room consumed a considerable amount of power and forced-draught ventilation had to be provided through the bottom of the bays to cool the equipment.[50]

By 1954 Light Entertainment were wanting to mount more programmes with audience reaction; the Shepherd's Bush Empire was taken over and was brought into service in June 1954. This was done very quickly by adopting a method that later became common when new studios had to be brought into use either temporarily or in advance of the time when they could be fully equipped; an MCR was stationed close to the building and cables were run from it to the cameras in the studio, so that the camera control units and other equipment in the van could be used as at an OB – hence the term 'drive-in studio'. In August of the same year, Television News began to operate from the old Studio A at Alexandra Palace.

These activities were not part of the long-term plan for studio expansion, but they afforded opportunities for experiment and the accumulation of experience that could be turned to good account in the planning of the Television Centre. To meet the long-term requirement, the BBC purchased in 1949 the 13½-acre site at the White City that had originally housed the buildings for the Franco-British Exhibition of 1908.[51] Graham Dawbarn of Norman & Dawbarn was appointed Architect in association with M. T. Tudsbery, then the BBC's Consulting Civil Engineer. A planning committee was set up, which included Tudsbery, C. H. Colborn and H. W. Baker as engineering representatives.

Peter Bax, then Television Design Manager, had advocated that television studios and their ancillary accommodation should be in the form of segments of a circle.[52] A scheme based on this concept was approved in principle in April 1951, but within a short time the project was 'frozen' because of Government restrictions on capital expenditure. It was, however, found possible to proceed with the scenery block, which could fulfil an immediate need in supplying scenery to the recently acquired Lime Grove studios, and this block (Stage 1 of the project) was completed and commissioned in 1953.

The delay provided an opportunity for a reappraisal of the planning that had already been done, and a Television Centre Development Committee met regularly, with the Architects, to advise on the specialised requirements and to study the sketch plans carefully as they were produced, so as to ensure that the building would be completely satisfactory from both the functional and aesthetic points of view. Stage 2, the laying of the foundations for the main block, was completed in mid-1954, but the further development of the Centre belongs to the next chapter.

In planning it, the Committee had to bear in mind two long-term requirements: the expected introduction of a second BBC Television Programme and the eventual introduction of colour television. The first requirement was straightforward and merely implied the provision of more studios and space in the central control room for a second presentation suite. The second was more difficult because the BBC at that time had no experience of colour working and of its needs for space, lighting, ventilation and power. A small working party was sent to the USA to study the CBS and NBC colour studios at Hollywood and Burbank. They found that, in comparison with black-and-white equipment, colour studio apparatus required $1 \cdot 5$ times as much floor space, and the apparatus rooms at the Television Centre were planned on this basis. After the return of the working party, a Studio Engineering Committee (Television) was set up to plan the technical facilities of the Television Centre. This Committee provided a forum at the right level for senior engineers of the specialist and operations and maintenance departments to deal with problems of technical design and installation, such as specifications for camera tubes and lenses, vision and sound signal distribution and switching arrangements, pulse timing and distribution, lighting and vision control, studio lighting arrangements and power supplies.

One of the trial grounds for the planning of the Television Centre was the Riverside Studios at Hammersmith. This was another film studio building, and the BBC acquired it in 1954.[51] These studios were needed to satisfy the pressing demand for more production space and also to enable the Lime Grove studios to be taken out of service, one by one, to enable the obsolescent equipment to be replaced. The two Riverside Studios, opened in 1956, were used to try out alternative methods of dealing with the finish of studio floors (a most important matter because of the need for camera dollies to be wheeled across the floor without any vibration that would be noticeable on the picture and without excessive noise), dimming controls for studio lighting (whether by thyratrons, rheostats or auto-transformers) methods of suspending studio lights, the location of the lighting control console (whether or not it should be adjacent to the vision control position), the layout of studio control rooms in relation to the studios, and the possibilities of one-man vision control. The last-mentioned problem was finally solved, as cameras became more stable and the control circuits more sophistiacted, so that one operator was able to control up to six camera channels.

Meanwhile, a start was made on the planning of Regional studios by converting a former chapel and a film studio in Dickenson Road, Manchester, to operate as a 'drive-in' television studio.

There was also a demand for the range and variety of OBs to be extended, especially in connection with sports of all kinds. An important development in this field was the introduction of microwave radio-link equipment. Up to about 1950 it had not been possible to do OBs from more than thirty miles from a suitable injection point on the television network; the radio-link equipment operated at VHF and there were no arrangements for putting a transmitter and receiver back-to-back and relaying over a second hop. The first microwave (i.e. SHF) equipment came from America and was an RCA 7000-MHz link. Marconi's, STC and EMI soon produced radio links operating on 4000 MHz and 7000 MHz. A special microwave section was set up at the OB base in the Palace of Arts to service this equipment. Very soon the range of OBs was much extended, as two or more links could be used in tandem, and extending-tower vehicles enabled aerials to be easily raised to the required height. Lines were usually available for transmitting the accompanying sound, but the sound could also be transmitted over the vision link on a sub-carrier.

Another important innovation was the use of mast-head receivers. These were SHF receivers mounted near the top of the masts of a number of the main television transmitting stations. These mast-head receivers could pick up OBs from fifty miles away or more. From the transmitting station the OB signals were fed over a contribution circuit to London or to the nearest switching point for distribution over the network. The adjustment of the mast-head receivers (developed by the Planning and Installation Department) and the swivelling of the parabolic dishes were remotely controlled from the ground, so that lining-up could be done quickly.

OB camera equipment, too, was evolving. The successors of the original Emitron camera after the war were the CPS Emitron and the Pye Photicon, but the former was not really rugged enough and the latter not sensitive enough for OB conditions, and they were both transferred to the studios where they could be worked under more closely controlled conditions. OBs then depended entirely on the 3-in. image orthicon, made by both Marconi's and Pye's, and this was used until the English Electric Valve Company's $4\frac{1}{2}$-in. image orthicon became available. This had an appreciably better signal-to-noise ratio and gave a cleaner and sharper picture, its main drawback being that because it was a bigger tube, the cameras tended to be bigger and heavier than ever.

In 1954 the need was felt for a mobile camera that could follow action over a comparatively wide area, and in that year the first of several such equipments was constructed by Designs Department in the Broadcasting House car park. It was named the 'Roving Eye', and consisted of an Austin van in which a camera was mounted in a gun ring on the roof; a petrol-electric generating set, the camera channel and sound equipment, and transmitters working in the VHF band were carried in the van. Even in built-up areas in Central London it was possible to achieve a range up to two miles. A gyro-compass was used to keep the aerial on bearing; the initial setting was done manually and the gyro-compass then held it regardless of the gyrations of the vehicle. This first Roving Eye and its successor were both designed and constructed by G. W. H. Larkby.[53]

A number of items of specialised apparatus, not then available commercially, were produced in this period. These included a test signal generator, TVTG/1, which was very advanced for its time, the type B waveform monitor to display test signals, and a range of video distribution amplifiers, pulse distribution amplifiers and stabilising amplifiers. Work was also done on the problem of synchronisation of signals from different sources, especially in view of the Coronation, for which many sources would be required. For this and other OBs, a manually-controlled synchronising system was devised, which depended on sending a locking tone at line frequency. There was provision for dividing this tone down to a frequency that could be carried by a telephone line, but in practice it was always found possible to transmit the 10,125-Hz line frequency over the line, and the division facility was never used.

Designs Department also developed a UHF 'starter link' for OBs in order to overcome the difficulty of obtaining an optically clear path from an OB point to a receiver point. The UHF link was not dependent upon an optically clear path between transmitter and receiver as are SHF links, and it was possible to get round obstacles provided they were not too large. Moreover, it was possible to obtain more power at UHF than at the higher frequencies.

There was also a continuing effort, in the field of measuring equipment.[54] Television waveforms could be examined, but there was still no systematic method of making a quantitative assessment of the performance of any circuit. In the early 1950s, however Dr N. W. Lewis of the Post Office suggested the use of sine-squared pulse and bar signals and produced apparatus to generate them. Designs Department helped Dr Lewis to establish the subjective picture quality corresponding to particular values of 'K-ratings', which represented deviations of the pulse and bar signals from their original shape, as determined by placing a graticule over an oscillographic display. A long series of subjective tests was carried out to determine these ratings for all the parameters of interest in the transmission of television signals. When this had been done, the method was taken up with enthusiasm and it has been registered by the CCIR as a standard testing method.

Experiments on colour television were started immediately after the war by Research Department in the old laboratories at Nightingale Square. Sequential scanning was used and, shortly after the move to Kingswood Warren, Surrey, the first demonstration was given with an iconoscope camera and a rotating colour disc. The system was not practicable, because of its dependence on mechanical moving parts and because of the amount of light required. But much was learned about colorimetry and lighting for television. In 1950 another colour disc system was proposed by CBS in America and was actually adopted by the FCC as the American standard system for a short time. Strong opposition to this system, however, caused it to be abandoned in 1953 in favour of the NTSC (National Television System Committee) system, the first demonstration of which was attended by F. C. McLean, then Deputy Chief Engineer. McLean brought back the NTS Committee reports, and Engineering Division decided that the system represented the right approach, and that experiments on it must be started immediately. By the beginning of 1954 an NTSC-type of signal adapted to the 405-line standard was being produced at Kingswood Warren and progress continued from there.

The achievement of the NTSC in developing their system in a remarkably short space of time was a good example of sustained co-operation to achieve a clearly-defined goal. It had been thought that colour television would require the transmission of three signals corresponding to three primary colours, each occupying about the same bandwidth as a monochrome system. This would have been extremely wasteful in spectrum space and would not have fulfilled the essential requirement that colour signals must be compatible. Fortunately, the eye is less sensitive to fine detail in colour than in black and white, so it was found unnecessary for all three primary colours to have the same standard of definition. The NTSC found a way of transmitting sufficient colour information to enable almost all colours in the spectrum to be reproduced by using only three signals, one corresponding to the brightness of the scene (the luminance signal) and two carrying all the additional information needed to portray colour (the chrominance signals). The two chrominance components were applied in quadrature to a colour sub-carrier within the video band. Thus, the composite colour signal occupied no more bandwidth than the equivalent monochrome transmission. Furthermore, the reproduction of the luminance signal alone produced a satisfactory black-and-white picture on a normal monochrome receiver. In later years the performance of the NTSC system in practical viewing conditions was substantially improved by two variations, the PAL and SECAM systems, based on the original NTSC system – which is itself still in use in the USA and several other countries.

Much work was done in Designs Department in testing equipment produced by Marconi's for scanning slides and 16-mm films, colour pictures from which were radiated by a standby 5-kW transmitter at Alexandra Palace. (The early colour transmissions were double-sideband and continued to be so until the Crystal Palace station opened in 1956. When radiating DSB colour, the 5-kW transmitter at Alexandra Palace gave an output of only 3 kW.) The signals were also sent round the SB system to Manchester and back, with surprisingly good results.

Encouraged by these experiments, a working party was sent to the United States to see the working of colour television in established studios. As a result of its report, an Experimental Colour Group was formed and S. N. Watson (later Chief Engineer, Television) was put in charge of it. This group, which included a producer, a make-up expert, and a lighting expert, set up experimental colour equipment in the old Studio A at Alexandra Palace and was soon able to radiate a series of programmes after the close of the television programme, beginning on 10 October 1955. A number of colour television receivers were distributed among observers, who sent in completed questionnaires covering various features such as colour accuracy, picture sharpness and compatibility (the Television Advisory Committee had laid down that whatever colour system was adopted must be compatible, that is the pictures must be receivable, in black-and-white, on the receivers then in general use).

Despite all the activity of BBC engineers in the post-war period – a period of financial stringency imposed by the Government – there was strong pressure from the programme side for a higher rate of progress in producing new types of equipment. On 3 February 1949 the OB Manager, C. I. Orr-Ewing (later Lord Orr-Ewing), who was about to leave the BBC, drew up a list of improvements that he considered necessary. He thought that the specialist engineering staff dealing with the supply of studio, film and OB equipment was too small and that the rate of delivery of telecine and film equipment, caption scanners, epidiascopes and back-projection equipment ought to be speeded up. He proposed that the whole of the television service should be placed under a single Director, with a Chief Engineer reporting to him. (This was done much later, in 1969, when the television operations and maintenance departments under the Chief Engineer, Television, were placed on the establishment of the Managing Director Television – though still answerable to the Director of Engineering for professional standards.) No doubt there was room for improvement, but the Engineering Division was taking the lead in many new developments to which a whole series of published papers by BBC engineers bear witness.[55-61]

Among these developments were several highly-sophisticated techniques to provide new facilities for the programme services. One of these was 'inlay', which by gating the picture signal at appropriate points in the line scan could make a hole of any desired shape or size in the television picture and fill it precisely with a picture from another source. This made it possible to show, for example, a view of a building with an open window, the area occupied by the window being filled by a picture from another camera. This equipment was introduced into service in the middle of 1953. The portion of the picture to be suppressed was determined by an opaque mask placed over the raster of a flying-spot scanner. The transitions between white and black operated an electronic switch, which substituted the second picture for the first. Later, the flying-spot scanner was replaced by a vidicon camera focused on a rectangular light source on which the mask was placed. The masks could be moved as required to produce a variety of 'wipes'.

In a more advanced technique, known as 'overlay', the portion of the first picture to be suppressed was determined by the shape and position of a particular object in the second picture. The object was viewed against a dark background so as to give the necessary sharp transitions between black and white. Overlay permitted a dancer to appear to be dancing on the rim of a wine glass. A coloured version of this technique was later widely used for many other purposes including the superimposition of a picture of a newsreader on a background from a different source.

Transparency scanners were also introduced for showing still pictures from single frames and film strips. The technique of back projection, already used in the film industry, was adapted for television so that action could take place in front of a large translucent screen on which a background scene was projected from a transparency or, later, by a film projector synchronised with the camera.

Although at this time most of the television output consisted of live pictures from the studios and from OBs, it was necessary also to televise 35-mm and 16-mm films. Telecine equipment for this purpose had been available since 1936, but a series of developments was needed to overcome the problems of the intermittent motion of conventional film projectors. In the flying-spot system, a raster of uniform brightness was produced on the screen of a cathode-ray tube and an image of this raster was passed through a moving film; the emergent light beam, varying in intensity according to the density of each part of the image, was picked up by a photo-cell. In the twin-lens flying-spot system, the film moved continuously and two images of the raster were focused on the film. As each film frame passed through the gate, the first image of the raster scanned the odd lines and when the film frame moved to the next image the raster scanned the even lines. A mechanical shutter blacked out each image alternately while the other was scanning the film. Good pictures were obtained from this equipment, but it took about 8 seconds for the mechanism to run up to synchronous speed before the picture could be transmitted. To obviate this delay, which was unacceptable when a film sequence had to be inserted into a live programme, a system was introduced using rotating and tilting mirrors to hold the image of the raster stationary relative to the movement of the film. So long as there was no soundtrack, the film could be transmitted while stationary or while running up to speed. In another method the same result was achieved by using a rotating glass polygon to hold the image of the raster stationary relative to the film. The problems inherent in these systems were finally overcome with the advent of the vidicon camera tube and of film mechanisms with very low inertia (and hence a quick pull-down time), which permitted the use of an intermittent-motion projector in conjunction with a camera tube. The relatively long storage time of the vidicon covered the intervals when the optical image was blacked out during the film pull-down.

The sound component of a film transmission was at first derived from an optical track on the film, but later a magnetic sound track was introduced, either on the same film as the picture or on a separate film synchronised with it. The use of a magnetic track gave a great improvement in sound quality compared with an optical sound-track, especially if the latter had undergone several stages of dubbing before reaching the final positive film.[62]

During this period a change was made in the visual aspect ratio of the television picture. On 3 April 1950 it was altered from the pre-war standard of 5:4 (width: height) to 4:3, thus bringing it into line with the format of standard cinema film.

6   TELEVISION TRANSMITTERS AND RECEPTION

The decision that the Television Service should be re-opened in 1946 on the 405-line standard necessitated intensive work on the sound and vision transmitters at Alexandra Palace, which had been modified for war-time purposes. H. W. Baker directed the rehabilitation of the transmitters and their feeder and aerial systems. New aerials were erected to the improved design he had used during the temporary resuscitation of the transmitters in June 1940.

The transmitters and the aerial system were ready for service towards the end of January 1946, using the pre-war frequencies of 45 MHz (vision) and 41·5 MHz (sound). On 1 February 'Trade Test' transmissions started using artificial bars for the vision signal and 400 Hz tone for the sound. These transmissions gave the television dealers an opportunity to install new receivers and rejuvenate old ones before programme transmissions started again. On 7 June 1946 at 1900 hours the Television Service was formally opened by the Postmaster General and on the following day an OB of the Victory Parade was shown. Owing to the high density of the population in the London area, the coverage of the Alexandra Palace transmitters amounted to about 25 per cent of the population of the United Kingdom.

The frequency bands allocated for television in Europe by the Atlantic City Conference of 1947 included VHF Band I (41 to 68 MHz).[63] There was considerable discussion at that time on the choice between double- and single-sideband transmission for television stations. Those in the USA were using asymmetric sideband characteristics, but there were staunch advocates of the double sideband mode in this country. Sir Edward Appleton suggested that the London Station should continue to radiate both sidebands so long as it was located at Alexandra Palace, but the new stations should be planned for asymmetric sidebands. By this means five channels could be obtained within Band I instead of the three channels that would have been available with the use of double sideband at all stations. When the Crystal Palace transmitter was being planned in 1955 to replace the Alexandra Palace station, the arguments were again brought forward in favour of retaining double-sideband operation in London, but the advocates of vestigial-sideband operation won the day – largely because the receiver manufacturers were naturally reluctant to produce different receivers for use in different parts of the country.

The allocation of frequencies for television in Band I is shown in the diagram. From this it will be noted that with the exception of the Alexandra Palace transmitters occupying Channel 1 and operating with a double sideband characteristic, the other four channels are spaced 5 MHz apart. The arrangement of these channels conformed

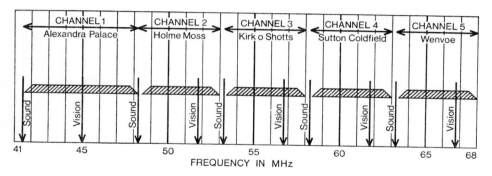

Television Channels in Band 1

with the system later known as System A, in which the spacing between vision and sound carrier frequencies on each channel is 3·5 MHz, the sound carrier being placed on the low frequency side of the vision carrier. The nominal width of the main sideband is 3 MHz and that of the vestigial sideband 0·75 MHz. The lower sideband of the vision signal is transmitted substantially unattenuated and with negligible phase distortion from a frequency 2·75 MHz below the carrier up to the carrier frequency. The vestigial sideband is attenuated by 10 dB at a frequency 1·5 MHz above the vision carrier frequency, i.e. at that of the sound carrier of the next channel. Both vision and sound transmissions are amplitude-modulated, positive modulation being employed for the vision signal.

Experience with the Alexandra Palace transmitters had shown that the average range was considerably greater than the thirty miles or so originally assumed and it was found that reception was often satisfactory, in the absence of interference, at field strengths as low as 40 dB μV/m. Nevertheless, in planning the new stations it was considered that an effective radiated power considerably greater than that of Alexandra Palace (34 kW) would be desirable. War-time developments had resulted in valves with considerably higher output power than those of the pre-war era. The first four of the new vision transmitters were ordered to a specification calling for an output power of 50 kW peak white. It was expected that an erp of about 100 kW would then be obtainable by using a design of aerial that gave a good compromise between bandwidth, mechanical rigidity and low wind resistance.[64] It was estimated that such transmitters sited in the Midlands, the North of England, Central Scotland and South Wales (or the West of England) would increase the television coverage to about 80 per cent of the United Kingdom population.[65]

The new stations were designed for eventual use as combined television and VHF/FM radio stations; the FM plant was to be installed in a separate part of the building and operated on a semi-attended basis. The aerials for the FM transmissions were to be of the cylindrical slotted type and it was arranged that these would be mounted on the masts immediately below the television aerials.

The four new high-power stations were opened between December 1949 and August 1952. The overall planning and engineering of the complete stations were carried out by the Planning & Installation Department in conjunction with Research Department and Building Department.

The first to be built was at Sutton Coldfield, where a site was chosen from several showing good predicted coverage as being the only one for which planning permission could readily be obtained. It was not considered necessary to test the site, which occupied some twenty-five acres near Hill Village, $2\frac{1}{2}$ miles north of Sutton Coldfield and about 10 miles north of Birmingham. It was approximately at the centre of gravity of the population of the Midlands and a first-class service was expected to be given to Birmingham, Coventry, Leicester, Derby, Stafford, Wolverhampton and Worcester.

The EMI/Metropolitan Vickers vision transmitter was high-power modulated, the modulation being applied to the grids of the valves in the final rf stage. The rf amplifiers were arranged in order of increasing power output from right to left, as seen from the front of the transmitter framework, and the four stages of the video modulator were arranged in order of increasing output from left to right. Thus, the modulator output stage was located next to the rf output stage. The modulator consisted of a pre-amplifier accepting an input of 1 V dap (double-amplitude peak, i.e. measured from the base of the sync. pulses to the peak of the picture signal) with a 70:30 picture-sync. ratio. An innovation in design of the pre-amplifier was the provision of means for adjusting the picture-sync. ratio and the curvature of the input/output amplitude characteristic to compensate for non-linearity in the later stages of the transmitter. The pre-amplifier was followed by a sub-sub-modulator with a cathode-follower coupling to the sub-modulator, a black-level clamp being applied to its input. The sub-modulator drove the modulator, which was connected as a cathode follower having a low impedance output capable of supplying the heavy grid current taken by the final rf stage and also the large capacitive input current to this stage at the highest video frequencies.

The pre-amplifier used receiver-type valves, but all other stages of the modulator used the ACM3 valve. This had high mutual conductance, which made it particularly suitable for use in cathode-follower circuits. It used forced-air cooling and had an anode dissipation of 2 kW.

The rf section of the transmitter comprised five stages of amplification after a self-contained crystal drive. The output stage originally had two CAT 21 triodes in push-pull with earthed grids. The output stage was cathode-driven and grid-modulated and was coupled to a 51-ohm transmission line through a triple-tuned, balanced-to-unbalanced coupling circuit. When BW 165 valves became available they replaced the CAT 21 valves and the power output was then 50 kW. The high voltage dc supply was derived from hot-cathode mercury-vapour rectifiers. The main ac power supply to the transmitter was voltage-stabilised and phase-balanced by using moving-coil regulators, one for each of the three phases.[66, 67, 68]

The vestigial-sideband filters at this and other stations had to have consistent characteristics, so that the overall response of the transmitters plus the receivers would not vary between one area and another. The filter was designed to give no more than 3 dB attenuation at $0 \cdot 75$ MHz above the vision carrier and more than

10 dB at 1·5 MHz. The response curve was published by the BBC to assist receiver manufacturers. [69]

The sound transmitter (type BD 259) was supplied by the Marconi Company. This had a high-power Class B modulator, the amplitude modulation being applied to the anode of the final rf stage. About 14 dB of negative feedback was applied over the last four of the six stages in the modulator; rectified rf feedback was used to reduce the level of hum. The rf section was driven by a self-contained crystal drive and had four stages of amplification. The final stage used a BR 128 triode in an earthed-grid circuit with a carrier output power of 12 kW. The rf output was coupled to a transmission line through a harmonic filter. [70, 71]

The transmitter control equipment was concentrated on a control desk in a room with windows giving a view of the transmitter hall. Because of the complex nature of the electrical and mechanical interlocks, mimic diagrams were used to give an indication at a glance of the state of the circuits. Both air and water cooling were used in the vision transmitter, but only air cooling in the sound transmitter. [66]

The power supply was obtained from the mains via duplicate feeders. The buildings were electrically heated and in addition the exhaust air from the heat exchanger of the vision transmitter valve-cooling system was used for warming the transmitter hall when required. Maintained lighting circuits were fed from an emergency battery in case of a complete failure of power supply to the station.

The site at Sutton Coldfield is only 560 ft AMSL and to increase the aerial height above the surrounding countryside, a 750-ft mast was erected carrying a Band I aerial system with a power gain of 3 dB. As the proposed VHF/FM sound aerial was to be of the slotted cylindrical type radiating horizontally polarised waves, the presence of mast stays was not thought to be likely to distort the radiation pattern appreciably and a stayed lattice mast was decided upon. The mast was of triangular cross-section for the first 600 ft and within this section was installed a small electrically-operated lift (since removed) for maintenance purposes. Above the 600-ft level, the cross-section was circular for the next 115 ft and carried the VHF/FM slot aerial system. Finally, a top mast of square cross-section, 35 ft high, carried the Band I television aerials, The latter consist of two tiers, each of four folded vertical dipoles. Both vision and television sound signals were radiated from the same aerial, but were carried on separate 51-ohm transmission lines to the top mast and there combined in a diplexer before being fed to the aerials through a distribution feeder system. Initially reserve aerials were provided on a separate 150-ft mast, but these were later removed and reserve aerials were mounted on the main mast. [66] (The aerial arrangements were modified later, when UHF aerials were added.)

The programme input equipment for the sound component of the television signal was of standard BBC design. The vision input equipment accepted the signals from a Post Office coaxial cable from Birmingham (which could be connected to the London–Birmingham cable) and included provision for distribution and comprehensive monitoring. A telecine machine was installed initially as a stand-by source with a disc reproducer for apologies in sound only, but later a monoscope (an electron-beam tube producing picture signals from a fixed pattern deposited on an electrode within the tube) and, still later, a transparency scanner were provided to replace the telecine equipment. A tape reproducer replaced the original disc reproducer. A special receiver was installed to check the overall performance of the station.

A microphone was provided in an acoustically treated quality checking room, which was used as a studio for the opening ceremony by the Postmaster General on 17 December 1949. As Sutton Coldfield was the first large transmitting station to be commissioned by the BBC after the war, the arrangements for the ceremonial opening were lavish by modern standards. Some 300 guests were invited and were shown round the station in relays before assembling at the Sutton Coldfield Town Hall to witness, on picture monitors, the opening ceremony with Sylvia Peters as commentator. Unfortunately a valve failure in the vision transmitter delayed the opening by minutes, which seemed to the waiting assembly to be hours. As the ceremony was also being carried by the Alexandra Palace transmitters this delay was particularly unfortunate. At all later main stations – and at Sutton Coldfield in April 1953 – reserve vision and sound transmitters were installed having output powers of one-tenth of those of the main transmitters.

When the Sutton Coldfield station was being planned, it was evident that the coming of television to the Midlands would face television dealers with many problems in getting their staff accustomed to the installation and adjustment of receivers and aerials, so as to obtain the best results and to be able to deal with any abnormalities in reception that might occur. To assist them, it was decided to use a mobile pilot vision transmitter for some months before the opening of the new station. This transmitter operated on the vision frequency allotted to Sutton Coldfield ($61 \cdot 75$ MHz) and was located in the Birmingham area during August 1949 and in the Wolverhampton and Coventry areas in September and October respectively.

Sutton Coldfield operated on Channel 4 (vision $61 \cdot 75$ MHz, sound $58 \cdot 25$ MHz), vertically polarised and without offsets from the start of the service. It increased the television coverage by about nine million people.

The next high-power television transmitting station to be built was at Holme Moss. It was opened on 12 October 1951 and brought a further 11 million people within range of television for the first time, thus increasing the coverage to 65 per cent of the population. It was intended to serve as large an area as possible in the North of England, beyond the service area of Sutton Coldfield, and would have to be sited at a high point in the Pennine Chain to serve both Lancashire and Yorkshire. An inspection of the map indicated a site in the triangle Leeds-Manchester-Sheffield. Three possible sites were considered and Research Department carried out extensive field tests using a mobile transmitter and an aerial supported by a balloon.[72] Field strength measurements were made in the principal towns in the projected service area and a site at Holme Moss was chosen at a height of 1718 ft.

The Holme Moss station was approved by the Postmaster General in October 1949 and work was begun immediately in order to make as much progress as possible on the exposed site before severe winter weather set in. Although the layout of the station followed that of Sutton Coldfield, there were important differences. For example, to avoid extensive blasting in the rock sub-soil, the foundations had to be built up on one side, leaving a basement area. The nearest water supply to the site was from a reservoir 800 ft lower down the hillside and a pumping station had to be provided to raise the water to the transmitting station. Sewage disposal had to be arranged clear of this reservoir's catchment area and a drain was provided to Holmfirth at a cost of £12,000 to meet the Local Authorities' requirements. The exposed site necessitated special arrangements for heating the building; these comprised a combination of thermostatically controlled electric heaters and the use of exhaust air from the valve-cooling heat exchangers when the transmitters were operating. An additional room was provided to accommodate staff who might be snowbound during severe weather and this has been used on many occasions. It was decided not to provide a telecine machine for stand-by programming, but reserve transmitters were installed from the outset in an annexe behind the transmitter building.

The vision signal was routed to Holme Moss from Manchester on a ⅜-in. diameter coaxial circuit provided by the Post Office, together with screened pairs and control circuits in a special cable. A second coaxial circuit was available for routing vision signals to Manchester from the television OB pick-up point at Holme Moss. For the radiation of apologies and test patterns, a monoscope was originally provided, but was later replaced by a transparency scanner. A receiver tuned to Sutton Coldfield on Channel 4 was installed as a stand-by, in case of failure of the programme circuits.

The arrangement of the technical equipment at Holme Moss was generally similar to that at Sutton Coldfield, but the vision transmitter had an earthed-cathode amplifier in the final rf stage; the object of this was to ensure stability of the rf drive voltage when the input impedance of the rf output stage varied with the modulation. The modulator was a shunt-regulated cathode-follower.[73, 74] The Marconi type BD 353 vision transmitter was high-power modulated and delivered an output of 45 kW on Channel 2 (vision carrier 51·75 MHz). The rf output stage used a pair of BW 165 water-cooled thoriated tungsten-filament triode valves in balanced-bridge, push-pull connection with drive applied to the grids. The crystal drive was followed by four stages of rf amplification, the last being a cathode-follower stage. The modulator comprised an input amplifier, sub-modulator and black level clamp unit and a main modulator stage with stabilised ht and bias supplies. The bandwidth of the modulator was approximately 7 MHz and the output impedance approximately 8 ohms, giving a high degree of linearity in the modulated amplifier. Circuits of particular interest in this transmitter are the shunt-regulated cathode followers and amplifiers, and the use of neon tubes in the interstage dc couplings and as high-voltage stabilisers.[74, 75] (Neon tubes are used in constant-impedance networks because, when one is inserted in a dc circuit, the potential difference across it remains constant, provided it exceeds the striking voltage.) Two types of black-level clamp were used. In one, a correction voltage was obtained from the rectified output of the transmitter and was used to clamp at line speed in the normal manner. In the other, a high-gain feedback system, with a long time-constant, was connected to the same source and varied the voltage of the negative bias supply line. The input amplifier was a three-valve amplifier with cathode feedback to give a characteristic as flat as possible, and circuits to stabilise the sync. pulses.[76] Compensation was included for any non-linearity in the picture

z

region of the waveform arising from the amplitude characteristics of the modulated amplifier. In view of its complexity, the input amplifier was duplicated to guard against faults. Other means to reduce breakdown time included the provision of interchangeable sub-assemblies, which allowed a faulty unit to be removed and repaired in the test room.

The television sound transmitter at Holme Moss was a Marconi type BD 259, as at Sutton Coldfield, delivering a carrier output power of 12 kW at 48·25 MHz.

The reserve transmitters had rated outputs of 5 kW and 2 kW respectively. The vision transmitter was low-power modulated and the modulated signal was amplified in two stages of linear amplification. No vsb filter was provided for these reserve transmitters; the necessary shaping of the output characteristics was effected in the tuned circuits of the linear amplifiers. The sound transmitter was high-power Class B modulated. The sound transmitter was used with its output power reduced to 1·25 kW to preserve the 4:1 ratio of vision-to-sound power.

At Holme Moss the output of the main transmitter (after passing through the vsb filter) and the output from the main sound transmitter were connected to a combining unit mounted behind the vision transmitter. To give the combining unit sufficient power-handling capacity, it was fed with high-pressure air to increase the voltage break-down rating. Some of this air was allowed to escape to carry away surplus heat. The output from the combining unit was passed to the aerials over a single 51-ohm transmission line. At the top mast the feeder was connected to a split drum distribution system driving the individual pairs of dipoles in anti-phase. This arrangement had several advantages over the method used at Sutton Coldfield. The combining unit was at ground level, so that the cost of the second feeder to the top of the mast was saved and work on the combining filter could be carried out much more conveniently. Any mismatch between the combining unit and the feeders could be corrected, but even if this were not done the time delay between the direct signal and the reflection was negligible, so that the visible effect on the received picture was unimportant.

The mast was similar to the one at Sutton Coldfield, except that it was designed to withstand higher wind-loading and ice-loading. The dipoles were heated to prevent ice formation as far as possible. No lift was provided, as it was thought that it would be immobilised by ice at the very time it might be needed for maintenance purposes. The Band I aerials were similar to those at Sutton Coldfield. At the top of the 600-ft lattice section of the mast a dipole array for stand-by reception of Sutton Coldfield was mounted. Reserve transmitting aerials were initially provided on a separate 150-ft mast, but later a single reserve aerial was mounted on the main mast at the 470-ft level and was fed with combined vision and sound outputs through a separate transmission line. As at Sutton Coldfield a circular section 115 ft long was mounted above the triangular section, forming the slot aerial system for the VHF/FM transmissions.

The power supply for Holme Moss was brought in at 11 kV over two separate routes. In a sub-station on the site, 500 kVA transformers provided 415-V supplies for the transmitters and for the low-voltage distribution system.

Kirk o'Shotts was the third of the post-war high-power television stations to be built. Its main objective was to cover the densely populated area in the Forth–Clyde belt and as much of the rural Lowlands as possible. Site tests made by Research Department during the summer of 1949 resulted in the choice of a site at Harthill about twelve miles from Glasgow and about twenty-four miles from Edinburgh at an elevation of 90 ft AMSL. The station brought in a further 4·1 million potential viewers and thereby increased the total coverage to 72 per cent of the UK population. The station went into service on 14 March 1952 using the reserve transmitters. It used Channel 3 (vision 56·75 MHz, sound 53·25 MHz) and the transmissions were vertically polarised. The main transmitters for Kirk o'Shotts and its sister station, Wenvoe, had been ordered in January 1950 and the Kirk o'Shotts high-power transmitters took over the service with a minimum of ceremonial on 17 August 1952.

The main vision transmitter was provided by EMI (type 5704) and the main sound transmitter by STC (type CTS–12). The medium-power reserve transmitters were provided by the Marconi Company and were of the same type as previously supplied to Holme Moss.

The layout of the building at Kirk o'Shotts again followed closely that of Sutton Coldfield, but the main vision transmitter was low-power modulated. Modulation was carried out at the 600-W level in the rf chain and the modulated signal was then amplifiers in three push-pull, earthed-grid, Class B linear wide-band rf power amplifiers in cascade, using triple-tuned circuits like those in the output circuit at Sutton Coldfield.[76] The BW 165 valves in the final amplifier gave a rated output power of 70 kW at peak white, but the transmitter was operated at 50 kW output to improve its reliability.

The low-level modulated transmitter had several advantages. It cost less than the earlier high-level designs and the transmitter was smaller in size. The overall conversion efficiency was higher, and there were fewer stages using transmitting-type valves – which improved reliability. The video modulator amplifier used receiving-type valves throughout and was simpler than its high-level counterpart.

The vsb filter was similar to that at Sutton Coldfield and its output was connected to a combining unit in the transmitter hall.

The 15-kW sound transmitter was operated at 12½ kW. It was air-cooled throughout and had a single-ended, co-axial, earthed-grid, final rf amplifier with high-power Class B modulation.

A common aerial system was used for vision and sound. The combining unit at Kirk o'Shotts was of the coaxial in-line type; a 'sound pass/vision stop' filter was inserted between the sound transmitter output and the common output and a 'vision pass/sound stop' filter between the vision transmitter output and the common output. The output of the combining unit was connected to the common feeder, which was of a new type with a characteristic impedance of approximately 78 ohms. The inner conductor of this coaxial transmission line, which was weighted at the lower end, consisted of a locked-coil winding rope as used in mining practice, but modified so as to have low electrical loss and a uniform diameter along its length.[77]

This type of inner conductor had the advantage that it was free from joints, which could cause impedance irregularities and bad contacts caused by expansion and contraction. It was, however, removed later when modifications had to be made to the mast to accommodate UHF aerials.

The mast at Kirk o'Shotts was similar to those at the earlier stations and carried a VHF/FM cylindrical slot aerial as well as the Band I television aerials. A reserve aerial was initially provided on a separate 150-ft mast, but was removed to the main mast later and fitted at the 468-ft level.

Wenvoe was the fourth and last of the post-war high-power Band I television stations to be erected. Its objective was to serve a large part of the population of South Wales and in the West of England (in the Bristol–Bath area). Research Department conducted extensive tests during the winter of 1949–50 and the spring of 1950 at three sites, one in South Wales and two in the West of England. The site chosen was at 425 ft AMSL and was about four miles west-south-west of Cardiff, near the A.48 Cardiff–Swansea road, and some twenty-nine miles west of Bristol. The estimated coverage of the Wenvoe station was 4·3 million people and it raised the total television coverage to 81 per cent of the population of the United Kingdom.

The plant at Wenvoe followed very closely that installed at Kirk o'Shotts, the transmitters, main and reserve, being supplied by the same three manufacturers and of the same types. The mast was similar and again used the locked-coil rope transmission line for the mast section. Wenvoe was allocated the highest frequency channel in Band I, namely Channel 5 (vision 66·75 MHz, sound 63·25 MHz), and the transmissions were vertically polarised. The station opened using the reserve, medium-power, transmitters, on 15 August 1952, and the high-power transmitters were brought into use on 20 December 1952.

It was decided that all the stations should operate with a ratio of 5:1 between the powers radiated on vision and sound. This value was adopted, after discussion with the industry, as the best compromise to reduce the risk of interference between sound and vision in the receiver.

The television coverage of 81 per cent reached with the completion of the first five high-power stations marked a significant stage, but it was by no means the end of the road. Plans were prepared for a further extension comprising five medium-power stations to be sited in the areas of Newcastle upon Tyne, Belfast, Plymouth, Aberdeen and the Isle of Wight. Later, two other medium-power stations were added to the list, one near Carlisle and another near Norwich. It was estimated that with these seven stations added to the initial five high-power stations, the coverage would be increased to about 97 per cent. Unfortunately restrictions on capital investment in the country as a whole made it necessary for the Assistant Postmaster General to announce in March 1951 that the construction of these medium-power stations would have to be postponed. Research Department nevertheless carried out an extensive programme of site testing, which continued until the summer of 1953 and included testing for the new station to replace the one at Alexandra Palace to serve the London area, and also for a station in the south-west of England.

The restrictions on capital investment were lifted early in 1953, but, unfortunately, this relief came too late for the new transmitters to be ready for the major event of that year – the televising of the Coronation Ceremony on 2 June 1953. However, in order to provide the maximum coverage for this important broadcast, the BBC obtained Government permission for temporary low-power stations to be erected near Newcastle upon Tyne, Belfast and Brighton, to provide additional, though restricted, coverage in these areas. For the first of these the temporary transmitters, which consisted of two pairs of converted RCA type ET 4336 transmitters, were installed in one of the pre-war television OB scanner vans, which was housed in a pre-fabricated building to protect it from the weather. This temporary building was sited on land at Pontop Pike acquired for the permanent station. A 250-ft mast was erected to support the three-stack 'Superturnstile' aerial. The programme was received on a short coaxial circuit from the nearby Post Office radio-link station on the route from Manchester to Kirk o'Shotts. The temporary station at Pontop Pike went into service on 1 May 1953, using Channel 5.

As the five channels in Band I were all being used by the five high-power stations, it was necessary for any further stations using that band to share channels with them. This raised the problem of co-channel interference. It was decided that some of the new stations should use horizontal polarisation so as to reap the advantage of about 10 dB discrimination that this would afford. The aerial at Pontop Pike was therefore arranged to give horizontal polarisation.

The temporary station to serve the Belfast area was erected at Glencairn, about $1\frac{1}{2}$ miles from the site chosen for the permanent station at Divis. The transmitters, mast and aerial were similar to those used for the temporary station at Pontop Pike. The programme feed was provided by rebroadcasting the Kirk o'Shotts signal picked up by the Post Office at nearby Black Mountain, and transmitted to the Glencairn Post Office station on a carrier channel. After demodulation there, the video signal was sent to the BBC Glencairn site on a short coaxial circuit. The Glencairn temporary station also went into service on 1 May 1953, on Channel 1.

The station to give temporary coverage to the Brighton, Hove and Worthing areas was sited at an ex-RAF site at Truleigh Hill on the crest of the South Downs north of Shoreham-by-Sea. The transmitters were again converted type ET 4336 units, mounted on a trailer. The Truleigh Hill transmitter went into service on 9 May 1953 using Channel 3, and used simple dipole aerials mounted on a 100-ft wooden tower, which already existed on the site.

The RCA type ET 4336 transmitters used for these temporary stations were originally designed for high-frequency communications with a power of 250 W; they were converted to deliver 500 W peak white power in Band I. The vision transmitters incorporated a completely new grid-modulated rf stage with a BBC-designed stabilising amplifier as the modulator. For the associated sound transmitters, a new rf stage was added and some improvements were made to the original modulator. The conversion of these transmitters and the production and installation of the temporary stations at Pontop Pike, Glencairn and Truleigh Hill was carried out jointly by the Designs Department and the Planning & Installation Department in three months.

On 20 December 1953 a similar temporary installation was put into service at Douglas, Isle of Man, and in 1954 low-power installations were completed at Redmoss, near Aberdeen, on 14 December, and at North Hessary Tor, Dartmoor, on 17 December. The Redmoss installation was similar to those at Pontop Pike and Glencairn, but was located in the Redmoss medium-wave transmitter building. The North Hessary Tor installation used a redundant 1-kW television OB mobile vision transmitter and a converted RCA type ET4336 transmitter for sound. The use of these temporary stations permitted a restricted service to be given in these areas, anticipating the permanent service by periods varying from ten months (at Aberdeen) to four years (at Douglas).

While the service was being carried on temporary equipment at a number of stations, work proceeded as fast as possible on the construction of the seven permanent medium-power stations. The site for the Pontop Pike station was at a height of about 1000 ft and about ten miles south-west of Newcastle upon Tyne. A first appraisal indicated that it would provide coverage of both Tyneside and Teesside. The latter area would be less well served than the former, but no other site appeared to give a more even coverage of these areas while still serving the other populous districts of Northumberland and Durham. This was confirmed by site tests. The building of the station and the erection of the mast raised problems, because the site was over a coalfield and subject to subsidence. Discussions with the National Coal Board established the position of the workings, including disused workings, and the expected rate of subsidence. In the disused workings the pit props had been left in place to rot away and collapse as the ground above subsided to fill in the tunnels. The building was therefore designed in five separate sections with flexible joints and special care was taken in the planning of the drainage system. These measures proved successful and the subsidence has taken place more or less as predicted. By 1971 it had almost ceased, having amounted to about 5 ft since the station was built. Frequent measurements of mast-stay tension were carried out during the first two years as a check on uneven subsidence of the stay-blocks, but this has also ceased and the mast stays are now subject to the same routine checks as other masts.

The permanent station at Pontop Pike went into service on 15 November 1955 using the same channel and polarisation as the temporary station. The medium-power transmitters were Marconi type BD 352 (vision) and type BD 263 (sound), as used for the reserves at the high-power stations.

In Northern Ireland it was evident from the topography that a site on the range of hills overlooking Belfast would be required to serve the most densely populated areas, while at the same time providing some coverage of the rural areas. A site at Divis, 1200 ft AMSL and some four miles north-west of Belfast was available and was considered satisfactory. The permanent station used Channel 1 with horizontal polarisation and came into service on 21 July 1955. The erp was at first 12 kW, but the aerial was later modified to give a directional pattern with a maximum of 35 kW.

The Divis station served 1·14 million people in Northern Ireland with minor coverage in England and Scotland of 42,500.

The first essential in the coverage of the South Hampshire area was that a high-grade service should be provided in Southampton, Portsmouth and Bournemouth, with Brighton, Winchester and Salisbury as desirable further targets. From an inspection of the map it appeared likely that the ridge of hills across the Isle of Wight might be a likely search area, with an alternative on the mainland near Southampton. Three possible sites were tested by Research Department and one was chosen at Rowridge Farm, some four miles west-south-west of Newport, Isle of Wight. The Rowridge site was at 450 ft AMSL and a temporary 200-ft lattice mast was erected to carry a BBC-designed two-stack experimental aerial mounted at a height of 175 ft, with a reserve aerial mounted lower down the mast. These aerials were directional to reduce unwanted coverage to the south and to enhance the signal northwards.

The transmitter installation at Rowridge was similar to that of the previous medium-power stations, but the provision of the vision signals presented a problem as the station was outside the reliable service area of both Wenvoe and Alexandra Palace. A programme feed was obtained from the Post Office on a radio link from Museum Exchange to a terminal at Rowridge itself with an intermediate relay station near Alton, Hampshire.

Rowridge used Channel 3 with vertical polarisation; the erp was initially 9 kW, but subsequently improvements were made to the aerial and a 450-ft mast was erected. In 1957 the erp was increased to 32 kW in the direction of maximum radiation.

It had been hoped that when the Rowridge station was operating it would be possible to close down the temporary installation at Truleigh Hill, near Brighton; but the coverage of Rowridge in the Brighton area was insufficient and it was decided to retain the station at Truleigh Hill. It could not, however, continue to work on Channel 3, which was used by Rowridge and it had therefore to be changed to work on Channel 2. The modification was made overnight by D. E. Todd (later Deputy Director of Engineering).

The station planned to serve Aberdeen was required to reach also a scattered population in north-east Scotland. The range of the Kirk o'Shotts high-power transmitter was known to extend as far north as Montrose, so that the new station could be sited to the north-west of Aberdeen; there was thus a good chance, using medium-power transmitters, of serving the coastal belt of the Moray Firth as far west as Elgin. A number of sites were considered, but only three were tested; the one chosen was at Core Hill, twenty miles north-west of Aberdeen at an altitude of 802 ft. Site tests indicated that Aberdeen would have a median field strength of about 2 mV/m and that the service area would extend to Elgin with a possibility that a secondary service would be given farther north. A temporary installation was commissioned at the Redmoss medium-wave station at Nigg, some two miles south of Aberdeen and the power was restricted so that the field strength in the centre of Aberdeen would be the same as would be given by the permanent station at Core Hill later. The temporary station, and the permanent one (to be known as Meldrum) that replaced it, both used Channel 4. To reduce interference from other stations on the same channel, horizontal polarisation was used and the carrier frequencies of the vision and sound transmitters were offset from the nominal values by $-6 \cdot 75$ kHz and −20kHz respectively. The effect of offsetting the vision carrier frequency by two-thirds of the line frequency was to reduce the visibility of the interference pattern in the received picture. The offset of the sound carrier was made 20 kHz so that the difference frequency was outside the audible range.

While the temporary station was in use, the programme from Kirk o'Shotts was received at a Post Office station at Craigowl and transmitted to Bruxie Hill and thence to a temporary Post Office terminal at Redmoss. With the opening of Meldrum, the programme was routed by SHF link from the intermediate station at Bruxie Hill to Granite Hill and thence to Meldrum. Further improvements in this link were made later.

The site for the Devon station was decided upon only after very careful consideration and tests at two sites. One was at Horner Down and the other, which was finally decided upon, at North Hessary Tor near Princetown on Dartmoor, and some thirteen miles north-north-east of Plymouth. The North Hessary Tor site was the only single site that would adequately cover Plymouth and its environs, and at the same time serve nearly all Cornwall, the Torbay district and Exeter. The proposal to build a broadcasting station with a 500-ft mast within the Dartmoor National Park raised serious objections from the Dartmoor Preservation Society, which led to a public inquiry being held in Exeter. The outcome was a decision in favour of the BBC and the North Hessary Tor site was acquired. The site was at a height of 1650 ft and was at first used for the temporary station, which went into service in December 1954. This used an aerial system consisting of single dipoles for vision (one for service and one as reserve) and another single dipole for sound. These aerials were supported on a square-section mast 150 ft in height. The vision transmitter was a converted television OB transmitter having an output power of 1 kW with a modified type ET 4336 transmitter as a spare. Type ET 4336 transmitters, modified, were also used for the television sound transmission – one service and one spare. The programme was obtained by direct pick-up from Wenvoe, and both the temporary and the permanent station radiated on Channel 2, vertically polarised, and with offsets of −16·875 kHz (vision) and −20 kHz (sound).

The permanent station at North Hessary Tor was similar to previous medium-power stations, though the elevation of the building was designed to harmonise with the surrounding landscape: the station was commissioned in May 1956 as described in the next chapter.

For the East-Anglian station a site seven miles south-west of Norwich at a height of 211 ft was acquired in 1954. This station, Tacolneston, was intended to provide a service to Norwich, Yarmouth and Lowestoft and to the population within a twenty-five-mile radius. For the permanent station an aerial with special directional properties was required to restrict the field strength in the Rowridge service area at its eastern limit towards Beachy Head, so as to reduce co-channel interference; it was also necessary to restrict radiation towards the service area of the Liège transmitter in Belgium. A temporary installation started service on 1 February 1955, using two pairs of STC type CG–1 transmitters accommodated in a wooden hut and using an aerial mounted on a 236-ft Post Office mast. The rural nature of this site may be

Sir Harold Bishop, Director of Technical Services/Director of Engineering, 1952–63

Above Marconi-Stille tape recorder, 1935

Left Philips-Miller film recorder, 1935

Top right MSS disc recorder, 1935

Right BBC Type D recorder, 1945

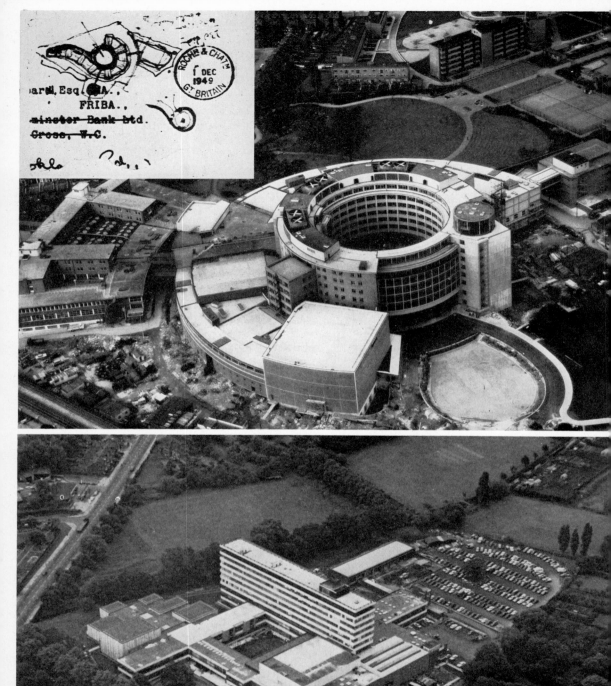

Inset Television Centre, London: The Dream, 1949

Top Television Centre, London: The Reality, 1960

Below Birmingham Broadcasting Centre, Pebble Mill, 1971

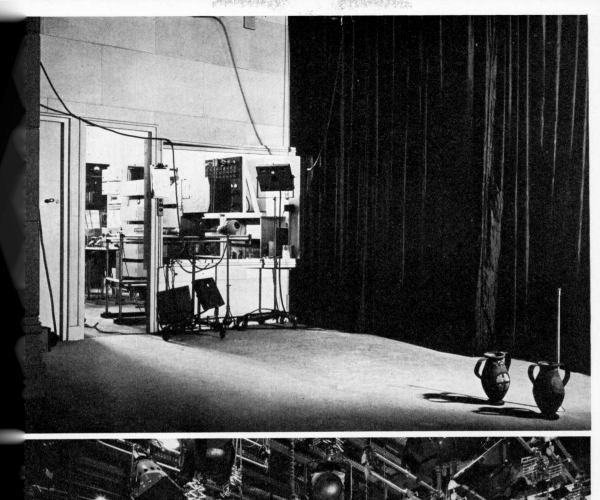

Top Television studio at 16 Portland Place, London, 1934
Below Studio 7 at Television Centre, 1965

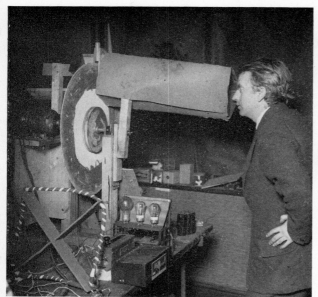

Above left J. L. Baird with 30-line scanning disc, 1925 (Photo: Radio Times Hulton Picture Library)

Above right Flying-spot scanner in Broadcasting House, 1932

Left Camera mounted on 'Iron Man', Alexandra Palace, 1950

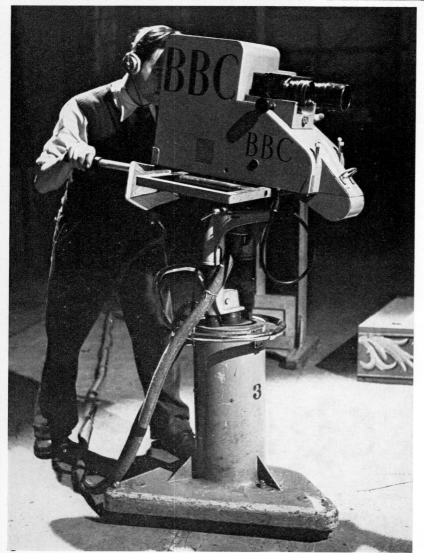

Right Image-Orthicon camera, 1960

Below Evolution of the camera tube

1 Iconoscope (standard Emitron)
2 Image Iconoscope (Pye Photicon)
3 Cathode-potential-stabilised Orthicon (CPS Emitron)
4 3-in. image orthicon (EEV)
5 4½-in. image orthicon (EEV)
6 Plumbicon (Philips)

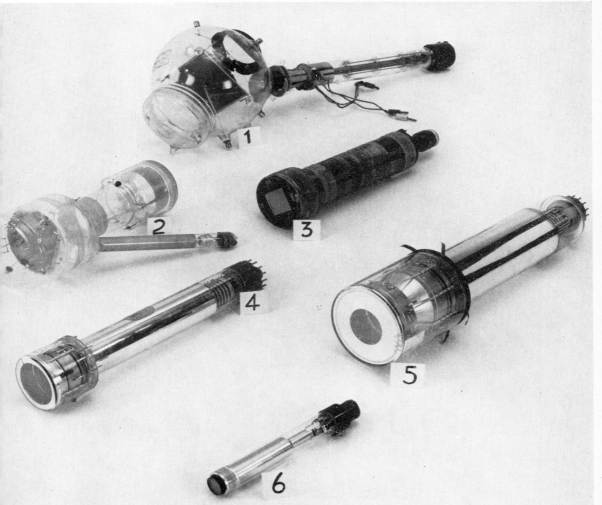

Alexandra Palace in wartime: cartoon by W. C. Pafford

judged from a comment of one of the original staff: 'It was not unknown for a gaggle of geese to stroll through the transmitter hut on a summer evening'. The permanent station was not commissioned until late 1956.

The vision programme feed was obtained initially by a temporary Post Office SHF link, which carried the Alexandra Palace signal picked up at Tye Green, near Saffron Walden, to a relay station at Depden Green near Bury St Edmunds, and thence on another SHF link to Tacolneston. This arrangement continued until 1959 when an improved link was provided from Sutton Coldfield.

Finally, in the period under review, a low-power installation was commissioned at Les Platons in Jersey. A site was found for this station at an elevation of 440 ft AMSL on the north coast of Jersey. It was fully tested by Research Department in 1952 and it was concluded that a station located there would provide reasonably good coverage of Jersey, Guernsey, Sark and Herm, but would not serve Alderney (some thirty-five miles away). The programme feed presented a difficult problem, as the only stations that could be used for rebroadcasting were North Hessary Tor and Wenvoe, and, at the time, North Hessary Tor was still a low-power temporary station. A receiving site was therefore acquired at Torteval in Guernsey, and an aerial system of sloping wires oriented on North Hessary Tor and Wenvoe was backed up by double 3-element Yagi aerials. The better of the two signals was selected manually and sent over the twenty-five miles to Les Platons on a 4-GHz BBC link. The receiving equipment at Torteval was accommodated in wooden huts for some years before being installed in a permanent building in 1960.

The Les Platons station used STC type CG–1 transmitters operating on Channel 4, horizontally polarised, with offsets of $\pm 6 \cdot 75$ kHz (vision) and $+20$kHz (sound). The mast was 165 ft in height and the erp was 1 kW. This was the first of the permanent low-power transmitting stations to be commissioned, and it was estimated that it served 106,300 people.

By the end of the year 1955 BBC television coverage had been increased to $93 \cdot 5$ per cent of the population of the United Kingdom. The addition of further stations raised the question how best to accommodate them within the five channels in Band I available to the BBC. The main problem was to avoid co-channel interference and the first step in planning was to separate stations using the same channel as widely as possible. The next step was to use vertical polarisation at one station and horizontal polarisation at another; this was of limited usefulness if more than two stations had to use the same channel.[78] A third measure, already mentioned, was to offset the carrier frequency of one station by a simple fraction of the line frequency, usually either plus two-thirds or minus two-thirds of the line frequency. This gave an improvement of about 10 dB. Another possibility of improving the results was to make the amount of offset extremely precise. Tests made by Research Department using the stations at Holme Moss and North Hessary Tor showed that, if the carrier frequencies could be controlled, so that the difference was less than about ± 2 Hz, a further advantage of about 7 dB could be obtained. During the experiment, the carrier frequency of Holme Moss was maintained accurately at its nominal value by using the 200 kHz transmissions from Droitwich as a reference frequency. The vision carrier of North Hessary Tor was then adjusted to give the precise value of offset required. This system required complicated equipment and it was not used in Band I except in special cases. Finally, resort was had to shaping the horizontal radiation patterns of the transmitting aerials where this could be done without unduly restricting the coverage. As the number of stations on the Continent using Band I increased, this technique became increasingly necessary to avoid international interference.

By 1955 the Alexandra Palace transmitters were nearly twenty years old and despite the many developments in the programme origination equipment, the transmitters had never restricted the overall performance of the Television Service. This is a remarkable tribute to those who were responsible for the original design and installation. However, when agreement was reached at the Stockholm Conference in 1952 for the use of 500 kW erp for the London station, it was decided to build a new high-power station to replace Alexandra Palace. The new station, which was to operate in the first instance with 200 kW erp, was to use the same channel as Alexandra Palace and, after considerable discussion, it was agreed that, unlike its predecessor, it should have a vsb characteristic. To obtain the desired coverage it was decided that the new station should be south of the Thames and in the winter and spring of 1952 Research Department carried out extensive site testing. It was predicted, and later confirmed by measurement, that to the $0 \cdot 1$ mV/m contour, the range of the Crystal Palace station would include $14 \cdot 5$ million people compared with the $12 \cdot 5$ million served by Alexandra Palace. Although site testing and a large part of the planning and constructional work[79] for the new London station took place in the closing years of the period under review, that station did not go into service until March 1956 and its commissioning belongs to the next chapter.

The reopening of the Television Service in 1946 and its subsequent extension to a large part of the country necessitated a major effort on the part of the receiver industry and the trade. Most of the pre-war receivers that survived the war had to be reconditioned and as television spread over the country new receivers had to be capable of working on any one of the five channels in Band I. Sales increased rapidly and the number of television licences increased from 14,560 in March 1947 to 4,503,766 in March 1955 – a three-hundredfold increase in eight years.

Soon after the war there was some interest in obtaining larger pictures comparable in size with those available from ciné projectors in the home. Some sets were sold that produced larger pictures by means of a projection system, using a very small tube giving a bright image in conjunction with an optical system. The projection screens had directional characteristics to improve the brightness of the display, so that the viewing angle was restricted. Projection receivers did not become popular, partly because the restricted viewing angle made it difficult for several people to watch the programme, partly because the brightness tended to be greater towards the centre of the screen than at the edges, and partly because direct-viewing tubes could give considerably brighter pictures. The latter eventually became universal.

The need for a bulky mains transformer and a rectifier to produce the eht supply for the picture tube was eliminated by using the high inductive voltages produced in the line-scanning transformer during the horizontal flyback period to generate the eht voltage. This development, together with the connection of the valve heaters in series rather than in parallel, led to the use of ac/dc receivers, which were lighter in weight and eased the problem of reducing mains hum in the displayed picture. In the ac/dc receiver the chassis could be live and care had to be taken in servicing to reduce the risk of shock.

When the television service reopened in 1946 many receivers cost more than £100 and it was surprising to note that quite a high proportion of them were in the homes of people with incomes in the region of £500 pa, many of them living in 'prefabs'. Increased production resulting from popular interest in television programmes and from the spread of the BBC transmitter network across the country (starting with the opening of the Sutton Coldfield station in 1949) enabled the price to be reduced to between £60 and £70, in spite of the introduction of purchase tax. It is much to the credit of the receiver industry and to modern production techniques that this price level was maintained into the 1970s, despite the complications resulting from multi-channel and dual-standard operation.

The first five high-power transmitters used vertical polarisation and most receiving aerials were vertical dipoles with reflectors, forming the large H aerials that were for many years a prominent feature of the landscape. Viewers in remote areas sometimes used high masts supporting aerials with more than one reflector to increase the directivity and so increase the available signal strength, while reducing co-channel interference from signals coming from directions remote from that of the wanted station. Mast-head amplifiers were occasionally used to overcome interference affecting the feeder, but, until transistors became available, such amplifiers were troublesome because the power supply, which had to be fed to the top of the mast, had to be of considerably greater capacity for valves than for transistors.

Ignition interference from motor cars and motor boats could be annoying, since few vehicles at this time incorporated suppressors. The trouble could usually be reduced by using a directional receiving aerial. Interference limiters were incorporated in receivers; these restricted the brightness of impulsive interference to that of peak white and so reduced the visibility of the dots and splashes of white produced by the interference. The limiter also reduced the size of the blemishes by preventing the defocusing of the tube that occurred when very bright pulses were reproduced.

Although the steps that were taken in planning the transmitter network to avoid co-channel interference were generally successful, viewers in fringe areas could still be troubled by it, especially when high-power transmitters came into service on the Continent. Co-channel interference can be caused by a high-power station at distances of some hundreds of kilometres by refraction in the troposphere, which is particularly likely to occur during periods of settled weather – that is during anti-cyclonic conditions. Such interference produces spurious patterns on the screen of the receiver. Another mode of propagation can produce interference in the VHF bands over distances of more than 1000 km by refraction in drifting clouds of ionised gases in the ionosphere known as 'sporadic-E'. Interference of this kind occurs mainly in the summer months. A third type of propagation that can occasionally cause interference over great distances is by refraction in the F_2 layer of the ionosphere. This type of propagation rarely produces serious trouble, but can occur during daytime in periods of maximum sunspot activity, when stations (including those used for communication purposes) as far away as the USA and South Africa, have caused interference in this country. Interference has also occasionally occurred from high-power communications stations using forward-scatter as the means of propagation, but steps to avoid such stations using frequencies in the neighbourhood of the television bands were taken at the Administrative Radio Conference at Geneva in 1959.[80]

Individual viewers might also be troubled by multiple images produced by multi-path propagation in areas where reflections from hills and tall buildings occur. This problem could often be eased by the use of directional aerials, which might, for best results, have to be directed at the source of reflection rather than at the wanted station. Local screening caused by obstructions could also reduce the available field strength and this problem again could be eased by the use of high-gain aerials, including those incorporating an amplifier at the mast-head.

The BBC's efforts to combat all these difficulties included giving advice to viewers on steps that could be taken at the receiving end and also the building of relay stations to increase the field strength available to viewers in the fringe areas of the main stations.

Other reception problems are of technical interest though not sufficiently wide-spread to constitute a general problem. These include, in some coastal areas where the receiver is screened from the transmitter by hills or cliffs, the appearance of delayed images varying in intensity with the roughness of the sea. A study of this phenomenon showed that it was caused by scattering of the radio waves by those of the sea. Another effect that could occur where the transmission path was over the sea was that the field strength varied with the state of the tide. Reflections from the surface of the sea set up a standing-wave pattern, which changed with the height of the reflecting surface and thus with the tide.

Since the early days of radio, interference had sometimes been caused by poor contacts in metalwork near the receiving aerial. These could produce a series of combination frequencies from two or more transmissions by inter-modulation and reradiation. This became known as the 'drain-pipe' or 'rusty bolt' effect. It also occasionally affected television reception and the cause was sometimes difficult to trace. In one particular instance, it was tracked down to a rusty back axle in a scrap-yard and hence became known also as the 'back-axle effect'. Spurious frequencies could also be radiated by the broadcasting stations themselves, and much care was taken to eliminate them.

The steps taken to combat interference from electrical machinery and appliances have been described in section 2 of this chapter. The types of interference particularly affecting television are those caused by the ignition systems of vehicles and by electro-medical and industrial equipment operating at radio frequencies. Ignition interference was the subject of a Statutory Instrument issued in 1952 and electro-medical equipment was similarly dealt with in 1963. Industrial rf equipment, such as is used for plastic welding and wood glueing, presents special difficulties because it often operates at high power and interference may be caused over a wide area. The makers and users of such equipment, and of electro-medical equipment, were exhorted by the Post Office to use one of a series of frequencies that were allocated by international agreement for this purpose. One of these frequencies is in Channel 1 of Band I and is not therefore available for general use in this country. In cases where it is necessary to use frequencies within or adjacent to the broadcasting bands to achieve the desired heating effect, the Post Office operates a zoning system by which users of potentially-interfering equipment are asked to employ frequencies other than those of interest to television viewers in the part of the country concerned.

The line-scanning oscillators and the local oscillators in television receivers could themselves cause interference. On the 405-line system the former operated at 10,125 Hz and its harmonics occasionally interfered with reception of Droitwich on 200 kHz. As most British television receivers designed for the 405-line standard in Band I had intermediate frequencies of 34·65 MHz for vision and 38·15 MHz for sound, the local oscillator frequency (being higher than that of the carrier) could fall within Band II and thus interfere with VHF/FM radio transmissions when they were introduced in 1955. Television reception itself sometimes suffered from local-oscillator interference when dual-band receivers came into use in 1955 with the start of the ITA service in Band III. Recommendations to receiver manufacturers on the limitation of these types of interference and on measures to be taken to reduce the susceptibility of receivers to interference were incorporated in a British Standard, first published in 1940.[81]

There were considerable improvements in the design of television receivers, brought about by improvements in valves and by the development of ferrite magnetic materials, which reduced the losses in transformers and deflector coils. The use of picture tubes with wide deflection angles reduced the dimensions of receivers.

The extension of the television service during this period and the peculiarities of propagation in the VHF bands made it more than ever necessary to maintain close co-operation between the BBC and the radio receiver manufacturers, represented by the British Radio Equipment Manufacturers Association (BREMA). They also made it necessary to build up technical liaison with viewers and with dealers, many of the latter being represented by the Radio and Television Retailers' Associations of England, Scotland, Wales, and Northern Ireland. The Engineering Information Department dealt with technical enquiries from viewers and advised them on their reception problems. For this purpose it was necessary to know about reception conditions in all parts of the country; this information was assembled partly from field-strength maps produced by the Research Department, partly from surveys undertaken by the Engineering Information Department, and partly from interviews with dealers and correspondence. The use of the VHF bands (and still more the later use of the UHF bands) implied that reception conditions, especially in hilly or built-up areas, could vary over a small area and even between one house and the next. It was therefore impossible for the BBC to give detailed instructions to individual viewers on the types of aerials they would need. This could be done only by dealers having local knowledge and experience. They have therefore played a major part in improving the general standard of reception. Naturally, some of them have shown greater skill and enthusiasm for this work than others – it is all too easy to blame the BBC transmission system for shortcomings that could be put right by expert attention to the receiving installation. One viewer who had been advised by the BBC to consult a local dealer, replied that this was useless because his dealer 'did not know the difference between a dipole and a tadpole'. Fortunately the enthusiasm of most dealers, aerial contractors, and servicemen, and the efforts of the Retailers' Associations, has brought about a general improvement, despite the increasing complexity of the problem resulting from the use of the VHF band and subsequently the introduction of colour television in the UHF bands. Improvements in the performance and reliability of receivers and in the design of aerials have also made great strides towards the goal of trouble-free reception. The annual number of letters received by the Engineering Information Department about television reception problems has varied as follows (the corresponding numbers of television licences are given in brackets):

1950	1600 (approx.)	—	(343,882)
1960	4694	—	(10,469,753)
1970	4230	—	(15,882,528)

7 RECORDING OF RADIO AND TELEVISION PROGRAMMES

The post-war decade was a period of striking changes in the recording world. Television recording made its first appearance. The Marconi-Stille and Philips-Miller systems of sound recording vanished from the scene. The BBC Type D disc recorder, although it was installed in only modest numbers, set a new standard of technical quality. The most far-reaching change in sound recording was the introduction of the magnetic tape system that had been put into a practicable form by the Germans during the war. At the beginning of 1945 there was not a single machine of this kind in the BBC; by 1955 over 200 of them were in operation and they were handling more than half the sound recording work.

The first undertones of disenchantment with the Philips-Miller film system had been heard as far back as 1943. By then $33\frac{1}{3}$-rpm disc recording was firmly established, and a direct comparison of the two systems was possible. It showed that the quality of recordings made on the two systems was about the same, but discs had a quieter background and considerably lower running costs than the Philips-Miller system. In fact, the cost per hour of film, sapphires, rental, and royalties for Philips-Miller were at least ten times as great as the cost of blank discs, cutters and depreciation for $33\frac{1}{3}$-rpm disc recording.

In April 1945, with the end of the war in sight, M. J. L. Pulling made an appraisal of the Philips-Miller system, pointing out that as a result of the ageing of the equipment and the great improvements in disc recording, it no longer held the pre-eminent position it had had before the war. He noted that the system still had some operational advantages and recommended that the BBC should continue to use it, but that the number of channels should be reduced as soon as possible, although at least one reproducing channel would have to be retained indefinitely to cope with the stock-pile of Philips-Miller recordings (some 10,000).

From then on there was a fairly rapid run-down of Philips-Miller equipment. The channel at Bristol was surrendered on 1 July 1945, and the three other channels that had been taken over at the beginning of the war were handed back to Philips by the end of June 1946. The BBC was then left with the two original pre-war sets at Maida Vale. In September 1948 one of these channels was bought from Philips and for the the time being the other set continued to be rented as a stand-by. Finally, in October 1950, all recording on Philips-Miller came to an end, and the stand-by channel was returned to Philips. The pair of machines that were bought in 1948 are now in the BBC's collection of engineering museum pieces, though regrettably the cutter-heads have been lost.

The run-down of Marconi-Stille was more rapid. One of the drawbacks of the system was the great weight of the reels of steel tape: 25 lb for half an hour's playing time. Two out of the four channels were withdrawn during 1945, and by 1946 there was only one channel, at Maida Vale, still in service. In 1952 the last four machines were written off. But two have survived – one in the Science Museum and the other in the BBC's engineering collection.

A curiosity of the post-war decade was the multiple mobile recording unit. Familiarly known as the 'octopus', because of its eight wire recorders, this unit was constructed (at a cost of £4650) for the European Services, and made its first appearance at the 1948 Olympic Games. The idea behind it was that several commentators of different nationalities could record their accounts of the same event simultaneously. The recorders were medium-quality machines made by Wirek Electronics Ltd, under licence from Boosey and Hawkes. In 1953 they were replaced by Ferrograph tape recorders.

In June 1945 the BBC Type D recorders (described in chapter IV, section 6) installed in Broadcasting House completed their two months' service trial. They proved a great success, although there were a few criticisms of details of the design, where compromises had had to be made to avoid prolonging the development work. H. L. Kirke gave his opinion that the Type D recorder represented a substantial advance over all other known disc recording machines, European or American, and he emphasised the importance of starting a production run as soon as possible.

By this time a large number of Presto channels were in use, and thoughts were turned to replacing them gradually by Type D recorders. A complete replacement programme would have needed something like thirty channels, but because of the possibility that the Magnetophon system might take over some of the load, quotations for only six, twelve, and twenty-four channels were invited from three firms. The contract was placed with EMI for twelve Type D channels (each comprising two machines), at rather more than £4000 per channel. One was completed in June 1948 and by the end of the year seven had been accepted. The first one to be installed went to Bristol, where it replaced a Presto channel at the beginning of 1949. Thereafter Type D recorders were commissioned at Broadcasting House, Bush House, and Oxford Street, and at Maida Vale (for the Transcription Service). The desirability of ordering another batch was mooted more than once, but was overtaken by the growth of magnetic tape recording. Thus, Type D recorders were installed in modest numbers, and did not, in the event, replace all the Presto recorders.

After the war mobile disc recording in London and the Regions became firmly established. The first of the Humber Pullman cars, which were to become a familiar feature of the recording scene, was commissioned in 1946 to replace the 18-hp Austins. By 1949 there were forty-three units in London and the Regions. Most of them were equipped with Type C recorders, though there were a few Presto transportable recorders as well. In 1951, five more units were added. This was the high-water mark, and from then on mobile disc recording gradually declined in quantity and importance as magnetic tape increasingly took over.

The development that had the most profound influence on post-war recording was the magnetic tape system perfected in Germany during the war and embodied in the Magnetophon recording/reproducing machine. This was developed in the 1930s by the Allgemeine Elektrizitäts Gesellschaft (AEG) and was first marketed about 1935 as a dictating machine. Instead of the steel tape or wire commonly used at that time for magnetic recording, the Magnetophon used paper tape impregnated with iron dust and later cellulose-acetate film, $6 \cdot 5$ mm wide, coated on one side with a thin layer ($0 \cdot 01$ to $0 \cdot 02$ mm) of ferric oxide. This was known as C tape. Before long the Reichs Rundfunk Gesellschaft (the German broadcasting organisation) became interested in the system and set about trying to improve its performance. In 1940 Dr Braunmühl, in collaboration with Dr Walter Weber (both of the RRG), made a fundamental discovery, or rather re-discovery, that was to have far-reaching consequences. This was that a dramatic improvement in performance could be achieved by applying a high-frequency signal to the tape in addition to the audio-frequency signals to be recorded. Up to this time dc bias had been used to displace the operating point to the linear portion of the curve relating flux density to magnetising force. The amplitude that could be recorded without distortion was limited to the straight portion of the curve. When hf bias (at about 100 kHz) was used, with an amplitude considerably greater than that of the af signal, it was found that the remanent magnetisation after several cycles of the hf was proportional to the af signal over a wide range of amplitudes.[82] As von Braunmühl said, 'The success of this expedient was quite astonishing in regard to extension of the frequency range, to reduction of non-linear distortion and, in particular, to elimination of background noise.' This advance led to wholesale adoption of the Magnetophon by the RRG. Before long, all their programmes, except news bulletins, were being pre-recorded, most of them on Magnetophons, and they were consuming 5000 km (5000 reels) of tape a month. (Von Braunmühl and Weber's invention of hf bias had been anticipated by a patent taken out in the USA by Carlson and Carpenter in 1921;[128] it does not appear to have made much impact at that time, presumably because the magnetic recording equipment and materials then in use were not good enough to show up the advantages of the discovery.)

By the end of the war several versions of the Magnetophon were available in

Germany, among them the K4, which was the original static broadcasting machine with dc bias and wiping, the HTS with hf bias and wiping that succeeded it, and the K7, the latest static machine for broadcasting, which had only just made its appearance. There were also transportable and portable models known as Tonschreibers.

In the course of the war, an improved kind of tape (L tape) was developed by I. G. Farben to replace the film, which tended to become rather brittle during storage. The new tape was a homogeneous combination of polyvinyl chloride and magnetite, which had good mechanical properties. Later, another tape, the LG, was produced, in which a polyvinyl chloride backing was coated with a magnetic layer. In contrast to the steel tapes used in the Blattnerphone and Marconi-Stille systems, the Magnetophon tapes were thin, light, easily cut and rejoined, and cheap to make.

The BBC had heard of the Magnetophon before the war, when the present writer inspected one in Germany. At that time the tape frequently broke, but it was obvious that the machine could have important applications in broadcasting if this defect could be remedied. The improvements resulting from the introduction of hf bias and the use of less brittle material for the tape occurred during the war. The extensive use that the Germans were making of the Magnetophon became known from an article entitled 'Radio Changed Over to Magnetic Steel Tape', which appeared in *Das Reich* at the end of March 1944. But it was not until the Allies had penetrated into Europe that any equipment came to hand. In November 1944, F. C. McLean, who had been seconded to the Psychological Warfare Division of SHAEF, was able to send home a sample recording from among the thousands he had found at Radio Luxembourg; but no recorder was available, as the Germans had not abandoned any when they retreated. However, by March 1945, the BBC had managed to borrow one machine, a Tonschreiber B as used by the German army, and this was followed in July as a broadcasting model, type HTS, with hf wiping and bias. These machines created a favourable impression.

By January 1946 the BBC had acquired seven Magnetophons. Six of them were RE3s, a static version with dc wiping developed for the German navy. Two of these and one HTS machine were sent to Research Department for evaluation. The rest were lent for examination and dissection to four manufacturing firms – BTH, EMI, Marconi's, and STC – with the idea that they might develop and manufacture something similar. In the meantime, a great deal of valuable information on the Magnetophon was obtained by the technical mission that visited Germany at the end of 1945 to investigate war-time developments in recording. M. J. L. Pulling (BBC) and E. M. Payne (EMI) were members of this mission.

During the summer of 1946, as plans for the new Third Programme began to take shape, it became clear that because of the unreliability of Continental circuits and restrictions on their use immediately after the war, live relays from abroad of musical programmes, including opera, could not be counted on. In the circumstances the best alternative seemed to be to use Magnetophon recordings made on the Continent, of which there was a generous supply, provided that Engineering Division could set up a reproducing channel. Although there were some misgivings about this, the two HTS machines that the BBC had acquired by then were pressed into service to make a reproducing channel at Maida Vale. This channel became operational with the start of the Third Programme on 29 September 1946, and was first used for a reproduction of *Der Rosenkavalier*, recorded by Radio Hamburg. The result was highly satisfactory, both from the operational and the technical points of view. (The Magnetophon channel had a six-year run, closing down on 3 November 1952, by which time British-made tape recording equipment was readily available.)

On 2 December 1946 a demonstration of the Magnetophon was staged at Nightingale Square. The model used was type K7, the current broadcasting model, which had the following specified performance figures:

Tape speed	77 cm/sec (30 in./sec)
Tape width	6·5 mm ($\frac{1}{4}$ in.)
Length of reel	1000 m
Playing time	20 minutes
Overall frequency response	within ± 2 dB from 50 to 50,000 Hz
Signal-to-noise ratio	50 dB
Distortion at 1000 Hz	3 per cent

These figures were not altogether substantiated in Research Department's tests of the machine. The signal-to-noise ratio was only 43 dB and the response was nearly 8 dB down at 50 Hz. Nevertheless, the K7 was appreciably better than its predecessor, the HTS, and Research Department conceded that, though its performance was not quite as good as the best obtainable from their own high-grade disc recorder (type D), it was quite good enough for most purposes. The engineers and programme heads who attended the demonstration concluded that the Magnetophon system had great advantages, and they recommended that, subject to a satisfactory service trial, it should be developed for general programme use, the ultimate aim being to confine recording to two systems only – tape and disc.

The setting up of two channels for the service trial proved much harder to achieve than anyone had imagined. The expectations of being able to get four K7 Magnetophons from Germany were not fulfilled, and the British manufacturers had a long way to go before they had anything comparable to offer. By February 1948, however, EMI had produced a first-grade static machine. They had in fact built three sample machines by then, and had staged a demonstration at the Royal Society, which BBC engineers had witnessed. In July 1948 they had progressed to the point where they could lend the BBC two of their static machines, Type BTR/1. These went first to Nightingale Square for examination by Research Department and then to Maida Vale for a four-month service trial. Research Department reported that the BTR/1 was comparable with the Magnetophon in performance, though some modifications would be needed to make it acceptable operationally. All hope of getting more Magnetophons having meanwhile evaporated, the money set aside for them was spent on four of the EMI machines, at about £600 each. They arrived before the end of the year. Designs Department had two of them, Research Department one, and one was kept by Recording Department.

This was a start, but more experience was needed before the BBC committed itself to magnetic recording. When the question was discussed in June 1949 Ashbridge forecast that magnetic recorders might eventually be so improved that they would be able to replace disc recorders, and it was agreed that the experiments should continue. To this end four more BTR/1 machines were ordered, and also a number of static and mobile machines made by Tolana in France.

In agreeing to the continuance of tests, the Board of Management had stipulated that a joint report by Engineering and Programme interests on the present capabilities and future potentialities of magnetic recording should be prepared in due course. This was presented in October 1949, after a BBC delegation had visited Brussels, Hamburg, Copenhagen, Stockholm and Oslo, to study recording practices there. The report reiterated the, by then, established view that there was a place for tape alongside disc in the BBC's operations. It was decided that magnetic tape should be tried out, at first experimentally and then in service, and that its application to programme requirements should be the subject of study by a committee. Thus, the stage was set for comprehensive service trials and a further report.

The committee was formed in January 1950, and the service trials started in February. By the end of March, A. P. Monson (then Superintendent Engineer, Recording) felt confident enough to broadcast a programme recorded on tape: an edition of *Much Binding in the Marsh*. A recording was made of the live performance on 12 April 1950, and this was transmitted as a recorded repeat on 14 April. It was an unqualified success, and from then on four or five repeat programmes from tape recordings were broadcast each week.

Three kinds of equipment figured in the service trials: static recorders for studio centres; mobile recorders, suitable for use in recording cars; and 'midget' recorders, small and light enough for a commentator to carry around and simple enough for him to work himself. The static equipment consisted of a pair of the EMI BTR/1 machines, which had been installed at Maida Vale. For the mobile tests, Tolana (French) equipment was used, there being no suitable British recorder available. There was a similar difficulty over the midget recorders; two British recorders had been ordered in March 1949, but when a prototype was produced, it was disappointingly heavy. By August 1949 hopes for a British design of midget recorder had waned. At about this time, however, the Stancil-Hoffman Corporation in America produced one; it was compact and light, 14 in. $\times$ $6\frac{1}{2}$ in. $\times$ $6\frac{1}{4}$ in. and weighing only $12\frac{1}{2}$ lb, and would run for about an hour before the batteries gave out. Features Department were keen that some of these should be provided for their contributors to the Christmas Day programme, but dollars were scarce and the suggestion was turned down. However, it was found possible to borrow one from the Columbia Broadcasting System in time for it to be sent after Colin Wills, who had by then left for Africa, and soon afterwards two more were obtained, again on loan, from Paris. In addition, four copies of the Stancil midget were made by a British firm under licence in 1950, but they were not a success. Luckily, however, the BBC still had the borrowed Stancil machines, and was able to use these for the service trials.

The committee's report, when it came out in September 1950, marked a turning-point in the evolution of recording in the BBC. From then on tape recording increasingly gained ground until eventually it swept the board and ousted every other system. The report's main conclusion was that tape recording should be introduced as soon as possible, with the expectation that in three to five years' time it could undertake 60 per cent of the recording work, with a resultant saving on discs of £50,000 pa. The report also included recommendations on tape speed, which should be 15 in./s for static recording (though the machines should be capable of $7\frac{1}{2}$ in./s as well), and both 15 and $7\frac{1}{2}$ in./s for mobile and midget work. The report was accepted on 6 November and an estimate was produced in October 1951. The scheme was an ambitious one: it included 66 static and 44 mobile tape recorders, 44 midgets, and 2000 reels of tape, at a total cost of just over £200,000. But the times were not propitious; capital expenditure was strictly controlled by the Government and the scheme had to be postponed until 1953. However, enough money was found to go ahead with 30 out of the 44 mobile recorders needed. The choice fell on the RGD recorder. The mobile version was in two units – recorder and amplifier – each weighing about 90 lb. Four of these machines had been obtained at the beginning of 1952 for the Royal Tour of Australia, which was abandoned. By the beginning of 1953 these four, and the thirty that followed later, had been installed as static machines in London and the main Regional centres.

Over the three years, 1950 to 1952, there were important developments in British equipment. In 1950, EMI decided to go ahead with a midget recorder. By February 1951 a first model appeared to be extremely promising and it soon became clear that EMI was the only British firm able and willing to develop a midget recorder to the BBC's requirements at that time.

An initial consignment of six EMI midget recorders was delivered early in 1952, at a cost of about £100 each. Several of them were put through their paces abroad, one with Wynford Vaughan Thomas in India, another in Africa, and three at the Olympic Games in Helsinki. In November 1952 the first big order – for thirty-eight of them – was approved. From then on the number of EMI midget recorders steadily increased until by 1955 there were over a hundred of them in service.

The EMI midget tape recorder was compact and light – it measured only 16 in. $\times$ 8 in. $\times$ 8 in., and weighed 16 lb (7·3 kg) when loaded. Originally the tape speed was 15 in./s, which gave a playing time of $7\frac{1}{2}$ minutes. The frequency response was within $\pm$ 2 dB from 50 to 3000 Hz, 6 dB down at 5 kHz and 12 dB down at 10 kHz. Harmonic distortion was low – about 0·85 per cent at maximum input level. In 1954 the tape speed was changed to $7\frac{1}{2}$ in./s, which extended the playing time to fifteen minutes, without any noticeable sacrifice of quality. Conversion to transistors in place of valves began in 1958. In addition to its role as a commentator's personal recorder, the EMI midget was widely used as a sound recorder for films intended for television.

Small and light, yet robust, the EMI midget held the field unchallenged for over fifteen years until the German-made Uher began to supersede it towards the end of the 1960s.

Another important development of the early 1950s was the EMI type BTR/2 static recorder, the successor to the BTR/1. This was a completely new design, which, unlike the BTR/1, lent itself to remote control. It also had a superior performance,

390

with an overall frequency response within $\pm$ 2 dB from 40 Hz to 10 kHz at a speed of 30 in./s. At 15 in./s the response was within these limits up to 8 kHz. Harmonic distortion at maximum input level was 1 per cent at 30 in./s and 1·5 per cent at 15 in./s. The unweighted signal-to-noise ratio was 54 dB at either speed, which was remarkably good. A prototype was obtained for tests by the Designs and Recording Departments at the beginning of 1952; production models began to appear early in 1953 and large orders were placed for this recorder during the summer. With improvements in the design of the machine and in the quality of the tape, the performance of the BTR/2 was considerably improved and for many years it was without a rival for static recording in the BBC. In terms of robustness, reliability and ease of operation and editing. Some machines were later modified for stereo operation. At the beginning of the 1950s EMI were also successful in their attempts to produce a tape with high coercivity – that is with high resistance to demagnetisation. The results were improved performance at the higher frequencies, lower noise level and less risk of print-through from one turn to the next during storage.

Another development was the Leevers-Rich portable recorder. A mains-driven design was on the stocks as early as September 1950, and this was followed by a battery-operated version in two units, together weighing just under 200 lb (90 kg) including the battery. These recorders established a reputation for themselves on their first assignment – the Royal Commonwealth Tour of 1953–4. From then on the Leevers-Rich recorder was increasingly used for mobile work, and it is still the BBC's main recorder in this field.

Originally all recording and reproducing machines were mains-driven, and this meant that the speed at which they ran depended on the frequency of the electricity supply. After the war the demand for electricity outstripped the installation of new generating equipment, and as a result the stability of the mains supply deteriorated, the frequency varying from about 48 Hz to 52 Hz between peak-load and light-load conditions. At worst this could cause a half-hour programme to overrun or underrun by as much as two and a half minutes. It also affected the pitch and Stanford Robinson, who was Opera Director, complained about this in December 1946; a Magnetophon recording of Smetana's opera *Dalibor* was, to his ear, 'more or less entirely ruined by the fact that the whole performance was put out a semi-tone sharp . . . The result of this was appalling . . . The singers' voices were radically changed in quality by such a marked error in pitch, and the whole performance took on a hectic atmosphere quite out of keeping with the composer's intentions.'

The problem was tackled in 1949 when a scheme for fitting the Transcription Unit with permanent frequency-stabilising equipment went ahead. This improvement was later extended to the main London and Regional centres. At the larger London centres a 12-kVA or 17·5-kVA frequency-stabilised motor alternator was provided to drive the recording equipment. In the Regions, where the load was lighter, a 1-kW power amplifier driven by a 50-Hz tuning fork was adopted. A variable-frequency supply was also developed so that speed errors in a recording could be corrected during reproduction.

For reproducing disc recordings and gramophone records at 78 rpm the pre-war

TD/7 desk had long been in use. After the war a new disc reproducing desk, type DRD/1, was designed by the BBC to take either 78- or 33⅓-rpm recordings. Special care was taken in the design to maintain constancy of speed and the desk incorporated a groove-locating unit with a parallel-tracking arm fitted with an EMI type 12 pick-up. By the end of the period under review, there was need for a new desk for reproducing fine-groove recordings at 45 and 33⅓ rpm. The DRD/5 designed for this purpose included an optical system to indicate the position of the pick-up on the disc and a novel form of quick-starting arrangement, designed to avoid damage to recordings and styli and to suppress the output until the correct speed had been reached. [83]

At the end of 1952 the 1951 scheme for a major investment in magnetic recording was revived and approved at an estimated cost of £225,000. It provided for a complement of 82 static, 35 mobile, and 50 midget recorders, with the implication that tape would eventually take up 60 per cent of the recording load. During 1953 good progress was made, and by the end of the year, 48 static, 30 mobile and 42 midget recorders were operational, spread over London and the Regions. By the end of 1954 about three-quarters of the equipment was delivered, and in 1955 the scheme was finally completed.

During the summer of 1953 A. P. Monson and Brian George, Head of Recorded Programmes, visited the United States and Canada to see what they could learn from the recording practices current there. Three things struck them in particular: the concept of central recording and reproducing rooms, the use of recording equipment in studio cubicles, and the generous scale of equipment for editing. Their report, issued in October 1953, recommended that the BBC should adopt these ideas. The recommendation for centralised recording areas was put into effect ahead of the rest of the expansion programme.

The first central recording area, in the form of a reproduction room for transmissions, was completed in 1954 in the basement of Broadcasting House. It was fitted with eight BTR/2 machines, which could be started and stopped by remote control from the continuity suite taking the reproduction. Tape speeds of 30, 15 and 7½ in./s were available. This centralised system had the great advantage that it made for clearer lines of communication, because the continuity suite had to deal with only one point and one engineer on everything to do with tape reproduction. It also helped to free staff for the more exacting task of tape editing.

This transmission reproduction room quickly proved its worth. It was soon handling most of the reproductions for the Home, Light and Third Programmes, and it was by no means uncommon for it to originate as many as four programmes simultaneously. Encouraged by this success, Recording Department embarked on centralised systems at Oxford Street and Bush House for the External Services. There the pattern of programme commitments made it possible to give these central areas the dual role of recording and reproducing. They were equipped on the same scale as the one at Broadcasting House, with eight BTR/2 machines. The Oxford Street installation went into operation at the end of May 1955 and the one at Bush House followed soon after.

During 1954 it became clear that programme demands for magnetic recording had reached the point where they could no longer be met in full, and a working party was set up to study the problem. Its report recommended a large increase in tape facilities for the Home Services and endorsed the recommendations resulting from the visit to the United States and Canada. A scheme estimated at £216,000 was authorised in November 1955, comprising 54 BTR/2 machines, 8 Leevers-Rich mobile recorders, and 38 EMI midget recorders.

When television started up again in 1946 it soon became evident to engineers and programme staff alike that it would be a great advantage to be able to record television programmes. They were thinking mainly of being able to repeat during the evening a programme that had been broadcast during the day; many important topical programmes, such as the Royal Weddings, the Olympic Games, and the Lord Mayor's Show, took place during the day when many people were unable to watch them. It was also appreciated that television recording would have other, and increasingly important, advantages for the export of programmes and for easing the demand on studios by relieving them of repeat performances and permitting several instalments of a series to be recorded in one session.

In 1947 a method suggested by Philip Dorté was tried out, using an ordinary 35-mm film camera to photograph the television pictures. It had the limitation that only one frame of each interlaced picture – half the picture information – could be recorded, the other frame being lost while the film was pulled down for the next scan. This gave rise to interference patterns when the film was subsequently transmitted by a telecine machine. Nevertheless, the first television recordings to be transmitted were made using this method in November 1947, one being of the Cenotaph service and the other of Princess Elizabeth's wedding.

In 1948 H. W. Baker tried modifying one of the Mechau 35-mm continuous-motion projectors used in telecine machines at Alexandra Palace to work in conjunction with a film camera. The experiment was a success, and after more development work had been done by W. D. Kemp, a telefilm channel comprising two of these machines went into operation at Alexandra Palace in November 1949. The following year the construction of a second channel, with three machines of improved design, was authorised at a cost of £30,000. Strenuous efforts were made by W. H. Cheevers, D. R. Morse and D. G. Packham to produce the new version before the Coronation, using improved Cintel display tubes and Mechau projectors specially adapted by W. Vinten Ltd for use as cameras. The improved Mechau channel was installed at Lime Grove before the end of 1952 and gave good results. An attempt to develop a 16-mm version was less successful.

At the same time it was resolved that another television recording channel must be ready in time for the Coronation the following year. This task was given to Research Department. With so little time for development work they decided to revive the 35-mm suppressed-frame system that Dorté had tried in 1947. A reappraisal had shown that the loss of vertical resolution resulting from the lack of half the lines in the picture was not as serious as had been thought. The interference patterns occurring when the film was scanned for transmission were avoided using the recently perfected technique of line-broadening, or 'spot wobble', in which each line of the display to be filmed was widened by applying an alternating vertical deflection to the scan. This telefilm channel, with two machines, was ready in time to record excerpts from the Coronation ceremony that were rebroadcast the same evening. The complete ceremony, lasting about seven hours, was recorded on the Mechau telefilm channel at Lime Grove. The suppressed-frame channel was installed initially at Alexandra Palace, but was later moved to Lime Grove where it continued to give reliable service until 1957, when it was substantially modified.

8 THE LINE NETWORK AND EUROVISION

As a result of the major changes in the system that were made during the war the network of programme circuits had grown by 1945 to many times its peace-time size; there was also an extensive communications network for telephony and telegraphy, but there were no television links at all. Peace-time brought the need for re-planning the entire network.

To take the programme circuits first, the SB system at the end of the war contained a preponderance of lines provided exclusively for the greatly expanded External Services, and it was clear that there would have to be considerable retrenchment, not only because of the run-down of many of the programmes that were broadcast during the war, but also because the scale on which reserve facilities and special routings had been provided to guard against the effects of enemy action would not be justified in peace-time. Although an entirely new network soon had to be set up for the Third Programme, one of the main preoccupations of the Lines Department during the period under review was to reorganise the SB system by reducing the number of lines and by routing those from the overseas studio centres direct to the appropriate transmitting stations rather than through BBC Regional Centres. Some changes would have been necessary in any case on account of the closing of the overseas studios at Aldenham and 200 Oxford Street and the concentration of all the External Services at Bush House, where they still remain.

The introduction of the carrier phantom circuits, described in section 5 of the previous chapter, into the SB system gave promise of considerable improvement in the quality of transmission, because in most cases it was found possible to achieve a transmitted frequency band of 50 to 11,000 Hz, whereas the pre-war upper limit had been about 7500 Hz on the most modern type of programme circuit then available. The velocity of propagation on the carrier phantom circuits was so high that phase distortion could be neglected. This was all to the good, because there were already some very vocal Hi-Fi enthusiasts who were critical of some of the BBC transmissions. (One of them, living in the neighbourhood of Newcastle upon Tyne, frequently commented on the quality of the transmissions from Stagshaw compared with those coming direct from London. There was little to be done about that, because, owing to the shortage of wavelengths, Stagshaw had to be synchronised with Lisnagarvey, and the programme had to be routed via Northern Ireland.)

The technique already mentioned for compensating temperature effects on the equalisation of long lines derived from carrier cables was consolidated and refined.[84] Although the quality achieved on the programme lines was much improved by these developments, the same could not be said about their reliability. A quarterly meeting was instituted in 1952, at which representatives of the BBC and the Post Office kept this problem under constant review. Statistics were compiled of the types of fault that occurred: interruptions, momentary breaks, sudden changes in level, overloading, noise and, occasionally, crosstalk. They established the fact that the carrier phantom circuits were not as reliable as had been hoped, and there was a clear connection between the number of faults per hundred miles of programme circuit over a given period and the number of access points in intermediate Post Office repeater stations. (The carrier systems had intermediate amplifiers at intervals of fifteen miles, whereas the older type of loaded circuit needed repeaters only at every fifty miles.) There was a great expansion of Post Office telephone facilities of all kinds after the war, and this necessitated the laying of large numbers of new carrier cables on many routes. These activities were apt to jeopardise the circuits already in service on the routes concerned, in spite of the efforts that the Post Office made to prevent this. The regular meetings helped to overcome these problems and to promote cordial relations; so much so that the meetings have continued, at a reduced frequency, ever since.

In 1949 television began to extend to the provinces with the opening of the Sutton Coldfield transmitting station, which had to be fed with programme from London. This was the beginning of the television SB system. Unfortunately it was also the beginning of heavy annual expenditure on vision links rented from the Post Office. Tentative planning of a distribution system for vision signals had begun long before the first Regional transmitting station was opened. In 1946 the BBC and the Post Office had agreed that a cable link to Birmingham should be provided, and the intention of the Post Office was to provide a number of coaxial tubes in a composite cable from London. Two of these tubes were to be 1-in. diameter and were intended to be capable of transmitting a bandwidth up to 10 MHz. (It was thought at that time that the definition of the television service might later have to be increased to about 1000 lines, so as to be comparable with that available in the cinema; this would have needed a bandwidth of at least 10 MHz.) Since the coaxial tubes could not be used efficiently at very low frequencies, the frequency band was transposed by using a carrier system. For 405-line transmissions between London and Birmingham, a vestigial sideband system was used with a carrier frequency of 6·12 MHz; the amplifiers covered the band 3 to 7 MHz, the upper sideband being partially suppressed. This arrangement avoided the problem of separating hum from the low-frequency video components and also eased the design of amplifiers, as the ratio of the highest to the lowest frequency was reduced.

There were delays in the completion of the cable with the result that when the BBC set a date for the opening of the television service in the Midlands from the Sutton Coldfield transmitter (December 1949), the Post Office had to provide an experimental radio link. This was a one-way link, which, however, could be reversed within a few seconds. Its performance did not meet the requirements that the BBC considered ought to be met by a chain of four or five links. The transient response was not good enough to prevent the obliteration of the suppression pulse preceding the line synchronising pulse, and this caused difficulty in synchronising receivers. Non-linearity was also a cause for concern. These results were not encouraging, because the planned network of vision circuits would include both $\frac{3}{8}$-in. coaxial tubes and radio links, and demodulation and remodulation at the junctions between them, would introduce additional distortion. Nevertheless, the subsequent development of the system was carried out successfully; this was due partly to the co-operation between the BBC and the Post Office and partly to the use of pulse and bar test signals, which played an important part in ensuring that the performance of the links was maintained.

By the end of the period under review the network had expanded to include the transmitting stations at Sutton Coldfield, Holme Moss, Pontop Pike, Kirk o'Shotts, Wenvoe, and Rowridge, all on what were described as 'fully-engineered' two-way links (i.e. with one uni-directional link in each direction). London–Birmingham transmissions used the 1-in. coaxial tubes in the new composite cable, which had come into service in late 1950. The subsequent extensions of the network in coaxial cable were on $\frac{3}{8}$-in. tubes with a carrier frequency of 1 MHz and the lower sideband partially suppressed, so that the bandwidth extended from 0·5 to 4 MHz. Such tubes were used in the Birmingham–Manchester composite cable with an extension, also in $\frac{3}{8}$-in. tubes, to Holme Moss. Between Manchester and Kirk o'Shotts there was a radio link with seven intermediate stations, one of which was at Pontop Pike, where demodulation took place to feed the Pontop Pike transmitter; the circuit between London and Wenvoe was provided by $\frac{3}{8}$-in. tubes and that between London and Rowridge by a radio link. As the network extended, other stations were connected to it either by picking up the signals from an existing transmitting station at a Post Office centre from which it could be passed over Post Office links to the new station, or by direct pick-up (rebroadcasting) at the new station. Although colour television was still in the future, tests were made to make sure that the network would be satisfactory for colour. Tests made over a loop from London to Manchester and back were reassuring on this point.

At this time discussions with the Post Office about the technical aspects of extensions to the vision network were done by Designs Department, whereas Lines Department became responsible as soon as the links were taken over for service and also negotiated rental agreements with the Post Office. A long series of discussions took place between the Lines Department, the BBC's Chief Accountant, and the Post Office on the amount of rentals and on the Post Office method of estimating.

The costs turned out to be substantially higher than the BBC had expected and they were subject to subsequent variation and also to an indemnity payment if the links were given up within forty years. As the vision links depended on the use of new techniques, the Post Office was naturally reluctant to quote firm figures in advance and the result was that when the rentals were finally fixed the BBC was faced with a bill that constituted a severe strain on its budget for the Television Service.

The upshot of this controversy was that in August 1955 the Post Office agreed that the process of assessing the costs was unsatisfactory. They then proposed that instead of levying a charge for each link based on its actual cost to the Post Office, the rental would be based on a fixed charge per circuit plus a mileage charge and that the rental for all the main two-way vision circuits, both cable and radio, for the BBC and the ITA should be averaged. Sir Ian Jacob, then Director-General of the BBC, welcomed the Post Office proposals and asked that before the construction of any new circuits was put in hand the BBC should be consulted about the method to be adopted; he also made suggestions about the way in which the accounts should be presented.

A most important development took place during the period under review. This was the start of 'Eurovision'. The exchange of radio programmes between different countries had become firmly established before the war. A corresponding development in television was much more difficult, because it necessitated the provision of international vision circuits and also because of differences in line standards. During the period just after the war the United Kingdom and France were the only countries in Europe that were actually operating television services; there was, therefore, a community of interest between them and programmes were exchanged in the only way then possible – by means of film – the French standards of 819 and 441 lines being different from the UK standard of 405 lines.

An international television relay of a rather special kind took place on 27 and 30 August 1950 when BBC cameras were sent to Calais to produce 405-line pictures for broadcasting in the United Kingdom. The vision signal was brought from the Hotel de Ville in Calais by a series of four radio links terminating at the Senate House of London University. The installation and operation of the radio links was planned and directed by the Planning & Installation Department and the OB arrangements in Calais by the Television Operations & Maintenance Department. The Designs Department also co-operated.

In spite of formidable difficulties, this pioneer venture was successful, though the picture quality was far from perfect. The radio links gave a great deal of trouble because of lack of measuring equipment at the intermediate stations, various forms of distortion and interference, and the fact that communications with the intermediate stations could be achieved only by simplex working over single-frequency links. The communication transmitter at one of the intermediate stations (Harvel, near Wrotham) had blocked the vision receiver working on $64 \cdot 75$ MHz and a harmonic of the crystal oscillator in the communication receiver caused patterning on the vision circuit. The communications link could not therefore be used while the vision circuit was being tested. There were also many administrative problems associated with an undertaking of this magnitude carried out in a foreign country. These were accentuated by the fact that the OB was to be done after dark, so that 90 kW of lighting equipment had to be sent from England and staging for it had to be erected. As the electricity supply in Calais was unsuitable for the lighting, which required dc, a mobile battery-electric generator had to be sent. A low voltage derived from the mains in the UK had to be transmitted over a control line to lock the frequency of the waveform generators in Calais to the frequency of the UK grid.

Link equipment provided by Standard Telephones and Cables was used between Calais and Swingate on 4700 MHz and between Swingate and Warren Street, near Lenham, on 4750 MHz. The cross-channel vision link was subject to severe fading, possibly caused by reflections from the sea. A mobile vision transmitter on 64·75 MHz provided the link between Warren Street and Harvel and a Marconi link on 6800 MHz completed the circuit to the Senate House in London. The communication links between adjacent stations were on 71·975 MHz.

The success of the Calais television broadcast led to a proposal that a series of OBs should be undertaken from Paris during the week 18 to 25 July 1951. It was evident, however, that in the short time available there would be no hope of being able to mount such a programme, which would have needed about eight radio-links in tandem, with all the technical problems that had already been experienced in the OB from Calais, and the administrative difficulties that would arise from the deployment of so much BBC equipment on French soil. It was therefore decided that the earliest date for such an ambitious project would be July 1952. The transmission of vision signals all the way from Paris to London would have placed a severe strain on the technical resources of the BBC; fortunately standards converters had become available by that time and this made it possible for the broadcast to be originated on 819 lines and broadcast both by the BBC and the RTF. The programmes were taken over by the BBC at Cassel in Northern France, where the BBC converter was installed. The four radio links, using Marconi, EMI and STC equipment and operating in the 7000 and 4500 MHz bands, brought the vision signals to the Senate House in London. At the same time a French firm produced an optical converter to enable the 819-line signals to be changed to 441 lines for the transmitter in Paris still working on that standard. The planning was done in close co-operation between the Engineering and Programme staff on both sides and a Franco-British Liaison Committee was formed for 'Franco-British Television Week 2 to 14 July 1952.[85, 86, 87] After a series of tests during the month of April the programme took place without any serious trouble. It was technically a complete success and it stimulated the regular inter-change of programmes that later developed into Eurovision and finally into world-wide exchanges through communications satellites.

The BBC optical standards converter had been developed by the Research Department earlier in 1952 using a cathode-ray tube to display the picture on the incoming standard and rescanning it with an image-orthicon camera operating on the receiving standard. It had seemed too much to hope that such a simple method would work, but by using a display phosphor with a delay time comparable with the time taken to scan a single television field, it was made to perform quite well when converting 819-line signals to 405 lines, both using the same field frequency.[88]

The success of the first attempts to relay television programmes between England and France led to the formation of an Anglo-French Television Liaison Committee to discuss further programme interchanges between the two organisations and when, in 1952, it became known that the Coronation of Queen Elizabeth would take place on 2 June 1953, this Committee considered the technical facilities that would be necessary to enable French viewers to see the ceremony. The success of the operation, described in the next section, led to further plans for international programme exchanges. Switzerland and Belgium started television in September and October 1953, respectively, and Italy and Denmark started early in the following year; all these television organisations adopted the standard of 625 lines, which had been recommended by the CCIR in July 1950 (see chapter IV, section 12). They were all keen to take part in programme exchanges. Close co-operation would be needed, and was indeed forthcoming, not only from the broadcasting organisations but also from the various Post, Telegraph and Telephone Administrations, which waived many of the normal formalities in order to ensure a good start for this new venture. The formalities were to come later, but at the beginning nobody worried about sending in bills or indeed about what charges were appropriate. It was decided that there would be one month of Eurovision, from 6 June to 4 July 1954; on any particular day one country would make one or more contributions, which meant setting up circuits to link the originating country with all the others. This venture was known as the 'Lille Experiment', because it was directed from a special control centre set up at Lille in France. The results were surprisingly good, although some of the links were far longer than any over which vision transmission had previously been attempted. Although some of the participating EBU Members were only beginning to develop their television services, they willingly co-operated in meeting the additional demands on their limited equipment and expert staff. Considerable difficulties had to be surmounted; international vision links were naturally less stable than national networks and many programme circuits had to be provided for commentaries in different languages as well as a large number of control circuits. It was during this experiment that the technique was evolved of using a single programme circuit to carry background sounds, so that each television service receiving the programme could super-impose a commentary in its own language.[87] The success of the Lille Experiment led to a larger venture, lasting three months – from 6 October to 31 December 1954.

The year 1954 thus marked the start of Eurovision.[89] The Technical Centre of the European Broadcasting Union (EBU) in Brussels, under the direction of the Technical Director (Henri Anglès d'Auriac until 31 January 1956 and afterwards Georges Hansen), took over the important function of technical co-ordination. BBC engineers played a major part: the chairman of all the *ad hoc* conferences for the planning of the programme exchanges was M. J. L. Pulling (one of the principal architects of Eurovision, who conceived it as an act of faith and carried it through by sheer momentum) and the BBC representative on them was T. H. Bridgewater, then Superintendent Engineer, Television OBs. The Chief Engineer of the Technical Centre at Brussels was J. Treeby Dickinson, seconded from Engineering Information Department, and the detailed planning and operation was done, first by E. F. Woods on a six-months' secondment from Lines Department, and later by E. Griffiths, who was transferred permanently from the engineering staff at Bristol.[90]

The growth of popularity of Eurovision has been spectacular. In 1954 the number of transmissions co-ordinated by the EBU's Control Centre in Brussels amounted to 55. In 1955 there were 91 transmissions, making a total of 115 hours; nine television services could be connected to the network.[89] The corresponding figures for 1970 were 3510 transmissions totalling 1772 hours (not counting 'unilateral' programme exchanges not requiring co-ordination by the EBU Technical Centre); 29 television services belonging to EBU Members then had access to the network as well as others in Eastern Europe and overseas. (In the figures for 1970 the twice-daily news exchanges are each counted as single transmissions, although each consists of several items coming from different points of origin.)

Immediately after the war, when Regional Broadcasting started again and communications between the Regions and London became important, traffic studies were undertaken to determine how many telephone and teleprinter channels should be provided on the main routes.[91] Data were at first hard to obtain, since the traffic developed only gradually, and as a consequence bold assumptions had to be made, some of which had to be modified later. During the war the BBC had developed a carrier system for deriving three telephone circuits from two programme circuits, one in each direction (see chapter IV, section 5). It was decided that the best way of meeting the post-war traffic requirements was to plan the required telephone channels as far as possible in groups of three and to provide them by means of the carrier system. Each telephone channel could also be made to carry a voice-frequency teleprinter channel if required, and would still comply with the requirement of a minimum bandwidth of 2300 Hz and a maximum overall loss of 15 dB between any stations that were likely to be interconnected over the system. The cost of renting two programme circuits was the same as that for three telephone circuits, so the teleprinter channels did not cost anything except the capital and running costs of the carrier equipment. In addition, it was possible to operate a number of such carrier systems on programme circuits that for fairly long periods – especially during the day when the telephone traffic was heaviest – were not required for programme. In the 'inward' direction, these were contribution circuits and some reserve circuits, and in the 'outward' direction they were distribution circuits for the Third Programme (which did not start until 1800 hours) and other reserve circuits. With this added consideration, the scheme fully justified itself financially. A further advantage was that the loss from end to end of each carrier telephone channel was only 3 dB, whereas the loss on a rented Post Office tariff 'D' circuit was never less than about 10 dB; thus, even if three carrier channels were connected in tandem through intermediate switchboards the loss would still be only of the same order as that on one tariff 'D' circuit. (The Post Office could quite easily provide low-loss circuits between Post Office terminals, but the local-ends between Post Office terminals and BBC premises brought the overall loss up to 10 dB or more.)

The electrical design of the carrier systems was straightforward. The channel filters were designed according to well-established principles,[92] the only unusual feature being that, in order to economise in bandwidth, it was found possible to use adjacent filters in channels 2 and 3 in which the cut-off frequency of the lower-frequency filter was slightly higher than the cut-off frequency of the higher-frequency filter. Where carrier telephone channels were permanently connected together (e.g. a channel of a London–Birmingham system to a channel of a Birmingham–Manchester system to form a London–Manchester PBX circuit) they could be lined up so that the overall loss was still only 3 dB.

Among the teleprinter services, an 'Engineering Teleprinter Network' was set up for the purpose of sending BBC engineering service messages. This involved the installation of a number of teleprinters in various control rooms on the main routes and, as it was obviously too expensive to have an individual connection from the London control room to each centre, they were connected together omnibus fashion, which meant that all messages were repeated at all stations on the network. Although the idea of the Engineering Teleprinter Network was welcomed by the Studio Operations & Maintenance Department, it was not a success, probably for two reasons: first, because it was not possible to provide operators in the control rooms who knew how to use the teleprinters and, secondly, because if a fault occurs on an omnibus circuit it is likely that all subsequent stations along its length will be affected. It was found that service messages were becoming more inaccurate and were taking longer to transmit than those passed by telephone. The Engineering Teleprinter Network was therefore discontinued – without, however, any waste of equipment, because by that time there was a demand for more teleprinter channels for inter-office purposes.

By the early fifties it had become apparent that the music channels being provided by the Post Office on carrier phantom circuits could generally be relied upon to transmit a frequency band up to 11,000 Hz, and the suggestion was put forward by F. C. Barrett of Lines Department that a fourth telephone channel could be added to the existing carrier systems to cater for the expanding demand. This suggestion was put into effect, with the result that a number of the carrier systems became four-channel systems.

Apart from the introduction of many long-distance circuits throughout the BBC network, great changes had to take place in the local internal networks at the different centres. Before and during the war all the telephones that could be connected to the Post Office system were dependent upon manual switchboards except the Midland Regional offices at Broad Street, Birmingham, where there was a small private automatic branch exchange installation (PABX). The staff of the BBC, however, had grown enormously during the war, particularly in London, with the result that immediately after the war there were large groups of staff at Broadcasting House, 200 Oxford Street, Bush House, Aldenham, Alexandra Palace and Maida Vale, and there were manual boards at all these places; these were of various sizes and types and were interconnected by a multiplicity of tie-lines, so that there were high overall losses on calls routed through switchboards in tandem. The manual switchboard at Broadcasting House in 1939 consisted of thirteen positions serving some 300 to 400 extensions, and was situated on the seventh floor. After the bombing incident in 1941 this switchboard was transferred to what was considered a safer place on the ground floor of Egton House, and from time to time it was enlarged by the addition of more operating positions until the total number, in 1952, was thirty-two. The service was unfortunately deteriorating all the time. The staff was still increasing in numbers and a number of buildings in the neighbourhood were taken over, some with their own separate small PBX switchboards, which introduced additional operations and more losses. It was no longer possible to give any relief by handling purely internal traffic on the PAX system, which had been in operation since the early 1930s, had only 750 extensions, could not be extended, and was coming to the end of its useful life. These problems had been foreseen before the end of the war, when, on 25 October 1944, they were discussed with the Post Office. In the following year, a recommendation was made by H. B. Rantzen that the BBC's future internal telephone requirements in London should be met by a Private Automatic Branch Exchange (PABX); he showed that this would be more economical than to continue with a large PBX installation supplemented by an equally large PAX system, which could not be connected to any outside line.

There were attempts to find accommodation for a PABX installation in various places, including The Langham and All Souls Church Hall, all of which were fraught with difficulties, and it was not until the end of 1954 that it was agreed that the installation should be housed in the new extension to Broadcasting House, with the switchroom on the second floor and the apparatus room in the basement. The ultimate capacity of the Broadcasting House installation does not differ materially from that envisaged in 1944. It is now the normal practice to have a PABX in each major centre, although before the war, there was some opposition to the PABX idea because it would mean the discontinuance of much of the helpful service that a good PBX operator could render.

Another effort that was made in connection with the PABX installation turned out to be unsuccessful. Detailed studies showed that the cost of maintaining the proposed installations could be greatly reduced if the BBC were permitted to undertake it with its own staff. This proposal was put twice to the Post Office, who turned it down, explaining that non-Post Office maintenance was permitted only to the telephone manufacturers and to the railways. The BBC therefore purchased equipment approved by the Post Office from one of the recognised major contractors and paid the Post Office the appropriate annual charge for its maintenance.

Circuits for outside broadcasts can be regarded as temporary extensions of the SB network. On the television side the Lines Department engineers, having built a great deal of apparatus for the purpose of taking television OBs over cable circuits, were ready to take up again the work they had done in this field before the war. However, the Post Office decided to do it themselves. They accordingly set to work to design their own equipment, which the BBC rented from them. The Post Office also provided injection equipment, which enabled OB signals, collected by local cable or by radio link, to be fed to London from an intermediate Post Office repeater station by the return leg of any one of the main two-way television links. This meant that, with the help of the mobile microwave links that had become available, OBs became possible from a very large part of the United Kingdom by the end of the period under review.[93] Northern Ireland was a notable exception, because as yet there was no return link to Great Britain. The decision of the Post Office to undertake this OB transmission work on cable circuits was a considerable stimulus to Designs Department in devising test equipment with which to check the transmission qualities of the circuits the Post Office provided (see section 5).

402

On the sound OB side, techniques of equalising and lining up cable circuits remained much as before the war. Overhead circuits had disappeared during the war except for isolated lines to villages. Non-loaded cable circuits and bunched cable pairs continued to be used in increasing numbers as the number of sound OBs increased. Up to the late 1940s the Lines Department were still using the pre-war portable equaliser repeaters, PER/3 and PER/4, already described, but by 1948 the old sets were replaced by type PER/5, which combined in three light boxes of equal size, designed for stacking, the various facilities that had hitherto required about five much heavier boxes. The top unit comprised a telephone set, a bridge megger and all the switches necessary for changing amplifiers, operating the telephone and carrying out tests. Each of the other two boxes comprised an amplifier and two equalisers of different types, operating between the three amplifier stages; all the valves were of type EF50. This equipment represented a great simplification and reduction of weight, and the soundness of its design can be judged by the fact that it is still in service some twenty-four years later. The other principle item of gear for OB circuits was a variable-frequency oscillator. After the war one such oscillator was produced for line-testing purposes, the PTS/10. This oscillator was continuously variable in frequency, the frequency-determining element being a Wien bridge in the feedback path; it was based on a design of S. N. Watson (later Chief Engineer, Television). Like the PER/5 repeater, it is still in service, the secret of its durability being, perhaps, its flimsy case, which looks so fragile that people take great care of it.

An important development in the post-war era has been the introduction by the Post Office of their 'OP Network' of occasional programme circuits. This they did by installing programme amplifiers in many places to form a network, parts of which they offered for use as required for OBs. At first these circuits were variable and it was often necessary to test them in the same way as circuits that the BBC were to equalise and line-up themselves. The troubles gradually receded, however, and the OP network was useful in providing replacement circuits for parts of the private wire network when faults occurred and also for occasional circuits between studio centres on the SB system as well as for OBs.

For sound OBs from remote locations, the Post Office might be able to provide only circuits suitable for telephony, with a bandwidth of perhaps 300 to 3000 Hz. In such cases the 'split band' technique already described was used; better-designed systems were constructed after the war and enabled difficult places such as the Channel Islands (immediately after the liberation), the Orkneys and Shetlands, and some remote places in Northern Ireland to be drawn into the programme catchment area.

9 OUTSTANDING BROADCASTS

Among outstanding broadcasts, those taken from outside the studios are usually of the most technical interest, because each one has to be treated individually and presents special engineering problems. In pre-war days the BBC had already earned a reputation for its presentation of events of public interest, and in the period under review this reputation was maintained and enhanced – television now playing a full part in the reporting of such events. As Sir Harold Bishop remarked of this period: 'Outside broadcasts . . . play a more important part in the BBC's television programmes than in those of any other broadcasting organisation.'[94] A few examples will be given of broadcasts that set a pattern for future undertakings of this kind.

The Fourteenth Olympiad – 29 July to 14 August 1948 – was at that time the most ambitious series of broadcasts ever undertaken by the BBC. The cost of the installations was nearly £130,000. It was necessary to build a complete broadcasting centre for both sound and television at Wembley, near to the Stadium and the Empire Pool – the two chief centres of activity. An old 1924 Exhibition building, the Palace of Arts, was converted into, virtually, a temporary 'Broadcasting House'.

A technical committee under L. Hotine, the Senior Superintendent Engineer, guided the planning of the broadcasting centre at Wembley and the arrangements at other venues, such as Harringay Arena, Henley and Torquay. Although the coverage for radio was considerably more extensive, television used two mobile control rooms (they were usually called 'scanners' then) at Wembley, one for the Stadium events and the other for those in the Empire Pool. It could be said, and was indeed said, that the Olympic Games put British television 'on the map'.

As this was an international event, the facilities to be provided were dictated largely by the requirements of the foreign broadcasting organisations. The final arrangements at the Palace of Arts broadcasting centre included the provision of eight sound studios, each equipped with two disc-reproducing turntables, eight disc-reproducing cubicles capable, if necessary, of being used as reserve studios, a record library, twenty disc-recording channels operating on 78 rpm and twelve mobile recording cars. On the television side, there were two production rooms for the control of material incoming from the two 'scanners' in the Stadium and the Empire Pool and a central control room with monitoring equipment, vision mixer, distribution amplifiers, etc.

The sound facilities had their own, much larger control room. A total of 121 microphone positions were installed for the commentators at the various venues, of which 32 were at the Stadium and 16 at the Empire Pool. Altogether 150 microphones and about 600 amplifiers were used, and nearly 300 engineers were deployed for this event. Lip microphones were used throughout. Red and green cue lights were provided at each microphone position and each broadcaster had earphones enabling him to take his cue, to listen to his own output or to receive messages from his 'controlling' engineer. In the Stadium and the Empire Pool he could switch his earphones to the Post Office time signal (TIM), to various BBC programmes and, in the Stadium, to the local public address announcements. During the sixteen days of the Games, 1500 live broadcasts were transmitted and 6000 recordings were made; the control room was the largest the BBC had ever built, although its working life was less than three weeks. A total of thirty-two control positions was provided, each with an OBA/8 amplifier, with its mixers, mounted on a bay, with one spare OBA/8 amplifier shared between every two positions.

The programme material had to be transmitted to many different destinations – some to the domestic networks, some to European countries over cable circuits, and some overseas by radiotelephone. The Post Office naturally played an important part in providing the outgoing circuits to all these destinations. It fell to the BBC to tackle the operational problem of feeding the foreign-language commentaries to the right destinations at the right times – some on a time cue and others on a cue spoken over a control circuit from the country to which the commentaries were addressed. Most of the commentaries were to be broadcast live by the receiving organisation and cueing was therefore important – not always easy because of language problems and because a single control line from Wembley might be connected successively to several destinations.

The provision of telephones alone for the whole Olympic Games project (not just for the BBC requirements) was such that the Post Office installed a special exchange, appropriately named 'Corinthian', and all telephone users were served from this exchange rather than through separate PBXs. It was decided that all the programme feeds from Wembley as well as those from the remote OB points should be routed into Broadcasting House, where the BBC would undertake the equalisation and amplification required. This arrangement was adopted after consultation with the Post Office, rather than the more obvious one of transmitting the programme feeds directly from the Palace of Arts to the network and to other countries, because the latter arrangement would have made it necessary to bring programmes from all the remote OB points into Wembley and also because the line loss between Wembley and London was so high that a large number of equalisers and amplifiers would have had to be provided by the Post Office, either at the Continental Traffic Exchange or at the Radio Terminal. It was necessary to set up a special switching centre in Broadcasting House, where almost 300 lines were terminated and where all the necessary equalisers and amplifiers could be accommodated. The construction of more than a hundred special equalisers, after the testing of the lines, gave the lines engineers plenty to do for some months before the Games began.

The broadcasting, in sound, of the Oxford-Cambridge Boat Race had already become a traditional event in the BBC calendar, but the televising of the Boat Race before the war had been a very modest event. In 1939 there were only two mobile television OB units in service and no more equipment was obtained until after the 1948 race had taken place, so that only the start and finish could be shown. In 1949, however, a more ambitious presentation was attempted; more outside broadcasting equipment had become available and, with the co-operation of the Planning & Installation Department and Designs Department in the provision and operation of radio links and camera channels, it was possible to cover the race with nine cameras, one of which was mounted in the launch *Consuta*.[95, 96, 97] Its success led to the formation in late 1949 of a Boat Race Committee to plan the 1950 event on a still more ambitious scale. (Many disrespectful jokes have been prevalent about the working of committees. It is fair to say that many of the BBC committees mentioned in these pages have done good service. It all depends on whether they have clearly defined objectives and are composed of people with the ability and authority to back up their decisions.) This committee worked out a comprehensive plan requiring the use of twelve television cameras.[95] The main features were:

(i) the deployment of more shore-based cameras to cover the long gap between Hammersmith and Chiswick and to safeguard the transmission in case of trouble with the camera on the launch *Consuta*;

(ii) the routeing of all camera unit outputs through a central control point at the Post Office Riverside Exchange to ensure supervision and co-ordination;

(iii) the provision of additional radio reception points for the pictures from the launch to ensure more consistent picture quality throughout the race and to allow local producers to select shore or launch pictures at will;

(iv) the provision of a link for communication between the launch and the central control point (in 1949 there had been almost no communication with the launch);

(v) the assignment of a special commentator to report exclusively for television viewers.

The four radio-link pick-up points for the vision signals from the launch were at Putney, Harrod's Depository, Church Wharf and Chiswick; these were linked, either by vision cable or by microwave link, to the central control point, except that Putney was linked by cable direct to Broadcasting House. The occasion marked the bringing into service for the first time of two microwave links, one on 6800 MHz, supplied by Marconi's, and one on 4800 MHz, supplied by STC. These links were used in tandem to transmit the pictures from the launch, which were received at Chiswick on a 187-MHz link, via the Queen's Head on the south bank to the mobile central control room at Riverside Exchange.

All the sound circuits for commentaries and communication were provided by line except those from the launch. As it was important that the sound commentary should originate from a point as close as possible to the foremost camera, a 77·3-MHz sound channel, supplied by Pye Telecommunications Ltd, was set up in the launch working to a receiving point on the roof of Riverside Exchange. Another Pye channel operating on 99·3 MHz in the reverse direction was provided to enable cues and instructions to be passed to the people in the launch.

The broadcast was a complete success, in spite of last-minute difficulties caused by the failure of the commentator's vision monitor on the *Consuta*, when the launch shipped a wave, and the failure of the vision receiver at Harrods on account of severe interference (apparently from the OB communications link between Harrods and the sound broadcasting service's launch *Enchantress*). It had demanded a great deal of effort from the specialist departments as well as the operating departments, and it was decided that, the major problems having been solved, the broadcasting of future Boat Races would be handled by the operating departments from their own resources.

Television played an important part in a General Election for the first time in 1950; by that time there were several mobile control rooms and the techniques of collecting OB material were becoming well established. On 9 December 1948 the Television OB Manager was already making suggestions about programmes that might be mounted, including OBs from a polling station and a Town Hall, and urging that planning should start in case an election occurred at short notice. Television coverage of public meetings was, however, regarded as altogether too hot a potato; the BBC had not yet learned the art of carrying one on a political tight-rope. The Controller Television agreed that the idea of showing results as they came through was an excellent one and this decision was the first step towards the elaborate set-up that now appears in television studios on a General Election night. After much deliberation it was decided that both studios at Alexandra Palace should be dedicated to the Election, when it came, with cameras giving views of a scoreboard, a clock, and a 'thermometer' showing the state of the parties, and commentators giving the results as they came in, with appropriate sidelights on them. In the event there was one outside broadcast from Trafalgar Square where the *Daily Mail* had a display screen. The results evidently caught the imagination of Television Management, because only five days after the election the Controller, Television, was already enquiring about plans for the next one.

In July 1951 there were several broadcasts in connection with the Festival of Britain, including OBs of the state drive from Buckingham Palace, the service in St Paul's Cathedral and the opening ceremony. Provision was made for twelve simultaneous commentaries in sound from points along the processional route and in the cathedral. At the site of the exhibition on the South Bank of the Thames a broadcasting centre was set up, including a control room, a television interview studio and two talks studios for sound broadcasting. A separate sound control room and three acoustically treated cubicles were installed in the Royal Festival Hall. The former aircraft-carrier *Campania*, which visited a number of ports as a travelling exhibition, was also equipped for broadcasting. During the Festival Year, the BBC showed several exhibits in the Transport Pavilion on the South Bank and it also mounted displays at the B.S.I. exhibition in the Science Museum and at its own exhibition at 201 Piccadilly. The last-mentioned included 'See Yourself on Television' and 'Hear your own Voice', which proved extremely popular.

Royal occasions have faced the BBC with many challenges, and great efforts have been made to treat them with appropriate dignity, combined with technical competence. When King George VI died suddenly in early February 1952, the BBC services were faced with urgent problems. Even the long-established Sound Services had had little experience of such occasions, since the funeral of King George V in 1936. In 1952 there was much interest in other European countries and in North America and the Far East, so that facilities had to be provided for many commentaries, either for live transmission or for recording. Commentaries in sound were given in the BBC Home, French, German, Italian, Greek, Scandinavian, North-American, Eastern, Far Eastern, Hungarian, Czech, Polish, Bulgarian and Spanish Services, and technical facilities were provided for commentators from France, Belgium, the Netherlands, Sweden and Switzerland, and from NBC, CBS, ABC and MBS in the USA. Commentary points in London for the funeral procession from Westminster to Paddington Station and in Windsor for the procession from the railway station to the Castle were provided, making a total of forty-six, and many of these had 'effects' and cue-light facilities. Four television mobile control rooms were deployed: one at New Palace Yard, Westminster, one in Whitehall, one at Hyde Park Corner and one at Windsor Castle.

The Coronation of Queen Elizabeth II on 2 June 1953 presented a formidable challenge to the BBC. There were seven television control points – Westminster Abbey; Abbey House, Tothill Street; the Colonial Office; the Victoria Memorial; Hyde Park (Grosvenor Gate); Westminster Pier, and Buckingham Palace. Signals from all these points were fed to a central control room that was specially set up in Broadcasting House, near to the Television Switching Centre. The schedule of circuits to be provided by the Post Office listed 18 vision and 84 sound circuits (programme lines, control lines, production control lines, microphone circuits, frequency-locking lines and reserves) for the BBC, 3 sound lines for the NTS (the Netherlands Television Service) and 27 for the RTF (the French Broadcasting Service). The resources of the BBC were stretched to the utmost and equipment, including radio links, had to be hired from manufacturers. In the nine years during which television had been operating between the Coronation of 1937 and the Coronation of 1953 the number of cameras covering the event had increased from three to twenty-two.

Because all the BBC's resources were fully deployed, it was necessary to enter into a contract with STC by which this firm undertook the transmission of the vision signal for the continental users from the Senate House tower of the University of London to Cassell in Northern France, the BBC being financially responsible for the section from London to the coast and the RTF for the portion from Swingate to Cassel, where the signal would join the French television network. From Cassel, the 405-line signal was routed in two directions, to Paris and to Breda in Holland, where conversion took place to the 819-line and 625-line standards respectively. The transmissions were very successful, and they were received on the Continent with enthusiasm.[98]

The Coronation was also notable for the first use of the manually controlled synchronising system mentioned in section 5 of this chapter. Each of the vision circuits was connected through a phase-shifter, with which the source could be manually steered into synchronism.

10 INTERNATIONAL RELATIONS

During this period many of the links with overseas broadcasting organisations that had been broken during the war years were re-established; co-operation with broadcasting authorities in Commonwealth countries and Colonial territories were developed and the BBC again played a full part in international radio conferences.

In 1946 a preliminary meeting was held in Moscow to prepare for an International Telecommunications Convention to be held at Atlantic City in the following year. The United Kingdom, the USA, the USSR, China and France were represented at Moscow; the UK delegation, led by Col. Angwin of the Post Office, included L. W. Hayes representing the BBC.

From May to October 1947 there were in effect three conferences working in

FREQUENCY BANDS ALLOTTED TO SOUND BROADCASTING AT ATLANTIC CITY, 1947
(including minor amendments by the Geneva Conference, 1959)

Band	Frequency range	Channels available to the BBC
Long Wave	150 – 285 kHz	1 channel
Medium Wave	525 – 1605 kHz	11 channels plus use of two International Common Frequencies for domestic services and 2 channels for services to Europe
Short Wave	3950 – 4000 kHz (75-m band) 5950 – 6200 kHz (49-m band) 7100 – 7300 kHz (41-m band) 9500 – 9775 kHz (31-m band) 11,700 – 11,975 kHz (25-m band) 15,100 – 15,450 kHz (19-m band) 17,700 – 17,900 kHz (16-m band) 21,450 – 21,750 kHz (13-m band) 25,600 – 26,100 kHz (11-m band)	126 channels
Band II (VHF)	87·5 – 100 MHz	40 channels between 88 and 95 MHz.

Atlantic City: the Plenipotentiary Conference (which amended the Convention), the Radio Conference and a High Frequency Broadcasting Conference. The last-mentioned made arrangements for the convening of a further HF Broadcasting Conference at Mexico City during 1948. The revised Radio Regulations allocated bands of frequencies to the various services in the range from 10 kHz to 10 GHz.[99] (The table lists the frequency bands allocated to sound broadcasting and applicable to the United Kingdom, and includes minor amendments made at the Geneva Conference of 1959.)

At Atlantic City the frequency tolerances specified in the Radio Regulations were tightened up, but the advances made in precision frequency control by the BBC during the war years enabled BBC stations to work within tolerances at least three orders better on long and medium waves and one order better on short waves than the revised requirements.

An important step taken at Atlantic City was the decision to set up the International Frequency Registration Board (IFRB). This was, initially, to have consisted of experienced radio engineers from five countries, but the number was later increased to eleven. The Board's terms of reference were to draw up and maintain a list showing global frequency usage in the range 14 kHz to 27·5 MHz for all phases of the solar cycle. The Board had no mandatory powers and was to act in a consultative capacity, advising Administrations of the likely interference that might result from the introduction of new services or from alterations to existing services.[100]

To implement the Atlantic City recommendations concerning the HF bands a conference was held in Mexico City from October 1948 to April 1949. It evolved a plan to cover one phase of the sunspot cycle which, at the time, was thought to represent average conditions of propagation (later it was found that the Mexico City Plan was based on far too optimistic a condition of sunspot activity). The plan was accepted by fifty-three countries (including the UK) and was taken as the basis for the production of additional plans to cover the remaining periods of the sunspot cycle. A Technical Committee to work out these plans was set up; it met in Paris from June 1949 until the end of that year, producing six additional plans to cover the worst periods of the sunspot cycle. However, it soon became clear that these plans would not be acceptable to a large number of countries because of their restrictive nature, and that it would be extremely difficult to improve them. Many countries were by then using short-wave broadcasting as an important means of making their voices heard in distant parts of the world so as to disseminate their own versions of world affairs. Each country needed a number of frequencies to reach all the target areas at appropriate times of day and the optimum frequencies varied with the season and with the sunspot cycle. (The BBC alone requires 126 different HF channels to cope with its needs over a period of years.) The task of reconciling the requirements of all the participating countries so as to avoid mutual interference was therefore a gigantic one, bearing in mind that all the short-wave bands together provide fewer than 270 9-kHz channels and some of these are rarely usable.

The Technical Committee met again in Florence in March 1950 and produced a further report in preparation for the third HF Broadcasting Conference, which opened in Florence on 1 April 1950 with F. C. McLean as the principal BBC representative. This conference continued at Rapallo. The principal non-signatories of the Mexico City Plan were the USA and the USSR, but both were represented at the Florence conference However, after two days the delegations of the USSR and its associated countries walked out and the conference continued without them. As the work proceeded it became obvious that each country's requirements – particularly at the sunspot minimum condition (when the highest of the HF bands are unusable) – greatly exceeded the spectrum space available under the Atlantic City Regulations. The final requirements having been reduced to what appeared to be an absolute minimum it was found that in some of the higher frequency broadcasting bands, and at certain phases of the solar cycle, they could just be accommodated. However, in the lower frequency bands during periods of reduced sunspot activity, the pressure was much greater; in the 6-MHz band at sunspot minimum the requirements amounted to nearly four times the spectrum space available.

This situation was apparent to some of the delegates as far back as the time of the early committee work in Paris, but others were reluctant to admit the inevitable and the Rapallo Conference carried on in an indecisive manner. Finally, the USA delegation proposed that there should be a postponement of the detailed implementation of the Atlantic City Plan and that the Rapallo Conference should admit its failure to solve the short-wave broadcasting problem and disperse forthwith. Despite the expenditure of a great deal of time and effort it had proved impossible to achieve agreement in this difficult and intricate field. All that remained was a large volume of statistics which showed quite clearly that the bands available for short-wave broadcasting under the Atlantic City Plan were quite inadequate. It was also evident that mutual interference between short-wave broadcasting stations would increase over the ensuing years and that some means to overcome this – such as the use of frequencies outside the broadcasting bands – would inevitably be exploited by the broadcasting authorities. Efforts were made continuously from 1949 onwards to find 'in-band' channels to replace the 'out-of-band' frequencies that were being used, but with limited success.

In an effort to save something from the wreck of the Atlantic City proposals for the regulation of HF broadcasting an Extraordinary Administrative Radio Conference was convened in Geneva in August 1951. After four months of intensive work, agreement was reached between all countries, except the USSR and those in the Soviet bloc, to produce a new Record of Frequency Usage to replace the old Berne Frequency List.

After the war there was growing congestion in the long- and medium-wave broadcasting bands also. Many new stations were being built in Europe, of which some were of very high power. In an attempt to overcome the impending chaos in these bands, a European Regional Conference was held in Copenhagen in 1948 at which F. C. McLean was again the BBC's principal representative. A new Wavelength Plan for Europe was agreed with an implementation date of 15 March 1950. Under this plan the BBC was allocated one long-wave channel, eleven medium-wave channels and the use of two International Common Frequencies for its Domestic Services, plus two medium-wave channels that were used by its European Service.[101]

The Copenhagen Plan had some success for a time in reducing interference, but chaos soon returned; this was largely because the plan was not adhered to by all the countries that participated in the conference and some countries had not participated at all. In particular the plan was not adopted by the Occupying Powers in Europe at that time. It provided for a total of some 520 stations, but nearly double this number were operating in the long- and medium-wave bands by the end of the 1950s. The resulting interference was accentuated by the advent of intentional jamming by several countries (though the BBC never resorted to it). The development of sound broadcasting on VHF offered a way out of these difficulties and it was introduced in West Germany and Italy (where the shortage of MF channels was particularly acute), and finally throughout Europe. In the UK, the BBC had already invited tenders for VHF/FM transmitters in 1946, although the introduction of the service was delayed until 1955, partly by the financial problems of the time and partly by the need for extensive field trials to ensure that the system adopted was the best that could be devised.

The realisation that the VHF broadcasting bands should be planned at the earliest possible stage in their exploitation resulted in the holding of a European Regional Conference in Stockholm in May and June 1952. (There were indeed those who thought that the time was not yet ripe for such a conference on the ground that 'it is …

ridiculous to formulate a code of traffic regulations for a desert.'[102]) Some thirty European countries participated; many of them had no immediate plans to start a VHF sound broadcasting service, but television services were rapidly expanding. The Stockholm Conference assigned channels in Band II to sound broadcasting stations and channels in Bands I and III for television. In view of the early stage of development, it proposed that a further conference should be convened in five years' time.[103] (This subsequent conference was again held in Stockholm, but later than planned – in 1961.) It is of interest to note that during the 1952 Stockholm Conference use was made for the first time of a computer in the preparation of a frequency assignment plan, the programming on this occasion being effected by staff of Nordwestdeutscher Rundfunk. The conference succeeded in producing a plan for the assignment of channels in Bands I, II, and III, which enabled the development of broadcasting in these bands to proceed in an orderly manner; its major weakness was that the Plan was not signed by the Eastern European countries. By 1961, the number of stations – actual or projected – had greatly increased and the need was already apparent for planning the UHF television bands (Bands IV and V). Fortunately, the Plan of 1961 was accepted by the Administrations of the Eastern European countries and this applied to the whole of the European Broadcasting Area, thus greatly strengthening and extending the foundations laid in 1952.

From its foundation in 1925 until the war the International Broadcasting Union (IBU/UIR) had provided a forum for the discussion of wavelength problems and other matters of major interest to broadcasting authorities. After hostilities in Europe had ended, a meeting was held at Stresa, to reactivate the UIR, but the political climate was unpropitious. The meeting at Stresa broke up because of the USSR's insistence that the Baltic States (Latvia, Estonia and Lithuania), which had been members of the old IBU should have individual votes and representation in any new union. This the Western countries refused to accept; they decided to form a new organisation and it fell to the UK representatives to suggest a venue for a meeting to further this aim. The meeting was held at Torquay in February 1950 and the Engineering Division was represented by Sir Noel Ashbridge.

At that meeting the European Broadcasting Union (EBU/UER) was formed, with Sir Ian Jacob – Director-General of the BBC – as its first President. Its administrative headquarters were in Geneva and its technical centre in Brussels. The first Director of the Technical Centre was Henri Anglès d'Auriac; the first Chairman of the Technical Committee was Cunha da Eça of Portugal.

The IBU was formerly dissolved in May 1950 and its staff and part of its property were transferred to the EBU.[104] The latter now includes as Active Members thirty-three broadcasting organisations in the European Broadcasting Area (which includes countries in North Africa and the Near East) and many Associate Members in other parts of the world.

One of the major contributions the BBC has made to the work of the EBU has been the secondment of experienced engineers to the Technical Centre. Among these was J. Treeby Dickinson who was seconded from the Overseas and Engineering Information Department in September 1950 'for an indefinite period' and remained

412

with the Union as Chief Engineer until his retirement in 1972. He and his BBC colleagues have played a substantial part in the development of the technical activities of the EBU. Many members of the Engineering Division served on the Technical Committee and its working parties and specialised sub-groups during the period under review in the mutual interests of the BBC and of the EBU as a whole. From 1 January 1953 until the end of 1970 E. L. E. Pawley was Chairman of the Technical Committee.

Until 1953 the work of monitoring broadcasting stations and measuring their frequencies was done at the Technical Centre in Brussels, but in that year a technical monitoring station was set up at Jurbise in south-west Belgium on land placed at the disposal of the EBU by the Belgian PTT. There was, and is, close co-operation between this station and the monitoring stations operated by EBU Members at Tatsfield (BBC), Monza (RAI), Limours (ORTF), Helsinki (Yleisradio) and Wittsmoor, Nurnberg and Cologne (ARD). These stations report on the occupancy of the broadcasting bands, study cases of mutual interference between stations, and contribute to long-term studies of propagation and of ionospheric cross-modulation.

In Eastern Europe, an organisation similar to the EBU was set up in 1950; this was the OIR (later OIRT) with its headquarters in Prague. This included the broadcasting authorities in the USSR and other countries in the Soviet bloc, including some in the Far East. There is an exchange of information between the EBU and the OIRT, and direct liaison between them on matters of mutual practical interest. Members of both organisations also meet in the study groups of the CCIR and the CCITT. The Finnish broadcasting organisation is a Member of both Unions.

During the period 1946 to 1955 the BBC also participated in the work of the ITU's Advisory Committees – the CCIR and the CCIF. Wherever it appeared that BBC interests were concerned. BBC engineers took part in the work of National and International Study groups and attended Plenary Meetings of these bodies. BBC engineers attended these meetings as members of the UK delegation – which was usually headed by a representative of the Post Office – but the BBC had the status of a recognised Private Operating Agency in the CCIR and has recently enjoyed the same status in the CCITT. (The CCIF and the CCIT, set up in 1925 were merged in the CCITT in 1956; the CCIR was established in 1927 and the IFRB in 1948.)

The BBC also continued to take part in the work of the CISPR, which deals with the control and suppression of interference caused by all forms of electrical equipment.

Before the end of the war, the need had been felt for some form of organised liaison on broadcasting among the Commonwealth countries and the Colonial Territories. The first Commonwealth Broadcasting Conference was held in London in 1945, while the capital was still under enemy attack. The technical sub-committee comprised H. Bishop (BBC), R Cahoon and G. W. Olive (Canada), H. Collett (South Africa), C. W. Goyder (India) and J. R. Smith (New Zealand). The need for co-operation of this kind was accentuated by the expansion of broadcasting overseas, particularly after 1949 when the British Government made funds available for setting up broadcasting services under the Commonwealth & Dominions Welfare Act. A second Commonwealth Broadcasting Conference was accordingly held in London in 1952 and a third in Sydney in 1956. The main purpose of these first conferences was to provide facilities for the major broadcasting organisations of the UK, Australia, Canada, New Zealand, South Africa and India to review the results of their war-time co-operation and to decide how best to expand and develop this co-operation in peace-time. The technical sub-committee dealt with the engineering and scientific side and useful papers were prepared by BBC Engineering Division staff for each of these conferences on a wide range of technical subjects.[100] In recent years the broadcasting organisations of many of the emergent countries of the Commonwealth have joined the conference, which provides a means by which the less developed countries can benefit from the experience of those with a longer history in the running of radio and television services. One of the most pressing problems is finding sufficient staff trained in the programme, administrative and engineering aspects of broadcasting. This need has been partially met by the secondment of staff from the BBC and other old-established organisations, but the emphasis is now on training local staff – either by accepting trainees on courses such as those offered by the BBC or by setting up local or regional training centres in Asia and Africa.

During this period, the BBC's assistance to broadcasters in the developing countries began to take a definite shape. The need was accentuated by the growing appreciation of the importance of radio services (and later of television) in these countries. Requests for aid came partly as a result of the Commonwealth Broadcasting Conferences and the personal contacts they encouraged and partly through visits by senior BBC people to territories overseas.

This aid, in which all branches of the BBC took part, included advice on the planning and staffing of broadcasting services, the secondment of advisers and executive staff, the provision of training facilities and the offer of programme material. Naturally, the advice given was influenced by the BBC's tradition of public service and tended towards absolute objectivity in the presentation of news and information, freedom from political control and freedom from commercial pressure – though many of the emerging radio and, especially, television services had to rely, at least in part, on revenue from advertising to keep them going.

On the engineering side the principal forms of assistance were:

(i)   The assignment of BBC engineers to conduct surveys and feasibility studies, and the giving of technical advice and information.

(ii) The secondment of BBC engineers, usually for two years at a time, to supervise the installation of new studios and transmitting stations and to set them to work, or to assist in the training of technical staff.

(iii) The training in the United Kingdom of engineering staff from overseas broadcasting organisations and the provision of training manuals and technical instructions.

(iv) The provision of items of equipment no longer required for BBC use.

A technical survey was made in East and Central Africa by W. E. C. Varley (of the headquarters staff of the Transmitter Department) between 18 December 1945 and

414

23 March 1946 to investigate the feasibility of establishing broadcasting services or extending existing services in Kenya, Uganda, Tanganyika, Zanzibar, Northern Rhodesia and Nyasaland. Recommendations for transmitting stations, studios, receiving stations, communal listening arrangements and staffing and organisation were required, together with estimates of capital and running costs, bearing in mind that the services were to be primarily for the indigenous population but also taking into account the needs of the non-African minorities. The resulting proposals were divided into two parts: those dealing with the East African territories (under the East African High Commission) and those dealing with the Central African Colonial territories. Although the recommendations were not accepted as a whole they were implemented in stages by individual territories in later years as funds became available; the embryo broadcasting service in Northern Rhodesia led the way in late 1946.

In February to May 1949 a broadcasting survey in West Africa was undertaken by L. W. Turner (of the same department) in association with F. A. W. Byron of the Telecommunications Department of the Crown Agents. The terms of reference of this survey were generally similar to those for the East and Central African Survey and applied to Nigeria, the Gold Coast, Sierra Leone and the Gambia. The aim was again to provide a broadcasting service primarily for the African population and to make recommendations for communal listening. The recommendations of the Turner/Byron report were implemented in all the territories surveyed, the speed of development being conditioned by the availability of funds for broadcasting purposes. Much use was made of BBC staff seconded from Engineering and Programme Departments, particularly in Nigeria and in the Gold Coast.

In 1950 W. A. Roberts (of Engineering Secretariat) was seconded to the Colonial Office to co-ordinate the development of broadcasting in all Colonial territories and during the five years from 1950 to 1955 he travelled extensively and produced thirty-six reports. Recommendations had already been made to the Colonial Office on broadcasting facilities for Aden, Mauritius, Trinidad, Fiji and Zanzibar.

Several other BBC engineers visited overseas countries to deal with specific technical problems. H. B. Rantzen (Head of Designs Department) went to New York in 1949 to advise on the equipment of the new broadcasting headquarters of the United Nations. H. V. Griffiths (EiC Tatsfield) visited Hamburg to advise the NWDR on the technical design of their new monitoring and frequency measuring station at Wittsmoor. Assistance was also given to the British Forces Network and the Canadian Forces Radio Unit in North-West Europe through the Allied Control Commissions for Germany and Austria, to the Union of South Africa (CSIR) on frequency standards; to RNF, Paris, on transmitter synchronisation, and to the South African Broadcasting Corporation on transmitter and receiving aerial design.

At least thirty-five long-term assignments of BBC engineers to posts abroad took place between 1945 and 1955, excluding those serving in BBC establishments overseas. The streamlining of BBC services made it possible to spare engineers of the right calibre and experience, though not without difficulty. As time went on and BBC activities became more specialised there were fewer engineers with the necessary all-round experience and most of those were in key posts at home. In April 1949 an internal advertisement was issued for engineers to join a pool of staff to be trained for overseas engineering assignments. There was limited response, but short lists were produced of suitable staff from which individuals were selected as requests for aid came in. Staff returning from secondments sometimes presented a resettlement problem. If they were away for more than two years, it was impossible to hold their BBC posts open for them (by filling them in the interim on an acting basis). Secondments enabled young engineers to gain experience in responsible positions, but it was not always easy for one who had been a big fish in a small pond to reconcile himself to the opposite role on his return.

BBC training for engineers from abroad may be said to have started when two Polish engineers were received for training in 1942. Immediately after the war, when travel restrictions were lifted, there was a continuous flow of trainees from overseas for both formal courses and on-the-job training by the BBC. During the period 1945 to 1955 an average of fourteen technical trainees each year from a total of twenty-seven countries were accepted. They were given lectures and some practical instruction at the Engineering Training School at Wood Norton, followed by a period of attachment to appropriate departments according to the jobs they were intended to do in their parent organisations. The scope of this effort can be judged by the countries of origin of the trainees accepted for training during the decade: Pakistan, Uganda, Indonesia, Ireland, Italy, Syria, Argentina, Hong Kong, Norway, Ceylon, Ethiopia, Uruguay, Australia, Cyprus, Greece, New Zealand, South Africa, Sudan, Sweden, Egypt, Israel, Korea, Malaysia, Mauritius, Thailand, Japan and Yugoslavia.

During this period, the trainees from abroad were fitted into the courses that were primarily intended for BBC staff; there were no engineering courses specially mounted for people from overseas. It had therefore to be insisted upon that they had a working knowledge of English and sufficient technical understanding to benefit from the courses. It was also required that they should be sponsored by bona-fide broadcasting organisations.

These various forms of aid cost money, and the cost could not be allowed to fall on licence-holders in Britain. The actual cost was charged either to the sponsoring broadcasting organisation or to the British Government under one of its overseas aid schemes; no charge was made, however, for technical advice that could be given without detriment to the day-to-day activities of the BBC engineers concerned.

II STAFF, ORGANISATION AND FINANCE

The stability in the senior ranks of the Engineering Division that had characterised the war period did not last long once it was over. By 1950 no fewer than five heads of departments, out of a total of eleven, had left for one reason or another. The first to go was B. N. MacLarty, who went back to the Marconi Company in 1947 as their Engineer-in-Chief. He was followed by L. W. Hayes, who resigned in 1949 to become Vice-Director of the CCIR, H. Wilkinson taking his place as Head of Overseas &

Engineering Information Department. In 1950 there were three more resignations, H. B. Rantzen, Head of Designs Department, L. Hotine, Senior Superintendent Engineer, and T. C. Macnamara, who had succeeded B. N. MacLarty as Head of Planning & Installation Department. Their successors were A. R. A. Rendall, E. G. Chadder (as Senior Superintendent Engineer, Sound), and A. N. Thomas. In 1953 F. M. Dimmock, who had long been Head of Equipment Department, was succeeded by E. C. Drewe.

Sir Noel Ashbridge had never wanted the post of Deputy Director-General, to which he was appointed in 1943, because his interests were on the technical side; in 1948 the post was abolished and Ashbridge became Director of Technical Services. He held this position until his retirement in August 1952. By then he had served twenty-six years with the BBC. All of them had been spent in positions of high responsibility, for he had joined as second in command to Eckersley, and for twenty-three years he had been in control of the Engineering Division and had shaped its course. In a tribute to him at the time R. T. B. Wynn wrote:

'Much could be written of the way his outlook has influenced the technical policy of the Corporation, the welfare of the engineers who serve it, and above all his qualities as a man outside the professional sphere. Those of us who have been fortunate enough to know Sir Noel as an immediate superior and as a friend have learned not only to respect his character but to recognise the deep affection in which he holds the Division and all those who work in it. A keen lover of music and outdoor sports, particularly the sea, a critic of the arts, a wise counsellor, with a vivid sense of humour and of the ridiculous – we are fortunate indeed in having served under him. He has always possessed the gift of helping and encouraging any member of the staff who was down, and trimming them up to their advantage when things were going too well with them. He rightly demanded a very high standard of professional practice within the Division, and was intolerant of an ill-considered proposal or anything which nowadays is known as a "line-shoot".'

In 1950, Wynn, who had been Assistant Chief Engineer until then, became Deputy Chief and H. L. Kirke, who had moved up to Broadcasting House from Kingswood Warren, became Assistant Chief Engineer. Unhappily this appointment was short-lived, for in January 1951 Kirke had a serious illness from which he never recovered. This was a grievous loss to the BBC. In Ashbridge's words, 'Mr Kirke had been responsible for engineering development in the BBC on the highly technical side from the very early days. It would be generally conceded in the profession that he contributed more in this field towards the development of broadcasting than anyone else in the country, or for that matter in Europe.' By 1952 it was clear that there was no hope of Kirke returning to duty, and F. C. McLean was appointed Assistant Chief Engineer. Meanwhile, in 1950, W. Proctor Wilson had taken over as Head of the Research Department.

Three new engineering departments were created during the post-war decade. The Engineering Training School was raised in status to become the Engineering Training Department in 1945, and Dr K. R. Sturley (subsequently Chief Engineer,

417

External Broadcasting and later professor at Ahmadu Bello University, Nigeria) was brought in from the Marconi Company to run it. In May 1947 the Designs Department was formed, with H. B. Rantzen as its head, from among engineers in the Lines Department and the Design & Installation Departments. The latter, having shed its responsibilities for equipment design, then became the Planning & Installation Department, and a post of Superintendent Engineer Lines was created to run the Lines Department. In 1949 the growing importance of television was recognised by the creation of a separate television operating department with M. J. L. Pulling as its Senior Superintendent Engineer.

There were also two new groupings of departments. In 1949 Engineering Training, Engineering Secretariat, and Overseas & Engineering Information Departments were affiliated to form the Engineering Services Group under F. C. McLean, and after him, E. L. E. Pawley. In 1950 an Engineering Projects Group, consisting of Planning & Installation Department and Designs Department, was created; McLean was put in charge of this group, but it was dissolved when he became Assistant Chief Engineer.

In August 1952 Bishop succeeded Ashbridge as Director of Technical Services, and Wynn became Chief Engineer, with McLean as Assistant Chief. In the 1955 Birthday Honours, Bishop received a knighthood.

In October 1952 Sir Ian Jacob succeeded Sir William Haley as Director General. Like Reith, Jacob was an engineer by training; he had served as an officer in the Royal Engineers.

During this period there were important developments in training and recruitment. It was fortunate that, once the war was over, there was no further use for Wood Norton as an operational centre. Bishop and Wynn recommended that it should become the headquarters of the Engineering Training Department, and that all technical training should be concentrated there. Engineering in broadcasting was so specialised a subject, and the apparatus for it so costly, that the BBC could not expect the Universities or the Technical Colleges to undertake anything more than basic instruction in it. The role of the Engineering Training Department would be to extend this basic instruction by more specialised training in engineering for broadcasting, particularly in the methods used in, and largely developed by, the BBC.

In April 1946 the move to Wood Norton was authorised. The department moved out of its temporary home at St Hilda's, Maida Vale, and established itself at Wood Norton. There was room for a hundred students at a time and in the first year two hundred students, made up of new recruits and staff seeking promotion, passed through the school. An important result of the move was that the school (later dignified by the title 'Engineering Training Centre') became entirely residential – a feature that had many advantages, but also created problems when students of many nationalities with diverse customs and religions had to be accommodated. Much attention was given to the welfare of the trainees; facilities for recreation were provided and also a surgery with a qualified nurse in attendance.

During 1954 recruitment was stepped up to match the ever-growing demands of television. Over two hundred junior staff would have to be taken on annually in order to keep pace. This was more than the training department could cope with, and it was decided to double its capacity so that it could take two hundred students at a time. Work on a new dormitory block costing just over £50,000 started at the beginning of 1955. By 1956 the department was running seven different kinds of course and accepting 700 students a year.

The possibility of reviving the pre-war student-apprenticeship scheme for university graduates was considered in 1947, but there were doubts about its efficacy, and the idea was shelved. The following year, however, Kirke, who was by then having difficulty in staffing the Research Department, pointed out that the demand for university graduates exceeded the supply, and that some energetic action must be taken to improve recruitment. Other organisations were more zealous than the BBC in visiting and keeping in touch with the universities, with the result that they were getting the pick of the graduates. Kirke insisted that the future strength of the BBC depended on its success in recruiting talented people. In May 1948 Wynn went to see Professor Moullin, head of the Engineering Faculty at Cambridge, to discuss this predicament. His visit amply confirmed all that Kirke had said. The BBC was up against competition for graduates and would have to make a greater effort to get its share of the available output from the universities.

Two steps were taken as a result of this visit. Senior engineers were nominated to make regular visits to the principal universities, in order to seek out talented graduates and try to attract them to the BBC. (By 1950 there were fourteen of these visitors, and they were in touch with twenty-three universities and colleges.) Secondly, a permanent pool of staff, on which the Research, Designs, Installation, and Equipment Departments could draw, was instituted; staff recruited to this pool would have about a year's training with one of the specialist departments, after which it was expected that they would find permanent posts. The pay on recruitment was £375 pa.

The results were disappointing. The graduates did not come forward in either the numbers or the quality required. They were on a sellers' market, and they could afford to pick and choose. They did not find the BBC's scheme, or the career prospects, as attractive as those offered by industry and the scientific civil service.

In an attempt to improve matters, a booklet extolling the attractions of an engineering career in the BBC was produced in 1950. It was well received by the appointments staff at the universities. In 1953 a graduate-apprentice scheme was instituted. The apprenticeships ran for two years and the training was more comprehensive and varied than before. It embraced ten different fields of BBC activity, including the operating side and a spell of workshop training. It proved to be a much more attractive training course and by this time the starting salary had gone up to £500 pa.

The first graduate-apprentice course started in September 1953; it had nine people on it, seven of whom came straight from university and the other two from within the BBC. For the next two years the aim was to fill twelve places on each course. To encourage interest in the scheme a week-end summer school for university appointments officers was held at Wood Norton during the summer of 1955. It was a resounding success.

Vacation courses for undergraduates during the summer, which had been popular during pre-war years, were started again in 1951. There were sixty on the first course, but this proved rather too many, and in subsequent years the number was limited to forty.

The difficulties resulting from the uncompetitive salaries in the BBC after the war were not confined to recruitment. There was dissatisfaction among staff, particularly in the specialist departments. This led to the resignation of about a dozen experienced engineers during 1948. Ashbridge pointed out that it would be necessary to raise the salaries of a small number of key men to stop them being tempted to leave, but that it would not be possible – without completely disrupting the general level of salaries – to raise even key men to the salary levels that were occasionally being offered outside. Two years later the problem was still acute and Ashbridge was concerned lest the loss of these engineers might put the big construction programme for television in jeopardy.

For the most part staff released by the Services after the war had been reabsorbed into the Engineering Division quite easily. In 1948, however, there were difficulties over this. At the end of the Olympic Games, and the burst of activity they had occasioned, about two hundred who had joined since the summer of 1948 had to be dismissed to make way for the reinstatement of staff who had been in the BBC earlier. The irony of the situation was that many of those who had to be dismissed had served longer with the BBC than the people displacing them.

In 1948 it was suggested by the Regional Controllers that the senior engineer in each of the main regional centres should be on the staff of the Controller rather than belong to the Engineering Division. This suggestion found no favour with Ashbridge and Bishop, and it was to be another twenty years before this transfer came about – though with safeguards to protect the interests of the engineers and to maintain professional standards. A step in this direction was, however, taken in 1952, when a senior engineer was assigned to each of the directorates concerned with programme output – Television, Home and External Broadcasting. This engineer's task was to concern himself with the problems of the directorate, to advise the Director on them and to represent his views to the Engineering Directorate. The aim was to give each of the output directors some measure of control over the engineering side of their operations as well as full control of the programme and administrative sides. In making this change the Board of Management sought to introduce some decentralisation of engineering work, but emphasised that all BBC engineers were still to be professionally responsible to, and administered by, the Director of Technical Services.

In 1952 E. G. Chadder was redesignated Senior Superintendent Engineer and two new senior superintendent engineers were created for the Home and External Services, as a result of the reorganisation. These posts were held by F. Williams and F. Axon respectively. Television had already had its Senior Superintendent Engineer since Pulling's appointment in 1949.

The passing of the Television Act in July 1954 and the setting up of the ITA and the first four programme companies the following year posed a real threat to the Engineering Division and to the Television Service. In order to get started, the ITA and the companies had to sign up experienced engineers and operators quickly, and the BBC was one of the few places where they could fine them. While realising that some losses would be inevitable, the BBC had hoped originally to be able to maintain its policy of grading staff in all departments according to the same scale based on objective assessments of the requirements of the posts. This hope was not realised. The inducements offered by the competitors to key staff during the spring of 1955 were on such a scale that they bid fair to bring the BBC's operations to a standstill. By May over fifty engineering staff had resigned, among them some senior engineers – including P. A. T. Bevan and R. H. Hammans, who became the Chief Engineers of the ITA and Granada Television respectively. By September nearly two hundred had left.

In this situation there was no choice but to offer enhanced salaries to staff who were essential for keeping the service going. This was done by offering special contracts to television staff on condition that they stayed with the BBC for three or five years. A number of these 'no-escape' contracts were offered to engineers and operators, the majority of whom accepted despite the fact that the Staff Association advised its members not to sign these contracts.

Inevitably, the singling out of a few people for higher salaries upset the relativities that the BBC had long sought to preserve, and led to some resentment and discontent. The disparity was partially offset by giving personal grades to the most deserving of the staff who had not been offered special contracts, but it took a considerable time for staff relations to recover fully from this set-back.

The number of staff in the Engineering Division increased from just over 3700 at the end of 1945 to 4827 in 1955. In 1945 the Television Service was not functioning, but by 1955 1203 of the Engineering staff were working in that service. The Engineering Division comprised the Operations & Maintenance Departments of the three output directorates (which were responsible to the Directors of those services for day-to-day working), the Operations & Maintenance staff for Transmitters, Recording and Lines, the five specialist departments (Designs, Planning & Installation, Research, Equipment and Building), and four service departments (Establishment, Engineering Information, Engineering Secretariat and Training, the last three forming, at the end of the period, the Engineering Services Group).

In the financial year 1944–5 the total income of the BBC was £8·35 million, of which £2·59 million was spent on running costs attributable to Engineering and only £0·148 million on capital expenditure. The total number of receiving licences increased from 9·71 million in 1945 to 13·98 million in 1955 and of these the number of television licences had risen from zero to 4·5 million. The BBC's total income in 1954–5 was £25·87 million. Running costs had increased correspondingly and the major expansion that was taking place had involved a great increase in the rate of capital expenditure, for most of which the Engineering Division was responsible. In 1954–5, revenue expenditure on Engineering amounted to £6 million and capital expenditure to £2·45 million. By the end of the period the income was apportioned between Sound, Television and External Broadcasting (this last being financed by a direct Grant-in-Aid) and the whole of the expenditure was charged against these three services; items that could not be directly attributable to one or other of them were fairly apportioned between them.

The increase in engineering running costs over the decade was largely accounted for by the restarting and expansion of the television service. The steep rise in capital expenditure, representing the increasing rate of investment in new stations and in studio and OB facilities, necessitated a major expansion of the specialist departments concerned with the planning, ordering and installation of buildings and plant.

12 RESEARCH AND DEVELOPMENT

The end of the war found the Research Department none too well poised to cope with the changed conditions of peace-time. For six years the department had had little opportunity of fulfilling its normal task of harnessing current scientific advances to the use of broadcasting, and of pushing forward the frontiers by investigating specialised problems. Instead, the department had had to concern itself with finding quick solutions to the many pressing problems thrown up by the war, few of which were relevant to peace-time broadcasting. It had also had to take on the design and production of equipment, a task outside its normal scope, and it had lost the services of some of its most talented people through their transfer to other BBC departments or to the Services. After the war, it had to adjust itself to its peace-time role, particularly in applying new techniques to television.

The transition inevitably took some time. In 1946 Kirke reported that it had been possible to re-orient the activities of the department, but that the change from war conditions to peace-time was far from complete. The introduction of a third medium-wave programme, the reopening of the Television Service, and the investigation of the feasibility of a VHF/FM service had thrown a heavy load on the department, which was still below strength. In the process of adaptation the acoustics, audio-frequency, and recording sections were combined to form an electro-acoustics group under T. Somerville. The equipment in the laboratories was augmented and brought up to date. More staff were recruited, and by the end of the year the complement was nearly up to full strength. This brought to a head the serious shortage of laboratory and office space under which the department was labouring. 'Operations have now been resumed on considerably more than the pre-war scale,' Ashbridge declared in a report to the Board, 'and the Nightingale Square building, already inadequate in 1939, is now still more so, while the house near Oxford (Bagley Croft) is neither large enough for a headquarters nor conveniently placed, though owing to lack of alternative accommodation it is still used.'

This nettle was grasped in 1947, when an intensive search for new premises to replace Nightingale Square and Bagley Croft was instituted. The search would have started earlier but for the fact that there had been some uncertainty over the future of the Monitoring Service, with the possibility that its premises at Caversham Park might become available for Research Department. By the beginning of 1947 it was clear that Caversham Park would not be available, and the search for a site in the neighbourhood of London began in earnest. Curiously enough, none of the local authorities within the desired area seemed eager to have a BBC research station within its boundaries, with the exception of Banstead Urban District Council. They were sympathetic, and the search was accordingly concentrated in their territory. Initially it produced only one property that looked at all suitable, Weston Acres. The house was rather small, but the grounds were big enough to take extensions and there was ample space for field-work. Negotiations went ahead, but in September it was learned that another property, Kingswood Warren, was on the market, having been given up by the Ministry of Works. With thirty acres of grounds and a bigger house than Weston Acres, this was a much more attractive proposition, and an option to purchase was secured at once. There was some difficulty over planning consents, because the property was in a residential neighbourhood and within the Green Belt, but approval was eventually obtained in January 1948.

The house, an essay in the Tudor style by an unknown architect, had been built between 1835 and 1837. Previous owners included Sir Cosmo Bonsor, the railway magnate and philanthropist, and Joseph Rank, the founder of the Rank milling fortune. The work of adapting and adding to it so as to fit it for its new purpose was carried out in three stages over a two-year period. The first task was to repair the house and carry out minor alterations. In January 1949 the alterations were complete, and the television, field-strength, and transmitting sections, which had been at Bagley Croft, were able to take up residence. At the same time Kingswood Warren became the Research Department's headquarters. Next, the stable block was converted to house the workshops and stores, this stage being completed in June 1949. There was then no further use for Bagley Croft, and it was sold to Oxford University. The third and final stage was the construction of new laboratories and offices adjoining the original house. Work started in July 1949, and just over a year later, in September 1950, the television and field-strength sections were able to move to the new block. In December the audio-frequency section and the drawing office took their place in the house, leaving only the recording and acoustics sections still at Nightingale Square. The completion of the Kingswood Warren project was marked by holding an open day on 20 June 1951 at which more than two hundred engineers and scientists were present. In 1955 plans were prepared for the addition of a building to house the acoustics section, but the need for economy at the time caused this project to be postponed.

In building up the department after the war it was thought advisable to obtain the benefit of the counsel and experience of scientists of repute, so as to correlate the BBC's research with what was going on outside. At the suggestion of Lord Simon of Wythenshawe, Chairman of the Governors at the time, an invitation was extended to Sir Edward Appleton to preside over a Scientific Advisory Committee (the name was changed to Engineering Advisory Committee in April 1961) consisting of Sir John Cockcroft, Professor Willis Jackson (later Lord Jackson of Burnley), Professor F. C. Williams, Dr R. L. Smith-Rose, and Dr H. C. Booker, with W. Proctor Wilson as secretary. This Committee was appointed in May 1948, and met about three times a year. The Committee gave valuable advice and guidance to the BBC on many fundamental problems and developments. The experience and knowledge of its members and their association with national and international committees proved particularly valuable on such matters as the television standards to be adopted on UHF and the choice of a colour television system. The Committee strengthened the BBC's links with the universities and with industry in the fields of research, development and training.

A broad idea of the trend of the Research Department's activities in the post-war decade can be gained from the fact that the average number of research reports produced each year went up by more than half compared with the war-time figures. Acoustics, which had been dormant throughout the war, showed a strong revival, and so, naturally, did television. The staff increased from 120 to 215 in ten years, and annual expenditure increased from £90,000 in 1945–6 to about £260,000 in 1954–5 (two-thirds of which represented the cost of staff). The latter figure, which included capital expenditure on laboratory equipment, was about 1 per cent of the BBC's total income – not an excessive investment in the future.

One of the first tasks to be undertaken at the conclusion of the war was an investigation of the relative virtues of frequency modulation and amplitude modulation for a broadcasting service on VHF. Four 1-kW transmitters were made up, and an elaborate series of field trials carried out on 45 and 90 MHz during 1945 and 1946. These trials demonstrated unequivocally the advantages of FM.[105] They were followed by a full-scale field trial with transmissions from Wrotham at an effective radiated power of 120 kW. The results led to the decision to go ahead with a three-programme VHF/FM network for the whole country. In parallel with this work the effects of ignition-interference from motor-vehicles on VHF reception were examined during 1946 and 1947.[106] Limiting field-strength for various conditions of reception were established, and it was concluded that horizontal polarisation was preferable to vertical for use in Band II.

Much of the work on acoustics after the war was concerned with the treatment of individual studios, but a good deal of research of a more general and fundamental character was also carried out. Membrane absorption units and Helmholtz resonators were developed for bass absorption in studios.[107, 108] A more sophisticated method of measuring reverberation time and investigating colorations was devised, the decay of pulses of sound of slowly varying frequency being displayed on a cathode-ray oscilloscope.[109] The acoustical behaviour of four well-known concert halls was studied, in an attempt to isolate the factors that contributed to a satisfactory acoustic.[110] An investigation was conducted into the maximum loudness preferred by various categories of people – non-specialist listeners, engineers, and musicians – for various kinds of programme; this was a subject of much controversy both at home and abroad.[111, 112]

The study of mast radiators for medium-frequency stations, which was begun during the war, culminated in the erection of aerials of this type at Brookmans Park and Daventry.[113] For investigations of VHF aerials a method using scaled-down models, with a corresponding increase in frequency, was developed. The designs for slot aerials for the VHF stations and dipole aerials for the main television stations were evolved with the aid of this technique.[114, 115]

A new version of the commentator's lip microphone was produced in 1951.[116] It was a considerable improvement on the original model, being lighter and capable of better speech quality. The following year a smaller and lighter version of the BBC ribbon microphone, which had done yeoman service for nearly twenty years, was developed. Known as the PGS (Pressure Gradient Single), this design began to go into service in 1954.[2]

In recording, the work of Research Department was concentrated on the more basic aspects of the subject. The mechanism of magnetic-recording and reproduction, the factors determining its overall frequency characteristic,[118] absolute measurements of surface induction,[119] and the properties of different kinds of tape, came under investigation. A long-term study of the possibility of recording television signals on magnetic tape was started in 1952, but was not to bear fruit until the second half of the 1950s.

Much effort went into the planning of the networks for national coverage of television and VHF radio, and the testing of transmitter sites for these services,[120] Some more general investigations were also undertaken, notably into the effect of aircraft on VHF reception,[121] and into the propagation of VHF signals over distances of up to three hundred miles in Great Britain and also over greater distances across the North Sea. In 1951 these investigations were extended to include the UHF bands.

In television the first task was to develop and construct equipment for the comprehensive appraisal of television systems. These investigations covered a wide range of factors, among them visual acuity, co-channel interference, the visibility of noise,[122] and the effects of bandwidth and the number of lines on definition.[123] Work on colour television started at the beginning of the 1950s and by 1954 it had become the major preoccupation of the Television Group. By 1955 experimental apparatus had been designed and built for an appraisal of the NTSC colour system, adapted to the UK standard of 405 lines/50 fields (see section 5 of this chapter). In October test transmissions in colour started, using a low-power transmitter at Kingswood Warren and a medium-power transmitter at Alexandra Palace.

Some highly practical work, with immediate operational applications, was also undertaken. In 1951 research into methods of recording television pictures on film began, and this culminated in the design and construction of two machines working on the suppressed-frame system in time for the Coronation in 1953.[124] The problem of converting signals from one television standard to another was tackled, and an optical line converter was produced in time for the first relay of a programme originated in Europe on another standard in July 1952.[125]

Another development of great practical value was the time-derivative equaliser.[126] It made use of the fact, implicit in the Heaviside operational calculus, that amplitude and phase equalisation can be achieved by treating the signal as a function of time rather than of frequency. The signal was differentiated repeatedly by means of simple circuits and the time derivatives so obtained were added to the signal in appropriate senses and proportions. This was a very flexible device, which could compensate for distortion in many forms of linear electrical or electro-mechanical systems. In particular it made possible the equalisation of an inadequately resolved picture by adjusting two or more controls from direct inspection of the picture.

Important work was done on the optical performance of lenses for television cameras. Visual methods of appraisal were abandoned in favour of photo-electric scanning using both square wave and sine wave test patterns.[117] This work laid the foundations for later developments including the design of a photo-electric optical test bench.

The series of reports issued by the Research Department, dealing with these and other investigations, maintained a high standard of style and perspicuity. The importance of this matter was appreciated in other departments: much care was taken to secure the utmost clarity in the instructions on the operation and maintenance of equipment that were prepared by the Engineering Information Department and later by the Engineering Training Department. J. W. Godfrey, then Editor, Technical Instructions, was co-author of a book on the presentation of technical literature.[127]

The Designs Department, formed in 1947 and based on Western House, near Broadcasting House, London, was concerned with the development of new items of equipment, the building and testing of prototypes, and the evaluation of apparatus produced by the industry. This work had to be done in the closest possible collaboration with the Operations and Maintenance Departments, which in turn were closely associated with the programme-producing departments and conversant with their needs. The need for a new piece of equipment, not already available from commercial sources, having been established the Designs Department must either find a manufacturer willing to produce it under its guidance or undertake the design work itself. In the latter case the potential demand from the BBC and from elsewhere might justify one or more manufacturers in going into production, in which case the design information was made available at a charge representing only the cost of producing the drawings. This method of working was intended to ensure that the BBC's requirements would be met, when possible, by commercial products and that the BBC's experience and needs would influence commercial designs.

The Designs Department found itself under pressure to cope with the ever-expanding variety of requirements for sound and television equipment for studios, control rooms and recording installations, for special types of receiver and for low-power unattended transmitters. Its size, in terms of staff and costs, grew until in the 1970s it is roughly the same as that of Research Department.

The Equipment Department, with its workshops and test-room at Avenue House, Chiswick, and its transport depot in south-west London, was (and is) responsible for manufacturing apparatus that cannot be obtained from industry, either because only small numbers are required or because of urgency. It also undertakes repair work and tests a great variety of equipment used in the BBC, whether obtained from outside or made or repaired by the department itself. It maintains stocks of components and of items of equipment that have been duly accepted and coded as suitable and necessary for BBC use. Standardisation is an important aspect of its work, and since March 1954 it has had a Standards Engineer on its staff. (The BBC has always fully supported, and taken part in, the work of the British Standards Institution, the International Electrotechnical Commission, and the International Standards Organisation in this field.) The Equipment Department also maintains a drawing office. One of its most important functions is the provision and running of the transport fleet, which by 1955 included 450 vehicles – many of them specially equipped as OB units, mobile transmitters or mobile power units for operational use in the radio and television services.

CHAPTER VI

The Years of Expansion: 1956–72

1 STUDIOS AND OUTSIDE BROADCASTS: RADIO SERVICES

A remarkable phenomenon in the development of broadcasting technology during this period was the renewal of interest in sound broadcasting and the application of new techniques to it. This could hardly have been expected, because evolution had already continued for forty years and now a large amount of effort was being put into the development of television. Television appealed to the pioneering spirit because it demanded a new and complex technology (largely derived from war-time experience with radar) and because it added a new and exciting dimension to broadcasting. Nevertheless, there was a continuing interest, and in some directions a sharpening of interest, in radio. It was marked by two significant milestones, namely the introduction of the VHF/FM service in 1955 and the beginning of regular stereophonic transmissions in 1966.

There were several factors favouring a revival of interest in the development of radio broadcasting:

1 On the programme side, it was realised that there had been a marked change in the listening habits of the public, resulting mainly from the growing popularity of television. There was still a large audience for radio, but it was largest in the early morning and midday periods and much reduced in the evening. There were marked trends, not only in this country but in many others, for each programme service to take on a more clearly defined character ('pop' music, 'light' music, information, culture) and for a greater diversification of news and information.[1]

2 On the technical side, the introduction of transistors and other solid-state devices, followed by printed circuits and integrated circuits, made it possible to design highly complex equipment of small physical size, with low power consumption and heat dissipation, and this in turn facilitated the spread of automation. At the same time, there was a steady increase in knowledge of radio propagation and in the exploitation of higher and higher frequencies in the radio spectrum. These developments helped to offset the effects of increasing difficulties arising from shortage of skilled staff, shortage of money, and the overcrowding of the available wavebands caused by a large increase in the number of stations operating in all parts of the world and in the power used by many of these stations.

The start of the period now under review was still a time of post-war austerity, when materials of all kinds were scarce, and severe restrictions on capital expenditure continued until the mid-1950s. The period nevertheless developed into one of expansion. The outward sign of an increased pace of development was that the BBC began once more, though modestly enough at first, to build. Although the biggest single development was the Television Centre, the Extension to Broadcasting House was also an important one. It was planned before the war and excavation work for the foundations had already been started when war broke out; the resulting large hole in the ground alongside Broadcasting House remained open for many years. During the war part of the site had been used to construct the 'Stronghold', which contained an emergency control room, with studios and transmitters for vital services. Now at last it became possible to put the pre-war plan into effect, but, because of the financial situation at the time, it was necessary to enter into an agreement with the Prudential Assurance Company by which they financed the construction of the building and leased it to the BBC. They were to provide the shell of the building, the BBC having specified its size, shape and quality. The BBC itself subsequently carried out the internal work to form studios, a control room and a large number of offices. The original plan for the Extension had followed the same architectural style as Broadcasting House itself, with a Portland stone facing, but the Prudential was concerned that the Extension should appear as a separate building in case the BBC ever vacated it and it became necessary to lease it to other occupants. It was therefore designed in a rather different architectural style from Broadcasting House itself. This precaution proved unnecessary, because the history of Broadcasting House was repeated; the BBC subsequently acquired the freehold and thus now owns the whole of the island site.

The Extension, completed in 1961, was designed primarily as an office block and there were originally to be no studios in it, but early in the planning stages it was decided to include them. In the basement, there are two of the best-equipped large drama studios in the country, and the Extension has nine other studios, two of which are small talks studios and the rest general-purpose studios for discussions, gramophone record programmes and talks. There are also several recording and editing areas on the fifth floor, two with small simple studios, which can be used to add narration during editing. A large new control room was constructed on the first floor. The Extension has direct access to Broadcasting House at several levels and its own set of automatic lifts.

Towards the end of the 1960s developments in the Regions were influenced by the changes in the Radio Services announced in July 1969.[2] Radio 1 remained a 'pop' music channel. Radio 2 became a channel for 'light' music, separate from Radio 1 except during the evening. Radio 3 was to comprise classical music with speech programmes in the evening. Radio 4 was to include news, current affairs, plays, discussions and light entertainment. Scotland, Wales and Northern Ireland would continue to produce programmes for their own listeners on Radio 4 as well as contributions to the other radio programmes. The three English Regions (North, Midlands and South & West) were replaced by eight smaller regions, which would produce more television programmes for their own audiences than the three former Regions. The main production centres for both radio and television contributions to the national networks would be at Birmingham, Manchester and Bristol. In addition there would be twenty Local Radio stations, each self-contained with its own studio and OB facilities.

However, before these plans took shape there had already been building developments in the Regions. Broadcasting House, Glasgow, was extended in two stages. The first, completed in the early 1960s, consisted of a new building on a former bowling green adjoining the existing studio and office block in Queen Margaret Drive. This extension houses up-to-date television facilities (converted in 1971 to colour operation). The second stage of the extension was a new administrative block. An interesting problem arose from the presence of very old coal-mining excavations, of which only scanty records were available. Because of the uncertainty about them, it was decided to pump cement into the ground under pressure to fill any remaining voids.

The most important of the new Regional buildings is the Birmingham Broadcasting Centre, on a site in Pebble Mill Road. Planning for it continued for some years, suffering many postponements because of financial stringency and because the plans of the Birmingham city authorities which could have caused the ejection of the BBC from the Broad Street premises were themselves frequently held up. In the summer of 1971, however, the new building was completed and occupied. It was formally opened by Princess Anne on 10 November 1971. It is a purpose-designed Broadcasting Headquarters containing both radio and television broadcasting facilities. The principal feature of the design is that there is a main central technical block with radio studios on one side and television studios on the other; an administrative block adjoins a third side of the technical block. In addition a small OB depot has recently been added. Planning of the Birmingham centre was begun in the 1950s with the old concept of Regional broadcasting in mind and with provision for continued expansion of activity. Because of the lapse of about fifteen years between the initial planning and the completion of the building, and because of the changing techniques of programme presentation and the replanning of the Regional structure, some of the radio studios have been left in carcass form. The drama studio has been made into a fully professional studio with up-to-date equipment; the design of the music studios has been changed to the modern 'specialist' type, one being intended for 'pop' music. The larger music studio was designed for the Midland Light Orchestra, but this orchestra now tends to divide up into groups for different kinds of music.

Another new Regional Headquarters is Broadcasting House, Llandaff, Cardiff. It at present houses the Administrative and Radio activities and was occupied on 7 November 1966, when the old premises at Park Place, which had been occupied since spring 1924 were vacated. The building was planned for radio only at first, with the intention that television facilities would be added later. It contains a Concert Hall and five other radio studios. The central areas were based on the traditional method of staffing and had a switching centre for television and a control room for radio to carry out all the switching and routeing for the networks in the studio premises. Efforts were made in both Cardiff and Birmingham, as the centres were being built, to integrate these two areas as closely as possible.

A new headquarters building has recently been designed for Manchester, to be erected on a site in Oxford Road. This will be on a smaller scale than the one at Birmingham, but will include radio studios, appropriate to its role as a 'network production centre', and a separate Local Radio station. A particular problem here is that the site is in a busy city centre, with an elevated trunk traffic route running nearby so that noise levels are excessive. To overcome this problem all the offices will have fixed windows and will be air-conditioned.

The BBC Building Department (recently renamed the Architectural and Civil Engineering Department) under its head, R. A. Brown, has been concerned with a number of other projects including modifications to existing and newly acquired premises, the formation of studios and technical areas in them, the solution of acoustical problems, the construction of masts for transmitting stations, and maintenance work on buildings and services.

It was noted in the previous chapter that the trend in studio planning was towards 'general-purpose' rather than specialised studios. In the period now under review, this trend was to some extent reversed and studios have been constructed specially for music and drama and even for programmes of gramophone records. More programmes are now recorded before transmission and few complete programmes are broadcast live, apart from public events and some performances; this has led to the gradual adoption of much larger studio cubicles because more recording is done there rather than in separate recording rooms; the tendency is to record the programme in short sections as it is built up. In the Regions the amount of material produced has not usually justified the provision of specialised studios, but such studios are now being included in the new buildings.

Studio desks have become more complicated because of changing techniques in the presentation of programmes. The tendency is to use more microphones, to separate out sounds from different instruments and to balance them individually. The trend since the mid-1950s has been to produce the kind of sound that the listener wants to hear rather than a faithful reproduction of the sound originating in the studio. Studios have therefore been equipped with devices for altering the frequency response or putting in 'presence', such as are used in commercial recording studios.

One of the problems in planning new buildings was the ever-increasing sound level of 'pop' music; studios must now be insulated against noise levels hitherto unimagined. An apt illustration of this problem comes from Broadcasting House, London, where, on the removal of the old war-time control room from the sub-basement area to the Extension, the area vacated was converted once more into a studio, to be used for dance music. It was intended to use it also for pop music, but it was found impossible to insulate it sufficiently from the Concert Hall above. Loudspeakers, too, are affected by the high sound level of pop music. Those who monitor it insist on such high levels (about 120 phons) that loudspeakers are sometimes damaged.

Since the Broadcasting House Extension came into service a new type of studio has been evolved for News and Current Affairs – indeed the whole technique of news-collecting has changed since that time. News material was formerly collected in the same way as any other; it was routed on lines into a communications or control room area, sent to a recording channel booked for the purpose, recorded and then sent to the news studio. When the Extension came into service, arrangements were made for all news dispatches from abroad to be recorded under remote control by traffic managers in an area adjacent to the news studio. The time required for the item to be broadcast was greatly reduced, and the correspondent did not have to wait until a channel was available. News from this country has since been brought into the same type of operation, and specialist studios are being developed for the *World at One* type of programme.

The increase in the scope of the programmes that took place in the 1960s and the advent of the Open University has meant that the four continuity suites that were provided when the Extension came into service had to be increased to six. The introduction of Radio 1 caused the greatest change in continuity operation. The disc jockeys were skilled operators, able to perform better by themselves than when they had somebody to assist them. This led to the majority of programmes for Radio 1 being originated in the continuity suite, with very little rehearsal. What rehearsal there is, is done in the continuity suite, so that two of them are required for Radio 1, one for rehearsals and the second for transmission, the two suites being switched alternately to the network. The London control room has thus become a centre of activity for producers, performers and operators rather than a sanctum for engineers, and contact between all those concerned in a programme has become much closer. This technique made it possible to introduce Radio 1 without building any new studios, and with very few extra technical staff. The disc jockey himself has much technical apparatus to manipulate, including compressors, cartridge recorders and artificial reverberation.

The changes in programme techniques, coupled with the possibilities of using pcm (pulse code modulation) on wide-band SHF links are leading to a more rigid distribution network, with little or no 'opting out' of the Regions from the networks, except on Radio 4. Even on Radio 4 access by the Regions is needed only for their own output – there is no need for them to control the network as such.

A major development during the period under review has been the introduction of stereophonic broadcasting. Like many other scientific developments it suddenly became popular after spasmodic attempts dating back to the nineteenth century. As long ago as 1881 arrangements were made at the Paris Opera, using ten microphones, to convey the programme in stereo by line to an exhibition at the Palace of Industry. This demonstration showed that 'auditory perspective' can lend a touch of magic to systems of quite modest performance.[3]

In this country, in 1925, a two-channel experiment took place in which the medium-frequency transmitter in London was paired with the long-wave transmitter at Daventry to provide an experimental stereophonic transmission of an opera from the Old Vic. At that time the left- and right-hand microphones were placed only a short distance apart – perhaps to imitate a pair of human ears – which made the result quite impressive for anyone listening on headphones, but not very effective when loudspeakers were used. Work on the problem continued in various countries, but it was A. D. Blumlein who first proposed the arrangement of two microphones close together and pointed half-left and half-right.

The first determined moves towards stereo were made towards the end of 1957, when the BBC decided that the increasing availability of stereophonic gramophone records and the public interest that was being aroused justified serious consideration of stereophonic broadcasting. Late in that year an experimental transmission took place at night, the left- and right-hand channels being transmitted by two of the VHF transmitters at Wrotham. The programme came from a tape supplied by EMI, with items recorded in this country and in America. The BBC was in the forefront of systematic research into the audio-frequency problems. Many subjective tests were carried out over a period of two and a half years – a laborious task, which established the tolerances applicable to phase-shift between channels and other parameters. This work was done in collaboration with the operational and programme staff; orchestras and artists had to be engaged to perform specially for the tests. It was an expensive exercise but it yielded valuable results,[3-9] which have contributed to international discussions on the audio-frequency standards for stereo that are still continuing, notably in the CMTT (Commission Mixte des Télégraphes et Téléphones).

Putting this accumulated knowledge into practice the BBC began to make experimental stereo transmissions, which on 18 October 1958 developed into regular fortnightly transmissions, on Saturday mornings. The Third Programme transmitters (VHF and MF), which were free at that time, were used for the left-hand channel and the television sound transmitters for the right-hand. An hour's programme was broadcast, consisting in part of discs issued by the recording companies but also including material produced by the BBC. Listeners had to use two receivers, a VHF or an MF receiver and a television receiver, placed suitably in the room. At locations well within the service range of the transmitters the stereo effect was very good. These experimental transmissions continued for some years and generated a great deal of correspondence from all parts of the country, although it was made clear that the system could not be used for a regular programme service because it was incompatible.

An early OB experiment in stereo was the Carol Service from King's College, Cambridge, on 24 December 1958. This was double-banked with the normal mono transmission. As it happened, there was some trouble on the line during the live monophonic broadcast in the afternoon. The stereo was recorded 'on location', and as there was to be a repeat broadcast in the evening the stereo tapes were rushed back to London, so that the appropriate parts of them could be cut into the mono version where the latter was imperfect. The result was a faultless recorded repeat.

The audio-frequency techniques were by this time well advanced, but two important decisions had still to be made before regular stereo broadcasting could be introduced to the public. One was the wave-band to be used. Since high quality and freedom from interference were essential to the appreciation of stereo transmissions there was no doubt that they should be in the VHF band (Band II) rather than in the long- or medium-wave bands. The second question was more complex, i.e. the method of coding to be used. Just as with colour television, compatibility was seen to be essential if the service was to be practicable on any wide scale: the stereo transmissions must be receivable as monophonic programmes, without any noticeable loss of quality, on ordinary VHF receivers. It was most desirable, as experience with television had shown, to reach world-wide agreement on a common system before a stereo service was introduced. After much experimental work had been done in this and other countries, the CCIR decided in 1966 to recommend (though not exclusively) the pilot-tone system as an international standard. On the recommendation of the TAC it was adopted in the UK. It is now in use in most countries of Western Europe. In this system, which was originally developed in the USA by Zenith-GE, half the sum of the right- and left-hand signals is transmitted as modulation of the main carrier and half their difference as amplitude modulation of a suppressed sub-carrier at 38 kHz. A pilot tone at 19 kHz is also incorporated in the waveform to enable stereo receivers to recover the difference signal from the sub-carrier. Both the modulated sub-carrier and the pilot tone are added to the sum signal to frequency-modulate the main carrier. As in monophonic transmission the frequency deviation is limited to $\pm$ 75 kHz. Monophonic receivers ignore the difference signal and the pilot tone, but respond to the sum signal as if it were a monophonic transmission. (An alternative system, known as polar-modulation, was adopted by the USSR; in it the amplitude-modulated sub-carrier is only partially suppressed and no pilot-tone is used.)

The stereo system is compatible, the additional equipment required in the receiver for stereo reception is relatively simple, and the multiplexed signal can be radiated from a single VHF transmitter. Experimental transmissions on this system started from the Third Programme transmitter at Wrotham in August 1962, and regular broadcasts in the same programme from the same station and its dependent relay stations started in July 1966. The service was extended to the Midlands and the North in 1968 and is expected to reach Central Scotland and the Bristol Channel area in 1974. By 1971 most programmes in Radio 3 were produced in stereo and in 1972 the system was being extended to Radio 2 and Radio 4.

With the coming of stereo there was revived interest in 'effects' of all kinds. There were many demonstrations, including a touring BBC one, in which express trains sped through the room or listeners swivelled their heads rapidly from side to side as they 'watched' a table tennis match. Some effects were more sophisticated: in a scene from *Sherlock Holmes* a dagger was thrown across the room to fix the door of a cupboard in which somebody had just been shut. This was done by swishing a stick in front of the microphone and synchronising it with a bang elsewhere in the room. It was soon evident, however, that the real value of stereo lay not in such tricks but in the added richness it could give to music and to almost every other kind of programme.

The fact that a stereo signal requires two identical paths up to the point where it is coded to go into the transmitter complicates the equipment and the links (unless wide-band circuits are available to carry the coded signal). This is by no means the only complication. Only seldom can a simple 'crossed-pair' of microphones (a coincident pair of directional microphones with axes at right angles) be used, because the right balance of direct and reverberant sound cannot be combined with the right width of 'picture'. Generally, therefore, stereo mixing panels are provided not only with ganged faders for the left and right channels, but also with means for fading in mono microphones, and perhaps other pairs of stereo microphones as well. When a mono microphone is used, its output is fed into both channels through a 'pan-pot' (a fader arranged to connect an input to two output channels in any desired proportion), so that the position of the image can be controlled according to the proportions that are fed to the left and right channels. On recent stereo panels there are three or more stereo channels and a much larger number of mono channels, up to sixteen or more. Pop music is, usually, more conveniently handled by a large number of mono microphones, each suitably steered by its pan-pot.

Transportable stereo desks have been designed for OBs, usually with three stereo channels, stereo echo and a number of mono channels. Valve-operated equipment was used at first, but subsequent models were transistorised. Outside London, only the new Pebble Mill studios in Birmingham have so far been equipped with special stereo desks. In other regions make-shift arrangements are used successfully. All the recordings of the BBC Scottish Symphony Orchestra in Glasgow Studio 1 for Radio 3 are now done in stereo. So too are all broadcasts from the Royal Festival Hall in London whether or not they are ultimately to be broadcast in stereo. Much of the output of drama is also done in stereo.

The large control room that was put into service in the Broadcasting House Extension building in 1961 still has valve-operated equipment; it has a good record for reliability, but produces more heat and takes up more room than would a modern transistorised installation. The switching equipment, based on the Siemens motor-driven uniselector, is still giving good service. When the studios in the extension were equipped the original type A equipment had already given place to type B, which had been given service trials in 1954. The type B equipment was valve-operated, but shortly after the Extension was opened, the type C equipment, using transistorised amplifiers, became available and this was used in the two drama studios. These first transistorised amplifiers tended to be noisy; improvement in this respect had to await the arrival of the field-effect transistor and a new generation of studio equipment – type D. This was in modular form and its electrical design proved excellent. It was, however, overtaken by events during the production period as it was not designed for stereo. Moreover, suitable commercial equipment was now becoming available. A desk produced by Rupert Neve & Co. was installed in the Concert Hall in Broadcasting House and gave good results with very little modification.

A useful development was the introduction of the reverberation plate, which has now almost entirely superseded the old type of echo room as a means of adding reverberation to a programme. This device was invented by W. Kuhl of IRT, Hamburg. It consisted of a steel sheet (originally 2 m² in area and 5 mm thick) with input and output transducers of very low mass.[10] Later models have successfully used much smaller plates. Those made by Elektromesstechnik Wilhelm Frank, AG, have a transducer near one corner to excite vibrations that are picked up by another transducer, acting as a microphone, near another corner of the plate. The assembly is suspended in a box with a damping plate, which can be moved closer or farther away to control the reverberation time. This plate can also be used for stereo echo; for classical music, the sum signal is put on to the plate and two pick-up points are used, one for the left-hand and the other for the right-hand channel. Another technique is to have two plates, one for left and the other for right, which enables the echo to be steered so that it comes from the same apparent position as the source.

Automatic volume compressors were increasingly used during this period, both at the sources of programmes and at the transmitters. About 6dB of compression was used on the long- and medium-wave transmitters from February 1961 as a means of increasing the average depth of modulation so as to reduce the effect of interference from foreign stations. In March 1964 the 'pirate' stations started to operate off the coasts of this country, giving stronger signals in some coastal areas than the BBC stations. The degree of volume-compression applied to the MF transmissions of the Home and Light Programmes was increased to 12 dB in February 1965 to improve their competitive effectiveness. By the end of 1971 MF transmissions of Radio 1 had compression at the source only; the LF transmissions of Radio 2 were subjected to 12 dB compression at the source, but some of the MF transmitters took their programme feeds from VHF stations and as the VHF output was not compressed, these stations had 12 dB of compression applied at the transmitter. Radio 4 had 12 dB compression applied at the MF transmitters. Radio 3, consisting mainly of music had only 4 dB compression applied at Daventry and 6 dB at other stations. No compression was applied to Radio 3 transmissions on VHF.

Compression was applied to Radio 1 at the source because the network was fixed and the amount of compression could be varied to suit the programme – none for gramophone records that were already compressed or for football matches where compression would cause unpleasant variations in the level of background effects. The techniques for the balance and control of pop music and dance music, and even for a full orchestra playing light music, now demand either compression or limiting, and this has led to the use of compressors in the studios themselves at the outputs of individual microphones.

Special techniques were also developed for broadcasting telephone calls from members of the public. Compressors were used to overcome the difference in level between the speech from the near and distant ends of a two-way telephone circuit. In a more sophisticated method the output from the microphone in the studio was used to cut down the level applied to the telephone circuit while the person in the studio was speaking.

There were also advances in producing effects in drama programmes to reduce the need for disc recordings for this purpose. An attack on the problem was made with the design of a 'Programme Effects Generator',[11] a machine playing match-box-sized cartridges of tape, each giving about ten seconds of playing time. The cartridges could be wound back at high speed, so that the same effect could be repeated quickly. A number of cartridges carrying pre-recorded effects could be held in the machine and any one of them could be instantly selected and put into operation by an ingenious mechanism.

Although this machine covered some of the requirements for effects in a production, there was still a requirement for background effects of relatively long duration, so that either conventional tape machines or long-playing records still had to be used. Increasing use has been made of gramophone records played at variable speed, which is essential where the effects have to be fitted into the timing of the activity; it also enables one recording to be used for different effects by varying the pitch to create such sounds as engines slowing down. A commercial unit, the Goldring-Lenco, has a conical drive to a rubber wheel, so that continuously variable speed is obtained as the wheel is moved from one part of the cone to another.

In the early 1960s the art of 'radiophonics' was developed for the generation of artificial sounds to be used as effects. The earlier processes in radiophonics were carried out mainly with variable-speed tape machines, which were used to manipulate either natural or electronically produced sounds. In recent years, however, more sophisticated electronic equipment has been devised, including synthesizers with keyboards that can be played like those of a conventional keyboard instrument and a 'gunfire effects generator' developed by the Designs Department. With this development the borderline between radiophonics and electronic music has become blurred, and the BBC Radiophonic Workshop now not only produces effects and noises but also, since the people working there are musicians as well as engineers, compositions such as musical introductions and incidental music to plays. The Workshop, started in 1958, now produces some two hundred compositions a year for the radio and television services.[12, 13]

From the earliest days of broadcasting much attention has been devoted to the monitoring of programmes. At first monitoring was done by ear at almost every point in the broadcasting chain, and the ideal was to maintain the highest quality that could be achieved at the time, and to ensure that any deviations from it were detected, logged, and remedied as quickly as possible. This was wasteful of manpower because there were long periods, especially at transmitting stations, where an engineer would do nothing else but listen to the programme and keep a careful log of events such as the ending of one programme and the beginning of another. After the war automatic methods of monitoring were developed, and since then the tendency has been to use fewer and fewer people on routine tasks and more and more automatic equipment. Two main types of automatic monitor have been developed in the BBC: the first an 'absolute' monitor, which checks the carrier or the level of the programme or of a pilot signal accompanying it, the second a 'comparison' monitor, which compares the programme signal at some particular point in the chain with that derived from another point. Comparison monitors were designed so that any difference that could be detected by the monitor between the two signals would represent a significant deterioration in the programme, such as noise, changes in level or changes in frequency response. If both the signals to be compared were not available at the same point, data derived from one of them could be transmitted over a control line to the distant point. The monitor then compared the data derived from the two signals. Either type of monitor could be arranged to sound an alarm at a manned point or to take executive action, e.g. by switching over to reserve equipment. As equipment became more and more reliable with increased use of solid-state devices the tendency was to use simpler monitors, especially at small translator stations, so as to detect failure of the programme rather than variations in quality.[14]

The increasing use of unattended stations made it necessary to develop methods of finding out whether they were operating normally. The Active Telephone Indicator (ATI), such as that marketed as the 'Datofonic' equipment, initiated a telephone call to a manned point when it received information about a fault or a change in operating conditions. The Passive Telephone Indicator (PTI), on receiving a telephone call, presented information to the caller in a simple code about the state of the equipment. A further development was the Telephonic Controller, which controlled the operation of distant equipment on receiving a coded signal over the public telephone network. When signals from a VHF/FM transmitter could be received at a staffed centre, information about the state of the transmitter could be sent automatically in the form of pulses of a pilot tone at 23 kHz; when the transmitter was operating normally the pilot tone was continuous. These methods could provide information for the analysis of faults by means of a computer.[14, 15]

Much attention was devoted to studio acoustics during the period under review. In the mid-1950s work was done on the development of sound absorbers for use in studio design, particularly on various forms of low-frequency absorber – the most difficult to make. Low-frequency absorbers were already in use, but various modifications were developed during the years 1955 to 1960 (e.g. using membranes consisting of hardboard bonded to roofing-felt); improvements were also made in absorbers for the medium and high audio-frequencies. These improvements resulted from tests made in the Research Department's reverberation rooms on various fabrics for covering the absorbers. The BBC also took part in an international series of measurements which led to the formulation of recommendations for the design and operation of reverberation rooms for measuring sound absorption. As a result of these investigations good agreement is now obtained between calculated and measured values in listening rooms; in studios, where the factors are not under such close control, variations up to 25 per cent from the calculated value are still commonly found.[16, 21]

The standards of noise level that are acceptable in various kinds of studio are kept continuously under review. Among the sources of noise it has been necessary to investigate are ventilation and heating systems, road and air traffic (including sonic booms),[22] and programmes taking place in neighbouring studios. In television it is also necessary to take account of noise made by the movement of camera cables and revolving stages, and also of electrical interference from thyristor lighting dimmers.

Steps taken to reduce the level of extraneous noise in studios include the design of the 'Camden' and 'double Camden' types of standard sound-insulating partition (now commonly used in BBC studios), special methods of construction of double- and triple-glazed windows, and the sealing of studio doors with magnetic seals or, occasionally, hydraulic seals. All these forms of sound-reducing construction have been tested in a variety of situations, and it is now possible to predict reasonably well the insulation that will be obtained from a particular type of construction. It has recently been found necessary to re-examine the requirements on account of the great increase in the noise level from pop groups, already mentioned, and from the use of electrical amplification in the studios.

During the last five years notable advances have been made by Research Department in the use of models to predict the acoustic characteristics of sound studios. Those of Studio 1 at Maida Vale were successfully reproduced in a 1/8 scale model, using sound at eight times the normal frequencies. (Plate XXX.)

Many commercial types of microphone came into use during this period and this necessitated an extensive programme of testing by Research Department. In the period 1957 to 1966 samples of some fifty different commercial microphones were tested, of which fifteen came into operational use. At the beginning of the period, the redesigned ribbon microphones (the studio type and the lip microphone) were in general use along with some commercial types. The redesigned studio microphone mentioned in the previous chapter, the PGS, was produced by STC and coded 4038; the consistency of its performance was very high and it has been used by broadcasting organisations throughout the world. The redesigned lip microphone was also manufactured by STC under the coding 4104. This was appreciably more sensitive than its predecessor and gave considerably better sound quality. In fact the improvement in sound quality produced by these two microphones was one of the factors causing a demand for better loudspeakers. The capacitative microphone has recently become increasingly popular, though the PGS microphone still holds the palm for consistency of performance.[23, 24]

Much work was done on loudspeakers during this period. The LSU/10 loudspeaker, based on a Parmeko model, was in wide use, but its response fell off above 7000 Hz. This limitation not only affected the sound quality but also made it impossible to hear the 10,125 kHz whistle produced by a 405-line television signal, which sometimes appeared as a blemish in both radio and television programmes. In 1956 the problem of extending the frequency range of the LSU/10 was solved by adding a Lorenz LPH/65 high-frequency unit, which, with a suitable filter and crossover unit, extended the range to about 15 kHz. The BBC applied critical tests to the units and the resulting loudspeaker showed a considerable improvement, one important advantage being that the sensitivity was so high that adequate sound levels could be obtained by using only a 10-W amplifier.

Meanwhile tests on commercial loudspeaker units continued. A monitoring loudspeaker was produced in 1955, using a GEC/Rola-Celestion direct-radiator high-frequency unit with a 15-in. Plessey unit. Tighter manufacturing tolerances were applied to these units, and the sound quality of the combination was extremely good; it was registered as an approved design, but did not go into production because the elaborate cabinet which was thought necessary made it too expensive, and only a few were made for experimental use. However, the need for an improved monitoring loudspeaker was still evident, and the design of this experimental loudspeaker was examined once again. This resulted in the LS5/1, which went into production in about 1960. It consisted of a Plessey 15-in. unit with a paper-pulp cone for the bass, with a cross-over frequency at 1500 Hz; two of the GEC/Rola high-frequency pressure units were used above this frequency to cover the whole range up to 13 kHz. The LS5/1 design continued through most of the 1960s and it was put into commercial production by KEF Electronics. Another loudspeaker, the LS3/1, was designed along similar lines for use on outside broadcasts.

To improve quality still further and to narrow the differences between samples of the same loudspeaker, an investigation was undertaken into the use of new materials for loudspeaker cones. The most successful of these was a solid polystyrene sheet damped by the addition of synthetic rubber. This could be quite simply vacuum-formed to the shape desired, and it was found that a 12-in. unit made with this material gave very good results. The new loudspeaker which resulted from these investigations, the LS5/5, had three units; a 12-in. unit, going up to 400 Hz; an 8-in. unit from 400 Hz to 3 kHz; and a high-frequency unit going from 3 kHz upwards. The use of plastics, besides giving a loudpeaker of good quality and free from coloration, improved the consistency of results, so that the tolerance on the frequency response could be reduced to ± 1 dB. It is thus impossible to detect any difference between samples that have passed the test.

In sound Outside Broadcasting the main development, apart from the stereo equipment already mentioned, has been the introduction of OB and recording equipment that can be operated by a speaker without engineers or programme staff in attendance. On the other hand major OBs have tended to become more elaborate. The number of music OBs has greatly increased, particularly with the growth of stereo. (The OB Department was equipped for stereo before the studios.) The technical equipment used was still the OBA/9, though a new design, the OT2/3, was produced during the early 1960s. This had high-level mixers providing a flexible number of channels; the output from these was fed into a level-raising unit with group faders and a main amplifier, and there were separate units for power supply and communications.

Another feature in the field of OBs is the increasing world interest in international events such as the Olympic Games and the World Cup. The facilities that the BBC has been called upon to provide at events taking place in this country have increased as more countries have taken part, and there is competition among broadcasters in different parts of the world in making the coverage as complete as possible. Whereas mixing and control always used to be done remote from the commentary positions there is now a tendency to have comprehensive facilities available at the commentary position itself. Techniques used in different countries have become more alike than they used to be, no doubt because each organisation learns from the experience of others through seeing them at work and through the exchange of information that takes place in the EBU and other international bodies. A special commentators' unit was standardised by the EBU for use at complex OBs with commentaries in many languages.

An event which caught the imagination of the world was the State Funeral of Sir Winston Churchill on 30 January 1965. Thought had been given to the planning some ten years ahead, and in considerable detail; it had to be done in strict secrecy and had to be continually kept up to date. In the event there were five sites for sound broadcasting, each with five commentary positions – apart from St Paul's Cathedral, which had twelve such positions. A large number of microphones had to be used for the service itself and the balance and control of them presented a difficult problem.

At midnight on 31 December 1971 there was a change in the Greenwich Time Signal, which had kept to its original form since it was introduced on 5 February 1924. The nature and purpose of the change was widely misunderstood despite careful publicity. It arose from the decision of the General Conference of Weights & Measures, 1971, to adopt the International Atomic Time Scale for time signals throughout the world. They would thus be of great value for many scientific purposes, being based on precisely equal time intervals as determined by atomic clocks. Greenwich Mean Time, based on astronomical observations, would, however, remain the standard civil time. Owing to slight irregularities in the motion of the earth, the time signals would have to be corrected occasionally to keep them in line with GMT within three-quarters of a second. The six short pips of the GTS were replaced by five short pips followed by one longer one starting at the exact minute and on 31 December and 30 June each year a positive or negative 'leap second' will be introduced to make the necessary correction. On those occasions there might, at midnight, be seven pips or five instead of six. The object of lengthening the last pip was to make it easily distinguishable. The GTS continued to be operated by an atomic clock at the Royal Greenwich Observatory at Herstmonceux Castle, Sussex, as it had been for the previous ten years, but instead of being corrected frequently to keep it to GMT within one-tenth of a second, it has now to be corrected only twice a year.

2 TRANSMITTERS FOR RADIO SERVICES

During this period the VHF/FM sound broadcasting network was expanded from three stations at the end of 1955, giving a coverage of about 33 per cent of the UK population, to seventy-seven stations in 1972 giving a coverage of 99·3 per cent with three programmes. The long- and medium-wave transmitters existing at the end of 1955 continued in service; wherever possible unattended or semi-attended operation was introduced at these stations and some of the older plant was replaced by modern high-efficiency equipment. Following the closure of the majority of the so-called 'pirate' stations in 1967, after their three years of activity, the BBC Light Programme was replaced by two programmes, Radio 1 and Radio 2; this necessitated the regrouping of the long- and medium-wave transmitters and supplementing them with additional stations. In 1967 'Local Radio' stations were introduced, each with its own facilities for producing programmes. These VHF/FM stations of limited range were brought into service in two stages – an experimental stage consisting of eight stations and a later expansion to a total of twenty stations. In July 1966 regular stereophonic transmissions were started for VHF/FM listeners in south-east England; two years later these transmissions were extended to the Midlands and the North of England, and in 1971 to the station at Rowridge, Isle of Wight.

The first of these developments had germinated in February 1954, when the Government accepted the recommendation of the Television Advisory Committee that VHF sound broadcasting should use frequency modulation,[25] and in July 1954, the BBC had been authorised to begin the construction of the first of the new VHF–FM stations.[26]

The three stations in service at the end of 1955 were:

Wrotham	Home, Light and Third Programmes	120 kW erp
Pontop Pike	Home, Light and Third Programmes	60 kW erp
Penmon	Welsh Home Service only	1 kW erp

Wenvoe was also operating, in a temporary condition, carrying the Welsh Home Service only. Six more high-power VHF/FM stations were commissioned at Holme Moss (1956), Sutton Coldfield, Tacolneston, Kirk o'Shotts, and Wenvoe (1957), and Sandale (1958). Of these, Sandale was the first VHF/FM station to radiate four programmes (North Home, Scottish Home, Light and Third). Wenvoe became the second four-programme station in 1959 radiating Welsh Home, West of England Home, Light and Third programmes. While the high-power stations were being built, five medium-power VHF/FM stations were also under construction at Divis, Meldrum, North Hessary Tor, Blaen Plwyf and Rowridge, the last of these, Rowridge, being commissioned in June 1957. The cylinders in which the VHF slot aerials were formed could offer desirable resting places for birds; at Rowridge in 1959 a colony of rooks was persuaded to leave by the use of netting and a scarecrow.

When the Sandale station had been brought into service in August 1958 the coverage on VHF/FM had been increased to an estimated 95 per cent and the objective was then to close the gaps by building a number of low-power relay stations throughout the country. The network was extended in five stages until it reached a total of seventy-seven stations, most of them radiating three programmes but a few carrying four.

The VHF/FM stations were co-sited with BBC television transmitting stations, except the high-power stations at Wrotham and the relay stations at Brecon and Llangollen. The transmitters were designed from the outset for unattended operation and reliability was ensured by operating the transmitters in pairs and by dividing the slot aerial system into two halves, connected by separate feeders to two combining units. Each of these combined the outputs of one of each pair of transmitters carrying each programme. This arrangement ensured that failure of any one transmitter unit would be hardly noticeable to most listeners, since the drop in the strength of the FM signal would merely result in a corresponding increase in background noise and interference. At the high-power stations, two 10-kW transmitter units were provided for each programme to produce a transmitter output power of 20 kW, which was radiated by a high-gain slot aerial to give an erp of 120 kW. Two types of transmitter, one manufactured by Marconi's and the other by STC, were used at the high- and medium-power stations, the main difference between the two being in the method of modulation. Marconi's used their 'FMQ' (Frequency Modulated Quartz) system.[27] This had a special type of crystal, the natural frequency of which could be 'pulled' by means of a susceptance modulator; the crystal operated in the range between 3 and 5 MHz and frequency multipliers increased the deviation and the mean carrier frequency to the required values. STC used an oscillator comprising a resonant circuit modulated by a reactance valve with its centre frequency controlled by a quartz-crystal oscillator.[28]

Transmitters, properly so-called, were used for stations with an output power down to about 1 kW. For lower powers transposers were used, with or without power amplifiers. These received the programmes from a main station and rebroadcast them on another group of frequencies without demodulation. Early transposers were equipped with valves, but later designs embodied solid-state circuitry throughout.

A considerable amount of development work was undertaken by the specialist departments as the VHF/FM network expanded, particularly in the design of transmitters, transposers, three- and four-programme combining units, feeders, aerials, and matching devices.[14, 15, 29, 30, 31] VHF aerials were designed to match the special requirements of many of the stations and a wide range of monitoring and surveillance equipment was designed.

The co-siting of VHF/FM and television stations facilitated construction work as common access roads and services could be used and a common mast for both sets of aerials. Major staff savings also resulted from this, because the staff necessarily required at the television stations were available to give 'first-aid' attention to the VHF/FM transmitters in the unlikely event of both transmitter chains failing simultaneously. A comprehensive alarm and monitoring system incorporated in the design of the VHF/FM stations gave clear indications of fault conditions.[15] Routine maintenance of the VHF transmitter plant at the high- and medium-power stations required only a single additional post at each television station.

Where VHF/FM installations are sited at unattended television relay stations – and this applies to most of the low-power relay stations – the restoration of service and routine maintenance are the responsibility either of Transmitter Maintenance Teams or of Engineers-in-Charge of near-by attended stations who have, where necessary, been provided with 'Assistants (Mobile)' specifically to undertake these duties.

Transmitter Maintenance Teams were first used early in 1951 when they were known as Mobile Maintenance Teams. Initially there were only two of these, one based at Moorside Edge and the other at Stagshaw. Each consisted of two engineers who were provided with a light estate car equipped with simple test equipment to service and maintain the few medium-wave unattended relay stations in operation at that time.[32] There are now thirteen of these teams in operation each consisting of three engineers, the senior of which is designated Team Manager. They are equipped with a four-wheel drive Land Rover and a light van. The former vehicle is used for normal visits and the latter when simultaneous faults make it necessary to split up the team. The teams are provided with a wide range of modern test equipment capable of making sophisticated performance measurements on the sound and television equipment at the various kinds of station. Originally the teams were also provided with equipment to enable them to make regular checks on the field-strength of MF stations in their area and compare them with data obtained by Research Department staff at selected points. With the increase in the number and complexity of the relay stations, this field-strength measurement work is now carried out by staff in the Site Acquisition Section of the Transmitter Group.

The transmission of programmes for the Open University, which started on 10 January 1971, were carried by the Radio 3 VHF transmitters during the early evenings on week-days and by the Radio 4 VHF transmitters during morning and afternoon periods on Saturdays and also on Sunday mornings. At these times the normal programmes of Radios 3 and 4 were carried by the MF transmitters only; the distribution networks and monitoring arrangements had therefore to be rearranged to permit this separation. Open University programmes in television were broadcast by the BBC-2 network at various times outside the programme hours of BBC-2. All the Open University programmes were presented from Alexandra Palace.

The introduction of the high-power VHF/FM transmitters into service raised some problems of local interference. For example, the West of England Home Service and Light Programme transmitters at Wenvoe were found to interfere with communication channels of the local ambulance service operating on an adjacent frequency band; this was overcome by offsetting the centre frequencies by $+$ 50 kHz and $+$ 25 kHz respectively. The Tacolneston Light Programme transmitter at first caused second-channel interference on some receivers and until local dealers had obtained and fitted suitable filters the power of the Tacolneston transmitter was held down to an acceptable level.

At some stations in remote parts of the country there were difficulties in providing programme feeds. The VHF/FM station at Rosemarkie, opened in late 1958, was the first to be programmed entirely by radio pick-up of a station earlier in the distribution chain, i.e. Meldrum. In case of failure of this link, the Scottish Home and Light Programmes could be received from Burghead on medium waves; the Third Programme could be received at Burghead from Meldrum and retransmitted over a VHF link to Rosemarkie. The VHF/FM station at Les Platons in Jersey was provided with receivers for reception of either North Hessary Tor or Rowridge and the television receiving station at Torteval in Guernsey was used as a reserve reception point with a radio link to Les Platons. The Londonderry VHF/VM station at Sherrif's Mountain was fed with the Northern Ireland Home Service by line through the Londonderry MF station, but the Light and Third Programmes were initially received at a receiving station at Glenderowen. In fact, direct reception proved to be satisfactory at Sherrif's Mountain and the use of Glenderowen became unnecessary. At the end of 1962 a VHF/FM station was opened at Fort William; this was fed with the Scottish Home Service by line from Glasgow via Oban and Ballachulish, while the Light and Third Programmes were received from Rosemarkie at a link station at Fort Augustus and thence by line. The opening of the unattended relay station at Oban by the Secretary of State for Scotland at the end of June 1963 marked the completion of the VHF/FM scheme for covering the South-West Highlands.

The Orkney station was established at an old RAF radar station site at Nether-button, near Kirkwall, in 1958 and was programmed by direct reception initially from the Meldrum station and later from Thrumster. The northward extension to Shetland was completed in 1964 with the commissioning of a station on Bressay, near Lerwick. The programmes were received direct from Orkney at a site on Fitful Head in the extreme south of Shetland and routed to the transmitters by line.

The first completely unattended television and VHF/FM station was built at Llandrindod Wells in 1961. This station employed transposers for the three sound programmes, the equipment being switched on and off by the Wenvoe VHF/FM transmissions. The first of the BBC-design of solid-state transposer was brought into service at Barnstaple in May 1968 and the last of the valved versions at Whitby in 1969.

At Les Platons a crystal-controlled clock system was installed in 1969 to provide for precision timing of opt-out switching in the Home Service (Radio 4). This clock used a 1-MHz crystal oscillator, phase-locked to the Droitwich 200-kHz trans-mission, followed by a frequency divider using integrated circuits and having a ratio of $2 \times 10^6 : 1$. An output pulse was thus produced every two seconds to drive a solid-state unit, which operated the slave dials.

In 1959 some preliminary work was done at Droitwich with the object of modi-fying the original 5XX series-modulated long-wave transmitter to use the Doherty high-efficiency modulation system. The proposal was dropped in favour of replacing the original transmitter with two 200-kW units recovered from Ottringham when it closed down in 1953. These were used in parallel giving a maximum power output of 400 kW and went into service on 18 September 1962; they are still in operation.

The frequency stability of the Droitwich 200-kHz carrier, which serves as a con-venient and widely-used sub-standard of frequency, was considerably improved during the period under review. In 1945, when this transmission was first publicised as a sub-standard of frequency, a short-term frequency stability of ± 2 parts in 10^8 was maintained using a BBC type CP-17E crystal drive, with a Post Office type W5 crystal operating at 1 MHz. This was replaced in 1963 by an improved crystal oscil-lator supplied by Henn Collins Associates and used a 5-MHz crystal in an oven with very accurate temperature control. This improved the frequency stability to $\pm 5/10^9$. Then, in late 1963, two Essen ring quartz oscillators operating at 100 kHz were obtained from the Post Office. These were installed in a specially screened room and were mounted on shock-absorbing plinths. Continuous adjustment of frequency was made automatically to counteract the known rate of drift of the oscillators. The short-term frequency stability was thereby improved to $\pm 1/10^{10}$. In 1967, the National Physical Laboratory made available to the BBC a rubidium gas cell oscillator, which improved the frequency stability still further to a long-term figure of one or two parts in 10^{11}, which is of the same order as that of the National Standard Frequency transmissions from the Post Office station at Rugby (MSF).

At the medium-wave stations the trend has been to replace obsolescent equipment by modern plant of higher overall efficiency and to introduce as much automation and unattended working as possible. With the advent of Radio 1 in 1967 the transmitters in the previous Light Programme distribution were transferred to this new programme and additional transmitters were included to improve the coverage.

The programming of low-power MF transmitters by direct reception of VHF transmissions was extended to most of them from 1958 onwards. This resulted in improved quality and reliability and in savings in line rentals; but later, with the introduction of Open University programmes, it became necessary to restore line feeds to the Radio 3 MF stations.

In 1961 the Droitwich 5GB, Midland Regional, transmitter was replaced by two 200-kW units recovered from Ottringham. These operated with an output of 150 kW and were used alternately until the introduction of Radio 1 in 1967 when one unit was allocated to that programme, operating on 1214 kHz, with the output power reduced to 30 kW.

In October 1962 the original Regional transmitter of 1929 carrying the Light Programme at Brookmans Park was replaced by a new design of Marconi 50-kW transmitter using a high-efficiency output amplifier. The overall efficiency of the new transmitter, when tested at full power, was 62 per cent compared with 20 per cent for the transmitter it replaced.

In January 1963 with the release by External Services of their medium frequency of 1340 kHz, it became possible to split the Northern England and Northern Ireland Home Services by changing the Lisnagarvey and Londonderry transmitters from 1151 kHz to 1340 kHz.

From 1965 onwards several MF stations were converted to unattended working. For instance, at Redmoss (autumn 1966), Bartley (January 1967) and Clevedon (August 1967), the Radio 4 transmitters were rebuilt by the staff of Transmitter Group to provide each station with duplicate units and automatic change-over switching. Air-cooled valves replaced water-cooled; solid-state circuitry was used in the low-power stages and silicon diode stacks replaced hot-cathode mercury-vapour rectifiers in the eht supply. Considerable modifications to the monitoring and alarm arrangements were made by Designs Department and Planning and Installation Departments. The traditional reliability of these stations was not impaired by the change to unattended working. In 1967 work began on the design and construction of a prototype transmitter to replace the 1939 Radio 4 transmitter at Start Point. The original design was for a conventional high-power Class B transmitter, but this was later changed to a high-efficiency Doherty circuit. At first the new transmitter provided an instantly available reserve unit in case of failure of the main plant, but it is proposed to build a second 50-kW unit to operate in parallel with the first, so as to allow the old 100-kW transmitter to be scrapped and staff savings made. It is proposed to make similar arrangements at Burghead, Lisnagarvey and Stagshaw, completing the work as soon as possible after 1972. The staff reductions intended have thus been preceded by a long period of notice, so as to allow phased withdrawals.

Unauthorised broadcasting stations transmitting programmes that appealed especially to young people, and carrying advertisements, started to operate in 1964 from ships in the North Sea or from platforms in shallow waters. Most of them used frequencies in the MF band and they caused interference to authorised broadcasting stations and to other services in several countries. By the end of 1964 there were seven of these stations giving substantial coverage in the UK and others started up in the following two years. The EBU encouraged its Members to press their governments to deal with the 'pirates' by legislation. By the spring of 1968 all except one, operating off the Dutch coast, had closed down, some as a result of legal action and others through the hazards of the sea.

The Radio 1 programme was introduced on 30 September 1967 after most of the pirate commercial broadcasting stations had closed down. Radio 1 was radiated by the transmitters previously carrying the Light Programme on 1214 kHz with the addition of transmitters at Washford (60 kW), Droitwich (30 kW), Brighton and Fareham (1 kW each), and Hull (0·15 kW). A 2-kW transmitter at Bournemouth was added in November 1968 operating on the common wave of 1484 kHz and using two Marconi 1-kW transmitters in parallel.

From 1968 onwards a great deal of work was done by the Research Department in collaboration with the EBU and the CCIR in preparation for the revision of the Copenhagen Plan of 1949, which is to be done at a new European Frequency Conference to be organised by the ITU, probably in 1974. The studies included tests to determine the optimum frequency-spacing in the LF and MF bands, to see whether a spacing less than the 9-kHz of the Copenhagen Plan would increase the total effective coverage, and experiments on the effect of using filters to limit the radiated bandwidth of transmitters to about half the channel spacing so as to reduce adjacent-channel interference. This was found to be beneficial in some cases, where foreign stations using channels adjacent to those of BBC stations adopted the same policy. Several stations took part in these tests and another series of tests was made on the rearrangement of the MF channels to make some available for Local Radio services. Additional low-power MF stations were brought into use to improve the coverage of Radio 2.

Experiments in Local Radio started on closed circuit in 1967, followed by a scheme using eight experimental Local Radio VHF transmitters.[2] Radio Leicester was the first of these VHF stations to be opened, on 8 November 1967. The last of them, Radio Leeds, was opened in June 1968. Following the success of these first eight stations, approval in principle was given by the Postmaster General in 1969 to the BBC's proposals for a permanent Local Radio system and plans were prepared for a total of forty stations, of which twenty were approved; these were completed by April 1971. No channels were available within the part of Band II that was already used by the BBC (88 to 94·6 MHz), but frequencies between 94·6 to 97·6 MHz were released by Home Office services.

At that time all the BBC's VHF/FM stations (and most of those in other countries, with the exception of the Republic of Ireland) used horizontal polarisation. The increased use of portable receivers and car radios raised the question whether the signal strength available to such receivers, e.g. in 'picnic situations' where a portable set was placed on the ground, could be improved by adopting some other form of polarisation. Investigations by Research Department, first at Kingswood Warren in

1968 and then at Radio Nottingham, led to the adoption of slant polarisation at Local Radio stations wherever it could be employed without undue complication of the transmitter aerial system.[33]

Most of the Local Radio stations are located at existing BBC transmitting stations and thus benefit from the availability of a built-in emergency service. The transmitters at the other stations are serviced by the engineers in charge of the Local Radio centres, backed up by the Transmitter Maintenance Teams. Operationally, these transmitters are the responsibility of the Chief Engineer, Radio Broadcasting, and his staff.

The early stereophonic broadcasts mentioned in the previous section developed into regular experimental transmissions; the right-hand channel was radiated by Wrotham (93·5 MHz) and Brookmans Park on 908 kHz, and the left-hand channel by Wrotham on 91·3 MHz and by the Crystal Palace television sound transmitter on 41·5 MHz.[34] In May 1958 the tests were extended to transmitters throughout the UK using VHF and MF channels for the left-hand component and Network 3 and television sound channels for the right-hand channel. In October, as stated in the previous section, the tests were put on a regular basis. They yielded valuable information, but it was obvious that a practicable system would have to be compatible and require only a single receiver. In August 1962 a full-scale test of the Zenith-GE multiplex pilot tone system began using the Radio 3 VHF channel at Wrotham; it continued until March 1965. The 19-kHz pilot tone used in this system necessitated changing the tone at 20 kHz that had been used for monitoring and switching purposes, because this would have caused receivers to switch to the stereo mode whenever it was transmitted; the monitoring tone was therefore changed to 23 kHz and it was automatically suppressed when the 19-kHz pilot tone was present. (i.e. during stereo transmissions). From July 1966 stereo programmes were broadcast regularly by Wrotham and its relay stations, using the pilot-tone system. There was increasing pressure to extend the coverage of stereo transmissions outside London and in 1968 the drives for the Radio 3 VHF/FM transmitters at Sutton Coldfield and Holme Moss were modified for stereo transmission. A link station was set up at Whipsnade, where the programme was received from Wrotham and sent over two SHF links in tandem to Sutton Coldfield. A link station at Macclesfield Forest, near Buxton, relayed the signals over an SHF link to Holme Moss. In July 1971 Rowridge started stereo transmissions, being programmed by direct pick-up from Wrotham.[6, 35] Plans for further extensions have been mentioned in the previous section.

During this period there were some violent incidents causing interruptions to the radio services. On 12 December 1956 a bomb exploded at the Londonderry MF station – fortunately when no staff were on duty – and caused considerable damage to the station. The service was restored using a mobile transmitter on the following day, but the station was not completely rehabilitated until the following summer. Bomb damage occurred at the Brougher Mountain transmitter near Omagh in Co. Tyrone on 7 January 1971. A more tragic incident followed on 9 February when two members of the Transmitter Maintenance Team based at Divis and three men employed by the building contractor were killed when their vehicle was blown up on the way to the Brougher Mountain station.

There is a risk of fire at unattended stations, but the only serious cases affecting the Radio Services during this period were both at the Newcastle (Wrekenton) station. Both were caused by equipment faults, the transmitters at Wrekenton being of a type designed for attended operation. Two fires at Droitwich occurred in the 11-kV circuit-breakers, which were thirty years old and may have deteriorated in store; both fires were extinguished by the automatic carbon-dioxide protection system.

The period under review included a mast failure at Brookmans Park where the 500-ft mast radiator collapsed on 29 September 1956 while in the hands of contractors for maintenance work. The service interruption was minimal as a reserve aerial was available; a replacement mast from Ottringham was taken into service on 1 July 1957.

Many of the transmitting station masts have been in service for many years and replacements have been considered advisable at Start Point and Moorside Edge. The Start Point masts were replaced one at a time during 1957 after eighteen years' service at this isolated coastal site. The three 500-ft masts erected at Moorside Edge in 1931 were replaced by two masts in 1970–1. The Moorside Edge Radio 4 transmitter now uses a 675-ft base-fed mast radiator and Radio 1 is radiated from a directional aerial system supported by a 500-ft mast.

The rapid increase in the number of transmitting stations led to a deluge of essential operational information, which required attention by the headquarters staff. In 1965 a pilot scheme was started for transferring the incoming data to punched cards; from October 1966 these data were processed on the BBC's ICT 1909 computer, from which a read-out was obtained summarising breakdowns and their causes. In 1970 an improvement in the handling of service messages from transmitting stations was introduced in the form of a telephone-answering recorder, which accepted messages sent after office hours for transcription by secretarial staff on the following morning.

An Engineering Automation Development Committee was set up to survey the potential applications of automation over the whole field of BBC engineering activities. One of the projects it initiated was code-named CEMAST (Control of Engineering Material, Acquisition, Storage and Transport); its aim was to devise a computer-controlled system to ensure that engineers were provided with materials and components in sufficient quantities at the time when they were needed, while the cost of supplying them and the amount of capital tied up in stocks were kept to a minimum. The Valve Stores were selected for a pilot study and this was very successful in reducing the levels of stocks of valves and semi-conductor devices of all kinds.[144, 145] By this time a bewildering variety of semi-conductor devices had been developed by a number of manufacturers. (By 1966 there were already 24,000 different types of valve and semi-conductor in use in the BBC and the number was growing as solid-state circuitry was increasingly adopted.)

Open Days at transmitting stations were introduced in 1957 to show the public something of the work and equipment in the last link of the transmission chain. At first there was no experience to indicate how popular these occasions might be and embarrassingly high attendances were recorded. Excellent co-operation from local authorities and services such as the police, RAC, AA and St John Ambulance Brigade helped station staff to handle large numbers of visitors, many of whom travelled long distances and waited patiently in long queues for a relatively short glimpse of the object of their pilgrimage. Nevertheless, the Open Days continued to be popular and the total attendance figures were 24,515 at six stations in 1957 (including 12,650 at Droitwich) rising to 33,736 at thirty-three stations in 1960 and falling to 17,854 in 1963 when there were Open Days at stations in Scotland, the Midlands and East Anglia only.

3 STUDIOS FOR EXTERNAL SERVICES

In 1955 planning and a large amount of construction work were started, which culminated in the gathering together of all the External Services in Bush House in November 1957, when the Overseas Services vacated 200 Oxford Street. This major change necessitated the building of a new control room on the sixth floor of the Centre Block at Bush House, and additional studios on various floors throughout the Centre Block. During the latter part of 1957 the General Overseas Service (Green Network), Arabic (Brown), Far Eastern (Red) and Overseas Regional Services (Purple), were all transferred from Oxford Street to Bush House. These networks were served by three new continuity suites, which were built on the seventh floor of the Centre Block and fitted with the recently designed type B equipment.[36]

Since the network-to-destination switching followed well-established patterns it could be carried out automatically, according to a prearranged schedule, by uniselector switches triggered by clock-controlled pulses at fifteen-minute intervals. The switching positions corresponding to the network transmission schedule were predetermined by a further group of uniselectors, which were 'programmed' by metal-toothed combs inserted between their contacts. These combs were colour-coded to correspond with the network colours. Manual override was provided to permit last minute changes. The switching equipment installed in the new control room, which is still in service, comprises Siemens motor-driven uniselectors, each with fifty outlets on sixteen levels, to effect remotely controlled switching of up to 150 sources to 132 routes via seventy-two channels. The circuit conditions are displayed on a large indicator panel in the control room, with indicator lamps showing the sources and routes selected at any time.[37]

Another feature of this control room is the centralisation of engineering communications by means of a manual telephone exchange. This consists of a cordless switchboard arranged in two positions, each of a hundred lines, with associated rack-mounted selector equipment. This exchange needs two operators at busy periods, but as each operator has full access to all lines in both positions, a single operator can cope with periods of light traffic.

Eleven new studios were built in the Centre Block at that time and equipped with type B equipment, Marks I and II; two of these studios were designed to work as large mixers with a total of ten lines from outside sources, and provision was made for remote control of recording and reproducing machines.

The new control room took over all operations on 3 November 1957 and the old control room in the basement of the south-east wing was kept running in parallel with it until it was closed down in October 1958.

For many years there were separate continuity positions for each of the External Services networks, of which, nowadays, up to fourteen may be running at the same time; each position required a man to control the corresponding network. During the latter part of the 1960s a multichannel control position with sequential monitoring was developed, so that one operator could control up to six networks at a time. This has proved very successful. A special suite was also constructed for dealing with programmes for the Voice of America suite. The signals picked up at Tatsfield from America are fed by line to Bush House, where they are controlled and switched to networks feeding the transmitting station; if necessary, alternative programmes can be injected.

The studios at Bush House are somewhat different from those usually to be found in sound broadcasting centres, being designed chiefly for talks and programmes on current affairs. They are small and are equipped with simple recording and reproducing apparatus, so that news material can be accepted up to the last moment. A news bulletin may not be completed until the programme is actually on the air, and the news is often illustrated by a talk or by 'actuality' material. The increasing demand for actuality has recently led to a reassessment of the equipment required, so as to permit, for instance, the inclusion of telephone calls from outside, which have long been a feature of domestic broadcasting.

The principal ingredient of the External Services has always been news, and many efforts have been made from time to time to streamline the flow of news from all outside sources to the news editors in the various sections. In 1958, the Bush House Centre Desk was reorganised so as to allow the news editors to work actually in the same room as twenty-five incoming and four outgoing teleprinters. This amalgamation of hitherto immiscible elements was rendered possible by the construction of special silencing cabinets, in which particular attention was paid to the avoidance of mechanical rattle, paper noise and rumble transmitted through mountings. So great was the reduction of noise that it is claimed that the twenty-nine teleprinters made less noise than six 'silent' typewriters. In the same reorganisation a loudspeaker system was installed to facilitate the passing of news information to all the programme departments and, later, a Lamson pneumatic tube was installed to permit the rapid transfer of duplicated news information.

As the current design of BBC studio equipment, the Type D, is too elaborate for the requirements of the External Services, the engineers at Bush House have recently designed a 'custom-built' desk, which has been accepted as a standard item of equipment under the coding DK4/12. This is used in small talks studios, and has proved so successful that it may have applications in regional centres.

EE

Because of the basic simplicity of the programmes in the External Services and the continuing pattern of programmes timed to exact quarter-hour intervals, efforts have always been made to introduce as much simplification and automation as possible into the operations. One of the first steps in this direction was the introduction of a 'do-it-yourself' news studio operated by the news reader without any programme assistant or engineer in attendance. There was some doubt whether programme levels would be subject to unacceptable fluctuations, but it was found that if a programme meter were placed on the announcer's desk just out of his normal line of vision, but still within view, he would speak at the right level. These considerations led to the development of a special talks table, on which were mounted a fader, facilities for the remote-control of two tape machines, and a peak programme meter. Production staff can operate this equipment themselves, and so far a total of thirteen such tables have been built; five of these are intended for use in the transmission chain, the others being used for the recording of interviews on closed circuit. This development may be taken a stage further by introducing a fully producer-operated cubicle with more sophisticated controls. An experiment on these lines showed that a producer could achieve smooth presentation of a programme, with inserts from disc and tape. Such a mode of operation could save much staff and time, provided that the problem of dealing with faults can be overcome.

A recent modernisation programme includes the improvement of supervisory facilities, the introduction of fully transistorised equipment and a new computer-controlled switching system using a magnetic drum memory.[38]

In 1971 the External Services broadcast a total of 730 hours of programme per week from the forty-eight studios at Bush House. This is twenty hours more than the output of the rest of the BBC and of the ITA in television and radio combined. The output of the External Services is divided into fourteen networks, which together embrace 39 languages, including English. The World Service is on the air for twenty-four hours each day, the Arabic Service for about eighteen hours each day, and other Services for lesser periods down to a quarter of an hour per week for programmes for the Falkland Islands. For the convenience of embassies and other organisations in London, several of the programmes are distributed to them by wire from Bush House.

The External Broadcasting Engineering Department is also responsible for studios in Berlin and Beirut where news items and talks can be recorded. The Berlin studio was modernised about 1965; the old one in Beirut has recently been replaced by a completely new one with modern equipment.

For many years an engineer has been attached to the BBC's office in New York. He now has the title of Senior Engineer, New York. His responsibilities are to operate and maintain the studio equipment in the New York office and to make technical arrangements with the American networks and the 'Common Carriers' for relays to and from the United Kingdom by cable, radio and satellite. He also keeps the Engineering Division informed of technical developments in North America over the whole field of broadcasting. The advent of public service broadcasting in the

USA by National Public Radio, which transmits educational and current affairs programmes, has led to a regular export of BBC programmes to that organisation. They are sent over a telephone circuit in the transatlantic cable, which is rented by the BBC and is used for this purpose for a quarter of an hour each day. During these periods, the circuit is automatically switched through to Washington, where the programme is recorded.

The BBC also has a studio in Paris, though this, like the one in New York, is administered by the Overseas and Foreign Relations Division and not by the External Broadcasting Directorate. The Paris Office moved to a new location in 1970 and the opportunity was taken to bring the studio facilities up to date.

Relays from other countries for BBC sound services are made under reciprocal arrangements with the broadcasting organisations abroad. Regular outgoing transmissions are made by line to European countries from studios at Bush House, and sometimes involve two-way working.

The major improvements that have been made in the transmitting facilities available to the External Services are described in the next section. Since the transmitters form an essential link with the audience, it is natural that a large part of the available money and effort has been spent on improving them. More needs to be done to improve the studios, particularly in the direction of securing a more efficient layout of them and of the various ancillary areas.

4   TRANSMITTERS FOR EXTERNAL SERVICES

The years from 1956 onwards were marked by a great expansion of the transmitting facilities for the External Services that resulted from the report of the Drogheda Committee.[39] New stations were built overseas, those in the United Kingdom were extended and brought up to date, equipment for the remote or automatic control of the transmitters was installed, and various steps were taken to improve reception in the target areas.

By the end of the 1960s there were seventy-eight high-power transmitters in use for the External Services, operating in the MF and HF bands. Forty-six of these were located in the United Kingdom at five separate sites and the remaining twenty-four were at relay stations overseas operated either by the BBC or the Diplomatic Wireless Service (DWS) of the Foreign and Commonwealth Office.

By the 1970s nearly half of the BBC's HF transmitters in the United Kingdom had an output power of 250 kW, the remainder being rated at 100 kW. Twenty-six of them are of modern design and the remainder have been in service since the Second World War. One hundred and ninety aerials are available, most of which could be used on any frequency within the two adjacent wavebands for which they are designed. The majority of these arrays are reversible and their transmission direction can be slewed by electrical means to 15° on either side of the central line. The latest designs of curtain array give a power gain of about 23 dB, giving an effective radiated power up to 50 MW in the favoured direction from a single transmitter.

An important development was the establishment of several relay stations in different parts of the world to reinforce the direct transmissions of BBC programmes. The success of the Far Eastern Relay Station had shown the value of retransmitting on short waves as a means of overcoming the vagaries of long-distance propagation. There were now cogent reasons for setting up relay stations in other parts of the world: the intense competition from other countries and the popularity of transistor receivers requiring a high signal strength and often capable of receiving medium waves only. The Eastern Relay Station, opened on 1 June 1969, provides a medium-wave service with a maximum power of 1500 kW to India, Pakistan, Iraq, the Arabian Peninsula and the Persian Gulf. The East Mediterranean Relay Station gives both medium-wave and short-wave services to the Near East. The Atlantic Relay Station on Ascension Island has four 250 kW short-wave transmitters serving Africa and South America. The Arabic Service is relayed by a medium-wave transmitter in Malta, and a station in Berlin relays BBC programmes on medium waves and also on VHF.[40]

The efficacy of the short-wave services was improved during this period by developments in aerial design resulting from a long series of experiments, and also by better use of the available frequencies resulting from the study of the occupancy of the short-wave bands by means of band-scanning receivers (which produce charts showing the extent of use of each channel at different times of the day) and by the use of back-scatter transmissions (which determine the state of the ionosphere by projecting pulses at various frequencies and measuring the delay and the intensity of the reflected signals). Information so obtained, plus reception reports from the target areas, enabled forecasts to be made of the optimum frequencies for use over each path with considerable confidence.

By 1960 126 frequencies were registered for BBC External Services use and on 4 September 1960 the first IFRB operational schedule was introduced.[41] By the end of 1971 over two hundred frequencies in the HF broadcasting band were registered for BBC use, of which about 180 are scheduled for operation in any one period.

With the approach of the sunspot maximum in 1956 higher frequencies came into scheduled use and new 26-MHz arrays were erected at Daventry, including a wide-angle array of type HR2/4/1·0/11m/160° centred on South Africa, but giving coverage from Egypt in the east to Sierra Leone in the west. Such an array produces a beam $\pm 24°$ wide to the half-power points, which is about twice as wide as that of the HR4 type. The erection of dual-band arrays followed for all wavebands; these could operate in either of two adjacent wavebands, e.g. the 9- and 11-MHz bands. In mid-1962 tests were made at Daventry of paralleling two high-power transmitters into one dual-band array system.

In June 1959 a frequency synthesiser was installed at Daventry, using the Droitwich 200 kHz radiation as a reference frequency. With the installation of similar equipment at Rampisham and Skelton late in 1960 and a second set at Daventry and Rampisham in late 1961, the synchronising of HF transmitters at the same or different sites – with its economical use of the limited number of frequencies available – became a routine operation at these stations. In 1961 a new control console and automatic switching unit was put into service at Daventry, so as to eliminate one duty position.

In May 1961 when two new 100-kW senders at Rampisham were in service, Senders 4 and 5 were closed down and removed to make way for the installation of two more 100-kW transmitters (Senders 12 and 13), which were brought into use on 2 September 1962. They were Marconi type BD 253 transmitters and were of the dual-channel, rapid wavechange type using evaporative cooling for the large valves. The original transmitters at Daventry, Senders 1 and 2, were closed down, together with Sender 6, on 7 October 1962. Sender 6 was then removed to make way for the new Sender 16. Space was also prepared at this time in the mercury arc rectifier room to take two new 250-kW transmitters – Senders 19 and 21.

On 1 September 1963 a third 100-kW transmitter, Marconi type BD 253 – Sender 14 – at Daventry took over the service carried by Rampisham Sender 33 to release it for modernisation work at that station. (Before taking full service, Sender 14 was used for a short series of test transmissions to enable the Canadian Broadcasting Corporation to make observations on ionospheric conditions over the North Atlantic path during the solar eclipse on 20 July 1963.) A fourth 100-kW transmitter – Sender 16 – was brought into service on 13 November 1963 and the first of the 250-kW transmitters (Sender 21), Marconi type BD 272A, was commissioned on 3 May 1964. A second 250-kW transmitter – Sender 19 – was opened on 6 September 1964. By this time one of the type SWB18 transmitters – Sender 10 – had been modified to permit it to be used for either double or single sideband transmission and SSB tests took place on the Cyprus and Singapore routes during September 1964 using a peak envelope power of 20 kW. During the latter part of September 1964, Sender 7 was taken out of service to modify it for dual-channel rapid-wavechange operation. Shortly afterwards a Marconi type H1200 SSB transmitter with a peak envelope power of 30 kW was commissioned at Daventry and designated SSB1.

The object of the SSB transmissions was to provide programme feeds to the relay stations overseas with a minimum of interference and with maximum economy in the use of the spectrum; such transmissions could be made outside the broadcasting bands, thus saving channels in those bands. The system was not compatible, i.e. the transmissions could not be received satisfactorily on ordinary DSB receivers, but there was no difficulty in using special receivers at the relay stations. Earlier tests made from Rampisham in May 1964 with a compatible SSB (CSSB) system had shown that such a system had no advantage over SSB for providing feeds to relay stations.

In February 1965 a new feeder and feeder switching system was brought into use at Daventry using feeders with a characteristic impedance of 330 ohms; the switching was controlled remotely from the Control Room and replaced the original gantry system, which was manually operated and had been installed in 1937. The new switching system permitted any sender to be connected to any one of eight preselected arrays.

The third and fourth 250-kW transmitters at Daventry – Senders 18 and 20 – were commissioned on 26 September 1966. In 1969 an additional Marconi type

H1200 SSB transmitter (Sender SSB2) was installed to replace the modified Sender 10. Both the Marconi SSB transmitters worked into rhombic aerials giving narrow beams suitable for providing radio links to the relay stations.

By March 1971 all the war-time variable-frequency drive equipment at Daventry had been replaced by frequency synthesisers of German manufacture, whose versatility and suitability for inter-station synchronising greatly improved the operational facilities. The type VFO/4 Drives, except for one set retained as a museum piece, were scrapped after thirty years' service.

In February 1968 new back-scatter equipment made in America was installed at Daventry. This produced a frequency shift of the carrier of very short duration and could thus be used with a normal AM HF transmitter without any modification. The amount of frequency shift was pre-set in multiples of $2 \cdot 5$ kHz and the keying rate adjusted to ten pulses per second. The signals reflected from the target area were received at Tatsfield and observed on a cathode-ray display whose time-base was calibrated as a range marker.

In the period 1968 to 1972 efforts were made to streamline the staffing of the short-wave stations so as to make substantial savings in operating costs by employing a smaller complement of engineers at higher grades and with increased responsibility.

At Rampisham in 1956 an automatic sequential monitoring and switching unit was installed, similar in design to that installed at Skelton in 1951.[37] The equipment incorporated uni-selectors, which switched the loudspeaker to a number of different programmes so as to sample them at 5-second intervals. Each programme could be monitored both at the output of the incoming line and at the output of the transmitter. This system has worked well for twenty years, because the staff become adept at noticing any change in one of the outputs, although they are not observing it continuously and may be engaged in other work at the same time.

In the years 1957 to 1960 a considerable programme of aerial work was carried out at Rampisham and tests were made to determine the vertical radiation pattern of selected arrays. Arrays were rebuilt in 1958 to handle the output of 250-kW transmitters, and tests were made using the 4/4/1 and 4/4/2 types, oriented on Singapore. These tests failed to establish the superiority of one type of array over the other and in 1960 tests were made with a rhombic aerial operating in the 13-m band. The forward gain of this aerial was estimated to be comparable with that of an HR/4/4/1 curtain array, but the vertical propagation angle was different. Tests of the rhombic aerial on the Rampisham-Singapore path failed to prove it superior to the curtain array for providing a signal for rebroadcasting.

On 5 March 1961 the first of the new 100-kW transmitters was put into service (Sender 35) at Rampisham. This was a Marconi transmitter, type BD 253C, and was the fore-runner of those installed later at Daventry. (The overall power efficiency of these transmitters was approximately 47 per cent which represented a substantial improvement over the older SWB18 type.) On 8 May 1961 a second new 100-kW transmitter – Sender 36 – was commissioned. Special attention was paid in the design of these transmitters to the need for screening and filtering to reduce interference to broadcast reception and communications in the VHF bands.

During the exceptionally bad weather of January and February 1963 Rampisham was the worst hit by ice and wind of all the BBC's short-wave stations. Strenuous repair work by the station staff limited the loss of transmission time to 1·2 per cent during the first week of severe weather.

On 17 August 1963 Sender 33 was withdrawn from service to make room for the first two 250-kW transmitters at Rampisham, which were commissioned on 6 September and 13 October 1964 – Senders 39 and 37. On 3 February 1965 Sender 34 was withdrawn from service to make way for the third and fourth 250-kW transmitters – Senders 40 and 38 – which were brought into service on 25 October 1966 and 27 February 1967 respectively. Senders 31 and 32 were taken out of use in April 1967, having given faithful service since 1941.

On 7 September 1969 a Marconi type H1200 SSB transmitter – Sender SSB3 – was installed at Rampisham to extend the relaying facilities.

Between 1956 and 1962 modifications were made to the war-time plant at Skelton to improve its operating characteristics particularly in rapid wave- and band-changing. Dual-band arrays replaced the original aerials and arrays capable of handling the output of 250-kW transmitters were erected in readiness for the new transmitters to be installed under the expansion scheme. In the late 1950s the STC transmitters at Skelton (OSE-9) were modified to take type 3Q 294E thoriated-filament valves, in place of the CAT 17C valves, with consequent savings in the cost of filament heating. In the early 1970s the 3Q 294E valves began to be replaced by STC 3QC 294J ceramic valves.

By the end of 1956 an extensive exercise in HF screening and filtering the Marconi SWB18 transmitters at Skelton (OSE-8) had been completed to reduce interference with broadcast reception and communications in the VHF bands.

In the summer of 1958 new feeder change-over switches were tested at Skelton. These switches, designed by the Planning & Installation Department, were operated by compressed air through remotely controlled electrically operated air valves. These tests were successful and by the end of 1959 all six 'B' channels of the STC transmitters at Skelton had been equipped with the new switches permitting aerials to be connected to transmitters in twenty seconds instead of the fifteen minutes previously needed for manual (bicycle-assisted) switching. In the spring of 1962 the 'A' channels of the OSE 9 transmitters were modified for quick waveband changing and throughout the decade from 1956 a continuing programme of array rebuilding was in progress.

The modernisation of OSE8 at Skelton began in January 1967 with the withdrawal of Senders 63, 65 and 66 to make way for the new installations. The new transmitters, Marconi type B6122 (Senders 51 to 56) were rated at 250 kW output power and were all commissioned between January 1968 and January 1969, replacing Senders 62 to 66, while Sender 61 remained in service.

In 1969 the use of 'OSE' numbers (the Overseas Station Extensions listed at the end of chapter IV, section 4) was discontinued and the station names were used instead; OSE8 became Skelton A and OSE9 Skelton B.

Early in 1971 a 'memory-assisted control system' was installed at Skelton A; it was later extended to Skelton B. This system takes charge automatically of all the aerial, feeder, transmitter and programme switching and the monitoring requirements of the Skelton complex.

Programmes of the Voice of America had been broadcast by BBC stations since 25 February 1942. On 28 September 1958 the short-wave station at Woofferton entered upon a new phase of operation, radiating from six transmitters through three shifts – the VOA programmes during the night shift and BBC External Service programmes during the day and evening shifts. This arrangement continued until 4 April 1964 when the use of the station for BBC programmes ceased and VOA took over the three shifts for their three programmes operating between 0200/0730 GMT and 1400/2200 GMT. Since 7 September 1964 Woofferton has carried VOA programmes with a few External Services programmes. New Marconi BD 272 250-kW transmitters (Senders 91 to 96) were put into service there for the VOA transmissions between September 1963 and October 1964. These replaced the old Senders 81 to 86, but Senders 85 and 86 were retained as spares. The modernisation programme was completed six weeks before the scheduled commissioning date and the BBC Engineering Division received a note of appreciation from the VOA authorities.

A difficult technical problem presented itself with the installation of six 250-kW transmitters at Woofferton, because the BBC-1 television signal strength from Sutton Coldfield in the Ludlow area was only about $0 \cdot 1$ mV/m and the presence of high-power short-wave transmitters was likely to cause interference from out-of-band radiation. It was decided to strengthen the television signal by erecting a low-power Band I translator station in the area and a site was selected at Mary Knoll, about three miles from Woofferton. However, the 250-kW short-wave transmitters were thoroughly screened and were also fitted with filters to suppress the harmonics; in in addition, notch filters were inserted in the output feeders to give additional suppression on the television channels used by the BBC and the ITA in the area. These measures proved so effective that the translator station became unnecessary and it was removed. Monitoring facilities were provided at Woofferton to detect any excessive out-of-band radiation that might occur.

The Far Eastern Relay Station at Tebrau was also brought up to date by the installation of four 250-kW and four 100-kW short-wave transmitters, which were brought into service from December 1970 onwards.

The Atlantic Relay Station, on Ascension Island, comprising four 250-kW short-wave transmitters was planned in 1964. The aim was to operate the station with the absolute minimum of staff, because of the cost of moving them and their families. Special efforts were made to make conditions of life on the island as attractive as possible and the staff undertaking a tour of duty were assured that their substantive posts at home would be held open for them on their return. In the event those selected for the initial tours were as keen as the BBC Management to make a success of the enterprise and they were assisted in no small measure by their families who went with them. The ABS co-operated in accepting the novel conditions of service for their members and the minimal establishment proposed by the BBC.

The station was equipped with four Marconi type B 6122 250-kW transmitters, which went into service between July 1966 and May 1967. Thirty aerial arrays of the latest dual-band design were provided with remote feeder-switching. The programme feed from the UK is by SSB links, with a cable circuit as a stand-by. Programmes are also available on tape to back up relays during poor reception conditions. Special problems that arose during the installation work included the provision of mast bases and stay block foundations in the volcanic rock of the island and the hazardous ship-to-shore journey for passengers and freight when the air link from the UK was not used. An interesting addition to the station is a low-power medium-wave transmitter (RCA Type ET 4336, modified by BBC), which radiates the World Service on 1484 kHz for the benefit of station staff and their families and for other expatriates on the island.

One of the most interesting of the projects that have been studied was one for a relay station in the Aldabra Islands, five hundred miles from Zanzibar. A survey party, organised by D. A. V. Williams and A. M. Bosworth of the Planning & Installation Department, visited the islands in 1966 on a chartered ship, which kept them in touch with London by means of a two-way radio link provided by an SSB transmitter on board and a transmitter at Daventry. A great deal of interest about the islands and their turtles was discovered by the expedition, which included ecologists and other experts, but the proposal to establish a broadcasting station there was abandoned.

The success of the existing relay stations overseas in bringing BBC programmes to audiences in remote parts of the world has encouraged proposals for additional relay stations to fill gaps in the coverage in Europe, Africa and Latin America. Surveys have been made in some romantic parts of the world so that definite plans can be put into effect when money is available.

Meanwhile, the possibility of direct broadcasting by satellite has been under review. The World Administrative Radio Conference for Space Telecommunications of June–July 1971 rejected a proposal to allocate frequencies in the 26-MHz shortwave band for satellite broadcasting. It is possible that higher frequencies may be used for sound broadcasting by satellite to reinforce the conventional services, but special aerials and special receivers, or adaptors, would be needed and the problem of transmitting a number of radio programmes to a large number of target areas by satellite at an economic cost is a formidable one. If television broadcasting by satellite is introduced on a major scale (e.g. in the 12-GHz band), it seems possible that channels for sound broadcasting might be incorporated in the system.

The External Services have, since 1940, made considerable use of broadcasting facilities owned and operated by other organisations than the BBC, particularly those operated by the Diplomatic Wireless Service of the Foreign & Commonwealth Office, and during the years 1956 to 1972 this activity has been expanded. In April 1962, when the MF transmitter at Norden in north-west Germany ceased to be used by the BBC, its frequency of 1295 kHz was transferred to the DWS station at Crowborough, with a power of 150 kW. The frequency formerly used by that station, 1340 kHz, was transferred to a transmitter at Brookmans Park until January 1963, when it was released by the External Services to permit Northern Ireland and north-east England programmes to be split. From March 1967 the transmitter at Crowborough was used on 809 kHz at certain times of the day for transmissions to France.

From June 1962, the External Services hired two 100-kW HF transmitters at Crowborough. On 4 September 1968 the power of the MF transmitter operating on 1295 kHz was increased to a nominal 500 kW and in November 1970 an improved aerial system was commissioned giving some 7 dB gain in the forward direction and improving the signal in north-west Germany. These measures helped to improve reception of the European Service on the Continent in the face of interference from high-power foreign stations.

The East Mediterranean Relay Station owned and operated by the DWS has been used for BBC programmes since March 1957. The original HF and MF transmitters were reinforced by the commissioning of four 100-kW short-wave transmitters in 1963 to 1965 and a 50-kW MF transmitter in 1969; there are now thirty-eight dual-band arrays.

A VHF transmitter in Berlin has been used by External Services since 1 January 1953. The MF transmitter in Berlin was operated on 1295 kHz in synchronism at first with Norden and, from April 1962, with Crowborough. In December 1968 the frequency was changed to 809 kHz to avoid interference from Crowborough at times when that station was working on 1295 kHz, especially if it was carrying a different programme.

A Central African Relay Station was brought into service on 30 December 1965, at the time of the unilateral declaration of independence in Rhodesia, with an MF transmitter and an HF transmitter. A second MF transmitter was installed in 1966. The operation ceased on 31 March 1968.

The Eastern Relay Station was put into operation on 1 June 1969, providing a high-power MF service to a large part of Asia.

Although direct reception of the External Services provides access to important audiences all over the world, the most effective means of reaching the general public is by relays from local stations to which the great majority of the population are accustomed to listen. The extent of the relaying of BBC programmes, either live or recorded, has greatly increased and now extends to over sixty countries.

From 1957 onwards much effort was put into technical developments to improve the intelligibility of BBC programmes in the target areas. This work included:

(*a*) the improvement of studio acoustics
(*b*) the provision of bass-cut filters and limiters at transmitters, and experiments with compression ratios and recovery time.
(*c*) the introduction of peak-clipping amplifiers at some transmitting stations to increase the effective depth of modulation (though the BBC prefers limiters, giving up to 16 dB compression, because they introduce less distortion).

Attention was also paid to the selection of announcing staff with suitable voices and to the special scoring of music intended for broadcasting on short waves. Observations of the effect of the new techniques were made and recorded by several broadcasting organisations abroad.

The Geneva Conference in 1959 reviewed the frequency tolerances for broadcasting transmitters in all bands; for stations operating between 4 and 29·7 MHz, the tolerance was tightened up to $\pm 15/10^6$ for new transmitters commisioned after 1 January 1964 and for all transmitters after 1 January 1966. As the BBC VF Drive equipment designed in the 1940s already met this specification, no additional expense was incurred by the BBC on account of the Geneva decision and the frequency synthesisers that replaced the VF Drive equipment had a frequency stability some two to three orders better than the international tolerance.

In December 1960 Research Department produced a new design of oscillator and receiver for use with HF impedance bridges operating within the range 3·5 to 30 MHz. The new equipment weighed less than one quarter as much as the apparatus it replaced. In March 1961 Research Department produced a new equipment for measuring the back-to-front ratio of curtain arrays for use in aligning them and their reflectors. The new design required no built-in power supply and its weight was only one third of that of the device it replaced. A new standing-wave indicator of lightweight construction was also produced.

In 1963 a fading simulator was constructed in Research Department for modulation studies over a range of carrier frequencies between 500 kHz and 20 MHz. The design was based on the fading machine used by the Post Office at their Dollis Hill Research Station, and enabled studies of signals subjected to fading to be made under strictly controlled conditions.

At the beginning of the 1970s the BBC's External Services were in competition with those of sixty other countries and the BBC was in sixth place in terms of hours of programme per week. Nevertheless, the BBC services were producing over a hundred hours of programme each day in forty languages, broadcast from forty-six transmitters in the UK and twenty-four overseas. All the programmes are produced in the forty-eight studios at Bush House. Reports on reception come from 250 locations and amount to up to 10,000 in a week. The results are collated by a computer, so that a comprehensive survey of the effects of introducing a new schedule is available within a few days. The automatic switching operations are being transferred to computer control, allowing switching every five minutes instead of every fifteen minutes and giving greater flexibility in programme planning. Transcriptions sent to other countries for local transmission are now distributed on stereo discs as well as on magnetic tape.

5 TELEVISION STUDIOS AND OUTSIDE BROADCASTS

Decisions vital to the future of television in this country were taken by the Government in July 1962, following the report of the Pilkington Committee.[62, 63] There was to be a second BBC programme on the 625-line standard, with colour; this was to be broadcast on UHF, and it was recognised that the existing BBC and ITA programmes on 405 lines might have to be duplicated on 625 lines in the UHF bands so as to facilitate an eventual transition to the use of 625 lines exclusively.

At the beginning of the period now under review these decisions had not been taken, but the planning of the new Television Centre in London was already in progress as described in the previous chapter. In practice, the estimate of space requirements – crucial element in the cost – turned out to be about right, with the benefit of the subsequent change from valve-operated to solid-state equipment, which helped to save space. The Studio Equipment Committee, Television (SECTel.), made recommendations on the whole range of design and installation problems previously mentioned. The technical facilities at the Television Centre, which resulted from these studies, have been fully described elsewhere.[42, 43, 44] There was sharp controversy about the type of camera to be used: whether the high-velocity type, such as the Emitron, or the low-velocity type typified by the image orthicon. It was decided to equip the Riverside Studios (which were used as a trial ground for some of the ideas for the Television Centre) with Marconi image-orthicon cameras, and after thorough tests the $4\frac{1}{2}$-in. image-orthicon was adopted as standard.

The first studio to go into service at the Television Centre was Studio 3 on 29 June 1960. An unexpected snag arose only a few weeks before the opening date for this studio. The floor finish, of heavy linoleum on asphalt, had been laid to a fine tolerance to provide a flat surface for fast-moving camera dollies, as had been done at the Riverside studios where the linoleum had been laid in long strips about 4 ft wide. In Studio TC3, however, it had been laid in 2-ft squares so as to facilitate the replacement of small areas when damaged by the movement of scenery. When the floor was finished the surface was found to be too uneven for tracking even at moderate speed and treatment by sanding machines proved ineffectual. Fortunately, however, in the next studio to come into service (TC4), the linoleum squares had not yet been laid; particular care was taken in this studio to get a very even asphalt surface and, by laying the linoleum in strips rather than squares, a satisfactory surface was achieved; the floor of studio TC3 was later relaid in the same way.

By the end of August 1961 four production studios had been opened at the Television Centre (Studios 2, 3, 4 and 5) and one presentation studio. In the two larger studios (TC3 and 4) six cameras could be deployed and in the two smallest (TC2 and 5) four. The largest studio (TC1) came into service on 15 April 1964 – a few days before the opening of BBC-2. (In 1970, ten years after the opening of the Television Centre, there were eight studios in use, all by then equipped for colour.)

BBC-2 was opened on 21 April 1964 only twenty-one months after the Government decision of July 1962 in favour of a second BBC television programme – surely an astonishing feat, bearing in mind that the new programme required a major increase in the output of programmes, with all the changes in technique and in equipment needed for operation on the new line standard, and with new transmitters operating in the UHF bands.

The Television Centre and other studios elsewhere required a great number of video amplifiers. The many advantages of transistors dictated their use, but there were difficulties in achieving the required degree of precision, linearity and absence of delay distortion for use in colour television. A range of transistor amplifiers suitable for colour was nevertheless developed by the Designs Department in 1960 and from then onwards, solid-state techniques obtained a firm foot-hold in video-frequency equipment of almost every kind. The use of printed circuits was already established, and integrated circuits were coming into use.

From about 1950 onwards increasing attention was devoted to the problems of producing programmes in colour. An experimental studio was set up in Studio A at Alexandra Palace (the original Marconi-EMI studio of 1936) with one colour camera (based upon the RCA camera) and a 16-mm film scanner designed by Research Department. When, later, a second camera was available, a series of programmes was mounted and radiated after the main service had closed down at night. The American NTSC system, adapted to 405 lines, was used in all these experiments. The programmes were critically observed by people who had been lent colour receivers to use in their homes. The analysis of the questionnaires that were completed by these observers showed that the picture quality was adequate for a public television service; indeed there was a confident expectation that colour television would be started within a year or two, but the Government of the day did not agree that the time was ripe for it, and the experimental team was disbanded. The film scanners (by this time a Cintel 35-mm film scanner had been added) were moved to the Lime Grove studios where they continued to provide, for the benefit of the industry, a regular series of day-time transmissions of colour films and slides.[46, 47]

The further series of tests and decisions leading to the choice of the colour system are described in section 13 of this chapter. The decision to adopt the PAL system was made in 1966, but there was a great deal of planning to be done before a colour service could be launched, and much of it had to be done in co-operation with industry. F. C. McLean, as Director of Engineering, directed this work with great vigour; he insisted that colour television must be *good* colour television and that the paramount consideration must be that viewers have reliable reception with a high standard of performance and at an economic cost. From the moment when colour was introduced, a high proportion of the programme material (eventually almost all of it) was to be in colour; colour was to be the rule, monochrome the exception.

The choice of system was not the only major decision that had to be made before the colour service could start. One major preoccupation was the choice of camera tube. The image-orthicon tubes that were used at first were not ideal for colour because of their non-linear light-transfer characteristics. The Philips Company introduced a lead-oxide photo-conductive tube under the trade name 'Plumbicon'. British manufacturers later produced lead-oxide photo-conductive tubes for use in colour cameras. Tubes employing this principle were small, and could be used in either a three-tube or a four-tube configuration. In the three-tube form one tube was used for each of the primary colours – red, green and blue; in the four-tube form one tube was used for the luminance and the other three for the colour information. The relative merits of the two types were much discussed and the tendency was to use the three-tube camera for OBs and the larger four-tube camera for studio productions.[48] Considerable numbers of colour cameras were obtained for use in studios, mostly the EMI type 2001 (with four lead-oxide tubes), the Marconi Mark VII (also with four tubes) and the Marconi Mark VIII (with three tubes and automatic line-up facilities).

For televising films, there were two basically different types of telecine equipment, one using a television camera to produce the picture and the other a flying-spot in conjunction with a photocell. The regional centres were equipped with the former type, made by Pye's in a cross-fire arrangement which could take either 16-mm or 35-mm film. The Television Centre in London had mainly the flying-spot type made by Rank Cintel, which lent itself readily to colour operation.

Improvements were made in the processing of films taken by BBC cameramen, but films made for the cinema were not ideally suited to colour television; the conditions for the viewing of films to establish their suitability, and the colour temperature of the light source, were standardised. Apparatus was developed for correcting colour errors by electronic means during transmission. Since 16-mm film was considerably cheaper than 35-mm film, efforts were directed towards obtaining the best possible performance with 16-mm film. The requirements were severe, because it was necessary to avoid any striking differences between the colour quality of films and of live studio performances, especially when filmed inserts were included in studio productions. Films shown in the news are often taken under difficult conditions and hastily processed. For reproducing them telecine equipment using either three-tube or four-tube photo-conductive cameras was preferred to the flying-spot machines. Telerecording also had to be done in colour as described in section 8 of this chapter.

By this time both commercial films and films specially taken by BBC cameramen had become an important ingredient of television programmes. Almost the whole film operation now had to be geared to colour. Facilities for making, editing, reviewing and dubbing films had been concentrated at the BBC Television Film Studios (formerly Ealing Film Studios) since the end of 1955. Facilities had been provided there for making documentary films for television as well as film inserts, captions and animated drawings. All the mobile film units in London were based at Ealing, apart from those used by the news services. Cameras and projectors were available for 35-mm and 16-mm films, with provision for the various types of sound track: optical or magnetic track recorded either on the picture film or on a separate film or tape. An existing film-dubbing suite was equipped for producing a sound-track, synchronised with the film, from the various components (dialogue, commentary, effects, background music, etc.) of which it might be composed. A separate building was constructed to house the film vaults.[46]

Before the BBC colour service could be launched in July 1967, there was great activity in installing and testing colour equipment. Operational and production techniques had to be adapted to the new medium and this could be done only by the closest collaboration between production staff and engineers. Two large studios and a smaller one at the Television Centre were made ready for colour and also a presentation studio, which was equipped with a flying-spot caption scanner. Further studios were converted to colour from time to time in readiness for the day (in 1969) when nearly all programmes on both BBC-1 and BBC-2 would be in colour.

Regular colour transmissions in BBC-2 started on 1 July 1967 and were thus the first in Europe. During the first few months – the 'launching period' – intense efforts were made to achieve the highest possible standard of performance. Different types of camera were used on a regular rota so that the quality of the pictures could be compared in the homes of observers, and many experiments were made in lighting and presentation to achieve the best possible results. On 2 December 1967 the full colour service in BBC-2 officially started. BBC-1 went into colour on 15 November 1969, following an announcement by the Postmaster General on 16 May of that year. This decision resulted from careful consideration by the Television Advisory Committee of the best method of achieving the final goal: the use of the 625-line standard for all television services in the country. The 405-line transmissions of BBC-1 and the ITA programmes were to be duplicated on 625-lines (with colour) in the UHF bands. It was envisaged that, when national coverage of the duplicated transmissions had been achieved, long-term notice might be given of the final withdrawal of the 405-line VHF services.

When the Television Centre was completed, the building was seen to be of astonishing grace and lightness, despite the exacting functional requirement it was required to fulfil. The central garden was surrounded by a ring containing the technical areas, with offices above the eight production studios (of which the largest was 108 ft by 100 ft and 54 ft high) radiated outwards from the ring, and goods and scenery could be moved around the perimeter without impeding the flow of artists and staff from the inner ring. The Central Apparatus Room, the nerve-centre of the main complex, was built on the third floor in the wedge between Studios 3 and 4. It was equipped for switching, routing, monitoring and communications and also for producing synchronising waveforms for distribution throughout the centre and to remote sources. Associated with each studio was a Production Control Room, the main mixer of which operated remotely the equipment in a nearby Vision Apparatus Room; in the larger studios up to six cameras could be used. Studio lighting and cameras were controlled from adjacent consoles in a separate control room, and there was also a sound control room with its own apparatus room.

The telecine suite was on the second floor of the central wedge and the telerecording suite in the basement. The two Presentation Suites were each provided with a Network Control Room, a Presentation Studio, a Continuity Room, and a Caption Room with a servo-controlled caption scanner. A separate International Control Room for Eurovision programmes and those transmitted by satellite was provided with standards converters and with facilities for twenty separate commentaries in sound.

Like the earlier installation at Broadcasting House, the ventilation system at the Television Centre was on a grand scale, as the bare figures show: 123 fans, 16 pumps, 151 electric motors, 1600 filter coils, 10 miles of air-ducts, 150 automatic controls and 900 dampers. The five oil-fired boilers could produce thirty tons of steam per hour and there were 1000 radiators and over twenty miles of circulating mains for heating and hot water supplies. The electricity supply was taken from the mains at 11 kV, with an ultimate capacity of 4 MW.

When the Television Centre was opened in 1960 news operations had remained at Alexandra Palace. With the start of the colour service one of the studios there was equipped with cameras, a film scanner and a video-tape recorder for colour. During the night of 19–20 September 1969 the whole operation with its colour cameras, dubbing equipment, libraries and files, was transferred to a newly built wing (the 'Spur') at the Television Centre.[50] A separate Central Apparatus Room was built into the Spur for the news services and two studios were each equipped with four remotely controlled colour cameras, caption scanners and overlay facilities. The remote-control system for the cameras was operated according to a pre-set sequence stored in a memory bank. The news facilities also included nine film scanners, four video-tape recorders, editing facilities, and a film processing and copying plant. Reversal film was used to obtain increased sensitivity and quicker processing.

The use of colour cameras with lead-oxide photo-conductive tubes in the Television Centre simplified studio operations, because their stability made it possible for all the cameras in one studio to be controlled by one man and the lighting controls could be placed alongside in the same room. The Centre was also provided with colour equipment for all the special effects (inlay, overlay, wipes and split screen) that had been available for black-and-white; in fact, overlay effects became more sophisticated by taking advantage of colour differences between foreground objects and the background. A method of 'colour-separation' overlay was first used in a black-and-white programme in September 1959; this avoided some of the difficulties that occurred when the separation depended solely on differences in brightness. The technique was further developed for colour television and was used very extensively to show a subject, usually standing against a blue background, the background being replaced by a picture from another source (usually a slide scanner) by the electronic equipment.[51] The design of equipment of this kind, and also of apparatus for synchronising remote services, was eased by the fact that the PAL system is tolerant of phase errors.

A factor that has an important effect on the capital cost, as well as the running costs, of a studio centre is the productivity that can be achieved from each studio (i.e. the number of hours of programme output as a fraction of the total time, including that required for setting and striking scenery, rehearsals, camera line-up and the arrangement of lighting.) Before the advent of colour the BBC had a reputation for studio productivity that was envied among broadcasters abroad. The productivity was maintained, despite the longer period needed for lining up cameras and adjusting lighting for colour. A large production studio operated $6\frac{1}{2}$ days per week (with half a day for maintenance work) and produced thirty minutes of programme each day – the same as had been achieved in black-and-white.[48]

The weight of cameras was important, because they had to be quickly manoeuvred, whether mounted on dollies or on elaborate cranes. The early colour cameras with three image-orthicon tubes weighed about 400 lb. Later cameras with photo-conductive tubes and zoom lenses were around 200 lb and the Marconi Mark VIII camera with three tubes weighs only 139 lb.

The development of electronic standards converters is described in section 13 of

466

this chapter. A number of line-store converters of this type were installed for converting the 625-line pictures to 405 lines for radiation by the VHF television transmitters, which were broadcasting on this standard. Field-store converters were installed in the Television Centre for converting in both directions between the 525-line 60-field standard and the 625-line 50-field standard. These were used for the exchange of live or video-taped programmes with the USA, Canada and Japan. Despite its high cost, the BBC-designed field-store converter was preferred to the optical type manufactured in Germany, because, being entirely electronic, it was quite stable and did not require staff to maintain its performance at the optimum.

In the Regions technical developments followed much the same pattern as in London; their needs were similar, though on a smaller scale, and there was not the same opportunity for local ingenuity as there had been in the pioneering days of sound broadcasting. The basic planning of all regional production and interview studios, except Aberdeen and Leeds, was carried out by a Television Studios Development Committee, which had been responsible for the planning of London television studios other than the Television Centre itself; its chairman was H. W. Baker, then Superintendent Engineer Television Studios. News interview studios at Aberdeen and Leeds were planned in 1962 by T. H. Bridgewater as Superintendent Engineer Television, Regions and Outside Broadcasts, with the help of the specialist engineering departments. Premises in Dickenson Road, Manchester, which had been a chapel and a film studio, were first brought into service for television on a 'drive-in' basis, a mobile control room being parked beside the building and the cameras deployed inside as required. Camera channels were later installed in the Dickenson Road studios, which went into service on 23 September 1957. Developments in the other regions followed similar lines, except at Belfast, where one of the existing large studios in Broadcasting House was equipped for use both as a production studio and as a news/interview studio. By the end of 1959 all the main Regional Centres had production studios and news/interview studios and a start had been made on the construction of news/interview studios at Newcastle, Southampton, Norwich, Plymouth, Leeds and Aberdeen; this work was completed by September 1962.

Meanwhile plans were taking shape for the building of Regional Centres. An extension was built to Broadcasting House Glasgow, with television studios, since converted for colour operation. The new headquarters building at Cardiff, mentioned in section 1 of this chapter, will have television studios added to it. The new broadcasting centre that is being built in Manchester will also include television studios.

As recorded in section 1 of this chapter, the new broadcasting headquarters in Birmingham were completed in 1971. The building was designed specifically for the purpose and includes two television studios: a general-purpose studio of 6500 sq. ft and an interview studio of 1050 sq. ft, both equipped for colour. The new centre is not only a comprehensive regional studio headquarters, but also a key point in the distribution network. Its communications centre, in which switching, routing and monitoring operations for the radio and television services are fully integrated, is therefore an important element in the whole complex, which also includes news and presentation facilities, telecine and video-tape areas, a film dubbing suite, a review theatre, and an area for processing colour films.[52]

In the period up to 1956 little development work had been done on television lighting equipment. Cameras were so insensitive that the major problem was to provide sufficient illumination and most of the lighting equipment had been designed for use in film studios. With the advent of the image-orthicon tube the situation changed and during the next fifteen years there was a remarkable rate of development, with two main objectives. The first was to improve the picture quality by giving the lighting supervisor the most flexible control of light intensity and distribution and the second to increase the productivity of the studios by reducing the time required for placing the luminaires and controlling their output. Simultaneously with these developments the 'hands off' technique was pioneered by the BBC, which reduced the number of operational controls on the cameras, so that the achievement of the required pictorial composition was greatly simplified.

From 1956 onwards the BBC drew on the practice of the theatre and installed sophisticated dimmer systems with group memories that enabled the lighting supervisor to change from one group of lighting to another, as the scene of interest changed, at the touch of a button. Early dimmers were motor-driven resistors and transformers or thyratrons, but today the thyristor is universal. The latest system, the 'Q-file' developed by Thorn Electrical Industries and installed in BBC studios, uses computer techniques and enables up to a hundred groups with a total of three hundred lighting circuits to be stored in a memory, together with information on the lighting intensities required, which can be recalled at will.

The tungsten lamp remains almost universal in television studios though in the 1970s discharge lamps have become attractive for OB sites. The advent of the tunsten halogen lamp has resulted in a marked reduction in size of the lamp envelope, with significant increases in optical and luminous efficiency. There has been steady development of luminaires up to the point where today most BBC studios are equipped with a multi-purpose unit, which can serve the function of either a spotlight or a softlight and can be switched from 5 kW to $2\frac{1}{2}$ kW in either function. All the larger BBC studios are equipped with electrically operated lighting bars, which vary in length from $1 \cdot 2$ m to 3 m. Each bar is equipped with a number of permanently wired circuits and the bars may be raised and lowered in unison or singly by electric hoists controlled from an operating panel on the studio floor. This method was preferred to the alternative of using individual telescopic suspensions for each luminaire. Similar electric hoists are also used for scenery suspension.

The large studios each required a maximum lighting load of 450 kW for colour and the ventilation system was designed for a continuous heat dissipation of 300 kW. The 'colour temperature' of the lamps was standardised at 2900° K ($\pm150°$). An incident-light level of 1600 lux was found to suit the photo-conductive cameras best and to give good reproduction of skin tones – the most critical subjects for pictures in colour. The contrast range of the scene had to be kept within 30:1 to give pictures of the highest standard – and by 1972 the standard had become very high indeed.

Cue dots have proved a useful aid to the smooth running of programmes. The dot appears in a corner of the picture 30 seconds before the next item is to start, giving a preliminary warning, and is removed ten seconds before as a cue for running up a telecine or tape machine. The dot reappears five seconds before the switch is to be made and is removed at the instant when the switch is required.

Test patterns have played an important part in television. One of the simplest, known as 'artificial bars' consisted of a black cross on a white ground and was electronically generated. From the early days of television, this pattern was useful when adjusting the focus, brightness and contrast of receivers. From 1946 onwards two series of test patterns were produced, one for testing cameras and caption scanners, and one for transmission over the whole chain to the display tube in the receiver. The first of the latter kind was 'Test Card A', produced in 1946 and mentioned in the previous chapter. Its use indicated any serious defects in definition, frequency response, and geometry. It was used only for engineering tests. Test Card B included coloured areas to indicate the panchromatic response of the monochrome system. Test Card C was used from 1947 to 1964 for trade transmissions. Its design, which had been discussed with the receiver manufacturers, included for the first time graduated grey areas to assist in achieving the correct transfer function. Test Card D, of 1964, was designed jointly by the BBC, the ITA and BREMA; a 625-line version, Test Card E, was also produced. The frequency bars were intended to correspond to sinusoidal, rather than rectangular, signals because rectangular bars at 3-MHz would be produced sharply only by a system that would transmit harmonics of this frequency. However, the appearance was unacceptable and work was started on a colour test card, Test Card F. This was suitable for viewing in black-and-white and in colour. It included six steps of grey, six rectangular frequency bars up to $5 \cdot 25$ MHz, coloured 'castellations' along the edges, and (most important) a coloured picture of a child carefully chosen to include flesh tones, black and white areas and some bright colours. (The little girl was the daughter of G. Hersee, who was also responsible for the test-card itself.) The difficult problem of reproducing such a test pattern accurately in considerable numbers were overcome. When the test card was transmitted, the four active lines at the top of the picture were replaced by an electronically generated colour-bar signal.[53]

In television outside broadcasts the ever-increasing demand for accommodation had to be met. The sheer bulk of a mobile control room (MCR) makes it necessary to have a considerable amount of space to house it and to allow for maintenance work on the vehicle and its equipment. Major OBs took some time to mount and to dismantle and there had to be an interval between one and the next to allow for this and for travelling. Pressures for more programmes diminished the interval between OBs to an alarming extent. In the Regions television programmes were at first entirely dependent upon the MCRs; at first some of them had to be shared between Regions, and they were also required for 'drive-in' work at newly acquired studio premises. Premises had to be found in the Regions for OB bases, the installations had to be planned and staff had to be recruited.

In 1958 premises were found at East Kilbride for an OB base for Scotland. An OB base at Bristol, with accommodation for forty vehicles, was opened in July 1964. A new London OB base and Transport Garage at Kendal Avenue, Acton, was occupied in January 1965 replacing the former accommodation at Wembley and elsewhere. It was conveniently placed and combined facilities for servicing all types of vehicles used in the television service with the special requirements for maintaining the equipment in the seventy vehicles used for OBs – MCRs, 'Roving Eyes', mobile video-tape vans, aerial towers and radio-link vehicles. At Cardiff accommodation for OBs was provided at the new Broadcasting House, and the new Birmingham Headquarters include an OB Maintenance Depot with a transport workshop, garage, stores and a mechanical workshop.[52]

The efficiency and flexibility of OB equipment was continually improved. The Taylor, Taylor and Hobson 'Varotal' zoom lens was introduced in the spring of 1956, with focal length ranges of 4–20 and 8–40 in. at maximum apertures of f/4·5 and f/8 respectively. Zoom and focus were manually controlled and the iris was remotely controlled by the camera control unit operator.

In the summer of 1956 a new radio link came into use for television OBs. This was the Philips 850-MHz link, with transmitter and receiver units of suitcase dimensions and helical transmitting and receiving aerials, which could be mounted on tripods. With a beam-width of 23°, the effective range was twelve miles. The frequencies used for radio links rose progressively from UHF into the SHF bands as the lower channels were required for other purposes. SHF links had the advantage that highly directional aerials of small dimensions could be used.[45] The 4000-MHz band came into use about 1952 with the acquisition of EMI ML6A equipment, incorporating klystrons. Receivers were installed on the masts at Sutton Coldfield, Holme Moss, Kirk o'Shotts and Wenvoe, below the VHF aerial cylinders. In 1959, 7000-MHz links were brought into service and the 'mast-head' receivers were converted to work in this band.

These links enabled OBs to be picked up from a distant point (up to fifty miles away) and fed into the permanent network. At first, radio-link equipment at the receiving points was brought along on each occasion, only the aerial dish and an oscillator being permanently attached to the mast. Permanent equipment was installed later at the high-power transmitting stations, and at some other stations; the receivers and the swivelling of the dishes were then remotely controlled from the ground, so that they could quickly be made ready for use.

In London the receiving point at Swains Lane, Highgate, was used as the terminal of the radio links until the Crystal Palace station became available for this purpose. The links working to the Crystal Palace used the 4000-MHz band until the first 7000-MHz solid-state equipment was installed there. The latest radio-link equipment is designed for fixed-frequency working. When a direct link to a BBC receiving point is not possible the signal may be relayed at an intermediate point by a second link without demodulation and remodulation. Alternatively, a mobile receiver may be used, feeding into the network at an intermediate point.

Television OBs made a stride forward in 1963, when the capability of the equipment and the conditions in which the engineers had to work, were improved by the delivery of a new generation of mobile control rooms. In August 1963 the first of ten new MCRs built by Pye TVT to BBC specifications went into service with four camera channels designed for multi-standard operation. The operating area was fully-air-conditioned and slightly pressurised to prevent draughts, and a foot-warming pad for each operator was let into the floor – welcome aids when OBs were taken from exposed sites in wintry weather.

For television OBs the cameras had to be capable of working in poor light. For this reason the $4\frac{1}{2}$-in. image-orthicon camera was used in the black-and-white era, in preference to the smaller and lighter camera with a 3-in. tube. Colour required about about four times as much light and when the colour service started sensitivity became even more vital; the light intensity could vary over a wide range and the winning goal might well be scored just when the light was failing. Fortunately the new photo-conductive tubes needed only about half as much light as the image-orthicon and were also more stable.[54] Philips three-tube cameras were used in some of the colour OB units and EMI four-tube cameras in others.

For certain types of OB, lightweight cameras were needed that could be carried by the cameraman and connected to the base unit by a thin cable or by a radio link operating in the 2-GHz band. The Minicam, designed by CBS and made by the Philips Broadcast Equipment Corporation in the USA, was modified by Pye TVT to operate on the British standards. The total weight, including the radio transmitter and batteries, was 55 lb and the camera could, if necessary, be operated by remote. control.

The first colour mobile control room (CMCR) was acquired in May 1967; it was equipped with three Plumbicon cameras. Operational experience with it, and con-sideration of OB sites, led to the conclusion that an even larger vehicle was needed to permit separation of the production control room, the vision apparatus and con-trol room, and the sound apparatus and control room. These considerations gave rise to the design of the type 2 CMCR that was being brought into service in 1972. This is a heavy vehicle, being 35 ft long compared with 28 ft for the first CMCR. The increased length enabled the production control room, the vision control room and the sound control room to be separated from each other.[48]

One of the OBs of outstanding international interest, though a melancholy one, was the State Funeral of Sir Winston Churchill on 30 January 1965. Like the sound OBs mentioned in section 1 of this chapter, the television operation was a very large one, for which a total of sixteen camera sites with thirty-three cameras was needed (four of these inside St Paul's Cathedral). Planning for this event began as soon as it was known that Sir Winston would be given a State Funeral. The plans naturally had to be kept secret and, to be sure that Post Office circuits would be available to the various commentary points when they were required, many of them were rented permanently. Moreover, the whole project had to be kept continuously under review because of changes in the Earl Marshal's plans and because of changes in Post Office plant. This great operation was carried through with all the dignity and sense of occasion that had for long been characteristic of the BBC. Had Sir Winston sur-vived into the age of colour television it would have been even more impressive. The magnitude of the resources needed in London was such that it was necessary to concentrate mobile control rooms and radio-link sets borrowed from all the Regions (though there was also an OB point in the Midland Region, at Bladon near Woodstock, where Sir Winston was buried) and there was only a short time in which to deploy all the resources.

Some of the most complicated outside broadcasts demanded a large number of OB points, widely spread throughout the country, and an extensive network of circuits through appropriate switching points – often involving two-way communication in vision and sound. The General Election of 1955 required VHF links, SHF links, telephone pairs, spare coaxial cable pairs, and balanced television cable pairs. This broadcast set a standard of complexity that was followed, and exceeded, at later General Elections.

Another outstanding programme entitled *Our World* took place on 25 June 1967. This was an exchange of programmes from forty different locations in various parts of the globe, including Japan, Mexico and Australia. Because of its technical resources and its central location in the communications world, the BBC was allotted by the EBU the task of linking and co-ordinating the programmes. It was necessary to set up a master control point in the gallery of Studio TC1 at the Television Centre and to organise three teams of commentators on the floor of Studio TC2 to give guide commentaries in English, French and German to the countries taking the programme. Transatlantic links were set up via the 'Early Bird' satellite.

Another milestone in OB history was the first public engagement of a CMCR in June 1967 at the Wimbledon Lawn Tennis Championships. In addition to the colour transmissions in BBC-2 this event was covered by monochrome cameras for BBC-1. Many viewers with dual-standard monochrome receivers remarked that the luminance characteristic of the pictures originated in colour was better than that of the black-and-white transmissions in BBC-1.

Much effort was devoted to the problems of automatic monitoring of television signals. Equipment introduced during this period included line sync pulse monitors, field sync pulse monitors, intercarrier monitors (detecting the 6-MHz beat between the sound and vision carriers in a Band IV or V television transmission), the television monitor major (which monitors a test line signal inserted in the field-blanking interval of the television waveform and alarms if the 'K-rating' falls outside the specified limits), and the television automatic monitor minor, a simplified version of the 'major'.[55] The most sophisticated of these was the latest form of Television Automatic Monitor Major, which, when a test signal is inserted at the source into the field-blanking interval of the television waveform, can assess twelve parameters of the television signal at a remote point in the transmission chain. At relay stations only the intercarrier monitor was required to check the performance of the translator itself, because neither the vision nor the sound signal was processed in any way by the transposer.

In 1968 a great deal of interest was aroused by the publication by NHK, Japan, of details of its TOPICS system; this was a 'Total On-line Programme and Information Control' for the automation of almost all aspects of broadcasting operations. Its development took five years. Automatic techniques have been introduced in other countries on a less ambitious scale, and to make the accumulated experience widely available the EBU organised a symposium that was held in Hamburg in October 1970 under the title 'Automation and Computers in Broadcasting'. Four papers were presented by BBC authors, one dealing with the BBC's television management information system, one with the automatic control of switching in the external services, one with the use of computers for allocating technical resources, and one with the general aspects of automation in the BBC Television Service.[38, 56, 57, 58] The management information system made use of computers for the control of programme resources and for keeping management informed of costs. A feasibility study had already been made of the use of a computer for scheduling and allocating studios, equipment, and other resources to programmes. The possibility of adopting a system that would link the programme-scheduling information with on-line switching was considered in the light of a visit that had been made to Japan by a team of engineers, programme production and administrative staff to study the TOPICS system. It was not thought to be directly applicable as a whole in the BBC, because of the nature of the output, the need to preserve flexibility and the cost of a fully automated system. It was, however, decided to introduce certain stages in automation. The switching and mixing of the contributions making up each of the two BBC television programmes could be done semi-automatically by an 'event-type' mixer. Remote control of camera operation had already been adopted in the news studios and remote control of film scanners had been applied to film inserts in studio programmes; this included the remote control of the TARIF settings for matching the filmed pictures to the studio pictures. The computer-based control system for studio lighting has already been mentioned. Consideration is also being given to the possibility of adopting digital techniques for the electronic editing of video-tape recordings.

In 1971 the series of ingenious electronic devices for creating special effects was supplemented by a technique for distorting the geometry of the television picture in a precisely controlled manner. The method, known as Geometrical Electronic Modulation, was first applied to a programme called *The Restless Earth* broadcast in February 1972. A scale model of the Atlantic Ocean 15 ft across was filled with water up to the equivalent of normal sea level. A film was taken while the water was gradually drained away until the contours of the ocean floor were revealed. As the model had to be flat, to retain the water, the curvature of the earth was shown by distorting the raster when the film was reproduced, so as to give the picture a pincushion shape. Trapezium distortion was also used, to give the required perspective, and both forms of distortion could be varied to suit different viewing angles. Other uses are foreseen for this technique.

6 TELEVISION TRANSMITTERS

Developments during this period included the extension of the 405-line coverage of BBC-1 in Bands I and III from 93·5 per cent of the population at the end of 1955, to 99·5 per cent in mid-1970; the introduction of BBC-2 on UHF in 1964 and the development of the 625-line network with colour for this programme, achieving a coverage of 91 per cent by the end of 1971; and the duplication of BBC-1 on 625 lines on UHF with colour from November 1969, reaching 87 per cent of the population by the end of 1971. There were also important developments in techniques during the period.

The total number of television transmitting stations carrying BBC programmes increased from fourteen at the end of 1955 to 187 at the end of 1971 and it is estimated that a total of 217 stations will be in service by the end of 1973. The planning of the UHF transmitter network envisaged the provision of about 55 main stations with erps ranging from 50 kW to 1 MW and about 450 relay stations with erps ranging between 20 W and 10 kW. It is expected that these stations will serve about 96 per cent of the people of the United Kingdom. Each will be equipped for three programmes (BBC-1, BBC-2 and ITA) with provision for a fourth later if required. Many more stations may be needed to reach the remainder, many of them in small isolated communities. All the main stations are expected to be completed by the mid-1970s, the 450 relay stations by about 1980, and the remaining relay stations should follow towards the end of the 1980s.

The UHF transmitting stations were designed for unattended working and the technical staff at all the television stations, plus those in London concerned with the management of these stations, numbered 262 (for 52 stations) at the end of 1963 and is expected to reach 302 (for 217 stations) by the end of 1973, apart from 34 temporary posts. This small increase in staff has been more than offset by a saving of some 88 posts at sound broadcasting stations during the period.

At the beginning of this period the 405-line transmitter network comprised Alexandra Palace, four new high-power stations, six medium-power stations, and three low-power stations. By the end of 1955 the Alexandra Palace transmitters were nearly twenty years old and were due for replacement. A new installation was therefore planned to serve London and the Home Counties using higher power but the same frequencies as Alexandra Palace (Channel 1 in Band I). The new London station was planned to complement the service areas of the other stations then in service and to provide a field strength of about 0·25 mV/M at the limit of the service area; it was to be designed to achieve a high degree of reliability with the minimum of staff. The station was to have duplicate vision and sound transmitters and a feeder and aerial system constructed in two separate halves, each of which would normally be connected to one vision and one sound transmitter. A fault in one chain would result in a 3 dB reduction of output power to the aerial and also a 3 dB reduction in power gain (as only one half of the aerial would be active), but there would be no interruption to the service. If the fault were prolonged the loss in erp could be reduced from 6 dB to 3 dB by switching the good pair of transmitters to the full aerial system. This concept differed from that of the earlier high-power stations where a 5-kW reserve vision transmitter and a 1·25-kW reserve sound transmitter were installed; this resulted in a power reduction of 10 dB when the main aerial was used with the reserve transmitters, and an emergency aerial on a 150-ft mast had to be provided. (Domestic receivers could tolerate a reduction in signal strength up to about

10 dB using the front-of-panel controls to compensate for the weaker input signal.)

Experience with the post-war television stations had shown that a service range of about fifty miles could be obtained with an erp of 100 kW and an aerial system about 1000 ft above the surrounding terrain. A compromise between cost and signal-to-interference ratio suggested an ultimate erp of 500 kW for the new London station. The station layout and power intake plant were accordingly designed for a maximum erp of 500 kW, although the station was operated with an erp of about 200 kW.

The station at Alexandra Palace had been the only BBC television station operating with double-sideband transmission. The post-war transmitters used a vestigial sideband characteristic to conserve spectrum space and all domestic receivers designed since about 1950 were built for VSB working. The use of a VSB characteristic for the new London station would save about 2 MHz of spectrum space for possible other uses, and the narrower frequency range would make it possible to design the aerial and feeder system with improved performance and would improve the efficiency of the transmitting equipment. The aerial system was designed to have a higher gain than that of earlier stations, so as to reduce the transmitter power required, but the more complex aerial system needed a more substantial supporting structure. The greater vertical height of a high gain aerial system (in this case, with eight tiers) requires a higher support structure to maintain the same mean aerial height above ground, and, as the vertical radiation pattern becomes sharper with higher aerial gain, the support tower must have greater mechanical stability to avoid variations in the angle of maximum radiation.

There appeared to be a good chance of covering Kent, Surrey and parts of Sussex in addition to the whole of the Greater London area from a site to the south of the Thames. Six possible sites were considered, including that of the Wrotham VHF station and one on Sydenham Hill where the Crystal Palace (the vast glazed structure that had been erected in Hyde Park for the Great Exhibition of 1851, moved to Sydenham, and burnt down in a spectacular fire in 1936) had once stood. Practical tests were undertaken first from the Crystal Palace site in January 1952, using a mobile transmitter and an aerial supported by a balloon at a height of 600 ft. For four months an exhaustive survey was made of field strengths up to a distance of seventy miles by mobile teams each provided with field-strength measuring equipment that could be used while on the move. The results of this survey were so satisfactory that it was decided not to proceed with any of the other possible sites. The tests were made on frequencies in Band I only as it was known that results in Band III would be similar if this band were used in the future. As the site was within quasi-optical range of the maximum possible population, it was also likely to be suitable for transmissions in Bands IV and V.

Each of the two vision transmitters had an output power of 15 kW (peak white) and the associated sound transmitter an output power of 4 kW (unmodulated carrier). As the transmitters were smaller than the earlier type for which the building was designed, space was available that was used later for UHF transmitters.[49, 60, 61]

The operating shift complement initially was two engineers and one technical assistant and even with the addition of four high-power UHF vision and sound transmitters for BBC-2 (1964) and BBC-1 (1969), the number of shift staff required for normal operational work on the station has not been increased, thanks to the wide range of automatic monitoring and control equipment provided.

The Crystal Palace station took over the BBC-1 service from Alexandra Palace on 28 March 1956, but as the support tower was not then completed, a temporary 250-ft mast was erected to the east of the main site. The mean height of this temporary aerial was only 190 ft agl and the erp was about 60 kW. On 10 September 1956 the service was transferred to the main tower, thus increasing the mean aerial height to 380 ft and increasing the erp to 120 kW. Finally on 18 December 1957 the mean aerial height was further increased to 426 ft and the erp to 200 kW.

The aerodynamic stability of the support tower was tested on 20 November 1957 by using six reaction rockets mounted in a frame located at the 630-ft level. Accelerometers measured the tower deflection when the rockets were fired so as to impart a thrust equivalent to 2·14 tons against the 450-ton structure. The amplitude of the oscillation at the thrust level was found to be about 8 in. on either side of the vertical.[116]

The coverage of the Crystal Palace station in Band I was most satisfactory, and it included a population of more than thirteen million. There were, however, some local difficulties at first because of a sharp null in the vertical radiation pattern. This affected a few viewers, particularly in the Penge area, and became known as the 'Penge effect'. In certain directions the radiation from the upper half of the aerial could arrive 180° out of phase with that from the lower half, thus resulting in cancellation. The trouble was overcome by combining the outputs of the two transmitter chains in a diplexer before they were fed to the aerial and dividing the power unequally between the two halves of the aerial. The relative phases of the currents in the aerial tiers were carefully adjusted to achieve the most uniform horizontal radiation pattern and also to fill gaps in the vertical radiation pattern.

Other Band I stations were brought into service in various parts of the country in quick succession: North Hessary Tor (February 1956), Rowridge (June 1956), Tacolneston (December 1957), Sandale (November 1956), Blaen Plwyf (April 1957), Rosemarkie (August 1957), Douglas (December 1957), Londonderry (December 1957), and Swingate (April 1958). Some of these stations were first opened in a temporary condition and later consolidated. Methods of feeding the programme to them varied; at Sandale the vision signals were received at a Post Office relay station at Haltwhistle and fed to Sandale on an SHF link, while the sound component was received directly from Holme Moss. Douglas in the Isle of Man received its programme from a link station on the summit of Snaefell, which had already been installed to improve the feed of BBC-1 to Divis in Northern Ireland.

Quite complex transmitting aerials were needed at some of these stations because of the need to reduce co-channel interference with other stations in this country or abroad using the same channel. The Research Department designed aerials that were put into fully engineered form by the Transmitter Planning & Installation Department and produced nulls in the direction of co-channel stations while providing enhanced gain in the populated areas that were to be served.

The stations so far built were of high or medium power; there was still a need for a number of low-power relay stations. Transposers were already in use in Germany and Italy which received the sound and vision signal, amplified them together, and re-transmitted them on another channel. In the 405-line system, however, the sound was AM rather than FM and it was therefore necessary to deal with the vision and sound signals separately. A transposer was produced by the Designs Department with an output power of about 2 W; it used valves throughout and was housed in a steel cubicle similar to those used for the control gear of traffic lights. The first transposer of this kind was installed at Folkestone and brought into service in July 1958 with a maximum erp of 2 W. In August 1963 it was replaced by an improved design giving an output power of 10 W and a maximum erp of 40 W. The transmitting and receiving aerials were supported by two 110-ft masts about 100 ft apart.

Coverage of the North of Scotland was extended by the opening of stations at Thrumster (December 1958) and Netherbutton in Orkney (December 1958). Thrumster received the signals by direct pick-up from Meldrum and they were relayed to Orkney through an intermediate link station. The station at Thrumster was the first at which the aerials for television in Band I and sound broadcasting in Band II were interleaved to economise in space on the mast. The link station at Thrumster however used a receiving aerial designed by Research Department to give protection against precipitation static. An improved version of this aerial was later used at the relay station at Newmarket Hill to feed the Band I station at White-hawk Hill, Brighton. A low-power station was opened at Peterborough in October 1959 and transposers at Sheffield and Hastings in May and December 1960.

By 1959 television had become extremely popular and there was mounting pressure in Parliament and elsewhere for relay stations in areas that were still unserved. These were provided in five stages, the first approved by the Postmaster General in June 1955 and the last in March 1966, comprising a total of eighty-five stations. In planning them, attention naturally had to be paid to places where a relatively large population could be served from one station and also to the fact that extensions to the network must be planned progressively so that programme feeds could be made available. At the same time, special efforts were made to serve some of the sparsely populated communities in the Highlands and Islands of Scotland and in Wales where other forms of entertainment were scarce.

One of the recommendations of the Pilkington Committee's Report,[62] published in June 1962, was that Band III should be used for certain BBC stations, there being no room for further high-power stations in the five channels in Band I. Band III was already in use by the ITA and it was decided that a high-power Band III transmitter should be installed at Wenvoe to enable a separate programme for BBC-Wales to be transmitted. A Band III transmitter was also installed at the ITA station at Winter Hill to improve BBC coverage in Lancashire. A third Band III transmitter was installed at Sandale to improve coverage in south-west Scotland and north-west England.

The last of the 405-line transmitting stations was opened at Llanelli in June 1970; by then there were 107 stations carrying this service and two of them were dual-programme stations (Wenvoe and Sandale). By that time a number of UHF stations carrying BBC-1 and BBC-2 on 625 lines had been built and it was decided not to construct any more VHF television stations as the 405-line system was obsolescent and it would not have been right to encourage new viewers to acquire 405-line receivers.

The final decision on the future television networks was taken by the Government in 1962, following the report of the Pilkington Committee[62, 63] (see section 5 of this chapter). It necessitated a major programme of transmitter construction to provide a national network of UHF stations, each capable of carrying four programmes in colour on 625 lines (BBC-1, BBC-2, the ITA programme and a fourth, still unspecified). In November 1957 Band V transmitters were installed at Crystal Palace radiating with an erp of 125 kW from a high gain aerial mounted on a cantilever extension at the top of the support tower. The transmitters worked on frequencies around 650 MHz and in the initial series of tests, which ended on 28 March 1958, monochrome television signals on 405 lines were compared with similar signals radiated in Band I. Then, later in 1958, 625-line test signals were radiated on one pair of vision and sound transmitters and compared with a 405-line transmission on the other pair. On 3 September 1962 a further series of field trials was begun from the Crystal Palace with colour transmissions on the NTSC and SECAM systems. These tests continued until 15 November 1963.

Long-distance propagation tests were made from a transmitter at Pontop Pike operating in Band V; field-strength recordings were made at Moorside Edge, Nottingham, Mursley, Kingswood Warren and Beddington. It was found that the UHF bands gave a smaller effective range than the VHF bands and that the coverage was less uniform because of the shadowing effect of hills and tall structures. This meant that about four times as many high-power stations would be required to provide UHF coverage equivalent to the VHF television coverage as well as a large number of relay stations. The high cost of such a network and the large effort that would be required from the industry and in the BBC would make it necessary to spread the construction programme over several years. Moreover, the number of channels available in Western Europe in the UHF bands was limited and those in the VHF bands were already fully committed. The UHF bands nevertheless offered considerable advantages: the field strength at long distances would be weaker, so that more channel sharing would be possible; interference from vehicle ignition systems and electrical equipment would be negligible; and the transmitting aerials could have greater directivity so as to permit higher erps to be obtained from transmitters of modest output power. Receiving aerials also could have more directivity and smaller size than those required for the VHF bands.

The planning of the UHF bands were based on the need eventually to provide four colour television programmes on 625 lines each having substantially national coverage. All the programmes were to be radiated from common sites (to reduce costs and to enable viewers to use a single receiving aerial for all of them) and the BBC prepared a series of outline plans for national coverage on this basis. With the forty-four channels available in the two UHF bands, each station being allocated four channels, it was clear that a great deal of channel sharing would be necessary. The fullest use would have to be made of directional transmitting aerials and of cross-polarisation in order to reduce co-channel interference, and the siting of the stations, as well as the assignment of channels to them, would have to be determined with meticulous care. Even so, the coverage would have been seriously reduced by co-channel interference had it not been for the use of carrier offsets; the vision and sound carrier frequencies of stations sharing a channel were offset from each other by a sub-multiple of the line frequency so as to reduce the visibility of interference patterns by the equivalent of some 15 dB. This technique was allowed for in the Stockholm Plan of 1961, and the optimum offsets were subsequently worked out in detail in a series of meetings arranged by the EBU in which the PTT Administrations and broadcasting organisations of EBU and OIRT countries participated. The BBC took a leading part in the technical preparations for this work.

The transmitter powers were standardised as $6\frac{1}{4}$ kW, 10 kW, 25 kW and 40 kW for the main stations and 2 W, 10 W, 50 W, 200 W and 1 kW for the relay stations. Wherever possible standard aerial designs would be used. It was estimated that the main four-programme stations would cost, on average, less than £1 per head of population covered, but that low-power relay stations in sparsely populated areas might cost as much as £40 per head of population. As the potential licence-holders number about one in three of the population, the extension of the service to such areas would be uneconomic and efforts would have to be made to reduce the cost of small relay stations.

As the BBC and ITA transmissions on UHF were to be co-sited, and were as far as possible to use the same sites as existing VHF stations, the planning involved co-operation between them, as well as consultation with the Post Office. In 1963 agreement was reached between the BBC and the ITA on the responsibility for the construction and maintenance of the stations that were to be built and on the way in which the costs should be shared. One of the two authorities was to be licensed by the Postmaster General to operate each station, but engineers of the other would be responsible for the running of the transmitters carrying its programmes. Thus a sort of landlord-and-tenant relationship was established, the BBC and the ITA each being 'landlord' of about half the UHF stations.

Since the main stations had to serve large numbers of viewers directly, and many others through their dependent relay stations, their design had to achieve high reliability while providing for unattended operation to keep down operating costs. At most of the main stations, two similar klystron amplifiers were used; one to radiate the vision and the other the sound component of the programme, the outputs being combined in a network before being fed to the aerial system. (The klystron is an electron beam tube in which the electron flow is periodically 'bunched' by an applied high-frequency field and passes through a series of resonant cavities; the name refers to the action of waves breaking on a beach.) Klystrons were preferred to triodes or tetrodes for this application mainly because their higher power gain permitted one klystron to do the work of three or more triodes or tetrodes, thus simplifying the circuitry and improving reliability. Klystrons have long lives and tend to fail slowly rather than catastrophically; on the other hand, they have lower power conversion efficiency and are more difficult to replace. (The travelling wave tube is another type of electronic beam tube, containing a delay line; it shares the advantages of the klystron as compared with triodes and tetrodes.) It is possible that developments in solid-state driving equipment and in triodes and tetrodes may swing the balance back in their favour for future relay stations.

The decisions to use klystrons for the main amplifiers was taken after a study of the economics and reliability of high-power unattended UHF transmitters. By using solid-state circuitry in the earlier stages a total of some eighty valves could be eliminated in a pair of transmitters. Klystrons can be cooled by forced air, liquid or vapour. Cooling by vapour, e.g. steam, is attractive for high-power unattended stations because it is immune from the effects of frost, uses very little water and avoids the need for handling large quantities of air at high velocity.[64]

In the later stations it was arranged that if one klystron amplifier failed, the vision and sound components were automatically combined at a low power level and the combined signal was then routed through the good klystron amplifier.[65] In this mode the output power was reduced by about 7 dB to ensure that intermodulation products did not exceed a tolerable level. Against this disadvantage there was a saving of some 20 per cent in capital cost compared with a fully duplicated station. At some of the earlier UHF stations full duplication was retained. Most of the relay stations are equipped with UHF transposers; the low power stages have solid-state circuitry and their output drives either a klystron or a travelling-wave-tube amplifier. The use of common amplifiers for the vision and sound signals reduces distortion, but makes it necessary to operate the final amplifier below its full power rating to avoid excessive intermodulation products.

At some of the main stations two aerials were used, each capable of radiating two television programmes; at others and at relay stations a single aerial was designed to radiate up to four programmes. To accommodate four channels it was necessary to design high-gain multi-channel aerials; different types are used at the main stations according to the supporting structure available. The outputs of up to four transmitters had to be combined to feed a single coaxial feeder and the design of combining units for high power at UHF presented many difficulties, which had to be overcome.[66] A. B. Shone received a Geoffrey Parr award from the Royal Television Society for his work in this field.

At one or two relay stations it was possible to use an 'active deflector' instead of a transposer. This amplifies the received signals and retransmits them on the same channel. This method can be used only where the viewers to be served are screened from the parent station, so that interference between the direct signal and the re-transmitted signal will not be troublesome. So far only one active deflector is in service, at Bethesda in North Wales.

As all the UHF stations are operated unattended, monitoring equipment had to be provided to take executive action in the event of a fault and to warn the nearest manned station of the action taken so that a transmitter maintenance team could be alerted to effect repairs and restore the service to normal power. The monitoring equipment varies in scope according to the coverage of the station and the type of plant installed, but the parameters monitored in the most complex case include the luminance and chrominance components of the colour television signal. To ensure a high degree of reliability the aerial systems at all UHF stations were built in two co-linear sections each with its own feed, so that in the event of a fault on one half of the system, the full output could be automatically switched to the other half.

The first high-power UHF transmitters to be commissioned were at the Crystal Palace. Trade tests were radiated from 4 January 1964 using two 10 kW EMI vision transmitters and two 2 kW Pye sound transmitters. The BBC-2 programme was to start on the evening of 20 April 1964, but owing to a major failure of London's public electricity supply that evening, which affected the Television Centre but not the Crystal Palace, the opening of BBC-2 was deferred until the following day. The Sutton Coldfield BBC-2 transmitter opened on 6 December 1964, using a temporary aerial giving an erp of 50 kW. The permanent aerial was put into service on 4 October 1965 and the erp then increased to 1000 kW. In 1965 the first of the UHF relay stations (dependent on the Crystal Palace) were opened at Hertford (11 October) and Tunbridge Wells (25 October). The installation of BBC-2 UHF stations then followed at a rapid rate in successive years. In 1969 alone, seven main stations and thirteen relay stations were commissioned and by the end of 1971 there were thirty-three main stations and forty relay stations in service, giving a population coverage of about 91 per cent.

Three different UHF aerials were erected at the Crystal Palace station at different times. An EMI helical aerial was used for radiating a single programme during the field trials of 1957–8 and 1962–3. At the start of the BBC-2 service in 1964, a Marconi aerial comprising arrays of three-element Yagis was installed. When the ITA decided that their UHF transmitters should also be at the Crystal Palace, while the VHF transmitters remained at Croydon, separate aerials were erected for the BBC and ITA services; as their gain was less than that of the previous aerial, the twin 25-kW transmitters had to be replaced by 40-kW transmitters to achieve the required erp of 1000 kW.

UHF transmitting aerials commonly comprised several tiers, each of three or four panels; there were four dipoles in each panel, so that the aerial could contain as many as 120 dipoles. A complicated assembly of feeders was needed to supply current at the required amplitude and phase to each dipole. As snow and ice could seriously affect the electrical characteristics of the aerials those at some of the high-power stations were protected by glass-fibre cylinders – a method that had been used successfully in the German Federal Republic. The cylinders had to be about 6 ft in diameter to permit a man to climb inside to work on the aerial; fortunately the wind resistance of a cylinder is considerably less than that of a lattice structure of the same projected area. The presence of a cylinder of dielectric material obstructed the radiation to some extent; models were made with two concentric cylinders a quarter of a wavelength apart in order to cancel this effect, but so far this artifice has not been applied in a practical form. Smaller glass-fibre cylinders were used at relay stations, where a diameter of 16 in. could be sufficient.

In order to achieve a unified television standard on 625 lines in the United King-

481

dom, the TAC accepted the BBC proposal that the BBC-1 and ITA programmes on 405 lines in Bands I and III should be duplicated on 625 lines in the UHF bands, the coverage of densely populated areas being given first priority. The long-term objective was to re-engineer Bands I and III for 625-line services. It was considered that an approach to national coverage could be achieved for four programmes in Bands IV and V, but, although the international allocation for broadcasting extends to an upper limit of 960 MHz, other services are using the part above 854 MHz in this country. It is hoped that some channels in this part of the band will be released to enable the UHF coverage to be extended.

The development of the UHF network for BBC-1 followed closely on that of the BBC-2 network. BBC-1 on 625 lines with colour started on 15 November 1969 from the main stations at the Crystal Palace, Sutton Coldfield, Winter Hill and Emley Moor, thus covering London, the Midlands and the North of England. Black Hill (in the Forth/Clyde belt) and Rowridge followed in December 1969 and the first relay station for the duplicated service opened at High Wycombe on 22 December 1969. Further installations followed until by the end of 1971, BBC-1 was being broadcast on UHF from twenty-seven main stations and nineteen relay stations, giving a coverage of about 87 per cent.

The finding and acquisition of sites for the large number of stations that had to be built under the UHF development scheme (half of which were to be the direct responsibility of the BBC) was a burdensome task because of the stringent technical requirements, the need to satisfy the Planning Authorities responsible for preserving the environment, and the difficulty of acquiring land in suitable and accessible areas. Until 1960 the planning of new BBC stations was the joint responsibility of the Research Department, the Planning & Installation Department and the Building Department, the first-mentioned making recommendations on suitable areas and, when necessary, making site tests. The search for sites and preliminary negotiations for their lease or purchase were carried out by members of the Transmitter Group, and the Legal Department finalised the acquisition of the land.

By 1960 the number of sites needed each year heavily over-taxed the part-time effort available from the staff of the Transmitter Group and a Site Acquisition Section was set up within that group; it was to devote its full time to the site finding work, in close co-operation with Research Department and the Planning & Installation Department. The Site Acquisition Section was provided with a Land Rover vehicle with field-strength measuring equipment and a 70-ft telescopic mast. The engineers of this unit made a detailed study in each area of the local topography, of planned residential developments and of difficulties that might arise in acquiring sites or obtaining planning consents. They had to find out whether the existence of mineral rights or commoners' rights might affect the construction of the proposed station and also whether an electricity supply and Post Office telephone facilities could be made available. In the case of a relay station they had to establish by measurement that a signal suitable for relaying was available at the selected site. The Research Department then had to pronounce upon the suitability of the site from a propagation point of view and the choice had to be confirmed in discussion with the ITA and the Post Office. When planning consent had been obtained by the Building Department, final Post Office approval by the Engineering Information Department and financial approval through the Engineering Secretariat, the BBC Solicitor was asked to complete the legal negotiations; when a high mast was required the consent of the Air Navigation Authorities also had to be obtained. In a few cases public inquiries had to be held before planning consent was given.

Apart from the actual transmitting equipment a great deal of miscellaneous technical apparatus had to be maintained at transmitting stations. Automatic monitoring equipment had to be provided at all unattended stations. Stations with tall masts were provided with SHF equipment for receiving OBs. Attended stations had facilities for radiating test cards or transparencies, together with sound from tape recorders, to allow test transmissions to be made without encumbering the distribution network from London. With the duplication of BBC-1 on 625 lines it was necessary to install line-store standards converters at a number of transmitting stations to provide a 405-line feed to the VHF transmitters.

Despite the complexity of the transmitting equipment, serious interruptions of service were very infrequent. There were, however, a few serious failures; one was the collapse in the early evening of 19 March 1969 of the 1265-ft mast at the ITA transmitting station at Emley Moor. This mast carried the BBC-2 UHF transmitting aerials and it provided the programme feed to the Belmont UHF station and the Sheffield relay stations. Thus, a large area of Yorkshire and Lincolnshire suffered an interruption of service. BBC-2 was restored on low power on 21 March by using a temporary aerial supported on a 60-ft mobile tower supplied by the television OB unit at Manchester and this enabled the services to be restored also from Belmont and Sheffield. On Easter Monday, 6 April, a temporary 300-ft mast, assembled from two 200-ft masts stored at Skelton was erected at Emley Moor and this extended the service to some two million viewers. As a permanent solution it was decided to erect a 900-ft self-supporting reinforced concrete tower weighing some 14,000 tons and to mount the UHF and VHF aerials on the top, enclosed in glass-fibre cylinders. The new UHF aerials for all three services were brought into service from this tower on 21 January 1971.

Fire damage occurred at the Sheffield BBC-2 relay station on 13 May 1970. The amplifier was badly damaged and a replacement travelling-wave-tube amplifier from the Reigate station was transferred to Sheffield early on 14 May. While this was being done, a transmitter maintenance team, assisted by members of the Holme Moss station staff, repaired the damage and the service was restored twenty-four hours after the fire, with reduced power of 70 W to the aerial. Fire damage also occurred at the Keighley BBC-1 UHF relay station on 15 August 1970.

7 RECEPTION PROBLEMS

Just as in 1922 the BBC and the receiver industry were mutually inter-dependent, so through succeeding years the BBC's licence income depended on the availability of reliable and efficient receivers at reasonable prices. In its turn the receiver industry depended on the BBC, and in recent years the ITA, to attract its customers. This interdependence made it necessary to establish close liaison between the BBC and the receiver manufacturing industry and the retailer to overcome the difficult problems that arose in 1964 with the introduction of BBC-2 on 625 lines in the UHF bands, in 1967 with the start of a regular service in colour on BBC-2, and in 1969 with the duplication of BBC-1 on that standard (also with colour). This liaison took place mainly in the Television Advisory Committee, in various international meetings organised by the CCIR and the EBU, in a BBC/BREMA technical liaison committee, and through the RTRA.

The use of the 625-line standard in the UHF bands for the BBC-2 network and subsequently for BBC-1 (while BBC-1 continued to be transmitted on 405 lines in the VHF bands) complicated the design of receivers because of the need for a UHF tuner and for operation on both 405 and 625 lines. Unlike the 405-line transmissions the 625-line system uses negative picture modulation and frequency-modulated sound, both of which complicated the switching from one standard to the other. By this time the design of tuners had developed from simple tuned circuits (one for each channel) to permeability tuners and, by 1970, to electronic tuners in which the capacitance of reverse-biased diodes was controlled by a direct voltage. From the point of view of the user, the most important development was the introduction of push-button tuning, which was made possible by the improved stability of the tuned circuits and the introduction of automatic frequency control.

The need for dual-standard operation greatly increased the complexity of the receiver and hence tended to detract from its reliability. But the decision to duplicate BBC-1 and ITV programmes on 625 lines made it possible, in 1969, to produce single standard 625-line sets; these were cheaper and more reliable and could be used, with a single UHF receiving aerial, in areas where all three programmes were provided on UHF. By the end of 1971 such areas included about three-quarters of the population.

The 625-line system not only produced better pictures, with markedly improved definition and with less noticeable patterning at nearly horizontal edges in the scene, but it was also effectively free from the line-frequency whistle produced by receivers when operating on 405 lines. The line frequency of the 405-line system was at 10,125 Hz, whereas for 625 lines it was at 15,625 Hz and was inaudible to most people.

The start of colour transmissions on BBC-2 in 1967 introduced a vast new problem for receiver designers, especially as it was necessary to keep down the cost of sets to attract a sufficient number of viewers to colour and at the same time to insist on high performance and good reliability to retain their allegiance. The introduction of colour transmissions was preceded by close and detailed consultations between the BBC, the ITA and the receiver industry. The Government decided in 1966 that colour should be on 625 lines only, using the PAL system. This fundamental decision was welcomed by the industry and by the broadcasting organisations, but many points of detail affecting both parties remained to be solved. For monochrome television a *modus vivendi* had been reached at an early stage to ensure that the contrast characteristic ('gamma') of receivers, when combined with that of the transmitted pictures, would give an acceptable result. The same problem arose with colour, but in a more complex form. It was also necessary to maintain compatibility, i.e. pictures transmitted in colour must be receivable in black-and-white on monochrome receivers, and pictures transmitted in black-and-white must be receivable on colour receivers.

The early shadow-mask colour tube developed by RCA in America had a round face; its deflection angle was 70°, so that a relatively deep cabinet was needed to house it. By the end of 1970 square-cornered colour tubes with a deflection angle of 90° had become popular and 110° colour tubes were being developed. Popular picture sizes (measured across a diagonal) were 19, 22 and 25 in., but 26-in. tubes were later preferred to 25 in. The presence of the shadow mask inevitably reduced the brightness of the pictures as compared with those of a black-and-white tube, but improvements in the phosphors helped to overcome this problem. Several attempts were made to produce tubes working on different principles, but the shadow-mask was almost without a rival until the 13-in. 'Trinitron' tube, which was claimed to give pictures nearly twice as bright as those of the shadow-mask tube, was put into production by the Sony Company of Japan in 1968; 625-line PAL receivers using this 13-in. tube became available in 1971.

Improvements in phosphors tended to change the colour-balance of the received pictures and a study was made by the BBC Research Department, which resulted in the adoption by the EBU of standard chromatic co-ordinates suitable for present-day colour receivers.

By the end of 1971 there were nearly $17\frac{1}{2}$ million television receivers in use in the UK, of which about $1\frac{1}{2}$ million were colour receivers. Many families had second sets, especially those which had acquired colour receivers and continued to use their black-and-white sets, often dual-standard models, as well.

The Engineering Information Department has received complaints through the years of the unsightliness of outside aerials. In the early 1930s the poles used to support medium-wave aerials often leaned crazily across back-gardens. The use of sensitive superheterodyne receivers with internal ferrite rod aerials reduced the need for outside aerials for medium-wave reception, except where electrical interference was troublesome, but television in Band I demanded aerials with elements some 10 ft long and spaced 5 ft apart, mounted on poles attached to chimneys. The problem reached a peak during the 1960s when many people needed separate aerials for television on VHF, television on UHF, radio on VHF and possibly radio on MF. The line that has been consistently taken is that aerials should be so designed and installed as to be as unobtrusive as possible, consistent with efficiency, but that local authorities and landlords should not prevent the use of effective individual aerials unless community aerials, or wire distribution, were provided. The problem was eased in the 1970s by the fact that in most parts of the country a single aerial could receive all three television programmes on UHF and another all the radio programmes on VHF (with the exception of Radio 1, which is available only on MF,

485

except when it is broadcast by Radio 2 and Local Radio stations). Furthermore, the aerial elements needed for television on UHF were no more than one-tenth as long as those for VHF, so that a highly directional aerial with up to eighteen elements was quite compact and much less obtrusive than the older types of VHF aerial. Many viewers in areas of high UHF field-strength could obtain good results with an aerial of four or five elements or even with an indoor aerial standing on the top of the receiver – provided that interference and multipath propagation were not troublesome. In general, however, set top aerials are not satisfactory, particularly for reception in colour.

The design and installation of UHF receiving aerials was greatly eased by the fact that the transmitters for BBC-1, BBC-2 and ITA programmes serving each area were co-sited and used channels within a group of neighbouring frequencies, so that aerial designs covering five standard frequency ranges sufficed for reception anywhere in the country.

The growth of wire distribution systems and the use of community aerials, especially in new residential areas, also helped to reduce the miscellaneous array of chimney-mounted aerials that threatened the urban landscape. In blocks of flats the landlord often provided an aerial with an amplifier feeding the three television programmes to each apartment. If there were many extensions the incoming UHF signals might be transposed to channels in the VHF bands to simplify the distribution problem. The individual tenants could not then receive BBC-2 unless they had modified receivers capable of taking 625-line pictures on VHF channels, or frequency-changers to transpose the signals back to UHF.

Wire distribution systems, operated by private firms, received the programmes at a central point by radio (or in a few cases by line direct from the television authorities' centres) and distributed them over either coaxial or multi-pair cables to the subscribers. In some systems the distribution was done at HF, in others at VHF. In the latter case care had to be taken not to use channels on which there were strong signals from BBC and ITA stations in the area, which might cause interference. Liaison on such matters was maintained with the Relay Services Association of Great Britain. By the end of 1971, there were some two million subscribers to wire distribution systems in the UK, most of them equipped for both television and radio.

Care was taken to brief local television dealers, either directly or through the RTRA and the National Television Rental Association, about new stations that were about to open in their areas, so that they could stock appropriate receivers and aerials and instruct their servicemen about any problems that might arise. The public also had to be informed so that they would be prepared with the appropriate equipment when the time came for them to take advantage of the new station. The coming of colour television required a special effort in these directions because of its greater technical complexity, and because, until the regular colour service started, few viewers appreciated the added excitement, and indeed beauty, that it could bring to their screens; it held a mirror up to life, nature and art and was not content merely to present a black-and-white simulacrum of them. Nation-wide publicity was not enough. The message had to be brought to the people in their own areas as colour

486

television spread across the country. Leaflets, booklets, lectures, discussions and exhibitions were supplemented by a specially equipped BBC demonstration vehicle, which contained several colour receivers and measuring equipment and was provided with a retractable telescopic aerial mast on the roof. The use of this vehicle showed that good colour reception was possible in some areas where local opinion thought otherwise. From 1967 to the end of 1971 the colour vehicle gave demonstrations at some fifty locations and over five million people saw them.

In the course of its efforts to enable viewers to take full advantage of the technical quality of its programmes, the BBC tried to persuade receiver manufacturers to make certain improvements to television receivers. One of these was the reproduction on black-and-white receivers of the full dc component in the transmitted pictures. There were technical difficulties in reproducing it in full (e.g. it was extinguished by the operation of agc derived from the mean level of the signal) and it was also difficult to show the customer that its presence made a great difference to the pictures on the screen. In the 1950s the BBC arranged demonstrations to show that the absence of the dc component made dimly lit scenes appear with a grey background, instead of black as the producer intended. There was a gradual improvement in this respect and colour receivers necessarily reproduced the dc component. The quality of sound produced by most television sets was generally rather poor, mainly because the loudspeakers were small. Some makers introduced receivers that showed a marked improvement in this respect, but relatively few customers showed much interest in the quality of sound or indeed could do so in the conditions in which the sets were demonstrated in many shops.

The introduction of colour receivers using EHT voltages up to 25 kV gave rise to some fears, especially in the USA, about the danger of radiation of X-rays, particularly from the voltage stabiliser tube. Since the effects of X-radiation are cumulative it was thought that there might be some danger for viewers who watched the screen for long periods each day. Although the risk was slight the British radio industry investigated the matter to ensure that the limit of radiation fixed by the Medical Research Council would not be exceeded either when the receiver was operating normally or in the case of any fault that would not result in loss of picture and thus cause the viewer to switch off. Steps were also taken to avoid danger to servicemen when making adjustments to receivers.

In sound broadcasting many of the reception problems had been overcome by the introduction in 1955 of the VHF/FM service, which, by the end of 1971, was available to more than 99·3 per cent of the population. The system provided markedly better sound quality than was possible in the long-wave and medium-wave bands, because of its greater audio bandwidth and its greater dynamic range; it was far less susceptible to interference from foreign stations – though for a small percentage of the time interference from other stations could occur in areas of weak field strength at times when conditions favoured tropospheric propagation; provided that effective aerials were used, where necessary, it was almost immune from electrical interference; and the network of VHF/FM stations could be used for stereo. Despite these outstanding advantages, efforts to encourage the purchase of VHF receivers met with only meagre success in the early years, although by 1972 nearly 50 per cent of homes possessed them. The reasons no doubt were that a large proportion of listeners were reasonably well satisfied with the standard of reception on long and medium waves, that VHF receivers had to compete with television receivers in the market, that the cost of the VHF facility somewhat increased the price of a set (although the difference was considerably narrowed in the early 1970s), and that the services available on VHF were also available on LF or MF, with the exception of Local Radio and the Open University programme. A minor factor was that in a few small areas the advantages claimed for VHF reception were not realised, because of distortion caused by multi-path propagation. As this was not easy to recognise, the BBC produced a special transportable receiver giving an oscilloscope display of the received signal amplitude as a function of the instantaneous carrier frequency; from this display it was possible to deduce the magnitudes and path differences of the principal delayed signals. The display could also be used to adjust the position of the receiving aerial to obtain the maximum ratio of direct to reflected signal.[67]

The coming of stereophonic broadcasting made it necessary to inform the public about it and about the best ways of getting good results from it. Since the system was compatible, listeners with monophonic receivers had no new problems. Stereophonic reception was, however, more susceptible, by some 12 dB, to electrical interference, e.g. from motor vehicles, and also considerably more sensitive to receiver 'hiss'. Listeners in areas of low field strength were advised to use good outside aerials; this was also necessary where multi-path propagation occurred, and could help to avoid co-channel or adjacent-channel interference. Fortunately the level of ignition interference from vehicles had been reduced since the introduction of regulations on the subject in 1952.

During this period the campaign against electrical interference, that is interference caused by electrical equipment of all kinds, continued on the same lines as before. It has already been described in chapter V, section 2, which indeed trespassed to some extent on this later period. There were, however, two new factors; the introduction of multi-channel television receivers with the start of the ITA service in 1955 created new problems of interference from the frequency-changing oscillators of those receivers and the spread of television on UHF from 1964 onwards tended to ease the problem of interference with television, because few kinds of electrical apparatus produced serious interference in the UHF bands.

8   RECORDING FOR SOUND AND TELEVISION

From 1956 onwards magnetic tape steadily increased its share of sound recording work at the expense of discs until tape had a virtual monopoly. In 1955 it had accounted for 60 per cent of the work; in 1960 the figure was nearer 80 per cent. By the mid-1960s, apart from one or two specialist uses, disc recording had come to an end and magnetic tape held the field unchallenged. Thus, in a little over thirty years, the wheel had turned full circle. The first recording system the BBC ever had, in 1930, was a magnetic one, using steel tape. Disc recording came in soon after and gained supremacy during the war and immediately after it. Thereafter disc recording declined and tape gained ground until it was once again, with one or two minor exceptions, the sole system of recording in the BBC's Radio and External Services.

There were two other significant developments from 1956 onwards. One was the increased use of recorded programmes. In 1960 about half the programmes for home audiences were broadcast live. By the second half of the decade nearly everything was being recorded. The principal exceptions were public events and concerts, and the news and current affairs programmes, though these latter drew heavily on recorded inserts. The other development was the gradual shift of recording operations from separate, and usually remote, recording rooms to the studio cubicles.

During 1956 and the early part of 1957 the scheme for extending tape recording, which had been launched the previous year, came to fruition. The Regions, benefited handsomely from this. Each headquarters was provided with an editing suite, with three BTR/2 recorders, and tape equipment was installed for the first time at the smaller studio centres, which had previously been entirely dependent on disc. In London more editing suites were provided and another big central recording room, on the top floor of Broadcasting House, was commissioned. This was equipped temporarily with BTR/2 recorders.

In 1957 a new tape recorder was produced by EMI; this was the TR90, a fully professional machine, but half the price of the EMI BTR/2. It was in two units, tape deck and amplifier, weighing just under 140 lb. between them. The TR90 was first used in the central recording room on the eighth floor of Broadcasting House, where sixteen of them, mounted on racks, were installed towards the end of 1957 to replace the temporary BTR/2s. A trolley-mounted version for recording in studio cubicles was developed at about the same time. This first appeared in some of the London studios in 1958. By 1959 trolley-mounted TR90s had spread to many of the London studios and to the Regions, and it was not long before they were an almost universal feature of studio cubicles. Ultimately something like two hundred were in use. A few of these recorders were later modified to two-track recording for the initial stereo transmissions.

In 1957 Designs Department were successful in developing a transistorised version of the EMI midget recorder. This owed something to the work they had already done on making a tape recorder sufficiently robust to withstand the rigours of a polar crossing with the British Commonwealth Transantarctic Expedition of 1957. In the valve-operated machine separate ht and lt batteries were required, but in the transistorised design a single battery of eight $1 \cdot 5$ V U2 cells operated both the motor and the amplifier, thus making a useful saving of weight. Another modification was the addition of a miniature loudspeaker, so that reporters could more readily check their recordings in the field. A start was made during 1958 on the task of modifying the two hundred or so midget tape recorders that were by then in service.

Towards the end of the 1950s Leevers-Rich mains-driven recorders came into general use for mobile work. In the early 1960s they were supplemented by the Nagra, a portable recorder of Swiss manufacture. Of modest size ($14\frac{1}{2}$ in. $\times$ $9\frac{1}{2}$ in. $\times$ $4\frac{1}{4}$ in.) and weight (16 lb.), the Nagra was a precision-built instrument with a remarkably high standard of performance, comparable to that of a high-grade studio machine. At about the same time another personal recorder, the Ficord, was introduced. This was a pocket-sized machine ($9\frac{5}{8}$ in. $\times$ 5 in. $\times$ $2\frac{3}{4}$ in.) weighing only 4 lb., with a playing time of $4\frac{1}{2}$ minutes. For two or three years the Ficord was widely used by news reporters.

By the early 1960s the increased activity in recording and the trend towards recording and editing in the studio cubicle created a demand for yet more tape equipment. The Philips EL3566 was chosen to meet this growing demand. Its two units, tape-deck and amplifier, were mounted on a trolley with a control panel. By 1965 over two hundred of these recorders were being used for home broadcasting, most of them in studio cubicles. In the External Services, which increasingly transferred recording to the studio cubicles at Bush House, the British-made Leevers-Rich machines were installed in large numbers.

In the mid-1960s Studer machines made in Switzerland were introduced. By 1965 there were over thirty of the C37 model in use, mainly in music studios and the Broadcasting House continuity suites. The C37 was a machine of very high quality, well suited for editing work and capable of meeting the most exacting demands. Another Studer model to be imported was the A62. This was about the same size as the Philips EL3566, but was in one unit, lighter, and fully transistorised. The A62 came in during the second half of the 1960s for mobile work, replacing the heavier and bulkier Leevers-Rich and TR90 machines that had been used hitherto. This period also saw the demise of the EMI midget, the BBC's most successful personal recorder which had first appeared in 1952. It was superseded by the much smaller Uher 4000, from Germany, with dimensions 11 in. $\times$ 8 in. $\times$ 3 in., which weighed only $8\frac{1}{4}$ lb. – half the weight of the EMI midget.

By the end of the 1950s tape speeds had settled down at 15 and $7\frac{1}{2}$ in. per second, though a nucleus of machines capable of 30 in./s was retained. The 15 in./s speed was used for stereo and music programmes, and $7\frac{1}{2}$ in./s for everything else. External Services wished to reduce their operating speed still further in order to economise in tape consumption; their Leevers-Rich machines were accordingly modified to include a speed of $3\frac{3}{4}$ in./s. The original tests at $3\frac{3}{4}$ in./s looked promising, but during a service trial at the beginning of 1971 several unforeseen snags appeared, mostly due to imperfections in the tape itself, and the attempt was abandoned for the time being. Meanwhile, the EBU had declared itself in favour of the adoption of 15 and $7\frac{1}{2}$ in./s as primary standards for the international exchange of recordings and recommended further study of the possibility of using $3\frac{3}{4}$ in./s as a secondary standard, i.e. one that may be used only by prior agreement between the parties.

In 1957 the Transcription Service at St Hilda's, Maida Vale, went over exclusively to fine-groove recording. Their BBC type D disc recorders were modified to cut up to 260 grooves per inch and provided with cutter-heads incorporating a heater-coil for the stylus. The procedure adopted was to record a master tape and then transfer the recording to 10- or 12-in. discs in transfer suites. There were two of these, each

Sir Francis McLean, Director of Engineering, 1963–8

Top left BBC 'VERA' television tape recorder, 1958

Top right 35-mm film telerecording (rapid pull-down) equipment, 1958

Videotape machines at Birmingham Broadcasting Centre, 1971

Control room A, Alexandra
Palace, 1946

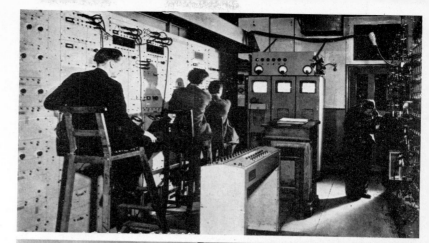

International control room,
Television Centre, 1968

Television apparatus room,
Birmingham Broadcasting
Centre, 1971

Right Extending mast vehicle for television OBs, 1954

Top left Televising the Naval Review, Spithead, 1953

Bottom left Television OB from submarine, 1956

Top left Colour mobile control room, 1968

Top right Telecine equipment at Alexandra Palace, 1949

Bottom left Flying-spot Mechau telecine machine, 1954

Bottom right Colour telecine machine, 1971

Left Electronic character generator, 1970

Right Receivers at Tatsfield, 1965

ANCHOR

BBC DESIGNS DEPARTMENT

CHARACTER GENERATOR

INPUT PICTURE

OUTPUT PICTURE

Left Acoustic tests on scale model of studio, 1969

Right Video switching matrix, 1970

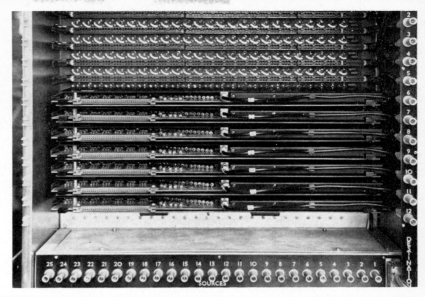

Left Digital line-store standards converter, 1971

Right Electronic field-store standards converter, 1968

James Redmond, Director of Engineering, 1968–

equipped with a BTR/1 tape machine and a type D disc recorder. In 1959 another transfer suite with a Neumann disc-cutting lathe and a Telefunken tape machine was set up. Automatic control of the groove pitch was provided, the pitch being expanded for loud passages and contracted for the quiet ones – thus enabling higher amplitudes to be recorded. This not only improved the signal-to-noise ratio of the recording, but also made it possible to record most half-hour programmes on one side of a 12-in. disc. In 1964 the original suites with their type D recorders were closed down and all transfer work was then handled by the Neumann machine. At the same time the BTR/1 tape recorders, which had been in service for several years, began to be replaced by Studer C37 machines. By the end of 1964, when the transcription recording unit moved to Kensington House, Shepherds Bush, a dozen C37 recorders had been installed.

Experiments with stereo transcriptions began in 1960. Programmes from the 1962 Edinburgh Festival were recorded in stereo on modified Leevers-Rich machines and then transferred to discs by the EMI and Decca companies. Stereo channels at Kensington House were commissioned in 1966 and equipped with two-track Studer C37 recorders; control desks were devised and made by the Transcription Service Engineers. A mobile stereo desk was completed in the same year for use with Studer A62 mobile recorders. It was put into service for the first time at the Aldeburgh Festival in June 1966. In 1968 the Neumann disc recorder was modified for stereo and the Telefunken tape machine associated with it replaced by a two-track Studer C37.

Two Studer type A80 tape recorders were obtained for transcription work in 1971. These were eight-track machines using one-inch tape. With these multi-track machines there was no longer any need to record a musical performance, classical or pop, at one go complete with all its component parts, instruments and soloists. They could be recorded separately as convenient, and the recording mixed and balanced later. This made the recording engineer's task less exacting, and often saved time and money as well. It also permitted reverberation to be added to the individual components of the programme, or modifications made to their frequency response, to suit the producer's intentions.

Throughout the history of sound recording the need has been felt to standardise the essential characteristics of the process so as to permit recordings made on any machine to be reproduced on any other. This proved particularly difficult in the case of the frequency characteristic of disc recordings, because it was desirable to embrace commercial gramophone records as well as recordings made by broadcasters. Some measure of agreement was finally reached and is incorporated in recommendations of the IEC for discs and of the CCIR for tapes.

To economise in the amount of recording tape that had to be purchased and stored. a tape reclamation service was set up in the BBC in the early 1960s, with equipment for testing old tapes and joining together parts of them that were still serviceable.[68] Equipment was also purchased for erasing tapes in bulk by subjecting them to strong magnetisation.[69]

In television recording the situation changed out of all recognition between 1956 and 1971. At the outset nearly every programme was transmitted live, and when recordings were made their technical quality left much to be desired. By 1971 live programmes, apart for public events and news, had become the exception, and the quality of the telerecordings had improved so much that they were indistinguishable from live transmissions.

During the opening years of the period the film system of telerecording was greatly improved and more channels were installed. In 1956 the Research Department developed a method of recording the full information in the television picture, rather than that in alternate fields. This was the 'stored-field' system. By means of a long-persistence phosphor in the display tube, the two fields making up a complete television picture were displayed simultaneously to the recording camera. The difference in brightness between the two fields was compensated by correction circuits in the video amplifier. This system was first applied to the two 35-mm suppressed-field machines that had been installed in 1953. The conversion was completed during 1957 and the system was in service by the end of the year.[70] At the same time much stricter control over the processing of telerecordings on film was instituted, and their quality was substantially improved.[71]

Additional film telerecording channels were installed over the next two years. In 1958 a 16-mm suppressed-frame channel with three machines developed by the Designs Department became operational and a Marconi 16-mm rapid pull-down machine was installed, initially at Lime Grove and later at Alexandra Palace. Six more of these were acquired later. During the summer of 1959 another full-information 35-mm channel with three machines was added using a camera made by Moy and a display unit by Cintel; this was intended to be a fast pull-down channel, but it proved impossible to make the pull-down between film frames so rapid that it could be contained within the field blanking period. The difficulty was overcome by storing about sixty lines at the start of each alternate field, which would otherwise have been lost during the pull-down period while the camera shutter was closed. An important advantage of this system was the the maximum storage period was only three milli-seconds, far less than in the stored-field system, and therefore much easier to compensate. Telerecordings of outstandingly high quality were produced by this channel.

By the summer of 1959 the BBC's complement of film telerecording equipment amounted to:

1 35-mm stored field channel (2 cameras)
1 35-mm rapid pull-down channel (3 cameras)
1 16-mm suppressed-field channel (3 cameras)
1 16-mm Marconi rapid pull-down machine.

A turning point came in 1958 with the emergence of the video-tape recorder, using magnetic film as the recording medium. That year the long-term investigation into the recording of television signals on magnetic tape, on which Dr P. E. Axon and his group in the Research Department had embarked in 1952, came to fruition. On 8 April VERA (Vision Electronic Recording Apparatus), the video-tape recorder they had developed, was demonstrated to the Press and the following week it made its début in Panorama.

VERA recorded on half-inch magnetic tape running at 200 in. per second. The tape was spooled on 1500-ft reels giving a playing time of a quarter of an hour. Three tracks were recorded. The vision signal, which was split into two frequency bands, 0 to 100 kHz and 100 kHz to 3 MHz, occupied two of them, with the sound occupying the third. The 100-kHz to 3 MHz band was recorded directly, but the lower vision band was made to frequency-modulate a 1-MHz carrier; the frequency-deviation was such that an instantaneous frequency of 1 MHz corresponded to the troughs of the synchronising pulses and 400 kHz to peak white. The modulated carrier was recorded on the track. The sound also was recorded in the form of a frequency-modulated carrier. The machine incorporated an elaborate electro-mechanical system for stabilising the tape speed at 200 in. a second.[72] The first broadcast performance in *Panorama* was not an unqualified success. Richard Dimbleby's opening of the programme was repeated within a few minutes, but the radio correspondents thought the picture rather fuzzy, and no better than the best film telerecording.

This gallant effort broke new ground, but its usefulness was short-lived. Almost simultaneously the Ampex Corporation in California unveiled their video-tape recorder, the VR1000A. Bishop and McLean happened to be in America at the time and managed to attend the demonstration. They were most impressed. Orders were placed and the first machines went into service at Lime Grove on 1 October 1958 with a trailer for *A Tale of Two Cities*. It was joined by a second machine in January 1959. Meanwhile VERA quietly faded out of existence; all that survives of it is one of the spools and some of the recording heads.

In the Ampex recorder the vision signal was recorded transversely on a two-inch tape by four heads rotating at 15,000 rpm on an axis parallel to the tape length. The tape wrapped round more than 90° of the periphery of the head, so that the head-to-tape velocity was nearly 1600 in./s, yet the tape speed was only 15 in./s as against the 200 in./s needed for VERA. An hour's programme could be accommodated on a 12-in. spool. The vision signal was recorded as a frequency-modulated 4-MHz carrier. In addition to the transverse vision track, two longitudinal tracks were recorded on the tape, one for the sound and the other carrying control information on the speed and position of the recording heads. A vacuum system was used to keep the tape in close contact with the head wheel. At first there was some trouble with 'head-banding', i.e. horizontal bands on the picture caused by differences between the outputs of the four heads (such as might be caused by clogging of the heads by particles of the tape coating), but this was overcome by a quick-acting compensator and is now rarely noticeable. 'Drop-outs' caused by minute imperfections in the tape produced white flashes on the screen. These were reduced by polishing the tapes before use and automatic methods were developed for assessing them.[73] The difficulty was finally overcome by means of an electronic compensator, which, on the onset of a drop-out switched to the previous line held in a store; the resulting repetition of one line did not show in the picture.[74, 75]

From the beginning of 1959 onwards more and more video-tape recorders were acquired. By September 1959 there were four in operation, all at Lime Grove. A mobile version, on a three-ton chassis, appeared in 1961; five of these were stationed in the Regions and the sixth in London.[76] During that year a central video tape recording area was set up at the Television Centre. By June 1962 it was equipped with six machines, which with another two at Lime Grove, one at Alexandra Palace, and seven in the Regions, made up a total of sixteen. Half of them were multi-standard machines, capable of recording 625-line and 525-line as well as 405-line signals.

In 1963 the first RCA video-tape recorders made their appearance. These were transistorised machines, type TR22. Three of them went into the central recording area at the Television Centre as part of the increase in facilities required for the launching of BBC-2 in April 1964. In 1965 the first of a second generation of video-tape recorders, the Ampex VR2000, became available. This was a multi-standard, high-band colour machine, with a vision bandwidth of 6 MHz as against the 4·2 MHz for the original 405-line low-band machines; seven of these were installed at Television Centre when colour programmes started in July 1967. (In the high-band machines the FM carrier frequency was raised so as to avoid the production of spurious low-frequency patterns by the colour sub-carrier. For a 625-line system the instantaneous frequencies corresponding to the synchronising signals and to peak white respectively were 4·95 and 6·80 MHz in the low-band recorders and 7·16 and 9·30 MHz in the high-band. These standards were adopted by the CCIR in 1970.)

For the World Cup series of 1966, Designs Department produced a slow-motion video-tape recorder, which could be run so as to give a still frame or a four-to-one reduction in speed.[77] This was superseded in 1968 by an Ampex HS100 recorder using two video discs 16 in. in diameter and rotating at 3000 rpm, which replayed at any speed from still frame to twice normal, in either the forward or the reverse direction. These machines proved extremely useful for televising sports, because any selected passage in the recording could be repeated in slow motion within a few seconds.

Video-tape operation is not cheap. The machines themselves are costly since they are built to a high standard of precision, and include complex servo mechanisms for maintaining the movement of the tape and of the head-wheel to the accuracy required for replaying in synchronism with other sources. Additional units are needed to maintain the even higher accuracy required for colour. The recording heads are expensive and have to be replaced after a few hundred hours. Running costs include the cost of tapes (which can, however, be reused many times), tape storage, maintenance and editing. At first editing was done by cutting and joining the tape, but electronic editing was provided with the second generation of video-tape recorders. This permitted the timing of cuts to be determined during the recording session, so that the producer was closely concerned with the editing. Electronic counting circuits switched the machine automatically at each editing point so that there was no loss of continuity in the video, sound or control signals on the tape.

Despite its cost, video-tape recording has become an essential part of the television system. Some 400 sessions for recording, play-back or editing are now mounted each week and 12,000 programme items are held in store.

By 1972 the BBC had a massive array of 53 video tape recorders, 42 of which were colour machines, 19 were in the Regions, and 11 were mobile.

These highly sophisticated video-tape machines with a transverse scan across the width of the tape are used for programmes intended for transmission. For less exacting requirements helical-scan recorders are adequate; they do not embody a rotating head-wheel and are considerably cheaper. Future improvements in recorders of this type may make them acceptable for use on programmes.

The various systems that are being developed for reproducing television programmes in the home, and in some systems also for recording them, do not come within the scope of this book; but they are of direct interest to the BBC because they could afford means for distributing its programmes in recorded form, especially to schools.

9 TELEVISION LINKS

During this period there were important developments in the networks of distribution and contribution links for television programmes. Among the factors contributing to these changes were: the acceptance of continuity working as normal; the inauguration of the second BBC television programme, BBC-2; the development of Eurovision and of satellite communication; the introduction of colour on both BBC-1 and BBC-2; the development of improved forms of test signal and better methods of using them; and the introduction of solid-state video switching matrices.

Towards the end of the previous period there was still some resistance on the part of the then Lines Department to the principle of continuity working, which had been used in the Radio Services for many years and was greatly desired by the Television Service. It would imply that all contributions to the network programme would be routed through the Central Control Room in London, so as to secure smooth presentation. The objection to it was that a programme item from Scotland, for example, would have to be sent to London and thence to the transmitters all over the country, including those in Scotland. Unless the performance of the network reached a very high standard, the degradation of quality resulting from the double journey would be appreciable. The earlier 'shortest route' method of working shortened the path, in some cases, by 400 miles, but at the cost of introducing complex switching operations, which had to be done extremely quickly. For instance, an OB from Manchester would make it necessary for the Manchester switching centre to connect the OB to the circuits going north and south and to Holme Moss. The Birmingham switching centre would have to transfer the feed for Sutton Coldfield from the circuit from London to the one from Manchester, and so on. At the end of the OB these operations had to be put into reverse. This method was cumbersome and far too slow to be acceptable by today's standards of presentation, but continuity working became practicable as the performance of the Post Office vision circuits improved and it had just been introduced at the beginning of the period under review.

At the end of 1959, before preparations had begun for the introduction of BBC-2, the network of vision links comprised a total of about 3000 route-miles: 1700 miles consisted of 'fully engineered' links rented from the Post Office (with one circuit in each direction) and 1300 miles of direct pick-up or pick-up plus one or more SHF links. The fully engineered links comprised roughly 660 miles of SHF links operating at 4000 MHz, and 1040 miles of coaxial cable links of various types:

   (i) coaxial tubes 1 in. in diameter between London and Birmingham, carrying a vestigial side-band carrier system with a carrier frequency of 6·12 MHz and a transmitted band from 3 to 7 MHz.

   (ii) coaxial tubes ⅜ in. in diameter, carrying a vestigial side-band system with a carrier at 1·056 MHz and transmitted band from 0·5 to 4 MHz.

   (iii) coaxial tubes 1 in. in diameter using a BBC-designed carrier system with a carrier at 15 MHz and transmitted frequency band from 12 to 18 MHz. (Some of these tubes carried simultaneously a video-frequency channel.)

   (iv) coaxial tubes 1 in. in diameter using video transmission, for distances up to about 12 miles.

   (v) coaxial tubes ⅜ in. in diameter using video-frequency transmission, for numerous short links up to about 8 miles.

In 1960, after the Television Advisory Committee had published its report advocating a change of line standards and the introduction of colour, it was clear that the 625-line standard would be adopted, and all the television transmission circuits that were put into the new Television Centre, then nearing completion, had to be suitable for this standard. The introduction of BBC-2 necessitated the immediate duplication of a large part of the network and the subsequent addition of many more links, all capable of operating on this standard. The addition of more transmitting stations, both for BBC-2 and for the duplicated BBC-1 625-line system, continually stretched the network farther and farther. The BBC-2 distribution network was formed, on all the main routes, by SHF links rented from the Post Office and working in the 2-, 4- and 6-GHz bands. Since the opening of BBC-2, the BBC-1 distribution network has been replaced by radio links in the same geographical configuration as the BBC-2 network, and contribution links towards London are carried on the same routes. Many of the feeds to the outlying or low-powered transmitters on the BBC-1 network and many of the contribution links from the smaller studio centres use equipment installed and maintained by the BBC with the agreement of the Post Office. Since 4 March 1964 all programmes produced by the BBC for its own use have been originated on 625 lines for BBC-1 as well as BBC-2. The distribution of both programmes is done on 625 lines, and standards converters are provided at the 405-line BBC-1 transmitting stations.[48]

Wherever possible the Post Office provides 'protection channels' to reinforce their operational links; these are reserves that can be brought into use if a normal link fails, whether one used by the BBC or another on the same route.

The change to the 625-line standard with colour made it necessary not only to widen the video bandwidth of the SB links from 3 MHz to 5·5 MHz but also to impose tighter limits on their performance – particularly in the region of the colour sub-carrier frequency (4·43 MHz). It therefore became important to have a method of measurement as informative and as easily applied as possible. Reference has been made in the previous chapter to the 'pulse and bar' test signals proposed by Dr N. W. Lewis of the Post Office and to the 'K-ratings' derived from them: these ratings express as a percentage the deviation from perfection of the shape of the received pulse and bar signal. More recently colour pulse and bar waveforms and various other test signals have been developed, some of which are inserted into the television waveform at the source on certain lines in the field-blanking interval. These signals have the great advantage that measurements can be made, without interrupting the programme, at any point in the chain where the signal is at video frequency.[78] As long as the insertion test signal is in good order at the point of junction with the programme and also at the test point the programme should also be in good order at that point. The monitoring and control devices now used operate on this assumption; they not only measure the amount of distortion in the waveform but also correct certain types of distortion, and send an alarm signal to a manned centre if other types exceed the tolerances. The latest device of this sort is the Television Automatic Monitor Major, which can measure twelve parameters of the television waveform. Errors in six of the most important characteristics of a colour television signal can now be corrected automatically. Many transmitters, and therefore the links feeding them, are now working under the surveillance of one or other of these automatic devices and are unattended except when an alarm calls for engineering attention.[15, 79, 80]

Test signals inserted in the television waveform are applied to international circuits and it is therefore important to standardise them. As a result of studies by an EBU working party and by the CCIR, a standard form of interval test signal has been recommended by the CCIR for use of 625-line systems; the form used in the UK differs in one respect from the international interval test signal, but is compatible with it.

A further development in the use of insertion signals has been to exploit them for the purpose of conveying information. Insertion communications equipment produced by Designs Department enables data to be transmitted in digital form on some of the lines in the field-blanking interval of the television waveform. The information-carrying capability of such a system is quite high; it can be used for network identification and for the synchronisation of remote sources. It seems likely that more and more use will be made of the television waveform in this way – there are still lines available in the field-blanking interval that might be used.[81]

An important feature of the television distribution and contribution network is the flexibility provided by the use of BBC switching centres in London, Birmingham, Manchester, Bristol, Glasgow, Cardiff and Belfast. (The Independent Television Companies, however, relied from the start on switching done by Post Office staff at the terminals of the main television links.) The London switching centre in Broadcasting House was originally put in as a repeater station for the OB balanced-pair cable to Alexandra Palace. When programme compilation was moved to Lime Grove, and later to the Television Centre, the main purpose of the switching centre was to economise in vision circuits between Broadcasting House and the Television Centre, since the extension of all the available programme sources to the Television

Centre would have been extremely expensive. The testing of OB circuits was also carried out at the switching centre.

As the network developed, the switching centres in the Regions were set up, their functions being to act as receiving points for outside broadcast circuits, to test and where necessary to equalise them, to feed contributions towards London when required, to maintain the prescribed performance standards on the permanent network and to collaborate with the Post Office in reporting faults. The pulse and bar waveforms are now commonly used for testing OB circuits.

Switching operations on vision circuits were at first done by coaxial plugs and cords. When the Television Centre was designed, an improvement in the switching arrangements was made by the use of motor-driven rotary switches and solenoid-operated wafer switches in a remote-control system, which had good capacity and reliability. The wafer switches, however, were slow to operate and noisy; moreover, crosstalk could arise when coaxial cables were terminated on them. With the introduction of 625-line television, and the continuing attempt to achieve better standards of transmission, systems using high-grade sealed relay units were brought into use and they are still giving satisfactory service. Colour, and the increasing sophistication of programme presentation, nevertheless demanded further improvements: to avoid any blemish in the picture at the moment of switching from one source to another the switching must be synchronised with the field sync pulses to an accuracy of a few microseconds, and the switch elements must make effective contact instantly and unfailingly. These problems were solved by the use of semiconductor switches, which were incorporated in a solid-state video switching matrix developed in the Designs Department and already produced in considerable numbers. The matrix is arranged in a cross-bar pattern, the vertical lines being connected to twenty-five sources and the horizontal lines to twelve destinations. At each crossing point there is a solid-state switch, operated by a control voltage derived from the video waveform. This equipment has proved highly reliable; the number of component and wiring failures have been fewer than ten in the first 50,000 hours of use of all the matrices in service. It can be used for fading and cutting between sources and permits the mixing of pictures from different sources, provided the sources themselves are synchronised.

By 1965 the Post Office was able to apply a standard tariff for television links. The tariff quoted annual rentals for vision circuits of various lengths, with a surcharge for colour television, and a connection charge. This system permitted accurate forecasts of circuit costs to be made by all users of television links, which was not possible with the 'control account' method of charging previously in force.

It has been apparent for some time that important economies in the cost of both vision and sound links could be made if the BBC were permitted to provide more of them itself. Already radio links installed and maintained by the BBC account for more than 1000 miles of the permanent vision network; Post Office radio links amount to about 3700 miles and Post Office cables to about 420 miles, making a total circuit-mileage of nearly 5200. Rebroadcast links account for a further 5100 route miles. A network of BBC SHF links, connected between transmitting station sites and making use of existing masts, could be integrated conveniently with the rest of the system, but would require the agreement of the Post Office and of the Ministry of Posts & Telecommunications.

The start of Eurovision has been described in the previous chapter. By 1956 the UK was connected to the network by a cross-channel radio link set up jointly by the BBC and the ORTF, which was used until July 1959, when a permanent Post Office radio link was brought into service.[43] It was clear that much work would have to be done to achieve standardised operating and testing procedures, common technical standards of transmission and agreement on the methods of sharing the costs. As soon as it was seen, from the success of the experimental programme exchanges of 1954, that Eurovision was going to be a permanent institution, it was agreed that the European Broadcasting Union should assume responsibility for co-ordinating Eurovision activities. The EBU therefore set up two working parties: one, Working Party M to deal with the fundamental technical principles and determine standards and the other, Working Party L, to deal with operational matters and to co-operate with the PTT Administrations on the provision of vision, sound and communication circuits. The BBC was represented on both these working parties; M. J. L. Pulling, who had been chairman of an *ad hoc* committee that had hitherto organised the television programme exchanges, became chairman of the new Working Party L. The EBU also set up a Television Programme Committee to deal, among other things, with programmes for Eurovision. The EBU Technical Centre in Brussels took over technical planning and co-ordination and established a Eurovision Control Centre in the building of the Palais de Justice in Brussels (where the PTT radio links terminated). Members of the various PTT Administrations were invited to attend meetings of the technical working parties and their co-operation was invaluable, since in most countries they were responsible for providing the television and sound links. Moreover, it was possible for the broadcasting representatives to bring to the notice of the PTT people any troubles that had been experienced on past transmissions and to secure their help in putting them right. Meetings are now rather more infrequent, but there can be no better evidence of their value than the success of European international television transmissions, which are now as much taken for granted as are international sound transmissions.[48, 82]

International collaboration on questions of television engineering brought together many engineers of great goodwill and ability and, in a common venture such as Eurovision, it was not only useful but essential. Yet it had failed to achieve uniform standards on two fundamental features of television: the line and field rates used in the waveform and the method of adding colour to it. The divergences could have remained a bar to the exchange of programmes between countries using different standards, but the development of standards converters and of colour transcoders (in both of which the BBC played a major part) reduced the difficulties, at a price, to no more than an operational inconvenience.

The value of Eurovision was most evident in the fields of news and sport. International exchanges of these types of programme grew to such an extent that the number of programmes co-ordinated by the EBU (that is, excluding simple relays from one country to another) increased tenfold in ten years. It thus became cheaper

HH

to rent some of the links permanently, rather than hire them temporarily for each programme. This would also tend to improve the performance of the links because they would always be available for testing by the broadcasters. A permanent network of vision links between countries in Western Europe was gradually built up and was complemented by a corresponding network of sound programme links and control circuits. Additions to these permanent networks are frequently made as the traffic over each link grows to the point where permanent renting is economical.

The method of sharing the costs of circuits provoked a great deal of discussion. At first this took place among the technical services, which started from the simple concept that each participant (i.e. each Television Service taking the programme for live transmission or for recording and subsequent transmission) should pay for the circuits immediately 'upstream' of its own country. But with the increase in traffic and the accession of the smaller Television Services, some of them being at the periphery of the network, the EBU Administrative Council, set up a 'Cost-sharing Group' under the chairmanship of S. G. Williams, Controller of Television Administration in the BBC, to advise on this difficult problem. It worked on the principle that each television service should pay according to the use it makes of the network, but its share of the cost should be weighted according to its ability to pay. As the present author has stated elsewhere 'the system includes a built-in feedback circuit that keeps it under control,'[82] because if any user's share is fixed at too high a level he will not be able to afford to take many programmes and the cost to be shared between all the others will be higher. In addition to its share of the circuit costs, calculated by a computer at the EBU Technical Centre for each programme, each participant shares in the EBU's expenditure on its Eurovision services.

In the BBC it was necessary to set up a Continental Control Point; it went into service in September 1955 on the ground floor of Broadcasting House, London. It had facilities for sending and receiving vision and test signals, for originating opening routine captions, for handling several simultaneous sound commentaries in different languages and for the routing of the associated control lines. When outgoing Eurovision transmissions required a number of sound programme lines for commentaries in different languages there was a danger of the sound circuits getting crossed at some point along a route. To assist the PTT personnel in the transit countries in setting up the sound circuits and to warn them not to break down the connections during the waiting period before the programme began, tape reproducers were installed to give announcements in different languages recorded on continuous loops of tape. Such an announcement might be: 'This is the commentary circuit for Budapest' repeated in English, French, German and Hungarian.

The arrangements for music lines, commentary lines, guide commentary lines (a guide commentary is one spoken in the language of the country of origin for the information of a commentator in the country of reception) and control lines (there were sometimes both technical and programme control lines) could be much more complex than those for the vision links. To deal with the resulting problems a Sound Sub-group of Working Party M was formed under the chairmanship of L. F. Mathews of ATV, who was formerly of the BBC Lines Department. The activities of the Sound Sub-group revealed incorrect line-up of the programme circuits, resulting in either overloading or noise, and the need for close co-operation with the PTT Administrations. It was necessary to ensure that the level of programme sent by the broadcasting organisations was not sufficient to cause intermodulation distortion on the PTT carrier systems. It was also necessary to overcome the difficulties caused by the fact that some organisations, the BBC included, measure programme volume with a peak-reading meter, while others use the VU-meter type of instrument with a much longer rise-time constant. The reporting of faults to PTT offices was standardised and difficulties in communication over control lines, especially between an OB point in one country and the commentator's headquarters in another, were eased by the provision of standard OB facilities for speech and signalling.

BBC engineers took part in all these measures, and G. Stannard, Chief Engineer, Communications, later became chairman of the Sound-Sub-group, which was also concerned in the study of the BBC sound-in-syncs system[83] already described.

When the permanent cross-channel vision link came into service in July 1959 the Post Office terminal was at Tolsford Hill near Dover, and the BBC standards converters were moved there. They were transferred to the Television Centre when all BBC standards converters were concentrated there in the early 1960s. The Continental Control Point was then moved from Broadcasting House to the Television Centre, where it became the International Control Room.

The coming of the 625-line standard to Britain, followed soon after by the introduction of colour, meant that the London-Tolsford Hill link was no longer adequate to meet the technical requirements of vision transmission; the Post Office accordingly set up an SHF route as in the other parts of the Television SB System. This was commissioned in July 1964, and normally provides one colour-capable circuit in each direction between London and the French network at Lille, though it is possible to double the capacity by hiring a Post Office 'protection' channel that is provided against breakdown of the normal facilities.

The OIRT operates among countries in Eastern Europe a network corresponding to Eurovision under the name 'Intervision'. In February 1960 a joint meeting of the EBU and the OIRT took place. Tentative arrangements for the interchange of programmes were made, and representatives of the OIRT were invited to colour demonstrations mounted by the BBC. Further contacts developed and practical steps were taken for the exchange of programmes between the two organisations. The Eurovision network now connects twenty-three Members in the European Broadcasting Area and can be extended not only to the Intervision network but to all the other continents by communication satellites.

One of the major Eurovision activities is the twice-daily news exchange, which demands the closest co-operation between news editors and technical staff and is organised by means of a daily telephone conference via Brussels, in which each editor offers any item that he thinks may be of interest to any of the others. At fixed times each day all the selected news items are transmitted over the network, so that each television service can take those it wants and record them on tape for use in its news period. As well as the permanent vision network already mentioned, there is now a permanent sound programme network and a permanent network of circuits for telephone and teleprinter communications. Rapid communication is vital to Eurovision operations and automatic switching equipment is being installed in Brussels to handle telephone calls from one national control centre to another as well as an automatic distribution system for teleprinter traffic.

It is necessary for the vision, sound and control circuits to be switched at strategic points in the network when the required configuration changes. Arrangements have been made for this switching to be done instantly by remote control from Brussels and it is hoped to provide means by which the switching operations will be reported automatically to the Control Centre so that the periods of use of each link can be fed to the EBU computer for use in calculating the apportionment of the costs.

The success of Eurovision stimulated interest in the possibility of world-wide transmission of live television programmes. This was impossible until the coming of communications satellites in 1962, but a 'Cablefilm' system, devised jointly by the BBC Research and Designs Departments, was used from 1959 to 1962, to send short film sequences across the Atlantic to illustrate important news events. By exchanging bandwidth for time it was possible to send the television signals over telephone circuits in the transatlantic telephone cable and re-form them at the receiving end. The original film was scanned slowly so that the bandwidth required was only $4 \cdot 5$ kHz, but the transmission time was then about a hundred times the normal running time of the film. Nevertheless, moving pictures could be sent more quickly than by using an aircraft to transport the film. The pictures were of sub-standard quality, with jerky movements, but the method enabled news items originated on either side of the Atlantic to be seen on the same day by viewers on the other side.[84]

The launching of Sputnik I by the USSR in 1957 heralded a new era in communications. The break-through came in July 1962, when the US satellite Telstar transmitted television pictures to Europe, where they were relayed in nine countries. This was done only thirteen days after the satellite was launched – an outstanding achievement when set against the long period of service trials and adjustments usually considered necessary before a new technique is put before the public.

Telstar moved in a 'non-synchronous', elliptical orbit, and the time available for transmission was limited to a few minutes during each orbit. Elaborate tracking arrangements had to be used to keep the aerials at the ground stations aligned on the satellite. Telstar, however, was an 'active' satellite, which retransmitted the signals, and it immediately put out of court earlier plans for passive systems, which merely reflect the incident signal and require enormous power to be transmitted from the ground station.

The next step was the launching of active satellites in synchronous orbits, so that they remained stationary with respect to earth (at a height of 22,300 miles). The first, those in the Syncom series, were of limited capacity, but a notable success in world-wide television was scored by one of them, Syncom III, over the Pacific; this was used in October 1964 for the transmission of recorded pictures of the Olympic Games from Tokyo to California, thence by terrestrial systems to Montreal and by aircraft to Hamburg, bringing the pictures to Europe by 2230 hours on the day the events occurred.

Intercontinental communications entered an organised commercial phase in April 1965, when the International Telecommunication Satellite Consortium (Intelsat) launched 'Early Bird' (Intelsat I). This was the first satellite to carry international television and telephone traffic on a commercial basis, and its greater power improved the linearity and signal-to-noise ratio considerably; a number of interesting programmes were taken during this period, including the launching and recovery of Gemini Titan IV, the inauguration of President Johnson and the Clay–Liston fight, which was seen by seven million viewers in the UK. Intelsat I could not carry the television sound component as well as the picture, so the sound was sent by cable. The delay in transmission via the satellite relative to that through the cable was about 200 ms and this was compensated by means of a tape recorder.

The adoption by Intelsat of the synchronous satellite as the basis for world-wide development greatly simplified the design of ground stations, because there were no longer any large variations in direction requiring complex tracking equipment at the ground stations such as was needed for working with Telstar in those at Andover (USA), Goonhilly (UK), Pleumeur Bodou (France) and Raisting (Germany). This simplification has encouraged a proliferation of ground stations all over the world. Meanwhile the USSR developed its own system of non-synchronous Molniya satellites, the orbits of which are designed to make the transmission times fit conveniently into the time zones into which the country is divided.

The immediate concern of those responsible for planning the first satellite systems was to provide circuits for telephony, together with facsimile and data transmission. The broadcasters have co-operated closely with them to secure first-class transmission of colour television with its sound component. This is now regarded as an essential requirement for world-wide satellite communication systems.

The Intelsat I series of satellites was followed by Intelsats II, III and IV, each with a considerably greater capacity than the last and, taking the expected life of the satellites into account, a lower cost per circuit-year. The first satellite in the Intelsat IV series was launched in January 1971. It carries twelve communication channels, each with an rf bandwidth of 36 MHz, and has a total capacity equivalent to 6000 two-way telephone circuits. It was built by the Hughes Aircraft Company in the USA for the COMSAT Corporation, an inter-governmental body that manages the Intelsat projects. Future satellites in the series are being assembled by the British Aircraft Corporation and parts of the equipment are being supplied by European firms. Each satellite has two steerable aerials, which can produce narrow beams so that the earth stations can use aerials of relatively low gain. The designed active life of each satellite is seven years. Satellites in the Intelsat III and Intelsat IV series are now operating over the Atlantic, the Pacific and the Indian Ocean and more than seventy earth stations are already in operation, most of them equipped for television transmission. Television traffic between Europe and the USA is carried on the 525-line system; the conversion to and from 625 lines is done at the European end and the BBC-designed field-store converter plays a major part in this operation.

These satellites have contributed greatly to the immediacy and impact of televised news, public events and sport and they have enabled vast numbers of viewers throughout the world to see such spectacular events as the visit of Pope Paul to Colombia in 1968, the Olympic Games in Mexico in the same year, the investiture of the Prince of Wales at Caernarvon, the series of Apollo moonshots, the Winter Olympics in Sapporo, Japan, and the Olympic Games in Munich in 1972.

Satellites afford other possibilities for television transmission besides the relaying of live programmes between continents. One such possibility is the distribution of programmes between television services within the European Area – a function now performed by the Eurovision network. A satellite system would be attractive for this purpose if it could compete on economic terms with the renting of terrestrial circuits and could be designed to reach Iceland and countries in Africa and the Near East that are beyond range of the present network, while complying with the EBU's other requirements. These include a capacity of two television channels, one high-quality sound channel, and twenty commentary channels, with control and communication channels. Specifications for such a system have been discussed with the European Space Research Organisation (ESRO) and the CEPT. Alternatively, the need for a flexible distribution system might be met by a modified Intelsat IV satellite or by one launched under the Franco-German Symphonie project.[82]

Another possibility is the use of satellites to broadcast directly to viewers and radio listeners. Much study has been devoted to means of doing this. A promising suggestion is to use narrow beams, $0 \cdot 5°$ to $1 \cdot 5°$ in width, which would cover individual countries.[85, 86] This would make it possible to use such a system for national services and would enable receiving aerials of manageable size to be used. The allocation of frequencies for this purpose is mentioned in section 12 of this chapter. The use of broadcasting satellites working in the SHF bands would offer a means of providing additional programmes, if needed, the channels in the present VHF and UHF bands being already fully committed in Europe. However, the development and launching of satellites capable of transmitting powers of the order of 400 W and the provision of special aerials and special receivers (or adapters), together with the high initial cost of the system, make it unlikely to be practicable for several years. If the receiving installation is not restricted to the size and cost that viewers in general could be expected to afford, broadcasting satellites become much easier to achieve. This is the basis of the plan for educational broadcasting in India by means of a satellite to be launched by NASA in 1974, with receiving points in schools and other community centres. Projects of this kind are also being planned for other parts of the world.

10 SOUND PROGRAMME CIRCUITS

Most of the permanent sound programme circuits constituting the BBC's SB network are rented from the Post Office, which has to provide telegraph and telephone channels in vast numbers to satisfy the diverse requirements of industry, commerce, and private subscribers. The type of 'music' circuit that has been available to the BBC has therefore always been dependent upon the type of telephone plant currently in use, and has generally been a by-product of the types of circuit most in demand. Thus, during the post-war decade the mainstay of the sound SB system was the 'carrier phantom' circuit, because the policy of the Post Office at the time was to provide large groups of telephone circuits by means of multi-channel carrier telephony systems. Unfortunately the reliability of the carrier phantom type of circuit left much to be desired.

At the beginning of the period under review, however, ferrite materials were becoming available for loading coils, and this enabled the Post Office to use coils small enough to be located in cable joints. They were thus able to introduce 16-mH coils on half spacing (1000 yards) and 22-mH coils on quarter spacing, which gave bandwidths of 11 to 12 kHz. These coils were included mainly in such 40-lb per mile screened pairs as were still available; they yielded sufficient bandwidth, with lower noise levels and greater reliability than the carrier phantoms.

The growing demands for channels not only for telephony, but also for data transmission of all kinds, caused the Post Office to turn more and more to coaxial cables, over which large numbers (up to about 1000) of telephone channels can be simultaneously transmitted. The old carrier phantom circuits were then either scrapped or converted to short-haul working. Programme circuits on coaxial carrier routes are derived by removing the channel filters from three adjacent telephone channels and combining them to give a programme channel of about 11-kHz bandwidths. Unfortunately such circuits are not entirely satisfactory because they are a by-product of a system designed for telephony, the signal-to-noise ratio of which is not necessarily good enough for programme. Moreover, the noise on these circuits is of a random nature, so that the noise power on a series of links in tandem is additive.

Because such circuits form part of a multi-channel telephone system with a very large number of channels, the Post Office has to take strict precautions about the maximum transmitted levels. The channels are fitted with pre-emphasis and de-emphasis circuits, which means that high frequencies are accentuated on entering the system; the Post Office therefore set a maximum test level of − 10 dBmW for frequency runs, and harmonic measurements are not allowed at all unless the tone is sent automatically in very short pulses. This led the BBC to consider other methods of measurement, and at the beginning of the 1970s Designs Department explored a method of measuring harmonic distortion on carrier circuits by transmitting a filtered band of white noise and measuring the intermodulation products in the remaining part of the frequency spectrum.

It has always been necessary, and still is, for the BBC to carry out its own periodic checks on the quality of the programme circuits. From very early days these checks took the form of manually transmitted frequency runs done by station staff, the levels being measured at each centre along the route. This required the co-operation of the engineers at each of the centres on each chain, and as the network expanded the making of such tests became very laborious. Before starting a frequency run it had to be ascertained that all centres were ready to co-operate and if there was a delay at a centre near the beginning of the chain the engineers' time at all the 'downstream' stations could be wasted. Tests on one chain could take as much as an hour to carry out. The first advance was the development of automatic sending equipment, which was able to send a series of discrete frequencies in about four minutes and required no active co-operation, beyond the initial setting up, from engineers along the route. The automatic sender was left on for several runs, so that if a centre was not ready at the start it still had an opportunity to obtain results.

In 1964 a further reduction in the time and effort required for testing audio circuits was made by the introduction of automatic testing with a sweep oscillator at the sending end to generate a continuous frequency run; pen recorders were used at the intermediate centres, and pulses of tone were transmitted for harmonic measurements. At first, the results were returned to London where they were laboriously analysed by means of a mask technique. By 1971, however, the interpretation of the charts was done by an automatic read-out machine, the results from which were fed into a computer, which analysed the performance of each link and put the results on to punched tape. They could then be fed directly over the teleprinter network to inform all the regional communications engineers of the performance of the network.

As the noise levels on the 'music in band' circuits (i.e. those derived by combining two or more telephone channels in a carrier system) were barely tolerable, investigations were made into the possibility of using compandors, comprising a volume compressor at the sending end of each circuit with a corresponding expander at the receiving end. Tests were made on various types of compandor that became available from time to time (including two that operated at carrier frequency), but none was entirely satisfactory for use on programme circuits. The expander, by reason of its fluctuating gain, caused unpleasant variations in the level of circuit noise and modulated the noise with the programme. (The Dolby compandor, by operating independently on different parts of the frequency band, largely overcame this problem, but was then considered too expensive for general use on the network.) Assessments were made on a grading scale of 'continuous impairment' to determine the acceptable levels of noise when these effects were present.

The adoption of pulse code modulation (PCM) affords a possible solution of the problem of transmitting high-quality sound over the network. In 1966 Research Department made a feasibility study of the use of PCM for transmitting the sound component of the television programme within the synchronising period of the vision signal. This application, known as 'sound-in-syncs' (SIS), had the dual advantage of removing the necessity for a separate sound programme circuit and at the same time improving the sound quality and reliability. In the application of the system to a 625-line signal the audio signal is sampled twice during each television line and each sample is converted to a ten-bit PCM signal. Two of these signals are combined and inserted into the next line-synchronising pulse. At the arrival end, before the signals are transmitted to the public the audio signal is extracted and decoded and the video waveform is restored to normal. Compandors operating on the audio signal before and after decoding enable the required signal-to-noise ratio to be achieved. As the

506

noise introduced by a PCM system is predominantly high-pitched, the compandor need operate only on the higher frequencies. Moreover, the compandor can be set to operate only when a fairly high level of programme is reached, so that any modulation of the noise by the programme will occur only when the higher-frequency components in the programme are strong enough to mask it. A pilot tone at half the sampling frequency is transmitted to enable the expander to follow variations in the level of the programme input to the compressor, even when the latter is acting as a limiter.[83, 87]

The SIS system gave an audio bandwidth of 14 kHz and a ratio of peak signal to peak weighted noise of 66 dB. It was adopted for use on the contribution and distribution networks for BBC-1 and BBC-2. For use over television links of poor quality, such as may have to be used for OBs, a more rugged version was devised in which the use of flywheel synchronisation and error detection circuits permitted its use on such links at the expense of some reduction in bandwidth and increase of noise.[88]

In 1969 the development work on the SIS equipment was taken over by Designs Department and it is expected that the whole of the distribution networks for BBC-1 and BBC-2 will be equipped with it by the the end of 1972. Apart from the saving in line rentals for the sound component, economies should result from the simplification of control, monitoring and switching operations. Broadcasting organisations and PTT Administrations abroad have shown interest in the system and three British firms have been licensed by the BBC to manufacture the equipment. The system was demonstrated to the EBU in 1968 at a meeting in Copenhagen, and to both the EBU and the CMTT in Holland in June 1970, when the sound was sent to Milan and back over a distance of 2500 km accompanying a colour television programme, without any audible distortion or any degradation of the pictures attributable to the presence of the sound component. The EBU undertook to make experiments to determine whether the system should be used on the Eurovision Network; the CMTT is concerned with the possible acceptance of the system for general use over international television circuits. (There is no question at present of using it for broadcasting to the public, because existing receivers could not accept it; the signal must therefore be decoded before transmission.)

The future of sound programme distribution may well lie with PCM used on wide-band links. By 1971 multi-channel PCM systems were already being planned on links about 6 MHz wide, giving a maximum capacity of thirteen channels, from London to Sutton Coldfield and Holme Moss, and also to Wrotham. Each programme channel would have an audio-frequency bandwidth of 15 kHz and the noise would be well within the limit that the Engineering Division now considers necessary. PCM is particularly advantageous for transmission over radio links because of its inherent immunity from noise and distortion (within limits) on the bearer channel. These advantages make it attractive for the BBC to develop its use for the distribution of sound programmes over wide-band links, whether rented from the Post Office or installed by the BBC. For this purpose a system based on a sampling frequency of 32 kHz giving a bandwidth of 14 kHz, and using an 11-digit or 12-digit code is practicable. The quantising noise (noise inherent in a PCM signal by reason of the discontinuous nature of the waveform) can be greatly reduced by the use of compandors in conjunction with pre-emphasis and de-emphasis.[89]

The spread of stereophony raised new problems in providing programme circuits, because it required either sufficient bandwidth (53 kHz) to carry the encoded signal or two separate channels with closely matched characteristics. At first the circuits connecting London, Wrotham, Sutton Coldfield and Holme Moss were a combination of rebroadcast links and SHF links, the latter being provided by the BBC with the agreement of the Post Office. These links all carried the encoded stereo signals. When the SHF links have been re-engineered for PCM, as mentioned above, the left- and right-hand signals will be transmitted over separate channels and encoded at the transmitting stations, thus taking advantage of the high performance and reliability of PCM, while avoiding the difficulty of transmitting the wide bandwidth necessary to carry the encoded signals.[115]

The provision of links for sound OBs has continued generally in the same tradition as during the earlier periods, but here too stereophony has made its impact. The techniques of equalisation and line-up are still the same, but there is a tendency for the Post Office, which normally provides the lines, to undertake the equalisation. Two factors have reduced, over the last two or three years, the number of OBs carried out by line. One is that the Post Office raised its tariffs considerably because of the high cost of setting up temporary circuits for OB use. The other factor is the increase in stereophonic OBs, which often have to be recorded on site because of the difficulty and cost of providing matched lines for the 'A' and 'B' channels. A number of live stereo OBs have nevertheless been carried out, e.g. from Glyndebourne and Aldeburgh – sometimes with two lines of different construction, which it has been possible to phase-equalise. Live stereo programmes have been done from Manchester, in which the 'A' and 'B' channels were multiplexed on a south-going vision circuit. The multiplexing equipment, known as the 'Rood' equipment, was of Dutch origin and has been equipped to provide three channels, though more could be obtained by the addition of extra modules.

Despite the advances in technique that have been made and the success achieved in providing wide-band international circuits for colour television, international sound links often leave much to be desired. (Even musicians have complained about the quality of some of the international music exchanges organised by the EBU, although musicians are notoriously tolerant of noise and distortion because their minds are attuned to the music to the exclusion of all else.) On the Continent, programme circuits are almost all derived from carrier systems (music-in-band) and are susceptible to noise. Changes in routing made by the PTT Administrations at the last minute make it difficult to rely on the results of tests made in advance of a broadcast. If the lines were permanently available to the broadcasters, they could be regularly tested and this would no doubt result in an improvement in performance. This is indeed so in the case of the permanent Eurovision sound network, but this is required primarily for television sound and is seldom available for radio programmes. Over the last few years, however, there has been considerable improvement in lines for sound relays as a result of negotiations in the EBU Sound Sub-group. A further marked improvement was made at the beginning of 1971 with the use of Dolby compandors. These compandors, which are now used by most of the recording companies in making their master tapes, were used during an orchestral tour of Germany and Switzerland early in 1971 and made a great improvement. The difficulty with conventional compandors has always been the 'hush-hush' effect resulting from the varying level of noise with the variations of gain in the expander at the receiving end. The Dolby compandor splits the frequency into four parts, each of which is companded separately, so that this effect is greatly reduced. It is considered that the Dolby compandor gives a 10-dB advantage in the 'white' noise level from which music-in-band circuits tend to suffer, and raises many of them from the 'marginal' to the 'high-quality' category.

Stereophonic transmissions on international circuits to or from the UK are envisaged, and tests have been made round a loop from London to Frankfurt and back via Paris, with no audible degradation of the stereo quality. Music-in-band circuits were used for these tests with Siemens-Halske equipment providing two 15-kHz channels on a 48-kHz group, with a compandor. At the time of writing the problem of noise had not been entirely overcome. The provision of a European network of stereo circuits would require heavy capital investment, which would have to be justified by a sufficient load factor.

The provision of SB circuits for feeding the stations used for the External Services affords scope for the use of special techniques, because a number of programme circuits are needed over each route. The six circuits from Bush House, London, to the station at Skelton are over 300 miles long and do not enter any BBC centres along the route. To improve reliability over this route it was decided to replace the existing circuits by a 48-kHz group rented from the Post Office; a 12-channel carrier telephone system is to be installed, pairs of telephone channels being combined using the split-band technique to form six programme circuits – each with a bandwidth of about 6 kHz. Some exchange of bandwidth for reliability is acceptable for Overseas Services; the programmes consist mainly of speech, and reliability is particularly important because the division into quarter-hour periods leaves no time for explanation, apology or repetition.

11 TELEPHONE AND TELEGRAPH CIRCUITS

From 1955 onwards the BBC internal telecommunications network was continuously expanded to satisfy the demand for more and more services, and automation was increasingly introduced in both telephony and telegraphy.

At the beginning of this period a decision was made to install Automatic Branch Exchanges at the two main London premises, Broadcasting House and the Television Centre, and a somewhat smaller PABX was installed at Bush House in 1956. The Bush House installation was the thin end of a wedge moving towards the general acceptance in the BBC of automatic operation, to which there had been opposition from some senior members of the staff, who had been used to the old style of helpful personal service which a good operator could give to a caller. There were outside influences as well; many organisations, public and commercial, considered automatic telephony an essential part of their system, and visits were made to a number of such installations by representatives of the Lines Department (later renamed Communications Department) and the Central Services Group, to see how these systems performed and how they could best be used in the BBC. The Bush House installation was purchased from Ericssons.

The first of the two larger installations, both supplied by STC, to go into service was that at the Television Centre, the first two hundred lines of which were ready in November 1959, followed in March by the remaining 2100 lines. In the meantime the installation in Broadcasting House Extension was proceeding, and it went into service in May 1960. It had, at first, a capacity of 3000 extensions, but by the end of 1961 most of these had been allocated as working extensions and the capacity had to be extended by 500. The ultimate capacity of this type of PABX (PABX No. 3) is limited, and to cater for the possibility of future extensions an idea was evolved of building into the PABX a satellite exchange of 1000 lines. This was a new departure and was specially approved by the Post Office. There was no access from the switchboard to the satellite extensions except by dialling through a dialling junction; they were called NMA (non-multiple-appearance) extensions. Since they caused more work to the operators, care was taken not to allocate NMA extensions to staff likely to create a large amount of traffic.

As the network expanded in the London area, each new building or group of buildings was provided either with its own PABX installation or with a satellite to an existing PABX installation. In a satellite installation access from the public network to any extension is available only through the operator at the parent exchange.

The fourteen PABX's and satellite exchanges installed in London and the Regions since 1956 have a total capacity of 12,740 extensions. In addition to STC the manufacturers include Ericssons, Telephone Rentals Ltd, AEI and Reliance.

Although many of the BBC's communication problems are similar to those of other large organisations its long-distance communications network is influenced by the related programme networks. At the beginning of this period the BBC had a network of low-loss telephone channels derived by carrier systems from programme circuits rented from the Post Office; these carrier systems had a minimum of three telephone channels, but more usually four. At the time this was an economical method of providing telephone channels, but two events occurred in the late 1950s, which made this no longer true. These were the introduction by the Post Office of STD (subscriber trunk dialling) and a large increase, also introduced by the Post Office, in the cost of renting private wires of all kinds. STD, with its almost no-delay working, caused many extension users to prefer the public telephone service to the BBC network, on which there were some delays. The result was an increase in cost and at that time there was neither staff nor equipment available to enable traffic data to be collected, so that steps might be taken to reorganise the methods of handling. Later a Traffic Analyst was appointed, reporting directly to the Superintendent Engineer Lines, but working closely with the Central Services Group. This proved successful and the two departments now work together very closely indeed. Traffic data have been collected, and a much more accurate idea is being obtained of the amount of traffic between the various BBC centres. The results of this study show that it will be not only possible but economical to increase considerably the number of channels between London and certain of the Regional centres, so as to provide an 'on-demand' service. This would not have been economical on carrier channels of the type hitherto used, but transistorised twelve-channel equipment has come on to the market, which can be applied to a Post Office 48-kHz group (now available for rental). Economically this is well worth while, and in January 1971 the first such twelve-channel (frequency-division multiplex) system went into service between London and Manchester; in April a further system was commissioned between London and Birmingham. These systems operate in the band of frequencies between 60 and 108 kHz, each of the twelve channels having a bandwidth from 300 to 3400 Hz. In addition to the economic advantage, the bandwidth for speech is improved and each channel provides an out-of-band signalling path at a frequency of 3875 Hz for dialling pulses. This last facility made it possible to introduce 'operator dialling' between London and Birmingham (the London operator dials the wanted extension in Birmingham and a Birmingham extension can dial the London operator direct). This opens up the prospect of ultimately introducing direct dialling from extension to extension in different centres, with the dual advantage of immediate connection and immediate clearing after the end of the call. Future developments are likely to be along these lines.[90]

The period under review saw a great expansion in the use of teleprinters in the BBC. They are used for three purposes: as receivers of news material from Agency sources, for transmitting monitored material from the Monitoring Department at Caversham to selected destinations in the London area, and for the transmission of scripts and written messages between BBC centres throughout the system.

In the mid-1950s proposals were being formulated for the replacement of many teleprinter machines rented from the Post Office by BBC-owned machines maintained by teleprinter mechanics engaged for this purpose. This policy promised considerable economies, and has been pursued through the years, with the result that today there are some four hundred items of telegraph equipment of various sorts owned by the BBC and maintained by staff of the Communications Department. The news agencies continued to supply feeds of news material, the BBC renting one teleprinter at each reception point and having the right to distribute the material as required within its own system. Successive new models of teleprinter introduced by Creeds increased the operating speed from 50 bauds (66 words per minute) to 75 bauds (100 words per minute). In 1967 a 'SAGEM' semi-electric teleprinter (manufactured by the Société d'Applications Générales d'Electricité et de Mécanique in France) was introduced. It uses electronic 'serial-parallel' conversion of the telegraph code (in which the code elements are received consecutively and stored for simultaneous application to the printer); this gives the machine an extremely good margin for accepting distorted incoming signals. This made it particularly suitable for use at Caversham for the reception of signals received by radio. In 1971 a new tele-

511

printer was introduced into the system; made by the Extel Corporation of America, it is almost entirely electronic, is capable of high speeds and shows promise of good reliability and low maintenance costs.

The inter-office teleprinter network, operating between BBC centres, was carried until the mid-1960s on channels derived by the use of BBC-designed equipment from programme circuits rented from the Post Office. The need for more teleprinter channels, the large increases in Post Office charges already mentioned, the availability of commercial equipment and the development of message-switching systems all combined to favour a change in the method of providing telegraph channels. In June 1969 equipment manufactured by the Telephone Manufacturing Company for deriving a number of telegraph channels from a speech-quality Post Office circuit was installed. There were two of these systems operating between Caversham and London, to carry the output of monitored material. Early in 1971, when a 48-kHz group was put into service between London and Manchester, some of the twelve derived 3400-Hz speech channels were fitted with TMC equipment, still leaving a speech band up to 2400 Hz wide. A teleprinter channel derived in this way costs considerably less than a rented telegraph circuit. In addition the circuits are expected to be more reliable because they are working within a Post Office system carrying several hundred other channels and therefore maintained to the highest standards. It seems likely that future requirements for teleprinter channels will be met in this way.

Switching facilities on the BBC inter-office network were located, at the beginning of this period, in The Langham. As much use as possible was made of tape perforators and re-perforators, so that outgoing messages could be dealt with immediately, being stored on tape until the channel for which they were intended became free, when they were transmitted by an automatic tape sender. Switching facilities were provided, but these were used in the main for the allocation of machines to channels rather than for routing through traffic to different destinations. The system was therefore, by modern standards, somewhat wasteful of operator effort.

Shortly after the opening of Broadcasting House Extension in 1960, the London Teleprinter Room was moved from The Langham to the second floor of the Extension. At the same time a new switchboard was built by Lines Department based on two manual switching positions of a type that had been in service in the Post Office network for many years. These boards were dismantled and completely rebuilt with modern equipment, though the old switching techniques were still used. Much of the BBC inter-office traffic was 'multi-destination', so an attempt was made to improve efficiency by providing 'broadcast' facilities, giving simultaneous transmission to a number of destinations in parallel; a number of broadcast 'patterns' could be set up by operating keys in appropriate combinations. To assist in the flow of messages around the teleprinter room a Lamson conveyor belt was installed, and a second Lamson conveyor was used to feed the teleprinter room with the output from the phonogram positions, to which senders of teleprinter messages could telephone them. Received messages could also be telephoned to the addressee, the printed text being sent on to him later. In spite of the improved facilities, it was apparent that circuit switching was not the real answer to the teleprinter communication problem, and that some form of automatic switching would soon be necessary on account of the growing traffic.

In the late 1950s a new 'store and forward' message-switching system was being introduced by STC. This system was known as STRAD (Switching, Transmission, Reception and Distribution of messages) and was based on a new principle; telegraph messages were accepted at a central point, stored by means other than paper tape and transmitted when the destination was able to receive them. It was clear at once that the introduction of such a system would enormously increase the traffic-handling capacity of the BBC teleprinter circuits, but unfortunately it was not possible to demonstrate that the capital cost could be saved within a reasonable period. STC engineers suggested that for such a system to be economic in the BBC it would be necessary to look at the total communication problem, including methods of dealing with spoken and written messages of all kinds.

In 1967 the appearance of a more sophisticated form of message-switching system known as Automatic Data Exchange (ADX)[91] reawakened interest, especially in view of the increasing congestion in the manually operated circuit-switching system. A new study was undertaken, and it was soon established that if the BBC were to invest in a modern message-switching system the cost could be amortised over a period of about five years. As a result of the investigation, STC were asked to design an ADX for the BBC, the system to have a maximum capacity of 150 incoming and 150 outgoing telegraph channels. The result was the ADX 6350, which is built around a central computer, type PDP 9, made by the Digital Equipment Corporation of America; it was put into operation in 1970.

Among the characteristics of the system are:

(i) It is capable of increasing sixfold the utilisation of the telegraph network.

(ii) It accepts immediately traffic presented to it by incoming channels and stores it, however briefly, until the destination is free.

(iii) Messages stored in the system are transmitted to each address immediately after the previous message to that address has ended; thus a continuous stream of traffic is offered to the outgoing channels and a high degree of circuit utilisation is achieved.

(iv) Originators of messages are required to use certain codes in the message 'header'; these codes are used by the ADX to extract the information it needs for routing and destination.

(v) Received messages are printed out on standard size A4 pages. The paging facility means that a long message is prevented from blocking the system; a priority message can be inserted between pages.

(vi) The ADX automatically reports possible faults and other information about the state of the system to the operators, and records all message transmissions.

(vii) A cathode-ray tube displays any message that the system cannot handle because of some irregularity in the address, so that the operator can correct it.

(viii) The Post Office has granted a licence for Telex circuits to be connected directly to the ADX equipment, so that the BBC has unrestricted access to the national and international networks, for its own business only.

(ix) If a power failure occurs, stored programmes and messages are protected; the system can be restarted without loss of information and with minimum delay.

The ADX has made it possible to introduce a news concentration scheme in London, which will considerably reduce the number of teleprinters that newsrooms need for receiving the intake from the agencies. This in turn will lead to a reduction in space requirements and in noise. Another development rendered possible by ADX is the introduction of a 'Rip-and-Read' news service for Regional and Local Radio use. Three minutes before the hour of a news broadcast the latest information is transmitted to those stations that it concerns, and it can be ripped off the teleprinter and read directly. The Rip-and-Read service is operated through Multi-Outstation Selector Units (MOSU) at the ends of the respective channels – at Newcastle, Leeds, Manchester, Birmingham, Bristol, Cardiff and London – for distribution to the Local Radio stations in the area. News material being sent from London to, say, the Birmingham newsroom can be directed to any or all the outstations connected to that particular switching unit: Birmingham newsroom, Radio Birmingham, Radio Leicester, Radio Nottingham, Radio Stoke, and Radio Derby.

The advantages of a message-switching system for routing teleprinter traffic have been fully demonstrated. The EBU is considering the installation of such a system at its Technical Centre in Brussels for handling the large amount of international traffic generated by Eurovision.

The BBC now has a flexible communication system, with considerable capacity for further exploitation, particularly on the telegraph side. If a reasonably priced typewriter became available that gave an additional output in coded form suitable for transmission over the system, and could be used as a piece of normal office equipment, the way in which the BBC conducts the business side of its activities could be completely revolutionised.

12 INTERNATIONAL RELATIONS

During this period BBC engineers continued to play a full part in international conferences and in the detailed work of study groups and working parties of the CCIR, CCITT, EBU, IEC, CISPR, and ISO concerned with broadcasting. Aid to overseas broadcasting authorities continued to be given in the form of secondments of BBC engineers to assist in the planning and establishment of sound broadcasting and television services and in the setting up of training facilities for indigenous staff. As a complement to this, the BBC Engineering Training Department in the UK accepted many overseas trainees for courses in various aspects of broadcasting engineering.

The Atlantic City Administrative Radio Conference organised by the ITU in 1947 had allocated bands of frequencies to the various radio services in the spectrum between 10 kHz and 10 GHz. The next Administrative Radio Conference was held in Geneva in 1959; it revised the Radio Regulations and extended the frequency allocation table upwards to 40 GHz. The BBC was represented at this conference by F. Axon, W. J. Chalk, G. A. Graham and, at intervals, by F. C. McLean. At this conference the growing influence of the African and Asian countries was noticeable.

The BBC was very much concerned with the problem of frequency assignments in the long- and medium-wave bands. The number of stations in Europe working in these bands increased to more than double the number provided for in the Copenhagen Plan of 1948 and many of them were of very high power. BBC engineers carried out a considerable amount of work, particularly on the question of the optimum channel spacing, in preparation for the next Regional Administrative Conference, which is expected to start in 1974. The use of these bands in Africa and Asia reacts on their use within the European Broadcasting Area. A conference was arranged in 1964 to assign frequencies in the African Region, but it broke up on account of political difficulties. A second attempt at such a conference was made in 1966 and it succeeded in agreeing upon a wavelength plan in the remarkably short time of three weeks. A computer at the ITU Headquarters in Geneva was used during the preparation of this plan.

The rapid growth of television and sound broadcasting in the VHF bands, and the impending use of the UHF band for television made it necessary to revise and extend the frequency assignments that had been adopted at the Stockholm Conference of 1952. A further conference was therefore held in Stockholm in 1961, preceded by meetings of experts. The BBC took part in this conference and in the preparations for it. The plan did not include stations with an erp of less than 1 kW in the VHF band or less than 10 kW in the UHF bands, but even so 8000 stations had to be accommodated, compared with about 2500 that were included in the first Stockholm Plan.

The next major conference affecting broadcasting was the World Administrative Radio Conference on Space Telecommunications held in Geneva in 1971. It considered the allocation of frequencies for both communications and broadcasting satellites. BBC engineers had taken part in earlier discussions in an EBU working party to establish the frequency requirements likely to be needed if satellites are used for direct broadcasting in the future. The conference allocated 800 MHz in the 12 GHz band for this purpose, shared with fixed and mobile services and with terrestrial broadcasting services. Parts of the spectrum in the regions of 42 and 85 GHz were also allocated to broadcasting-satellite services.[92]

The CCIR is concerned with technical problems over the whole field of radio-communications. The BBC Engineering Division was strongly represented at all the Plenary Assemblies, which are held every four years, and also in the intermediate meetings of Study Groups – particularly those directly concerned with sound and television broadcasting, which include the recording of sound and of television pictures for broadcasting. The XIth Plenary Assembly held in Oslo in June 1966 was notable for the discussion of the choice of a colour television system for the European Area. The European countries attending were almost equally divided in their support for the PAL and SECAM III systems and the Assembly decided to recognise both systems. At this Assembly L. W. Hayes finally retired from his post as Director Ad Interim and was succeeded by J. Herbstreit of the USA.

The CCIR, and the other agencies of the ITU, are world-wide organisations supported primarily by governments and concerned with a very wide field of activity. The EBU provides a forum for the discussion of technical, as well as programme, administrative and legal problems that are of special interest to its Members in the European Broadcasting Area; its activities are strictly confined to broadcasting. It has been able to make valuable contributions to technical developments in sound and television broadcasting because it is able to arrange joint studies, demonstrations and measurement campaigns by co-operation among small groups of experts who are well known to each other. BBC engineers continue to take an active part in the technical work of the EBU and several of them have been chairmen of working parties and sub-groups. The importance that the BBC attaches to the EBU is indicated by the fact that the Director-General, Charles Curran, like his predecessor Sir Hugh Greene, is a member of the Administrative Council and the BBC's principal representative on the Technical Committee is the present Director of Engineering, J. Redmond.

The Asian Broadcasting Union (ABU) was formed in October 1964. BBC engineers have taken part in its conferences and presented papers to them. They have also taken part in seminars organised for the benefit of members of the Union of National Radio and Television Organisations of Africa (URTNA) founded in 1962 and of the Arab States Broadcasting Union (ASBU) formed in 1969. They have also co-operated in the work of the OIRT through joint meetings between that organisation and the EBU.

The first of the Commonwealth Broadcasting Conferences was held in London in 1945 and the ninth is planned for October 1972 in Kenya. At all the conferences BBC engineers have contributed to the technical aspects of the work and representative papers have been presented, many of them dealing with the problems facing the developing countries. These conferences have cemented valuable personal contacts between broadcasting engineers of the countries of the Commonwealth.

During this period, the BBC Engineering Division continued to devote a substantial effort to assistance to broadcasting organisations in the developing countries. This assistance has included the detachment of staff for surveys and feasibility studies, secondment of staff for tours of duty abroad and the training of staff from overseas at the Engineering Training Centre. As one of the most difficult problems facing the developing countries is to find sufficient trained staff to operate their radio and television services, stress has been laid on advising them how to set up their own training facilities and train potential teachers among their engineers.

Between 1956 and 1971 the number of BBC engineers on secondment overseas, usually for two years at a time, averaged sixteen; the peak figure in 1958 having been thirty-three. As many of these engineers had experience over the whole field of broadcasting, their absence constituted an appreciable drain on the BBC's resources of manpower.

In 1957 D. B. Weigall visited Kenya to advise on the development of radio broadcasting there. In 1959 W. A. Roberts went to Kenya and Uganda as a member of a commission to make recommendations for the setting up of a television service. H. W. Baker visited the Republic of Ireland in October 1959 to advise on the project for a television centre in Dublin. Other visits included those by D. E. Todd to Saudi Arabia and to Nigeria and by R. F. Vigurs to New York to exchange experience with CBS on the launching of a colour television service.

In January 1965 E. L. E. Pawley made a survey in Libya and produced a plan for a major project for the development of the existing radio broadcasting facilities and for the introduction of a television service. A. C. Rothney of the Transmitter Group later visited Libya to make recommendations on sites for transmitting stations and H. Henderson made plans for the training of local staff. Another BBC engineer, N. C. Davey, was appointed as Project Supervisor for the installation work and four other BBC engineers were seconded to assist in starting the new services and in training local staff in operational work. Davey succeeded, by a prodigious effort, in getting the television station in Tripoli working by 25 December 1968 – the date of the King's birthday.

Several BBC engineers have held senior posts in broadcasting organisations abroad; for instance, D. B. Weigall was Chief Engineer of the Malaya Broadcasting Corporation from 1940 to 1942 and A. W. Busby was Chief Engineer of the Ghana Broadcasting Service from 1953 to 1958. BBC engineers have also served in Ceylon, Gilbert & Ellice Islands, Guyana, Iran, Kenya, Laos, Lesotho, Malaysia, Malawi, Nepal, Qatar, Southern Yemen, Thailand, Uganda and Zambia.

The first Overseas Management Conference was held by the BBC at Wood Norton in 1970. In addition to talks by BBC staff, including engineers, eminent guest speakers gave the visitors the benefit of their experience of various aspects of broadcasting.

The BBC receiving station at Tatsfield is an important link with the outside world. Transmissions from the USSR satellite Sputnik I were first observed there on 5 October 1957 after the Monitoring Service at Caversham had heard a report of the launching from Moscow. Frequency measurements and tape recordings of the signals were made at Tatsfield and information was supplied to the BBC News Services. The information provided by Tatsfield created great interest in the British Press. All the later Sputniks were watched and, later, speech was received from the manned 'Vostok' satellites. At a time when it was widely believed that only one Vostok was in operation, Tatsfield recorded conversations between the crews of two of these space vehicles.

13 RESEARCH AND DEVELOPMENT

Television, and colour television in particular, attracted a great deal of research and development effort during this period. There were extensive field trials and laboratory tests to evaluate the various colour systems and establish their potential, and much detailed research as well.

A demonstration of the NTSC system adapted to 405 lines was given in April 1956 to a CCIR working party that had been set up to determine what colour television system should be used in Europe. Demonstrations were also given by the BBC to the Postmaster-General, the Television Advisory Committee, and the BBC Board of Management. At the end of January 1957, a further demonstration was given to both Houses of Parliament at Westminster. Experimental colour transmissions in Band I were made with this system in 1957–8.[93, 94] The results were assessed by non-technical as well as technical observers viewing the transmissions at home. The tests established the soundness of the NTSC system, and in the process a great deal of valuable experience in the operation of a colour service was gained. During the same period extensive field trials were made to determine the relative performance of 405-line and 625-line transmissions in black-and-white and the relative advantages of the VHF and UHF bands.[96]

The Television Advisory Committee issued a report on 17 May 1960, in which it concluded that the existing 405-line system would not be adequate for all purposes for the next twenty-five years, that a 625-line system on 8-MHz channels would offer worth-while improvements over the 405-line system, and that a fully compatible colour system was required. The Committee recommended that a system of the NTSC type could be used, but colour should be introduced only on the line standards to be ultimately adopted for monochrome television. A decision on colour would therefore have to await a decision on line standards.[95] The Committee on Broadcasting (the Pilkington Committee) considered these conclusions in detail and the Government decided that colour should be introduced on 625 lines only; a new programme, BBC-2, and duplicated transmissions of BBC-1 and the ITA programme were to be broadcast on UHF.[62, 63]

The 'battle for the system' had not yet been fought out. By early 1963 three systems were in being: the original NTSC system, which has been described in chapter V, section 5, and two variants of it PAL and SECAM, which will be mentioned later in this section. A great deal of careful investigation was done in the early 1960s by the BBC Research and Designs Departments to determine their relative merits. The results of this work were presented in no fewer than seventy technical documents, many of them describing highly complex experiments, to the EBU Ad-hoc Group on Colour Television. This group was set up in November 1962 and included representatives of the broadcasting organisations in France, Germany, Italy, Norway, Holland and the UK (BBC and ITA), together with representatives of the PTT Administrations and of the industry in Western Europe. The Ad-hoc Group was under the chairmanship of Prof. R. Theile, Director of the IRT, Munich; the BBC representatives, F. C. McLean and Dr R. D. A. Maurice, played an active part in it, supported by the impressive efforts made by the Engineering Division to establish the merits of the three systems by extensive experiments and theoretical work.

In September 1962 the BBC had started another series of colour transmissions on 625 lines, which were radiated from the Crystal Palace station with an erp of 125 kW in Bands IV and V. At first only the NTSC system was used, but in 1963 comparative tests were made with all three systems, using slides, films and still pictures. These trials, and the intensive background studies associated with them, established that the PAL system was acceptable.

The results of the two series of field trials, in which the Post Office, the DSIR, the ITA and the Industry co-operated, were published in two substantial volumes, in the same format as the series of Engineering Monographs; one volume compared the results obtained with 405-line monochrome transmissions in Bands I and V with those on 625 lines in Band V, concluding that the 625-line standard would be preferable; the other compared 625-line monochrome with colour transmissions on the NTSC, PAL and SECAM systems. Both series of trials were concerned with standards of reception, taking propagation factors into account.[96, 97]

To illustrate the performance of the three systems under all circumstances likely to exist in practice, demonstrations had to be arranged under carefully controlled conditions. The first was given by the BBC in London in November 1962 and others took place in Hanover, Paris, Eindhoven, Berne and Rome in 1963. A second demonstration in London in July 1963 to EBU and OIRT delegates was organised by the BBC, the GPO, the ITA/ITCA and British industry. Further demonstrations were given to the TAC and other interested bodies, and later to the Colour Sub-group of Study Group XI of the CCIR.

A notable demonstration was given in Moscow at the end of 1964, as the result of a request from the USSR to the BBC. A competitive demonstration of the SECAM system was given by French engineers. Complete coding equipment was taken by the BBC team to Moscow, with a Cintel slide scanner as a source of pictures; a successful demonstration was also given of pictures sent from London on all three systems, PAL, SECAM, and NTSC, through the Eurovision and Intervision networks. It subsequently came to light that the USSR was already committed to the SECAM system.

The EBU Ad-hoc Group on Colour Television studied every aspect affecting the choice of colour system through six sub-groups concerned with the general characteristics of the systems, receivers, propagation, transmitters, distribution networks, and studio and recording equipment. The massive amount of data that it produced was placed at the disposal of the CCIR, which ultimately had the task of making recommendations on the subject to the government agencies throughout the world that constituted its membership.

Within the United Kingdom six committees had been set up to study the various aspects of the problem; these included representatives from the BBC, the ITA/ITCA, the Post Office, BREMA, EEA, RECMF, DSIR and Mullard Research. The basic principles of all three systems were the same, namely the transmission of the luminance signal on the main carrier with two colour components transmitted on a subcarrier within the luminance band. Most of the equipment, including the cameras and display tubes, was common to all three systems, only the method of coding and decoding and equipment that depended on those methods, being different. The BBC was, at that time, strongly in favour of adopting the NTSC system, because it was the only one that had proved itself in a public service, as it had done in the USA. There was clearly a wide gap between a reliable and effective public service and a successful series of laboratory experiments. The SECAM and PAL variants therefore came as unwelcome complications. The principal object of the alternative systems was to avoid two of the shortcomings of the NTSC system, namely its susceptibility to phase errors (such as could occur in transmission over long circuits) and the need for a hue control in the receiver.

The SECAM system was developed in France from a suggestion by Henri de France that the vertical definition of the colour components need not be as high as that of the black-and-white picture.[98] In the original SECAM (Séquentiel Couleur à Mémoire) system the two colour components were transmitted alternately during successive lines using amplitude modulation of a sub-carrier, and the receiver was provided with a delay line to permit the simultaneous display of the information derived from both chrominance components. In 1960 the SECAM system was modified by using frequency modulation of the sub-carrier for the chrominance components instead of amplitude modulation; this greatly improved the performance in fringe areas. Further modifications intended to improve the compatibility of the system resulted in SECAM II and SECAM III; by 1965 SECAM III was the preferred form.

At a late stage the USSR introduced a further variant known as SECAM IV or NIIR. It arrived too late to be adopted internationally. The idea on which it was based had been put forward by a BBC engineer, B. W. B. Pethers, some years earlier, but not published. In this system all the colour information is sent on alternate lines and a reference sub-carrier on the other lines, thus avoiding the need for a colour burst such as is inserted in the back porch of the horizontal scanning in the other systems to maintain colour synchronisation. The suggestion was not pursued when it was first put forward in the BBC because there were already three competing systems and another would have introduced further delay into the final choice.[48, 99]

Early in 1963 the German Federal Republic put forward the PAL (Phase Alternation Line) system, which had been invented by Dr Walter Bruch of the Telefunken Company.[100, 101] In this system the polarity of one of the two chrominance components was reversed during alternate line periods. This reversal could be compensated by the use of a delay line in the receiver.

It was unfortunate from the BBC point of view that the three competing systems involved the national prestige of the countries where they originated: the USA, France and the German Federal Republic. The BBC's main interest was to choose a system that would give the best possible service to viewers at the minimum cost to them; any complications that might arise in the origination and transmission of programmes were a secondary consideration.

At the Eleventh Plenary Assembly of the CCIR in Oslo in 1966 the UK delegation supported the PAL system in the hope that this would be adopted in at least a large number of countries in Europe. The Postmaster General had previously announced that unless agreement was reached at Oslo on some other system for general use in Europe the UK would adopt PAL. The Oslo meeting was unable to reach agreement on a single system for Europe and it had to content itself with specifying the characteristics of the three systems. This result created a dramatic moment in the meeting of the General Assembly of the EBU that was being held in Dublin at the same time as the Plenary Assembly of the CCIR. The Chairman of the Technical Committee was in the middle of presenting his report when he was called away to take an urgent telephone message from Oslo. On returning to the meeting he was greeted with undeserved applause, but had to report that no agreement had been reached.

The CCIR debate brought the long saga to an end and the BBC formerly introduced colour into its BBC-2 transmissions in December 1967 using the PAL system, after a six-month launching period. Subsequent experience has amply confirmed the wisdom of the decision. The system has proved to be thoroughly practical in operation, resistant to phase and differential phase distortion and capable of producing excellent colour pictures. It is well-adapted to reception in difficult conditions and gives satisfactory black-and-white pictures on monochrome receivers.

By 1972, although the USA, Canada and Japan had naturally retained the NTSC system on the 525-line standard, most countries in Western Europe and also Turkey Iran, Australia, Brazil and some Asian countries, had decided for PAL, while France, the USSR, some of the Eastern European countries and some others in the Near East, had opted for SECAM.

From 1963 onwards there was a great deal of interest in electronic standards converters using solid-state techniques. Both Research and Designs Departments developed line-store converters, working on the same principles, but with different instrumentation.[102, 103] They sampled the incoming signal, stored it, and then re-sampled the stored signal to give an output at the other standard. This was a most important development; with the start of BBC-2 the following year two line-standards would be current, 405 for BBC-1 and 625 for BBC-2, and it was vital to be able to convert readily from one to the other without loss of quality. BBC converters were the first all-electronic standards converters in the world. One was demonstrated to the Press on 20 August 1963. P. Rainger received the Geoffrey Parr award of the Royal Television Society for his part in this achievement. Both converters were installed at the Television Centre in 1964 for conversion from 625 to 405 lines. The Research Department model was adapted to work in either direction in June of that year.

Neither of these line-store converters could cope with different field frequencies and there was a need for a converter that would enable video-tape recordings or live pictures to be exchanged in colour with countries using the 525-line 60-field standard. Development work to this end was begun in 1963 by two teams, one in Research and the other in Designs Department. This was a far more difficult task, calling for much longer storage periods. However, by August 1967 Rainger's team in the Designs Department had solved the problem and produced a field-store converter that accepted American NTSC colour pictures on the 525/60 standard and transformed them to the European PAL 625/50 system, though with a slight reduction in picture height and width. This was the first electronic field-store converter, an outstanding achievement which earned no fewer than three awards – an 'Emmy' (given by the National Academy of Television Arts & Sciences in the USA), a J. J. Thomson premium (awarded by the IEE) and a Geoffrey Parr award (from the Royal Television

Society). Two converters of this type were installed at the Television Centre in time for the Mexico Olympics in October 1968.

An even more advanced design was produced by E. R. Rout and his team in the Research Department.[104, 105] Described as the most intricate and sophisticated piece of equipment the BBC had ever used for television, this converter was the complete solution to the problem, producing full-sized pictures and having many other advantages. It made its début for the Mexico Olympic Games in 1968, producing colour pictures on the 625/50 PAL standard for Europe and for the BBC's transmitter network from the American NTSC transmissions received by satellite across the Atlantic. A second model, for converting 625/50 PAL pictures to 525/60 NTSC, was ready at the end of June, and was used when the Investiture of the Prince of Wales was shown in colour in America and Japan on 1 July 1969.

The advanced field-store converter won for the BBC its first Queen's Award to Industry in 1969. Field-Marshal Sir Gerald Templer made the presentation to the Chairman, Lord Hill, on 22 July 1969. It also earned Rout a Geoffrey Parr award, and R. E. Davies, one of the Research Department team, a Pye award.

In 1971 an experimental line-store standards converter using digital processing techniques for converting from 625 to 405 lines was demonstrated by the Research Department.[106] This was one of the first-fruits of a fundamental study of the application of digital techniques to television signals. An analogue-to-digital converter and a digital-to-analogue converter had been developed first, followed by means for processing the digital signals so as to re-form them on a different line standard. The converter was demonstrated most successfully and will, no doubt, be the basis for the next generation of line-store converters. The advantages of digital operation suggest that it will be applied in the future to other processes, such as video-tape recording.

Digital methods were also applied to sound signals. During 1966 work started in the Research Department on what came to be known as Sound-in-Syncs; a method of incorporating the sound component of a television programme in the vision waveform for transmission over the distribution and contribution networks, using pulse-code modulation. In 1968 field trials were successfully carried out between London and the Kirk o'Shotts transmitter, near Falkirk, and also between London and Copenhagen via Brussels and Frankfurt. The practical advantages of this system have been mentioned in section 10 of this chapter. Equipment working on this principle was developed for use on the network and in 1971 it was successfully adapted for television OBs.[88, 89, 107, 108, 109]

Cablefilm, a method of transmitting film pictures over two telephone channels in the Atlantic cable, together occupying a band between 0·5 and 5·6 kHz, was perfected jointly by the Research and Designs Departments in 1959. At the sending end a film was scanned at low speed (about one-hundredth of normal speed), at the receiving end the pictures were displayed on a tube with a very long delay time and photographed on another film.[110, 111] The practical applications of this system are mentioned in section 9 of this chapter.

At the beginning of the period much work was done on methods of recording television on film. In 1957 Research Department produced the stored field system, in which the full picture information was recorded. An improved version of this, using a rapid pull-down camera, was produced by the Planning and Installation Department in 1959.[70] Another development, which initially showed great promise but was overtaken by a gifted competitor, was VERA, the video-tape recorder designed and made by the Research Department in 1958.[72] All these advances have been dealt with in section 8 of this chapter.

It was important that the pictures derived from the three, or four, tubes in a colour camera were accurately registered. The advantages of achieving this automatically were obvious and both the Research and the Designs Departments developed techniques for it. The problem was also tackled by the industry and the Marconi Mark VIII camera included this feature.[112]

Two types of apparatus were produced for improving the colour rendering of televised films. They resulted in pictures much better than those obtained by optical projection of the film and helped to eliminate the difference between the colour values of film inserts and those of live pictures from the studio. One of these electronic equipments was TARIF (television apparatus for the rectification of inferior film) which enabled an operator to remove colour casts by making adjustments according to settings determined during a pre-view of the film; the equipment could also be programmed by a punched tape. A second type of equipment used a matrix to correct errors caused by the characteristics of the dyes used in the film to produce the negative colour primaries (cyan, magenta, and yellow).[113] Both these devices were adopted by the industry for commercial sale. Negative film was preferred for transmission, because the colour quality and definition were impaired when prints were made; but the use of negative film was restricted because the single original had to be for transmission.

Work on colour television necessitated the development of specialised laboratory equipment. An example of this was the tristimulus spot colorimeter, which enabled objective measurements to be made of colours displayed on the screen of a monitor.[114]

Methods had been devised for synchronising pictures coming from different sources, for instance, from a remote OB point and from a local studio. Even with black-and-white television the synchronisation had to be sufficiently accurate to permit split-screen working; for colour the requirements were even more severe and the synchronisation was achieved by the use of pulse-generators, controlled by extremely accurate crystal oscillators, the frequency of which was locked to the spectrum frequency of rubidium.

An inherent limitation to the definition of television pictures is the size of the scanning spot used in cameras and telecine machines. As a result of work done largely in the Research Department, vertical aperture correctors were produced which, by electronic means, sharpen the edges of horizontal lines in the picture.

Meanwhile, research in the traditional fields was continuing. The Research Department took a leading part in the development of high-quality loudspeakers for monitoring.[149] For this purpose a simple method was developed of making loudspeaker cones of repeatable performance from a plastic material.

523

The Acoustics Section of Research Department moved from Nightingale Square to Kingswood Warren in May 1961, the last unit to do so. A new 'dead' room for sound measurement was completed there in 1963.[17] In 1967 the pulse method of determining the reverberation times of studios was carried a stage further by using recordings for the test signal and recording the response of the studio; the results were processed on a computer.[21] A versatile tool for the solution of problems in the acoustic design of studios was the use of one-eighth scale models, in conjunction with miniature microphones and loudspeakers; the sounds used for the experiments were at frequencies eight times those in the normal audio-frequency range. This method, which had been pioneered in Germany, was applied to the redesign of the studios at Maida Vale.[117]

Important work was done in the Research Department on the propagation of television signals at UHF. A series of measurement campaigns was mounted to determine the characteristics of propagation over long paths, including those over the sea, to determine the strength of interfering signals at considerable distances. A comprehensive study[96] was also made of propagation within the service area; the strength of the received signal depends not only on the distance between the transmitting and receiving aerials, and on their respective heights, but also upon the intervening topography. The results of the measurements were translated into formulae, which have since been adopted as international recommendations; the BBC Research Department has indeed been a major contributor for many years to the work of the CCIR in this field. Computer programs have been developed that make use of empirical formulae, both for the calculation of interference at long distances and for the computation of the wanted field strength within the service area of the transmitting station.

The results of these studies were applied to the planning of the fifty main UHF stations and 450 relay stations that had to be established to carry BBC-1, BBC-2 and the ITV programmes, with a fourth channel still unallocated. The choice of sites was done in close co-operation with the Site Acquisition Unit of the Transmitter Group and with the ITA and the Post Office.[118, 119, 120]. The foundations for this work had been laid in 1957–8 when extensive VHF and UHF field trials were carried out from the Crystal Palace station.[96, 121, 122]

Much work was done on the design of VHF and UHF aerials. A sixteen-tier vertically polarised aerial was developed for mounting inside a cylinder of glass-fibre (glass-reinforced plastic) 16 in. in diameter. This was widely used at UHF relay stations. The use of larger cylinders would have permitted the aerial to be inspected or repaired *in situ*, but reflections from the surface of a large cylinder were found to affect the characteristics of the aerial to an unacceptable extent.[123-127] (Cylinders up to 6 ft in diameter were used at main stations where the aerial elements were symmetrically disposed in relation to the central supporting structure.) An aerial in the form of a printed panel was developed for UHF relay stations.[128] At the same time important work was being done on sky-wave propagation at medium frequencies.[129, 130]

Reference has been made in the previous section to the forthcoming conference on the revision of the Copenhagen Plan for frequency assignments to long- and medium-wave broadcasting stations in the European Broadcasting Area. The Research Department is much concerned with the preparatory work for this conference because, if it is to be a success, it is essential to explore every possibility of reducing mutual interference between stations by the application of new knowledge on the effects of the terrain on propagation, the use of directional transmitting aerials, the reduction of the bandwidth occupied by a broadcast transmission and the increased use of sky-wave propagation to serve large areas at night. The Research Department is contributing to international studies of these possibilities. Experimental work has shown that limitation of the bandwidth of long- and medium-wave transmissions to about half the channel-spacing could be advantageous, but that the use of single-sideband transmission in these bands must be relegated to a more distant future, since it would be incompatible with existing receivers.

Preliminary theoretical work was done on the possible conditions of use for broadcasting satellites, particularly for television. It was evident that it would be many years before the use of satellites would be practicable for this purpose (see section 9 of this chapter) and even then the cost seems likely to be very great. The preliminary work was mainly directed towards the World Administrative Radio Conference on Space Telecommunications held in 1971.

Research into stereophonic broadcasting started in 1958 and continued with a thorough investigation into every aspect of the subject, including a series of full-scale field trials from Wrotham, using the compatible Zenith-GE pilot-tone system. The steps leading up to the introduction of stereophonic broadcasting have been described in section 1 of this chapter.[6-9]

The Designs Department put into practical form many of the developments that had been made in Research Department and elsewhere, and also put into effect many of their own ideas. They produced a VHF/FM crystal-controlled stereo receiver of such high quality that it could be used for rebroadcasting without any significant deterioration in the signal. Towards the end of the 1950s they developed a complete range of transistorised amplifiers for sound broadcasting, which were widely used in sound control rooms and studios and gradually replaced the valve amplifiers of an earlier era.[131] A programme effects generator was produced that enabled a wide range of sound effects to be reproduced from tapes stored in cassettes, which could be instantly brought into use by means of an ingenious electro-mechanical system.[11] Since the beginning of broadcasting it has been necessary for an operator to control the volume of programmes at or near the source so as to keep the dynamic range within prescribed limits. The problem of devising automatic equipment to carry out this function had proved intractable for many years because of the difficulty of matching in an electronic apparatus the judgement and foresight of a skilled operator. A considerable advance was made by the development of an automatic control system, which was used in 'self-operated' sound studios and also in television studios.[132] It is widely used in Local Radio studios.

Early in this period the Designs Department developed an improved model of the 'Roving Eye', a single-camera self-contained mobile television OB unit for obtaining live news material.[133] During 1961–2 they designed a range of transistorised television amplifiers for use in studio centres. Their work on automatic monitors for both sound and television continued throughout this period.[14, 15] In 1967 a slow-motion video-tape recorder was produced, which filled an urgent need at the time,[77] but was supplanted by the later development of the video disc. A particularly interesting application of new techniques was an electronic character generator, known as ANCHOR, which produced captions by electronic means.[135] A major advance in the switching of television signals was the development of a solid-state video switching system, sufficiently rapid in operation to permit switching during the field sync period and meeting stringent requirements for linearity and crosstalk.[136] Fifty of these matrices were manufactured between 1968 and 1970.

To complete the VHF and UHF transmitter networks, a great many relay stations were required and it was important that they should be simple and reliable, and able to work unattended. Whenever possible transposers were used, which received the signals from a parent station and re-transmitted them on another group of channels without demodulation. The Designs Department developed a range of transposers for television and others for sound broadcasting. The early designs used valves[137] but in 1964 a transistorised UHF translator was designed.[138] A transportable UHF radio-link equipment for television OBs was produced in 1957–8.[139]

An advance in sound studio facilities was the RP2/6 disc reproducer, which had a 'jump-start' facility; the starting point on a record was located with the needle on the disc and the turntable, already rotating, was raised up to the record by pressing a button to give an instant start on the cue.

Much of the work of the Research and Designs Departments is directed towards the production of specialised equipment. Early in the period a procedure was set up to ensure that any equipment, whether designed by the BBC or purchased from a manufacturer, that was to be included in the transmission chain or permanently associated with it, was approved and registered. (Transmitters and some other items of radio and television equipment purchased from outside were exempted from this procedure.) The approval has to be given by the Design Co-ordination Committee, which was set up in 1947, to avoid any unproductive duplication between the work of the specialist departments or between them and the industry, and also to ensure that any equipment brought into use would be acceptable to the users and would conform with BBC standards of performance, reliability, robustness and ease of maintenance. Most of the equipment required is purchased from the industry, but the Equipment Department manufacturers specialised items to BBC designs that are not available commercially. Its workshops and stores continued to keep pace with modern requirements and its test rooms were equipped to deal with a wide range of items.[140] The department is also responsible for the BBC's transport fleet; by 1972 it included 876 vehicles, which travelled seven million miles in a year.

Standardisation within the BBC, and with the world outside, was necessary to simplify maintenance and reduce costs. During this period BBC engineers continued to co-operate with the organisations concerned with standards in various fields: the BSI and the industrial associations (BREMA and EEA) in this country, and the IEC, EBU, ITU, CCIR, CMTT and IFRB on the international plane. Dimensional standards for many items of equipment and components were essential; performance standards facilitated the testing and acceptance of equipment; agreed standards of operation, testing and acceptance of equipment; agreed standards of operation, testing and terminology were essential for the international exchange of programmes. Following the recommendations of the BSI published in 1964 the BBC adopted the International System of Units (SI Units) for scientific work.[141, 142] The system is founded on six basic units (metre, kilogramme, second, ampere, degree Kelvin and candela) from which all others, and preferred multiples and sub-multiples of them, are derived. In the field of terminology, a glossary of technical terms had been published in the *BBC Handbook* as early as 1929 and the *BBC Glossary* embracing the whole field of broadcasting had been produced during the war. It has not been found possible to publish a more up-to-date version of the latter (now out of print), but many of the technical terms that would have been included in it have been defined in BSI publications.[143] Some help was given to the ARD in the preparation of an Anglo-German dictionary of broadcasting terms to be published on the occasion of the Olympic Games in Munich in 1972.

An important function of the specialist departments is to provide the BBC Management with advice necessary for the formulation of engineering policy. Another is to make the results of their work widely available by publication and by participating in the work of societies concerned with the advancement of professional standards in the application of engineering to broadcasting. BBC engineers have played an active part in the work of these societies. The Engineering Division has provided two Presidents of the IEE (Sir Noel Ashbridge in 1941 and Sir Harold Bishop in 1953), and five chairmen of the Electronics Division and its predecessors: H. Bishop (1941), H. L. Kirke (1944), R. T. B. Wynn (1949), M. J. L. Pulling (1959) and G. G. Gouriet (1964). Other BBC engineers have been members of the IEE Council and of its committees and nearly two hundred papers have been contributed by BBC authors to the publications of the Institution.

At the International Television Conference held in London in 1962 by the IEE, the IRE of America, the Television Society and the British Kinematograph Society, thirty of the 123 papers were presented by BBC engineers. The Faraday Lecture of 1948 was given by Sir Noel Ashbridge and H. Bishop on 'Television' and that of 1963–4, on 'Colour Television', by F. C. McLean and M. J. L. Pulling. The close association between the BBC and the IEE over the years was described on the occasion of the IEE's Centenary in 1971 in an article by the BBC's Director of Engineering.[144]

The BBC was associated with the British Institution of Radio Engineers (now the Institution of Electronic and Radio Engineers) from its foundation in 1925. BBC engineers have played a prominent part in its activities and have contributed some thirty papers to its journal.

Sir Harold Bishop was President of the Royal Television Society in 1961–2 and four BBC engineers have been chairman of its Council. T. H. Bridgewater has served as its Hon. Treasurer since 1957. Thirty papers have been contributed to the Society's Journal by members of the Engineering Division. Sir Harold Bishop was President of the Association of Supervising Electrical Engineers from 1956 to 1958; he was also the first President of the Institution of Electrical & Electronic Technician Engineers, founded in 1965, and other BBC engineers have taken part in its work. J. Redmond, the present Director of Engineering, was President of the Society of Electronic & Radio Technicians in 1970.

BBC engineers have also contributed widely to the technical press. A long series of papers appeared in the *BBC Quarterly* from April 1946 to October 1954, in the eighty *BBC Engineering Monographs* published between June 1955 and December 1969, and in the periodical *BBC Engineering* from January 1970 onwards. 'Information Sheets' on technical matters have been issued by the Engineering Information Department whenever the need has arisen for guidance to be given to the public or to radio dealers on reception problems and other points of interest. Lists of BBC stations and service area maps are also issued from time to time. The department keeps in touch with the Press on technical matters and also takes part in exhibitions and demonstrations illustrating BBC activities. The Technical Publications Section of the Engineering Training Department has, through the years, produced an impressive series of technical instructions for the guidance of BBC engineers concerned with the operation and maintenance of equipment. Several retired members of staff have been re-employed part-time to assist in this work. A series of 'BBC Engineering Training Manuals' by BBC staff has been issued by a commercial publisher (see list of references).

Since 1926 some 350 British patents have been granted for inventions by BBC staff, almost all of them members of the Engineering Division. Between sixty and seventy of these patents are still in force and further applications continue at the rate of about twenty each year. Occasionally, applications have also been filed abroad. Licences are granted to manufacturers on agreed conditions to make use of BBC patents. Among the most important, in their time, have been those relating to acoustics and sound absorbers, transmitting aerials (including slot aerials (1949)), receiving aerials, circuits (including a cathode-follower circuit (1938), various types of modulator, and applications of negative feedback), transformers, filters and attenuators, several forms of automatic monitor, frequency-dividers and multipliers, measuring equipment, limiters and volume compressors, loudspeakers, microphones (including the ribbon (1934) and lip (1937) microphones), oscillators, sound recording and reproducing equipment (including radius compensation (1934)), video-tape equipment (including a drop-out compensator (1964)), television recording on film, bandwidth compression, several types of television standards converter, pulse-code systems and digital techniques.

14 FINANCE, STAFF AND ORGANISATION

Methods of budgeting, financial control, stores control and the allocation of resources were strengthened and streamlined during this period by increasing use of computers, of which the BBC had six in operation in 1972.[145, 146] Computers were also increasingly used for engineering calculations, notably in connection with field-strength studies, and aerial design. The progress of capital projects was kept under close scrutiny with the aid of modern techniques.

Capital expenditure by the BBC, for most of which the Engineering Division was responsible, amounted to £4·028 million in 1955–6 and rose (though by no means uniformly) to £13·216 million in 1970–1. The number of Engineering staff rose from 4997 in 1956 to 7051 in 1969. The increase was a modest one, when compared with the massive expansion of programme output and transmitter coverage, and the increase in the scale of capital projects, that took place during the period. It was contained by economies in manpower, mainly achieved by introducing automatic methods of working – especially at transmitting stations; more and more stations were automated so as to do without staff altogether. This policy released skilled staff from routine duties for more rewarding activity.

The 1960s marked the end of an era. The senior people who had guided the Engineering Division for so long gradually vanished from the scene to be replaced by the new men. The first of the old guard to go was R. T. B. Wynn, who had been Chief Engineer since 1952 and had in 1958 become the Hon. R. T. B. Wynn; he retired in 1960, to be succeeded by F. C. McLean (as Deputy Director of Engineering rather than Chief Engineer). M. T. Tudsbery, the BBC's Civil Engineer since 1926, also retired in 1960 and R. H. S. Howell became Head of Building Department. Sir Harold Bishop who had become Director of Technical Services in 1952 (the title was changed to Director of Engineering in 1956), withdrew into very active retirement in 1963; he had completed forty years' service with the BBC, the first man ever to have done so. In its Annual Report for that year, the BBC paid him this tribute – 'Sir Harold Bishop has been responsible during his long service for helping to provide great pleasure for many millions of listeners and both the country and the BBC owe him a great debt of gratitude. He has also laid firm foundations for the future developments which are to take place.'

Many other familiar figures in the upper levels of the Engineering Division, some of them with service going back to the days of the Company, left the scene during the period. Among those with the longest service were E. G. Chadder, who joined in 1923 and had been Senior Superintendent Engineer since 1952; E. F. Wheeler, who joined in 1924 and had been Superintendent Engineer, Transmitters, for seventeen years; F. Williams, who joined a year later and had been in charge of Operations and Maintenance (Sound Broadcasting) for twelve years; and W. Proctor Wilson, who had come to the BBC in 1927 and had been Head of the Research Department for fourteen years. Out of the twenty-four most senior people in the Engineering Division in 1963 – directors, heads of departments, and superintendents – only one (J. Redmond, now Director of Engineering) was still among them nine years later.

In 1962 the engineering management team was enlarged by the addition of an Assistant Director and from then on it continued as a triumvirate. M. J. L. Pulling was the first Assistant Director of Engineering. On Sir Harold Bishop's departure in 1963, F. C. McLean became Director of Engineering with Pulling as his deputy, and D. B. Weigall became Assistant Director. Sir Francis McLean received his knighthood in the New Year Honours of 1 January 1967. Pulling's turn to retire came in

1967, and J. Redmond, who had been Senior Superintendent Engineer, Television, since 1963, then joined the triumvirate as Assistant Director. The following year, on McLean's retirement, he became Director of Engineering, with Weigall as Deputy Director and D. E. Todd as Assistant Director. When Weigall's time was up in 1971 Todd became Deputy Director and T. B. McCrirrick, who had been Chief Engineer Radio Broadcasting since 1970, was appointed Assistant Director.

The first significant reorganisation during the period took place in 1957, when the Recording Department, which had been set up under Pulling in 1942, was merged with the operating departments for home and external radio. In the early days of recording the equipment required a good deal of watchful attention, and considerable expertise to get the best results. But with the move from disc to tape recording equipment and the gradual improvement in its performance and reliability over the years, recording ceased to need a separate specialised staff. At the same time there was more work requiring operational skill and experience, and less requiring fundamental engineering knowledge. A new category of technical operators was therefore introduced and staff in the engineer and technical assistant categories were thenceforth engaged solely on maintenance work. A. P. Monson, who was Superintendent Engineer, Recording, at the time, became Superintendent Engineer, Sound Broadcasting, upon this reorganisation.

In 1964 the time-honoured division of engineers in the Regions into three groups – television, sound and lines – which had evolved naturally over the years, was abolished. A new pattern with three strands – operations, services, and communications – was adopted. Communications embraced radio links as well as line transmission, and services included the maintenance of equipment, transport, and minor building work. The intension was to eliminate some overlapping that had existed in the original structure, to create an organisation better matched to the work it had to do, and to cut down on the number of staff needed. This reorganisation brought with it a measure of devolution. Previously all the engineering staff in the Regions had reported to the corresponding Superintendent Engineers in London. This close control from London was loosened a little; all the engineering staff in a Region reported to the Regional Head of Engineering and he in turn was responsible to the Chief Engineers, Television and Radio. At the same time a new section in the Engineering Personnel Department was created to administer the staff in the Regions.

During 1967 there were changes in the television organisation under T. H. Bridgewater, then Chief Engineer, Television. With the translation of Redmond to the engineering direction team in May, the post of Senior Superintendent Engineer, Television, lapsed and two Assistant Chief Engineers were created, one responsible for operations and the other for developments. Under them came six Heads of Engineering, dealing with studios, recording, outside broadcasts, the network, news, and services.

During 1968 the firm of McKinsey, management consultants, was engaged by the BBC to examine its operations. They recommended that managerial responsibilities should be defined with more precision and that the accountability of managers for their use of resources should be stressed. These recommendations were accepted, and as a result all the technical staff working in the television, radio, and external broadcasting services were transferred from the Engineering Division to the television, radio, and external broadcasting directorates. This took place in February 1969. The Managing Directors of the three output directorates then became responsible for the economic deployment of their technical staff. The Director of Engineering, however, continued to be responsible for their professional and technical standards. About 2600 people out of a total of 7050 were directly involved in this move. The Transmitter Group, the Communications Department and the Chief Engineer, Regions, with all the specialist, personnel and service departments, remained on the establishment of the Director of Engineering.

During the following year the same policy was followed in the English Regions (South & West, Midland, and North), when the technical staff were placed on the Regional establishments. Two of the national Regions – Scotland and Northern Ireland – followed suit in 1971, and Wales in 1972. The continued use of preferred types of equipment and of uniform operational methods throughout the BBC was assured by the fact that all the engineers were still responsible to the Director of Engineering for professional standards.

The title of Chief Engineer, which had lapsed on R. T. B. Wynn's retirement in 1960, was revived in 1962. Previously it had always been an exclusive title, but in that year five Chief Engineers were created, for television, radio, external broadcasting, transmitters, and communications. More were added later – research and development, external relations, capital projects, and, for a time, administration.

The new equipment, buildings and methods that were being introduced in the BBC evoked much interest abroad. Engineers from broadcasting organisations in other countries were welcome visitors in considerable numbers. In 1959 an Engineering Liaison Officer was appointed to organise these visits and international meetings of engineers held in this country at the invitation of the BBC. He was also expected to put the visitors in touch with British firms that could supply equipment to meet their needs. The first holder of the post was Brigadier W. G. Tucker, who had just retired as Deputy Signal Officer-in-Chief at the War Office. He carried out his new duties with great éclat until his retirement in 1970. One of his toughest assignments was to find a new propeller for an ocean-going cruiser belonging to a distinguished visitor– not an easy task on a Sunday morning in Edinburgh.

The graduate apprenticeship scheme, which had been launched in 1953 gained momentum as the years went by. Numbers mounted until fifty or sixty new entrants a year were being taken on, compared with only a dozen or so at the beginning. In 1956 the scope of the scheme was extended to cater for graduates destined for the operating departments; a new course of two years duration, which complied with the IEE's requirements for practical training, was introduced for them in that year. Most of the recruits came immediately after they had graduated, but a few had had useful experience in industry. Early in the 1970s, however, when the decline in employment released a number of graduates from industry, the apprenticeship scheme was replaced by the recruitment of 'graduate trainees', who spent a year in either the

Research or the Designs Departments and could then apply for vacancies as they arose.

Another training scheme, leading to a Higher National Diploma and graduate membership of the IEE, was instituted in 1958. This was a three-year sandwich course for eighteen-year-olds just out of school and was divided equally between practical training in the BBC and theoretical training at the Hendon Technical College. Eight technical trainees embarked on the first of these courses in October 1958. By 1963 there were over seventy-five of them, and two more technical colleges (Plymouth and Southampton) had been brought in to supplement the theoretical instruction. These trainees were intended mainly for the operations and maintenance departments. However, by 1972 so many graduates became available that there was no difficulty in filling vacancies by the 'direct entry' of engineers already qualified.

To encourage research that might contribute to the advancement of broadcasting techniques, the BBC endowed two research scholarships in 1956. They ran for two years and afforded an opportunity to work for a higher degree, such as a Ph.D. From then on two of these scholarships were offered every year.

Much thought was given during this period to the career prospects of staff, and with considerable success. In accordance with the BBC's policy, vacant posts were filled as far as possible by promotion from within – usually through internal advertisements. From 1958 onwards efforts were made to encourage weekly-paid staff with suitable qualifications and experience to transfer to the grades of Technical Assistant and Technical Operator. Internal advertisements were issued almost every year offering such transfers.

The pattern of engineering recruitment changed over the years. Three factors were chiefly responsible for this. One was the gradual run-down of National Service from 1958 onwards, leading to the recruitment of eighteen-year-olds direct from school. In 1958 there were nearly fifty of these youngsters among the 365 technical assistants and operators who joined that year. The following year there were over a hundred of them, and by 1963 they were a majority of the intake. Another factor was the increasing complexity of equipment, which in turn created a demand for more people with good academic qualifications. At the same time the proportion of technical assistants declined. From 1953 to 1961, for example, the proportion of engineers to technical assistants more than doubled. A side effect of this trend was that the BBC found itself unable to meet all its needs for engineers by promotion from within, and so had to go outside for more of them.[147] The third factor was the increase in the rate of retirements, a phenomenon that was bound to overtake an organisation before its fiftieth birthday.

The period was one of expansion for the Engineering Training Department at Wood Norton. The residential accommodation for students was stepped up from 200 to 250, and the training facilities were developed to keep pace with changes and advances in broadcasting. In 1956 a laboratory was added for optical work. In 1959 a new studio for television training was provided, and in 1962 a laboratory for colour television. The laboratory facilities were improved again in 1963 by the addition of a transmitter wing, and in 1967 by a colour television training area.

After experiments with modern teaching techniques during 1966 it was decided to introduce programmed learning methods into the basic training for new entrants. Two 'feedback' classrooms equipped for this technique were in use by the end of 1967, and a third was added in 1970.

In 1956 700 students passed through Wood Norton. By the end of the period the annual figure was nearer 1500, and about seventy courses a year were being staged. Before the introduction of colour television in 1967 intensive colour courses were mounted and by the end of that year over 500 staff had attended them.

From early days the BBC had prided itself on its standards of welfare and safety. In addition to all the standards set by the Central Medical and Welfare Department for all staff, the Engineering Division issued a booklet of safety regulations for engineering staff, which by 1970 had reached its eighth edition. The regulations had to be kept under review, latterly by an Engineering Safety Committee, to take account of hazards introduced by new types of equipment, especially those producing rf radiation or X-rays. The procedures had to be modified in some respects in the mid-1960s when it was decided that the Factories Act 1961, and the Offices, Shops & Railway Premises Act, 1963 (and the corresponding legislation in Northern Ireland) should apply to certain BBC premises, or to parts of them. Many of the necessary changes applied to administrative matters, such as the keeping of records and the reporting of accidents, rather than to the actual safety standards, but the process of revising the internal regulations brought to light the need for some rethinking about methods of operation and testing.

Some of the problems were not easy to resolve. For instance, it is generally accepted that the testing of electrical equipment should be done in an 'earth-free situation'; but when ac/dc receivers are being tested, and are operated directly from the mains, the mains voltage can exist between the chassis of adjacent receivers. This would create a danger even if the tests were done in an 'earth-free situation'. It was therefore considered safer to supply each receiver through a separate isolating transformer and to earth the chassis of each receiver. Any mains-operated testing equipment must also be supplied through a transformer and the exposed metalwork of mains-operated tools must be earthed. Although these rules departed from the traditional ideal of an earth-free situation, they proved practicable and were accepted by the Factory Inspectorate as complying with the Electricity Regulations issued under the Factories Acts.

There was much concern abroad in questions of safety and an EBU monograph on the subject, incorporating experience in the BBC and in other organisations, aroused considerable interest and was translated into other languages.[148]

Broadcasting is totally dependent on its engineers for its very existence; they depend upon it for more than a livelihood – for work that is continually extending its frontiers and has an objective worthy of their toil. We have recorded some of the achievements of BBC engineers. We have done far less than justice to the great body of technicians, draughtsmen, craftsmen, clerical staff and secretaries, as well as engineers, who during the fifty years have kept the BBC services going through all the vicissitudes of peace and war, and have – with their colleagues who create the programmes – developed a vital means of communication and set standards of excellence that future generations may find a challenge and an inspiration.

References

Acknowledgments have been made in the Foreword to some of the sources used in compiling this book, many of which are not available to the public. The numbered references apply to published works: the list is selected and far from complete. The books and reviews of progress mentioned have been particularly helpful.

Mention should also be made of the following series of books by BBC authors:

D. J. Corbett, *Motion Picture and Television Film Image Control and Processing Techniques*, Focal Press.

S. W. Amos, *Principles of Transistor Circuits*, Butterworth.

K. R. Sturley, *Sound and Television Broadcasting: General Principles*, Butterworth.

D. C. Birkinshaw, S. W. Amos and K. H. Green, *Television Engineering: Principles and Practice*, Vols. 1 to 4, Butterworth.

H. Burrell Hadden, *High-quality Sound Production and Reproduction*, Butterworth.

A. E. Robertson, *Microphones*, Butterworth.

H. V. Sims, *Principles of PAL Colour Television and Related Systems*, Butterworth.

The references listed below are given partly to enable anyone interested to pursue the study of particular items, and partly by way of acknowledgment, not only of the material derived from the papers but also, in many instances, of the work done by the authors on the developments they describe.

References relating to Chapter I

1 *Radio Regulations*, International Telecommunication Union, Geneva, 1968, pp. 6–8
2 *Little Oxford Dictionary*, Clarendon Press, Oxford
3 *From Semaphore to Satellite*, ITU, Geneva, 1965, p. 96
4 Asa Briggs, *The History of Broadcasting in the United Kingdom*, Vol. I, p. 43
5 G. R. M. Garratt, 'David Edward Hughes', *World Radio*, 6 May 1938. (One of a series of articles on 'Pioneers of Broadcasting')
6 Rollo Appleyard, 'Heinrich Rudolf Hertz', *Electrical Communication*, October 1927, p. 63. (One of a series of articles on 'Pioneers of Electrical Communication')
7 W. J. Baker, *A History of the Marconi Company*, p. 69
8 Ibid., p. 32
9 Heinz Gartmann, *Science as History*, p. 148
10 *Telecommunication Journal*, ITU, March 1971, p. 133
11 Heinz Gartmann, op. cit., p. 152
12 P. P. Eckersley, *The Power Behind the Microphone*, pp. 30–8
13 W. J. Baker, op. cit., p. 184
14 *Handbook of the Collections Illustrating Electrical Engineering*, II Radio Communication, Science Museum, 1934

References

15 S. R. Mullard, 'Early Days of the Thermionic Valve Industry', *IEE Journal*, No. 16, 1970
16 Asa Briggs, *The History of Broadcasting in the United Kingdom*
17 J.-J. Fahie, *A History of Wireless Telegraphy 1839–1899*, 1899
18 J. A. Fleming, *The Principles of Electric Wave Telegraphy*, 1906
19 G. G. Blake, *History of Radio Telegraphy and Telephony*, 1926
20 *Wireless World* (60th Birthday Issue), April 1971
21 Letter from G. Gourski, *EBU Review*, 116B, July 1969, p. 43
22 Heinz Gartmann, op. cit., p. 153
23 N. Tj. Swierstra, 'The Birth of Broadcasting', *EBU Review*, 114B, March 1969, pp. 10–15
24 *EBU Review*, 117B, September 1969, p. 19
25 Asa Briggs, op. cit., Vol. I, p. 47
26 W. J. Baker, op. cit., p. 186
27 *Wireless World*, 25 June 1921
28 J. Clarricoats, *World at their Fingertips*, Ch. 9
29 W. J. Baker, op. cit., p. 192
30 Asa Briggs, op. cit., Vol. I, p. 85

References relating to Chapter II

1   Asa Briggs, *The History of Broadcasting in the United Kingdom*, Vol. I, p. 307
2   Op. cit., Ch. III
3   *Wireless World*, 3 September 1924, p. 662
4   *BBC Year Book*, 1930, p. 152
5   R. H. Coase, *British Broadcasting: a Study in Monopoly*
6   J. Clarricoats, *World at their Fingertips*
7   Asa Briggs, op. cit., Vol. I, Ch. IV
8   *The Times*, 18/19 October 1923, quoted by Asa Briggs, op. cit., Vol. I, p. 187
9   *Wireless World*, February 1971, p. 95
10 Asa Briggs, op. cit., Vol. I, p. 202
11 P. P. Eckersley, *The Power Behind the Microphone*, Ch. IV
12 EBU Technical Monograph No. 3109, *Technical Advice to Listeners and Viewers*
13 *Wireless World*, April 1961, pp. 168–9
14 Ibid. (60th Birthday Issue), April 1971, p. 158
15 BS 905: British Standards Institution
16 P. P. Eckersley, op. cit., p. 76
17 Cmd 1951, *Report of the Broadcasting Committee* (Sykes Committee) 1923
18 W. E. C. Varley, 'Synchronous Operation of BBC Transmitters', *World Radio*, 18 August 1939
19 *Wireless World*, 18 March 1925, p. 196
20 Ibid., 6 May 1925, p. 424
21 Asa Briggs, op. cit., Vol. I, p. 395
22 P. P. Eckersley, op. cit., p. 116
23 Cmd 2599, *Report of the Broadcasting Committee* (Crawford Committee) 1925
24 Asa Briggs, op. cit., Vol. I, p. 384
25 Arthur Burrows, *The Story of Broadcasting*, pp. 148 and 156
26 George Burnett (Ed.), *Scotland on the Air*, Moray Press, 1938 (contributions by George Burnett and L. Hotine)
27 Arthur Burrows, op. cit., p. 144
28 Asa Briggs, op. cit., Vol. I, p. 389
29 A. G. D. West, 'A Tour Round Savoy Hill', *Wireless World*, 9–23 February 1927 (inclusive)

30 A. G. D. West, 'Studio Equipment', loc. cit., 2 March 1927, p. 253
31 A. C. Shaw, 'The Control Room', loc. cit., 9 March 1927, p. 299
32 H. Bishop, 'Twenty-five Years of Broadcast Engineering', *BBC Year Book*, 1948, p. 23
33 *Wireless World*, 1 August 1923, p. 594
34 *Time in Broadcasting* (booklet produced by the BBC for the Centenary Exhibition of the British Horological Institute, October 1958)
35 E. K. Sandeman, 'The Development of Simultaneous Broadcasting, *Wireless World*, 21 May 1924, p. 225, and 21 May 1924, p. 257
36 H. Bishop, 'Thirteen Years of Technical Progress', *World Radio*, 15 November 1935, p. 15
37 P. P. Eckersley, op. cit., p. 69
38 Asa Briggs, op. cit., Vol. I, p. 217
39 *Wireless World*, 27 October 1926
40 C. A. Lewis, *Broadcasting from Within*, p. 32
41 Arthur Burrows, op. cit., p. 105
42 *Popular Wireless*, 3 May 1924
43 Asa Briggs, op. cit., Vol. I, p. 290
44 *Radio Times*, 30 May 1924; *Wireless World*, 8 July 1925
45 *Wireless World*, 17 June 1925, p. 624
46 *World Radio*, 11 November 1927, p. 490
47 EBU Technical Monograph No. 3102, *Receiving and Measuring Stations*, p. 11
48 J. Clarricoats, op. cit., Ch. 12 and 13
49 P. P. Eckersley and A. B. Howe, 'The Operation of several Broadcasting Stations on the same Wavelength', *Journal IEE*, Vol. 67, No. 390, June 1929
50 *Twenty Years of Activity of the International Broadcasting Union*, IBU, Geneva, 1945, pp. 7–8
51 Asa Briggs, op. cit., Vol. I, p. 310
52 Ibid., pp. 312–14
53 P. P. Eckersley, op. cit., pp. 81–92
54 Asa Briggs, op. cit., Vol. I, p. 412
55 Ibid., p. 11
56 P. P. Eckersley, op. cit., Ch. IV, pp. 62–80
57 Asa Briggs, op. cit., Vol. I, p. 200
58 F. Gill and W. W. Cook, 'Principles involved in Computing the Depreciation of Plant', *Journal IEE*, 55, p. 137, 1917
59 F. Gill, Presidential Address, loc. cit., 61, 1922, p. 2
60 F. Gill, 'Engineering Economics', loc. cit., 90, 1943, pp. 373–86

References relating to Chapter III

1 Asa Briggs. *The History of Broadcasting in the United Kingdom*, Vol. II, p. 424
2 *Wireless World*, 31 August 1927, p. 285 and 26 October 1927, p. 585
3 *BBC Year Book*, 1931, pp. 269–79
4 P. P. Eckersley and N. Ashbridge, 'A Wireless Broadcasting Transmitting Station for Dual Programme Service', *Journal IEE*, 68, 1930, p. 1149
5 P. P. Eckersley, *The Power Behind the Microphone*, p. 122
6 W. E. C. Varley, 'Synchronous Operation of BBC Transmitters', *World Radio*, 18 and 25 August 1939
7 P. P. Eckersley, *The Service Area of Broadcasting Stations*, BBC, 1929
8 *BBC Year Book*, 1931, pp. 254–7
9 Ibid., 1933, pp. 234–40
10 Ibid., 1934, pp. 169–278

11 *BBC Year Book*, 1934, pp. 318–22
12 N. Ashbridge H. Bishop and B. N. MacLarty 'The Droitwich Broadcasting Station', *Journal IEE*, 77, 1935, p. 437
13 *BBC Year Book*, 1937, pp. 75–6
14 H. S. Black, 'Stabilised Feedback Amplifiers', *BSTJ*, January 1934
15 F. C. McLean, 'Negative Feedback as applied to Radio Transmitters', *World Radio*, 27 May 1938
16 P. P. Eckersley, T. L. Eckersley and H. L. Kirke, 'The Design of Transmitting Aerials for Broadcasting Stations', *Journal IEE*, Vol. 67, No. 388, April 1929
17 *Wireless World*, April 1961, pp. 170–5
18 A. J. Gill and S. Whitehead, 'Electrical Interference with Radio Reception', *Proc. Wireless Section IEE*, September 1938, Vol. 13, No. 39, p. 209
19 Asa Briggs, op. cit., Vol. II, p. 458 et seq.
20 Carrier Engineering Company Ltd., *A description of the Air-conditioning Equipment in Broadcasting House*
21 C. P. Williams, 'Buildings for Broadcast Transmitters', *World Radio*, 25 March 1938
22 R. E. Springett, 'Broadcasting House, Glasgow', *World Radio*, 11 Nov. 1938
23 *BBC Year Book*, 1932, p. 89 et seq.
24 *BBC Sound Broadcasting: its Engineering Development*, BBC, August 1962
25 *BBC Year Book*, 1932, p. 331
26 *A Technical Description of Broadcasting House*, BBC, 1932
27 J. McLaren, 'The Acoustical Design of Broadcasting Studios', *World Radio*, 4 November 1938
28 *BBC Year Book*, 1928, p. 182
29 Ibid., p. 278
30 W. J. Stentiford, 'The Production Panel', *World Radio*, 21 April 1939
31 *BBC Year Book*, 1932, pp. 355–65
32 C. G. Mayo, 'Programme Meters', *World Radio*, 24 June 1938
33 T. Somerville and S. F. Brownless, 'Listeners' Sound Level Preferences', *BBC Quarterly*, Vol. III, No. 4, January 1949 and Vol. V, No. 1, Spring 1950
34 E. R. Wigan, 'The Relative Merits of the VU-Meter and the Peak Programme Meter', *EBU Review* 79–A, January 1963
35 D. G. H. Mills, 'The Problem of Loudness Level in Broadcasting', ibid., 126–A, April 1971
36 K. Ilmonen, 'Investigation of Listeners' Programme-volume Preferences', ibid., 109–A, June 1968
37 F. W. Alexander, 'Ribbon Microphones', *World Radio*, 13 May 1938
38 *A Technical Description of Broadcasting House*, BBC, 1932, p. 79
39 Ibid., pp. 88–9
40 F. W. Alexander, 'Microphone Amplifiers', *World Radio*, 28 October 1938
41 H. S. Walker and C. G. Mayo, 'A new Valve-Testing Set', *World Radio*, 8 and 15 April 1938
42 E. G. Chadder, J. McLaren and W. J. Stentiford, 'Broadcasting House, Glasgow', *World Radio*, 18 and 25 November 1938 and 2 December 1938
43 Asa Briggs, loc. cit., Vol. II, p. 98
44 BS 880: 1950, British Standards Institution
45 'Pitch', *The Oxford Companion to Music*, OUP
46 C. van Loo, 'On the Standardization of Musical Pitch', *EBU Review* 76–A, December 1962
47 F. W. Alexander, 'Standard Musical Pitch', *BBC Quarterly*, Vol. VI, No. 1, Spring 1951, p. 62
48 *Wireless World*, April 1971, p. 173
49 J. Clarricoats, *World at their Fingertips*, pp. 130–2

50 J. C. W. Reith, *Into the Wind*, p. 113
51 Asa Briggs, op. cit., Vol. II, pp. 370–1
52 Ibid., Vol. I, p. 324
53 Ibid., Vol. II, p. 371
54 *BBC Year Book*, 1938, pp. 297–8
55 Asa Briggs, op. cit., Vol. II, pp. 374–9
56 *BBC Year Book*, 1933, pp. 275–87
57 L. W. Hayes and B. N. MacLarty, 'The Empire Service Broadcasting Station at Daventry', *Journal IEE*, Vol. 85, 513, September 1939
58 T. W. Bennington, 'Seasonal Effects in Short-wave Communication', *World Radio*, 3 February 1939
59 T. W. Bennington, 'Long-period Effects in Short-wave Communication', ibid., 14 July 1939
60 *Nature*, 18 June 1908
61 Asa Briggs, op. cit., Vol. II, p. 537
62 *Handbook of the Collections Illustrating Electrical Engineering* II, Radio Communication, Science Museum, 1934
63 Asa Briggs, op. cit., Vol. II, p. 544
64 Cmd. 4793, 'Report of the Television Committee' (Selsdon Committee) 1935
65 P. P. Eckersley, op. cit., p. 239
66 *BBC Television: A British Engineering Achievement*, BBC, 1961
67 'Berlin Begins Television', *World Radio*, 29 March 1935
68 Asa Briggs, op. cit., Vol. II, p. 606
69 Ibid., p. 579
70 Ibid., p. 566 et seq.
71 *The Times*, 21 March 1934 (quoted by Asa Briggs)
72 A. Rosen, 'The London Television Cable', *Siemens Magazine* (Engineering Supplement), No. 145, June 1937
73 S. H. Padel, 'Television Transmission by Telephone Cable', *World Radio*, 28 April and 5 May 1939
74 A. R. A. Rendall, 'Television via Telephone Cables', *World Radio*, 12 and 19 August 1938
75 *POEEJ*, Vol. 64, Part 2, July 1971, p. 135
76 T. C. Macnamara, 'Outside Broadcasts in Television', *World Radio*, 22 July 1938
77 D. C. Birkinshaw, 'Operating Technique in Television', *World Radio*, 13 January 1939
78 T. C. Macnamara and D. C. Birkinshaw, 'The London Television Service', *Journal IEE* Vol. 83, No. 504, December 1938, p. 729
79 *Wireless World*, April 1971, p. 163
80 *POEEJ*, Vol. 32, January 1940
81 A. B. Hart, 'The London-Glasgow Trunk Telephone Cable and its Repeater Stations' *POEEJ*, Vol. 19, 1926
82 E. K. Sandeman, 'Simultaneous Broadcasting in Czechoslovakia', *Electrical Communication*, Vol. 6, 1928, p. 171
83 E. K. Sandeman, 'Control of "Quality" in a Broadcasting System', *Electrical Communication*, Vol. 7, 1928, p. 33
84 Comité Consultatif International des Communications Téléphoniques à grande distance, Plenary Session, Paris, 11–18 June 1928, p. 132
85 *BBC Annual Report*, 1931
86 *BBC Year Book*, 1933, p. 401
87 'A Glimpse of Gloucester', *Wireless Constructor*, April 1932
88 'At the BBC – How the S.B. System Works', *Amateur Wireless*, March 1932
89 F. A. Peachey, 'Simultaneous Broadcasting System', *World Radio*, 12 and 19 May 1939
90 W. G. Edwards, 'Simultaneous Broadcasting System', *World Radio*, 3 June 1938

91 *Wireless World*, 9 March 1927
92 Asa Briggs, op. cit., Vol. I, p. 265
93 R. T. B. Wynn, 'The Coronation Broadcast', *World Radio*, 7 May 1937
94 'The Coronation Broadcast: an outline of the Technical Arrangements', *World Radio*, 23 April 1937
95 O. H. Barron, 'Portable Repeaters', *World Radio*, 1 July 1938
96 O. H. Barron, 'Audio-frequency Oscillators', *World Radio*, 24 March 1939
97 E. F. Woods, 'Lines for Outside Broadcasts', World Radio 7, 14 and 21 October 1938
98 F. W. Alexander, 'Ribbon Microphones: the underlying principles of their design', *World Radio*, 13 May 1938
99 D. E. L. Shorter, 'Testing Ribbon Microphones', *World Radio*, 20 May 1938
100 A. E. Barrett, C. G. Mayo and H. D. McD. Ellis, 'New Equipment for Outside Broadcasts', *World Radio*, 21 and 28 July 1939
101 R. D. Petrie, 'New Equipment for Outside Broadcasts', *World Radio*, 4 August 1939
102 G. G. Blake, 'History of Radio Telegraphy & Telephony', p. 212
103 A. E. Barrett and C. J. F. Tweed, 'Some Aspects of Magnetic Recording and its Application to Broadcasting', *Proc. IEE*, Wireless Section, Vol. 13, No. 38, June 1938
104 J. W. Godfrey, 'The History of BBC Sound Recording', *BSRA Journal*, Vol. 6, No. 1, 1959
105 Asa Briggs, op. cit., Vol. II, p. 101
106 J. E. Lock, 'Mobile Recording Equipment', *World Radio*, 2 October 1936
107 'The BBC makes Records', *Empire Broadcasting*, 19 and 25 September 1937
108 M. J. L. Pulling, 'Sound Recording as applied to Broadcasting', *BBC Quarterly*, Vol. III, No. 2, July 1948
109 A. E. Barrett, 'The BBC Sound-Recording Service', *World Radio*, 2 June 1939
110 J. A. Miller, 'Mechanographic Recording for Motion Picture Sound Tracks', *Journal SMPE*, Vol. XXV, 1935, pp. 50–64
111 R. Vermeulen, 'The Philips-Miller System of Sound Recording', *Philips Technical Review*, May 1936
112 R. Vermeulen, 'The Philips-Miller Method of Recording Sound', *Journal SMPE*, Vol. XXX, No. 6, 1938, pp. 680–93
113 E. Bruce, A. C. Beck and L. R. Long, 'Horizontal Rhombic Antennas', *Proc. IEE*, Vol. 23, January 1935, p. 24
114 H. Bishop, 'The War-time Activities of the Engineering Division of the BBC', *Journal IEE*, Vol. 94, Part IIIA, No. 11, 1947, p. 184
115 N. Ashbridge, 'The Tatsfield Receiving Station of the BBC', *UIR Monograph No. 2*, August 1932
116 'The Tatsfield Checking Station', *World Radio*, 7 and 14 April 1933
117 'Tatsfield Relaying Receivers', *World Radio*, 5 and 12 May 1933
118 H. V. Griffiths, 'The BBC Measurement and Technical Receiving Station at Tatsfield', *BBC Quarterly*, Vol. 9, 1954
119 'Receiving and Measuring Stations for Broadcasting Purposes', *EBU Technical Monograph No. 3102*, p. 43
120 P. P. Eckersley, *The Power Behind the Microphone*, p. 152
121 *Daily Worker*, 23 May 1935
122 Asa Briggs, op. cit., Vol. II, p. 451
123 Cmd 5091, Report of the Ullswater Committee 1936
124 Asa Briggs, op. cit., Vol. II, p. 513
125 Ibid., p. 514
126 *BBC Handbook*, 1929, p. 42
127 Siffer Lemoine, 'Allocation of European Broadcast Wavelengths – some new points of view', *Electrical Communication*, Vol. 7, 1928–9, p. 200 (reprinted from *Experimental Wireless & The Wireless Engineer*)

128 P. P. Eckersley, op. cit., Ch. V
129 'Twenty Years of Activity of the International Broadcasting Union', IBU, Geneva, 1945, p. 20
130 *ABU Newsletter*, December 1970, p. 14
131 Asa Briggs, op. cit., Vol. II, p. 347
132 'Wavelength Changes – how the Lucerne Plan came into Operation', *World Radio*, 19 January 1934
133 'Christmas Over Europe', *World Radio*, 23 December 1938
134 Asa Briggs, op. cit., Vol. II, p. 625
135 H. Bishop, 'The War-time Activities of the Engineering Division of the BBC', *Journal IEE*, Vol. 94, Part IIIA, No. 11, 1947, p. 169
136 J. C. W. Reith, op. cit., p. 192
137 Asa Briggs, op. cit., Vol. II, p. 629
138 Ibid., p. 630
139 Ibid., p. 631
140 W. E. C. Varley, 'Improvements in synchronisation of BBC Transmitters 1938–1946', *BBC Quarterly*, Vol. II, No. 1, April 1947
141 Maurice Gorham, *Forty Years of Irish Broadcasting*, p. 19

References relating to Chapter IV

1 Max Barnes, 'Miniature BBC in Avon Rocks', *Bristol Evening World*, 20 March 1946
2 Asa Briggs, *The History of Broadcasting in the United Kingdom*, Vol. III, pp. 294–5
3 'From Peace to War', *BBC Handbook*, 1940, p. 41
4 L. W. Hayes, 'Never Off the Air', *Radio Times*, 14 December 1945
5 H. Bishop, 'The War-time Activities of the Engineering Division of the BBC', *Journal IEE*, Vol. 94, Part IIIA, No. 11, 1947, p. 169
6 W. E. C. Varley, 'Improvements in Synchronization of BBC Transmitters 1938–1946', *BBC Quarterly*, Vol. II, No. 1, April 1947
7 Asa Briggs, op. cit., Vol. III, p. 177
8 T. C. Macnamara, A. B. Howe and P. A. T. Bevan, 'Design and Operation of High-Power Broadcast Transmitter Units with their Outputs Combined in Parallel', *Journal IEE*, Vol. 95, Part III, 1948, p. 183
9 Asa Briggs, op. cit., Vol. III, p. 427
10 Sefton Delmer, *Black Boomerang* (1962)
11 L. W. Hayes and B. N. MacLarty, 'The Empire Service Broadcasting Station at Daventry', *Journal IEE*, Vol. 85, No. 512, 1939, p. 321
12 F. C. McLean and F. D. Bolt, 'The Design and Use of Radio-Frequency Open-Wire Transmission Lines and Switchgear for Broadcasting Systems', *Journal IEE*, Vol. 93, Part III, 1946, p. 191
13 W. E. C. Varley, 'BBC Variable-Frequency Drive Equipment for Transmitters', *BBC Quarterly*, Vol. II, No. 4, January 1948
14 H. Page, 'The Measured Performance of Horizontal Dipole Transmitting Arrays', *Journal IEE*, Vol. 92, Part III, June 1945, p. 68
15 P. A. T. Bevan, 'The Application of High-Voltage Steel-Tank Mercury-Arc Rectifiers to Broadcast Transmitters', *Journal IEE*, Vol. 92, Part II, 1945, p. 469
16 Asa Briggs, op. cit., Vol. III, p. 95 (Table)
17 Ibid. p. 656
18 H. B. Rantzen and J. H. Holmes, 'BBC Communications Network: Proposed Developments', *BBC Quarterly*, Vol. III, No. 1, April 1948

References

19 J. W. Godfrey and S. W. Amos, 'Sound Recording and Reproduction' (*BBC Engineering Training Manual*), p. 83 *et. seq.*

20 H. Davies, 'Design of a High-Fidelity Disc Recording Equipment', *Journal IEE*, Vol. 94, Part VIII, p. 275, 1947

21 S. R. Lance, 'Recording and Reproducing Styli', *Journal BSRA*, Vol. 3, No. 5, August 1948

22 W. J. Lloyd and D. E. L. Shorter, 'New Portable Sound Recording Machine developed by the BBC', *Electrical News & Engineering* (Electronic Supplement), January 1945

23 Asa Briggs, op. cit., Vol. II, pp. 403 and 652

24 Ibid., Vol. III, p. 188

25 R. D. A. Maurice and C. J. W. Hill, 'The Development of a Receiving Station for the BBC Monitoring Service', *BBC Quarterly*, Vol. II, No. 2, July 1947

26 Asa Briggs, op. cit., Vol. III, pp. 361–3

27 H. Bishop, op. cit., pp. 169–85

28 A. Price, *Instruments of Darkness*, p. 34

29 Ibid., pp. 21–2 and 47–9

30 Ibid., p. 104

31 Asa Briggs, op. cit., Vol. III, p. 646

32 Ibid., pp. 664 and 712

33 Ibid., p. 640 *et. seq.*

34 Ibid., p. 679

35 Ibid., p. 652–3

36 *War Report*, OUP, 1946, pp. 11–12

37 Asa Briggs, op. cit., Vol. III, pp. 655–6

38 *War Report*, OUP, 1946, p. 20

39 Ibid., pp. 439–40

40 Sefton Delmer, op. cit., p. 161

41 *War Report*, op. cit., p. 34

42 Asa Briggs, op. cit., Vol. III, Ch. II

43 H. L. Kirke, 'Radio-Frequency Bridges', *Journal IEE*, No. 92, Part I, 1945, p. 39

44 R. T. B. Wynn, 'Continuity Working', *BBC Quarterly*, Vol. I, No. 4, January 1947

45 F. J. Stringer and G. Stannard, 'Compensation of Temperature Effects on music Circuits', *BBC Quarterly*, Vol. II, No. 1, April 1947

46 Report of the Television Committee (1943), (Hankey Committee), H.M.S.O., 1945

47 *The Times*, 9 March 1945

48 *Electronic Engineering*, April 1945

49 *Wireless World*, May 1945

50 *Proc. IEE*, Vol. 101, Part 1, No. 127, January 1954

51 *EBU Bulletin*, 15 September 1950, p. 271

References relating to Chapter V

1 D. E. L. Shorter, 'The Evolution of the high-quality Microphone', *BSRA Journal*, Vol. 4, No. 7, November 1954

2 D. E. L. Shorter and H. D. Harwood, 'The Design of a Ribbon-Type Pressure-gradient Microphone for Broadcast Transmission', *BBC Engineering Monograph*, No. 4, December 1955

3 *Sound Broadcasting: its Engineering Development*, BBC, 1962, p. 44

4 A. E. Robertson, *Microphones*, BBC Engineering Training Manual

5 'The Design of a high-quality Commentator's Microphone insensitive to Ambient Noise', *BBC Engineering Monograph*, No. 7, June 1956

6 H. J. von Braunmühl and W. Weber, *Einführung in die Angewandte Akustik*, 1936

7 A. E. Robertson, *Microphones*, BBC Engineering Training Manual, p. 168

8 H. D. Ellis, 'Studio Equipment: a new Design', *BBC Quarterly*, Vol. I, No. 1, April 1946, p. 21

9 R. T. B. Wynn, 'Continuity Working: a new method of presenting Broadcast Programmes', *BBC Quarterly*, Vol. I, No. 4, January 1947, p. 184

10 J. McLaren, 'The Acoustical Planning of Broadcasting Studios', *BBC Quarterly*, Vol. I, No. 4, January 1947, p. 194

11 F. L. Ward, 'Helmholtz Resonators as Acoustic Treatment at the new Swansea Studios', *BBC Quarterly*, Vol. VII, 1952–3, p. 174

12 C. L. S. Gilford, 'Membrane Sound Absorbers and their application to Broadcasting Studios, *BBC Quarterly*, Vol. VII, 1952–3, p. 246

13 T. Somerville, 'A comparison of the Acoustics of The Philharmonic Hall, Liverpool, and St Andrew's Grand Hall, Glasgow', *BBC Quarterly*, Vol. IV, No. 1, April 1949, p. 41

14 T. Somerville and C. L. S. Gilford, 'Cathode-ray Displays of Acoustic Phenomena and their Interpretation', *BBC Quarterly*, Vol. VII, spring 1952, p. 41

15 C. L. S. Gilford and M. W. Greenway, 'The Application of Phase-coherent Detection and Correlation Methods to Room Acoustics', *BBC Engineering Monograph*, No. 9, November 1956

16 P. E. Axon, C. L. S. Gilford and D. E. L. Shorter, 'Artificial Reverberation', *Proc. IEE*, Vol. 102, Part B, No. 5, September 1955

17 F. Williams, 'The Trend of Design of Broadcasting Control Rooms', *BBC Quarterly*, Vol. II, No. 3, October 1947

18 S. D. Berry, 'New Equipment for Outside Broadcasts', *BBC Quarterly*, Vol. VII, No. 2, summer 1952

19 F. C. McLean and R. Toombs, 'Unattended Low-Power Transmitting Stations with Remote Control', *BBC Quarterly*, Vol. III, No. 2, July 1948, p. 122

20 R. T. B. Wynn, Chairman's Address to IEE Radio Section, *Proc. IEE*, Vol. 97, Part III, No. 45, January 1950, p. 1

21 R. T. B. Wynn and F. A. Peachey, 'The Remote and Automatic Control of Semi-attended Broadcasting Transmitters', *Proc. IEE*, Vol. 104B, No. 18, November 1957, p. 529

22 W. J. Morcom and D. F. Bowers, 'The Design of High- and Low-Power Medium-Frequency Broadcasting Transmitters for Automatic and Semi-Attended Operation', *Proc. IEE*, Vol. 104B, No. 18, November 1957, p. 540

23 H. B. Rantzen, F. A. Peachey and C. Gunn-Russell, 'The Automatic Monitoring of Broadcast Programmes', *Proc. IEE*, Vol. 98, Part III, September 1951, p. 329

24 R. W. Holmes, 'Technical Monitoring of Transmitters and Programme Links', *BBC Engineering*, No. 85, January 1971, p. 10

25 N. Ashbridge, 'Broadcasting and Television (A Review of Progress)', *Journal IEE*, Vol. 84, 1939, p. 380

26 H. Chireix, 'High-power out-phasing Modulation', *Proc. IRE*, Vol. 23, November 1935, p. 1370

27 W. H. Doherty, 'A new high-efficiency Power Amplifier for Modulated Waves', *Proc. IRE*, Vol. 24, September 1936, p. 1163

28 *Twenty Years of Activity of the IBU*, IBU, Geneva, 1945

29 W. E. C. Varley, 'Improvements in Synchronisation of BBC Transmitters', *BBC Quarterly*, Vol. II, No. 1, April 1947, p. 51

30 E. L. E. Pawley, 'BBC Sound Broadcasting 1939–1960', *Proc. IEE*, Vol. 108, Part B, No. 39, May 1961, p. 279

31 H. Page and G. D. Monteath, 'The Vertical Radiation Pattern of Medium-wave Broadcasting Aerials', *Proc. IEE*, Vol. 102, Part B, No. 3, May 1955, p. 279

32 H. L. Kirke, 'Frequency Modulation: BBC Field Trials', *BBC Quarterly*, Vol. I, No. 2, July 1946, p. 62

33 'The BBC Scheme for VHF Broadcasting', *BBC Quarterly*, Vol. VI, No. 3, autumn 1951, p. 171

34 E. W. Hayes and H. Page, 'The BBC Sound Broadcasting Service on Very High Frequencies', *Proc. IEE*, Vol. 104, Part B, No. 15, May 1957, p. 213

35 H. Bishop, Presidential Address to IEE, *Proc. IEE*, Vol. 101, Part I, No. 127, January 1954

36 W. S. Mortley, 'Frequency-modulated quartz oscillators for Broadcasting Equipment', *Proc. IEE*, Vol. 104, Part B, No. 15, May 1957, p. 239

37 C. O. Boyce, 'Radio Masts and Towers', Joint Engineering Conference, 1951: Part 8

38 C. H. Hill, 'Masts for Transmitting Stations', *World Radio*, 17 March 1939, p. 14

39 *Wireless World*, April 1961, p. 178

40 A. J. Gill and S. Whitehead, 'Electrical Interference with Radio Reception', *Proc. IEE*, Vol. 13, No. 39, September 1938, p. 209

41 BS 905:1969, British Standards Institution

42 'Technical Advice for Listeners and Viewers', *EBU Technical Monograph*, No. 3109, 1968

43 EBU document R1–P, 27 April 1955

44 H. D. M. Ellis and J. C. Taylor, 'The Design of Automatic Equipment for Programme Routing and Sequential Monitoring', *BBC Quarterly*, Vol. VI, No. 4, 1951, p. 241

45 R. D. Petrie and J. C. Taylor, 'Programme Switching, Control and Monitoring in Sound Broadcasting', *BBC Engineering Monograph*, No. 28

46 Summary of the Report of the Independent Committee of Enquiry into the Overseas Information Services, April 1954, HMSO, Cmd 9138

47 Heinz Gartmann, *Science as History*, Hodder & Stoughton, 1960, p. 164

48 K. R. Sturley, *Sound and Television Broadcasting – General Principles'*, BBC Engineering Training Manual

49 S. W. Amos, D. C. Birkinshaw and J. L. Bliss, *Television Engineering*, Vol. I, BBC Engineering Training Manual

50 D. C. Birkinshaw, 'The Television Studio', *BBC Quarterly*, Vol. IV, No. 2, summer 1949

51 *BBC Television: a British Engineering Achievement*, BBC, 1961, p. 18

52 Peter Bax, 'A Plan for Television Studios', *BBC Quarterly*, Vol. I, No. 2, July 1946, diagram, p. 51

53 *BBC Television: a British Engineering Achievement*, BBC, 1961, p. 41

54 S. H. Padel, A. R. A. Rendall and S. N. Watson, 'Test Equipment for Television Transmission Circuits', *Proc. IEE*, Vol. 99, Part IIIA, September 1952, p. 821

55 D. C. Birkinshaw and D. R. Campbell, 'Studio Technique in Television', *Journal IEE*, Vol. 92, Part III, No. 19, September 1945, p. 165

56 D. C. Birkinshaw, 'Television Programme Origination – an Engineering Technique', *Proc. IEE*, Vol. 99, Part IIIA, September 1952, p. 43, and a companion paper by I. Atkins, 'Television Programme Production Problems in relation to the Engineering Technique', p. 74

57 R. F. Pottinger, 'Problems of Sound in Television Programmes', *Proc. IEE*, Vol. 99, Part IIIA, September 1952, p. 145

58 H. O. Sampson, 'Television Lighting Technique', *Proc. IEE*, Vol. 99, Part IIIA, September 1952, p. 150

59 G. J. Phillips, 'VHF Aerials for Television Broadcasting', *Proc. IEE*, Vol. 102, Part B, September 1955, p. 687

60 F. C. McLean, A. N. Thomas and R. A. Rowden, 'The Crystal Palace Television Transmitting Station', *Proc. IEE*, Vol. 103, Part B, No. 11, 1956, p. 633

61 A. R. A. Rendall and S. H. Padel, 'The Broadcasting House/Crystal Palace Television Link', ibid, p. 644

62 *BBC Television: a British Engineering Achievement*, BBC 1961, pp. 26–27

63 International Radio Regulations, annexed to the International Telecommunication Convention, Atlantic City, ITU, 1947

64 H. Cafferata, C. Gillam and J. F. Ramsay, 'Television Transmitting Aerials', *Proc. IEE*, Vol. 99, Part IIIA, No. 18, April–May 1952

65 R. A. Rowden, 'Television Coverage of Great Britain', *Journal Television Society*, Vol. 7, No. 11, July–September 1955

66 P. A. T. Bevan and H. Page, 'The Sutton Coldfield Television Broadcasting Station', *Proc. IEE*, Vol. 98, Part III, No. 56, November 1951, p. 416

67 E. A. Nind and E. McP. Leyton, 'The Vision Transmitter for the Sutton Coldfield Television Station', *Proc. IEE*, Vol. 98, Part III, No. 56, November 1951, p. 442

68 P. A. T. Bevan, 'Television Broadcasting Stations', *Proc. IEE*, Vol. 99, Part IIIA, September 1952, p. 179

69 E. C. Cork, 'The Vestigial-Sideband Filter for the Sutton Coldfield Television Station', *Proc. IEE*, Vol. 98, Part III, No. 56, November 1951, p. 460

70 P. A. T. Bevan, 'Earthed grid power amplifiers for VHF vision and Sound Transmitters', *Wireless Engineering*, No. 26, 1949, p. 182

71 C. E. Strong, 'The Inverted Amplifier', *Electronics*, July 1940, p. 14

72 L. F. Tagholm and G. I. Ross, 'The Selection and Testing of Sites for Television Transmitters in the United Kingdom, *Proc. IEE*, Vol. 99, Part IIIA, No. 18, April–May 1952, p. 300

73 V. J. Cooper, 'Shunt-regulated Amplifiers', *Wireless Engineer*, May 1951

74 V. J. Cooper, 'High-power Television Transmitter Technique, with particular reference to the transmitter at Holme Moss', *Proc. IEE*, Vol. 99, Part IIIA, No. 18, April–May 1952, p. 231

75 V. D. Landon, 'Cascade Amplifiers with maximal flatness', *RCA Review*, Vol. 5, 1941

76 P. A. T. Bevan, 'The BBC Television Transmitting Stations', *BBC Quarterly*, Vol. VII, No. 4, winter 1952–3, p. 235

77 E. C. Cork, 'Suspended Locked-Coil Rope Television Feeder Systems', *Proc. IEE*, Vol. 99, Part IIIA, April–May 1952, p. 243

78 J. A. Saxton and B. N. Harden, 'Polarization Discrimination in VHF Reception', *Proc. IEE*, Vol. 103, Part B, No. 12, November 1956, p. 757

79 F. C. McLean, A. N. Thomas and R. A. Rowden, 'The Crystal Palace Television Transmitting Station', *Proc. IEE*, Vol. 103, Part B, No. 11, 1956, p. 633

80 'Technical Advice for Listeners and Viewers', *EBU Technical Monograph*, No. 3109, 1968

81 BS 905:1959, British Standards Institution

82 J. W. Godfrey and S. W. Amos, *Sound Recording and Reproduction*, BBC Training Manual, p. 159

83 G. V. Buckley, W. R. Hawkins, H. J. Houlgate and J. N. B. Percy, 'Reproducing Equipment for Fine-Groove Records', *BBC Engineering Monograph*, No. 5, February 1956

84 F. J. Stringer and G. Stannard, 'Compensation of Temperature Effects on Music Circuits', *BBC Quarterly*, Vol. II, No. 1, April 1947

85 *BBC Television: a British Engineering Achievement*, BBC, 1961, p. 43

86 E. L. E. Pawley, 'BBC Television 1939–1960', *Proc. IEE*, Vol. 107, Part B, No. 40, July 1961, p. 391

87 M. J. L. Pulling, 'Eurovision Technical Operations: a Survey', *EBU Review*, No. 55A, June 1959

88 A. V. Lord, 'Conversion of Television Standards', *BBC Quarterly*, Vol. VIII, No. 2, p. 108

89 *This is the EBU*, EBU, 1965

90 M. J. L. Pulling, 'The Development of Eurovision', *Journal IEE*, Vol. 6, No. 62, February 1960, pp. 96–100

91 H. B. Rantzen and J. H. Holmes, 'BBC Communications Network: Proposed Developments', *BBC Quarterly*, Vol. III, No. 1, April 1948

92 T. E. Shea, *Transmission Networks and Wave Filters*, Van Nostrand, 1929

93 A. R. A. Rendall and W. N. Anderson, 'Temporary Linkages for Television Outside Broadcasting Purposes', *Proc. IEE*, Vol. 99, Part IIIA, 1952, p. 323

94 H. Bishop, 'Twenty-five Years of BBC Television', *BBC Engineering Monograph*, No. 39, October 1961

95 T. H. Bridgewater, R. H. Hammans and S. N. Watson, 'Televising the Boat Race 1950', *BBC Quarterly*, Vol. V, No. 2, summer 1950

96 T. C. Macnamara, 'Engineering prelude to the Boat Race', *Radio Times* (Television Edition), 25 March 1949

97 T. C. Macnamara and P. A. T. Bevan, 'Televising the 1949 Oxford and Cambridge Boat Race', *Electronic Engineering*, May 1948

98 W. S. Proctor, M. J. L. Pulling and F. Williams, 'Technical Arrangements for the Sound and Television Broadcasts of the Coronation Ceremonies, 2 June 1953', *Proc. IEE*, Vol. 101, Part I, 1954, p. 57

99 International Radio Regulations, annexed to the International Telecommunication Convention, Atlantic City, ITU, 1947

100 E. L. E. Pawley, 'BBC Sound Broadcasting 1939–1960', *Proc. IEE*, Vol. 108, Part B, No. 39, May 1961

101 European Broadcasting Convention, Copenhagen, 1948, ITU

102 *EBU Bulletin*, Vol. III, No. 15, 15 September 1952, p. 459

103 European Broadcasting Conference, Stockholm, 1952, Final Acts, ITU

104 *EBU Bulletin*, 15 July 1950, p. 164

105 H. L. Kirke, 'Frequency Modulation: BBC Field Trials', *BBC Quarterly*, Vol. I, No. 2, July 1946

106 H. Page and G. G. Gouriet, 'An experimental investigation of Motor-vehicle Ignition Interference', *BBC Quarterly*, Vol. III, No. 3, October 1948

107 C. L. S. Gilford, 'Membrane Sound Absorbers and their application to Broadcasting Studios', *BBC Quarterly*, Vol. VII, No. 4, winter 1952–3

108 F. L. Ward, 'Helmholtz Resonators as Acoustic Treatment at the new Swansea Studios', *BBC Quarterly*, Vol. VII, No. 3, autumn 1952

109 T. Somerville and C. L. S. Gilford, 'Composite Cathode-Ray Oscillograph Displays of Acoustic Phenomena and their Interpretation', *BBC Quarterly*, Vol. VII, No. 1, spring 1952

110 T. Somerville, 'Subjective Comparison of Concert Halls', *BBC Quarterly*, Vol. VIII, No. 2, summer 1953

111 T. Somerville and S. F. Brownless, 'Listener's Sound-level Preferences', *BBC Quarterly*, Vol. III, No. 4, January 1949, and Vol. V, No. 1, spring 1950

112 K. Müller, 'What Dynamic Range does the Listener wish to have?' *EBU Review*, No. 124A, December 1970

113 H. Page, 'Anti-fading Series-loaded Mast Radiators', *BBC Quarterly*, Vol. II, No. 3, October 1947

114 G. D. Monteath, 'Wide-band Folded-slot Aerials', *Proc. IEE*, Vol. 97, Part III, No. 50, November 1950, p. 412

115 P. A. T. Bevan and H. Page, 'The Sutton Coldfield Television Broadcasting Station', *Proc. IEE*, Vol. 98, Part III, November 1951, p. 416

116 H. D. Harwood, 'The Design of a High-quality Commentator's Microphone insensitive to Ambient Noise', *BBC Engineering Monograph*, No. 7, June 1956

117 W. N. Sproson, 'The Measurement of the Performance of Lenses', *BBC Quarterly*, Vol. VIII, No. 1, spring 1953

118 P. E. Axon, 'Overall Frequency Characteristic in Magnetic Recording', *BBC Quarterly*, Vol. V, No. 1, spring 1950

119 E. D. Daniel and P. E. Axon, 'Absolute measurements in Magnetic Recording', *BBC Engineering Monograph*, No. 2, September 1955

120 L. F. Tagholm and G. I. Ross, 'The Selection and Testing of Sites for Television Transmitters in the UK', *Journal IEE*, Part IIIA, 1952, p. 300

121 R. A. Rowden and G. I. Ross, 'The Effects of Aircraft on the Reception of Transmissions in the 45-MHz Band', *BBC Quarterly*, Vol. III, No. 4, January 1949

122 R. D. A. Maurice, M. Gilbert, G. F. Newell and J. G. Spencer, 'The Visibility of Noise in Television', *BBC Monograph*, No. 3, October 1955

123 H. L. Kirke, 'Television Definition and Bandwidth', *BBC Quarterly*, Vol. III, No. 3, October 1948

124 C. B. B. Wood, A. V. Lord and E. R. Rout, 'The Suppressed Frame System of Telerecording', *BBC Engineering Monograph*, No. 1, June 1955

125 A. V. Lord, 'Conversion of Television Standards', *BBC Quarterly*, Vol. VIII, No. 2, summer 1953

126 G. G. Gouriet, 'Spectrum Equalisation', *Wireless Engineer*, May 1953

127 J. W. Godfrey and G. Parr, *The Technical Writer*, Chapman & Hall, 1959

128 P. Ford, 'History of Sound Recording', *Recorded Sound*, April–July 1963

References relating to Chapter VI

1 R. Wangermée, Series of Articles on the Evolution of Radio Programmes, *EBU Review*, 119B, January 1970; 122B, July 1970; 128B, July 1971

2 *Broadcasting in the Seventies*, BBC, July 1969

3 D. E. L. Shorter, IEE Electronics Division Lecture, 11 December 1968

4 T. Somerville, 'A Survey of Stereophony', *Proc. IEE*, Vol. 106, Part B, 1959, p. 201

5 D. E. L. Shorter, 'A Survey of Stereophony as applied to Broadcasting', *Proc. IEE*, Vol. 106, Part B, 1959, p. 226

6 D. E. L. Shorter and G. J. Phillips, 'A Summary of the Present Position of Stereophony', *BBC Engineering Monograph*, No. 29, April 1960

7 D. E. L. Shorter, 'Operational Research on Microphone and Studio Techniques in Stereophony', *BBC Engineering Monograph*, No. 38, September 1961

8 H. D. Harwood and D. E. L. Shorter, 'Stereophony: the Effect of Cross-talk between Left and Right Channels', *BBC Engineering Monograph*, No. 52, March 1964

9 D. E. L. Shorter and H. D. Harwood, 'Stereophony: the Effect of Inter-channel Differences in the Phase/Frequency and Amplitude/Frequency Characteristics', *BBC Engineering Monograph*, No. 56, December 1964

10 N. F. Spring, 'Progress in Acoustics', *Wireless World*, November 1971, p. 522

11 H. Davies, 'The Programme Effects Generator', *BBC Engineering Monograph*, No. 71, November 1967

12 F. C. Brooker, 'Radiophonics in the BBC', *BBC Engineering Monograph*, No. 51, November 1963

13 F. C. Brooker, 'The BBC Radiophonic Workshop', *Electronics & Power*, Vol. 11, January 1965

14 F. A. Peachey, 'Automatic Monitoring', *BBC Engineering Monograph*, No. 62, April 1966

15 R. W. Holmes, 'Technical Monitoring of Transmitters and Programme Links', *BBC Engineering*, No. 85, January 1971

16 C. L. S. Gilford and M. W. Greenway, 'The Application of Phase-coherent Detection and Correlation Methods to Room Acoustics', *BBC Engineering Monograph*, No. 9, November 1956

17 D. E. L. Shorter, C. L. S. Gilford and H. D. Harwood, 'The Acoustic Design and Performance of a new Free-field Sound Measurement Room', *BBC Engineering Monograph*, No. 59, September 1965

18 A. N. Burd, C. L. S. Gilford and N. F. Spring, 'Data for the Acoustic Design of Studios', *BBC Engineering Monograph*, No. 64, November 1966

19 D. K. Jones and H. D. Harwood, 'Recent research on Studio Sound Problems', *BBC Engineering Monograph*, No. 68, July 1967

20 N. F. Spring and K. E. Randall, 'Permissible Bass Rise in Talks Studios', *BBC Engineering*, No. 83, July 1970

21 M. E. B. Moffat and N. F. Spring, 'An Automatic Method for the Measurement of Reverberation Time', *BBC Engineering Monograph*, No. 80, December 1969

22 A. N. Burd and M. E. B. Moffat, 'Sonic booms and other Aircraft Noise in Studios', *BBC Engineering Monograph*, No. 73, April 1963

23 D. E. L. Shorter and H. D. Harwood, 'The Design of a Ribbon-type Pressure-gradient Microphone for Broadcast Transmission', *BBC Engineering Monograph*, No. 4, December 1955

24 H. D. Harwood, 'The Design of a High-quality Commentators' Microphone insensitive to Ambient Noise', *BBC Engineering Monograph*, No. 7, June 1956

25 *Second Report of the Television Advisory Committee*, 1952, HMSO, 1954

26 E. W. Hayes and H. Page, 'The BBC Sound Broadcasting Service on Very High Frequencies', *Proc. IEE*, Vol. 104, Part B, 15 May 1957, p. 213

27 W. S. Mortley, 'F.M.Q.', *Wireless World*, 1951, No. 57, p. 399 (see also ref. 36 of Chapter V)

28 A. C. Beck, F. N. Norbury and J. L. Storr-Best, 'Frequency-modulated UHF Transmitter Technique', *Proc. IEE*, Vol. 104B, November 1956, p. 225

29 G. D. Monteath, 'An Aerial for VHF Broadcasting', *BBC Quarterly*, No. 6, 1951, p. 122

30 P. Knight and G. D. Monteath, 'The Power Gain of Multi-tiered VHF Transmitting Aerials', *BBC Engineering Monograph*, No. 31, July 1960

31 J. E. Packman, 'The Variable Inductance Frequency Modulator', *BBC Engineering Monograph*, No. 76, December 1968

32 R. T. B. Wynn and F. A. Peachey, 'The Remote and Automatic Control of Semi-attended Broadcasting Transmitters', *Proc. IEE*, Vol. 104, Part B, No. 18, November 1957, p. 529

33 J. G. Spencer, 'Tests of Mixed Polarisation for VHF Sound Broadcasting', *BBC Engineering*, No. 83, July 1970

34 'Convention on Stereophonic Sound Recording, Reproduction and Broadcasting', *Proc. IEE*, Vol. 106B, Supp. 14, March 1959

35 'Stereophonic Broadcasting in the United Kingdom', Editorial, *BBC Engineering*, No. 88, October 1971

36 F. Axon and O. H. Barron, 'Planning and Installation of the Sound Broadcasting Headquarters for the BBC's Overseas and European Services', *Proc. IEE*, Vol. 107, Part B, No. 36, November 1961, p. 485

37 H. D. M. Ellis and J. C. Taylor, 'The Design of Automatic Equipment for Programme Routing and Sequential Monitoring', *BBC Quarterly*, Vol. VI, No. 4, winter 1951–2, p. 241

38 R. M. Woodbridge, 'Control of Switching in the External Services of the BBC', *EBU Technical Monograph*, 3092

39 *Summary of the Report of the Independent Committee of Enquiry into the Overseas Information Services*, Cmd 9138, HMSO, April 1954

40 D. A. V. Williams, 'BBC External Services Engineering', *Sound & Vision Broadcasting*, spring 1971

41 E. L. E. Pawley, 'BBC Sound Broadcasting 1939–1960', *Proc. IEE*, Vol. 108, Part B, No. 39, May 1961

42 F. C. McLean, H. W. Baker and C. H. Colborn, 'The BBC Television Centre and its Technical Facilities', *Proc. IEE*, Vol. 109, Part B, No. 45, May 1962, p. 197

43 Sir Harold Bishop, 'Twenty-five Years of BBC Television', *BBC Engineering Monograph*, No. 39, October 1961

44 *The BBC Television Centre*, BBC, 1960

45 'Radio Relays for Television', an *EBU Technical Monograph*, No. 3110, 1969

46 W. N. Sproson, S. N. Watson and M. Campbell, 'The BBC Colour Television Tests: an Appraisal of Results', *BBC Engineering Monograph*, No. 18, May 1958

47 I. R. Atkins, A. R. Stanley and S. N. Watson, 'A new Survey of the BBC Experimental Colour Transmissions', *BBC Engineering Monograph*, No. 32, October 1960

48 J. Redmond, 'Television Broadcasting 1960–1970: BBC 625-line Services and the Introduction of Colour', *IEE Reviews, Proc. IEE*, Vol. 117, Special Issue, August 1970

49 N. F. Chapman, 'The Equipment of the BBC Television Studios at Ealing', *BBC Engineering Monograph*, No. 27, January 1960

50 H. C. J. Tarner, 'BBC Television News – Alexandra Palace and the Television Centre Spur', *BBC Engineering*, No. 81, January 1970

51 C. R. Longman, 'Experience in the Operation of Colour Studios', *BBC Engineering Monograph*, No. 81, January 1970

52 R. A. Sparks, 'Regional Studio Centre, Birmingham: Part I, Architectural Aspects' and D. R. Kinally, 'Regional Studio Centre, Birmingham: Part II, Technical Facilities', *BBC Engineering*, No. 87, July 1971

53 G. Hersee, 'A Survey of the Development of Television Test Cards used in the BBC', *BBC Engineering Monograph*, No. 69, September 1967

54 'From Iconoscope to Plumbicon', Editorial, *BBC Engineering*, No. 82, April 1970

55 I. J. Shelley and D. L. Smart, 'Automatic Measurement and Control using Insertion Test Signals', IEE Conference Publication, No. 69, 1970 International Broadcasting Convention, pp. 249–52

56 C. Lashmar, 'The BBC's Television Management Information System (TIMS)', *EBU Technical Monograph*, 3092, 1970

57 G. L. Pexton, 'Computer-based scheduling of Technical Resources in BBC Television', ibid.

58 D. M. B. Grubb, 'Automation in the BBC's Television Service', ibid.

59 F. C. McLean, A. N. Thomas and R. A. Rowden, 'The Crystal Palace Television Transmitting Station', *Proc. IEE*, Vol. 103, Part B, No. 11, September 1956, p. 633

60 V. J. Cooper and W. J. Morcam, 'Band I Television Transmitter Design with particular reference to the transmitters at Crystal Palace', *Proc. IEE*, Vol. 103, Part B, No. 11, September 1956, p. 651

61 A. R. A. Rendall and S. H. Padel, 'The Broadcasting House–Crystal Palace Television Link', *Proc. IEE*, Vol. 103, Part B, No. 11, September 1956, p. 644

62 *Report of the Committee on Broadcasting*, 1960, Cmnd 1753, HMSO, 1962

63 *Memorandum on the Report of the Committee on Broadcasting*, Cmnd 1770, HMSO 1962

64 A. L. Hands, 'Transmitters for Unattended High-power UHF Stations' and R. W. Leslie, 'Planning Automatic Transmitting Stations', IEE Conference on Automatic Operation and Control of Broadcasting Equipment, Publication No. 25, November 1966, p. 124

65 R. W. Leslie, 'Multiplex System for Stand-by Operation of UHF Television Transmitters', *BBC Engineering*, No. 85, January 1971

66 A. B. Shone, 'Channel Combining Units for UHF Transmitting Stations', International Broadcasting Convention Publication 46, Part 1, Paper 5/4, 1968

67 'Technical Advice for Listeners and Viewers', *EBU Monograph*, 3109, 1968

68 E. M. Sayer and J. R. G. Vernon, 'BBC Tape Reclamation Service', IEE Conference on Magnetic Recording, 6–10 July 1964

69 H. J. Houlgate, 'The Erasure in Bulk of Magnetic Tape and Film', ibid.

70 D. R. Morse, L. H. Griffiths and F. W. Nicholls, 'A full information Television Recording System', ibid.

71 J. Redmond, 'Television Recording', *Journal IEE*, Vol. 6, No. 70, October 1960

72 P. E. Axon, 'The BBC Vision Electronic Recording Apparatus', *EBU Review*, 49A, May 1958

73 W. K. E. Geddes, 'A Meter for the Assessment of Drop-outs in Video-tape Recording', *EBU Review*, 104A, August 1967

74 J. Nash, 'Twelve Years of Video Tape', *BBC Engineering*, No. 81, January 1970

75 W. K. E. Geddes, 'Drop-out in Video Tape Recording', *BBC Engineering Monograph*, No. 57, June 1965

76 L. H. Griffiths, R. E. Nether and A. E. Berry, 'Mobile Video-tape Recording Equipment', IEE Conference Report, Series No. 5, International Television Conference, July 1963

77 P. Rainger, 'The Slow-motion Video Tape Recorder', *Electronics & Power*, Vol. 12, November 1966

78 N. W. Lewis, 'Waveform Responses of Television Links', *Proc. IEE*, Vol. 101, Part III, No. 72, July 1954

79 D. C. Savage and D. A. Carter, 'The Application of Insertion Test Signal Techniques to Television Transmission Chain Operation', Joint IEE/IERE/RTS/IEEE Conference on Television Measuring Techniques, May 1970

80 I. J. Shelley and G. E. Williamson-Noble, 'The Automatic Measurement of Insertion Test Signals', ibid.

81 'Insertion Communication Equipment: Field Trial', *BBC Engineering*, No. 87, July 1971

82 E. L. E. Pawley, 'International Aspects of Television Broadcasting', *RTSJ*, Vol. 13, No. 2, March–April 1970

83 D. E. L. Shorter, 'The Distribution of Television Sound by Pulse-code Modulation Signals incorporated in the Video Waveform', *EBU Review*, No. 113A, February 1969

84 C. B. B. Wood and I. J. Shelley, 'Cablefilm', *Journal IEE*, 1960, No. 6, p. 634

85 G. Hansen, 'Direct Broadcasting from Satellites', Editorial, *EBU Review*, 128A, August 1971, p. 142

86 G. J. Phillips, 'General Problems of Broadcasting from Satellites', *ITU Journal* (Special Issue), May 1970

87 'Waveform Specification of the BBC Sound-in-Syncs Equipment', *EBU Review*, 121A, June 1970

88 C. J. Dalton, 'A P.C.M. Sound-in-Syncs System for Outside Broadcasts', *BBC Engineering*, No. 86, April 1971

89 D. E. L. Shorter, J. R. Chew, D. Howorth and J. R. Sanders, 'Pulse-code Modulation for High-quality Sound-Signal Distribution', *BBC Engineering Monograph*, No. 75, December 1968

90 J. M. Chorley and J. S. Norwell, 'The Development of BBC Internal Communications', *BBC Engineering Monograph*, No. 48, May 1963

91 D. V. Lywood, 'Modernisation of the BBC Telegraph System with an Automatic Data Exchange', *BBC Engineering*, No. 83, July 1970

92 *EBU Review*, 128A, August 1971, p. 172

93 W. N. Sproson, S. N. Watson and M. Campbell, 'The BBC Colour Television Tests: an appraisal of results', *BBC Engineering Monograph*, No. 18, May 1958

94 I. R. Atkins, A. R. Stanley, S. N. Watson, 'A new survey of the BBC Experimental Colour Transmissions', *BBC Engineering Monograph*, No. 32, October 1960

95 *Report of the Television Advisory Committee 1960*, HMSO, 1960

96 *Television Field Trials of 405-line and 625-line systems in the UHF and VHF Bands: 1957–8*, BBC

97 *Television UHF Trials with 625-line Monochrome and Colour Television Systems: 1962–3*, BBC

98 R. Chaste and P. Cassagne, 'The Henri de France Colour Television System', *Proc. IEE*, Vol. 107, Part B, 1960, pp. 499–511

99 'BBC Man anticipates Russian Colour Television System', *Wireless World*, 1966, No. 72, p. 75

100 W. Bruch, 'PAL – a variant of the NTSC Colour Television System' (Series of papers), *Telefunken Zeitung*, 1964 and 1966

101 H. V. Sims, *Principles of PAL Colour Television and Related Systems*, Butterworth, 1969

102 A. V. Lord and E. R. Rout, 'A Review of Television Standards Conversion', *BBC Engineering Monograph*, No. 55, December 1964

103 P. Rainger, 'A new System of Standards Conversion', IEE Conference Report Series No. 5, International Television Conference, July 1963

104 E. R. Rout and R. E. Davies, 'Electronic Standards Conversion for Transatlantic Colour Television', *Journal SMPTE*, Vol. 77, No. 1, January 1968

105 S. M. Edwardson, 'An Advanced Form of Field-store Standards Converter', IEE International Broadcasting Convention, September 1968, Vol. 46, Part 1

106 A. V. Lord, P. Rainger and E. R. Rout, 'Digital Line-store Standards Conversion', IEE Conference Publication, No. 69, 1970 International Broadcasting Convention

107 J. R. Sanders, 'Pulse Sound: a System of Television Sound Broadcasting using pulses in the Video Waveform', *BBC Engineering Monograph*, No. 67, May 1967

108 J. M. Chorley and D. E. L. Shorter, 'P.C.M. Sound-in-Syncs: Operational Systems for Video Distribution and Contribution Networks', IEE Conference Publication, No. 69, 1970 International Broadcasting Convention

109 C. J. Dalton, 'The Distribution of Television Sound Signals by PCM Signals incorporated in the Vision Waveform', IEE International Broadcasting Convention, September 1968, Vol. 46, Part 1

110 S. N. Watson, 'Cablefilm Equipment', *Journal Brit. IRE*, Vol. 20, No. 10, October 1960

111 S. H. Padel, P. Rainger, C. B. B. Wood, 'Cablefilm Equipment', *Journal SMPTE*, Vol. 70, No. 7, July 1961

112 C. B. B. Wood, 'Automatic Registration of Colour Television Cameras', *Journal SMPTE*, Vol. 80, No. 6, June 1971

113 C. B. B. Wood, J. R. Sanders, F. A. Griffiths, 'Electronic Compensation for Colour Film Processing Errors', *Journal SMPTE*, Vol. 74, No. 9, September 1965

114 H. A. S. Philippart, 'Tristimulus Spot Colorimeter', *BBC Engineering Monograph*, No. 65, December 1966

115 D. E. L. Shorter, 'Progress in the use of Pulse-code Modulation for High-quality Sound Links', *BBC Engineering*, No. 81, January 1970

116 'Towers and Masts for VHF and UHF Transmitting Aerials', *EBU Technical Monograph*, 3103, 1965

117 A. N. Burd and H. D. Harwood, 'Acoustic Modelling of Studios', IEE Conference Publication, No. 69, 1970 International Broadcasting Convention

118 H. Page, 'Television Broadcasting on UHF: Planning the Transmitter Chain', *Journal IEE*, Vol. 9, November 1963

119 R. W. Lee, J. H. Causebrook and R. S. Sandell, 'Service Area Planning by Computer', *BBC Engineering*, No. 86, April 1971

120 R. S. Sandell and J. H. Causebrook, 'Field-strength Prediction in the Planning of a Television Transmitter Network', IEE International Broadcasting Convention, September 1968, Vol. 46, Part 1

121 F. W. Taylor and L. C. Munn, 'A Mobile Laboratory for UHF and VHF Television Surveys', *BBC Engineering Monograph*, No. 34, February 1961

122 G. J. Phillips, P. T. W. Vance and R. V. Harvey, 'A Band V signal-frequency unit and a Correlation Detector for a VHF/UHF Field-strength Recording Receiver', *BBC Engineering Monograph*, No. 44, October 1962

References

123 H. Page and D. J. Whythe, 'Corona and Precipitation Interference in VHF Television Reception', *Proc. IEE*, Vol. 114, No. 5, May 1967

124 G. H. Millard and A. B. Shone, 'UHF Transmitting Aerial Design', *IERE Conference Proceedings*, No. 6, International Conference on UHF Television, November 1965

125 P. C. J. Hill, 'Methods of Shaping the Vertical Radiation Patterns of VHF and UHF Transmitting Aerials', *Proc. IEE*, Vol. 116, No. 7, July 1969

126 P. Knight and R. E. Davies, 'VHF Aerial Gain Calculations', *BBC Engineering Monograph*, No. 66, February 1967

127 P. Knight and G. D. Monteath, 'The Power Gain of Multi-tiered VHF Transmitting Aerials', *BBC Engineering Monograph*, No. 31, July 1960

128 G. H. Millard, 'A Printed Panel Aerial for UHF Relay Stations', *BBC Engineering*, No. 84, October 1970

129 P. Knight and R. C. Thoday, 'The Influence of the Ground on MF Sky-wave Propagation', *Proc. IEE*, Vol. 116, No. 6, June 1969

130 P. Knight, 'The Effect on MF Sky-wave Propagation of the Conductivity of the Ground near the Transmitting Aerial', IEE Conference Publication, No. 36, Conference on MF, LF and VLF Radio Propagation, November 1967

131 S. D. Berry, 'Transistor Amplifiers for Sound Broadcasting', *BBC Engineering Monograph*, No. 26, August 1959

132 D. E. L. Shorter and W. I. Manson, 'The Automatic Control of Sound-Signal Level in Broadcasting Studios', *BBC Engineering Monograph*, No. 77, March 1969

133 T. Worswick and G. W. H. Larkby. 'An improved Roving Eye', *BBC Engineering Monograph*, No. 12, April 1957

134 F. A. Peachey, 'Automatic Monitoring', *BBC Engineering Monograph*, No. 62, April 1966

135 R. J. Taylor and R. H. Spencer, 'ANCHOR – A new Electronic Character Generator', *BBC Engineering*, No. 84, October 1970

136 W. T. Shelton, 'Solid-state Video Switching Matrix', *BBC Engineering*, No. 83, July 1970

137 F. A. Peachey, R. Toombs and D. L. Smart, 'Apparatus for Television and Sound Relay Stations', *BBC Engineering Monograph*, No. 42, July 1962

138 G. G. Johnstone, E. K. Barratt and B. C. Taylor, 'UHF Translator Design, *IERE Conference Proceedings*, No. 6, International Conference on UHF Television, November 1965

139 K. C. Quinton. 'A UHF Television Link for Outside Broadcasts', *BBC Engineering Monograph*, No. 19, June 1958

140 F. R. Temple, 'Testing Facilities of the BBC's Equipment Department', *EBU Review*, No. 92A, August 1965, p. 64

141 BS 3763:1964, BSI

142 *The Use of SI Units*, BSI

143 BS 204:1960 (and supplements), BSI

144 J. Redmond, 'British Broadcasting and the IEE' *Electronics & Power*, April–May 1971, p. 152

145 S. Kandiah, 'Inventory Control Forecasting at the BBC', *Data Processing*, July–August 1968

146 R. C. Evens, 'The BBC Central Computer Complex', *BBC Engineering*, No. 84, October 1970, p. 10

147 G. Dunkerley, 'Technical Staffing in the BBC', *EBU Review*, 83A, February 1964, p. 2

148 'Safety Regulations for the Staffs of Broadcasting Organisations', *EBU Technical Monograph*, 3105, 1966

149 D. E. L. Shorter, 'A Survey of Performance Criteria and Design Considerations for high-quality Monitoring Loudspeakers', *Proc. IEE*, 105B, April 1958, p. 607

Abbreviations

used in the text (excluding those of SI units)

ABS	Association of Broadcasting Staff	CCIR	Comité Consultatif international des Radiocommunications (International Radio Consultative Committee)
ABSIE	American Broadcasting Station in Europe		
ABU	Asian Broadcasting Union		
ac	alternating current	CCITT	Comité Consultatif international télégraphique et téléphonique (International Telegraph and Telephone Consultative Committee)
ADX	automatic data exchange		
AEG	Allegemeine Elektrizitäts Gesellschaft		
af	audio frequency	CEPT	Conférence Européenne des administrations des postes et télécommunications (European Conference of Postal and Telecommunications Administrations)
AFN	American Forces Network		
AGL	above ground level		
AM	amplitude modulation (-ed)		
AME	Assistant Maintenance Engineer		
AMSL	above mean sea level	CISPR	Comité international spécial des perturbations radioélectriques (International Special Committee on Radio Interference)
ARD	Arbeitsgemeinschaft der öffentlich —rechtlichenRundfunkanstaltender Bundesrepublik Deutschland		
ASBU	Arab States Broadcasting Union	Cmd	*Command Paper*
ATI	active telephone indicator	CMTT	Commission Mixte CCIR/CCITT pour les transmissions télévisuelles (CCIR/CCITT Joint Commission for television transmissions)
BBC	British Broadcasting Company, British Broadcasting Corporation (see footnote p. 11)		
B & C	balance and control	COMSAT	Communications Satellite Corporation
BFEBS	British Far Eastern Broadcasting Service	CSIR	Council of Scientific and Industrial Research (South Africa)
BFN	British Forces Network		
BREMA	British Radio Equipment Manufacturers' Association	CSSB	compatible single sideband
Brit.IRE	British Institution of Radio Engineers	dap	double-amplitude peak
		dB	decibel
BS	British Standard	dBmW	decibels relative to one milliwatt (in 600 ohms)
BSI	British Standards Institution		
BSRA	BritishSoundRecordingAssociation	dBμV	decibels relative to one microvolt per metre
BSTJ	*Bell System Technical Journal*		
CAM	cooled-anode modulating (valve)	dc	direct current
CAR	cooled-anode rectifier (valve)	DSB	double sideband
CAT	cooled-anode transmitting (valve)	DSIR	Department of Scientific and Industrial Research
CBS	Columbia Broadcasting System (USA)	DWS	Diplomatic Wireless Service
CCI	Comité Consultatif international des Communications téléphoniques à grande distance (International Consultative Committee on long-distance telephony)	EBU	European Broadcasting Union
		EEA	Electronic Engineering Association
		eht	extra high tension
		EiC	Engineer in Charge
		EMI	Electric and Musical Industries, Ltd
		erp	effective radiated power
CCIF	Comité Consultatif international téléphonique (International Telephone Consultative Committee)	FCC	Federal Communication Commission (USA)
		FM	frequency modulation (-ed)

ft	foot, feet
HF	high frequency (see table, p. 2)
HMSO	His/Her Majesty's Stationery Office
ht	high tension
IBU	International Broadcasting Union
IEC	International Electrotechnical Commission
IEE	Institution of Electrical Engineers
IEEE	Institute of Electrical and Electronic Engineers (USA)
IERE	Institution of Electronic and Radio Engineers
IFRB	International Frequency Registration Board
if	intermediate frequency
in.	inch
Intelsat	International Telecommunications Satellite Consortium
IRE	Institute of Radio Engineers (USA)
ISO	International Organisation for Standardisation
ITA	Independent Television Authority (changed to Independent Broadcasting Authority, July 1972)
ITCA	Independent Television Companies Association
ITT	International Telephone and Telegraph Corporation
ITU	International Telecommunication Union
lb	pound (weight)
LF	low frequency (see table, p. 2)
lt	low tension
MCR	mobile control room
MF	medium frequency (see table, p. 2)
MSC	mile of standard cable
MSS	Marguerite Sound Studios
NASA	National Aeronautics and Space Administration (USA)
NBC	National Broadcasting Company (USA)
NMA	non-multiple-access
NTS	Nederlandse Televisie Stichting
NTSC	National Television System Committee (USA)
NWDR	Nordwestdeutscher Rundfunk
OB	Outside Broadcast(ing)
OIRT	Organisation Internationale de Radiodiffusion et Télévision. (International Radio and Television Organisation)
ORTF	Office de Radiodiffusion-Télévision Française
OSE	Overseas Station Extension
pa	per annum
PABX	Private Automatic Branch Exchange
PAL	Phase Alternation Line
PBX	Private Branch Exchange
pcm	pulse code modulation
POEEJ	*Post Office Electrical Engineers Journal*
PTI	passive telephone indicator
PTT	Post, Telegraph and Telephone (Administration)
PWD	Psychological Warfare Division
RCA	Radio Corporation of America
RECMF	Radio and Electronic Components Manufacturers Association
rf	radio frequency
RRG	Reichs Rundfunk Gesellschaft
RNF	Radiodiffusion Nationale Française
RTF	Radiodiffusion-Télévision Française
RTRA	Radio and Television Retailers Association
RTSJ	Royal Television Society Journal
SB	Simultaneous Broadcast(ing)
SCRE	Senior Control Room Engineer
SE	Superintendent Engineer
SECAM	Séquentiel Couleur à Mémoire
SHAEF	Supreme Headquarters Allied Expeditionary Force
SHF	super high frequency (see table, p. 2)
SICUIR	Société Immobilière du Centre de Contrôle Technique de l'UIR
SI	Système International d'Unités
SIS	sound-in-syncs
SME	Senior Maintenance Engineer
SMPE	Society of Motion Picture Engineers (USA)
SMPTE	Society of Motion Picture and Television Engineers (USA)
SSB	single sideband
SSE	Senior Superintendent Engineer
STC	Standard Telephones and Cables
STD	Subscriber Trunk Dialling
TAC	Television Advisory Committee
TARIF	television apparatus for the rectification of inferior film
TOPICS	total on-line programme and information control system
UER	Union Européenne de Radiodiffusion (EBU)
UHF	ultra high frequency (see table, p. 2)
UIR	Union Internationale de Radiophonie (later Radiodiffusion) (IBU)
URTNA	Union of National Radio and Television Organisations of Africa
USIS	United States Information Service
VERA	vision electronic recording apparatus
VFO	variable-frequency oscillator
VHF	very high frequency (see table, p. 2)
VOA	Voice of America
wpm	words per minute

Index